SECOND EDITION

LEGAL AND ETHICAL
ESSENTIALS of
HEALTH CARE
ADMINISTRATION

GEORGE D. POZGAR, MBA, CHE
AUTHOR, SPEAKER, CONSULTANT
GP HEALTH CARE
ANNAPOLIS, MARYLAND

LEGAL REVIEW
NINA SANTUCCI, JD

JONES & BARTLETT
LEARNING

World Headquarters
Jones & Bartlett Learning
5 Wall Street
Burlington, MA 01803
978-443-5000
info@jblearning.com
www.jblearning.com

Jones & Bartlett Learning books and products are available through most bookstores and online booksellers. To contact Jones & Bartlett Learning directly, call 800-832-0034, fax 978-443-8000, or visit our website, www.jblearning.com.

Substantial discounts on bulk quantities of Jones & Bartlett Learning publications are available to corporations, professional associations, and other qualified organizations. For details and specific discount information, contact the special sales department at Jones & Bartlett Learning via the above contact information or send an email to specialsales@jblearning.com.

Production Credits
Publisher: Michael Brown
Managing Editor: Maro Gartside
Editorial Assistant: Sean Fabery
Editorial Assistant: Chloe Falivene
Associate Production Editor: Rebekah Linga
Senior Marketing Manager: Sophie Fleck Teague
Manufacturing and Inventory Control Supervisor: Amy Bacus
Composition: Aptara, Inc.
Cover Design: Michael O'Donnell
Cover Image credit: Top: © Jerric Ramos/ShutterStock, Inc.; Bottom: © iStockphoto/Thinkstock
Printing and Binding: Edwards Brothers Malloy
Cover Printing: Edwards Brothers Malloy

Library of Congress Cataloging-in-Publication Data
Pozgar, George D.
    Legal and ethical essentials of health care administration / George D. Pozgar.—2nd ed.
        p. ; cm.
    Rev. ed. of: Legal essentials of health care administration / George D. Pozgar ; legal review, Nina M. Santucci. c2009.
    Related ed. of: Legal aspects of health care administration / George D. Pozgar ; legal review, Nina M. Santucci. 11th ed. c2012.
    Includes bibliographical references and index.
    ISBN-13: 978-1-4496-9434-0 (pbk.)
    ISBN-10: 1-4496-9434-9 (pbk.)
    I. Pozgar, George D. Legal essentials of health care administration.   II. Pozgar, George D. Legal aspects of health care administration.   III. Title.
    [DNLM: 1. Delivery of Health Care—legislation & jurisprudence—United States.   2. Delivery of Health Care—ethics—United States.
    3. Legislation, Medical—United States.   W 32.5 AA1]
    KF3821
    344.7304'1—dc23

2013010477

6048

Printed in the United States of America
17 16 15 14 13   10 9 8 7 6 5 4 3 2

Dedication

Mary Ann Pozgar-Berkebile

My Sister

Precious moments when she took my hand,

And said,

Let's Dance.

At that moment,

I knew from her touch,

How much she loved me.

Contents

Epigraph

 In civilized life, law floats in a sea of ethics.
—EARL WARREN, CHIEF JUSTICE OF THE UNITED STATES (1891–1974)

 I consider ethics, as well as religion, as supplements to law in the government of man.
—THOMAS JEFFERSON, PRESIDENT OF THE UNITED STATES (1743–1826)

 *In law a man is guilty when he violates the rights of others. In ethics he is guilty if he only thinks of doing so.*
—IMMANUEL KANT, PHILOSOPHER (1724–1804)

 It is curious—curious that physical courage should be so common in the world, and moral courage so rare.
—MARK TWAIN, AMERICAN AUTHOR AND HUMORIST (1835–1910)

Preface

 He has achieved success who has lived well, laughed often and loved much; who has gained the respect of intelligent men and the love of little children; who has filled his niche and accomplished his task; who has left the world better than he found it, whether by an improved poppy, a perfect poem, or a rescued soul; who has never lacked appreciation of earth's beauty or failed to express it; who has always looked for the best in others and given them the best he had; whose life was an inspiration; whose memory a benediction.

—BESSIE STANLEY

Legal and Ethical Essentials of Health Care Administration, Second Edition has become more than an abridged version of *Legal Aspects of Health Care Administration, Eleventh Edition.* The content has been updated and fully expanded to bring excitement into the learning process. This *Second Edition* delivers to the reader a comprehensive updated review of both health law and ethics. The substantive material in the *Second Edition* has been carefully selected based on the common legal and ethical issues the practitioner will face during his or her career. Although this book is mandatory reading for many students enrolled in health management and patient care courses, it is particularly valuable as a supplemental reading in the curricula of many healthcare programs. The *Second Edition* is also an invaluable desk reference for those in managerial positions and professionals providing direct patient care.

The author's unique experience in health care includes consulting and surveying more than 1,000 hospitals and ambulatory sites from Alaska to Puerto Rico, as well as his experience as administrator, educator, consultant, and speaker. Every attempt has been made to arm the student with the knowledge gained through his extensive healthcare experiences.

As a result of his background, one of the unique features of this book is that in each chapter the focus on the various issues includes more than merely definitions or descriptions of words. There is an infusion of life into the material by using cases that have been litigated or discussed in the press, as well as real-world events through reality checks experienced by healthcare professionals. In that way, the law and ethics spring to life and inspire dynamic discussion and excitement in the learning process, thus creating an atmosphere of interest and participation, which is conducive to learning.

The study of *Legal and Ethical Essentials of Health Care Administration, Second Edition* affords health professionals with the opportunity to apply the concepts learned to what they will face on a daily basis in a practical way. It details the actions healthcare providers can take to help prevent the wide variety of harmful events that occur in patient care settings. Although there will always be a next time for human error, the reader who synthetizes the contents in this book and understands its lessons will better understand how failures can turn to success and the pain of past mistakes can turn to hope.

About the Book Layout

Legal and Ethical Essentials of Health Care Administration, Second Edition lays a strong foundation in both health law and ethics. Chapter 1 begins with an introduction to government organization, sources of law, and government ethics and Chapter 2 progresses to a discussion of ethical theories, principles, virtues and values, and related topics. Chapter 3 provides an overview of the historical development of hospitals as influenced by medical progress, allowing the reader to look at their successes and failures through the centuries, and then drawing conclusions about what can be done to avoid repeating the failures of the past. In Chapter 4, the reader is introduced to negligent and intentional torts, progressing to criminal acts in Chapter 5, and contract law in Chapter 6 as they relate to health care. The reader is then introduced to civil procedure and trial practice in Chapter 7. The journey continues with a discussion of legal issues involving corporations in Chapter 8, medical staff organization and physician liability in Chapter 9, nursing and the law in Chapter 10, and a discussion of various hospital departments and allied health professionals in Chapter 11.

The first 11 chapters provide a solid basis for a more complete understanding of the following remaining chapters: Chapter 12 provides an overview of patient rights and responsibilities; Chapter 13 patient consent; Chapter 14 procreation and ethical issues; Chapter 15 end-of-life issues; Chapter 16 AIDS; Chapter 17 legal reporting requirements; Chapter 18 medical records; Chapter 19 national health insurance and managed care; Chapter 20 professional liability insurance; Chapter 21 labor relations; Chapter 22 employment at will and discharge; Chapter 23 employee rights and responsibilities; Chapter 24 tort reform; Chapter 25 culture of safety; Chapter 26 world wide search; Chapter 27 the journey to excellence; and a glossary of common legal and ethics vocabulary.

The practical application of ethics in the healthcare setting is accomplished by interspersing the thoughts of great minds through *Quotes*, applicable *Newspaper Clippings*, provider and organizational experiences through *Reality Checks* designated by a ✓ symbol, and patient experiences through legal rulings and summaries through *Case Law*. When reviewing the various cases in this book, the reader should consider both the ethical and legal implications of a dilemma and how they intertwine with one another. It is important to recognize that the decisions in the cases described are generally governed both by applicable state and federal statutes and common-law principles. When reviewing a case, the reader must keep in mind that the case law and statutes of one state are not binding in another state.

There is no one magic legal or ethics book that can possibly compress the plethora of issues that have bombarded the healthcare industry into one book. This book is merely a beginning of the study of legal and ethical issues and is an adventure that all caregivers should take. Although there is always much more that could be discussed on any one topic, the good student will understand that this book provides a solid foundation for practical everyday use as well as further study.

 Each life is like a novel. Filled with moments of happiness, sadness, crisis, defeat, and triumph. When the last page has been written, will you be happy or saddened by what you read?

—AUTHOR UNKNOWN

The reader is presented in the *Second Edition* with real-world life experiences that bring the reader through a journey of learning that provides an effective transitional stage from the classroom to the reality of the everyday work environment.

When people consider matters of law and ethics they are usually considering matters of freedom in regard to personal choices, one's obligations to other sentient beings, or judgments about human character and the right to choose. The author's objective is to equip the reader with the background knowledge necessary to understand that legal and ethical behavior begins with understanding that we have alternatives and choices in our behavior. To make good decisions, we must first understand that they will be only as good as our knowledge of what is *right* and what is *wrong*. This book is not an indictment of any profession or organization. There is a deluge of ethical issues in every aspect of human existence. Although cultural differences, politics, and religion influence who we are, it is all of life's experiences that affect who we will become. If we are compassionate it is most likely compassionate people have influenced us.

Author's Note: This book is not a definitive treatise but is a portrait of the ever-evolving story of health care through the study of law and ethics. It is educational in nature and should not be considered a substitute for legal advice on any particular issue. Moreover, each chapter presents an overview, rather than an exhaustive treatment, of the various topics discussed.

The author, legal reviewers, and/or publisher cannot be responsible for any errors or omissions, including: additions to, interpretations of, and/or changes in the regulations presented in this book.

Acknowledgments

The author especially acknowledges the staff at Jones & Bartlett Learning whose guidance and assistance was so important in making this *Second Edition* a reality. Special thanks to Mike Brown, Publisher at Jones & Bartlett Learning, who has once again been truly an amazing leader and mentor over the years. I would like to thank Chloe Falivene, Editorial Assistant, who worked diligently and tirelessly with me on this *Second Edition*. I would also like to thank the other Jones & Bartlett staff, including Rebekah Linga, Associate Production Editor; Sean Fabery, Editorial Assistant; and Sophie Teague, Senior Marketing Manager; who have also worked with me on this *Second Edition*. Thanks for allowing me to leave behind this legacy of writing.

I am grateful to the very special people in the more than 1,000 hospitals and ambulatory sites from Alaska to Puerto Rico with whom I have consulted, surveyed, and provided education over many years. Their shared experiences have served to remind me of the importance to make this book more valuable in the classroom and as a reference for practicing healthcare professionals.

To my students in healthcare law and ethics classes at the New School for Social Research, Molloy College, Long Island University–C.W. Post Campus, Saint Francis College, and Saint Joseph's College; my intern from Brown University; my resident in hospital administration from The George Washington University; and those I have instructed through the years at various seminars, I will always be indebted for your inspiration.

Many thanks are also extended to all those special people at the National Library of Medicine and the Library of Congress for their guidance over the years in locating research materials.

As the patriots of seventy-six did to the support of the Declaration of Independence, so to the support of the Constitution and Laws, let every American pledge his life, his property, and his sacred honor— let every man remember that to violate the law, is to trample on the blood of his father, and to tear the character of his own, and his children's liberty. Let reverence for the laws, be breathed by every American mother, to the lisping babe, that prattles on her lap—let it be taught in schools, in seminaries, and in colleges; let it be written in Primers, spelling books, and in Almanacs—let it be preached from the pulpit, proclaimed in legislative halls, and enforced in courts of justice. And, in short, let it become the political religion of the nation; and let the old and the young, the rich and the poor, the grave and the gay, of all sexes and tongues, and colors and conditions, sacrifice unceasingly upon its altars.

—ABRAHAM LINCOLN

1

Government, Law, and Ethics

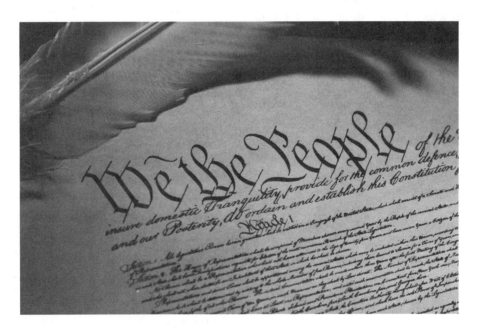

Figure 1–1 United States Constitution   © James Steidl/ShutterStock, Inc.

Learning Objectives

The reader upon completion of this chapter will be able to:

- Discuss the three branches of government, and the importance of *separation of powers*.
- Describe the organization structure of the Department of Health and Human Services.

- Explain the development of case law and how it differs from statutory and administrative law.
- Describe the function of various government ethics committees herein presented.

This chapter introduces the reader to the purpose and sources of law, the functioning of the legal system, and the roles of the three branches of government in creating, administering, and enforcing the law. There is also a brief overview of the Department of Health and Human Services and selected agencies within the department.

GOVERNMENT ORGANIZATION

The three branches of the federal government are the legislative, executive, and judicial branches (**Figure 1–2**). A vital concept in the constitutional framework of government on both federal and state levels is the *separation of powers*. Essentially, this principle provides that no one branch of government is clearly dominant over the other two; however, in the exercise of its functions, each can affect and limit the activities, functions, and powers of the others.

Executive Branch

The primary function of the *executive branch* of government on the federal and state level is to administer and enforce the law. The chief executive, either the president of the United States or the governor of a state, also has a role in the creation of law through the power to approve or veto legislative proposals.

The president serves as the administrative head of the executive branch of the federal government. The executive branch includes 15 executive departments, as well as a variety of agencies, both temporary and permanent. Each department is responsible for a different area of public affairs, and each enforces the law within its area of responsibility.

On a state level, the governor serves as the chief executive officer. The responsibilities of a governor are provided for in the state's constitution. The Massachusetts State Constitution, for example, describes the responsibilities of the governor as presenting an annual budget to the state legislature, recommending new legislation, vetoing legislation, appointing and removing department heads, appointing judicial officers, and acting as Commander-in-Chief of the state's military forces (the Massachusetts National Guard).

Legislative Branch

On the federal level, legislative powers are vested in the *Congress* of the United States, which consists of the *Senate* and the *House of Representatives*. The function of the *legislative branch* is to enact laws that can amend or repeal existing legislation and to create new legislation. The legislature determines the nature and extent of the need for new laws and for changes in existing laws. Committees of both houses of Congress are responsible for preparing federal legislation.

Judicial Branch

 As I have said in the past, when government bureaus and agencies go awry, which are adjuncts of the legislative or executive branches, the people flee to the third branch, their courts, for solace and justice.[1]

—JUSTICE J. HENDERSON,
SUPREME COURT OF SOUTH DAKOTA

The function of the *judicial branch* of government is adjudication—resolving disputes in accordance with law. As a practical matter, most disputes or controversies that are covered by legal principles or rules are resolved without resort to the courts.

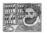 *Scarcely any political question arises in the United States that is not resolved, sooner or later, into a judicial question.*
—ALEXIS DE TOCQUEVILLE (1805–1859)

The decision as to which court has jurisdiction—the legal right to hear and rule on a particular case—is determined by such matters as the locality in which each party to a lawsuit resides and the issues of a lawsuit. Each state in the United States provides its own court system, which is created by the state's constitution and statutes. Most of the nation's judicial business is reviewed and acted on in state courts. Each state maintains a level of trial courts that have original jurisdiction, meaning the authority of a court to first conduct a trial on a specific case as distinguished from a court with appellate jurisdiction, where appeals from trial judgments are held. This jurisdiction can exclude cases involving claims with damages less than a specified minimum, probate matters (i.e., wills and estates), and workers' compensation. Different states have designated different names for trial courts (e.g., superior, district, circuit, or supreme courts). Also on the trial court level are minor courts such as city, small claims, and justice of the peace courts.

Each state has at least one appellate court. Many states have an intermediate appellate court between the trial courts and the court of last resort. Where this intermediate court is present, there is a provision for appeal to it, with further review in all but select cases. Because of this format, the highest appellate tribunal is seen as the final arbiter for the particular state's system of jurisprudence.

The trial court of the federal system is the *U.S. District Court*. There are 94 district courts in the 50 states (the larger states have more than one district court) and one in the District of Columbia. The Commonwealth of Puerto Rico

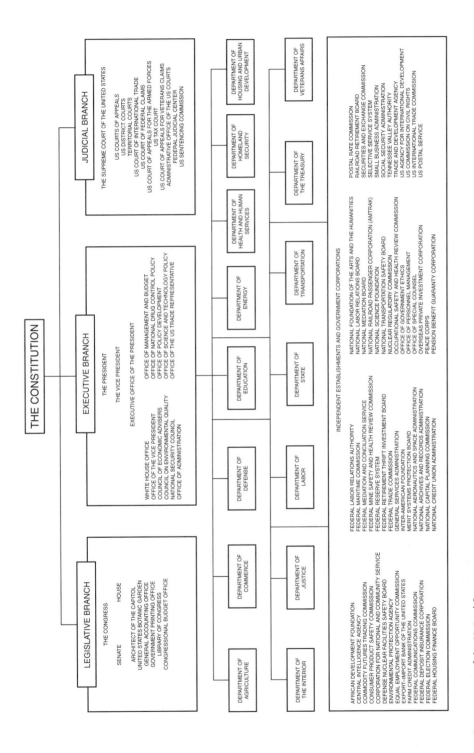

Figure 1-2 Government of the United States

also has a district court with jurisdiction corresponding to that of district courts in the different states. Generally, only one judge is required to sit and decide a case, although certain cases require up to three judges. The federal district courts hear civil, criminal, admiralty, and bankruptcy cases.

The *U.S. Circuit Court of Appeal* is an appellate court. There are 12 regional courts in various cities and the 13th judicial circuit is located in Washington, DC. Their main purpose is to review cases tried in federal district courts within their respective circuits, but they also possess jurisdiction to review orders of designated administrative agencies and to issue original writs in appropriate cases. These intermediate appellate courts were created to relieve the U.S. Supreme Court of deciding all cases appealed from the federal trial courts.

The *Supreme Court*, the nation's highest court, is the only federal court created directly by the Constitution. Eight associate justices and one chief justice sit on the Supreme Court. The court has limited original jurisdiction over the lower federal courts and the highest state courts. In a few situations, an appeal will go directly from a federal or state court to the Supreme Court, but in most cases, review must be sought through the discretionary writ of certiorari, an appeal petition. In addition to the aforementioned courts, special federal courts have jurisdiction over particular subject matters. The *U.S. Court of Claims*, for example, has jurisdiction over certain claims against the government. The *U.S. Court of Appeals* for the Federal Circuit has appellate jurisdiction over certain customs and patent matters. The *U.S. Customs Court* reviews certain administrative decisions by customs officials. Also, there is a *U.S. Tax Court* and a *U.S. Court of Military Appeals*.[2] The federal court system is illustrated in **Figure 1–3**. A comparison of federal and state courts can be found at the following website: http://www.uscourts.gov/EducationalResources/FederalCourtBasics/CourtStructure/ComparingFederalAndStateCourts.aspx.

Separation of Powers

The concept of *separation of powers*, a system of checks and balances, is illustrated in the relationships among the branches of government with regard to legislation. On the federal level, when a bill creating a statute is enacted by Congress and signed by the president, it becomes law. If the president vetoes a bill, it takes a two-thirds vote of each house of Congress to override the veto. The president also can prevent a bill from becoming law by avoiding any action while Congress is in session. This procedure, known as a pocket veto, can temporarily stop a bill from becoming

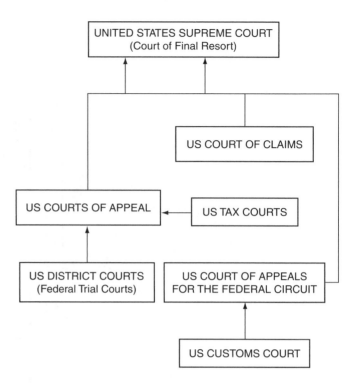

Figure 1–3 Federal Court System

law and can permanently prevent it from becoming law if later sessions of Congress do not act on it favorably. If enacted by Congress, the Supreme Court can declare a bill invalid if it violates the U.S. Constitution.

Even though a Supreme Court decision is final regarding a specific controversy, Congress and the president can generate new, constitutionally sound legislation to replace a law that has been declared unconstitutional. The procedures for amending the Constitution are complex and often time consuming, but they can serve as a way to offset or override a Supreme Court decision.

Department of Health and Human Services

The *Department of Health and Human Services* (DHHS), a cabinet-level department of the executive branch of the federal government, is concerned with people and is most involved with the nation's human concerns (**Figure 1–4**). The DHHS is responsible for developing and implementing appropriate administrative regulations for carrying out national health and human services policy objectives. It is also the main source of regulations affecting the healthcare industry. The secretary of the DHHS, serving as the department's administrative head, advises the president with regard to health, welfare, and income security plans, policies, and programs.

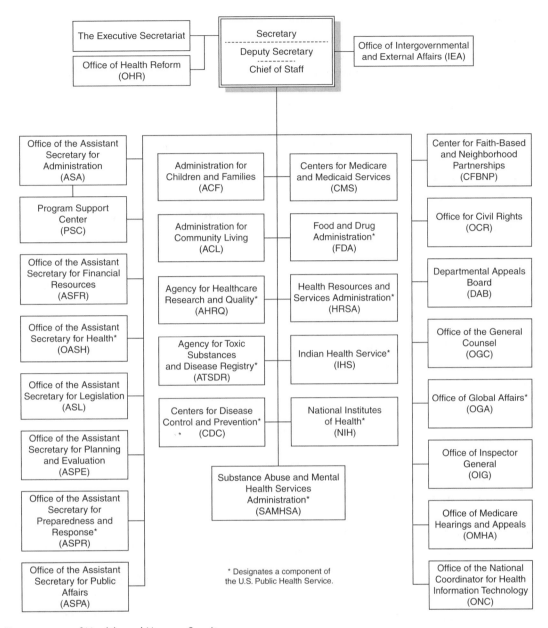

Figure 1–4 Department of Health and Human Services

The DHHS also is responsible for many of the programs designed to meet the needs of senior citizens, including Social Security benefits (e.g., retirement, survivors, and disability), Supplemental Security Income (which ensures a minimum monthly income to needy persons and is administered by local Social Security offices), Medicare, Medicaid, and programs under the Older Americans Act (e.g., in-home services, such as home health and home-delivered meals, and community services such as adult day care, transportation, and ombudsman services in long-term care facilities).

The Centers for Medicare and Medicaid Services

The *Centers for Medicare and Medicaid Services* (CMS), formerly the Health Care Financing Administration, was created to combine under one administration the oversight of the Medicare program, the federal portion of the Medicaid program, the State Children's Health Insurance Program, and related quality-assurance activities.

Medicare is a federally sponsored health insurance program for persons older than 65 and certain disabled persons. It has two complementary parts: *Medicare Part A* helps cover the costs of inpatient hospital care and, with qualifying preadmission criteria, skilled nursing facility care, home health care, and hospice care. *Medicare Part B* helps pay for physicians' services and outpatient hospital services. It is funded through Social Security contributions (Federal Insurance Contributions Act payroll taxes), premiums, and general revenue. The program is administered through private contractors, referred to as intermediaries, under Part A and carriers under Part B. The financing of the Medicare program has received much attention by Congress because of its rapidly rising costs.

Medicaid, Title XIX of the Social Security Act Amendments of 1965, is a government program administered by the states that provides medical services (both institutional and outpatient) to the medically needy. Federal grants, in the form of matching funds, are issued to those states with qualifying Medicaid programs. In other words, Medicaid is jointly sponsored and financed by the federal government and several states. Medical care for needy persons of all ages is provided under the definition of need established by each state. Each state has set its own criteria for determining eligibility for services under its Medicaid program.

Public Health Service

The *Public Health Service* (PHS) is responsible for the protection of the nation's physical and mental health. The PHS accomplishes its mission by coordinating with the states in setting and implementing national health policy and pursuing effective intergovernmental relations; generating and upholding cooperative international health-related agreements, policies, and programs; conducting medical and biomedical research; sponsoring and administering programs for the development of health resources, the prevention and control of diseases, and alcohol and drug abuse; providing resources and expertise to the states and other public and private institutions in the planning, direction, and delivery of physical and mental healthcare services; and enforcing laws to ensure drug safety and protection from impure and unsafe foods, cosmetics, medical devices, and radiation-producing objects. Within the PHS are smaller agencies that are responsible for carrying out the purpose of the division and DHHS. The PHS is composed of the offices and agencies described below.

• *National Institutes of Health*

The National Institutes of Health (NIH) is the principal federal biomedical research agency. It is responsible for conducting, supporting, and promoting biomedical research.

• *Centers for Disease Control and Prevention*

The Centers for Disease Control and Prevention (CDC) is recognized as the lead federal agency for protecting the health and safety of people at home and abroad, providing credible information to enhance health decisions, and promoting health. The CDC serves as the national focus for developing and applying disease prevention and control, environmental health, and health promotion and education activities.

• *Food and Drug Administration*

The Food and Drug Administration (FDA) supervises and controls the introduction of drugs, foods, cosmetics, and medical devices into the marketplace and protects society from impure and hazardous items.

• *Substance Abuse and Mental Health Services Administration*

The agency's mission is to reduce the impact of substance abuse and mental illness on America's communities.

• *Health Resources and Services Administration*

The primary federal agency for improving access to healthcare services for people who are uninsured, isolated, or medically vulnerable. Its mission is to improve health and achieve health equity through access to quality services, a skilled health workforce, and innovative programs. HRSA takes a comprehensive approach to addressing HIV/AIDS with activities taking place across multiple bureaus and offices designed to deliver care to people living with HIV or AIDS, expand and strengthen the HIV care workforce, and improve access to and the quality of HIV care and treatment.

• *Agency for Healthcare Research and Quality*

The Agency for Healthcare Research and Quality (AHRQ) provides evidence-based information on healthcare outcomes, quality, cost, use, and access. Information from AHRQ's research helps people make more informed decisions and improve the quality of healthcare services.

• *Agency for Toxic Substances and Disease Registry*

The mission of the Agency for Toxic Substances and Disease Registry (ATSDR) is to prevent or mitigate harmful exposures and related disease by applying science, taking responsive action, and providing trustworthy health information.

- *Indian Health Service*

The Indian Health Service (IHS), part of the U.S. Department of Health and Human Services,* provides a comprehensive health service delivery system for approximately 2 million American Indians and Alaska Natives (AI/AN) who belong to 566 federally recognized tribes in 35 states.

▍ SOURCES OF LAW

 The very essence of civil liberty certainly consists in the right of every individual to claim the protection of the laws, whenever he receives an injury. One of the first duties of government is to afford that protection. [The] government of the United States has been emphatically termed a government of laws, and not of men. It will certainly cease to deserve this high appellation, if the laws furnish no remedy for the violation of a vested right.

—Chief Justice John Marshall[3]

Scholars often define the law as a system of principles and processes by which people in a society deal with disputes and problems, seeking to solve or settle them without resorting to force. Simply stated, *laws* are rules of conduct enforced by government, which imposes penalties when prescribed laws are violated.

Laws govern the relationships between private individuals and organizations and between both of these parties and government. *Public law* deals with relationships between individuals and government; *private law* deals with relationships among individuals.

One important segment of public law, for example, is *criminal law*, which prohibits conduct deemed injurious to public order and provides for punishment of those proven to have engaged in such conduct. In contrast, private law is concerned with the recognition and enforcement of the rights and duties of private individuals. Tort and contract actions are two basic types of private law. In a *tort action*, one party asserts that the wrongful conduct of another has caused harm, and the injured party seeks compensation for the harm suffered. A *contract action* usually involves a claim by one party that another party has breached an agreement by failing to fulfill an obligation. Either remuneration or specific performance of the obligation can be sought as a remedy.

*See the website www.hhs.gov/ for more information on the Department of Health and Human Services and its various agencies.

Public Policy as a Principle of Law

Public policy is the principle of law that holds that no one can lawfully do that which tends to be injurious to the public or against the public good. The sources of public policy "include legislation; administrative rules, regulations, or decisions; and judicial decisions. In certain instances, a professional code of ethics may contain an expression of public policy."[4]

Common Law

Common law refers to the body of principles that evolve and expand from judicial decisions that arise during the trial of court cases. Many of the legal principles and rules applied today by courts in the United States have their origins in English common law.

Because a law will never cover every potential human event that might occur in society, the judicial system was developed to serve as a mechanism for reviewing legal disputes that arise in written law. It is also an effective review mechanism for those issues on which the written law is silent or in instances of a mixture of issues involving both written law and common-law decisions.

During the colonial period, English common law began to be applied in the colonies. After the Revolution, each state, with the exception of Louisiana, adopted all or part of the existing English common law and added to it as needed. Louisiana civil law is based to a great extent on the French and Spanish laws and, especially, on the Code of Napoleon. As a result there is no national system of common law in the United States, and common law on specific subjects can differ from state to state.

Judicial review became part of the law in the decade before the federal Constitution was adopted. Courts began to assert their power to rule on the constitutionality of legislative acts and to void unconstitutional statutes.

Today, legal cases are tried by applying common-law principles unless a statute governs. Even though statutory law has affirmed many of the legal rules and principles initially established by the courts, new issues continue to arise, especially in private-law disputes, which require decision making according to common-law principles. Common-law actions are initiated mainly to recover money damages or possession of real or personal property.

When a higher state court has enunciated a common-law principle, the lower courts within the state where the decision was rendered must follow that principle. A decision in a case that sets forth a new legal principle establishes a *precedent*. Trial courts or those on equal footing are not bound by the decisions of other trial courts. Also, a principle established in one state does not set precedent for another state. Rather, the rulings in one jurisdiction can be used by the courts of other jurisdictions as guides to the legal analysis of a particular legal problem.

The decisions of the U.S. Supreme Court are highest in the hierarchy of decisional law with respect to federal legal questions. Because of the parties or the legal question involved, most legal controversies do not fall within the scope of the Supreme Court's decision-making responsibilities. On questions of purely state concern—such as the interpretation of a state statute that raises no issues under the U.S. Constitution or federal law—the highest court in the state has the final word on proper interpretation. The following are explanations of some of the more important common-law principles:

- *Precedent*: A precedent is a judicial decision that can be used as a standard in subsequent similar cases. A precedent is set when a court decision is rendered that serves as a rule for future guidance when deciding similar cases.
- *Res judicata*: In common law, the term *res judicata*—which means the thing is decided—refers to that which has been previously acted on or decided by the courts. According to *Black's Law Dictionary*, it is a rule where "a final judgment rendered by a court of competent jurisdiction on the merits is conclusive as to the rights of the parties and their privies, and, as to them, constitutes an absolute bar to subsequent action involving the same claim, demand, or cause of action."[5]
- *Stare decisis*: The common-law principle *stare decisis* (let the decision stand) provides that when a decision is rendered in a lawsuit involving a particular set of facts, another lawsuit involving an identical or substantially similar situation is to be resolved in the same manner as the first lawsuit. New lawsuits are thus resolved by applying rules and principles of preceding cases. In this manner, courts arrive at comparable rulings. Sometimes slight factual differences can provide a basis for recognizing distinctions between the precedent and the current case. In some cases, even when such differences are absent, a court might conclude that a particular common-law rule is no longer in accord with the needs of society and can depart from precedent. Principles of law are subject to change, whether they originate in statutory or in common law. Common-law principles can be modified, overturned, abrogated, or created by new court decisions in a continuing process of growth and development to reflect changes in social attitudes, public needs, judicial prejudices, or contemporary political thinking.

Statutory Law

Statutory law is written law emanating from a legislative body. Although a statute can abolish any rule of common law, it can do so only by express words. The principles and rules of statutory law are set in hierarchical order.

The Constitution of the United States adopted at the Constitutional Convention in Philadelphia in 1787 is highest in the hierarchy of enacted law. Article VI of the Constitution declares:

> This Constitution, and the Laws of the United States which shall be made in Pursuance thereof; and all Treaties made, or which shall be made, under the Authority of the United States, shall be the supreme Law of the Land; and the Judges in every State shall be bound thereby, any Thing in the Constitution or Laws of any State to the Contrary notwithstanding.[6]

The clear import of these words is that the U.S. Constitution, federal law, and federal treaties take precedence over the constitutions and laws of the states and local jurisdictions.

Statutory law can be amended, repealed, or expanded by action of the legislature. States and local jurisdictions can only enact and enforce laws that do not conflict with federal law. Statutory laws can be declared void by a court; for example, a statute can be found unconstitutional because it does not comply with a state or federal constitution, because it is vague or ambiguous, or, in the case of a state law, because it is in conflict with a federal law.

In many cases involving statutory law, the court is called on to interpret how a statute applies to a given set of facts. For example, a statute can state merely that no person can discriminate against another person because of race, creed, color, or sex. A court can then be called on to decide whether certain actions by a person are discriminatory and therefore violate the law.

Administrative Law

Administrative law is the extensive body of public law issued by either state or federal agencies to direct the enacted laws of the federal and state governments. It is the branch of law that controls the administrative operations of government. Congress and state legislative bodies realistically cannot oversee their many laws; therefore, they delegate implementation and administration of the law to an appropriate administrative agency. Healthcare organizations in particular are inundated with a proliferation of administrative rules and regulations affecting every aspect of their operations.

The *Administrative Procedures Act*[7] describes the different procedures under which federal administrative agencies must operate.[8] The act prescribes the procedural responsibilities and authority of administrative agencies and provides for legal remedies for those wronged by agency actions. The regulatory power exercised by administrative agencies includes power to license, power of rate setting (e.g., Centers for Medicare and Medicaid Services [CMS]), and power over business practices (e.g., National Labor Relations Board [NLRB]).

Administrative agencies have legislative, judicial, and executive functions. They have the authority to formulate rules and regulations considered necessary to carry out the intent of legislative enactments. Regulatory agencies have the ability to legislate, adjudicate, and enforce their own regulations in many cases.

Rules and regulations established by an administrative agency must be administered within the scope of authority delegated to it by Congress. Although an agency must comply with its own regulations, agency regulations must be consistent with the statute under which they are promulgated. An agency's interpretation of a statute cannot supersede the language chosen by Congress. Executive regulations that define some general statutory term in a too-restrictive or unrealistic manner is invalid. Agency regulations and administrative decisions are subject to judicial review when questions arise as to whether an agency has overstepped its bounds in its interpretation of the law.

Recourse to an administrative agency for resolution of a dispute is generally required prior to seeking judicial review. The Pennsylvania Commonwealth Court held in *Fair Rest Home v. Commonwealth, Department of Health*[9] that the department of health was required to hold a hearing before it ordered revocation of a nursing home's operating license. The department of health failed in its responsibility when "in a revocation preceding it did not give careful consideration to its statutorily mandated responsibility to hear testimony."[10]

Conflict of Laws

When state and federal laws conflict, resolution can be sought in the appropriate federal court. The following case illustrates how federal and state laws can be in conflict. The plaintiff in *Dorsten v. Lapeer County General Hospital*[11] brought an action against a hospital and certain physicians on the medical board alleging wrongful denial of her application for medical staff privileges. The plaintiff asserted claims under the U.S. Code for sex discrimination,

violations of the Sherman Antitrust Act, and the like. The plaintiff filed a motion to compel discovery of peer-review reports to support her case. The U.S. District Court held that the plaintiff was entitled to discovery of peer-review reports despite a Michigan state law purporting to establish an absolute privilege for peer-review reports conducted by hospital review boards.

GOVERNMENT ETHICS

 I weep for the liberty of my country when I see at this early day of its successful experiment that corruption has been imputed to many members of the House of Representatives, and the rights of the people have been bartered for promises of office.

—ANDREW JACKSON

The words of Abraham Lincoln and Andrew Jackson, so eloquently spoken, resonate true today. Political corruption, antisocial behavior, declining civility, and rampant unethical conduct have heightened discussions over the nation's moral decline and decaying value systems. The numerous instances of questionable political decisions, executives with shocking salaries, dishonesty at work and in school, and the entertainment media have contributed to this decline. Legislators, investigators, prosecutors, and the courts have been quick to speak moral truths but continue to be slow in action. The question remains: Can the decline in ethical behavior be reversed as citizens struggle with a broken legal system inundated with new laws? The answer is more likely to be a return to practicing the virtues and values upon which this nation was founded. Ethics and the law are not mutually exclusive—they are intertwined throughout the text, providing an overview of government agencies designed to protect each individual's rights (e.g., the right to privacy and self-determination).

Office of Government Ethics

The *Office of Government Ethics* (OGE) is an agency within the executive branch of government. The agency was established by the Ethics in Government Act of 1978. Originally within the Office of Personnel Management, OGE became a separate agency on October 1, 1989. The Office of Government Ethics exercises leadership in the executive branch to prevent conflicts of interest on the part of government employees, and to resolve those conflicts of interest that do occur. In partnership with executive branch agencies and departments, OGE fosters high ethical standards for

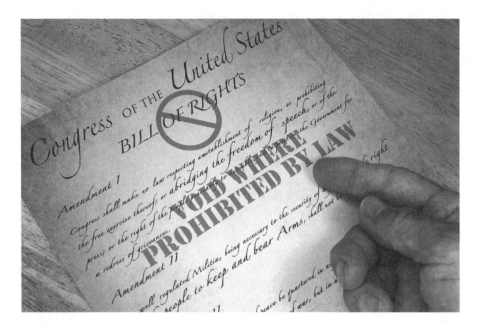

Figure 1–5 Constitution in Jeopardy   © iStockphoto/Thinkstock

employees and strengthens the public's confidence that the government's business is conducted with impartiality and integrity.[12]

The OGE website provides information about the agency and services it provides. The site helps people understand the executive branch ethics program and its effort to reach federal employees and the general public. Common ethical issues discussed on the website include gifts from outside sources, gifts between employees, conflicting financial interests, remedies for financial conflicts of interest, impartiality in performing official duties, seeking other employment, misuse of position, outside activities, postemployment, representation to government agencies and courts, supplementation of salary, financial disclosure, informal advisory letters and memorandum and formal opinions, DAEOgrams (memoranda to agency ethics officials providing guidance on how to interpret and comply with modifications or new issuances of ethics laws, policies, and procedures; copies of the memoranda released since 1992 are available in the DAEOgrams section of the OGE website), and contractors in the workplace.

U.S. House of Representatives Committee on Ethics

The Committee on Ethics is designated the "supervising ethics office" for the House of Representatives. The jurisdiction of the Committee on Ethics is derived from authority granted under House Rules and federal statutes.

The Committee on Ethics is unique in the House of Representatives. Consistent with the duty to carry out its advisory and enforcement responsibilities in an impartial manner, the Committee is the only standing committee of the House of Representatives with its membership divided evenly by party. These rules are intended to provide a fair procedural framework for the conduct of the Committee's activities and to help ensure that the Committee serves the people of the United States, the House of Representatives, and the Members, officers, and employees of the House of Representatives.[13]

The scope of the Committee's jurisdiction under the various authorizing rules and statutes involves duties and responsibilities related to:

- Jurisdiction over all bills, resolutions, and other matters relating to the Code of Official Conduct.
- Recommend administrative actions to establish or enforce standards of official conduct.
- Investigate alleged violations of the Code of Official Conduct or of any applicable rules, laws, or regulations governing the performance of official duties or the discharge of official responsibilities.
- Report to appropriate federal or state authorities substantial evidence of a violation of any law applicable to the performance of official duties that may have been disclosed in a committee investigation.
- Consider requests for written waivers of the gift rule.

- Oversight over foreign gifts and gifts to superiors and other Federal employees.
- Prohibits members, officers, and employees of the House of Representatives from soliciting or receiving gifts.[14]

U.S. Senate Select Committee on Ethics

(a) The ideal concept of public office, expressed by the words, "a public office is a public trust," signifies that the officer has been entrusted with public power by the people; that the officer holds this power in trust to be used only for their benefit and never for the benefit of himself or of a few; and that the officer must never conduct his own affairs so as to infringe on the public interest. All official conduct of Members of the Senate should be guided by this paramount concept of public office.[15]

The U.S. Senate Select Committee on Ethics consists of six members of the Senate, of whom three shall be selected from members of the majority party and three shall be selected from members of the minority party.[16] The committee is responsible for investigating complaints involving a violation of the Franking statute, Financial Disclosure Statements and for Outside Employment with respect to members, officers, and employees of the Senate, foreign gifts and decorations, gifts to an official superior or receiving gifts from employees with a lower salary level, prohibitions against members, officers, and employees of the Senate soliciting or receiving gifts.[17]

> The Senate Select Committee on Ethics is authorized to receive and investigate allegations of improper conduct which may reflect upon the Senate, violations of law, violations of the Senate Code of Official Conduct, and violations of rules and regulations of the Senate; recommend disciplinary action; recommend additional Senate rules or regulations to insure proper standards of conduct; and report violations of law to the proper federal and state authorities.[18]

Office of Congressional Ethics

The Office of Congressional Ethics (OCE) was created in March of 2008 as an independent, nonpartisan office governed by a board comprised of private citizens that provides more public review and insight into the ethical conduct of members of the House of Representatives. The OCE reviews allegations of misconduct against members, officers, and staff of the House and, when appropriate, refers matters to the House Committee on Ethics. The

OCE is not authorized to determine if a violation occurred nor it is it authorized to sanction members, officers, or employees of the House or to recommend sanctions. The OCE is not able to provide advice or education on the rules and standards of conduct applicable to members, officers, and employees of the House.[19] The mission of the OCE and its board is to assist the House in upholding high standards of ethical conduct for its members, officers, and staff and, in so doing, to serve the American people. The board of directors consists of eight members, which are private citizens and cannot serve as members of Congress or work for the federal government.[20] As the reader will note, there are a variety of laws and agencies that provide oversight and regulations that are designed to protect the right and safety of all citizens. Government is a reflection of the people it serves. Failure of the many to participate in the political process leads to government for the few who do.

Political Malpractice

> *The tragedy of society is not the noisiness of the so-called bad people, but the appalling silence of the so-called good people.*
> —Martin Luther King, Jr.

Like medical malpractice, political malpractice involves a failure to offer professional services to help prevent the travesties that take place daily, as illustrated by the following anonymous true story.

 REALITY CHECK: The Coal Miner

This is a story about a coal miner who had black lung disease. I had introduced myself to him as the administrator. He introduced himself to me as Jimmy. He then turned to a man who was on the opposite side of his bed and said, "This is my brother Bill." I asked, as he turned looking back at me, "Are we taking good care of you?" He said, "Yes." Bill, looking at me, choked up and asked, "Can you help my brother? He has given up the will to live. Please help my brother want to live." I looked at Jimmy lying there in his bed, fragile and struggling to breathe between each word, as he said, "I can no longer carry on this way. I am ready to move on. I'm a tired old man. I have fought so long. I've needed benefits for so many years for my family and myself. No one was able to help me. You see, I

(continued)

REALITY CHECK: The Coal Miner (continued)

have black lung disease. I can barely breathe." He then turned, looking over to Bill, and said, "My brother also has black lung disease. We worked together in the coalmines for many years. This is our reward." I looked at Jimmy and slowly back to Bill and said, "I will help you." As we said our goodbyes, I thought to myself, as I left the room, this man has fought so long. He has asked for so little, a man forgotten by a cruel system of corrupt government and greedy corporations. I remember this day all too well. It brings tears to my eyes as I recall the sadness of that day.

Discussion

1. What government agencies might be of help to Jimmy (e.g., OSHA).
2. Explain what action you would take to help Jimmy.
3. Describe the ethical principles that apply to this case.

 NEWSPAPER CLIPPINGS: Congressional Job Approval Ties Historic Low of 13%

Disapproval rating of 84% highest in Gallup annals

Americans' evaluation of the job Congress is doing is the worst Gallup has ever measured, with 13% approving, tying the all-time low measured in December 2010. Disapproval of Congress is at 84%, a percentage point higher than last December's previous high rating.

—*Jeffrey M. Jones,* Gallup, *August 16, 2011*

The failure of Congress to act when there is a duty to act by playing partisan politics is unconscionable to the citizens of the United States. It has occurred, for example, in financial and healthcare policy decision-making or lack thereof. Just indiscriminately objecting to every issue of the sitting president on a partisan basis continues to fall on the backs of the citizen whom Congress was elected to represent.

Ethicists in Public Service

Although not all cities may need to hire an ethicist in order to set priorities, it may be helpful in certain types of decisions. An independent, unbiased, professionally trained decision from an "outsider" may be more acceptable to councils, mayors, citizens, employees, or the press than one derived from inside the political process. This is particularly helpful in the decision to reduce or eliminate services to the public, especially services to the elderly, disabled, or less fortunate.[21]

✚ Notes

1. *Heritage of Yankton, Inc. v. South Dakota Dep't. of Health,* 432 N.W.2d 68, 77 (S.D. 1988).
2. United States Courts, Understanding Federal and State Courts, http://www.uscourts.gov/EducationalResources/ FederalCourtBasics/CourtStructure/UnderstandingFederalAndStateCourts.aspx.
3. *Marbury v. Madison,* 5 U.S. (Cranch) 137, 163 (1803).
4. *Pierce v. Ortho Pharmaceutical Corp.,* 417 A.2d 505, 512 (N.J. 1980).
5. *Black's Law Dictionary* (6th ed. 1990), 1305.
6. U.S. Constitution, art. 6, § 1, cl. 2.
7. 5 U.S.C.S. §§ 500–576 (Law. Co-op. 1989).
8. An "agency means each authority of the Government of the United States, . . . but does not include (A) the Congress; the Courts of the United States; . . ." 5 U.S.C.S. § 551(1) (Law. Co-op. 1989).
9. 401 A.2d 872 (Pa. Commw. Ct. 1979).
10. *Id.* at 873.
11. 88 F.R.D. 583 (E.D. Mich. 1980).
12. U.S. Office of Government Ethics, http://www.usoge.gov.
13. Committee on Ethics, Committee Rules, http://ethics. house.gov/about/committee-rules.
14. Committee on Ethics, Jurisdiction, http://ethics.house. gov/jurisdiction.
15. United States Senate Select Committee on Ethics, Jurisdiction, http://www.ethics.senate.gov/public/index.cfm/ jurisdiction.
16. U.S. Senate Select Committee on Ethics, Rules of Procedure, http://www.ethics.senate.gov/public/index.cfm/files/ serve?File_id=551b39fc-30ed-4b14-b0d3-1706608a6fcb.
17. U.S. Senate Select Committee on Ethics, Jurisdiction, http:// www.ethics.senate.gov/public/index.cfm/jurisdiction.
18. *Id.*
19. Office of Congressional Ethics, Frequently Asked Questions, http://oce.house.gov/faq.html.
20. *Id.*
21. Ethics in Public Service, "Alexandria hires ethics consultant," April 9, 2009; http://urpa5358group2.wordpress. com/2009/01/31/alexandria-hires-ethics-consultant/.

2
Healthcare Ethics

To laugh often and love much; to win the respect of intelligent persons and the affection of children; to earn the approbation of honest citizens and endure the betrayal of false friends; to appreciate beauty; to find the best in others; to give of one's self; to leave the world a bit better, whether by a healthy child, a garden patch or a redeemed social condition; to have played and laughed with enthusiasm and sung with exultation; to know even one life has breathed easier because you have lived—this is to have succeeded.

—BESSIE ANDERSON STANLEY

Figure 2–1   Socrates the Teacher   © Photos.com/Thinkstock

Learning Objectives

The reader upon completion of this chapter will be able to:

- Describe the concepts of ethics and morality.
- Describe how an understanding of ethical theories, principles, virtues, and values are helpful in resolving ethical dilemmas.
- Explain the relationship between spirituality and religion.
- Discuss *situational* ethics and how one's moral character can change as circumstances change.
- Explain how one's reasoning skills influence the decision-making process.

This chapter provides the reader with an overview of healthcare ethics and moral principles. Ethics and morals are derivatives from the Greek and Latin terms (roots) for custom. The intent here is not to burden the reader with the philosophical arguments surrounding ethical theories and moral principles, virtues, and values; however, as with the study of any new subject, "words are the tools of thought." Therefore, sufficient new vocabulary is presented to the reader in order to lay a foundation for applying the abstract theories and principles of ethics and make practical use of them.

ETHICS OVERVIEW

I expect to pass through this world but once. Any good therefore that I can do, or any kindness I can show to any creature, let me do it now. Let me not defer it, for I shall not pass this way again.

—Stephen Grellet[1]

Ethics is that branch of philosophy that seeks to understand the nature, purposes, justification, and the founding principles of moral rules and the systems they comprise. Ethics deals with values relating to human conduct. It focuses on the rightness and wrongness of actions, as well as the goodness and badness of motives and ends. Ethics encompasses the decision-making process of determining ultimate actions: What should I do, and is it the right thing to do? It involves how individuals decide to live, how they exist in harmony with the environment.

Ethics is also referred to as moral philosophy, the discipline concerned with what is morally good and bad, right and wrong. The term is also applied to any theoretical system of moral values or principles. Ethics is less concerned with factual knowledge than with virtues and values—namely, human conduct, as it ought to be, as opposed to what it actually is.

Microethics involves an individual's view of what is right and wrong based on life experiences.

Macroethics involves a more global view of right and wrong. Although no person lives in a vacuum, solving ethical dilemmas involves consideration of ethical issues from both a micro and macro perspective.

The term ethics is used in three different but related ways, signifying (1) philosophical ethics, which involves inquiry about ways of life and rules of conduct; (2) a general pattern or "way of life," such as religious ethics (e.g., Judeo-Christian ethics); and (3) a set of rules of conduct or "moral code," which involves professional ethics.

Bioethics addresses such difficult issues as the nature of life, the nature of death, what sort of life is worth living, how we should treat people who are especially vulnerable, and the responsibilities that we have to other human beings. It is about making the right judgments in difficult situations.

We study ethics to assist us in making sound judgments, good decisions, and right choices, or if not right choices, then better choices. To those in the healthcare industry, ethics is about anticipating and recognizing healthcare dilemmas and making good judgments and decisions based on the patient's needs and wishes and the universal values that work in unison with the laws of the land, our Constitution, and where the Constitution remains silent, we rely on the ability of caregivers to make the right choices using the wisdom of Solomon to do good.

MORALITY

Morality is a code of conduct. It is a guide to behavior that all rational persons put forward for governing their behavior. Morality describes a class of rules held by society to govern the conduct of its individual members.

Morals are ideas about what is right and what is wrong; for example, killing is wrong, whereas healing is right, and causing pain is wrong, whereas easing pain is right. Morals are deeply ingrained in culture and religion and are often part of its identity. Morals should not be confused with cultural habits or customs, such as wearing a certain style of clothing.

Moral judgments are those judgments concerned with what an individual or group believes to be the right or proper behavior in a given situation. It involves assessing another person's moral character based on how he or she conforms to the moral convictions established by the individual and/or group. What is considered to be right varies from nation to nation, culture to culture, religion to religion, as well as from one person to the next. In other words, there is no universal morality.

When it is important that disagreements be settled, morality is often legislated. Law is distinguished from morality by having explicit rules and penalties and officials who interpret the laws and apply the penalties as provided by law. There is often considerable overlap in "conduct" governed by morality and that governed by law. Laws are created to set boundaries for societal behavior. They are enforced to ensure that expected behavior is followed.

Making a *moral judgment* is being able to choose an option from among choices. It involves assessing another person's moral character based on how he or she conforms to the moral convictions established by the individual and/ or group. A lack of conformity can result in moral disapproval and possibly ridicule of one's character.

Codes of Conduct

Codes of conduct generally prescribe standards of conduct, states principles, expresses responsibilities, and defines rules expressing the duties of professionals to whom they apply. Most members of a profession subscribe to certain "values" and moral standards written into a formal document referred to as a *code of conduct*. Codes of conduct often require interpretation by caregivers as they apply to the specific circumstances surrounding each dilemma. Michael D. Bayles, a famous author and teacher, describes the distinction between standards, principles, and rules:

- *Standards* (e.g., honesty, respect for others, conscientiousness) are used to guide human conduct by stating desirable traits to be exhibited and undesirable ones (dishonesty, deceitfulness, self-interest) to be avoided.
- *Principles* describe responsibilities that do not specify what the required conduct should be. Professionals need to make a judgment about what is desirable in a particular situation based on accepted principles.
- *Rules* specify specific conduct; they do not allow for individual professional judgment.

▌ ETHICAL THEORIES

Ethics, too, are nothing but reverence for life. This is what gives me the fundamental principle of morality, namely, that good consists in maintaining, promoting, and enhancing life, and that destroying, injuring, and limiting life are evil.

—ALBERT SCHWEITZER

Ethical theories attempt to introduce order into the way people think about life and action. They are the foundation of ethical analysis and provide guidance in the decision-making process. The various theories present varying viewpoints that assist caregivers in making difficult decisions that impact the lives of others.

Ethics seeks to understand and to determine how human actions can be judged as right or wrong. Ethical judgments can be made based upon our own experiences or based upon the nature of or principles of reason. The following paragraphs provide a review of the more commonly discussed ethical theories.

Normative

The *normative theory* of ethics is the attempt to determine what moral standards should be followed so that human behavior and conduct may be morally right. Normative ethics is primarily concerned with establishing standards or norms for conduct and is commonly associated with general theories about how one ought to live. One of the central questions of modern normative ethics is whether human actions are to be judged right or wrong solely according to their consequences.

General normative ethics is the critical study of major moral precepts of such matters as what things are right, what things are good, and what things are genuine. General normative ethics is the determination of correct moral principles for all autonomous rational beings.

Applied ethics is the application of normative theories to practical moral problems. It attempts to explain and justify specific moral problems such as abortion, euthanasia, and assisted suicide.

Descriptive ethics, also known as comparative ethics, deals with what people believe to be right and wrong, whereas normative ethics prescribes how people ought to act.

Meta-ethics seeks to understand ethical terms and theories and their application.

Consequential

The *consequentialism theory* of ethics emphasizes that the morally right action is whatever action leads to the maximum balance of good over evil. From a contemporary standpoint, theories that judge actions by their consequences have been referred to as consequential ethics. Consequential ethical theories revolve around the premise that the rightness or wrongness of an action depends upon the consequences or effects of the action. The goal of a consequentialist is to achieve the greatest good for the greatest number of people. It involves asking the following questions:

- What will be the effects of each course of action?
- Will the effects be positive or negative?
- Who will benefit?
- What will do the least harm?

Utilitarian

Utilitarian ethics involves the concept that the moral worth of an action is solely determined by its contribution to overall usefulness. It describes doing the greatest good for the most people. It is thus a form of consequential ethics, meaning that the moral worth of an action is determined by its outcome, and thus, the ends justify the means.

Nonconsequential

The *nonconsequential theory* of ethics denies that the consequences of an action are the only criteria for determining the morality of an action. Under this theory, and as applied to healthcare decision-making, each situation may have a different fact pattern, thus resulting in moral decisions being made on a case-by-case basis. In this theory, the rightness or wrongness of an action is based on properties intrinsic to the action, not on its consequences.

The values held ever so strongly in one situation may conflict with the same values given a different set of facts. For example, if your plane crashed high in the Andes mountains and the only source of food for survival would be the flesh of those who did not survive, you may, if you wish to survive, have to give up your belief that it is morally wrong to eat the flesh of another human being. Given a different set of circumstances, given an abundance of food, you would most likely find it reprehensible to eat human flesh. Thus, in nonconsequential ethics, there are no effective hard and fast rules or guidelines to govern ethical behavior.

Deontology

Deontological ethics is commonly attributed to the German philosopher Immanuel Kant (1724–1804). Kant believed that although doing the right thing is good, it might not always lead to or increase the good and right thing sought after. It focuses on one's duties to others and others' rights. It includes telling the truth and keeping your promises. Deontological ethics is often referred to as *duty-based ethics*. It involves ethical analysis according to a moral code or rules: religious or secular. Deontology is derived from the Greek word meaning duty. Kant's theory differs from consequentialism in that consequences are not the determinant of what is right; therefore, doing the right thing may not always lead to an increase in what is good.

Ethical Relativism

"Ethical relativism is the theory that holds that morality is relative to the norms of one's culture. That is, whether an action is right or wrong depends on the moral norms of the society in which it is practiced. The same action may be morally right in one society but be morally wrong in another."[2] What is acceptable in one society may not be considered as acceptable in another society. Slavery may be considered an acceptable practice in one society and unacceptable and unconscionable in another. The administration of blood may be acceptable as to one's religious beliefs and not acceptable to another's religious beliefs.

The legal rights of patients vary from state to state, as is well borne out, for example, by Oregon's Death with Dignity Act. Caregivers must be aware of cultural, religious, and legal issues that can affect the boundaries of what is acceptable and what is unacceptable practice, especially when delivering health care to persons with beliefs different from their own. As the various cultures of the world merge together in common communities, the education and training of caregivers become more complex. Not only must the caregiver grasp the clinical skills of his or her profession, but he or she must also have a basic understanding of various cultures, what is right and what is wrong from both a legal and ethical point of view.

PRINCIPLES OF ETHICS

An army of principles can penetrate where an army of soldiers cannot.

—THOMAS JEFFERSON

Ethical principles are universal rules of conduct, derived from ethical theories that provide a practical basis for identifying what kinds of actions, intentions, and motives are valued. Ethical principles assist caregivers in making choices based on moral principles that have been identified as standards considered worthwhile in addressing healthcare related ethical dilemmas. As noted by the principles discussed in the following sections, caregivers, in the study of ethics, will find that difficult decisions often involve choices between conflicting ethical principles.

Autonomy

No right is held more sacred, or is more carefully guarded, by the common law, than the right of every individual to the possession and control of his own person, free from all restraint or interference of others, unless by clear and unquestioned authority of law.

—UNION PAC. RY. CO. V. BOTSFORD,
141 U.S. 250, 251 (1891)

The principle of autonomy involves recognizing the right of a person to make one's own decisions. *Auto* comes from a Greek word meaning "self" or "individual." In this context, *autonomy* is recognizing an individual's right to make his or her own decisions about what is best for him or herself. Autonomy is not an absolute principle, meaning that the autonomous actions of one person must not infringe upon the rights of another.

Each person has a right to make his or her own decisions about health care. A patient has the right to refuse to receive health care even if it is beneficial to saving his or her life. Patients can refuse treatment, refuse to take medications, refuse blood or blood by-products, and refuse invasive procedures regardless of the benefits that may be derived from them. They have a right to have their decisions followed by family members who may disagree simply because they are unable to let go. Although patients have a right to make their own choices, they also have a concomitant right to know the risks, benefits, and alternatives to recommended procedures.

Autonomous decision-making can be affected by one's disabilities, mental status, maturity, or incapacity to make decisions. Although the principle of autonomy may be inapplicable in certain cases, one's autonomous wishes may be carried out through an advance directive and/or an appointed healthcare agent in the event of one's inability to make decisions.

Life or Death: The Right to Choose

A Jehovah's Witness executed a release requesting that no blood or its derivatives be administered during hospitalization. The Connecticut Superior Court determined that the hospital had no common law right or obligation to thrust unwanted medical care on the patient because she had been sufficiently informed of the consequences of the refusal to accept blood transfusions. She had competently and clearly declined that care. The hospital's interests were sufficiently protected by her informed choice, and neither it nor the trial court in this case was entitled to override that choice.[3]

Beneficence

Beneficence describes the principle of doing good, demonstrating kindness, showing compassion, and helping others. In the healthcare setting, caregivers demonstrate beneficence by balancing benefits against risks. Beneficence requires one to do good. Doing good requires knowledge of the beliefs, culture, values, and preferences of the patient— what one person may believe to be good for a patient may

in reality be harmful. For example, a caregiver may decide that a patient should be told frankly, "There is nothing else that I can do for you." This could be injurious to the patient if the patient really wants encouragement and information about care options from the caregiver. Compassion here requires the caregiver to explain to the patient, "I am not aware of new treatments for your illness; however, I have some ideas about how I can help treat your symptoms and make you more comfortable. In addition, I will keep you informed as to any significant research and clinical trials that may be helpful in treating your disease processes."

Paternalism is a form of beneficence. People sometimes believe that they know what is best for another and make decisions that they believe are in that person's best interest. It may involve, for example, withholding information, believing that the person would be better off that way. Paternalism can occur due to one's age, cognitive ability, and level of dependency.

 REALITY CHECK: Paternalism and Breach of Confidentiality

Vicky traveled with her husband, Dan, to a work assignment in Michigan. While visiting with her brother in Michigan, Vicky believed that her potassium was low, which was a frequent occurrence with her for many years. Vicky's brother suggested she could have her blood tested at a local blooddrawing station. Dan later learned Vicky's potassium was low.

Later that morning, while at work, Joan, Dan's colleague, called Bill, Dan's supervisor, to discuss Vicky's health. Bill, however, had overslept and had not yet arrived at work. Joan decided to speak to the supervisor on call. After that conversation, Joan, being led by three staff members from the organization, tracked Dan down on several occasions that morning. On the first occasion, at approximately 10:15 A.M., Dan was surveying the organization's family practice center when Joan arrived. She rudely called Dan aside, excusing the organization's staff from the immediate area. Joan said, with surprise, "Dan, you are working?" Dan, even more surprised at the question, "Yes, I have been working." Joan replied, "Well, anyway, the corporate office wants to speak to you." Dan said he would call during lunch hour. Joan, somewhat agitated, walked away.

Joan again tracked Dan down with an entourage of the organization's staff at 11:30 A.M. She located Dan

(continued)

REALITY CHECK: Paternalism and Breach of Confidentiality (continued)

while he was in the organization's transfusion center. Again she rudely entered the conference room where Dan was discussing the care being rendered to a cancer patient. She once again asked in a stern tone of voice, "Could everyone please leave the room. I need to talk to Dan." The organization's staff left the room and the nurse said, "I finally reached Bill and he wants you to call him." Dan inquired, "Is he pulling me off this assignment?" The nurse replied, "Yes, he is. I spoke to Bill, and he has decided that out of concern for Vicky you should be removed from this particular assignment. He wants you to call him." Dan replied, "I don't understand why you did this, calling Bill and continuously interrupting my work and sharing with others confidential information about my wife. I will wrap up with the staff my review of this patient and call Bill." As Joan left the conference room Dan said, "I trusted you and you shared confidential information about my wife?" Joan, realizing that she had no right to share the information quickly walked away.

Dan called Bill during his lunch break. During that call Bill said, "I am going to remove you from your assignment because I think your wife's health needs should be addressed, and this could be disruptive to the survey." Dan replied, "The only disruption has been the nurse tracking me down with staff from the organization and not conducting her work activities." Bill said, "My decision stands. You can opt to take vacation time for the remainder of the week."

Discussion

1. Discuss what examples of paternalism you have gleaned from this case.
2. Do you think Dan was treated fairly? Discuss your answer.
3. Discuss the issues of trust, confidentiality, and fairness as they relate to this case.

Medical paternalism involves making decisions for patients who are capable of making their own choices. Physicians often find themselves in situations where they can influence a patient's healthcare decision simply by selectively telling the patient what he or she prefers based on personal beliefs. This directly violates patient autonomy. The problem of paternalism involves a conflict between the principles of autonomy and beneficence, each of which may be viewed and weighed differently, for example, by the physician and patient, physician and family member, or even the patient and a family member.

Nonmaleficence

Nonmaleficence is an ethical principle that requires caregivers to avoid causing patients harm. It derives from the ancient maxim *primum non nocere*, translated from the Latin, "first, do no harm." Physicians today still swear by the code of Hippocrates, pledging to do no harm. Medical ethics require healthcare providers to "first, do no harm." In *In re Conroy*, 464 A.2d 303, 314 (N.J. Super. Ct. App. Div. 1983), a New Jersey court found that "the physician's primary obligation is . . . First do no harm." Telling the truth, for example, can sometimes cause harm. If there is no cure for a patient's disease, you may have a dilemma. Do I tell the patient and possibly cause serious psychological harm, or do I give the patient what I consider to be false hopes? Is there a middle ground? If so, what is it? To avoid causing harm, alternatives may need to be considered in solving the ethical dilemma.

The caregiver, realizing that he or she cannot help a particular patient, attempts to avoid harming the patient. This is done as a caution against taking a serious risk with the patient or doing something that has no immediate or long-term benefits.

The principle of nonmaleficence is broken when a physician is placed in the position of ending life by removing respirators, giving lethal injections, or by writing prescriptions for lethal doses of medication. Helping patients die violates the physician's duty to save lives. There needs to be a clearer distinction between euthanasia and allowing a patient to die.

Justice

Justice is the obligation to be fair in the distribution of benefits and risks. Justice demands that persons in similar circumstances be treated similarly. A person is treated justly when he or she receives what is due, deserved, or can legitimately be claimed. Justice involves how people are treated when their interests compete with one another.

Distributive justice is a principle requiring that all persons be treated equally and fairly. No one person, for example, should get a disproportionate share of society's resources or benefits. There are many ethical issues involved in the rationing of health care. This is often due to limited or scarce resources, limited access due to geographic remoteness, or a patient's inability to pay for services combined with many physicians who are unwilling to accept patients who are perceived as "no pays" or high risks for legal suits.

VIRTUES AND VALUES

Virtues focus on the inherent character of a person rather than on the specific actions that he or she performs. Virtues are those characteristics that differentiate good people from bad people. A morally virtuous person is one who does the good and right thing by *habit.*

Values are standards of conduct. They are used for judging the goodness or badness of some action. Values are the standards by which we measure the goodness in our lives. *Intrinsic value* is something that has value in and of itself (e.g., happiness). *Instrumental value* is something that helps to give value to something else (e.g., money is valuable for what it can buy).

The emphasis one places on a particular value may change as needs change. If one's basic needs for food, water, clothing, and housing have not been met, one's values may change such that a friendship, for example, might be sacrificed if one's basic needs can be better met as a result of the sacrifice. If mom's estate is being squandered at the end of her life, the financially well-off family member may want to take more aggressive measures to keep mom alive despite the financial drain on her estate. Another family member, who is struggling financially, may more readily see the futility of expensive medical care and find it easier to let go. Values give purpose to each life. They make up one's moral character.

All people make value judgments and make choices among alternatives. Values are the motivating power of a person's actions and necessary for survival, both psychologically and physically.

We begin our discussion here with an overview of those virtues commonly accepted as having value when addressing difficult healthcare dilemmas. The reader should not get overly caught up in the philosophical morass of how virtues and values differ but should be aware that virtues and values have been used interchangeably.

Whether we call compassion a virtue or a value or both, the importance for our purposes in this text is to understand what compassion is and how it is applied in the healthcare setting.

Pillars of Moral Strength

 I am part of all I have met.
—ALFRED TENNYSON

What are the pillars that build one's moral strength? What sets each person apart? In the final analysis, one's moral character and strength can be determined by the degree to which he or she has embraced the virtues and values discussed below. Look beyond the words and ask, "Do I know their meanings?" "Do I apply their concepts?" "Do I know their value?" "Are they part of me?"

This book and this chapter are not about memorizing words but about applying what we learn for the good of all whose lives we touch. Discussion here begins with an overview of those virtues commonly accepted as having value when addressing difficult dilemmas.

Figure 2–2 Pillars of Moral Strength

Courage

Courage is the greatest of all virtues, because if you haven't courage, you may not have an opportunity to use any of the others.

—Samuel Johnson

Courage is the mental or moral strength to persevere and withstand danger. "Courage is the ladder on which all the other virtues mount."[4] Courage is the strength of character necessary to continue in the face of fears and the challenges in life. It involves balancing fear, self-confidence, and values. Without courage, we are unable to take the risks necessary to achieve the things most valued. A courageous person has good judgment and a clear sense of his or her strengths, correctly evaluates danger, and perseveres until a decision is made and the goal that is being sought has been achieved.

REALITY CHECK: My Journey—How Lucky Am I?

No words can be scripted to say what I have been through, so I will just speak from my heart and off the cuff. From the day the Dr. said to me, "Denise, you have a rare cancer and we are sorry there is nothing we can do. I did not waver in my faith in God. He was in me, he was thru me and he was around me. I just asked the Dr., "What Do I Do?" And yet, although he said a whole bunch of words, I wasn't focused so much on what was being said. It's like a calmness was over me, not much worry, just a feeling of I will never be ALONE on this new journey I'm about to experience. I felt calm. Not until I looked at my loved ones FACES did I realize, oh my, this can be bad. But again, a feeling came over me that I will not face this ALONE. God has plans for me and I will surrender in his grace and as time past, I realized how lucky and blessed I am, for most people who may feel that death may be close by, I didn't feel that way. What I felt was WOW!! Everyone gets to show me their love in the NOW and not in the later when I am no longer HERE. How lucky am I.

—Denise

Courage, in differing degrees, helps to define one's character (the essence of one's being) and offers the strength to stand up for what is good and right. It crosses over and unites and affects all other values. Courage must not be exercised to an extreme, causing a person to become so foolish that his or her actions are later regretted.

When the passion to destroy another human being becomes such an obsession that one is willing to sacrifice the lives of others, that person has become a bully and a coward and not a person of courage. History is filled with those men and women who have hidden their fears by inciting others to do evil. Such people are not the models of character that we wish to instill thoughts of in the minds of our children.

Wisdom

You can't inherit wisdom, You can't be taught wisdom. You can't learn wisdom. Wisdom is a God given gift.

—GP

True wisdom comes to each of us when we realize how little we understand about life, ourselves, and the world around us.

—Socrates

Wisdom is the judicious application of knowledge. Marcus Tullius Cicero (106–43 bc), a Roman philosopher and politician, is reported to have said, "The function of wisdom is to discriminate between good and evil." In the healthcare setting, when the patient's wishes and end-of-life preferences are unknown, wisdom along with good judgment without bias or prejudice is mandatory.

Temperance

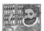
Being forced to work, and forced to do your best, will breed in your temperance and self-control, diligence and strength of will, cheerfulness and content, and a hundred virtues, which the idle will never know.

—Charles Kingsley[5]

Temperance has to do with orderliness and moderation in everything that is said and done.

Commitment

I know the price of success: dedication, hard work, and an unremitting devotion to the things you want to see happen.

—Frank Lloyd Wright

Commitment is the act of binding oneself (intellectually or emotionally) to a course of action. It is an agreement or pledge to do something. It can be ongoing or a pledge to do something in the future.

Compassion

Compassion is the basis of morality.
—Arnold Schopenhauer

Compassion is a moral value expected of all caregivers. Those who lack compassion have a weakness in their moral character. Dr. Linda Peeno's compassion was evident when she testified before the Committee on Commerce on May 30, 1996. She stated that she had been hired as a claims reviewer for several health maintenance organizations (HMOs). Here is her story in part:

> I wish to begin by making a public confession. In the spring of 1987, I caused the death of a man. Although this was known to many people, I have not been taken before any court of law or called to account for this in any professional or public forum. In fact, just the opposite occurred. I was rewarded for this. It brought me an improved reputation in my job and contributed to my advancement afterwards. Not only did I demonstrate that I could do what was asked, expected of me, I exemplified the good company employee. I saved a half a million dollars.
>
> Since that day, I have lived with this act and many others eating into my heart and soul. The primary ethical norm is do no harm. I did worse, I caused death. Instead of using a clumsy bloody weapon, I used the simplest, cleanest of tools: my words. This man died because I denied him a necessary operation to save his heart. I felt little pain or remorse at the time. The man's faceless distance soothed my conscience. Like a skilled soldier, I was trained for the moment. When any moral qualms arose, I was to remember, "I am not denying care; I am only denying payment."[6]

Although Dr. Peeno came forward with her story, the lack of compassion for others plagues the healthcare industry in a variety of settings.

Detachment, or lack of concern for the patient's needs, is what often translates into mistakes that often result in patient injuries. As with all things in life, there needs to be a comfortable balance between compassion and detachment.

REALITY CHECK: Compassion Comes in Different Forms

Annie, a 27-year-old woman with two children, began experiencing severe pain in her abdomen while visiting her family in May 2002. After complaining of pain to Mark, her husband, in June 2002, he scheduled Annie an appointment with Dr. Roberts, a gastroenterologist, who ordered a series of tests. While conducting a barium scan, a radiologist at Community Hospital noted a small bowel obstruction. Dr. Roberts recommended surgery, and Annie agreed to it.

After the surgery, on July 7, Dr. Brown, the operating surgeon, paged Mark over the hospital intercom as he walked down a corridor on the ground floor. Mark, hearing the page, picked up a house phone and dialed zero for an operator. The operator inquired, "May I help you?" "Yes," Mark replied. "I was just paged." "Oh, yes. Dr. Brown would like to talk to you. I will connect you with him. Hang on. Don't hang up." (Mark's heart began to pound.) Dr. Brown asked, "Is this you, Mark?" Mark replied, "Yes, it is." Dr. Brown replied, "Well, surgery is over. Your wife is recovering nicely in the recovery room." Mark was relieved but for a moment. "That's good." Mark sensed Dr. Brown had more to say. Dr. Brown continued, "I am sorry to say that she has carcinoma of the colon." Mark replied, "Did you get it all?" Dr. Brown reluctantly replied, "I am sorry, but the cancer has spread to her lymph nodes and surrounding organs." Mark, as he within the tears, asked, "Can I see her?" Dr. Brown replied, "She is in the recovery room." Before hanging up, Mark told Dr. Brown, "Please do not tell Annie that she has cancer. I want her to always have hope." Dr. Brown agreed, "Don't worry, I won't tell her. You can tell her that she had a narrowing of the colon."

Mark hung up the phone and proceeded to the recovery room. After entering the recovery room, he spotted his wife. His heart sank. Tubes seemed to be running out of every part of her body. He walked to her bedside. His immediate concern was to see her wake up and have the tubes pulled out so that he could take her home.

Later, in a hospital room, Annie asked Mark, "What did the doctor find?" Mark replied, "He found a narrowing of the colon." "Am I going to be okay?" "Yes, but it will take a while to recover." "Oh, that's good. I was so worried," said Annie. "You go home and get some rest." Mark said, "I'll be back later," as Annie fell back to sleep.

Mark left the hospital and went to see his friends, Jerry and Helen, who had invited him for dinner. As Mark pulled up to Jerry and Helen's home, he got out of his car and just stood there looking up a long

(continued)

REALITY CHECK: Compassion Comes
in Different Forms (continued)

stairway leading to Jerry and Helen's home. They were standing there looking down at Mark. It was early evening. The sun was setting. A warm breeze was blowing, and Helen's eyes were watering. Those few moments seemed like a lifetime. Mark discovered a new emotion, as he stood there speechless. He knew then that he was losing a part of himself. Things would never be the same.

Annie had one more surgery two months later in a futile attempt to extend her life. In November 2002, Annie was admitted to the hospital for the last time. Annie was so ill that even during her last moments she was unaware that she was dying. Dr. Brown entered the room and asked Mark, "Can I see you for a few moments?" "Yes," Mark replied. He followed Dr. Brown into the hallway. "Mark, I can keep Annie alive for a few more days, or we can let her go." Mark, not responding, went back into the room. He was now alone with Annie. Shortly thereafter, a nurse walked into the room and gave Annie an injection. Mark asked, "What did you give her?" The nurse replied, "Something to make her more comfortable." Annie had been asleep; she awoke, looked at Mark, and said, "Could you please cancel my appointment to be sworn in as a citizen? I will have to reschedule. I don't think I will be well enough to go." Mark replied, "Okay, try to get some rest." Annie closed her eyes, never to open them again.

Discussion

1. Do you agree with Mark's decision not to tell Annie about the seriousness of her illness? Explain your answer.
2. Should the physician have spoken to Annie as to the seriousness of her illness? Explain your answer.
3. Describe the ethical dilemmas in this case (e.g., how Annie's rights were violated).
4. Place yourself in Annie's shoes, the physician's shoes, and Mark's shoes, and then discuss how the lives of each may have been different if the physician had informed Annie as to the seriousness of her illness.

Conscientious

 The most infectiously joyous men and women are those who forget themselves in thinking about and serving others.

—ROBERT J. MCCRACKEN

A *conscientious* person is one who has moral integrity and a strict regard for doing what is considered the right thing to do. An individual acts conscientiously if he or she is motivated to do what is right, believing it is the right thing to do. *Conscience* is a form of self-reflection on and judgment about whether one's actions are right or wrong, good or bad. It is an internal sanction that comes into play through critical reflection. This sanction often appears as a bad conscience in the form of painful feelings of remorse, guilt, shame, disunity, or disharmony as the individual recognizes that his or her acts were wrong.

Discernment

 Get to know two things about a man. How he earns his money and how he spends it. You will then have the clue to his character. You will have a searchlight that shows up the innermost recesses of his soul. You know all you need to know about his standards, his motives, his driving desires, and his real religion.

—ROBERT J. MCCRACKEN

Discernment is the ability to make a good decision without personal biases, fears, and undue influences from others. A person who has discernment has the wisdom to decide the best course of action when there are many possible actions to choose from.

Fairness

 Do all the good you can, By all the means you can, In all the ways you can, In all the places you can, At all the times you can, To all the people you can, As long as you ever can.

—JOHN WESLEY[7]

In ethics, fairness requires each person to be objective, unbiased, dispassionate, impartial, and consistent with the principles of ethics. *Fairness* is the ability to make judgments free from discrimination, dishonesty, or one's own bias. It is the ability to be objective without prejudice or bias. We often tolerate mediocrity. We sometimes forget to thank those who just do their jobs, and we often praise the extraordinary, sometimes despite questionable faults. To be fair, it is important to see the good in all and to reward that good.

REALITY CHECK: Integrity has Limits

Bill, a quality improvement consultant hired by the board, was praised during the presentation for his quality improvement report. He was treated with kindness and assurances as to how well he helped the staff and how employees appreciated his suggestions for improvement. Prior to exiting the conference room, Bill asked whether there were any questions about his report. No questions, just smiles, accolades, and good-byes. Jeff thought to himself, wow, it is good to see good people take suggestions and be so willing to make the changes that Bill suggested.

Hold on; it turns out Bill wasn't as wonderful as he had been applauded to be. The group was now disgruntled with his report. Bill was gone and now criticized and berated. Jeff, who was still in the room, was not scheduled to finish his assignment for another 2 weeks, asked, "Why didn't you ask questions while Bill was here?" Carol, the finance director replied, "I spent 2 weeks with Bill. He just made up his mind. There was just no changing his mind." Jeff said, "Are you saying that you disagree with Bill's report?" Carol, replied, "Yes, I do disagree with it." Jeff continued, "But you did not state that while he was here. You told him you liked his suggestions and that you were already in the process of implementing them." Carol replied, "That's true, but since we made the suggested changes while he was here, he did not have to include them in his report. Now I look bad in that report." Jeff replied, "It speaks well of your organization that you have done so; however, it is the board that asked for the audit. We must report what we found." Carol, disgruntled, said, "Well Jeff you are doing a super job and the feedback from staff has been nothing but praise, but as to Bill, ugh."

Discussion

1. Were Carol's remarks during and after Bill left the conference room a fair representation of her integrity? Discuss your answer.
2. Discuss Bill's responsibilities to the board, which had hired the consulting team to evaluate the organization's operations.

3. What is Jeff thinking? He has to be in the organization another 2 weeks. How would you write your report? Keep in mind that Carol and her fellow department managers also evaluate the consultants as well with Bill and Jeff's managers.

Fidelity

Nothing is more noble, nothing more venerable, than fidelity. Faithfulness and truth are the most sacred excellences and endowments of the human mind.

—CICERO

Fidelity is the virtue of faithfulness, being true to our commitments and obligations to others. A component of fidelity, *veracity*, implies that we will be truthful and honest in all our endeavors. It involves being faithful and loyal to obligations, duties, or observances. The opposite of fidelity is infidelity, meaning unfaithfulness.

Freedom

You can only protect your liberties in this world by protecting the other man's freedom. You can only be free if I am free.

—DOROTHY THOMPSON

Freedom is the quality of being free to make choices for oneself within the boundaries of law. Freedoms sometimes forgotten and taken for granted but always cherished include freedom of speech, freedom of religion, freedom from want, and freedom from physical aggression.

Honesty/Trustworthiness/Truth Telling

Lies or the appearance of lies are not what the writers of our Constitution intended for our country, it's not the America we salute every Fourth of July, it's not the America we learned about in school, and it is not the America represented in the flag that rises above our land.

—AUTHOR UNKNOWN

Speaking the truth in times of universal deceit is a revolutionary act.

—GEORGE ORWELL

Honesty and trust involve confidence that a person will act with the right motives. It is the assured reliance on the character, ability, strength, or truth of someone or something. To tell the truth, to have integrity, and to be honest are most honorable virtues. Veracity is devotion to and conformity with what is truthful. It involves an obligation to be truthful.

REALITY CHECK: 36,000 Feet over Texas

A few weeks before Frank was to travel to Dodge City, Texas, for a work assignment, he received a call from Dr. Layblame: "Hi Frank. This is Dr. Layblame. Can you be ready for an early afternoon departure from Dodge City on Friday?" Frank replied, "Well you know we have been instructed not to leave early, and the last flight leaves at 4:30 P.M. Anyway, I don't mind flying out Saturday morning." Dr. Layblame replied, "Well, it's only an hour early. If you do most of your work the night before and during lunch on Friday, we should be able to finish up work by 2:30 P.M. The airport is small and close to the hospital. Besides, my team has to drive to Louisiana and we would like to get there early and go to dinner and enjoy the evening. I am the tour leader, so it should not be a problem." Frank said OK and scheduled a 4:30 P.M. return flight.

While Frank was on a flight to Washington, DC following his work assignment, Ronald, Frank's supervisor was dictating a voicemail message to him. When Frank returned home at about 10:30 that evening, he retrieved his voice mail messages. Ronald had left Frank a message at 4:30 P.M. earlier that day asking Frank, "Call me as soon as you get this message. I will be in my office until about 5:30 P.M. If you miss me, you can reach me over the weekend. My cell phone number is xxx/xxx-xxxx."

Frank called Ronald that evening and the next morning; however, Ronald never answered, nor did he return his call. Frank called Ronald Monday morning. As luck would have it, Ronald was out of the office for the day. Frank called Ronald again on Tuesday morning and Ronald answered. Frank asked, "Ronald, you called?" He replied, "Yes, I did. How were you able to get to the airport on Friday and catch a 4:30 P.M. flight without leaving your job early? I had your flight schedule and you left the survey early. You could not possibly have traveled to the airport in time to catch your flight without leaving early."

Frank replied, "I did not schedule the exit time from the survey. The physician team leader determined the time of the exit. He said that he was conducting a system tour and would like to get the exit briefing started as soon as possible. He asked for everybody to be ready to exit by having draft reports ready the night before." Ronald replied,

"Dr. Layblame told me the team had to exit early because you scheduled an early flight."

Frank asked, "Just one question Ronald, why would leave a message for me at 4:30 P.M. to call you at 5:30 P.M. when you knew I was 36,000 feet high in the sky? And why didn't you call the team leader at the beginning of the assignment and not after it was completed? Since you know flight schedules, why would you wait until the assignment was completed to raise this issue? Sounds a bit peculiar, don't you think? Sort of like observing a protocol not being followed in the OR and then chastising the OR team after the surgery is completed for not following protocol. This is a serious business we are in. You need to ask yourself why you would allow an event to occur if you believed it to be wrong."

Discussion

1. Discuss the ethical issues involved in this case.
2. Discuss what you would do if you found yourself in Frank's situation.
3. What should Frank have said if his manager said, "You should have reported Dr. Layblame"?
4. How would you describe Ronald's management style?

Truth telling, from a patient's perspective, involves providing enough information so that a patient can make an informed decision about his or her health care. Intentionally misleading a patient to believe something that the caregiver knows to be untrue may give the patient false hopes. There is always apprehension when one must share bad news; the temptation is to retreat from the truth for fear of being the bearer of bad news. To lessen the pain and the hurt is only human, but in the end, truth must triumph over fear.

Integrity

 Nearly all men can stand adversity, but if you want to test a man's character, give him power.
—ABRAHAM LINCOLN

Integrity involves a steadfast adherence to a strict moral or ethical code and a commitment not to compromise this code. A person with integrity has a staunch belief in and faithfulness to, for example, his or her religious beliefs, values, and moral character. Patients and professionals alike often make healthcare decisions based on their integrity and their strict moral beliefs. For example, a Jehovah's Witness generally refuses a blood transfusion because it is against his or her religious beliefs, even if such refusal may result in death. A provider of health care may refuse to participate in an abortion because it is against his or her moral beliefs. A person without personal integrity lacks sincerity and moral conviction and may fail to act on professed moral beliefs.

 REALITY CHECK: Employee Satisfaction Survey

The human resources department manager was reporting on an employee satisfaction survey at a leadership roundtable session with the organization's employees. To maintain employee confidentiality, a third-party consulting firm had conducted the survey. Approximately 49% of employees had responded to the survey, compared with 47% 3 years earlier. The HR manager commented that it is was the first satisfaction survey conducted in 3 years and that the results were excellent, with a 4.2% rise in overall employee satisfaction. Management was all smiles as they sat listening to the report. The HR manager had actually briefed the organization's leadership prior to the roundtable session. Following the report, she asked if there were any questions. The silence was deadly—no one responded. Finally, one employee, Richard, placed his hands on the table to stand up, but he felt a nudge on his right shoulder from Phil, a physician friend. Phil whispered, "Richard, are you sure you want to ask any questions? There is nothing to gain here." Richard, looking down with a smile, said, "I agree, but I can't help myself." Richard then stood up and asked the HR manager, "Do you know what the employee turnover rate has been during the past 3 years?" She responded, "Well, ugh, yes, it was about 30%." Richard replied, "So, then, does this report reflect that we have had a 30% turnover?" The manager replied, "Good point, I will have to get back to you on that." When he returned to his seat, Phil said, "Do you really think you will ever hear back an answer to your question?" Richard smiled and replied, "Not really." Richard was right; she never did get back to him.

Discussion

1. Discuss why employees are often reluctant to ask questions when their questions are solicited by leadership.
2. Knowing that the HR manager never followed up with Richard, should he have followed up with the manager as to the validity of the survey data? Explain your answer.

Kindness

 When you carry out acts of kindness, you get a wonderful feeling inside. It is as though something inside your body responds and says, yes, this is how I ought to feel.

—Harold Kushner

Kindness involves the quality of being considerate and sympathetic to another's needs. Some people are takers, and others are givers. If you go through life giving without the anticipation of receiving, you will be a kinder and happier person.

Respect

 Respect for ourselves guides our morals; respect for others guides our manners.

—Laurence Sterne

Respect is an attitude of admiration or esteem. Kant was the first major Western philosopher to put respect for persons, including oneself as a person, at the center of moral theory. He believed that persons are ends in themselves with an absolute dignity, which must always be respected. In contemporary thinking, respect has become a core ideal extending moral respect to things other than persons, including all things in nature.

Hopefulness

 Hope is the last thing that dies in man; and though it be exceedingly deceitful, yet it is of this good use to us, that while we are traveling through life, it conducts us in an easier and more pleasant way to our journey's end.

—Frans de la Rochefoucauld

Hopefulness in the patient care setting involves looking forward to something with the confidence of success. Caregivers have a responsibility to balance truthfulness while promoting hope. The caregiver must be sensitive to each patient's needs and provide hope.

Tolerance

 There is a criterion by which you can judge whether the thoughts you are thinking and the things you are doing are right for you. The criterion is: Have they brought you inner peace? If they have not, there is something wrong with them—so keep seeking! If what you do has brought you inner peace, stay with what you believe is right.

—Peace Pilgrim

Tolerance can be viewed in two ways, positive or negative. (1) *Positive tolerance* implies that a person accepts differences in others and that one does not expect others to believe, think, speak, or act as him or herself. Tolerant people are generally free of prejudice and discrimination. Recognizing this fact, Thomas Jefferson incorporated theories of tolerance into the U.S. Constitution. (2) *Negative tolerance* implies that one will reluctantly put up with another's beliefs. In other words, they simply tolerate the view of others.

Although tolerance can be viewed as a virtue, not all tolerance is virtuous. For example, it is more virtuous to have intolerance for governments that slaughter its own people than tolerating such despicable acts.

Education as a Value

It is expected and required that healthcare professionals have a current understanding of one's area of specialization and practice. Every professional is responsible to be current in his or her knowledge and skills. Competency comes by participating in one's professional organization, staying current by reading one's professional journals, attending in-services and continuing education programs, and mentoring.

▌ SPIRITUALITY AND RELIGION

Spirituality in the religious sense implies that there is purpose and meaning to life; spirituality generally refers to faith in a higher being. For a patient, injury and sickness are frightening experiences. Healthcare organizations can help reduce patient fears by making available to them appropriate emotional and spiritual support and coping resources. It is a well-proven fact that patients who are able to draw on their spirituality and religious beliefs tend to have a more comfortable and often improved healing experience. To assist both patients and caregivers in addressing spiritual needs, patients should be provided with information as to how their spiritual needs can be addressed.

Religion serves a moral purpose by providing codes of conduct for appropriate behavior through revelations from a divine source. These codes of conduct are often enforced through fear of pain and suffering in the next life and/or reward in the next life for adhering to religious codes and beliefs. The prospect of divine justice helps us to tolerate the injustices in this life where goodness is no guarantee of peace, happiness, wellness, or prosperity.

NEWSPAPER CLIPPINGS: Many Think God's Intervention Can Revive the Dying

When it comes to saving lives, God trumps doctors for many Americans. An eye-opening survey reveals widespread belief that divine intervention can revive dying patients. And, researchers said, doctors "need to be prepared to deal with families who are waiting for a miracle."

—*Lindsey Tanner, The Capital, August 19, 2008*

Religion should be a component part of the education, policy development, and consultative functions of ethics committees. Some hospitals provide staff with materials that describe various religious beliefs and how those beliefs might affect the patient's course of care while in the hospital.

Religion is often used as a reason to justify what, otherwise, could be considered unjustifiable behavior. Political leaders often use religion to legitimize and consolidate their power. Leaders in democratic societies speak of the necessity to respect the right to "freedom of religion."

Political leaders often use religion to further their political aspirations. They have often used religion to justify their actions. Religious persecution has plagued humanity from the beginning of time. The world today, with the aid of the news media, is able to see firsthand the results of what can happen to innocent people in the name of religion. The atrocities of evil people strapping bombs to the mentally deficient with the purpose of blowing themselves up in public places, killing and maiming men, women, and children, are but a few of the numerous atrocities of what has occurred throughout the ages.

Difficult questions regarding a patient's spiritual needs and how to meet those needs are best addressed by first collecting information about the patient's religious or spiritual preferences. Caregivers often find it difficult to discuss spiritual issues for fear of offending a patient who may have beliefs different from their own. If caregivers are aware of a patient's religious beliefs, they can share with the patient pertinent religious and spiritual resources available in the hospital and community.

A variety of religions are presented in the following sections for the purpose of understanding some of the basic tenets of these religions. They are presented here to note the importance of better understanding why patients differ in decision-making processes and how religion affects one's beliefs and to encourage further study of how each religion affects the decision-making process. Hospitals should maintain a directory of various religions that includes contacts for referral and consultation purposes.

Judaism

Jewish Law is the unchangeable 613 mitzvah (commandments) that God gave to the Jews. Halacha (Jewish Law) comes from three sources: (1) the Torah (the first five books of the Bible); (2) laws instituted by the rabbis; and (3) long-standing customs. The *Jewish People* is another name for the Children of Israel, referring to the Jews as a nation in the classical sense, meaning a group of people with a shared history and a sense of a group identity rather than a specific place or political persuasion.[8]

Judaism is a monotheistic religion based on principles and ethics embodied in the Hebrew Bible (Old Testament). The notion of right and wrong is not so much an object of philosophical inquiry as an acceptance of divine revelation. Moses, for example, received a list of 10 laws directly from God. These laws were known as the Ten Commandments. Some of the Ten Commandments are related to the basic principles of justice that have been adhered to by society since they were first proclaimed and published. For some societies, the Ten Commandments were a turning point, where essential commands such as "thou shalt not kill" or "thou shalt not commit adultery" were accepted as law.

When caring for the dying, family members will normally want to be present and prayers spoken. If a rabbi is requested, the patient's own rabbi should be contacted first.[9]

Hinduism

Hinduism is a polytheistic religion with many gods and goddesses. Hindus believe that God is everything and is infinite. The earliest known Hindu Scriptures were recorded around 1200 BC. Hindus believe in reincarnation and that one's present condition is a reflection of one's virtuous behavior or lack thereof in a previous lifetime.

When caring for the dying, relatives may wish to perform rituals at this time. In death, jewelry, sacred threads, or other religious objects should not be removed from the body. Washing the body is part of the funeral rites and should be carried out by the relatives.[10]

Buddhism

Buddhism is a religion and philosophy encompassing a variety of traditions, beliefs, and practices, largely based on teachings attributed to the Indian prince named Siddhartha Gautama (563–483 BC). He had gone on a spiritual quest and is said to have become enlightened at the age of 35, and he took the name Buddha. Simply defined, Buddhism is a religion to some and a philosophy to others that encourages one "to do good, avoid evil, and purify the mind."

When caring for the dying, Buddhists like to be informed about their health status in order to prepare themselves spiritually.[11]

Falun Gong

Falun Gong, also referred to as *Falun Dafa*, is a traditional Chinese spiritual discipline belonging to the Buddhist school of thought. It consists of moral teachings, a meditation, and four exercises that resemble tai chi and are known in Chinese culture as *qigong*. Falun Gong does not involve physical places of worship, formal hierarchies, rituals, or membership and is taught without charge. The three principles practiced by the followers are *truthfulness*, *compassion*, and *forbearance/tolerance* toward others. The followers of Falun Gong claim a following in 100 countries.

Taoism

Taoists believe that ultimate reality is unknowable and unperceivable. The founder of Taoism is believed to be Lao Tzu (6 BC). Taoism doctrine includes the belief that the proper way of living involves being in tune with nature. Everything is ultimately interblended and interacts.

Zen

Zen evolved from Buddhism in Tibet. It emphasizes dharma practice (from the master to the disciple) and experiential wisdom based on learning through the reflection, going beyond scriptural readings. In Zen, Buddhism learning comes through a form of seated meditation known as *zazen*, where practitioners perform meditation to calm the body and the mind, experience insight into the nature of existence, and thereby gain enlightenment.

Christianity

Christianity is based on the Bible's New Testament teachings. Christians accept both the Old and New Testament as being the word of God. The New Testament describes Jesus as being God, taking the form of man. He was born of the Virgin Mary and ultimately sacrificed his life by suffering crucifixion, and after being raised from the dead on the third day, he ascended into Heaven from which he will return to raise the dead, at which time the spiritual body will be united with the physical body. His death, burial, and resurrection provide a way of salvation through belief in Him for the forgiveness of sin. God is believed to be manifest in three persons: the Father, Son, and Holy Spirit.

The primary and final authority for Christian ethics is found in the life, teachings, ministry, death, and resurrection of Jesus Christ. He clarified the ethical demands of a God-centered life by applying the obedient love that was required of Peter. The Ten Commandments are accepted and practiced by both Christians and Jews.

Christians, when determining what the right thing to do is, often refer to the Golden Rule, which teaches us to "do unto others as you would have them do unto you," a common principle in many moral codes and religions.

There have been and continues to be numerous interpretations of the meaning of the scriptures and its different passages by Christians over the centuries. This has resulted in a plethora of churches with varying beliefs. As noted later, such beliefs can affect a patient's wishes for health care.

However, the heart of Christian belief is found in the book of John:

For God so loved the world, that he gave his only begotten and Son, that whoever believeth in him should not perish but have everlasting life.
                                        —KING JAMES VERSION, JOHN 3:16

The Apostle Paul proclaimed that salvation cannot be gained through good works but through faith in Jesus Christ as savior. He recognized the importance of faith in Christ over good works in the pursuit of salvation.

Jehovah's Witnesses

Religious beliefs and codes of conduct sometimes conflict with the ethical duty of caregivers to save lives. Many Jehovah's Witnesses, for example, believe that it is a sin to accept a blood transfusion since the Bible states that we must "abstain from blood" (Acts 15:29). Current Jehovah's Witness doctrine, in part, states that blood must not be transfused. In order to respect this belief, bloodless surgery is available in a number of hospitals to patients who find it against their religious beliefs to receive a blood transfusion.

Every attempt should be made to resolve blood transfusion issues prior to any elective surgery. In the case of emergent unconscious patients, a blood transfusion may be necessary to save the patient's life. Emergent transfusions are generally acceptable by the courts. When transfusion

of a minor becomes necessary and parental consent is refused, it may be necessary to seek a court order to allow for such transfusions. Time is of the essence in many cases, making it necessary for hospitals to work out such issues in advance with legislative bodies and the judicial system in order to provide legal protection for caregivers who find it necessary to transfuse blood in order to save a life. In those instances in which the patient has a right to refuse a blood transfusion, the hospital should seek a formal signed release from the patient.

Anointing of the Sick

When caring for the dying, services of the in-house chaplain must always be offered. A Catholic priest should be offered in those instances where last rites need to be administered.

Islam

The Islamic religion believes there is one God: Allah. Muhammad (570–632 AD) is considered to be a prophet/messenger of God. He is believed to have received revelations from God. These revelations were recorded in the Qur'an, the Muslim Holy Book. Muslims accept Moses and Jesus as prophets of God. The Qur'an is believed to supersede that of the Torah and the Bible. Muslims believe that there is no need for God's Grace and that their own actions can merit God's mercy and goodness. Humans are believed to have a moral responsibility to submit to God's will and to follow Islam as demonstrated in the Qur'an. The five pillars of the practice of Islam are: believing the creed, performing five prayers daily, giving alms, fasting during Ramadan, and making a pilgrimage to Mecca at least once in a lifetime.

When caring for the dying, patients may want to die facing Mecca (toward the southeast) and be with relatives. In death, many Muslims follow strict rules in respect of the body after death.[12]

SECULAR ETHICS

Unlike religious ethics, secular ethics are based on codes developed by societies that have relied on customs to formulate their codes. The Code of Hammurabi, for example, carved on a black Babylonian column 8 feet high, now located in the Louvre in Paris, depicts a mythical sun god presenting a code of laws to Hammurabi, a great military leader and ruler of Babylon (1795–1750 BC). Hammurabi's code of laws is an early example of a ruler proclaiming to his people an entire body of laws. The Code of Hammurabi, for example provides, "215: If a physician make a large incision with an operating knife and cure it, or if he open a tumor (over the eye) with an operating knife, and saves the eye, he shall receive ten shekels in money."

Atheism

Atheism is the rejection of belief in any god, generally because atheists believe there is no scientific evidence that can prove God exists. They argue that there is no objective moral standard for right and wrong and that ethics and morality are the products of culture and politics and are subject to individual convictions.

Those of various religious faiths, however, believe there is overwhelming evidence that there is reason to believe that God does exist and that the evidence through historical documents, archeological finds, and the vastness of space and time clearly supports and confirms the existence of God. Christians often refer to the Old Testament and cite the Book of Isaiah:

It is He that sitteth upon the circle of the earth . . .

—KJV ISAIAH 40:22

Christians argue when citing this verse, that Isaiah could not possibly have known that the earth is the shape of a circle. He presents no magical formula or scientific argument in his writings as to why the earth is round. Furthermore, Isaiah does not belabor the fact that the earth is round. The argument continues in the Book of Job:

He stretcheth out the north over the empty place, and hangeth the earth upon nothing.

—KJV JOB 26:7

The obvious question arises as to how Job knew 3,000 years before it became a scientific verifiable fact the earth hangs upon nothing.

SITUATIONAL ETHICS

Be careful how you judge others. . . . As Scottish author J.M. Barrie said, 'Never ascribe to an opponent motives meaner than your own.' We tend to judge others based on their behavior, and ours based on our intent. In almost all situations, we would do well to recognize the possibility even the probability of good intent in others . . . sometimes despite their observable behavior.
—STEPHEN M.R. COVEY, *THE SPEED OF TRUST* (FREE PRESS)

Situational ethics is concerned with the outcome or consequences of an action in which the ends can justify the means. Why do good people behave differently in similar situations? Why do good people sometimes do bad things? The answer is fairly simple: One's moral character can sometimes change as circumstances change; thus the term *situational ethics*. A person, therefore, may contradict what he believes is the right thing to do and do what he morally considers wrong. For example, a decision not to use extraordinary means to sustain the life of an unknown 84-year-old may result in a different decision if the 84-year-old is one's mother. To better understand this concept, consider the desire to live, and the extreme measures one will take in order to do so. Remember that *ethical decision-making* is the process of determining the right thing to do in the event of a moral dilemma.

REASONING AND DECISION-MAKING

Reason guides our attempt to understand the world about us. Both reason and compassion guide our efforts to apply that knowledge ethically, to understand other people, and have ethical relationships with other people.

—MOLLEEN MATSUMURA

The logical application of reasoning is important in the decision-making process. "Knowing" ethical theories, principles, values, and morals, and "understanding" how to apply them must go hand in hand. Reason includes the capacity for logical inference and the ability to conduct inquiry, solve problems, evaluate, criticize, and deliberate about how we should act and to reach an understanding of other people, the world, and ourselves.[13] *Partial reasoning* involves bias for or against a person based on one's relationship with that person. *Circular reasoning* describes a person who has already made up his or her mind on a particular issue and sees no need for deliberation.

Ethics in decision-making involves the process of deciding the right thing to do when facing a moral dilemma. Decision-making is not easy when there is more than one road, an alternative route, to take. *Ethical dilemmas* occur when ideas of right and wrong conflict. They arise in situations where a choice must be made between unpleasant alternatives. They occur whenever a choice must be made that involves giving up something good and suffering something bad, no matter what course of action is taken. Ethical dilemmas often require caregivers to make decisions that may break some ethical norm or contradict some ethical value. They involve conflict between values, rights, duties, and loyalties. Consequently, not everyone is satisfied with a particular decision.

Healthcare Dilemmas

Healthcare dilemmas often occur when there are alternative choices, limited resources, and differing values among patients, family members, and caregivers. Coming to an agreement may mean sacrificing one's personal wishes and following the road where there is consensus. Consensus building can happen only when the parties involved can sit and reason together. The process of identifying the various alternatives to an ethical dilemma, determining the pros and cons of each choice, and making informed decisions requires a clear unbiased willingness to listen, learn, and, in the end, make an informed decision.

Healthcare dilemmas arise when, for example, the principles of autonomy and beneficence conflict with one another. The following case illustrates how one's right to make his or her decision can conflict with the principle of doing no harm.

REALITY CHECK: A Patient's Journey: Need for Change

During the past 5 years, I have filled out numerous standardized forms requiring answers to questions that have been repeatedly asked by a wide variety of physician specialists and other caregivers. I've been told that my most recent specialist had great credentials. He came highly recommended. I grew more hopeful as I drove to his office during the early morning rush hour in Washington, DC. I would finally meet someone who cared and understood my disease processes. As I walked into his office, I noted that my medical chart was lying on the desk in front of him. The sight of it on his desk comforted me, thinking that he had actually read the answers. His staff had said he wanted them several weeks prior to my appointment because he needed time to familiarize himself with my case. I soon realized several minutes into the conversation that he had not reviewed my medical chart. The forms that I had so painstakingly completed, hoping for an answer to my illness, had not been read. He inquired as to what medications I was taking. My husband accompanied me that day and noticed that the list of medications was laid in front of him; he didn't hesitate to point

that out to the physician. The doctor asked questions within a predetermined range, one was, "What is your pain on a scale of 1 to 10?" How do I answer that? I am off your scale. I cannot remember not being in pain for the past 5 years. I sometimes wonder what it must have been like to be pain-free. I don't know that feeling anymore. Hello, is anyone out there?

Eventually, I was admitted to the hospital for the first time. My nerve endings felt frayed, my stomach churned, worries were multiplying, and my thoughts turned to, "Is it time to get more bad news?" I was extremely ill. The sitting area in the admissions office was uncomfortable and uninviting. Privacy was minimal and soft music was nonexistent. I wondered what was going to happen to me.

Things got worse when I was finally admitted to a room. Now, I had to stay in an unfamiliar room staring at drab, nondescript walls, and was dependent upon people who hardly had the time to dispense medications. Most physicians and other staff members were rushing about, engaged in their everyday tasks. No one seemed to have time for me.

Confusion set in, and the fear of being in a strange place caused me tremendous anxiety. Unfamiliar people looked at me, touched me, and repeatedly asked me the same questions over and over again. The questioning seemed never ending. And then I wondered, "Do these people ever talk to each other?" The surroundings were sterile and unfriendly, adding to my uneasy feelings.

Why can't healthcare facilities be more patient-friendly to those they serve? Why must I worry about complaining and fear of retribution? Provisions should be made for a serene environment with calming colors and carefully chosen people to gently ease answers from a frightened patient. More attention is needed in making a patient's room a calm and inviting place, which would help to soothe and carry the patient through troubling times.

—Anonymous

SUMMARY THOUGHTS

 The world is a dangerous place. Not because of the people who are evil; but because of the people who don't do anything about it.

—ALBERT EINSTEIN

Political corruption, antisocial behavior, declining civility, and rampant unethical conduct have heightened discussions over the nation's moral decline and decaying value systems. The nation's "moral compass has gone astray." Legislators, investigators, prosecutors, and the courts are finally stepping up to the plate and are taking action. The question, however, remains: Can this boat be turned around, or are we just plugging the holes with new laws and creating more leaks in a misdirected sinking boat? The answer is more likely to be a return to practicing the values upon which this nation was founded. If the lessons of history are ignored, society is destined to repeat the mistakes of the past.

 Be careful of your thoughts, for your thoughts inspire your words. Be careful of your words, for your words precede your actions. Be careful of your actions, for your actions become your habits. Be careful of your habits, for your habits build your character. Be careful of your character, for your character decides your destiny.

—Chinese Proverb

Although you cannot control the amount of time you have in this lifetime, you can control your behavior by adopting the virtues and values discussed in this chapter that will define who you are, what you will become, and how you will be remembered or forgotten.

Become who you want to be and how you want to be remembered. The formula is easy and well described in the previous quote in what has been claimed to be a Chinese proverb. Read it. Reread it. Write it. Memorize it. Display it in your home, at work, and most of all, practice it, always remembering it all begins with thoughts.

 My words fly up, my thoughts remain below: Words without thoughts never to heaven go.

—William Shakespeare

Control your thoughts, and do not let them control you. As to words, they are the tools of thought. They can be sharper than any double-edged sword and hurt, or, they can do good and heal.

It is never too late to change your thoughts, as long as you have air to breathe. Your legacy may be short, but it can be powerful.

The Final Analysis

 People are often unreasonable, illogical and self-centered; forgive them anyway. If you are kind, people may accuse you of selfish, ulterior motives; be kind anyway. If you are successful, you will win some false friends and some true enemies; succeed anyway. What you spend years building, someone may destroy overnight; build anyway. The good you do today, people will often forget tomorrow; do good anyway. Give the world the best you have, and it may never be enough; give the world the best you have anyway. You see, in the final analysis, it is between you and God; It was never between you and them anyway.

—Mother Teresa

Notes

1. French/American religious leader (1773–1855).
2. Santa Clara University, "Ethical Relativism," http://www.scu.edu/ethics/practicing/decision/ethicalrelativism.html (accessed October 13, 2010).
3. *Stamford Hosp. v. Vega*, 674 A.2d 821 (Conn. Super. Ct. 1996).
4. Albert Schweitzer, *Cultural Philosophy II: Civilization and Ethics* (London: A. & C. Black, 1929).
5. British Anglican clergyman, teacher, and writer (1819–1875).
6. "Important Issue Facing House-Senate Conference on Health Care Reform," http://www.fenichel.com/Ganske.shtml (accessed October 13, 2010).
7. Evangelist and founder of Methodism (1703–1791).
8. Tracey R. Rich, "Halakhah: Jewish Law," http://www.jewfaq.org/halakhah.htm (accessed October 13, 2010).
9. St. George's Healthcare, "A Guide to Faith and Culture," http://www.stgeorges.nhs.uk/docs/Diversity/MultiFaithGuidance2006.pdf (accessed October 13, 2010).
10. *Id.*
11. *Id.*
12. *Id.*
13. George Lakoff and Mark Johnson, *Philosophy in the Flesh* (New York: Basic Books, 1999), 3–4.

I was created at the end of the Renaissance, watched pirates rule the oceans as Ivan the Terrible ruled Russia, and witnessed the arrest of Galileo for believing the earth revolved around the sun.

—I AM HISTORY

3
Reflections on the Past

Figure 3–1   Hospital Ward   © chippix/ShutterStock, Inc.

Learning Objectives

The reader upon completion of this chapter will be able to:

- Explain how the conflicts of society due to politics, religion, and warfare have often impeded the growth of hospitals and at times contributed to their progression and many successes.
- Describe how the advances in medicine led to the rise of the modern day hospital and improved upon the quality of patient care.
- Explain the purpose of the *Patient Protection and Affordable Care Act.*

- Describe how advances in medicine over the centuries have not consistently been followed and continue to serve as reminders of the need to understand and build upon best practices.

This chapter provides the reader with a brief overview of the advance of civilization as disclosed in the history of hospitals, including some of the many milestones in medicine, as well as religious and political influences through the centuries to the present day. A study of the past often reveals errors that can often be avoided, customs that persist only because of tradition, and practices that have been superseded by others that are more effectual.

The importance of the study of history is undeniable. The Spanish philosopher George Santayana (1863–1952) recognized this all too well when he said, "Those who cannot remember the past are condemned to repeat it." George Bernard Shaw (1856–1950) an Irish dramatist and socialist recognized the tragedies of the history of civilization when he said, "If history repeats itself, and the unexpected always happens, how incapable must man be of learning from experience." Yes, Santayana and Shaw are right; if we don't learn from the mistakes of the past we are doomed to repeat them. Progress in health care will only prevail as long as advances in medicine are remembered and practiced by each new generation.

The past can bring to light some long-abandoned practices, which can be revived to some advantage. The story of the birth and evolution of the hospital portrays the triumph of civilization over barbarism and the progress of civilization toward an ideal characterized by an interest in the welfare of all humanity. Although the struggle to progress is a road filled with many pitfalls, hope still looms.

 We can learn from history how past generations thought and acted, how they responded to the demands of their time and how they solved their problems. We can learn by analogy, not by example, for our circumstances will always be different than theirs were. The main thing history can teach us is that human actions have consequences and that certain choices, once made, cannot be undone. They foreclose the possibility of making other choices and thus they determine future events.

—GERDA LERNER[1]

EARLY HINDU AND EGYPTIAN HOSPITALS

Two ancient civilizations, India and Egypt, had crude hospitals. Hindu literature reveals that in the 6th century BC, Buddha appointed a physician for every 10 villages and built hospitals for the crippled and the poor. His son, Upatiso, built shelters for the diseased and for pregnant women. These examples most likely moved Buddha's devotees to erect similar hospitals. Historians agree that hospitals existed in Ceylon as early as 437 BC.

During his reign from 273 to 232 BC, King Asoka built 18 hospitals that hold historical significance because of their similarities to the modern hospital. Attendants gave gentle care to the sick, provided patients with fresh fruits and vegetables, prepared their medicines, gave massages, and maintained their personal cleanliness. Hindu physicians, adept at surgery, were required to take daily baths,

keep their hair and nails short, wear white clothes, and promise that they would respect the confidence of their patients. Although bedside care was outstanding for those times, medicine was only beginning to find its way.

Egyptian physicians were probably the first to use drugs such as alum, peppermint, castor oil, and opium. In surgery, anesthesia consisted of hitting the patient on the head with a wooden mallet to render the patient unconscious. Surgery was largely limited to fractures, and medical treatment was usually given in the home. Therapy away from home was often available in temples, which functioned as hospitals.

GREEK AND ROMAN HOSPITALS

The term "hospital" derives from the Latin word *hospitalist*, which relates to guests and their treatment. The word reflects the early use of these institutions not merely as places of healing but as havens for the poor and weary travelers. Hospitals first appeared in Greece as *aesculapia*, named after the Greek god of medicine, Aesculapius. For many centuries, hospitals developed in association with religious institutions, such as the Hindu hospitals opened in Sri Lanka in the 5th century BC and the monastery-based European hospitals of the Middle Ages (5th century to 15th century). The Hotel-Dieu in Paris, France a monastic hospital, was founded in 660 and is located next to Notre Dame. Although there were disastrous fires and financial crises over the centuries, it was rebuilt and remains in operation today.

In early Greek and Roman civilization, when medical practices were rife with mysticism and superstitions, temples were also used as hospitals. Every sanctuary had a sacred altar before which the patient, dressed in white, was required to present gifts and offer prayers. If a patient was healed, the cure was credited to miracles and divine visitations. If the patient remained ill or died, he or she was considered to be lacking in purity and unworthy to live.

Greek temples provided refuge for the sick. One of these sanctuaries, dedicated to Aesculapius, is said to have existed as early as 1134 BC at Titanus. Ruins attest to the existence of another, more famous Greek temple built several centuries later in the Hieron, or sacred grove, at Epidaurius. Here physicians ministered to the sick holistically in body and soul. They prescribed medications such as salt, honey, and water from a sacred spring. They gave patients hot and cold baths to promote speedy cures and encouraged long hours of sunshine and sea air, combined with pleasant vistas, as an important part of treatment. The temple hospitals housed libraries and rooms for visitors, attendants, priests, and physicians. The temple at Epidaurius even boasted what might be described as the site of the first clinical records. The columns of the temple were inscribed with the names of patients, brief histories of their cases, and comments as to whether or not they were cured.

The aesculapia spread rapidly throughout the Roman Empire as well as through the Greek world. Although some hospitals were simply spas, others followed the therapy outlined by the leading physicians of the day. Hippocrates, for example, a physician born about 460 BC, advocated medical theories that have startling similarity to those of the present day. He employed the principles of percussion and auscultation, wrote intelligently on fractures, performed numerous surgical operations, and described such conditions as epilepsy, tuberculosis, malaria, and ulcers. He also kept detailed clinical records of many of his patients. Physicians like Hippocrates not only cared for patients in the temples but also gave instruction to young medical students.

HOSPITALS OF THE EARLY CHRISTIAN ERA

Christianity and the doctrines preached by Jesus stressing the emotions of love and pity gave impetus to the establishment of hospitals, which, with the advance of Christianity, became integral parts of the church institution. These Christian hospitals replaced those of Greece and Rome and were devoted entirely to care of the sick, and they accommodated patients in buildings outside the church proper.

The decree of Constantine in 335 closed the aesculapia and stimulated the building of Christian hospitals, which, during the 4th and 5th centuries, reached the peak of their development. Many were erected by the rulers of the period or by wealthy Romans who had converted to Christianity. By the year 500, most large towns in the Roman Empire had erected hospitals. Nursing during this period was inspired by religion. It was gentle and considerate of patients. The medical precepts of Hippocrates, Antyllus, and other early Greek physicians were eventually discarded because of their pagan origins. Instead, health care turned toward mysticism and theurgy (the working of a divine agency in human affairs) as sources of healing. No provision appears to have been made for care of the thousands of helpless paupers who had been slaves and were later set free when Christianity was introduced into the Roman Empire.

Hospitals rarely succeeded during the centuries leading to the Middle Ages. Only a few existed outside Italian cities. Occasional almshouses in Europe sheltered some of the sick, while inns along the Roman roads housed others.

ISLAMIC HOSPITALS

The followers of Mohammed were almost as zealous as the Christians in caring for the sick. In Baghdad, Cairo, Damascus, Cordova, and many other cities under their control, luxurious hospital accommodations were frequently provided. Harun al-Rashid, the glamorous caliph (a title for a religious or civil ruler claiming succession from Muhammad) of Baghdad (786–809), built a system of hospitals. Medical care in these hospitals was free. About four centuries later, in 1160, a Jewish traveler reported that he had found as many as 60 dispensaries and infirmaries in Baghdad alone. The Persian physician Rhazes, who lived from about 850 to 923, was skilled in surgery. He was probably the first to use the intestines of sheep for suturing and cleansing patient wounds with alcohol.

Islamic physicians like Rhazes received much of their medical knowledge from the persecuted Christian sect known as the Nestorians. Nestorius (Archbishop of Constantinople from April 428 to August 431) was driven into the desert with his followers and took up the study of medicine. The school at Edessa in Mesopotamia, with its two large hospitals, eventually came under the control of the Nestorians in which they established a remarkable teaching institution. Eventually driven out of Mesopotamia by the orthodox bishop Cyrus, they fled to Persia, establishing the famous school at Gundishapur, which is conceded to be the true starting point of Islamic medicine. Gundishapur was home to the world's oldest known teaching hospital and also contained a library and a university. It was located in the present-day province of Khuzistan, in the southwest of Iran, not far from the Karun river.

Islamic medicine had flourished until the 15th century. Physicians were acquainted with the possibilities of inhalation anesthesia. They instituted precautions against adulteration of drugs and developed a vast number of new drugs. Islamic countries also built asylums for the mentally ill a thousand years before such institutions appeared in Europe. The people of Islam made a brilliant start in medicine but never fulfilled the great promise that glowed in their early work in medical arts and hospitalization. Wars, politics, superstitions, and a nonprogressive philosophy stunted the growth of a system that had influenced the development of hospitals.

LY MILITARY HOSPITALS

Engraved on a limestone pillar dating back to the Sumerians (2920 BC) are pictures, which, among other military procedures, show the assemblage of the wounded. The Biblical books of Deuteronomy and Leviticus record that Moses provided rules of military hygiene. Out of the urgency of care for the wounded in battle came much of the impetus for medical progress. Hippocrates is quoted as saying that "war is the only proper school for a surgeon." Under the Romans, surgery advanced largely because of experience gained through gladiatorial and military surgery.

Throughout the centuries, warfare has been a two-edged sword, producing tragic events and at the same time providing an environment for the advancement of surgery and medicine. From an ethical point of view, the question arises, what surgical and medical advancements have been lost due to the failure of mankind to sit at the table of peace and compromise on differences based on logic and reason? Arguments between individuals and nations are best settled through a positive approach that must have as its basis, reasonable compromise, as opposed to a negative approach, often involving who has the most lethal weapons.

MEDIEVAL HOSPITALS

Religion continued to dominate the establishment of hospitals during the Middle Ages. A number of religious orders created *hospitia* or travelers' rests and infirmaries adjacent to monasteries that provided food and temporary shelter for weary travelers and pilgrims. One of these, the famous alpine hospice of St. Bernard founded in 962, gave comfort to the weary and sent its renowned dogs to the rescue of lost mountain climbers.

The hospital movement grew rapidly during the Crusades, which began in 1096. Military hospital orders sprang up, and accommodations for sick and exhausted crusaders were provided along well-traveled roads. One body of crusaders organized the Hospitallers of the Order of St. John, which in 1099 established in the Holy Land a hospital capable of caring for 2,000 patients. Knights of this order took personal charge of service to patients and often denied themselves so that the sick might have food and medical care. For years, these institutions were the best examples of hospitals of that period.

Although physicians cared for physical ailments to afford relief, they rarely attempted to cure the sick. Dissection of a human body would have been sacrilege because the body was created in the image of God.

Religion continued to be the most important factor in the establishment of hospitals during the Middle Ages. A number of religious orders created travelers' rests and infirmaries adjacent to monasteries that provided food and temporary shelter for weary travelers and pilgrims.

Finally, an active period of hospital growth came during the late 12th and early 13th centuries. In 1198, Pope Innocent III urged that hospitals of the Holy Spirit be provided for the citizenry of many towns. He set an example by founding a model hospital in Rome, known as Santo Spirito in Sassia. Built in 1204, it survived until 1922 when it was destroyed by fire. In Rome, nine other hospitals were founded shortly after completion of the one in Sassia. It is estimated that in Germany alone 155 towns had hospitals of the Holy Spirit during early medieval times.

Although most hospitals erected during the Middle Ages were associated with monasteries or founded by religious groups, a few cities, particularly in England, built municipal institutions. Like all hospitals of the period, the buildings were costly, often decorated with colorful tapestries and stained glass windows, but the interiors often consisted of large, drafty halls with beds lining each side. A few of the better institutions were arranged on the ward plan, usually built in the shape of a cross. Floors were made of red brick or stone, and the only ventilation came from the cupola in the ceiling.

With the spread of leprosy during the 12th and 13th centuries, lazar houses sprang up, supplying additional hospital facilities. Crude structures, lazar houses were usually built on the outskirts of towns and maintained for the segregation of lepers rather than for their treatment. Special groups of attendants, including members of the Order of St. Lazar, nursed the patients. The group represented an important social and hygienic movement because their actions served to check the spread of epidemics through isolation. The group is credited for virtually stamping out leprosy.

During the same period of hospital growth, three famous London institutions were established: St. Bartholomew's in 1137, St. Thomas's before 1207, and St. Mary of Bethlehem in 1247. St. Bartholomew's cared for the sick poor, but unlike like many hospitals of that day, it was well organized. A woman who was later canonized as St. Mary Overie founded St. Thomas's Hospital. It burned in 1207, was rebuilt 6 years later, and constructed again on a new site in 1228. St. Mary of Bethlehem was the first English hospital to be used exclusively for the mentally ill.

The Hotel-Dieu of Paris is portrayed as one of the better hospitals of the Middle Ages. The current architecture has been dated back to 1877. The hospital provided four principal rooms for patients in various stages of disease, as well as a room for convalescents and another for maternity patients. Illustrations by artists of the time show that two persons generally shared one bed. Heavy curtains sometimes hung from canopies over the bed to afford privacy, but this advantage was more than offset by the fact that the draperies, never washed, spread infection and prevented free ventilation. The institution was self-contained, maintaining a bakery, herb garden, and farm. Often, patients who had fully recovered remained at the hospital to work on the farm or in the garden for several days in appreciation for the care they had received.

THE "DARK AGE" OF HOSPITALS

Pictures and records of many hospitals during the Middle Ages illustrate how many hospitals commonly crowded several patients into one bed regardless of the type or seriousness of illness. A mildly ill patient might be placed in the same bed as an occupant suffering from a contagious disease. A notable exception to the general deterioration in medicine during this era was the effort of those monks who copied by hand and preserved the writings of Hippocrates and other ancient physicians.

The great Al-Mansur Hospital, built in Cairo in 1276, struck a contrast to the European institutions of the Middle Ages. It was equipped with separate wards for the more serious diseases and outpatient clinics. The handful of hospitals like Al-Mansur would lay the groundwork for hospital progress to come in later centuries.

HOSPITALS OF THE RENAISSANCE

During the revival of learning around the close of the 14th century, hundreds of medical hospitals in Western Europe received the new, more inquiring surgeons that the Renaissance produced. New drugs were developed, anatomy became a recognized study, and ancient Greek writings were printed. Leonardo da Vinci, known as the originator of cross-sectional anatomy, and Vesalius, performed dissection. Hospitals also became more organized. Memoranda from 1569 describe the duties of the medical staff in the civil hospital of Padua, a city that was home to the most famous medical school during the 16th century. These read:

> There shall be a doctor of physic upon whom rests the duty of visiting all the poor patients in the building, females as well as males; a doctor of surgery whose duty it is to apply ointments to all the poor people in the hospital who have wounds of any kind; and a barber who is competent to do, for the women as well as the men, all the other things that a good surgeon usually does.[2]

The practice of surgery during the Renaissance became more scientific. The long-robe surgeons practiced surgery, were educated in the universities, and were permitted to perform all types of operations. The short-robe barber surgeons were allowed only to leech and shave the patient, unless permission was granted to extend the scope of treatment. Both groups were regarded as inferior to physicians.

In 1506, a band of long-robe surgeons organized the Royal College of Surgeons of Edinburgh. By 1540, both the long- and the short-robe surgeons in England joined to form the Company of Barber-Surgeons of London. In 1528, Thomas Linacre, physician to Henry VIII, organized the Royal College of Physicians of England.

During the 16th century, King Henry VIII of England ordered that hospitals associated with the Catholic Church be given over to secular uses or destroyed. The sick were turned out into the streets. Conditions in hospitals became so intolerable that the king was petitioned to return one or two buildings for the care of patients. He consented and restored St. Bartholomew's in 1544. Practically the only hope for the sick poor among outlying towns was to journey many miles to London.

The dearth of hospitals in England continued throughout the 17th century, when the medical school was developed. The French and the English quickly accepted what had originated in Italy: the first attempt to make medical instruction practical. St. Bartholomew's took the lead in education by establishing a medical library in 1667 and permitted apprentices to walk the wards for clinical teaching under experienced surgeons.

In 1634, an outstanding contribution was made to nursing by the founding of the order of the Daughters of Charity of St. Vincent de Paul. Originating at the Hotel-Dieu of Paris as a small group of village girls who were taught nursing by the nuns, the order grew rapidly and was transplanted to the United States by Mother Seton in 1809.

HOSPITALS OF THE 18TH CENTURY

During the 18th century, the building of hospitals revived partially. Because of poverty, at first the movement made slow progress in England, but a few hospitals were built and supported jointly by parishes. By 1732, there were 115 such institutions in England, some of them a combination of almshouse and hospital.

The Royal College of Physicians established a dispensary where medical advice was given free and medicines were sold to the needy at cost. Controversies and lawsuits, however, brought an untimely end to this early clinic. Not discouraged by this experience, the Westminster Charitable Society created a similar dispensary in 1715. The same organization in 1719 founded Westminster Hospital, an infirmary built by voluntary subscription, in which the staff gave its services gratuitously. Ten years later, the Royal College of Physicians in Edinburgh opened the Royal Infirmary. London Hospital, another notable, had its origin in 1740. Admission of charity patients to the London Hospital was apparently by ticket because among its historical relics is an admission card. On the back of that card is a representation of a biblical scene drawn by the artist Hogarth.

As hospitals worked to provide services to more people, scientists worked to provide better services. Filling a need in hospitals at the time was Desaguliers's invention in 1727 of a machine for pumping fresh air into and foul air out of rooms. Used at first for prisons and public buildings, it later was installed in hospitals.

In the Elizabethan period, however, the deterioration of hospital service that had set in under Henry VIII continued. Despite advances made during the 18th century and the steady growth in population and wealth, hospital progress was uneventful.

Antony van Leeuwenhoek (1632–1723) succeeded in making some of the most important discoveries in the history of biology. Although Leeuwenhoek did not invent the first microscope, he was able to perfect it. Many of his discoveries included bacteria, free-living and parasitic microscopic protists, sperm cells, blood cells, and microscopic nematodes. His research opened up an entire world of microscopic life. Leeuwenhoek had a pronounced influence on the creation of the sciences of cytology, bacteriology, and pathology. His discoveries have forever affected not only the delivery of health care in hospitals, but also the way health care is delivered in all settings.

EARLY HOSPITALS IN THE UNITED STATES

Manhattan Island claims the first account of a hospital in the New World: a hospital that was used in 1663 for sick soldiers. Fifty years later, in Philadelphia, William Penn founded the first almshouse established in the American colonies. The Quakers supported the almshouse, which was open only to members of that faith. However, Philadelphia was rapidly growing and also in need of a public almshouse. Such an institution for the aged, the infirm, and the mentally ill was established in 1732. The institution later became the historic Old Blockley, which in turn evolved into the Philadelphia General Hospital.

Philadelphia was the site of the first incorporated hospital in America, the Pennsylvania Hospital. Dr. Thomas Bond wanted to provide a place where Philadelphia physicians might treat their private patients. With the aid of Benjamin Franklin, Bond sought a charter for the Pennsylvania Hospital, which was granted by the crown in 1751. The first staff consisted of Dr. Phineas Bond, Dr. Lloyd Zachary, and the founder, Dr. Thomas Bond, all of who gave their services without remuneration for 3 years.

Rich in the history of hospitals, Philadelphia must also be credited with the first quarantine station for immigrants (created in 1743) and the first lying-in hospital (established in 1762), a private institution owned by the noted obstetrician William Shippen. The quality of American health care seemed to be improving.

Dr. John Jones, an American, published a book in 1775 charging that hospitals abroad were crowded far beyond capacity, that Hotel-Dieu of Paris frequently placed three to five patients in one bed—the convalescent with the dying and fracture cases with infectious cases. He estimated that one-fifth of the 22,000 patients cared for at Hotel-Dieu died each year. Wounds were washed daily with a sponge that was carried from patient to patient. The infection rate was said to be 100%. Mortality after amputation was as high as 60%. Jones's call to action had a positive effect on American health care.

As late as 1769, New York City, with nearly 300,000 inhabitants, was without hospitals. In 1771, a small group of citizens, Dr. Jones among them, formed the Society of the New York Hospital. The society purchased a 5 acre site and made plans for a model hospital, which fell into the hands of British troops during the Revolution.

During postwar reconstruction, the New York Hospital broadened its services. Under the supervision of Dr. Valentine Seaman, the hospital began providing instruction in nursing, and in 1779 it introduced vaccination in the United States and established an ambulance service.

Other early American hospitals of historic interest include the first psychiatric hospital in the New World, founded in Williamsburg, Virginia, in 1773, and a branch of federal hospitals created by passage of the U.S. Marine Hospital Service Act in 1798. Under this act, two marine hospitals were established in 1802, one in Boston and another in Norfolk, Virginia.

The Massachusetts General Hospital, which pioneered many improvements in medicine, originated in Boston. Its first patient, admitted in 1821, was a 30-year-old sailor.

> The original building, designed by Boston's leading architect Charles Bulfinch, is still in use. One of the world's leading centers of medical research and treatment has grown up around it. The original domed operating amphitheater, where anesthesia was first publicly demonstrated in 1846, is now a Registered National Historic Landmark. MGH has achieved countless medical milestones, including the first successful reattachment of a human limb.[3]

In 1832, the Boston Lying-In Hospital opened its doors to women who were unable to afford in-home medical care. It was one of the nation's first maternity hospitals, made possible because of fundraising appeals to individuals and charitable organizations.

Despite the increased volume of institutions providing care for the sick, the first half of the 19th century stands as a dark period in hospital history. Surgeons of the day had sufficient knowledge of anatomy to lead them to perform many ordinary operations, and as a result more surgery was probably undertaken than during any previous era. While surgeons had sought to keep wounds clean, even using wine in an attempt to accomplish this purpose, 19th-century surgeons believed suppuration (the production and discharge of pus) to be desirable and encouraged it. Hospital wards were filled with discharging wounds. Nurses of that period are said to have used snuff to make conditions tolerable. Surgeons wore their operating coats for months without washing. The same bed linens served several patients. Pain, hemorrhage, infection, and gangrene infested the wards. Mortality from surgical operations rated as high as 90–100%.

▌LATE 19TH-CENTURY RENAISSANCE

Florence Nightingale, the famous English nurse, began her career by training at Kaiserswerth on the Rhine in a hospital and deaconess home established in 1836 by Theodor Fliedner and his wife. Florence Nightingale wrote disparagingly of her training there, particularly of the hygiene practiced. Returning to England, she put her own ideas of nursing into effect and rapidly acquired a reputation for efficient work.

By 1854, during the Crimean War, the English government, disturbed by reports of conditions among the sick and wounded soldiers, selected Florence Nightingale as the one person capable of improving patient care. Upon her arrival at the military hospital in Crimea with a small band of nurses whom she had assembled, she found that the sick were lying on canvas sheets in the midst of dirt and vermin. She proceeded to establish order and cleanliness. She organized diet kitchens, a laundry service, and departments of supplies, often using her own funds to finance her projects. Ten days after her arrival, the newly established kitchens were feeding 1,000 soldiers. Within 3 months, 10,000 soldiers were receiving clothing, food, and medicine.

As the field of nursing continued to progress, so did medicine. Crawford Long, for example, first used ether as an anesthetic in 1842 to remove a small tumor from the neck of a patient. He did not publish any accounts of his work until later, however, so the discovery is often attributed to W.T.G. Morgan, a dentist who developed sulfuric ether and arranged for the first hospital operation under anesthesia at Massachusetts General Hospital in 1846. Although not put to practical use immediately, ether soon took away some of the horror that hospitals had engendered in the public mind. Chloroform was first used as an anesthetic in 1847 for an obstetrical case in England by Sir James Simpson.

The year 1847 also brought about the founding of the American Medical Association (AMA) under the leadership of Dr. Nathan Smith Davis. The association, among its main objectives, strived to improve medical education, but most of the organization's tangible efforts in education began at the close of the century. The AMA was a strong advocate for establishing a code of ethics, promoting public health measures, and improving the status of medicine.

The culmination of Florence Nightingale's work came in 1860 after her return to England. There she founded the Nightingale School of Nursing at St. Thomas's Hospital. From this school, a group of 15 nurses graduated in 1863. They later became the pioneer heads of training schools throughout the world.

In 1886, the Royal British Nurses' Association (RBNA) was formed. The RBNA worked toward establishing a standard of technical excellence in nursing. A charter granted to the RBNA in 1893 denied nurses a register, although it did agree to maintain a list of persons who could apply to have their name entered thereon as nurses.

The first formally organized American nursing schools were established in 1872 at the New England Hospital for Women and Children in Boston (Brigham and Women's Hospital), and then in 1873 at Bellevue, New Haven, and Massachusetts General Hospital. In 1884, Alice Fisher was appointed as the first head of the nurse training at Philadelphia Hospital's (renamed as the Philadelphia General Hospital in 1902) nurses' training school. She had the distinction of being the first Nightingale-trained nurse recruited to Philadelphia upon recommendation by Florence Nightingale.

Mrs. Bedford Fenwick, a nurse leader in the English nurse registration movement, traveled to Chicago in 1893 to arrange the English nursing exhibit. As part of the Congress on Hospitals and Dispensaries, a nursing section included papers on establishing standards in hospital training schools, the establishment of a nurses' association, and nurse registration. The group formulated plans to improve nursing curriculum and hospital administration in the first-concerted attempt to improve hospitals through a national organization.

Progress in Infection Control

Ignaz Philipp Semmelweis of Vienna, Austria, unknowingly laid the foundation for Pasteur's later work. In 1847, at the Vienna Lying-in Hospital, Europe's largest teaching obstetrical department, he declared that the alarming number of deaths from puerperal fever was due to infection transmitted by students who came directly from the dissecting room to take care of maternity patients. Semmelweis noted that Division 1 of the hospital was a medical student teaching service; Division 2 was utilized for midwife trainees. Maternal deaths for Division 1 averaged 10%; Division 2 averaged 3%. Medical students performed autopsies; midwives did not. As a result of these findings, an order was posted on May 15, 1847, requiring all students to scrub their hands in chlorinated lime until the cadaver smell was gone. *The order was later revised to include hand washing between patients.*

Semmelweis had the satisfaction of seeing the mortality rate in his obstetrical cases drop from 9.92% to 1.27% in little more than a year as a result of an aseptic technique that he devised. A few years later, Louis Pasteur demonstrated the scientific reason for Semmelweis's success when he proved that bacteria were produced by reproduction and not by spontaneous generation, as was then generally believed. From his work came the origin of modern bacteriology and clinical laboratories.

Also of great importance to hospitals and infection control was Bergmann's introduction of steam sterilization in 1886 and William Stewart Halstead's introduction of rubber gloves in 1890.

By the end of the century, Lister carried Pasteur's work a step further and showed that wound healing could be hastened by using antiseptics to destroy disease-bearing organisms and by preventing contaminated air from coming into contact with these wounds. Lister was not content with obtaining better results in his own surgical cases; he devoted his life to proving that suppuration is dangerous and that it should be prevented or reduced by use of antiseptics. Despite his successful work and eloquent pleas, his colleagues persisted in following their old methods. As time went on and antiseptics and the techniques of using them were improved, even the skeptical were impressed by the clinical results. Surgeons eventually realized that they could undertake major operations with less fear of morbidity and mortality.

The Continuing Problem

Unfortunately, infections continue to be a major concern in the home and healthcare setting. With an estimated 99,000 deaths yearly from preventable hospital acquired infections, organizations must ask themselves, have we learned anything from the history of hospitals and how much progress have we really made?

 NEWSPAPER CLIPPINGS: 99,000 Die Yearly from Preventable Hospital Infections, CDC Finally Gets Data as State Laws Force Hospitals to Count Infections

May 27, 2010—As some 99,000 Americans die yearly from hospital-acquired infections, state laws are finally forcing hospitals to report the infections.

Early data released by CDC today suggest this is cutting infection rates. But the data paints a bigger picture. Despite the huge size of the problem, most hospitals in most states still haven't come to grips with it.

That's going to change, says Health and Human Services Secretary Kathleen Sebelius . . .[4]

—*Daniel J. DeNoon, WebMD, May 27, 2010*

In a special issue of *Emerging Infectious Diseases*, Dr. William R. Jarvis, Associate Director for Program Development, Division of Healthcare Quality Promotion (currently Hospital Infections Program), Centers for Disease Control and Prevention (CDC), writes:

Over the past two decades, acute-care facilities have become smaller and fewer, but the hospitalized patient population has become more severely ill and more immunocompromised and thus at greater risk for hospital-acquired infections. At the same time, the proportion of the U.S. population 65 years of age has increased, as have the number of long-term care facilities and the number of beds in these facilities. This trend is expected to continue for the next 50 years. Similarly, delivery of health care in the home has become the most rapidly growing sector of the health-care system. Currently, nearly as many patients are receiving care in the home as in the inpatient setting. Provision of health care in managed-care and outpatient and ambulatory-care settings continues to expand. Thus, the spectrum of health-care delivery in 2000 is larger than ever before. Because of the severely ill and immunocompromised populations in these settings, prevention of infections and other adverse events is a major component of providing quality care . . . .

Infection control personnel will need to expand their efforts to match the expansion of the healthcare delivery system. Enhanced administrative support for programs to prevent infections and medical errors will be needed if we are to reduce the risk of infection and other adverse events and improve the quality of care in the entire spectrum of healthcare delivery. Now, instead of the acute-care facility being the center of the infection control universe, the infection control department has become the center of the diverse healthcare delivery system. Infection control departments will need to expand their surveillance of infections and adverse events and their prevention efforts to all settings in which health care is delivered.[5]

Discovery of Anesthesia

As the 19th century neared its close, surgery was becoming more frequent. The discovery of anesthesia and the principle of antiseptics are to be regarded as two of the most significant influences in the development of surgical procedures and the modern hospital. Anesthesia improved pain control, and hygiene practices, which helped reduce the incidence of surgical site infections.

Modern Hospital Laboratory

The study of cytology originated during the middle of the 19th century and influenced the development of the modern hospital clinical laboratory. The cell theory was first advanced in 1839 by the German anatomist Theodor Schwann and was further developed by Jacob Henle, whose writings on microscopic anatomy appeared about 1850. Rudolph Virchow was the most eminent proponent of the cell theory. His studies in cellular pathology sped research in the etiology of disease.

Changing Hospital Structure

With nursing, anesthesia, infection control, and cytology under way, a change in hospital structure began in the last quarter of the 19th century. Buildings of the Civil War days continued with as many as 25–50 beds in a ward, with little provision for segregation of patients. In New York City in 1871, construction of Roosevelt Hospital, built on the lines of a one-story pavilion with small wards, set the style for a new type of architecture that came to be known as the American plan. A noteworthy feature was ventilation by means of openings in the roof, a definite improvement upon earlier hospitals that were characterized by a lack of provision for ventilation. Dr. W.G. Wylie, writing in 1877, said he favored this type of building, but he advocated that it be a temporary structure only, to be destroyed when it became infected.

Changing Hospital Function

Promoted by the wealth of bacteriological discoveries, hospitals began to care for patients with communicable diseases. During the decade 1880–1890, the tubercle bacillus was discovered; Pasteur vaccinated against anthrax; Koch isolated the cholera bacillus; diphtheria was first treated with antitoxin; the tetanus bacillus and the parasite of malarial fever were isolated; and inoculation for rabies was successful. Treatment of patients with some of the infections necessitated isolation, and hospitals were the logical place for observation of communicable diseases. Consequently, at the end of the century, in addition to their many surgical cases, hospitals were crowded with large numbers of patients suffering from scarlet fever, diphtheria, typhoid, and smallpox.

Discovery of the X-ray

Wilhelm Konrad Roentgen's discovery of the X-ray in 1895 was a major scientific achievement. The first use of the X-ray symbolizes the beginning of the period that necessitated equipment so costly that the average practitioner could not afford to install it. The natural result was the founding of community hospitals in which physicians could jointly use such equipment. Nineteenth-century inventions also included the clinical thermometer, the laryngoscope, the Hermann Helmholtz ophthalmoscope, and innumerable other aids to accurate diagnosis. Although the medical and nursing professions of the later half of the 19th century did not reap the full reward of their discoveries, they provided the 20th century with a firm foundation upon which to build.

20TH-CENTURY PROGRESS

The treatment of metabolic diseases, nutritional deficiencies, the importance of vitamins, and the therapy of glandular extracts played an important role in the advancement of medicine in the 20th century. As early as 1906, Gowland Hopkins began investigations of vitamins. Two years later, Carlos Finlay produced experimental rickets by means of a vitamin-deficient diet. This, in turn, was followed by Kurt Huldschinsky's discovery that rickets could be treated successfully with ultraviolet light. In quick succession came Casimir Funk's work with vitamins, Elmer McCollum's discovery of vitamins A and B, Joseph Goldberger's work in the prevention of pellagra, and Harry Steenbock's irradiation of foods and oils. Other outstanding contributions to the science of nutrition include Frederick Banting's introduction of insulin in 1922, the studies in anemia carried out by George Hoyt Whipple and Frieda Robscheit-Robbins, and the Minot and Murphy liver extract.

Willem Einthoven's invention of the electrocardiograph in 1903 marked the beginning of an era of diagnostic and therapeutic aids. Shortly after that invention came the first basal metabolism apparatus, then the Wassermann (August Von) test in 1906, followed by tests for pancreatic function, and the invention of the fluoroscopic screen followed in 1908. Subsequently, the introduction of blood tests and examinations of numerous body secretions required well-equipped and varied laboratories. Concurrent with this progress in the field of internal medicine was the introduction of radium for the treatment of malignant growths, increasing the use of the clinical laboratory for microscopic examination of pathological tissue, and developments in antibiotics. The result of these many new aids was the conquest of diseases formerly regarded as incurable, which in turn resulted in improved public confidence in hospitals.

The 20th century is also characterized by rapid growth in nursing education. The earlier schools were maintained almost entirely for the purpose of securing nursing service at a low cost. The nurses' duties were often menial, the hours long, and classroom and laboratory study almost entirely lacking. Nurses themselves had begun to organize for educational reforms. By 1910, training increasingly emphasized theoretical studies. This movement was largely due to the work of organizations such as the American Nurses Association and the National League for Nursing, along with the organization of the Committee on the Grading of Nursing Schools. In 1943, the U.S. Cadet Nurse Corps was organized to spur enrollment of student nurses in nursing schools to help meet the shortages due to enlistment of graduate nurses for military service. As a result, efforts increased to train practical nurses and nurses' aides to relieve the shortage of graduate nurses.

Reform in medical education began early in the century and was due almost wholly to the efforts of the Council on Medical Education and Hospitals, which was established in 1905 by the American Medical Association. Immediately after its organization, this council began inspection of medical schools. The council, by establishing standards and by grading the schools, brought about gradual elimination of most of the unethical, commercial, and unqualified institutions.

A great stimulus to the profession of hospital administration has been the work of the American Hospital Association. Organized in 1899 as the Association of Hospital Superintendents, it took its present name in 1907. Since its inception, the organization has concerned itself particularly with the problems of hospital management. As early as 1910, the association held educational programs for hospital chief executive officers and trustees.

The American College of Surgeons was founded in 1913 under the leadership of Dr. Franklin H. Martin, the first director general of the organization. One of the most dramatic achievements of the College was the hospital standardization movement that began in 1918. The founders drew up what was known as the "minimum standard," a veritable constitution for hospitals, setting forth requirements for the proper care of the sick. An annual survey of all hospitals having 25 or more beds made the standard effective. In 1918, when the first survey was conducted, only 89 hospitals in the United States and Canada could meet the requirements.

The hospital standardization movement focused its efforts on the patient, with the goal of providing the patient with the best professional, scientific, and humanitarian care possible. The growth of this movement is remarkable, given that participation in hospital standardization programs is euphemistically voluntary. Following several name changes over the years, *The Joint Commission* today conducts unannounced accreditation surveys with emphasis on ongoing improvements in the quality of patient care.

The years following 1929 will be remembered as a trying period in the history of hospitals. Due to critical economic conditions, many institutions found it difficult to keep their doors open. Lowered bed occupancy and increased charity load, coupled with steadily decreasing revenues from endowments and other sources of income, created hardships on private institutions.

In the later half of the 20th century, competition among hospitals began to grow as for-profit hospital chains began to spring up and compete with nonprofit organizations. Advances in medical technology, such as computed tomography (CT), magnetic resonance imaging (MRI), and positron emission tomography (PET) scanners and robotic surgery, as well as an ever-growing list of new medications, have revolutionized the practice of medicine. During this period, less invasive surgical procedures and a trend toward care in outpatient settings and home care have reduced the need for lengthy stays in hospitals and nursing facilities.

HEALTH CARE IN THE 21ST CENTURY

Grading Hospital Safety

About 180,000 Medicare patients die each year from hospital accidents, errors and infections, according to the U.S. Department of Health and Human Services. Another 1.4 million are seriously hurt by their hospital care. So how safe is your hospital? Two new rating systems help you check before you check in. Hospital safety score (hospitalsafetyscore.org), launched in June, assigns grades of A, B, C, D or F to more than 2,600 U.S. hospitals based on 26 safety measures and standards–from hand-washing policies to foreign objects left in body cavities after surgery. Nearly half of the hospitals received a C or lower.
—BILL HOGAN, AARP BULLETIN, NOVEMBER 2012

The delivery of health care in the modern hospital continues to be the revolutionary product of a long and arduous struggle. The continuing stream of new medicines and treatments, as well as, legal, financial, and human resource issues continue to test the healthcare system. Some of today's healthcare challenges have carried over from the 20th century, including exorbitant malpractice awards, skyrocketing insurance premiums, high expectations of society for miracle drugs and miracle cures, fairly balancing the mistakes of caregivers with the numerous successful events, negative press that increases public fear, as well as numerous ethical dilemmas such as the distribution of limited resources, abortion, and human cloning.

National Health Reform

At the beginning of the 21st century, there were nearly 49 million uninsured Americans. It was estimated that by the year 2015, 56 million Americans would be uninsured, with this number increasing to 61 million by 2020. The *Patient Protection and Affordable Care Act* (PPACA), passed by Congress and signed by President Barack Obama on March 23, 2010, is designed to ensure that more Americans receive healthcare benefits. The costs, however, associated with health care will continue to soar. Taxes will continue to increase, bureaucracy will become more complex, and discontent with the healthcare system will continue well into the 21st century.

Boutique Medicine

NEWSPAPER CLIPPINGS: The Red-Carpet Treatment, for a Fee

In 2014 about 14 million people will leave the ranks of the uninsured. The U.S already faces a shortage of primary-care physicians. The influx of newly insured patients when the Patient Protection and Affordable Care act kicks in promises to strain an already stressed system, resulting in a projected shortfall 45,000 primary-care doctors.

…people who struggled for years without health insurance might find themselves grappling with a whole new problem, adequate insurance, but no one to accept it.

—*Marvin Lipman, M.D.*, Consumer Reports, *February 2013*

The problem of accessibility to care is further exacerbated by an increasing number of physicians who turn to *boutique medicine*, a plan of care whereby a patient pays an annual retainer fee in exchange for immediate access to a physician for health care. As a result, physicians who elect to practice boutique medicine find it necessary to limit the number of patients they can treat due to the need to be readily available to patients in their practice. In other words, increased access leads to fewer patients, and arguably better care for those who can afford the fees.

History's Common Theme: Infection Related Deaths

One reoccurring theme throughout the ages has been infection control issues in healthcare settings. As noted in the case below and depicted in the above **Figure 3–2**, hospitals of the 20th century continue to be plagued with hospital-acquired infections.

Figure 3–2   Drawing of a Hospital Room   Courtesy of Brittany Salzone, Forest, VA

 REALITY CHECK: Failure to Follow Hand Hygiene Guidelines

Smith was a healthy young lady until suddenly she experienced neck pain and needed surgery. She was admitted to a post-surgical care unit at a major teaching hospital. Upon entering her assigned 4-bedded room, she and her husband observed a bloody suction bottle hanging from a wall at the head of her assigned bed. The bed rails were rusting with dried body fluids from previous patients. They were uneasy about having a surgical procedure performed but they decided the physician's skills were more important then an unclean room. The morning following surgery, a physician entered the room with three residents and examined each of four post-surgical patients. The first patient examined was a post-surgical amputee, who was later diagnosed with a staph infection. Mrs. Smith was the fourth patient to be examined in the room to have her surgical site checked. Even though each of the patients' wounds had been examined and dressings changed, the physicians failed to change their gloves between patients. Following examination of Mrs. Smith, they proceeded to remove their gloves and tossed them in Mrs. Smith's bedside wastebasket. All four patients contracted a staff infection. History repeated itself. CDC hygiene recommendations, though adopted by the hospital, were not followed, to the patients' detriment.

The Centers for Disease Control and Prevention has estimated that "nosocomial [hospital-acquired] bloodstream infections are a leading cause of death in the United States. If we assume a nosocomial infection rate of 5%, of which 10% are bloodstream infections, and an attributable mortality rate of 15%, bloodstream infections would represent the eighth leading cause of death in the United States."[6] It is believed that such infections have resulted in as many as 100,000 deaths and billions of dollars in additional health-care costs. These numbers do not reflect nonhospital-acquired infections that have occurred in physicians' offices.

THE CHALLENGE AHEAD

Dr. Makary, a surgeon at Johns Hopkins Hospital and a developer of the surgical checklists adopted by the World Health Organization, writes:

 NEWSPAPER CLIPPINGS: How to Stop Hospitals From Killing Us

Medical errors kill enough people to fill four jumbo jets a week.

. . . To do no harm going forward, we must be able to learn from the harm we have already done.

—*Martin Makary,* The Wall Street Journal, *September 21, 2012*[7]

The pinnacle of the hospital evolution has not been reached nor has the final page of its colorful history been written. As long as there remains a humanitarian impulse and as long as a society feels compassion, love, and sympathy for its neighbors, there will be hospitals. In the past, hospitals changed as conditions changed. In the future, they will continue to change to meet the needs of their communities. Healthcare leaders of the 21st century must understand their roots and the historical value of knowing the past, have the vision to preserve the good, and have the passion to create an even better healthcare system to provide superior care for all.

The greatest challenge of the 21st century requires that each member of society take a more responsible and proactive role in his or her health and well being through healthy living, which includes eating healthy, exercising, reducing stress, and eliminating bad habits such as smoking and over-indulging in alcohol consumption. Yes, *History is relevant to understanding the past, defining the present, and influencing our future.*

Notes

1. Wisdom Quotes, "Gerda Lerner Quote," http://www. wisdomquotes.com/002320.html (accessed October 13, 2010).

2. Malcolm T. MacEachern, *Hospital Organization and Management* (Berwyn, IL: Physician's Record Company, 1957), 10.

3. Mass Moments, "Massachusetts General Hospital Admits First Patient, September 3, 1821," http://www. massmoments.org/moment.cfm?mid=256 (accessed June 21, 2006).

4. Daniel J. DeNoon, "99,000 Die Yearly from Preventable Hospital Infections, CDC Finally Gets Data as State Laws Force Hospitals to Count Infections" WebMD, http:// www.webmd.com/news/20100527/99-thousand-die-yearly-from-preventable-hospital-infections (accessed August 31, 2010).

5. William R. Jarvis, "Infection Control and Changing Health-Care Delivery Systems," *Emerging Infectious Diseases,* Centers for Disease Control and Prevention, http:// www.cdc.gov/ncidod/eid/vol7no2/jarvis.htm (accessed August 31, 2010).

6. Richard P. Wenzel and Michael B. Edmond, "The Impact of Hospital-Acquired Bloodstream Infections," http:// www.cdc.gov/ncidod/eid/vol7no2/wenzel.htm (accessed October 15, 2010).

7. Marty Makary, "How to Stop Hospitals From Killing Us," *Wall Street Journal,* Friday, September 21, 2012. http:// online.wsj.com/article/SB100008723963904446201045 78008263334441352.html?mod=googlenews_wsj.

4
Tort Law

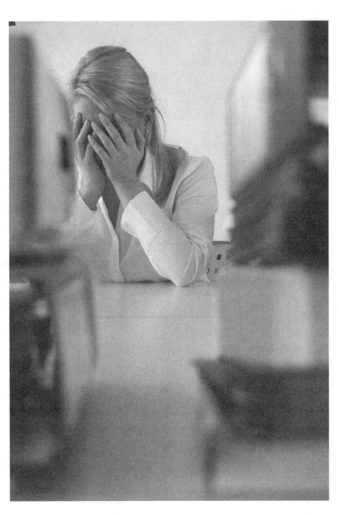

Figure 4–1 What Went Wrong   © F1online/Thinkstock

Learning Objectives

The reader upon completion of this chapter will be able to:

- Describe what a tort is and the purpose of tort law.
- Identify, understand, and describe the elements of negligence.
- Identify and describe intentional torts.
- Explain the theories a plaintiff could use in pursuing a products liability case and the defenses a manufacturer might use to defend itself.

This chapter introduces the reader to the study of tort law, with an emphasis on negligence in health settings. A *tort* is a civil wrong committed against a person or property for which a court provides a remedy in the form of an action for damages. The basic objectives of tort law are:

1. *preservation of peace* between individuals;
2. *determining fault* for wrongdoing;
3. *deterrence* by discouraging the wrongdoer from committing future tortious acts; and
4. *compensation* for the person/s injured.

NEGLIGENCE

Negligence is a tort. It is the unintentional commission or omission of an act that a reasonably prudent person would or would not do under the same or similar circumstances. *Commission of an act* would include, for example:

- administering the wrong medication
- administering the wrong dosage of a medication
- administering medication to the wrong patient
- performing a surgical procedure without patient consent
- performing a surgical procedure on the wrong patient
- performing the wrong surgical procedure

Omission of an act would include, for example:

- failing to conduct a thorough history and physical examination
- failing to assess and reassess a patient's nutritional needs
- failing to administer medications as prescribed
- failing to order diagnostic tests
- failing to follow up on critical lab tests

Negligence is a form of conduct caused by heedlessness or carelessness that constitutes a departure from the standard of care generally imposed on reasonable members of society. It can occur when, after considering the consequences of an act, a person: does not exercise the best possible judgment; fails to guard against a risk that was foreseeable; or, engages in behavior expected to involve unreasonable danger to others. Negligence or carelessness of a professional person (e.g., nurse practitioner, pharmacist, physician) is generally described as *malpractice*.

Malpractice suits can allege various mistakes made by medical professionals, including misdiagnosis, mistreatment, delayed diagnosis, failure to diagnose, and surgical errors. Although the actual number is unknown, studies suggest that there are 100,000 or more deaths per year due to medical errors. Not all errors in medical diagnosis and treatment are considered to be malpractice. Any medical or surgical intervention will involve some degree of risk. It is the responsibility of the treating professional to inform his or her patient as to the inherent risks, benefits, and alternatives of a proposed treatment or procedure.

Forms of Negligence

The three basic forms of negligence shown in **Figure 4–2** are:

1. *Malfeasance*: performance of an unlawful or improper act (e.g., performing an abortion in the third trimester when such is prohibited by state law)
2. *Misfeasance*: improper performance of an act, resulting in injury to another (e.g., wrong-sided surgery, such as removal of the healthy left kidney instead of the diseased right kidney, mistakenly administering a lethal dose or potentially lethal dose of a medication)
3. *Nonfeasance*: failure to act, when there is a duty to act as a reasonably prudent person would under similar circumstances (e.g., failing to administer medications as ordered by the treating physician)

Degrees of Negligence

The use of the terminology "degrees of negligence" more aptly describes three generally accepted "degrees of care" that can affect the amount of damages in a negligence case:

1. *Slight*: minor deviation of what is expected under the circumstances.
2. *Ordinary*: failure to do what a reasonably prudent person would or would not do under the circumstances.
3. *Gross negligence*: the intentional or wanton omission of required care or performance of an improper act.

Figure 4–2 Forms of Negligence

Elements of Negligence

The elements that must be present for a plaintiff to recover damages caused by negligence are:

1. *Duty to care*
   - There must be an obligation to conform to a recognized standard of care.
2. *Breach of duty*
   - There must be a deviation from the recognized standard of care.
   - There must be a failure to adhere to an obligation.
3. *Injury*
   - Actual damages must be established.
   - If there are no injuries, no damages are due the plaintiff(s).
4. *Causation*
   - The departure from the standard of care must be the cause of the plaintiff's injury.
   - The injury must be foreseeable.

All four elements must be present in order for a plaintiff to recover damages suffered as a result of a negligent act (**Figure 4–3**). When the four elements of negligence have been proven, the plaintiff is said to have presented a *prima facie case of negligence*, thus enabling the plaintiff to prevail in a lawsuit.

The *burden of proof* in a negligence case is not as great as the beyond-a-reasonable-doubt standard borne by a prosecutor in a criminal case. Therefore, if a plaintiff supports a negligence claim with evidence sufficient to outweigh the evidence presented by the defendant, the defendant will be found liable for the negligent act. The defendant then will be ordered by the court, in accordance with the verdict rendered by the jury or by the court itself, to compensate the plaintiff monetarily for the harm that the plaintiff suffered. *Compensatory damages* seek to restore the injured party's financial situation to match the party's financial state before suffering harm. *Punitive damages* can also be awarded to the plaintiff for pain and suffering caused by conduct that would be considered egregious.

The foundation of the columns in Figure 4–3 illustrates examples of negligent acts. The pillars represent each element of negligence that must be proven in order to establish that a negligent act has occurred. Any unproven element of negligence will defeat a lawsuit based on negligence.

Duty to Care

The first requirement in establishing negligence is that the plaintiff must prove the existence of a legal relationship between himself or herself and the defendant/s. *Duty* is a legal obligation of care, performance, or observance imposed on one to safeguard the rights of others. As

☑ Wrong Site Surgery (e.g., wrong side brain surgery: 3 occasions, same hospital, same year)
☑ Wrong Medication Dosage (e.g., Quaid twins given 20,000 units of heparin instead of 20)

Figure 4–3   Elements of a Negligence Case

---

depicted in **Figure 4–4,** the pharmacy manager leaving for the day is assigning responsibility to the pharmacist behind the counter, telling her, "You're in charge." Her duties of that responsibility are outlined in her job description.

Duty can arise from a special relationship such as that between a physician, nurse, or pharmacist, and a patient. Duty to care can arise from a simple telephone conversation or out of a physician's voluntary act of assuming the care of a patient. Duty also can be established by *statute* or *contract* between the plaintiff and the defendant.

Standard of Care

A duty of care carries with it a corresponding responsibility not only to provide care, but also to provide it in an acceptable manner. The *standard of care* describes what conduct

Figure 4–4   You're In Charge   Courtesy of Brittany Salzone, Forest, VA

is expected of an individual in a given situation. The fact that an injury is suffered is not sufficient for imposing liability without proof that the defendant deviated from the standard practice of competent fellow professionals. A nurse, for example, who assumes the care of a patient has the duty to exercise that degree of skill, care, and knowledge ordinarily possessed and exercised by other nurses.

The actual performance required of a caregiver in a given situation will be measured against what a reasonably prudent person would or would not have done. The reasonableness of conduct is judged in light of the circumstances apparent at the time of injury and by reference to different characteristics of the actor (e.g., age, sex, physical condition, education, knowledge, training, mental capacity). Deviation from the standard of care will constitute negligence if it can be shown that the resulting damages are caused by the breach of one's duty to care.

Traditionally, in determining how a reasonably prudent person should perform in a given situation, the courts often rely on the testimony of an expert witness as to the standard of care required in the same or similar communities. Expert testimony is necessary when the jury is not qualified to determine what the reasonably prudent professional's standard of care would be under similar circumstances. Most states hold those with special skills (e.g., physicians, nurses, nurse practitioners, physician assistants, pharmacists, and dentists) to a standard of care that is reasonable in the light of their education and training.

An organization's policies and procedures, regulatory requirements, and accreditation standards (e.g., The Joint Commission) can be used to help establish the standard of care required of the defendant/s in a negligence suit.

Failure to Treat Emergency Patient

In *O'Neill v. Montefiore Hospital*,[1] the duty owed to a patient was clear. The plaintiff sought recovery against the hospital for failure to render necessary emergency treatment and against a physician for his failure and refusal to treat her spouse. The deceased, Mr. O'Neill, had been experiencing pain in his chest and arms. He walked with his wife to the hospital at 5:00 A.M. He claimed that he was a member of the Hospital Insurance Plan (HIP). The emergency department nurse stated that the hospital had no connection with HIP and did not take HIP patients. The nurse indicated that she would try to get a HIP physician for O'Neill. The nurse called Dr. Graig, a HIP physician, and explained the patient's symptoms to the doctor. It was suggested by Dr. Graig that Mr. O'Neill see a HIP physician at 8:00 A.M. The nurse then handed the phone to Mr. O'Neill, who said, "Well, I could be

dead by 8 o'clock." Mr. O'Neill concluded his phone conversation and spoke to the nurse, indicating that he had been told to go home and come back when HIP was open. Mrs. O'Neill asked that a physician see her husband. The nurse again requested that they return at 8:00. Mr. O'Neill again commented that he could be dead by 8:00. He eventually left with his wife, after being denied treatment to return home, pausing occasionally to catch his breath. Shortly after arriving home, Mr. O'Neill suddenly fell to the floor and died. Dr. Graig claimed that he had offered to come to the emergency department, but that Mr. O'Neill had said he would wait and see another HIP physician at 8:00 that morning.

The New York Supreme Court, Appellate Division held that a physician who abandons a patient after undertaking examination or treatment can be held liable for malpractice. The proof of the record in this case indicated that the physician undertook to diagnose the ailments of the deceased by telephone, thus establishing at least the first element of negligence—duty to use due care.

Duty to Stabilize Patient in Hastings Case

In a similar case, the surviving parents in *Hastings v. Baton Rouge Hospital*[2] brought a medical malpractice action for the wrongful death of their 19-year-old son. The action was brought against the hospital; the emergency department physician, Dr. Gerdes; and the thoracic surgeon on call, Dr. McCool. The patient had been brought to the emergency department at 11:56 P.M. because of two stab wounds and weak vital signs. Dr. Gerdes decided that a thoracotomy had to be performed. He was not qualified to perform the surgery and called Dr. McCool, who was on call that evening for thoracic surgery. Dr. Gerdes described the patient's condition, indicating he had been stabbed in a major blood vessel. At trial, Dr. McCool claimed that he did not recall Dr. Gerdes saying that a major blood vessel could be involved. Dr. McCool asked Dr. Gerdes to transfer the patient to the Earl K. Long Hospital. Dr. Gerdes said, "I can't transfer this patient." McCool replied, "No. Transfer him." Kelly, an emergency department nurse on duty, was not comfortable with the decision to transfer the patient and offered to accompany him in the ambulance. Dr. Gerdes reexamined the patient, who exhibited marginal vital signs, was restless, and was draining blood from his chest. The ambulance service was called at 1:03 A.M., and by 1:30 A.M. the patient had been placed in the ambulance for transfer. The patient began to fight wildly, the chest tube came out, and bleeding increased. The patient virtually bled to death.

The duty to care in this case cannot be reasonably disputed. Louisiana, by statute, imposes a duty on hospitals licensed in Louisiana to make emergency services available to all persons residing in the state regardless of insurance coverage or economic status. The hospital's own bylaws provide that patient transfer should never occur without due consideration for the patient's condition. The 19th Judicial District Court directed a verdict for the defendants, and the plaintiffs appealed. The court of appeals affirmed the district court's decision. On further appeal, the Louisiana Supreme Court held that the evidence presented to the jury could indicate the defendants were negligent in their treatment of the victim. The findings of the lower courts were reversed, and the case was remanded for trial.

Duties Created by Statute

Some duties are created by statute, which occurs when a statute specifies a particular standard that must be met. Many such standards are created by administrative agencies under the provisions of a statute. To establish liability based on a defendant's failure to follow the standard of care outlined by statute, the following elements must be present:

1. the defendant must have been within the specified class of persons outlined in the statute;
2. the plaintiff must have been injured in a way that the statute was designed to prevent; and,
3. the plaintiff must show that the injury would not have occurred if the statute had not been violated.

Duties Created by Policy

Duties can also be created by an organization through its internal policies, procedures, rules, and regulations. The courts hold that such internal rules are indicative of the organization's knowledge of the proper procedure to follow and, hence, create a duty. Thus, if an employee fails to follow an operating rule of an organization and, as a result, a patient is injured, then the employee who violated the rule could be considered negligent for causing the injury.

Duty to Hire Competent Employees

Courts recognize that employers have a duty to hire competent employees, especially if they are engaged in an occupation that could be hazardous to life and limb and requires skilled or experienced persons.

A Texas court in *Deerings West Nursing Center v. Scott*[3] determined that an employer negligently hired an incompetent employee that it knew or should have known was incompetent, thereby causing unreasonable risk of harm to others.

In this case, an 80-year-old visitor had gone to Deerings to visit her infirm older brother. During one visit, Nurse Hopper, a 6-foot-4-inch male employee of Deerings, confronted the visitor to prevent her from visiting. The visitor recalled that he was angry and just stared. She stated that upon his approach she had thrown up her hands to protect her face, but he hit her on the chin, slapped her down onto the concrete floor, and got on top of her, pinning her to the floor.

Hopper testified that he was hired sight unseen over the telephone by Deerings' director of nursing. Even though the following day, Hopper completed an application at the nursing facility, he still maintained that he was hired over the phone. In his application, he falsely stated that he was a Texas *licensed vocational nurse* (LVN). Additionally, he claimed that he had never been convicted of a crime. In reality, he had been previously employed by a bar, was not a LVN, had committed more than 56 criminal offenses of theft, and was on probation at the time of his testimony.

Deerings showed a clear duty to care. The appellant violated the very purpose of Texas licensing statutes by failing to verify whether Hopper held a current LVN license. The appellant then placed him in a position of authority by allowing him to dispense drugs and by making him a shift supervisor. This negligence eventually resulted in the assault on an elderly woman. The employee's failure to obtain a nursing license was the proximate cause of the visitor's damages. Deerings's hiring of Hopper showed a heedless and reckless disregard of the rights of others.

The court pulled no punches when it determined it is common knowledge that the bleakness and rigors of old age, drugs, and the diseases of senility can cause people to become confused and cantankerous. It is predictable that elderly patients will be visited by friends and family. It is reasonable to anticipate that a man of proven moral baseness would be more likely to commit a morally base act on an 80-year-old woman. Fifty-six convictions for theft is some evidence of mental aberration. Hopper was employed not only to administer medicine but also to contend with the sometimes erratic behavior of the decrepit. The investigative process necessary to the procurement of a Texas nursing license would have precluded the licensing of Hopper. In the hiring of an unlicensed and potentially mentally and morally unfit nurse, it is reasonable to anticipate that an injury would result as a natural and probable consequence of that negligent hiring.[4]

Breach of Duty

When a duty to care has been established, the plaintiff must demonstrate that the defendant breached that duty by

Figure 4–5 Was This Diluted Correctly?   Courtesy of Brittany Salzone, Forest, VA

failing to comply with the accepted standard of care. *Breach of duty* is the failure to conform to or the departure from a required duty of care owed to a person. The obligation to perform according to a standard of care can encompass either performing or failing to perform a particular act. **Figure 4–5** illustrates a pharmacist checking the work of a pharmacy technician but fails to follow-up on his concern as to whether or not she correctly diluted the medication to be administered intravenously (IV).

Breach of Duty in Hastings Case

The court in *Hastings v. Baton Rouge Hospital*,[5] discussed earlier, found a severe breach of duty when the patient did not receive adequate care. Hospital regulations provided that when a physician cannot be reached or refuses a call, the chief of service must be notified so that another physician can be contacted for assistance. This was not done. A plaintiff need not prove the patient would have survived if proper treatment had been administered, only that the patient would have had a chance of survival. As a result of Dr. Gerdes's failure to make arrangements for another physician and Dr. McCool's failure to perform the necessary surgery, the patient had no chance of survival. The duty to provide for appropriate care under the circumstances was breached.

Breach of Duty—Bariatric Surgery

The plaintiff, Barbara Jupiter, in *Barbara Jupiter v. United States of America*[6] brought a suit against the defendant, United States of America, for the wrongful death of her husband Warren, who had bariatric surgery at a veterans hospital. The procedure involved stapling the stomach so that its functional area would be reduced to limit the amount of food that the patient could consume. The surgical procedure included removal of the distal area of the stomach.

Warren was released from the veteran's hospital after a 1-month stay. During the following 4 weeks, he developed fevers and severe weight loss, which necessitated a return to the hospital. A CT scan was ordered but not immediately performed because it was determined that his presurgical weight of 500 pounds exceeded the tolerance of the CT scanner. A CT scan was eventually performed and showed a stomach abscess with leakage of gastric fluids leading to an extensive infection, which led to the death of Warren.

The plaintiff contended the defendant was vicariously liable for the doctors' negligent acts. Specifically, it was alleged that the doctors did not perform the surgery correctly, and they failed to provide proper postsurgical treatment, both constituting malpractice. Warren passed away after filing suit, but his wife continued the lawsuit.

At a bench trial, the plaintiff asserted that the doctors should not have removed the distal area of the stomach since according to their experts; bariatric surgery may cause complications that require supplemental nutrition. That nutrition is normally provided through a tube placed in the distal region of the stomach. Alternatively, an intravenous catheter may be used, but the plaintiff claimed that the intravenous delivery of nutrition creates an unacceptable risk of infection. The plaintiff argued that the intravenous delivery caused an infection that resulted in brain and stomach abscesses, which lead to severe and incapacitating pain, culminating in his death. Further, the plaintiff asserted that the hospital's staff failed to timely diagnose Warren's infection in spite of postsurgical tests that his blood contained an abnormally large concentration of leukocytes, which indicate that an infection is present. The plaintiff's experts testified that a CT scan would have revealed an infection, and the hospital's equipment could have accommodated Warren.

The U.S. District Court Judge found that the staff strayed from the accepted *standard of care*, and in light of their actions, Warren suffered resultant fatal effects. He awarded $5.9 million dollars in damages ($5 million for wrongful death to the survivors, and $900,000 for wrongful death based upon the loss of parental assistance, guidance, and nurture).

Injury/Actual Damages

Injury is any harm or damages suffered by a person as a result of the defendant/s breach of duty. It includes physical harm, pain, suffering, loss of income, and reputation. A defendant may be negligent and still not incur liability if no injury or actual damages result to the plaintiff. Without harm or injury, there is no liability. The mere occurrence of an injury does not necessarily establish negligence for which the law imposes liability because the injury might be the result of an unavoidable accident or Act of God, such as a lighting strike that is the direct cause of an injury. **Figure 4–6** portrays the death of an infant due to the administration of an incorrect dose of an IV medication that had been improperly diluted in the pharmacy.

Injury in the Hastings Case

Hastings went into cardiac arrest. An attempt to revive him was futile and the patient died after having been moved back to the emergency department. The patient virtually bled to death, thus establishing the third element required to establish proof that a negligent act had been committed.

Failure to Render Care

Injury was obvious in *Lucas v. HCMF Corp.*,[7] where the patient had been transferred to a nursing facility following hospitalization for several ailments, including early decubitus ulcers. The resident was returned to the hospital 24 days later. An ulcer on her buttocks had grown from 1 inch in diameter to 8 inches in diameter and extended to the bone. The standard of care required in preventing and treating decubitus ulcers required that the resident be mobilized and turned every 2 hours to prevent deterioration of tissue. Treatment records reflected that the resident was not turned from September 22 through October 1, nor was she turned on October 4, 7, or 12. Failure to periodically turn the resident and move her to a chair had caused the deterioration in her condition.

Figure 4–6 Oh No! Courtesy of Brittany Salzone, Forest, VA

Causation

The element of *causation* requires that there be a reasonable, close, and causal connection or relationship between the defendant's negligent conduct and the resulting damages. In other words, the defendant's negligence must be a substantial factor causing the injury. *Proximate cause* is a term that refers to the relationship between a breach of duty and the resulting injury. The breach of duty must be the proximate/direct cause of the resulting injury. The mere departure from a proper and recognized procedure is not sufficient to enable a patient to recover damages unless the plaintiff can show that the departure was unreasonable and the proximate cause of the patient's injuries.

The courts generally apply the *but-for rule* to determine if the injury is directly the result of a defendant's act or omission of an act. A finding that an injury would not have occurred "but for" a defendant's act establishes that the particular act or omission is the proximate cause of the harm. If an injury would have occurred regardless of a defendant's negligent act, liability cannot be assigned to the defendant.

Causation in the Hastings Case

Causation was well established in *Hastings v. Baton Rouge Hospital.*[8] In the ordinary course of events, Hastings would not have bled to death in a hospital emergency department over a 2-hour period if surgical intervention had been introduced in a timely manner to save his life, thus, establishing the fourth element required in a negligence case.

Negligent Misreading of CT Scan

The patient–plaintiff in *Dic v. Brooklyn Hospital Center*[9] was admitted into the hospital complaining of a severe headache, an inability to open her eyes, and the absence of feeling in her legs. A CT scan was taken and read by a staff physician as normal. After discharging the plaintiff, the hospital's radiologist reviewed the CT scan and concluded it was "not" normal. The defendant did not contact the plaintiff to alert her about the revised finding. The hospital conceded that its employee's initial misreading of the CT scan and its failure to alert the plaintiff to the misreading were departures from accepted medical practice. The jury found that those departures were the proximate causes of the plaintiff's injury.

Delay in Diagnosing Breast Cancer

The plaintiff, while in the custody of a penal institution, alleged that because the institution's employees failed to timely diagnose her breast cancer, her right breast had to be removed. Pursuant to the institution's policy of medically evaluating all new inmates, on May 26, 1989, Dr. Evans gave the plaintiff a medical examination. He testified that his physical evaluation of the plaintiff's breasts was cursory.

The day following her examination, the plaintiff examined her own breasts. At that time she discovered a lump in her right breast, which she characterized as being about the size of a pea. The plaintiff then sought an additional medical evaluation at the defendant's medical clinic. Testimony indicated that fewer than half of the inmates who sign the clinic list are actually seen by medical personnel the next day. Also, those not examined on the day for which the list is signed are given no preference in being examined on the following day. The evidence indicated that after May 27, the plaintiff constantly signed the clinic list and provided the reason she was requesting medical care. A nurse examined the plaintiff on June 21. The nurse noted in her nursing notes that the plaintiff had a "moderate large mass in right breast." The nurse failed to measure the mass. She testified that no measuring device was available. The missing measuring device was a simple ruler. The nurse concluded that Dr. Evans should again examine the plaintiff.

On June 28, Dr. Evans again examined the plaintiff. He recorded in the progress notes that the plaintiff had a mass on her right wrist. "Will send her to hospital and give her Benadryl for allergy she has." Dr. Evans meant to write "breast" not "wrist." He again failed to measure the size of the mass on the plaintiff's breast.

The plaintiff was transferred to the Franklin County Prerelease Center (FCPR) on September 28. On September 30, a nurse at FCPR examined the plaintiff; the nurse recorded that the plaintiff had a "golf ball" sized lump in her right breast. The plaintiff was transported to the hospital on October 27, where Dr. Walker treated her. The plaintiff received a mammogram examination, which indicated that the tumor was probably malignant. This diagnosis was confirmed by a biopsy performed on November 9. The plaintiff was released from confinement on November 13.

On November 16, a surgeon examined the plaintiff. He noted the existence of the lump in the plaintiff's breast and determined that the size of the mass was approximately 4 to 5 cm and somewhat fixed. He performed a modified radical mastectomy upon the plaintiff's right breast.

The Ohio Court of Appeals was appalled that the physician had characterized his evaluation as a medical examination or had implied that what he described as a "cursory breast examination" should be considered to be a medically sufficient breast examination. It was probable that an earlier procedure would have safely and reliably conserved a large part of the plaintiff's right breast. Through inexcusable delays, the plaintiff lost this option. The court concluded that the defendant's negligence was the sole and *proximate cause* of the plaintiff's losses.[10]

Failure to Administer Proper Nourishment

Under the Illinois Nursing Home Care Reform Act, the owner and licensee of a nursing home are liable to a resident for any intentional or negligent act or omission of their agents or employees that injures a resident. The act defines neglect as a failure in a facility to provide adequate medical or personal care or maintenance, when failure results in physical or mental injury to a resident or in the deterioration of the resident's condition. Personal care and maintenance include providing food, water, and assistance with meals necessary to sustain a healthy life.

The nursing facility in this case maintained no records of the resident's fluid intake and output. A nurse testified that such a record was a required nursing facility procedure that should have been followed for a person in the resident's condition but was not. The resident's condition deteriorated after staying 6.5 days at the facility. Upon entering a hospital, the resident was diagnosed as suffering from severe dehydration. The nursing facility offered no alternative explanation for the resident's dehydrated condition. As a result of the facility's failure to maintain adequate records, the resident suffered severe dehydration that required hospital treatment. The evidence demonstrated that the proximate cause of the resident's dehydration was the nursing facility's failure to administer proper nourishment.[11]

Foreseeability

Foreseeability is the reasonable anticipation that harm or injury is likely to result from an act or failure to act. The test for foreseeability is whether a reasonable person should have anticipated the danger that caused the injury. The test is not what the wrongdoer believed would occur; it is whether he or she ought reasonably to have foreseen that the event in question would occur.

When a defendant's action/s breech the standard of care and injury is the result of the breech, the jury must make two determinations. First, was it foreseeable that harm would occur from the failure to meet the standard of care? Second, was the carelessness or negligence the proximate or immediate cause of the harm or injury to the plaintiff?

As noted in the following case, there is no expectation that a person can guard against events that cannot reasonably be foreseen or that are so unlikely to occur that they would be disregarded.

Patient Fails to Provide Known Allergies

For example, in *Haynes v. Hoffman*,[12] the plaintiff brought a medical malpractice action against the defendant–physician for his alleged negligence in prescribing a medication to which the plaintiff suffered an allergic reaction. The trial court returned a verdict in favor of the defendant, and the plaintiff appealed. The evidence at trial revealed that the plaintiff had not disclosed her history of allergies to the physician. The physician testified that, at the time of the physical examination of the plaintiff, she denied having any allergies. The physician testified that he would not have prescribed the drug had he known the plaintiff's complete history. By failing to disclose her allergies to the physician, the plaintiff, through her negligence, contributed to her own injury. Foreseeability involves guarding against that which is probable and likely to happen, not against that which is only remotely and slightly possible. Generally, the issue of foreseeability is for the trial court to decide. A duty to prevent a wrongful act by a third party will be imposed only where those wrongful acts can be reasonably anticipated.

Summary Case

The elements necessary to establish negligence were well established in *Niles v. City of San Rafael*.[13] On June 26, 1973, at approximately 3:30 P.M., Kelly Niles, a young boy, got into an argument with another boy on a ball field. After being hit on the right side of his head, he rode home on his bicycle and waited for his father, who was to pick him up for the weekend. At approximately 5:00 P.M., his father arrived to pick him up. By the time they arrived in San Francisco, Kelly appeared to be in a great deal of pain. His father then decided to take him to Mount Zion Hospital, which was a short distance away. He arrived at the hospital emergency department at approximately 5:45 P.M. On admission to the emergency department, Kelly was taken to a treatment room by a registered nurse. The nurse obtained a history of the injury and took Kelly's pulse and blood pressure. During his stay in the emergency department, he was irritable, vomited several times, and complained that his head hurt. An intern who had seen Kelly wrote, "pale, diaphoretic, and groggy," on the patient's chart. Skull X-rays were ordered and found to be negative except for soft tissue swelling that was not noted until later. The intern then decided to admit the patient. A second-year resident was called, and he agreed with the intern's decision. An admitting clerk called the intern and indicated that the patient had to be admitted by an attending physician. The resident went as far as to write "admit" on the chart and later crossed it out. A pediatrician who was in the emergency department at the time was asked to look at Kelly. The pediatrician was also the paid director of the Mount Zion Hospital Pediatric Out-Patient Clinic. The pediatrician asked Kelly a few questions and then decided to send him home. The physician could not recall what instructions he gave the patient's father, but he did remember giving the father his business card. However, he could not recall giving the father a copy of the emergency department's head injury instructions that was required by hospital policy to be given to patients with head injuries. The sheet explained that an individual should be returned to the emergency department should any of the following signs appear: a large, soft lump on the head; unusual drowsiness (cannot be awakened); forceful or repeated vomiting; a fit or convulsion (jerking or spells); clumsy walking; bad headache; and/or one pupil larger than the other. As noted above, Kelly had already experienced several of these signs while he was in the emergency department.

Kelly was taken back to his father's apartment at about 7:00 P.M. A psychiatrist friend stopped by the apartment at approximately 8:45 P.M. and examined Kelly, noting that one pupil was larger than the other. Because the pediatrician could not be reached, Kelly was taken back to the emergency department. A physician on duty noted an epidural hematoma during his examination and ordered that a neurosurgeon be called.

Today, Kelly can move only his eyes and neck. A lawsuit against the hospital and pediatrician for $5 million was filed. Expert testimony by two neurosurgeons during the trial indicated that the patient's chances of recovery would have been very good if he had been admitted promptly. This testimony placed the proximate cause of the injury with the hospital. The final judgment was $4 million against the medical defendants, $2.5 million for compensatory damages, and another $1.5 million for pain and suffering. The *Niles* case is a reminder to caregivers that an erroneous diagnosis and/or treatment can lead to the premature dismissal of a case and result in liability for both the organization and physician.

Case Lessons

Each case presented in this book illustrates actual experiences of plaintiffs and defendants, enabling the reader to apply the lessons learned to real-life situations. The many lessons of the *Niles* case, as well as other cases in this book, involves gathering information and making best decisions/choices based on that information:

- *Perform* thorough and well-documented patient assessments.
- *Monitor vital signs* closely and document findings.
- *Adhere to best practices*, protocols, policies, and procedures.
- *Collaborate* across disciplines.
- *Order* appropriate tests according to patient needs, not insurance carrier requirements.
- *Accurately interpret* and review all test results.
- *Conduct a complete review* of a patient's medical record including test results, and any and all entries by nurses, interns, residents, consultants, and other caregivers who participated in the patient's care.
- *Determine and render appropriate treatment* prior to discharge.
- *Provide follow-up* care instructions.

Medical decisions are made numerous times every day, and some of those decisions do not always have a lot of thought behind them. Therefore, caregivers must develop a habit of carefully processing information in order to make intelligent decisions. We have physicians because we need an intuitive yet cognitive, intelligent knowledgeable decision-making process that only medical expertise can provide in order to synthetize all the information available to provide an accurate diagnosis and treatment plan.

Protocols and best practices are helpful tools along the way, but in the final analysis, the physician must review ALL the information available and take responsibility for making a timely decision as to a diagnosis and treatment plan that meets each individual patient's needs. Therefore, based on a full review of the information gathered, the attending physician's judgment at times will necessarily trump protocols and best practices.

INTENTIONAL TORTS

There are two main differences between intentional torts and negligence. The first is intent, which is an element of intentional torts but not in negligence. For a tort to be considered intentional, the act must be committed intentionally, and the wrongdoer must realize to a substantial certainty that harm would result. The second difference is less obvious. In negligence, a wrong can simply be the failure to act when there is a legal duty to act. An intentional wrong always involves a willful act that violates another's interests. Intentional wrongs include such acts as assault, battery, false imprisonment, defamation of character, fraud, invasion of privacy, and infliction of emotional distress **(Figure 4–7)**.

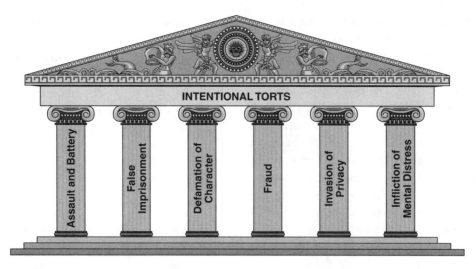

Figure 4–7   Intentional Torts

Assault and Battery

It has long been recognized by law that a person possesses a right to be free from aggression and the threat of actual aggression against one's person. The right to expect others to respect the integrity of one's body has roots in both common and statutory law. The distinguishing feature between assault and battery is that assault effectuates an infringement on the mental security or tranquility of another whereas battery constitutes a violation of another's physical integrity.

Assault

An *assault* is defined as the deliberate threat, coupled with the apparent present ability, to do physical harm to another. No actual contact is necessary. To commit the tort of assault, two conditions must exist: First, the person attempting to touch another unlawfully must possess the apparent present ability to commit a battery; second, the person threatened must be aware of or have actual knowledge of and fear of an immediate threat of a battery.

Battery

Battery is the intentional touching of another's person in a socially impermissible manner, without that person's consent. The law provides a remedy if consent to a touching has not been obtained or if the act goes beyond the consent given. Therefore, the injured person can initiate a lawsuit against the wrongdoer for damages suffered.

In the healthcare context, the principle of law concerning battery and the requirement of consent to medical

and surgical procedures is critically important. Liability of organizations and healthcare professionals for acts of battery is most common in situations involving lack of patient consent to medical and surgical procedures.

It is of no legal importance that a procedure constituting a battery has improved a patient's health. If the patient did not consent to the touching, the patient might be entitled to such damages as can be proved to have resulted from commission of the battery.

In *Perna v. Pirozzi*,[14] the New Jersey Supreme Court held that a patient who consents to surgery by one surgeon and is actually operated on by another has an action for battery. Proof of unauthorized invasion of the plaintiff's person, even if harmless, can entitle one to nominal damages.

False Imprisonment

False imprisonment is the unlawful restraint of an individual's personal liberty or the unlawful restraint or confinement of an individual. The personal right to move freely and without hindrance is basic to the legal system. Any intentional infringement on this right can constitute false imprisonment. Actual physical force is not necessary to constitute false imprisonment; false imprisonment can occur when an individual who is physically confined to a given area reasonably fears detainment or intimidation without legal justification. Both intimidation and forced detainment can be implied by words, threats, or gestures. Excessive force used to restrain a patient can produce liability for both false imprisonment and battery.

To recover for damages for false imprisonment, a plaintiff must be aware of the confinement and have "no" reasonable means of escape. Availability of a reasonable means of escape can bar recovery. To lock a door when another is reasonably available to pass through is not imprisonment. However, if the only other door provides a way of escape that is dangerous, the law might consider it an unreasonable way of escape and, therefore, false imprisonment can be a cause of action.

Some circumstances allow for a person's confinement, such as when there is a danger to oneself or other person/s. Criminals are incarcerated, as are sometimes the mentally ill who can present a danger to themselves or others. Patients are sometimes restrained to prevent falls. In this example, the right to move about freely has been violated, but the infringement occurs for reasons that are justifiable under the law.

Physically Violent Persons

In *Celestine v. United States*,[15] the right to move about freely had been violated; however, the infringement was permissible for reasons justifiable under the law. In this case, the plaintiff had brought an action alleging battery and false imprisonment because security guards had placed him in restraints. The plaintiff–appellant sought psychiatric care at a Veterans Affairs (VA) hospital. He became physically violent while waiting to be seen by a physician. The VA security guards placed him in restraints until a psychiatrist could examine him. The U.S. Court of Appeals for the Eighth Circuit held that the record supported a finding that the hospital was justified in placing the patient under restraint. Under Missouri law, no false imprisonment or battery occurred in view of the common-law principle that a person believed to be mentally ill could be restrained lawfully if such was considered necessary to prevent immediate injury to that person or others.

Contagious Diseases

Protocols should be instituted for handling patients diagnosed as having contracted a highly contagious disease. Detaining such patients without statutory protection constitutes false imprisonment. State health codes generally provide guidelines for caring for such patients.

Behavioral Health Patients

Statutes in many states allow mentally ill and intoxicated individuals to be detained if they are found to be dangerous to themselves or others. Those who are mentally ill, however, can be restrained only to the degree necessary to prevent them from harming themselves or others. If a mentally ill patient cannot be released, procedures should be followed to provide commitment to an appropriate institution for the patient's care.

Restraints

Restraints generally are used to control behavior when patients are disoriented or can cause harm to themselves (e.g., from falling, contaminating wounds, or pulling out intravenous lines) or others. The use of restraints raises many questions of a patient's rights in the areas of autonomy, freedom of movement, and the accompanying health problems that can result from continued immobility. In general, a patient has a right to be free from any physical restraints imposed or psychoactive drugs administered for purposes of discipline or convenience and that are not required to treat a patient's medical symptoms.

Although the motivations for using restraints appear to be sound, there has been a tendency toward overuse. The fear of litigation over injuries sustained because of the failure to apply restraints further compounds the problem of overuse. As a result, regulations governing the use of restraints under the Omnibus Budget Reconciliation Act of 1987 make it clear that restraints are to be applied as a last resort rather than as a first option in the control of a resident's behavior. Because prescription drugs are sometimes used to restrain behavior, the regulations represent the first time that prescription drugs must by law "be justified by indications documented in the medical chart."[16]

To avoid legal problems, healthcare organizations should implement policies aimed at eliminating or reducing the use of restraints. Programs for the effective use of restraints should include the following:

- written policies that conform to federal and state guidelines (e.g., a policy prescribing that the least-restrictive device will be utilized to maintain the safety of the patient, a policy requiring the periodic review of patients under restraint, and a policy requiring physician orders for restraints)
- procedures for implementing organizational policies (e.g., alternatives to follow before restraining a patient can include family counseling to encourage increased visitations, environmental change, activity therapies, and patient counseling)
- periodic review of policies and procedures, with revision as necessary
- education and orientation programs for the staff
- education programs for patients and their families
- a sound appraisal of each patient's needs

- informed consent from the patient or legal guardian
- application of the least-restrictive restraints
- constant monitoring of the patient to determine the continuing need for restraints, injury to the patient, and complaints by the patient
- documentation that includes:
  - the need for restraints
  - time-limited orders ("as needed" PRN orders are not acceptable)
  - consents for the application of restraints
  - patient monitoring
  - reappraisal of the continuing need for restraints

Discharge Against Medical Advice

Patients who decide to leave a facility against medical advice should be requested to sign a discharge against advice form. Should a patient refuse to sign such a form, such refusal should be noted in the patient's record.

Defamation of Character

Another type of intentional tort comes in the form of defamation of character. *Defamation of character* is a communication to someone about another person that tends to hold that person's reputation up to scorn and ridicule. To be an actionable wrong, defamation must be communicated to a third person; defamatory statements communicated only to the injured party are not grounds for an action. *Libel* is the written form of defamation and can be presented in such forms as signs, photographs, letters, and cartoons. *Slander* is the verbal form of defamation and tends to form prejudices against a person in the eyes of third persons.

Slander

Slander lawsuits are rare because of the difficulty in proving defamation, the small awards, and high legal fees. With slander, the person who brings suit generally must prove special damages; however, when any allegedly defamatory words refer to a person in a professional capacity, the professional need not show that the words caused damage. It is presumed that any slanderous reference to someone's professional capacity is damaging.

Professionals who are called incompetent in front of others have a right to sue to defend their reputation. However, it is difficult to prove that an individual comment was injurious. If the person making an injurious comment cannot prove that the comment is true, then that person can be held liable for damages.

Libel

In a libel or slander per se (on its face) action, a court will presume that certain words and accusations cause injury to a person's reputation without proof of damages. Words or accusations that require no proof of actual harm to one's reputation are: (1) accusing someone of a crime, (2) accusing someone of having a loathsome disease, (3) using words that affect a person's profession or business, and (4) calling a woman unchaste. Healthcare professionals are, however, legally protected against libel when complying with a law that requires, for example, reporting of venereal or other diseases. Damages typically consist of economic losses, such as loss of business or employment.

Defenses to a Defamation Action

Essentially, the two defenses to a defamation action are truth and privilege. When a person has said something that is damaging to another person's reputation, the person making the statement will not be liable for defamation if it can be shown that the statement is true. A privileged communication differs from a defamatory statement in that the person making the communication has a responsibility to do so. For example, many states have statutes providing immunity to physicians and healthcare institutions in connection with peer review activities. The person making the communication must do so in good faith, on the proper occasion, in the proper manner, and to persons who have a legitimate reason to receive the information.

An administrator's statements made to a physician's supervisor regarding the physician's alleged professional misconduct are not grounds for a defamation action as long as the statements are made in good faith. The administrator has a duty to report complaints about alleged professional misconduct of physicians working in the hospital. The administrator has qualified privilege to report such complaints to the physician's supervisor and other hospital officials as necessary.[17]

It is important to note that public figures have more difficulty in pursuing defamation litigation than the average individual. Legal action against a public figure generally will be denied in the absence of any showing of actual malice in connection with alleged defamatory references to a plaintiff. Actual malice applies only in cases involving public figures and encompasses knowledge of falsity or recklessness as to truth.

Performance Appraisals Not for General Publication

A statement in a hospital newsletter regarding the discharge of a nursing supervisor constituted libel per se in

Kraus v. Brandsletter.[18] The newsletter indicated that the hospital's medical board had discharged the nursing supervisor after a unanimous vote of no confidence. Couching the board's determination in terms of a vote gave the impression that the board's determination had been based on facts that justified the board's opinion. The statement tended to injure the nurse's reputation as a professional because it did not refer to specifics of her performance but rather to her abilities as a professional in general. The reasonable interpretation of the statement in the newsletter was that the supervisor was incompetent in her professional capacity, thus giving rise to a cause of action for libel per se.

On the flip side in the same case, an alleged statement that a physician said, "You nurses will receive your Christmas bonus early, your boss is going to get fired," was not slander per se in that it did not injure the nurse in her professional capacity.[19] In addition, the statement that she was going to be fired was true.

Performance Appraisal Statements Not Libelous

In *Schauer v. Memorial Care System*,[20] the plaintiff applied for and was given a supervisory position at Memorial Hospital's new catheterization laboratory. In March 1989, she received an employment appraisal for the period June 1988 through December 1988. At that time, Schauer's supervisor rated her performance as "commendable" in two categories and "fair" in eight categories, with an overall rating of "fair." Although Schauer did not lose her job as a result of the appraisal, she brought an action against the hospital and her former supervisor for libel and emotional distress as a result of the appraisal. The hospital moved for summary judgment on the grounds that the employment appraisal was not defamatory as a matter of law, the hospital had qualified privilege to write the performance appraisal, and the claim for emotional distress did not reach the level of severity required for a claim for intentional infliction of emotional distress. The trial court granted the hospital's motion for summary judgment, and Schauer appealed.

The Texas Court of Appeals held that the statements contained in the performance appraisal were not libelous and that the appraisal was subject to qualified privilege. Moreover, the hospital's conduct and the statements contained in the appraisal did not support the claim for intentional infliction of emotional distress.

To sustain her claim of defamation, Schauer had to show that the hospital published her appraisal in a defamatory manner that injured her reputation in some way. A statement can be unpleasant and objectionable to the plaintiff without being defamatory. The hospital argued

that the statements contained in the appraisal were truthful, permissible expressions of opinion and not capable of a defamatory meaning. Schauer's supervisor prepared the appraisal as part of her supervisory duties. The appraisal was not published outside the hospital and was prepared in compliance with the hospital policy for all employees. Schauer disputed her overall rating of "fair" as being libelous. "Clearly, this is a statement of her supervisor's opinion and is not defamatory as a matter of law."[21]

In her performance appraisal, Schauer objected to the statement, "Ms. Schauer was not sensitive to employee relations."[22] Schauer conceded in her deposition that there were a number of interpersonal problems in the catheterization laboratory and that she did not get along with everyone. The court found that given these admissions, the statement was not defamatory.

Newspaper Articles

A libel suit was brought against the Miami Herald Publishing Company more than 2 years after its publication of an editorial cartoon depicting a nursing facility in a distasteful manner.[23] The cartoon was described in the following manner:

> On October 29, 1980, *The Herald* published an editorial cartoon which depicted three men in a dilapidated room. On the back wall was written "Krest View Nursing Home," and on the side wall there was a board, which read "Closed by Order of the State of Florida." The room itself was in a state of total disrepair. There were holes in the floor and ceiling, leaking water pipes, and exposed wiring. The men in the room were dressed in outfits resembling those commonly appearing in caricatures of gangsters. Each man carried a sack with a dollar sign on it. One of the men was larger than the other two and was more in the forefront of the picture. One of the others addressed him. The caption read: "Don't Worry, Boss, We Can Always Reopen It As a Haunted House for the Kiddies."[24]

The court held that the newspaper's editorial cartoon depicting persons resembling gangsters in a dilapidated building, identified as a particular nursing facility that had been closed by state order, was an expression of pure opinion and was protected by the First Amendment against the libel suit alleging that the cartoon defamed the owner of the facility.

Fraud

Fraud is defined as willful and intentional misrepresentation that could cause harm or loss to a person or property.

Fraud includes any cunning, deception, or artifice used, in violation of legal or equitable duty, to circumvent, cheat, or deceive another. The forms it can assume and the means by which it can be practiced are as multifarious as human ingenuity can devise, and the courts consider it unwise or impossible to formulate an exact, definite, and all-inclusive definition of the action.

To prove fraud, the following facts must be shown:

- an untrue statement known to be untrue by the party making it and that it was made with the intent to deceive
- justifiable reliance by the victim on the truth of the statement
- damages as a result of that reliance

Concealment of Information from Patient

The plaintiff in *Robinson v. Shah*[25] was a long-time patient of defendant, Dr. Shah, from 1975 to 1986. During that period of time, the defendant treated the plaintiff for various gynecological disorders. On November 9, 1983, the defendant performed a total abdominal hysterectomy and bilateral salpingo-oophorectomy on the plaintiff. Approximately 1 week following surgery, the plaintiff was discharged from the hospital and was assured that there were no complications or potential problems that might arise as a result of the surgery. On the day after the plaintiff was discharged from the hospital, she began to experience abdominal distress. She consulted the defendant about these symptoms, and the defendant ordered X-rays to be taken of the plaintiff's kidneys, ureter, and bladder in an effort to explain her discomfort.

The X-rays were taken at a hospital and were read and interpreted by Dr. Cavanaugh, presumably a radiologist associated with that facility. After reading the X-rays, Cavanaugh called the defendant and reported that the slides showed the presence of surgical sponges that had been left in the plaintiff's abdomen after surgery. Cavanaugh also sent the defendant a copy of a written report that reflected the findings.

The defendant fraudulently concealed from the plaintiff the findings of the X-rays. The defendant told the plaintiff that the X-rays were negative and that there were no apparent or unusual complications from the recent abdominal surgery, and she assured the plaintiff that she did not require further treatment. At no time did the defendant reveal to the plaintiff the fact that she had left surgical sponges in her abdomen.

Over the next several years, the plaintiff continued to see the defendant for gynecological checkups. She continued to experience abdominal pain and discomfort. The defendant, however, continued to conceal from the plaintiff the existence of the surgical sponges left in the plaintiff's abdomen. The plaintiff ceased seeing the defendant as her physician in 1986. However, she consulted other physicians and continued to experience frequent pain and discomfort in her abdomen as well as intestinal, urological, and gynecological problems. Although the plaintiff brought her complaints to the attention of other physicians, no one was able to diagnose the source of her problems.

In 1993, one of the physicians attending to the plaintiff's problems diagnosed a pelvic mass, which he felt could be causing some discomfort. The plaintiff underwent pelvic sonograms and X-rays, which revealed the existence of retained surgical sponges. The plaintiff contended that the defendant, from and after November 18, 1983, had knowledge of the presence of the retained surgical sponges in her abdomen and knew the potential of future complications that could arise from this condition. Despite this knowledge, the plaintiff contended, the defendant fraudulently concealed the existence of this condition from the plaintiff.

The appeals court held that although the action in this case was filed more than 10 years after the fraud was perpetrated, the statute of limitations was not tolled because of the defendant's fraudulent concealment of information from the patient.

Invasion of Privacy

The right to privacy is implied in the Constitution. It is recognized by the law as the right to be left alone—the right to be free from unwarranted publicity and exposure to public view, as well as the right to live one's life without having one's name, picture, or private affairs made public against one's will. Healthcare organizations and professionals can become liable for invasion of privacy if, for example, they divulge information from a patient's medical record to improper sources or if they commit unwarranted intrusions into a patient's personal affairs.

The information in a patient's medical record is confidential and should not be disclosed without the patient's permission, with the exception of occasions when there is a legal obligation or duty to disclose the information (i.e., reporting of communicable diseases, gunshot wounds, and child abuse). Those who come into possession of the most intimate personal information about patients have both a legal and an ethical duty not to reveal confidential communications.

Intentional Infliction of Mental Distress

The intentional or reckless infliction of mental distress is characterized by conduct that is so outrageous that it goes beyond the bounds tolerated by a decent society. Mental distress includes mental suffering resulting from painful emotions such as grief, public humiliation, despair, shame, and wounded pride. Liability for the wrongful infliction of mental distress can be based on either intentional or negligent misconduct. A plaintiff may recover damages if he or she can show that the defendant intended to inflict mental distress and knew or should have known that his or her actions would give rise to it.

Mother Shown Her Premature Infant

The mother of a premature infant who died shortly after birth went to her physician for a 6-week checkup. She noticed a report in her medical chart that stated that the infant was past the 5th month in development and that hospital rules and state law prohibited disposal of the infant as a surgical specimen. The mother questioned her physician, who then requested that his nurse take the mother to the hospital. An employee at the hospital took the mother to a freezer. The freezer was opened and the mother was handed a jar containing her premature infant child. The circuit court found that the hospital, through its employees, committed intentional infliction of emotional distress. On appeal, the court of appeals held that the jury could find that the hospital's conduct in displaying the infant was outrageous conduct.[26]

Verbal Abuse of a Patient

In another mental distress case, the patient and his wife brought an action in *Greer v. Medders*[27] against the physician. The defendant–physician had been covering for the attending physician who was on vacation. When the hospitalized plaintiff had not seen the covering physician for several days, he called the physician's office to complain. The physician later entered the patient's room in an agitated manner and became verbally abusive in the presence of the patient's wife and a nurse. He said to the patient, "Let me tell you one damn thing, don't nobody call over to my office raising hell with my secretary. . . . I don't have to be here every damn day checking on you because I check with physical therapy. . . . I don't have to be your damn doctor."[28] When the physician left the room, the plaintiff's wife began to cry, and the plaintiff experienced episodes of uncontrollable shaking for which he received psychiatric treatment. The Georgia Court of Appeals held that the physician's abusive language willfully caused emotional upset and precluded summary judgment for the defendant.

PRODUCTS LIABILITY

NEWSPAPER CLIPPINGS: Pharmacy Linked to U.S. Meningitis Outbreak Files for Bankruptcy

(Reuters)—The Massachusetts pharmacy linked to a deadly U.S. meningitis outbreak filed for Chapter 11 bankruptcy on Friday and said it would establish a fund to compensate victims.

According to the Centers for Disease Control and Prevention, 39 people have died and more than 600 have been injured from injections of methylprednisolone acetate, a drug typically used to ease back pain.

New England Compounding Center, the specialty pharmacy, shut down in October after shipping tainted vials of the steroid, and filed for bankruptcy with between $1 million to $10 million in assets, court documents show.

—*Tim McLaughlin*, Reuters, *December 21, 2012*

Products liability is the accountability of a manufacturer, seller, or supplier of chattels to a buyer or other third party for injuries sustained because of a defect in a product. An injured party may proceed with a lawsuit against a seller, manufacturer, or supplier on three legal theories: (1) negligence, (2) breach of warranty (express or implied), and (3) strict liability. The three types of product defects that incur liability are (1) design defects, (2) manufacturing defects, and (3) defects in marketing (e.g., providing improper instructions for the product's use).

Strict liability is a legal doctrine that makes some persons or entities responsible for damages their actions or products cause, regardless of "fault" on their part. Strict liability often applies when people engage in inherently hazardous activities, such as blasting in a city. If the blasting injures a person, no matter how careful the blasting company is, it can be liable for any injuries suffered. Strict liability also applies in the case of manufactured products such as drugs. This section focuses on products liability.

Negligence

Negligence, as applied to products liability, requires the plaintiff to establish duty, breach, injury, and causation. The manufacturer of a product is not liable for injuries suffered by a patient if they are the result of negligent use by the user. Product users must conform to the safety standards provided by the manufacturers of supplies and equipment. Failure to follow proper safety instructions can prevent recovery in a negligence suit if injury results from improper use.

Because manufacturers are liable for injuries that result from unsafe product design, they generally provide detailed safety instructions to the users of their products. Failure to provide such instructions could be considered negligence on the part of the manufacturer.

Selling Equipment with a Known Hazardous Design

An action in *Airco v. Simmons National Bank, Guardian, et al.*[29] was brought against a physician partnership that provided anesthesia services to the hospital and Airco, Inc., the manufacturer of an artificial breathing machine used in the administration of anesthesia. It was alleged that the patient suffered irreversible brain damage because of the negligent use of the equipment and its unsafe design. The machine had been marketed despite prior reports of a foreseeable danger of human error brought about by the presence of several identical black hoses and the necessity of connecting them correctly to three ports of identical size placed closely together. The machine lacked adequate labels and warnings, according to the reports. The jury awarded $1,070,000 in compensatory damages against the physician partnership and Airco, Inc. Punitive damages in the amount of $3 million were awarded against Airco, Inc. On appeal of the punitive damages award, the Arkansas Supreme Court held that the evidence for punitive damages was sufficient for the jury. The manufacturer acted in a persistent reckless disregard of the foreseeable dangers by continuing to sell the machine with the known hazardous design.

Tainted Tylenol Capsules

Negligence, as well as breach of warranty and strict liability, was not established in the well-publicized case of the 1980s involving a woman who died after ingesting Tylenol capsules tainted with potassium cyanide. The decedent's estate in *Elsroth v. Johnson & Johnson*[30] sued the manufacturer and the retail grocery store that sold the over-the-counter drug. The defendants moved for a summary judgment. The U.S. district court held that the retailer did not have a duty to protect the decedent from acts of tampering by an unknown third party. The manufacturer was not liable under an inadequate warning theory. Manufacturers are under a duty to warn of the dangers that might be associated with the normal and lawful use of their products, but they need not warn that their products might be susceptible to criminal misuse.

Failure to Warn

Merck pulled its painkiller Vioxx off pharmacy shelves, a drug it manufactures for the treatment of arthritis, after participants in a study experienced adverse cardiovascular events compared to those taking a placebo. Merck officials had argued that Vioxx was not the cause of users' heart attacks and the company had properly warned doctors and consumers about its risks. Following a 3-year battle, Merck announced in November 2007 that it would pay $4.85 billion to settle plaintiff claims over injuries linked to Vioxx. The company paid the money into a fund, and people who claimed Vioxx injured them could petition for monetary relief.

Breach of Warranty

A warranty is a particular type of guarantee (a pledge or assurance of something) concerning goods or services provided by a seller to a buyer. Nearly everything purchased is covered by a warranty. To recover under a cause of action based on a breach of warranty theory, the plaintiff must establish whether there was an express or implied warranty.

Express Warranty

An *express warranty* includes specific promises or affirmations made by the seller to the buyer, such as "X" drug is not subject to addiction. If the product fails to perform as advertised, it is a breach of express warranty. For example, in *Crocker v. Winthrop Laboratories*,[31] the patient, Mr. Crocker, was admitted to the hospital for a hernia operation. His physician prescribed both Demerol and Talwin for pain. After discharge from the hospital, Crocker developed an addiction to Talwin and was able to obtain prescriptions from several physicians to support a habit he had developed. He was eventually admitted to the hospital for detoxification. After 6 days, Crocker walked out of the hospital and went home. He became agitated and abusive, threatening his wife, who eventually called a physician at his request. The physician arrived and gave Crocker an injection of Demerol. Crocker then retired to bed and subsequently died. Action was brought against the drug company for the suffering and subsequent wrongful death that occurred as the proximate result of the decedent's addiction to Talwin.

The district court rendered a judgment for the plaintiff, and the court of appeals reversed. On further appeal, the

Texas Supreme Court held that when a drug company positively and specifically represents its product to be free and safe from all dangers of addiction and when the treating physician relies on such representation, the drug company is liable when the representation proves to be false and injury results.

Implied Warranty

An *implied warranty* is a guarantee of a product's quality that is not expressed in a purchase contract. An implied warranty assumes that the item sold can perform the function for which it is designed. Implied warranties are in effect when the law implies that one exists by operation of law as a matter of public policy for the protection of the public.

Strict Liability

Strict liability refers to responsibility without fault and makes possible an award of damages without any proof of manufacturer negligence. The plaintiff needs only to show that he or she suffered injury while using the manufacturer's product in the prescribed way.

The following elements must be present for a plaintiff to proceed with a case on the basis of strict liability:

- The product must have been manufactured by the defendant.
- The product must have been defective at the time it left the hands of the manufacturer or seller. The defect in the product normally consists of a manufacturing defect, a design defect in the product, or an absence or inadequacy of warnings for the use of the product.
- The plaintiff must have been injured by the specific product.
- The defective product must have been the proximate cause of injury to the plaintiff.

Negligent Blood Handling

A blood bank was strictly liable in *Weber v. Charity Hospital of Louisiana at New Orleans*[32] when a hospital patient developed hepatitis from a transfusion of defective blood during surgery. Evidence established that the blood bank collected, processed, and sold the blood to the hospital. Although the hospital administered the blood, absent any negligence in its handling or administration, it was not liable for the patient's injury. Many states have enacted statutes to exempt blood from the product category and thus removed blood products from the theory of strict liability.

Res Ipsa Loquitur

Liability also can be based on the concept of *res ipsa loquitur* (the thing speaks for itself) if the plaintiff can establish the following evidence:

- The product did not perform in the way intended.
- The product was not tampered with by the buyer or third party. The defect existed at the time it left the defendant manufacturer.

Mislabeled Drugs

A manufacturer mislabeled a box of Duragesic patches, a strong prescription medication for moderate to severe chronic pain, marking the box as containing 25 mcg patches. In actuality, the box contained 100 mcg patches. The patient placed a patch on her back to provide relief of severe back pain. Instead of receiving the 25 mcg dosage recommended by her physician, she received 100 mcg, four times the recommended dosage. The patient went into a coma and eventually died.

Products Liability Defenses

Defenses against recovery in a products liability case include:

- assumption of a risk (e.g., voluntary exposure to such risks as radiation treatments and chemotherapy treatments)
- intervening cause (e.g., an intravenous solution contaminated by the negligence of the product user, rather than that of the manufacturer)
- contributory negligence (e.g., use of a product in a way that it was not intended to be used)
- comparative fault (e.g., injury is the result of the concurrent negligence of both the manufacturer and the plaintiff)
- disclaimers (e.g., manufacturers' inserts and warnings regarding usage and contraindications of their products)

Courts often invalidate disclaimers and waivers of liability for products as being against public policy. Warranties are limited so that manufacturers and retailers are held responsible for personal injuries caused by the use of a product.

⬥ Notes

1. 11 A.2d 132 (N.Y. App. Div. 1960).
2. 498 So. 2d 713 (La. Ct. App. 1986).
3. 787 S.W.2d 494 (Tex. Ct. App. 1990).
4. *Id.* at 496.
5. 498 So. 2d 713 (La. Ct. App. 1986).
6. No. CV-05 4449, (U.S. District Ct, Eastern District, NY, 12-20-2012).
7. 384 S.E.2d 92 (Va. 1989).
8. 498 So. 2d 713 (La. Ct. App. 1986).
9. No. 2003-01976 (N.Y. App. Div. 2004).
10. *Tomcik v. Ohio Dep't of Rehabilitation & Correction*, 598 N.E.2d 900 (Ohio Ct. App. 1991).
11. *Caruso v. Pine Manor Nursing Ctr.*, 538 N.E.2d 722 (Ill. App. Ct. 1989).
12. 296 S.E.2d 216 (Ga. Ct. App. 1982).
13. 116 Cal. Rptr. 733 (Cal. Ct. App. 1974).
14. 457 A.2d 431 (N.J. 1983).
15. 841 F.2d 851 (8th Cir. 1988).
16. J. Garrard, et al. "Evaluation of Neuroleptic Drug Use by Nursing Home Elderly under Proposed Medicare and Medicaid Regulations," *JAMA* 265, no. 4 (1991): 463.
17. *Miller-Douglas v. Keller*, 579 So. 2d 491 (La. Ct. App. 1991).
18. 562 N.Y.2d 127 (N.Y. App. Div. 1990).
19. *Id.* at 129.
20. 856 S.W.2d 437 (Tex. Ct. App. 1993).
21. *Id.* at 447.
22. *Id.*
23. *Keller v. Miami Herald Publishing Company*, 778 F.2d 711 (11th Cir. 1985).
24. *Id.* at 713.
25. 936 P.2d 784 (Kans. App. 1997).
26. 527 S.W.2d 133 (Tenn. Ct. App. 1975).
27. 336 S.E.2d 329 (Ga. App. 1985).
28. *Id.*
29. 638 S.W.2d 660 (Ark. 1982).
30. 700 F. Supp. 151 (S.D.N.Y. 1988).
31. 514 S.W.2d 429 (Tex. 1974).
32. 487 So. 2d 148 (La. Ct. App. 1986).

Although the legal and ethical definitions of right are the antithesis of each other, most writers use them as synonyms. They confuse power with goodness, and mistake law for justice.

—CHARLES T. SPRADING[1]

Figure 5–1 Criminal Law © Pixelbliss/ShutterStock, Inc.

Learning Objectives

The reader upon completion of this chapter will be able to:

- Explain what criminal law is, the classification of crimes, and its purpose.
- Describe the criminal procedure process from arrest through trial.
- Describe several of the more common crimes that occur in the healthcare setting.

Criminal law (also known as penal law) is the body of statutory and common law that deals with crime and the legal punishment of criminal offenses. Criminal law represents society's expression of the limits of acceptable human behavior. A *crime* is any social harm defined and made punishable by law.

Crimes are classified as misdemeanors or felonies, dependent upon the severity of the crime. A *misdemeanor* is an offense generally punishable by less than 1 year in jail and/or a fine (e.g., petty larceny). A *felony* is a much more serious crime (e.g., rape or murder) and is punishable by imprisonment in a state or federal penitentiary for more than 1 year.

Criminal law distinguishes crimes from civil wrongs such as tort or breach of contract. The intent of criminal law is to regulate the behavior of individuals and groups in relation to societal norms at large whereas civil law is aimed primarily at the relationship between private individuals and their rights and obligations under the law.

The objectives of criminal law are to:

- maintain public order and safety;
- protect the individual;
- use punishment as a deterrent to crime; and
- rehabilitate the criminal for return to society.

Particular to healthcare organizations is the fact that patients are often helpless and at the mercy of others. Healthcare facilities are far too often places where the morally weak and mentally deficient prey on the physically and sometimes mentally helpless. The very institutions designed as a place for healing can sometimes provide the setting for criminal conduct. The Department of Justice and state prosecutors vigorously pursue and prosecute healthcare organizations and individuals for criminal conduct.

CRIMINAL PROCEDURE

Criminal procedure regulates the process for addressing violations of criminal law. The process begins with an alleged crime. A complainant makes an accusation, which is investigated by the police who act as agents of the government. When necessary, detectives can be assigned to a case to gather evidence, interview crime suspects and witnesses, and assist in preparing a case for possible trial. When a misdemeanor or felony has been committed, evidence is gathered, a target defendant identified, and an arrest by a police officer is made. Upon arrest, the defendant is taken to the appropriate law enforcement agency for processing, which includes paperwork and fingerprinting. The police prepare and file accusatory statements, such as misdemeanor or felony complaints with a court in the appropriate jurisdiction. After processing has been completed, the defendant is either detained or released on bond. If the alleged offense is classified as a felony, the

U.S. Constitution requires that the case be referred to a grand jury for an indictment. An *indictment* is the official charging instrument accusing the defendant of criminal conduct.

A prosecuting attorney represents the interests of the state. The defendant's attorney represents the interests of the defendant. Although the specific process varies according to local law, in virtually every jurisdiction the process culminates with a trial, a verdict, and sometimes followed by an appeal to a higher court.

Criminal statutes spell out what constitute a crime. The prosecutor must prove each element of a crime charged beyond a reasonable doubt. Otherwise, the defendant is not guilty of the alleged offense. The three components of a crime include the:

1. act itself (the *actus reus* or guilty act);
2. requisite mental state/intent (the *mens rea* or guilty mind); and
3. attendant circumstances.

A prosecutor presents criminal cases to a grand jury. When the grand jury is presented with the prosecution's evidence, it may indict the target if members of the grand jury find in the evidence reasonable cause to believe that all the elements of a particular crime are present. Before indictment, the grand jury may request that in addition to the witnesses presented by the prosecutor, additional witnesses be subpoenaed to testify. Finally, actions of a grand jury are handed to a judge, after which the defendant is notified if indicted to appear to be arraigned for the crimes charged in the indictment.

Arraignment

The arraignment is a formal reading of the accusatory instrument (a generic term that describes a variety of documents, each of which accuses a defendant of an offense) and includes the setting of bail. After the charges are read, the defendant pleads guilty or not guilty. On a plea of not guilty, the defense attorney and prosecutor make arguments regarding bail. After the defendant's arraignment, the judge sets a date for the defendant to return to court. Between the time of arraignment and the next court date, the defense attorney and the prosecutor confer about the charges and evidence in the possession of the prosecutor. At that time, the defense will offer any mitigating circumstances it believes will convince the prosecutor to lessen or drop the charges.

Conference

If the defendant does not plead guilty, both felony and misdemeanor cases are taken to conference, and plea-bargaining commences with the goal of an agreed-upon disposition. If no disposition can be reached, the case is adjourned, motions are made, and the case is set for trial.

Criminal Trial

Most of the processes of a criminal trial are similar to those of a civil trial and include jury selection, opening statements, presentation of witnesses and other evidence, summations, instructions to the jury by the judge, jury deliberations, verdict, and, if necessary, opportunity for appeal to a higher court. In a criminal trial, the jury verdict must be unanimous, and the standard of proof must be beyond a reasonable doubt, not all doubt. Criminal trials involving healthcare professionals include healthcare identify theft, fraud, falsification of records, misuse and theft of drugs, patient abuse, and murder. A variety of such cases are reviewed here.

▮ HEALTHCARE FRAUD

NEWSPAPER CLIPPINGS: Health Care: A 'Goldmine' for Fraudsters

NEW YORK (CNNMoney.com)—There's a group of people who really love the U.S. healthcare system—the fraudsters, scammers and organized criminal gangs who are bilking the system of as much as $100 billion a year.

Healthcare identity theft dominated all other crimes in the sector last year, according to Louis Saccoccio, executive director of the National Health Care Anti-Fraud Association (NHCAA), an advocacy group whose members include insurers, law enforcement, and regulatory agencies.

Increasingly, criminal groups are hacking into digital medical records so that they can steal money from the $450 billion, 44-million-beneficiary Medicare system—making the government, by far, the "single biggest victim" of healthcare fraud, according to Rob Montemorra, chief of the FBI's Health Care Fraud Unit.

—*Parija Kavilanz*, CNNMoney, *January 13, 2010*[2]

NEWSPAPER CLIPPINGS: Doctor Gets 20 Years in Miss. Cancer Center Fraud

JACKSON, Miss. (AP)—A federal judge on Friday sentenced a doctor to 20 years in prison and ordered her to repay nearly $8.2 million for fraud at a former Mississippi cancer center she ran. U.S. District Judge Daniel P. Jordan III said he was "appalled" at how Dr. Meera Sachdeva treated patients at a vulnerable time of their lives.

Syringes were re-used and different patients' chemotherapy drugs were drawn from the same bag at Rose Cancer Center in the small town of Summit, Jordan said. He said prosecutors were unable to prove drugs were watered down, as they originally believed.

"It's a very small thing to send this woman to jail for the next 20 years when you compare it to the damage she has done," Jordan said from the bench.

—*Emily Wagster Pettus*, Associated Press, *December 7, 2012*[3]

False Claims Act—1986

NEWSPAPER CLIPPINGS: N.J. System Pays $12.6 Million to Settle Whistle-blower Case

Cooper Health System in Camden, N.J., has agreed to pay $12.6 million to settle whistle-blower allegations that it inappropriately encouraged cardiologists to refer patients to its hospitals by paying them $18,000 a year to serve on a local advisory board.

The system, which operates 493 beds among two hospitals, agreed to pay the Justice Department $10.2 million and the state of New Jersey $2.3 million for alleged violations of the state and federal false claims acts, which prohibit hospitals from paying doctors to refer patients to their facilities for treatment.

—*Joe Carlson*, ModernHealthCare.com, *January 26, 2013*

The False Claims Act of 1986 prohibits: knowingly presenting, or causing to be presented, to the government a false claim for payment; knowingly making, using, or causing to be made or used a false record or statement to get a false claim paid or approved by the government;

Figure 5–2   Identity Theft   © Keith Bell/ShutterStock, Inc.

conspiring to defraud the government by getting a false claim allowed or paid; and knowingly making, using, or causing to be made or used a false record to avoid or decrease an obligation to pay or transmit property to the government.

As part of the effort to reduce fraud and abuse in federal healthcare programs, the Office of Inspector General (OIG) can impose monetary penalties as well as exclude providers that violate the False Claims Act from participation in Medicare and other federal healthcare programs. Where the best interests of the programs are served by allowing continued participation by the provider, the OIG will often require that the provider adopt specific measures to better ensure its integrity. These measures are set forth in a corporate, institutional, or individual integrity agreement (collectively referred to as a corporate integrity agreement or CIA).

Anti-Kickback Statute—1987

The Medicare and Medicaid Patient Protection Act of 1987, as amended, 42 U.S.C. §1320a7b (the "Anti-Kickback Statute"), provides for criminal penalties for certain acts impacting Medicare and state healthcare (e.g., Medicaid) reimbursable services. The Anti-Kickback Statute, as amended, prohibits certain solicitations or receipt of remuneration. The statute penalizes anyone who knowingly and willfully solicits, receives, offers, or pays anything of value as an inducement in return for: referring an individual to a person for the furnishing or arranging for the furnishing of any item or service payable under the Medicare or Medicaid programs; and purchasing, leasing, or ordering or arranging for or recommending purchasing, leasing, or ordering any good, facility, service, or item payable under the Medicare or Medicaid programs.

The OIG investigates violations of the Medicare and Medicaid Anti-Kickback Statute. Violators are subject to criminal penalties or exclusion from participation in the Medicare and Medicaid programs. The OIG specifically targets four billing practices:

- claims for services not provided;
- claims for beneficiaries not homebound;
- claims for visits not made; and,
- claims for visits not authorized by a physician.

Ethics in Patient Referral Act—1989

The Ethics in Patient Referral Act prohibits physicians who have ownership interest or compensation arrangements with a clinical laboratory from referring Medicare patients to that laboratory. The law also requires all Medicare providers to report the names and provider numbers of all physicians or their immediate relatives with ownership interests in a provider entity.

HIPAA—1989

NEWSPAPER CLIPPINGS: Spat of Medical Data Breaches Raises Alarm

Keeping records secure is a challenge that doctors, public health officials, and the regulators are just beginning to grasp. And, as two incidents at Howard University Hospital show, inadequate data security can affect huge numbers of people.

One May 14, federal prosecutors charged one of the hospital's medical technicians with violating the Health Insurance Portability and Accountability Act (HIPAA). Prosecutors allege that over a 17-month period, Laurie Napper used her position at the hospital to gain access to patients' names, addresses, and Medicare numbers to sell their information.

—*David Schultz*, The Washington Post, *June 3, 2012*

The Health Insurance Portability and Accountability Act of 1996 (HIPAA), provides new criminal and civil enforcement tools and funding dedicated to the fight against healthcare fraud. In addition, HIPAA requires the U.S. Attorney General and the U.S. Secretary of the Department of Health and Human Services (DHHS), acting through the Office of Inspector General (OIG), to establish a national healthcare fraud and abuse control program. The program provides a coordinated national framework for federal, state, and local law enforcement agencies; the private sector; and the public to fight healthcare fraud. To combat fraud in home care settings, the DHHS announced Operation Restore Trust, which is an antifraud enforcement initiative targeted at home care agencies, nursing homes, and durable equipment suppliers. DHHS provided a toll-free telephone number (800-HHS-TIPS) to gather allegations of healthcare fraud from the public as well as from organizational whistle-blowers.

Fraud and Ethics

Behind every act of healthcare fraud lies a lapse in ethics. One particular type of fraud occurs when physicians refer their patients to hospitals and ancillary healthcare providers where the physician owns a financial interest in the provider to which the patient has been referred. The ethical risks inherent in physician self-referral were first noted in a 1986 Institute of Medicine study, and then again in a 1989 Health and Human Services inspector general study. The 1989 study concluded that physicians who owned or invested in independent clinical laboratories referred Medicare patients for 45% more laboratory services than did physicians without financial interests. It was in 1989 that the Ethics in Patient Referral Act was enacted, prohibiting unethical referrals, which were further defined in 1991, when the American Medical Association (AMA) Council on Ethical and Judicial Affairs concluded that physicians should not refer patients to a healthcare facility in which they have a financial interest and they do not directly provide services. In the following year, the AMA House of Delegates voted to declare self-referral to be unethical in most instances.

The Omnibus Budget Reconciliation Act of 1989 (which took effect January 1, 1992) backed the AMA's position on self-referral, barring the referral of Medicare patients to clinical laboratories by physicians who have, or whose family members have a financial interest in those laboratories. The scope of the ban on self-referral was expanded with the enactment of the Omnibus Reconciliation Act of 1993 (effective January 1, 1995), which added 10 additional designated health services, including physical therapy; occupational therapy; radiology services; radiation therapy services and supplies; durable medical equipment and supplies; parenteral and enteral nutrients, equipment, and supplies; orthotics, prosthetics, and prosthetic devices and supplies; home health services; outpatient prescription drugs; and inpatient and outpatient hospital services. The 1993 law also expanded and clarified exceptions and applied the referral limits to Medicaid.

Laboratory Kickback

In the case of *United States v. Katz*,[4] the owner of a diagnostic medical lab agreed to kickback 50% of Medicare payments received by the lab for referrals from Total Health Care, a medical service company. Under the scheme, Total Health Care collected blood and urine samples from medical offices and clinics in southern California and sent them to the medical lab for testing. The lab billed Total Health, which in turn billed the private insurance carrier or the government-funded insurance programs Medi-Cal and Medicare for reimbursement. The lab then kicked back half of its receipts to Total Health. The owners of the lab and Total Health arranged an identical scheme with a community medical clinic; Katz, the appellant, subsequently purchased a 25% interest in the clinic and began collecting payments under the scheme. Katz was convicted of conspiracy to commit Medicare fraud and of receipt of kickbacks in exchange for referral of Medicare patients. Although he appealed the decision, the Court of Appeals affirmed the charges against him.

Architectural Contract Kickback

Three members of a county council were convicted by a jury for soliciting and receiving kickbacks from architects in *United States v. Thompson*.[5] The architects testified that the appellants and others sought a 1% kickback on a hospital project, financed by federal funds, in return for being awarded the architectural contract. Mr. Galloway, of the architectural firm of Galloway and Guthrey, had delivered $6,000 to appellant Campbell at the Knoxville airport. The architects had informed the FBI, and an investigation was conducted. After the investigation, indictments, and trial by jury, the defendants were each sentenced to 1 year in prison. On appeal, the U.S. Court of Appeals for the Sixth Circuit held that the receipt of a kickback constituted an overt act in furtherance of a conspiracy to obstruct lawful government function and was a violation of the general conspiracy statute and a crime against the United States. It had been previously observed that "to conspire to defraud the United States means primarily to cheat the government out of property or money, but it also means to interfere with or obstruct one of its lawful governmental functions by deceit, craft, or trickery, or at least by means that are dishonest."[6] Proof that part of the architects' fee was reimbursed with federal funds was not necessary for a conviction. The criminal convictions were affirmed.

Scheme to Defraud Medicare and Medicaid

The defendant–physician in *United States v. Raithath*[7] owned and operated two clinics. The defendant was convicted for making false statements and scheming to defraud. The defendant, sentenced to 27 months of imprisonment, appealed his conviction and sentence.

The indictment filed against the defendant included charges for instructing billing staff to raise the current procedural terminology (CPT) codes on invoices when the physician reported a lower level of service; submit invoices to insurance companies for services performed by other physicians as if the defendant had performed them; submit claims with a diagnosis listing an illness when the patient did not have an illness; and causing patients to present themselves for medically unnecessary visits by refusing to authorize refills on prescriptions and preventing employees from authorizing refills of prescriptions.

Charges also included making unannounced home visits to patients; approaching people on the street and ushering them into the clinic for unscheduled examinations; examining people who had come into the clinic for nonmedical reasons, such as to pay debts owed to the defendant; ordering medical tests not related to patients' conditions; falsely representing that other physician employees had specialties so that patients would be examined an additional time by a "specialist"; and refusing to give test results until an additional appointment was kept.

The defendant was also charged with defrauding Medicare/Medicaid by submitting a cost report for 1997 that included personal expenses unrelated to patient care. Included in those expenses was money that was actually spent to furnish the defendant's home.

The defendant, on appeal, argued that there was insufficient evidence to sustain his conviction for defrauding or attempting to defraud. The defendant's staff members testified that the defendant instructed them to bill office visits covered by private insurance under CPT codes 99213 or 99203, regardless of the CPT code entered by the attending physician on the encounter form. Staff members were aware that this "up-coding" scheme resulted in higher reimbursement from private insurance companies.

Staff also testified that the defendant routinely ordered tests unrelated to his patients' conditions and supported the tests with false diagnoses. Zeren, a nurse practitioner working at the McKee clinic, testified that after she performed sports physicals on children at local schools and found no indication of upper-respiratory infections, the defendant, who had not been present at the examinations,

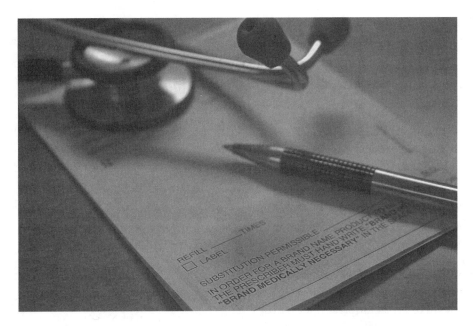

Figure 5–3   Generics Billed as Brand Name Drugs   © Cyrus J Cornell/ShutterStock, Inc.

falsely diagnosed them as having upper respiratory infections.

A reasonable juror could have reasonably found the defendant–physician guilty of defrauding or attempting to defraud Medicare/Medicaid. The conviction and sentence of the district court was affirmed.

False Medicaid Claims by Physician and Office Manager

In *United States v. Larm*,[8] a physician and his office manager were convicted on charges that they violated 42 U.S.C. § 139h(a)1 by submitting false Medicaid claims for medical services they never rendered to patients. Claims sometimes were submitted even when patients administered allergy injections themselves. In addition, sometimes more expensive serums were billed rather than those that were actually administered.

Pharmacist Submits False Drug Claims

The pharmacist in *State v. Heath*[9] submitted claims for reimbursement on brand-name medications rather than on the less-expensive generic drugs that were actually dispensed. A licensed pharmacist and former employee of the defendant contacted the Medicaid Fraud Unit of the Louisiana Attorney General's office and reported the defendant's conduct in substituting generic drugs for brand-name drugs. As a result of the complaint, the Medicaid Fraud Unit conducted a call out, in which the unit sent letters to Medicaid recipients in the pharmacy's surrounding area.

> In a recipient call out, the Medicaid Fraud Unit sends letters to Medicaid recipients in the general area of the pharmacy involved and asks them to bring all their prescription drugs to the welfare office on a specific date. The call out revealed that some of the prescription vials issued by the aforesaid pharmacies contained generic drugs while the labels indicated that they should contain brand name drugs. The pharmacist was convicted on three counts of Medicaid fraud.[10]

Inflating Insurance Claims

The North Carolina Court of Appeals held that a chiropractor's license was properly suspended for 6 months in *Farlow v. North Carolina State Board of Chiropractic Examiners*[11] for inflating the insurance claims of victims of an automobile accident. Dr. Farlow prescribed a course of treatment for several patients that were not justified by the injuries they received, instead the treatment had been prescribed to inflate insurance claims.

Falsification of Records

As with healthcare fraud, falsification of medical and business records is grounds for criminal prosecution. Anyone who suffers damage as a result of falsification of records can claim civil liability, which could result in the provider's loss of Medicare and Medicaid funding.

Misuse and Theft of Drugs

Perhaps one of the most tempting and accessible crimes for a healthcare professional involves the misuse or theft of drugs. Drugs can offer significant financial gain when they fall into the hands of the wrong people.

Internet Pharmacy

Such was the case in *United States v. Nelson*,[12] where a doctor cooperated in an Internet pharmacy and had the proceeds transferred to an offshore account. Fuchs, an unindicted coconspirator, operated an Internet pharmacy called NationPharmacy.com, where customers could obtain prescription and nonprescription drugs. In accord with federal law, all requests for prescription drugs were first reviewed by a physician, defendant Nelson, who either approved or denied the request. Nelson, however, approved 90–95% of all prescription drug requests and did so without ever examining his purported patient. Customers who used Fuchs's Internet pharmacy would have their orders routed through a brick-and-mortar pharmacy called Main Street Pharmacy. Nelson would physically visit Main Street Pharmacy to sign the prescription requests, and customers would receive prescriptions by mail and pay Fuchs directly. The prescribing physician (Nelson) was never paid by customers. Instead, Nelson received a total of $175,000, which was wired directly from Fuchs into an offshore account.

Nelson was charged and convicted of both conspiracy to distribute controlled prescription drugs outside the usual course of professional practice, in violation of 21 U.S.C. § 846, and conspiracy to launder money, in violation of 18 U.S.C. § 1956(h). Nelson appealed his conviction, arguing that there was insufficient evidence to support a conviction because there was no evidence of a conspiracy.

The most significant evidence came from testimonies by Weeks, the person who set up the website; Shadid, the resident pharmacist at Main Street Pharmacy; Thompson, another pharmacist at Main Street Pharmacy; and Dupes, the office manager for Fuchs. Weeks's testimony described the general workings of the Fuchs website. He testified he established this website at Fuchs's behest as a means of providing prescription and nonprescription drugs over the Internet. Weeks testified that only those orders for prescription drugs that were specifically approved by Nelson were processed. He testified that he provided Nelson the means to review and approve prescription drug requests with a unique user name and password that enabled Nelson to access the medical history questionnaires required to be filled out by all customers who requested prescription drugs, which Shadid and Thompson testified as to Nelson's participation in the scheme. Both men were pharmacists at Main Street Pharmacy, which processed all orders taken through NationPharmacy.com. Both testified that on numerous occasions, Nelson would personally come to Main Street Pharmacy to sign prescriptions and that Nelson signed "thousands" of prescriptions for NationPharmacy.com. Finally, Dupes testified she transferred money, a total of $175,000, from an account controlled by Fuchs to an offshore account controlled by Nelson.

The evidence described a scheme that depended upon the participation of Nelson. Without his approval, requests for controlled prescription drugs taken on the website would not have been filled. Given the concert of action between Nelson and Fuchs in the common purpose of operating a website pharmacy, a reasonable jury could infer the existence of an agreement constituting a conspiracy to distribute prescription drugs outside the usual course of professional practice and to launder the proceeds of that distribution.

Physicians Can Be Victims of Fraud

Physicians are not immune from being the victims of fraud. The detection, investigation, and prosecution of financial crimes against physicians are not uncommon occurrences. They involve such areas as computer billing crime, bookkeeper/office manager theft, insurance fraud, cash larceny, checkbook scams, and patient record tampering.

Physicians should be aware of how to analyze larcenous transactions, identify embezzled funds, and recognize the criminal employee. Physicians should be wary of bookkeepers who make themselves indispensable because of their perceived ability to operate the office computer system. To avoid being victimized by employee fraud, physicians should:

- familiarize themselves with patient billing and record keeping practices
- avoid having one person in charge of both the billing and collection process
- arrange for an annual audit of office procedures and records by a qualified auditor

PATIENT ABUSE

NEWSPAPER CLIPPINGS: Granny Cams

Gale . . . wasn't prepared for the rough treatment and cruel taunts she says her ailing mother suffered at the nursing home. She cried as a nurse's aide upbraided her mother for failing to straighten her arthritis-stricken legs. And she watched in disbelief as an assistant jerked her mother off her rubber bed pad and pushed her into the bed's metal rails.

All of these images were caught . . . by a "granny cam"—a camera hidden in her mother's room.

— *Deborah Sharp*, USA Today, *September 14, 1999*

Patient abuse is the mistreatment or neglect of individuals who are under the care of a healthcare organization. Abuse is not limited to an institutional setting and can occur in an individual's home as well as in an institution. Abuse can take many forms: physical, psychological, medical, and financial. To compound the issue, abuse is not always easy to identify because injuries often can be attributed to other causes, especially in elderly patients with their advanced age and failing health. In the hospital setting, patients are not generally as dependent upon the facility operator in the same manner as a resident in a nursing facility is. Persons are usually hospitalized for only brief periods of time, whereas nursing facility residents might be dependent upon the facility operator for a period of years. Thus, the potential for long-term abuse and neglect is far greater for nursing facility residents than hospital patients.

The abuse of the elderly is not a localized or isolated problem. Unfortunately, it permeates society. Behind Closed Doors, a landmark book on family violence stated that the first national study of violence in American homes estimated that one in two homes is the scene of family violence at least once per year.[13]

The plaintiffs in *In re Estate of Smith v. O'Halloran*[14] instituted a lawsuit in an effort to improve deplorable conditions at many nursing homes. The court concluded that:

The evidentiary record . . . supports a general finding that all is not well in the nation's nursing homes and that the enormous expenditures of public funds and the earnest efforts of public officials and public employees have not produced an equivalent return in benefits. That failure of expectations has produced frustration and anger

among those who are aware of the realities of life in some nursing homes, which provide so little service that they could be characterized as orphanages for the aged.[15]

Abuse of nursing facility residents gave impetus to the strengthening of resident rights under the Omnibus Budget Reconciliation Act of 1989. The act provides that a "resident has the right to be free from verbal, sexual, physical, or mental abuse, corporal punishment, and involuntary seclusion."[16] Although resident rights have been significantly strengthened, resident abuse is often in the headlines. For example, the headline "Nurse's Aide Jailed for Punching Patient" topped a story about a nurse's aide who was jailed for punching a 91-year-old senile man in the nose.[17] The aide had been previously convicted of resident abuse.

CRIMINAL NEGLIGENCE

Criminal negligence is the reckless disregard for the safety of others. It is the willful indifference to an injury that could follow an act. The defendants in *State v. Brenner*[18] were charged with cruelty to the infirm. The state alleged that the administrator of the nursing facility neglected and mistreated residents by failing to ensure: the facility was maintained in a sanitary manner, necessary health services were performed, staff were properly trained, there were adequate medical supplies and sufficient staff, records were maintained properly, and the residents were adequately fed and cared for. In addition to allegations of neglect and mistreatment of residents, other allegations charged the director with failing to properly train the staff at the facility in correct nursing procedures. The controller was alleged to have failed to purchase adequate medical supplies for proper treatment. The admissions director allegedly failed to exercise proper judgment regarding admissions procedures, and the physical therapist allegedly failed to provide adequate physical therapy services. The defendants asserted that the term "neglect" was unconstitutionally vague. The Louisiana Supreme Court, on appeal by the defendants from two lower courts, held that the phrases "intentional or criminally negligent mistreatment or neglect" and "unjustifiable pain and suffering" were not vague and that they were sufficiently clear in meaning to afford a person of ordinary understanding fair notice of the conduct that was prohibited.[19]

Neglect of Residents

The defendant in *State v. Cunningham*[20] was the owner and administrator of a residential care facility that housed 30 to

37 mentally ill, mentally retarded, and elderly residents. The Iowa Department of Inspections and Appeals conducted surveys at the defendant's facility. A grand jury charged the defendant with several counts of resident neglect in violation of Iowa Code section 726.7 (1989).

The district court held that the defendant had knowledge of the dangerous conditions that existed in the healthcare facility but willfully and consciously refused to provide or exercise adequate supervision to remedy or attempt to remedy the dangerous conditions. The residents were exposed to physical dangers, unhealthy and unsanitary physical conditions, and were grossly deprived of much-needed medical care and personal attention. The conditions were likely to and did cause injury to the physical and mental well being of the facility's residents. The defendant was found guilty on five counts of neglect. The district court sentenced the defendant to 1 year in jail for each of the 5 counts, to run concurrently. The district court suspended all but 2 days of the defendant's sentence and ordered him to pay $200 for each count, plus a surcharge and costs, and to perform community service. A motion for a new trial was denied, and the defendant appealed.

The Iowa Court of Appeals held that there was substantial evidence to support a finding that the defendant was responsible for not properly maintaining the facility, which led to prosecution for wanton neglect of the facility's residents. The defendant was found guilty of knowingly acting in a manner likely to be injurious to the physical or mental welfare of the facility's residents by creating, directing, or maintaining the following five hazardous conditions and unsafe practices:

1. There were fire hazards and circumstances that impeded safety from fire. For example, cigarette stubs were found in a cardboard box, and burn holes were found in patient clothing, on furniture, and in nonsmoking areas. Also, exposed electrical wiring was found, along with a bent and rusted fire door that could not close or latch.

2. The facility was not properly maintained and demonstrated many health and safety violations, including broken glass in patients' rooms, excessively hot water in faucets, dried feces on public bathroom walls and grab bars, no soap in the kitchen, insufficient towels and linens, dead and live cockroaches and worms in the food preparation area, and debris, bugs, and grease throughout the facility.

3. Dietary facilities were unsanitary and inadequate to meet the dietary needs of the residents. In one particular case, an ordered "no concentrated sweets" diet for a diabetic patient was not followed, subjecting the patient to life-threatening blood sugar levels.

4. There were inadequate staffing patterns and supervision in the facility. No funds were spent on employee training, and the defendant did not spend the minimum amount of time at the facility, as required by administrative standards.

5. Improper dosages of medications were administered to the residents. For example, physicians distributed an ongoing overdose of heart medication to one resident while failing to administer medication to another (which resulted in a seizure).[21]

The defendant argued that he did not create the unsafe conditions at the facility. The court of appeals disagreed. The statute does not require that the defendant create the conditions at the facility to sustain a conviction. The defendant was the administrator of the facility and responsible for the conditions that existed.

Abuse and Revocation of License

The operator of a nursing facility appealed an order by the department of public welfare revoking his license because of resident abuse in *Nepa v. Commonwealth Department of Public Welfare.*[22] Substantial evidence supported the department's finding. Three former employees testified that the nursing facility operator had abused residents in the following incidents: he unbuckled the belt of one of the residents, causing his pants to drop, and then grabbed a second resident, forcing the two to kiss (the petitioner's excuse for this behavior was to shame the resident because of his masturbating in public); on two occasions he forced a resident to remove toilet paper from a commode after she had urinated and defecated in it (denying that there was fecal matter in the commode, the petitioner's excuse was that this was his way of trying to stop the resident from filling the commode with toilet paper); and he verbally abused a resident who was experiencing difficulty in breathing and accused him of being a fake as he attempted to feed him liquids.[23]

The nursing facility operator claimed that the findings of fact were not based on substantial evidence and that even if they were, the incidents did not amount to abuse under the code. The court held that there was substantial evidence supporting the department's decision and that the activities committed by the operator were sufficient to support revocation of his license.

> We believe Petitioner's treatment of these residents as found by the hearing examiner to be truly disturbing. These residents were elderly and/or mentally incapacitated and wholly dependent on Petitioner while

residing in his home. As residents, they are entitled to maintain their dignity and be cared for with respect, concern, and passion.[24]

Abusive Search

A nurse in *People v. Coe*[25] was charged with a willful violation of the public health law in connection with an allegedly abusive search of an 86-year-old resident at a geriatric center and with the falsification of business records in the first degree. The resident, Mr. Gersh, had heart disease and difficulty in expressing himself verbally. Another resident claimed that two $5 bills were missing. Nurse Coe assumed that Gersh had taken them because he had been known to take things in the past. The nurse proceeded to search Gersh, who resisted. A security guard was summoned, and another search was undertaken. When Gersh again resisted, the security guard slammed a chair down in front of him and pinned his arms while the defendant nurse searched his pockets, failing to retrieve the two $5 bills. Five minutes later, Gersh collapsed, gasping for air, in a chair. Coe administered cardiopulmonary resuscitation but was unsuccessful, and Gersh passed away.

Coe was charged with violation of Section 175.10 of the New York Penal Law for falsifying records because of the defendant's "omission" of the facts relating to the search of Gersh. These facts were considered to be relevant and should have been included in the nurse's notes regarding this incident. "The first sentence states, 'Observed resident was extremely confused and talks incoherently. Suddenly became unresponsive. . . .' This statement is simply false. It could only be true if some reference to the search and the loud noise was included."[26] A motion was made to dismiss the indictment at the end of the trial.

The court held that the search became an act of physical abuse and mistreatment, the evidence was sufficient to warrant a finding of guilt on both charges, and the fact that searches took place frequently did not excuse an otherwise illegal procedure. It may well be that this incident reached the attention of the criminal justice system only because, in the end, a man had died. In those instances where residents' rights are violated contrary to standards of common decency, but that do not result in visible harm to a patient, the acts are nevertheless subject to criminal prosecution. A criminal act is not legitimized by the fact that others have, with impunity, engaged in that act.[27]

Medication Violations and Resident Abuse

The revocation of a personal care home license was found to be proper in *Miller Home, Inc. v. Commonwealth,*

Department of Public Welfare[28] because of repeated medication violations and resident abuse. Evidence was presented that the son of the personal care home's manager was hired as a staff member after having acted as a substitute, even though he had physical altercations with residents at the home. On one occasion, the manager's son punched a female resident, resulting in her hospitalization for broken bones around the eye, and on two prior occasions he had been involved in less-physical altercations that required police intervention.

The nursing facility resident in *Stiffelman v. Abrams*[29] died from:

> . . . blows, kicks, kneeings, or bodily throwings intentionally, viciously, and murderously dealt him from among the facility's staff over a period of approximately two to three weeks prior to his death"; that the "beatings were repeated and were received by the decedent at ninety years of age and in a frail, defenseless, and dependent condition"; that the beatings so administered to the decedent were "physically and mentally tortuous"; that he was caused by them to live out his final days in agony and terror; and that his physical injuries included thirteen fractures to his ribs, subpleural hemorrhaging, and marked lesions to his chest, flanks, abdomen, legs, arms, and hands; that during and following the period of the beatings the decedent lay at the facility for days unattended and unaided as to the deterioration and grave suffering he was undergoing.[30]

The executors of the estate had brought suit against the operator and individual and corporate owners of the facility for damages for personal injuries resulting in the death of the resident. The executors were requesting under Count I, $1.5 million in survival damages because of the physical and mental pain and suffering of the decedent, as well as $3 million for punitive damages, and under Count II, $1,504,084 in contractual breaches of the resident's admission contract with the facility. The executors claimed that certain standards of care and personal rights contained in the contract were violated. The trial court sustained the nursing facility's motion for dismissal of the case on the grounds that the plaintiffs failed to state a claim on which relief could be granted. On appeal, the judgment of the trial court was reversed with respect to Count I, and the dismissal of Count II was sustained. The case was remanded, requiring the executors to proceed under appropriate statutory authority and not under contract.

Assisted Living Facilities

NEWSPAPER CLIPPINGS: They Call It Assisted Living, But It Can Take the Life Out of You

"That's not fair," I told him. "You get to go home every day at 5 P.M., but this is my home." He stood up, pointed his finger at me, and roared: "This is NOT your home. You just lease an apartment here like everybody else."

I realized right then that the residents of "their" assisted living facility, among whom I now numbered, didn't have a voice . . .

We then can find ourselves silenced by, and subjected to, a top-down management team whose initial goal seems to be to strip us of our autonomy. And it is in this environment that most of us will die . . .

Administrators represent the whims of those who own the facility.

—*Martin Bayne*, BDN Maine Health, *July 11, 2012*

█ MURDER

NEWSPAPER CLIPPINGS: Napa State Hospital Psychiatric Worker Slain

A mentally ill patient with a long criminal history was arrested Sunday morning on charges that he robbed and killed a veteran employee at Napa State Hospital.

Donna Gross, a 54-year-old psychiatric technician from Concord who had worked at the hospital for 14 years, was found at 6:18 P.M. Saturday in a courtyard on the grounds. The staff became concerned when she failed to return to her unit from a dinner break.

—*Stacy Finz and John King*, San Francisco Chronicle, *October 21, 2010*

The tragedy of murder in institutions that are dedicated to the healing of the sick has been an all-too-frequent occurrence. The all too often occurrences of murder involve patient, family, visitors, and staff.

Unusual Number of Deaths

As was the case in *People v. Diaz*,[31] where the defendant, a registered nurse working nights at a community hospital, had an unusual number of deaths on her shift. During a three-and-a-half-week period, 13 patients on the night shift had seizures, cardiac arrest, and respiratory arrest; 9 died. The unit closed

and the defendant went to work at another hospital. Within 3 days, a patient died after exhibiting the same symptoms as those in the previous hospital while the defendant was on duty. The defendant was arrested and tried for 12 counts of murder.

The testimony revealed that the defendant injected the patients with massive doses of Lidocaine (a rhythm-controlling drug). Evidence showed that the defendant assisted the patients before they exhibited seizures, providing opportunity for the nurse to administer the drug. She was observed acting strangely on the nights of the deaths, and high concentrations of Lidocaine were found in the patients' syringes. Moreover, syringes containing the drug and Lidocaine vials were discovered in the defendant's home.

Pretrial investigation revealed that 26 other patients had died at the defendant's first hospital while under the nurse's care. All had the same symptoms. The defendant, who waived her right to trial by jury, was found guilty of the 12 counts of murder. The nurse appealed the judgment of death.

The California Supreme Court upheld the convictions. The expert testimony about the levels of Lidocaine in the patients' tissue, coupled with the nurse's testimony concerning the symptoms prior to the deaths, confirmed that the patients died from overdoses given to them by the defendant. Testimony showed that the defendant was the only nurse on duty the night each patient was poisoned, and only the defendant had the opportunity to administer the fatal doses.

Nurse Sentenced for Diabolical Acts

From 1993 to 1995, Majors worked as a licensed practical nurse (LPN) in the intensive care unit (ICU) of a county hospital. He might have been a competent nurse, but he had one problem: An incredibly high number of elderly patients died under his watch. By 1995, after rumors started to circulate that he was euthanizing patients, the hospital suspended him, and the state board of nursing suspended his license.

In 1994, 100 of the 351 people admitted to the hospital's 4-bed ICU died. A large percentage of those who died were elderly. In comparison, during the previous 4 years, an average of only 27 patients per year passed away, out of an average of 354 admitted to the ICU each year.

An analysis was conducted that showed Majors was present for more deaths than any other nurse, almost twice as many as the nearest contender. The hospital's president and chief executive officer, Ling, suspended Majors from work. Later, Ling asked the police to investigate. Majors was subsequently prosecuted and sentenced to spend the rest of his life in prison for murdering six elderly patients, a crime the judge referred to as a paragon of evil at its most wicked. Majors had been entrusted with these people's care. In response, he committed diabolical acts that extinguished the frail lives of six people.[32]

Fatal Injection of Pavulon

In a case involving the defendant–registered nurse Angelo on the cardiac/intensive care unit at a Long Island hospital, the defendant was found guilty of second-degree murder for injecting two patients with the drug Pavulon. He was found guilty of the lesser charges of manslaughter and criminally negligent homicide in the deaths of two other patients. Angelo committed the murders in a bizarre scheme to revive the patients and be thought of as a hero.[33]

▊ THEFT

NEWSPAPER CLIPPINGS: Employees Buy Luxury Lifestyle Pilfering Printer Cartridges

NEW YORK—Manhattan hospital clerk Marque Gumbs was doing so well moonlighting as a peddler of stolen property that he drove a BMW, shopped at designer stores like Burberry, and vacationed in Las Vegas and Mexico.

But unlike other more common thieves brazenly living beyond their means, his contraband wasn't jewelry or electronics, it was toner for copiers and printers.

The $1.5 million scheme at the prestigious Memorial Sloan-Kettering Cancer Center exploited what New York City authorities describe as a largely overlooked, yet lucrative black market for toner cartridges and other office supplies.

—*Marc A. Hermann*, Associated Press,
January 28, 2013

NEWSPAPER CLIPPINGS: Are Patients Stealing from Hospitals?

IRVING, TX—A new survey from VHA, Inc., a national healthcare group purchasing organization, reveals that patients take numerous items from hospital rooms when they are discharged, costing hospitals at least $52 million annually.

VHA officials say the $52 million figure was extrapolated from a survey of nearly 100 hospital supply executives. Almost two-thirds (64%) of the hospitals surveyed reported that patients and/or family members stole items ranging from towels and linens to lightbulbs, TV remotes, and telephones.

—*Richard Pizzi*, Healthcare Finance News,
February 10, 2010[34]

Healthcare organizations must be alert to the potential ongoing threat of theft by unscrupulous employees, physicians, patients, visitors, and trespassers. The theft of patient or resident valuables, supplies, and equipment is substantial and costs healthcare organizations millions of dollars each year.

The evidence presented in *People v. Lancaster*[35] was found to have provided a probable cause foundation for information charging felony theft of nursing home residents' money by the office manager. Evidence showed that on repeated occasions the residents' income checks were cashed or cash was otherwise received on behalf of residents; that the defendant, by virtue of her office, had sole responsibility for maintaining the residents' ledger accounts; and that cash receipts frequently were never posted to the residents' accounts.

In another case, there was sufficient evidence in *Miller v. Dunn*[36] to hold that a nurse assistant had misappropriated $15,000 from an 83-year-old nursing home resident. The record indicated that the funds were taken during those times the resident made visits to the hospital for respiratory problems. The patient had been diagnosed with dementia, and the resident's confusion was increasing. The nursing assistant actively procured the check in question filling in the date, amount, and her name as payee.

REALITY CHECK: OR Locker Room Thefts

It all started in the OR locker room. At first it was $2 from someone's wallet and $5 from another. It was sporadic when it first occurred. Then the frequency of the thefts increased. Employees would look at one another with suspicion. Finally management was able to make a difficult decision. A theft detection powder was dusted on some of the money and it was placed in a purse in an open locker. Greed finally took over the person as her thefts became more frequent and brazen. She eventually took the money that was marked with the powder that cannot easily be washed off. Being unaware that the money had been dusted, the employee, an OR transporter, who is responsible for wheeling patients into and out of the OR on a stretcher, eventually went to the hospital's coffee shop to spend some of the money. The cashier had noticed the greenish color on her hand and realized that she was the one who had been taking money from her coworkers

(continued)

REALITY CHECK: OR Locker Room Thefts (continued)

and notified administration. The transporter admitted to taking the money, not only from the OR staff, and her coworkers, but when she would transport patients to and from their rooms, she would take money and other items from their bedside cabinet. She admitted that patients often, having been recently anesthetized, were groggy and it made it easy for her to take money from them. The employee was discharged without charges being pressed against her.

The legal and ethical issues swirling around this incident became a hot topic for discussion amongst the OR staff.

Discussion

1. Should charges have been pressed?
2. Did the potential impact on public relations concerns rightfully mitigate the willpower of management to press charges?
3. What actions should healthcare facilities take to prevent theft?

✚ Notes

1. Charles T. Sprading, *Freedom and its Fundamentals*, (Los Angeles, CA: The Libertarian Publishing Company, 1923).
2. Parija Kavilanz, "Health Care: A 'Goldmine' for Fraudsters," *CNN Money*, January 13, 2010, http://money.cnn.com/2010/01/13/news/economy/health_care_fraud/.
3. Emily Wagster Pettus, "Doctor Gets 20 Years in Miss. Cancer Center Fraud," *Associated Press*, December 7, 2012, http://news.yahoo.com/doctor-gets-20-years-miss-cancer-center-fraud-231430553.html.
4. 871 F.2d 105 (9th Cir. 1989).
5. 366 F.2d 167 (6th Cir. 1966).
6. 265 U.S. 182, 188 (1924).
7. 385 F.3d 1013 (C.A. 6, Ky. 2004).
8. 824 F.2d 780 (9th Cir. 1987).
9. 513 So. 2d 493 (La. Ct. App. 1987).
10. *Id.* at 495.
11. 322 S.E.2d 696 (N.C. Ct. App. 1985).
12. No. 02-6183 (C.A. 10, Okla. 2004).
13. Richard J. Gelles, Murray A. Strauss, & Suzabbe K. Steinmetz, *Behind Closed Doors: Violence in the American Family*, (Anchor Books, NY, New York, 1981).
14. 557 F. Supp. 289 (D. Colo. 1983).
15. *Id.* at 293.
16. 42 C.F.R. § 483.13 (1989).
17. "Nurse's Aide Jailed for Punching Patient," *The Baltimore Sun*, June 29, 1990, §D, at 2.
18. 486 So. 2d 101 (La. 1986).
19. *Id.* at 101, 104.
20. 493 N.W.2d 884 (Iowa Ct. App. 1992).
21. *Id.* at 887–888.
22. 551 A.2d 354 (Pa. Commw. Ct. 1988).
23. *Id.* at 355.
24. *Id.* at 357.
25. 501 N.Y.S.2d 997 (N.Y. Sup. Ct. 1986).
26. *Id.* at 1001.
27. *Id.*
28. 556 A.2d 1 (Pa. Commw. Ct. 1989).
29. 655 S.W.2d 522 (Mo. 1983).
30. *Id.*
31. 834 P.2d 1171 (Cal. 1992).
32. *Majors v. Engelbrecht*, 149 F.3d 709 (1998).
33. Carolyn Colwell, "The Verdict of Angelo," *Newsday*, 50(103) 1989, 3.
34. Richard Pizzi, "Are Patients Stealing from Hospitals?" *Healthcare Finance News*, February 10, 2010, http://www.healthcarefinancenews.com/news/are-patients-stealing-hospitals.
35. 683 P.2d 1202 (Colo. 1984).
36. 184 S.W.3d 122 (Mo. App. 2006).

6
Contracts

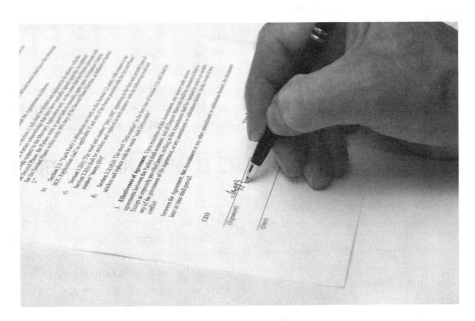

Figure 6–1 Contracts © Yevgen Timashov/ShutterStock, Inc.

✚ Learning Objectives

The reader upon completion of this chapter will be able to:

- Explain what a contract is.
- Describe the elements of a contract.
- Discuss independent contractors, as they apply to contract law.
- Describe how a hospital can be liable for the acts of a physician based on the concept of contract law.

- Explain the possible defenses and remedies for nonperformance of a contract.
- Describe under what circumstances an employee handbook could be considered a contract and how to avoid that assumption.

The intention here is to focus on providing the reader with a general understanding of the purpose, types, elements, and importance of contracts as they pertain to healthcare organizations and caregivers. Attention is also given to the defenses and legal remedies for nonperformance of a contract.

WHAT IS A CONTRACT?

A *contract* is a special kind of voluntary agreement, either written or oral, that involves legally binding obligations between two or more parties. A contract serves to provide one or more of the parties with a legal remedy if another of the parties does not perform his or her obligations pursuant to the terms of the contract.

The major purpose of a contract is to specify, limit, and define the agreements that are legally enforceable. A contract forces the participants to be specific in their understandings and expectations of each other. Contracts, particularly those in writing, serve to minimize misunderstandings and offer a means for the parties of a contract to resolve any disputes that might arise.

TYPES OF CONTRACTS

The following is a general description of the various types of contracts and a brief definition of each. Healthcare professionals should be knowledgeable of each as they are commonly used in the healthcare setting.

Express Contract

An *express contract* is one in which the parties have an oral or written agreement. Both written and oral contracts are generally recognized and are equally legal and binding. A written contract is always desirable over a verbal contract.

Implied Contract

An *implied contract* is one that is inferred by law. It is based on the conduct of the parties, such as a handshake or similar conduct. Much of the litigation concerning excesses of corporate authority involves questions of whether a corporation has the implied authority—incidental to its express authority—to perform a questioned act. In *Hungerford Hosp. v. Mulvey*, for example, even though its certificate of incorporation did not authorize a particular act specifically, a hospital was permitted to construct a medical office building on land that had been donated for maintaining and carrying on a general hospital. The court, in recognizing a trend to encourage charitable hospitals to provide private offices for rental, in this case, to staff members, held that such an act was within the implied powers of the hospital and that such offices aid in the work of a general hospital even though it went beyond the hospital corporation's express powers.[1]

A test for an implied contract can result from the conduct of the parties. An implication of contract could be argued based on the evidence even if nothing was said or written, even though most contracts are either oral or in writing. The conduct of the parties alone could imply that an offer was made and accepted if for example, (1) an independent contractor presented a work product (e.g., consulting report) to a hospital's agent that could reasonably be understood by the agent as an offer to enter into a contract and (2) if the hospital's agent accepted the consulting report, from which the hospital benefited, it could be reasonably understood that the acceptance of the consulting report was an acceptance of the consultant's offer. Such a contract would fail if the parties would or might have acted exactly as they did in the absence of a contract.

Voidable Contract

A *voidable contract* is one in which one party, but not the other, has the right to escape from its legal obligations under the contract. It is considered to be a voidable contract at the option of that party. For example, a minor, not having the capacity to enter into a contract, can void the contract. However, the competent party to the contract may not void the contract.

ELEMENTS OF A CONTRACT

The law will enforce contracts only when they are executed between persons who are competent; that is, those with the legal and mental capacity to contract. Certain classes of persons, such as minors, the insane, and prisoners, traditionally have been considered to be unable to understand the consequences of their actions and have been deemed incompetent, or lacking in legal capacity, to make a binding contract. Whether contracts are executed in writing or agreed to orally, they must contain the following elements to be enforceable.

Offer/Communication

An *offer* is a promise by one party to do (or not to do) something if the other party agrees to do (or not do) something. Preliminary negotiations are not offers. An offer must be communicated to the other party so that it can be accepted or rejected.

Consideration

Consideration requires that each party to a contract give up something of value in exchange for something of value. No side can have a free way out or the ability to obtain something of value without providing something in exchange. Only when legal consideration has been given will a court treat the agreement as a contract. The adequacy or inadequacy of consideration, or the price paid, will not normally affect the formation of a contract.

Acceptance

Upon proper acceptance of an offer, a contract is formed. A valid acceptance requires the following:

- *Meeting of the minds*: Acceptance requires a meeting of the minds (mutual assent); in other words, the parties must understand and agree on the terms of the contract. This means that each side must be clear as to the details, rights, and obligations of the contract.
- *Definite and complete*: Acceptance requires mutual assent to be found between the parties. The terms must be so complete that both parties understand and agree to what has been proposed.
- *Duration*: Generally, the offeror (the one who makes the offer) may revoke an offer at any time prior to a valid acceptance. When the offeror does revoke the proposal, the revocation is not effective until the offeree (the person to whom the offer is made) receives it. When the offeree has accepted the offer, any attempt to revoke the agreement is too late and is invalid.
- *Complete and conforming*: The acceptance must be a mirror image of the offer. In other words, the acceptance must comply with all the terms of the offer and not change or add any terms.

▌ BREACH OF CONTRACT

A *breach of contract* occurs when there is a violation of one or more of the terms of the contract. To be successful in a breach of contract lawsuit, the plaintiff must show: (1) a valid contract was executed; (2) the plaintiff performed as specified in the contract; (3) the defendant failed to perform as specified in the contract; and (4) the plaintiff suffered an economic loss as a result of the defendant's breach of contract.

▌ CORPORATE CONTRACTS

The ability of a corporation to enter into a contract is limited by its powers as contained in or inferred from its articles of incorporation (sometimes called a charter) or conferred upon it by general corporation law. Whenever a contract of any consequence is made with a corporation, appropriate corporate approval and authorization must be obtained. In the event that a contract is entered into with a corporation without the appropriate authority, the contract nevertheless can be ratified and made binding on the corporation by subsequent conduct or statements made on its behalf by its representatives.

When the chief executive officer (CEO) of an organization exceeds the limits of his or her authority, the question of whether the organization will be responsible for the CEO's acts might arise. If the actions of the governing body give rise to a third party's reasonable belief that the CEO acts with the authority of the organization, and such belief causes the third party to enter into an agreement with the CEO, expecting that the organization will be obligated under the contract, then the organization generally is responsible under the concept of apparent authority (the appearance of being the agent of another [employer or principal] with the power to act for the principal). However, if a third party contractor makes an agreement with the CEO in the absence of indications of the CEO's authority created by the governing body and thereby unreasonably assumes that the CEO possesses the authority to bind the organization to a contract, then such third party deals with the CEO in an individual capacity and not as an agent of the organization. There are times when the CEO clearly can exceed the limitations of his or her authority. The governing body, however, can subsequently approve such actions through ratification by accepting any resulting responsibility as though it had been authorized previously.

▌ PARTNERSHIPS

A *partnership* comprises two or more persons who agree to carry on a business for profit and to share profits and losses in some proportion. A partnership, unlike a corporation, can be created by the parties' actions without a written or oral agreement.

▌ AGENTS

An *agent* is one who has the power to contract for and bind another person, who is known as the principal. Corporations can act only through agents (e.g., their officers).

Apparent Agent or Ostensible Agent

An *apparent* or *ostensible agent* is one who a third person believes is acting on behalf of the principal. If a hospital undertakes to provide physician services to a community, and the community reasonably believes that the physician is employed by the hospital to deliver services, then the hospital would generally be liable for the physician's negligent acts.

Right to Assume Hospital Is Medical Provider

In *Jennison v. Providence St. Vincent Med. Ctr.*,[2] Jennison, having severe abdominal pain, was taken to the hospital emergency department. Unsure of the cause of Jennison's medical problems, Cook, Jennison's assigned physician, recommended surgery. Prior to surgery Cook asked Nunez, a member of an independent anesthesiology group at the hospital, to place a central venous catheter in Jennison.

An X-ray had been taken to confirm the correct placement of the central line. The X-ray showed that the tip of the central line had gone into the pericardial sac of Jennison's heart. A procedure had not been established to timely notify the treating physicians that the central line had been dangerously misplaced.

Upon the eventual discovery that the central line had been misplaced, it was pulled back to its proper position. Unfortunately fluids had already infused through the central line and into the space between Jennison's heart and pericardial sac. The pressure of the fluid against her heart kept it from filling adequately. Jennison's blood pressure dropped, and she went into cardiac arrest. The doctors attempted to remove the excess fluid. During the procedure, Jennison suffered a second cardiac arrest. The doctors were again able to resuscitate her. However, due to the lack of oxygen to her brain, Jennison suffered a severe brain injury.

The jury returned a verdict in favor of the plaintiffs, finding the hospital 100% negligent, and the hospital appealed. The Court of Appeals of Oregon affirmed the findings of the trial court. The hospital presented itself as providing radiology services to the public. The public, looking to the hospital to provide such care, is unaware of and unconcerned with the technical complexities and nuances surrounding the contractual and employment arrangements between the hospital and the various medical personnel operating therein. Public policy dictates that the public has every right to assume and expect that the hospital is the medical provider it purports to be.

INDEPENDENT CONTRACTOR

An *independent contractor* is an individual who agrees to undertake work without being under the direct control or direction of another. Independent contractors are personally responsible for their own negligent acts. Whether a physician is an employee or an independent contractor is of primary importance in determining liability for damages. Generally, a healthcare organization is not liable for injuries resulting from negligent acts or omissions of independent physicians. There is no liability on the theory of respondeat superior, whereby a physician is an independent contractor as long as the physician is not an employee of the organization, is not compensated by the organization, maintains a private practice, and is chosen directly by his or her patients. The mere existence of an independent contractual relationship, however, is not sufficient to remove an organization from liability for the acts of certain members of its professional personnel if the independent contractor status is not readily known to the injured party.

Hospital Liable for Physician's Negligence

A hospital can be liable for a physician's negligence, even if the physician is under contract to provide services to the hospital. The appellate division of the New York State Supreme Court in *Mduba v. Benedictine Hospital*[3] held that the hospital was liable for the emergency department physician's negligence whether the physician was an independent contractor or, even if under contract, the physician was considered to be an independent contractor. The court held that the patient had no way of knowing of the existence of a contract and relied on the relationship between the hospital and the physician in seeking treatment in the emergency department.

LEGALITY OF OBJECT

To be a valid contract, the purpose or object of the contract must not be against state or federal policy and must not violate any statute, rule, or regulation. If the subject or purpose of the contract becomes illegal by some statute, rule, or regulation before actual formation of the contract, the parties no longer can form the contract.

CONDITIONS

A *condition* precedent is an act or event that must happen or be performed by one party before the other party has any responsibility to perform under the contract. An express condition is formally written into the contract in specific terms. An *implied condition* is one in which, although the parties might not have specifically mentioned the condition, it can reasonably be assumed that the parties intended the condition to be enforced.

PERFORMANCE

Performance is the act of doing what is required by a contract. Each party to a contract is bound to perform the promises according to the stipulated terms of a contract. The effect of successful performance by each party to a contract is to discharge the parties bound to the contract from any future contractual liability.

NONPERFORMANCE DEFENSES

Under some circumstances the law gives a person a right not to perform under a contract. Defenses permitting nonperformance of a contract include fraud, mistakes, duress, illegal contract, impossibility, and statute of limitations.

Fraud

A victim of fraud will not have to perform under a contract. Fraud occurs when one party intentionally misrepresents a material fact or term of the contract and intends that the other party rely on that misrepresentation. The second party must rely on the misrepresentation and suffer some damage before it will be excused from performing.

Mistake of Fact

Mistakes often occur in contracts. However, a party will be allowed to claim mistake as a defense in only certain instances. There are two types of mistakes: mistake of fact and mistake of law. A *mistake of fact* is an incorrect belief regarding a fact. Both parties must have made the mistake. If only one is in error (and it is not known to the other), mistake of fact is not a defense. *Mistake of law*, on the other hand, is an incorrect judgment of the legal consequences of known facts. If the parties to a suit make a mistake as to the law involved, they usually must accept their plight without any remedy.

Duress

Duress is the use of unlawful threats or pressure to force an individual to act against his or her will. An act performed under duress is not legally binding.

Illegal Contract

An *illegal contract* is a contract whose formation, object, or performance is against the law or contrary to public policy that no court would uphold or enforce. No individual can recover damages when a contract is formed for illegal purposes.

Impossibility

Contracts can become impossible to perform because (1) certain facts might have existed at the time the contract was executed or (2) they might have arisen subsequent to the formation of the contract. Contracts that are impossible to perform do not have to be carried out by the parties to a contract.

Statute of Limitations

A party to a contract who does not, within a period of time known as the statute of limitations, take action to enforce contract rights by suing for damages caused by a breach of the contract or taking other action can be barred from doing so.

REMEDIES

What can a party do when another has breached the contract and refuses to or cannot perform? The general rule is that legal redress will attempt to make the injured party whole again.

Specified Performance

When an aggrieved party has subsequently complied with his or her obligations pursuant to the agreed-upon terms of a contract, that party might seek specific performance as a remedy rather than monetary remuneration. The most satisfactory remedy available to an injured party might be to require specific performance by the other party to the contract.

Monetary Damages

Money damages, sometimes called compensatory damages, are awarded in an attempt to restore to the aggrieved party the money that it would have had if the other party had not breached the contract. This can include the cost of making a substitute contract with another party and the expense of delays caused by the breach.

General and Consequential Damages

General damages are those that can be expected to arise from a breach of a contract. They are foreseeable and common in the circumstances. *Consequential damages* are those that occur because of some unexpected, unusual, or strange development involved in the particular contract in dispute. The distinction between the two types is one of foreseeability. If it is found that the party who breached a contract could have foreseen the damages that followed, that person could be liable for consequential as well as general damages.

Duty to Mitigate Damages

When someone has breached a contract, the other party cannot stand idly by and let damages build indefinitely. Every injured party has a duty to mitigate (lessen) damages caused by the breach of another person or entity. Failure to do so will prevent the aggrieved party's full recovery of damages that could have been mitigated.

▌ EMPLOYMENT CONTRACTS

An *employment contract* is an agreement between an employee and employer that specifies the terms of employment. The conditions of employment including wages, hours, and type of work are generally described in an employment contract. Depending on the level of employment and the responsibility of the new employee, the conditions of employment should include the terms of employment; the duties and responsibilities of the employee; compensation; confidentiality requirements (e.g., trade secrets and proprietary information); a noncompete clause; and provisions for termination of the agreement (e.g., an inability to perform one's duties and responsibilities).

A contract can be express or implied. Most employees work under employment contracts. For example, if an employee signs a document promising to abide by company policy and procedures, it likely constitutes an employment contract. Certain categories of employees (e.g., radiologists) often have the ability to negotiate their employment contracts. An employer's right to terminate an employee can be limited by express agreement with the employee or through a collective bargaining agreement to which the employee is a beneficiary.

The rights of employees have been expanding through judicial decisions in the different states. Court decisions have been based on verbal promises, historical practices of the employer, and documents such as employee handbooks and administrative policy and procedure manuals that describe employee rights.

Breaches of Contract: Repayment of Tuition Required

The registered nurse in *Sweetwater Hosp. Ass'n v. Carpenter*[4] was found to have breached her contract with the hospital under which the hospital agreed to pay for her schooling as a nurse anesthetist in exchange for her agreeing to work for the hospital for 5 years following completion of her studies. The nurse agreed that if she failed to work at the hospital following completion of her studies, she would be responsible for cash advances by the hospital plus interest. Upon completion of her studies, the nurse sought employment elsewhere because it appeared to her that there were no nurse anesthetist positions available at the hospital.

As consideration for the loan, the contract provided that the defendant agree to become or remain an employee of the hospital. The contract did not state in what capacity the defendant would become or remain an employee. There was nothing in the language of the contract stating that the hospital had an obligation to offer the defendant a nurse anesthetist position.

In this case, there was no proof by the defendant that the hospital breached the contract. The defendant breached her own contract by taking a job elsewhere without specifically getting proof that she was not going to be offered a job by the hospital. The defendant did not present herself for employment at the hospital after graduation. She accepted a position elsewhere. Because she did not become employed at the hospital, she was not entitled to rely upon the forgiveness provisions contained in the contract. She was, therefore, obligated to repay the hospital.

No Express Agreement: Right to Terminate

No express agreement was found to exist in *O'Connor v. Eastman Kodak Co.*,[5] in which the court held that an employer had a right to terminate an employee-at-will at any time and for any reason or no reason. The plaintiff did not rely on any specific representation made to him during the course of his employment interviews nor did he rely on any documentation in the employee handbook, which would have limited the defendant's common-law right to discharge at will. The employee had relied on a popular perception of Kodak as a "womb-to-tomb" employer.

Restrictive Covenant Enforceable

The plaintiff–hospital, in *Sarah Bush Lincoln Health Ctr. v. Perket*,[6] sued its former director of physical medicine and rehabilitation to enforce a restrictive covenant in the employment contract precluding the director from accepting similar employment in the same county within 1 year of termination of employment. The parties to the complaint entered into a contract whereby the defendant was employed as the plaintiff's director of physical medicine. The contract provided that during the director's employment and for a period of 1 year thereafter, the director would not, directly or indirectly, invest in, own, manage, operate, control, be employed by, participate in, or be connected in any manner with the ownership, management, operation, or control of any person, firm, or corporation engaged in competition with the hospital in providing health services or facilities within Coles County, including the provision of services in a private office, without prior written consent of the hospital. Following the termination, the defendant engaged in the business of providing physical medicine and rehabilitation services in Coles County. The plaintiff argued that unless the defendant was enjoined, the hospital would suffer irreparable injury. The circuit court granted the hospital's motion for preliminary injunction.

On appeal, the Illinois Appellate Court held that the grant of the preliminary injunction was proper and that the defendant was engaging in the business of providing physical medicine and rehabilitation services in Coles County. By hiring the defendant, the hospital was thereby bringing him in contact with a clientele that the hospital had established over a period of years. The hospital was naturally interested in protecting its clients from being taken over by the defendant as a result of these contacts.

Restrictive Covenant Not Enforceable

Not every restrictive covenant is enforceable; for example, a restrictive covenant in an employment contract between a hospital and neurosurgeon was found to be geographically too restrictive whereby the neurosurgeon was not to practice within a 30-mile radius of the hospital. This restriction was determined to be excessive. Such a restriction was considered to be detrimental to public interest in that the restricted area was plagued with a shortage of neurosurgeons.[7]

The reader should understand that employment contracts that contain a restrictive covenant between a physician and a hospital, although not favored, are not per se unreasonable and unenforceable. The trial court must determine whether the restrictive covenant protects the legitimate interests of the employer, imposes no undue hardship on the employee, and is not adverse to the public interest.[8]

Handbook Considered a Contract

For an employee handbook to constitute a contract, thereby giving enforceable rights to the employee, the following elements must be present:

1. A policy statement that clearly sets forth a promise that the employee can construe to be an offer.

2. The policy statement must be distributed to the employee, making him or her aware of the offer.
3. After learning about the offer and policy statement, the employee must "begin" or "continue" to work.

Hospital Violates Provisions of Employee Handbook

In *Watson v. Idaho Falls Consolidated Hospitals, Inc.,*[9] a nurse's aide was awarded $20,000 for damages when the hospital, as employer, violated the provisions of its employee handbook in the manner in which it terminated her employment. Although the nurse's aide had no formal written contract, the employee handbook and the hospital policies and procedures manual constituted a contract in view of evidence to the effect that these documents had been intended to be enforced and complied with by both employees and management. Employees read and relied on the handbook as creating terms of an employment contract. They were required to sign for the handbook to establish receipt of a revised handbook that explained hospital policy, discipline, counseling, and termination. A policy-and-procedure manual placed on each floor of the hospital also outlined termination procedures.

Handbook Not a Contract Due to Disclaimer

The employee handbook in *Churchill v. Waters*[10] was not considered to be a contract because of a disclaimer in the handbook. A nurse brought a civil rights action against the hospital and hospital officials after her discharge. The federal district court held for the defendants, finding that the hospital employee handbook did not give the nurse a protected property interest in continued employment: "Absent proof that the handbook contained clear promises which indicated the intent to bind the parties, no contract was created."[11] The "handbook contained a disclaimer" expressly disavowing any attempt to be bound by it and stated that its contents were not to be considered conditions of employment. The handbook was presented as a matter of information only, and the language contained therein was not intended to constitute a contract between McDonough District Hospital and the employee. Although an employee handbook can delineate specific disciplinary procedures, that fact does not in and of itself constitute an enforceable contract.[12]

Termination of Contract Due to Insubordination

The physician in *Trieger v. Montefiore Med. Ctr.*[13] circulated a memorandum to department chairs at the hospital strongly criticizing management and urging his cochairs "to set things right and reclaim their prerogatives and responsibilities." The appellate court found that the trial court correctly determined that the memorandum was insubordinate and that it gave just cause for termination of the physician's employment contract. In addition, the physician's age discrimination claim was dismissed for lack of evidence sufficient to raise an issue of fact as to whether the hospital's reason for the doctor's dismissal, circulation of the insubordinate memorandum, was a pretext for discrimination. The doctor was terminated immediately after circulating the insubordinate memorandum, and there was no other evidence in the record to support the claim that the hospital's actions were pretextual.

Medical Staff Bylaws Considered a Contract

Medical staff bylaws can be considered a contract. The plaintiff, Dr. Bass, in *Bass v. Ambrosius*,[14] alleged that the hospital's termination of his staff privileges violated its own bylaws. The hospital contended that its bylaws did not constitute a contract between itself and Bass, and, therefore, any violation of those bylaws would not support a breach-of-contract claim. The general rule that hospital bylaws can constitute a contract between the hospital and its staff is consistent with Wisconsin law that an employee handbook written and disseminated by the employer, and whose terms the employee has accepted, constitutes a contract between the employer and the employee. For example, in *Ferraro v. Koelsch*,[15] an employee handbook was management's statement of what the company offered its employees and what it expected from its employees in return. It thus contained the essential elements of a binding contract: the promise of employment on stated terms and conditions by the employer and the promise by the employee to continue employment under those conditions. The court noted that a promise for a promise, or the exchange of promises, constitutes consideration to support any contract of this bilateral nature.

The bylaws at issue in *Bass v. Ambrosius*, required by Wis. Admin. Code § HSS 124.12(5) and approved by the hospital's board of directors, had the same contractual elements as did the handbook in Ferraro. *First*, the bylaws state that they provide the rules that govern the physicians and dentists practicing at the hospital. *Second*, members of the hospital's medical–dental staff must continuously meet the qualifications, standards, and requirements set forth in the bylaws. *Third*, an appointment to the medical–dental staff confers only those privileges provided by the letter of appointment and the bylaws. *Fourth*, all applicants for appointment to the medical–dental staff must submit a signed application acknowledging the requirement to familiarize themselves with the bylaws. Each applicant for appointment to the medical–dental staff must submit a signed application attesting that he or she has read and agreed to accept and abide by the provisions and directives in the bylaws. Thus, Bass's application to the medical–dental staff acknowledged by his signature that he would conduct his professional activities according to the bylaws and rules and regulations of both the hospital and the medical–dental staff of the hospital. In a separate letter, part of the application process, Bass agreed to conduct his activities according to the bylaws of the hospital, as well as the bylaws and rules and regulations of the hospital's medical–dental staff. For its part, the hospital promised that the medical–dental staff would be guided and governed by rules and regulations consistent with the bylaws, and it promised that any adverse action against a member of the medical–dental staff would comply with various procedural safeguards. The bylaws constituted a contract between Bass and the hospital. Accordingly, Bass was entitled to an order holding that the hospital had to comply with its bylaws before it could terminate his staff privileges.

EXCLUSIVE CONTRACTS

An organization often enters into an exclusive contract with physicians or medical groups for the purpose of providing a specific service to the organization. Exclusive contracts generally occur within a variety of hospital departments (e.g., radiology, anesthesiology, pathology, and emergency). Physicians who seek to practice at organizations in such departments but who are not part of the exclusive group have attempted to invoke the federal antitrust laws to challenge various exclusive contracts. These challenges generally have been unsuccessful.

In *Jefferson Parish Hospital v. Hyde*,[16] the defendant hospital had a contract with a firm of anesthesiologists that required all anesthesia services for the hospital's patients be performed by that firm. Because of this contract, the plaintiff–anesthesiologist's application for admission to the hospital's medical staff was denied. Dr. Hyde commenced an action in the federal district court, claiming the exclusive contract violated Section 1 of the Sherman Antitrust Act. The district court rejected the plaintiff's complaint, but the U.S. Court of Appeals for the Fifth Circuit reversed, finding the contract illegal per se. The Supreme Court reversed the Fifth Circuit, holding that the exclusive contract in question does not violate Section 1 of the Sherman Antitrust Act. The Supreme Court's holding was based on the fact that the defendant hospital did not possess "market power," and therefore patients were free to enter a competing hospital and to use another anesthesiologist instead of the firm. Thus, the court concluded that the evidence was insufficient to provide a basis for finding that the contract, as it actually operates in the market, had unreasonably restrained competition.

NONCOMPETITIVE CONTRACT CLAUSES

The respondent–hospital in *Washington County Memorial Hospital v. Sidebottom*[17] employed the appellant–nurse practitioner from October 1993 through April 1998. Prior to beginning her employment, the nurse entered into an employment agreement with the hospital. The agreement included a noncompetition clause providing, in part that the nurse, during the term of the agreement and for a period of 1 year after the termination of her employment, would not within a 50-mile radius directly or indirectly engage in the practice of nursing without the express direction or consent of the hospital. In February 1994, the nurse requested the hospital's permission to work for the Washington County Health Department doing prenatal nursing care. Because the hospital was not then doing prenatal care, the hospital gave her permission to accept that employment but reserved the ability to withdraw the permission if the services the nurse was providing later came to be provided by the hospital. In January 1996, the nurse and the hospital entered into a second employment agreement that continued the parties' employment relationship through January 9, 1998. This agreement included a noncompetition clause identical to the 1993 employment agreement. It also provided for automatic renewal for an additional 2 years unless either party gave written termination notice no less than 90 days prior to the expiration of the agreement.

On March 11, 1998, the nurse gave the hospital written notice of her resignation effective April 15. On April 16, the nurse began working as a nurse practitioner with Dr. Mullen at his office. The office was located within 50 miles of the hospital.

The Circuit Court, on October 16, prohibited the nurse from practicing nursing within a 50-mile radius of the hospital for a period of 1 year from April 15.

The noncompetition clause in the nurse's employment agreement was found to be clear and unambiguous. The nurse obtained legal advice before signing her original employment agreement and before resigning. The hospital had notified the nurse that the noncompetition clause would be enforced. On appeal, the judgment of the circuit court was affirmed.

TRANSFER AGREEMENTS

Healthcare organizations should have a written transfer agreement in effect with other organizations to help ensure the smooth transfer of patients from one facility to another when the attending physician determines such is appropriate. A *transfer agreement* is a written document that sets forth the terms and conditions under which a patient can be transferred to a facility that more appropriately provides the kind of care required by the patient. It also establishes procedures to admit patients of one facility to another when their condition warrants a transfer.

Transfer agreements should be written in compliance with and reflect the provisions of federal and state laws, regulations, and standards affecting healthcare organizations. The parties to a transfer agreement should be particularly aware of applicable federal and state regulations.

Agreements that will aid in bringing about the maximum use of the services of each organization and in ensuring the best possible care for patients should be established. The basic elements of a transfer agreement include:

1. *identification of each party to the agreement*, including the name and location of each organization to the agreement;
2. *purpose of the agreement*;
3. *policies and procedures for transfer of patients* (Language in this section of the agreement should make it clear that the patient's physician makes the determination as to the patient's need for the facilities and services of the receiving organization. The receiving organization should agree that, subject to its admission requirements and availability of space, it will admit the patient from the transferring organization as promptly as possible.);
4. *organizational responsibilities for arranging and making the transfer* (Generally, the transferring organization is responsible for making transfer arrangements. The agreement should specify who will bear the costs involved in the transfer.);
5. *exchange of information* (The agreement must provide a mechanism for the interchange of medical and other information relevant to the patient.);
6. *retention of autonomy* (The agreement should make clear that each organization retains its autonomy and that the governing bodies of each facility will continue to exercise exclusive legal responsibility and control over the management, assets, and affairs of the respective facilities. It also should be stipulated that neither organization assumes any liability by virtue of the agreement for any debts or obligations of a financial or legal nature incurred by the other.);

7. *procedure for settling disputes* (The agreement should include a method of settling disputes that might arise over some aspect of the patient transfer relationship.);

8. *procedure for modification or termination of the agreement* (The agreement should provide that it can be modified or amended by mutual consent of the parties. It also should provide for termination by either organization on notice within a specified time period.);

9. *sharing of services* (Depending on the situation, cooperative use of facilities and services on an outpatient basis [e.g., laboratory and X-ray testing] can be an important element of the relationship between organizations. The method of payment for services rendered should be carefully described in the agreement.);

10. *publicity* (The agreement should provide that neither organization will use the name of the other in any promotional or advertising material without prior approval of the other.); and,

11. *exclusive versus nonexclusive agreement* (It is advisable for organizations—when and where possible—to have transfer agreements with more than one organization. The agreement can include language to the effect that either party has the right to enter into transfer agreements with other organizations.).

INSURANCE CONTRACT

Insurance is a form of risk management used primarily to hedge against the risk of potential loss. In an *insurance contract*, the insurer has an obligation to indemnify the insured for losses caused by specified events. In return, the insured must pay a fixed premium during the policy period. As noted, the interpretation of an insurance contract can give rise to a legal action when the insurer refuses to indemnify the insured.

Notes

1. *Hungerford Hosp. v. Mulvey*, 225 A.2d 495 (Conn. 1966).
2. 25 P.3d 358 (2001).
3. 384 N.Y.S.2d 527 (N.Y. App. Div. 1976).
4. 2005 WL 249695 (Tenn. App. Ct. 2005).
5. 492 N.Y.S.2d 9 (N.Y. 1985).
6. 605 N.E.2d 613 (Ill. App. Ct. 1992).
7. *Community Hosp. Group, Inc. v. More*, No. A75 September Term 2003 (N.J. 2005).
8. *Pierson v. Medical Health Ctrs.*, 869 A.2d 901 (N.J. 2005).
9. 720 P.2d 632 (Idaho 1986).
10. 731 F. Supp. 311 (D. Ill. 1990).
11. *Id.* at 321–322.
12. *Chesnick v. Saint Mary of Nazareth Hosp.*, 570 N.E.2d 545 (Ill. App. Ct. 1991).
13. 789 N.Y.S.2d 42 (N.Y. App. Div. 2005).
14. 520 N.W.2d 625 (Wis. App. 1994).
15. 368 N.W.2d 666, 668, 674 (1985).
16. 466 U.S. 2 (1984).
17. 7 S.W.3d 542 (Mo. App. 1999).

Law is not law, if it violates the principles of eternal justice.

—Lydia Maria Child, speech, 1861

7
Civil Procedure and Trial Practice

Figure 7–1   The Court Room   Courtesy of Brittany Salzone, Forest, VA

Learning Objectives

The reader upon completion of this chapter will be able to:

- Explain each stage of civil procedure.
- Discuss the pretrial discovery process.
- Describe the trial process.
- Explain the purpose of the judge's charge to the jury.
- Describe the types of damages and how they are awarded.
- Discuss the appeals process and execution of judgments.

This chapter in particular is valuable to readers in understanding the law and its application in the courtroom. Although many of the procedures leading up to and followed during a trial are discussed in this chapter, civil procedure and trial practice are governed by each state's statutory requirements. Cases on a federal level are governed by federal statutory requirements.

PLEADINGS

The pleadings of a case are the written statements of fact and law filed with a court by the parties to a lawsuit. Pleadings generally include such papers as a complaint, demurrer, answer, and bill of particulars.

A *complaint* is the first pleading filed by a plaintiff that initiates a lawsuit. It sets forth the relevant allegations of fact that give rise to one or more legal causes of action along with the damages requested. A *demurrer* is a pleading filed by a defendant challenging the legal sufficiency of a complaint. An *answer* to a complaint is a pleading that admits or denies the specific allegations set forth in a complaint and constitutes a general appearance by a defendant. A *bill of particulars* is a request for a written itemization of the claims, which a defendant can demand from the plaintiff to determine what the details of a claim are.

A defendant can also file a cross-complaint and bring other parties into a lawsuit by the process. If only questions of law are at issue, the judge will decide the case based on the pleadings alone. If questions of fact are involved, a trial is conducted to determine those facts.

Summons and Complaint

The parties to a controversy are the plaintiff and the defendant. The *plaintiff* is the person who initiates an action by filing a complaint; the *defendant* is the person against whom a lawsuit is brought. Many cases have multiple plaintiffs and defendants.

The first pleading filed with the court in a negligence action is the complaint. The *complaint* identifies the parties to a suit, states a cause of action, and includes a demand for damages. It is filed by the plaintiff and is the first statement of a case by the plaintiff against the defendant. In some jurisdictions, a complaint must accompany a summons (an announcement to the defendant that a legal action has been commenced). The essential elements contained in a complaint are: (1) a short statement of the grounds on which the court's jurisdiction depends (the court's authority to hear the case); (2) a statement of the claim demonstrating that the pleader is entitled to relief; and (3) a demand for judgment for the relief to which the plaintiff deems him- or herself entitled. All these elements apply to any counterclaim, cross claim, or third-party claims.

The complaint can be served on the defendant either with the *summons* or within a prescribed time after the summons has been served. Specific formalities must be observed in the service of a summons so that appropriate jurisdiction over a defendant is obtained. Such formalities dictate the manner in which a summons is to be delivered, such as, the time period within which the delivery must occur and the geographic limitations within which service must be made.

Improper service of a summons occurred on March 14, 1989, when the sheriff attempted to serve the writ on the defendant by leaving a copy with the receptionist at the hospital where he had worked. The defendant had terminated his relationship with the hospital on February 22, 1988. The plaintiff's attempted service of the writ of summons was defective because the defendant was not affiliated with the hospital at which service was attempted. A copy of the complaint was left with a nurse on the intensive care unit of the hospital where the defendant was then a patient. The intensive care unit of a hospital, however, cannot be deemed the defendant–patient's place of residence, nor can it be said that the defendant–patient resides there.[1]

Demurrer

Upon receiving the plaintiff's complaint the defendant can file preliminary objections prior to answering the complaint. A *demurrer*, for example, can be filed by one of the parties to a lawsuit claiming that the evidence presented by the other party is insufficient to sustain an issue or case.

Answer

After service of a complaint, a response is required from the defendant in a document termed the answer. The *answer* to a complaint requires the defendant to respond to each of the allegations contained in the complaint by stating his or her defenses and by admitting to or denying each of the plaintiff's allegations. If the defendant fails to answer the complaint within the prescribed time, the plaintiff can seek judgment by default against the defendant. However, in certain instances, a default judgment will be vacated if the defendant can demonstrate an acceptable excuse for failing to answer.

Personal appearance of the defendant to respond to a complaint is not necessary. To prevent default, the defendant's attorney responds to the complaint with an answer. The defense attorney attempts to show through evidence that the defendant is not responsible for the negligent act claimed by the plaintiff to have occurred. The answer generally consists of a denial of the charges made and specifies a defense or argument justifying the position taken. The defense can show that the claim is unfounded because: (1) the period within which a suit must be instituted has run out; (2) there is contributory negligence on the part of the plaintiff; (3) any obligation has been paid; (4) a general release was presented to the defendant; or (5) a contract was illegal and therefore null and void. The original answer to the complaint is filed with the court having jurisdiction over the case, and a copy of the answer is provided to the plaintiff's attorney.

Counterclaim

A *counterclaim* is generally filed with the *answer* denying the plaintiff's claims by alleging that it was the plaintiff and not the defendant who committed a wrongful act and, therefore, it is the defendant who is entitled to damages. For example, the plaintiff could sue a hospital for personal injuries and property damage caused by the negligent operation of the hospital's ambulance. The hospital could also file a counterclaim on grounds that its driver was careful and that it was the plaintiff who was negligent and is liable to the hospital for damage to the ambulance.

Bill of Particulars

The defense attorney can request a *bill of particulars*, seeking more specific and detailed information than is provided in the complaint. If a counterclaim has been filed, the plaintiff's attorney can request a bill of particulars from the defense attorney.

More specifically, a bill of particulars for a malpractice suit might request from the plaintiff's attorney: (1) the date and time of day when the alleged malpractice and injury allegedly occurred; (2) if the claim involves misdiagnosis or failure to perform a test; (3) if administration of a medicine or treatment or performance of a test or surgical procedure was conducted in a manner contrary to accepted standards of medical practice; (4) where the alleged malpractice occurred; (5) a listing of injuries claimed to have been caused by the defendant's alleged malpractice; (6) a listing of any witnesses to the alleged malpractice; (7) the length of time the plaintiff was confined to bed; (8) the weekly earnings of the plaintiff, and so on.

▋ DISCOVERY

Discovery is the process of investigating the facts of a case before trial. The objectives of discovery are to: (1) obtain evidence that might not be obtainable at the time of trial; (2) isolate and narrow the issues for trial; (3) gather knowledge of the existence of additional evidence that might be admissible at trial; and (4) obtain leads to enable the discovering party to gather further evidence.

Discovery can be obtained on any matter that is not privileged and that is relevant to the subject matter involved in the pending action. The parties to a lawsuit have the right to discovery and to examine witnesses before trial.

Attorney–Client Privilege

Attorney–client privilege protects confidential communications between a client and his or her attorney. There are three elements required to successfully assert attorney–client privilege:

1. Both parties must agree that the attorney–client relationship does or will exist.
2. The client must seek advice from the attorney in his or her capacity as a legal advisor.
3. Communication between the attorney and client must be identified to be confidential.

Preparation of Witnesses

The manner in which a witness handles questioning at a deposition or trial is often as important as the facts of the case. Each witness should be well prepared prior to testifying. Preparation should include a review of all pertinent records. Helpful guidelines for witnesses undergoing examination in a trial or a court hearing include the following:

- Review the records (e.g., medical records and other business records) from which you might be questioned.
- Do not be antagonistic in answering the questions. The jury might already be somewhat sympathetic toward a particular party to the lawsuit; antagonism might only serve to reinforce such an impression.
- Be organized in your thinking and recollection of the facts regarding the incident.
- Answer only the questions asked.
- Explain your testimony in simple, succinct terminology.
- Do not overdramatize the facts you are relating.
- Do not allow yourself to become overpowered by the cross-examiner.
- Be polite, sincere, and courteous at all times.
- Dress appropriately and be neatly groomed.
- Pay close attention to any objections your attorney might have as to the line of questioning being conducted by the opposing counsel.
- Be sure to have reviewed any oral deposition in which you might have participated during an EBT.
- Be straightforward with the examiner. Any answers designed to cover up or cloud an issue or fact will, if discovered, serve only to discredit any previous testimony that you might have given.

- Do not show any visible signs of displeasure regarding any testimony with which you are in disagreement.
- Be sure to have questions that you did not hear repeated and questions that you did not understand rephrased.
- If you are not sure of an answer, indicate that you are not sure or that you just do not know the answer.

Incident Reports

Hospital *incident and investigation reports* are generally not protected from discovery. The burden rests upon the hospital to demonstrate that incident and investigation reports are protected from discovery under attorney–client privilege and work–product doctrine. Attorney–client privilege is intended to ensure that a client remains free from apprehension that consultations with a legal advisor will not be disclosed. Such privilege further encourages a client to talk freely with his or her attorney so that he or she can receive quality advice. Likewise, with regard to the work–product doctrine, not even the most liberal of discovery theories can justify unwarranted inquiries into the files and the mental impressions of an attorney. Courts are required to protect the integrity and fairness of the fact-finding process by requiring full disclosure of all relevant facts connected with the impending litigation while, at the same time, promoting full and frank consultation between a client and a legal advisor by removing the fear of compelled disclosure of information.

If in connection with an accident or an event, a business entity, in the ordinary course of business, conducts an investigation for its own purposes, the resulting investigative report is producible in civil pretrial discovery. The distinction between whether a defendant's in-house report was prepared in the ordinary course of business or was a work product in anticipation of litigation is an important one. The fact that a defendant anticipates the contingency of litigation resulting from an accident or event does not automatically qualify an in-house report as a work product. *A document that is not privileged does not become privileged by the mere act of sending it to an attorney.*

Examination Before Trial

Examination before trial (EBT) is one of several discovery techniques used to enable the parties of a lawsuit to learn more regarding the nature and substance of each other's case. An EBT consists of oral testimony under oath and includes cross-examination. A deposition, taken at an EBT, is the testimony of a witness that has been recorded in a written format. Testimony given at a deposition becomes part of the permanent record of the case. Each question and answer is transcribed by a court stenographer and can be used at the subsequent trial. Truthfulness and consistency are important because answers from an EBT that differ from those given at trial will be used to attack the credibility of the witness.

MOTIONS

The procedural steps that occur before trial are specifically classified as pretrial proceedings. After the pleadings have been completed, many states permit either party to move for a judgment on the pleadings. When this motion is made, the court will examine the entire case and decide whether to enter judgment according to the merits of the case as indicated in the pleadings. In some states, the moving party is permitted to introduce sworn statements showing that a claim or defense is baseless. This procedure cannot be used when there is substantial dispute concerning the facts presented by the affidavits.

Motion to Dismiss

A defendant can make a motion to dismiss a case, alleging that the plaintiff's complaint, even if believed, does not set forth a claim or cause of action recognized by law. A motion to dismiss can be made before, during, or after a trial. Motions made before a trial can be made on the basis that the court lacks jurisdiction, that the case is barred by the statute of limitations, that another case is pending involving the same issues, and other similar matters. A motion during trial can be made after the plaintiff has presented his or her case on the grounds that the court has heard the plaintiff's case and the defendant is entitled to a favorable judgment as a matter of law. In the case of a motion made by the defendant at the close of the plaintiff's case, the defendant normally will claim that the plaintiff has failed to present a prima facie case (i.e., that the plaintiff has failed to establish the minimum elements necessary to justify a verdict even if no contrary evidence is presented by the defendant). After a trial has been completed, either party can move for a directed verdict on the grounds that he or she is entitled to such verdict as a matter of law.

Dismissal Denied

Procedural issues can result in a case being referred back to the trial court for further proceedings as noted in the following case, where Jean Pierrot, as personal representative of the deceased, filed a complaint alleging that Farrah, a 25-year-old pregnant woman, went to a hospital in the afternoon with complaints of abdominal pain. The hospital transferred Farrah involuntarily that evening to Park Place, a behavioral health facility. The involuntary transfer of Farrah was allowed under Florida's Baker Act. When Farrah arrived at Park Place she was in distress, complaining of severe abdominal pain and other symptoms. Over the next 2 days, Park Place employees committed various acts and omissions that resulted in her death.

The complaint alleged a wrongful death claim for violations of Farrah's rights as a patient under the *Baker Act.* Park Place, in response, disagreed and moved to dismiss Pierrot's wrongful death claim, arguing that the claim was one for medical malpractice and that Pierrot failed to comply with the pre-suit requirements of the Medical Malpractice Act.

The trial court dismissed Pierrot's claim, deciding that the main point of the claim was that Park Place failed to properly respond to Farrah's physical symptoms of severe abdominal pain, and therefore, the claim was one for medical negligence. Thus, the court ruled Pierrot could not avoid the pre-suit requirements of the Medical Malpractice Act by pleading the claim under the Baker Act.

On appeal, Pierrot argued that a plaintiff claiming only violations of a mental health patient's rights under the Baker Act is not required to comply with the medical malpractice pre-suit requirements. Additionally, Pierrot contends the pre-suit requirements do not apply to his claim because Park Place was not a healthcare provider. The Court of Appeal of Florida agreed with both arguments.

According to the complaint, Park Place was a licensed mental health facility and not a healthcare provider. The court found that Park Place failed to establish that it was a healthcare provider for purposes of the pre-suit requirements. The case was reversed and remanded back to the trial court for further proceedings.[2]

This case illustrates the importance of preserving all causes of action and positions that the plaintiff's attorney may wish to argue at trial. The question arises, based on the limited information provided in this court document, "Why was a medical malpractice complaint not filed in addition to the Florida Baker act?"

What often happens to a case that is referred back to the trial court? Why is it so difficult to find follow-up on a case after pretrial procedures are exhausted? The answer is that in many cases further deliberations would most likely prove to be more damaging than helpful. Defendants may decide that a settlement is less costly than a lawsuit that could drag on for years and gain the attention of the news media. The "Newspaper Clippings" dispersed throughout the text, often high profile cases, are often settled out of the courtroom due to the negative impact they can have on the reputation of the healthcare provider.

Summary Judgment

A *motion for summary judgment* can be made when either party to a lawsuit might believe that there are no triable issues of fact and only issues of law need to be decided. This motion asks the court to rule that there are no facts in dispute and that the rights of the parties can be determined as a matter of law, on the basis of submitted documents, without the need for a trial. Summary judgment is generally granted when the evidence demonstrates that there are no genuine issues of material fact and the moving party is entitled to judgment as a matter of law. Although the courts are reluctant to look favorably on motions for summary judgment, they will grant them if the circumstances of a particular case warrant it.

The plaintiff in *Thomas v. New York University Med. Ctr.,*[3] while under general anesthesia, slid off the operating table during a surgical procedure. The plaintiff's head was pulled out of a head-stabilizing device, causing his head to be lacerated by one of the pins. The plaintiff suffered trauma to his neck and required mechanical assistance to breathe for 6 days following the accident. The Supreme Court, Appellate Division, on motion by the plaintiff, determined that summary judgment on the issue of liability was warranted. It could easily be reasoned that anesthetized patients do not fall from operating tables in the absence of negligence. The defendants, who were in joint and exclusive control of the plaintiff, failed to explain their conduct in the operating room, and their failure to do so mandated summary judgment.

▌ PRETRIAL CONFERENCE

In many states, a pretrial conference will be ordered at the judge's initiative or on the request of one of the parties to the lawsuit. The *pretrial conference* is an informal discussion during which the judge and the attorneys eliminate matters not in dispute, agree on the issues, and settle procedural matters relating to the trial. Although it is not the purpose of the pretrial conference to compel the parties to settle the case, it often happens that cases are settled at this point.

▌ NOTICE OF TRIAL

The examination before trial can reveal sufficient facts that would discourage the plaintiff from continuing the case, or it might encourage one or both parties to settle out of court. When a decision to go forward is reached, the case is placed on the court's calendar. The trial court then issues a *notice of trial* to the parties of the lawsuit as to the date and time of the trial.

Postponement of the trial can be secured with the consent of both parties and the consent of the court. A case may not be postponed indefinitely without being dismissed by the court. If one party is ready to proceed and another party seeks a postponement, a valid excuse must be shown. Should a defendant fail to appear at trial, the judge can pass judgment against the defendant by default. A case also can be dismissed if the plaintiff fails to appear at trial.

MEMORANDUM OF LAW

A *memorandum of law* (or trial brief) presents to the court the nature of the case, cites case decisions to substantiate arguments, and aids the court regarding points of law. Trial briefs are prepared by both the plaintiff's and the defendant's attorneys. A trial brief is not always required, but it is a recommended strategy. It provides the court with a basic understanding of the position of the party submitting the brief before the commencement of the trial. It also focuses the court's attention on specific legal points that might influence the court in ruling on objections and on the admissibility of evidence in the course of the trial.

THE COURT

A case is heard in the court that has jurisdiction over the subject in controversy. The judge decides questions of law and is responsible for ensuring that a trial is conducted properly in an impartial atmosphere that is fair to both parties of a lawsuit. The judge informs the jury of what the defendant's conduct should have been, thereby making a determination of the existence of a legal duty.

The judge decides whether evidence is admissible, charges the jury (defines the jurors' responsibility in relation to existing law), and may take a case away from the jury (by directed verdict or making a judgment notwithstanding the verdict) when he or she believes that there are no issues for the jury to consider or that the jury has erred in its decision. This right of the judge with respect to the role of the jury narrows the jury's responsibility with regard to the facts of the case. The judge maintains order throughout the trial, determines issues of procedure, and is generally responsible for the conduct of the trial.

THE JURY

The right to a trial by jury is a constitutional right, but an individual may waive the right to a jury trial. If this right is waived, the judge acts as judge and jury, becoming the trier of facts and deciding issues of law.

Members of the jury are selected from a jury list. They are summoned to court by a paper known as the summons. Impartiality is a prerequisite of all jurors. The number of jurors who sit at trial is 12 in common law. If there are fewer than 12, the number must be established by statute.

Counsel for both parties of a lawsuit questions each prospective jury member for impartiality, bias, and prejudicial thinking. This process is referred to as the *voir dire*, the examination of jurors. When members of the jury are selected, they are sworn in to try the case.

The jury makes a determination of the facts that occurred, evaluating whether the plaintiff's damages were caused by the defendant's negligence and whether the defendant exercised due care. The jury makes a determination of the particular standard of conduct required in all cases in which the judgment of reasonable people might differ. The jury must pay close attention to the evidence presented by both sides to a suit to render a fair and impartial verdict. Jurors who fall asleep during the trial can be replaced with an alternate juror, as was the case in *Richbow v. District of Columbia*.[4]

The jury also determines the extent of damages, if any, and the degree to which the plaintiff's conduct might have contributed to his or her injury, thereby mitigating the responsibility of the defendant (see *contributory negligence* and *comparative negligence* discussed later in this chapter).

A Jury Decision

A New York City jury awarded $26 million to a boy injured during surgery. What was it that so disturbed the jury that caused it to grant such a huge award? According to an article written by an alternate juror, who invited the jurors to his home 3 weeks after the trial:

> For seven weeks, the jury had sat in that courtroom listening to the defense lawyers belittle Stephen's problems. We saw the doctors refuse to acknowledge Stephen's handicaps or to accept responsibility for them. To the jury at least, it seemed that the doctors had made mistakes, refused to admit them, and then tried to cover them up.[5]

SUBPOENAS

A *subpoena* is a legal order requiring the appearance of a person and/or the presentation of documents to a court or administrative body. Attorneys, judges, and certain law enforcement and administrative officials, depending on the jurisdiction, may issue subpoenas. Subpoenas generally include: a reference number; names of plaintiff and defendant; date, time, and place to appear; name, address, and telephone number of opposing attorney; and documents requested if a subpoena is for records.

Some jurisdictions require the service of a subpoena at a specified time in advance of the requested appearance (e.g., 24 hours). In other jurisdictions, no such time limitation exists. A court clerk, sheriff, attorney, process server, or other person as provided by state statute can serve a subpoena.

A *subpoena ad testificandum* orders the appearance of a person at a trial or other investigative proceeding to give testimony. Witnesses have a duty to appear and can suffer a penalty for contempt of court should they fail to appear. They may not deny knowledge of a subpoena if they simply refused to accept it. The court can issue a bench warrant, ordering the appearance of a witness in court, if a witness fails to answer a subpoena. Failure to appear may be excused if extenuating circumstances exist.

A subpoena for records, known as a *subpoena duces tecum*, is a written command to bring records, documents, or other evidence described in the subpoena to a trial or other investigative proceeding. The subpoena is served on one who is able to produce such records. Disobedience in answering a subpoena *duces tecum* is considered to be contempt of court and carries a penalty of a fine or imprisonment or both.

BURDEN OF PROOF

The burden of proof in a criminal case requires that evidence presented against the defendant must be beyond a reasonable doubt. Note the terminology: reasonable doubt—not "all" doubt. The burden of proof in a criminal case lies with the prosecution. In a civil suit, the evidence presented by the plaintiff need only tip the scales of justice.

The *burden of proof* in a civil case is the obligation of the plaintiff to persuade the jury regarding the truth of his or her case. A preponderance of the credible evidence must be presented for a plaintiff to recover damages. Credible evidence is evidence that, in the light of reason and common sense, is worthy of belief. A preponderance of credible evidence requires that the prevailing side of the case carry more weight than the evidence on the opposing side.

In a negligence case the burden of proof requires that the plaintiff's attorney show that the defendant violated a legal duty by not following an acceptable standard of care and that the plaintiff suffered injury because of the defendant's breach. If the evidence presented does not support the allegations made, the case is dismissed. Where a plaintiff, who has the burden of proof, fails to sustain such burden, the case can be dismissed despite the failure of the defendant to present any evidence to the contrary on his or her behalf. The burden of proof in some states shifts from the plaintiff to the defendant when it is obvious that the injury would not have occurred unless there was negligence.

RES IPSA LOQUITUR

Res ipsa loquitur ("the thing speaks for itself" or "circumstances speak for themselves") is the legal doctrine that shifts the burden of proof in a negligence case from the plaintiff to the defendant. It is an evidentiary device that allows the plaintiff to make a case legally adequate to go to the jury on the basis of well-defined *circumstantial evidence* even though *direct evidence* is lacking. This does not mean that the plaintiff has fully proven the defendant's negligence. It merely shifts the burden of going forward in the lawsuit to the defendant who must argue to dismiss the circumstantial evidence presented.

In a medical malpractice case, a plaintiff is required to establish that an act or omission by the defendant was not in keeping with the degree of skill and learning ordinarily used under the same or similar circumstances by members of the defendant's profession and that such negligence or omission caused the plaintiff's injury. However, under the doctrine of *res ipsa loquitur* the need for direct proof, including expert testimony, of negligence is not necessary, thus allowing a case to be submitted to the jury in the absence of direct proof of negligence. In other words, an inference of negligence is permitted from the mere occurrence of an injury when the defendant owed a duty and possessed the sole power of preventing the injury by exercise of reasonable care. For example, the presence of severe burns on a patient's body after being bathed by an employee raises the question of negligence without the need for expert testimony. Negligence is considered so obvious that expert testimony is not necessary. It lies within a layperson's realm of knowledge that patients generally do not suffer burns from a bath, absent negligence. That alone is sufficient to require a defendant to come forward with a rebuttal.

The three elements necessary to shift the burden of proof from the plaintiff to the defendant under the doctrine of *res ipsa loquitur* are as follows:

1. the event would not normally have occurred in the absence of negligence;
2. the defendant must have had exclusive control over the instrumentality that caused the injury; and,
3. the plaintiff must not have contributed to the injury.

To further illustrate this, a patient who is sedated, has surgery, and awakes with burns on her body allegedly from an instrument used during surgery, can proceed with a lawsuit on the basis of *res ipsa loquitur* because: (1) the burns did not occur in the absence of negligence (meaning there was a duty to care, there was a breach of duty, injury occurred, and the cause of the injury resulted from the improper placement of the heating instrument next to the patient's body during surgery); (2) the instrumentality used during surgery was under the exclusive control of the surgical team; and (3) the patient was unconscious at the time the burns occurred and, therefore, could not have contributed to the cause of the injury.

In another example, the oxygen mask discussed in *Gold v. Ishak*[6] caught fire during surgery. In performing surgery, the physician used an electrocautery unit provided by the hospital. At some point during surgery the oxygen mask caught on fire and the patient was injured. The trial court refused to apply the doctrine of *res ipsa loquitur*. On appeal, the trial court was found to have erred by refusing to apply the doctrine of *res ipsa loquitur*. The evidence presented at trial, as described here, clearly shows that the elements necessary *res ipsa loquitur* can be inferred.

1. A fire under these circumstances is such that in the ordinary course of things would not have occurred if the medical providers had used proper care in relation to the electrocautery unit and oxygen mask. Expert testimony is not required because a fire occurring during surgery where an instrument that emits a spark is used near a source of oxygen is not beyond the realm of the layperson to understand. It is easily understandable to the common person that careless use of the two could cause a fire and result in bodily injury.
2. The plaintiff had exclusive control over the electrocautery unit.
3. The patient was undergoing surgery and did not participate in the procedure or in any way contribute to the injury that occurred.

OPENING STATEMENTS

During opening statement, the plaintiff's attorney attempts to prove the wrongdoing of the defendant by presenting credible evidence favorable to his or her client. The opening statement by the plaintiff's attorney provides in summary: (1) the facts of the case; (2) what the attorney intends to prove by means of a summary of the evidence to be presented; and, (3) a description of the damages to his or her client.

The defense attorney makes his or her opening statement indicating the position of the defendant and the points of the plaintiff's case he or she intends to refute. The defense attorney explains the facts as they apply to the case for the defendant.

EXAMINATION OF WITNESSES

After conclusion of the opening statements, the judge calls for the plaintiff's witnesses. An officer of the court administers an oath to each witness, and direct examination begins. The attorney obtains information from each witness in the form of questions. On cross-examination by the defense, an attempt is made to challenge or discredit the plaintiff's witness. Redirect examination by the plaintiff's attorney can follow the cross-examination, if so desired. The plaintiff's attorney may at this time wish to have his or her witness review an important point that the jury might have forgotten during cross-examination. The plaintiff's attorney may ask the same witness more questions in an effort to overcome the effect of the cross-examination. Recross-examination can take place, if necessary, for the defense of the defendant.

A sampling of preliminary questions that a physician might expect to be asked can take the following form:

1. Please state your name, residence, and any prior residences.
2. Where did you attend medical school?
3. Are you licensed in this state?
4. Where did you serve your internship?
5. Where did you serve your residency?
6. Is your practice general or special?
7. Are you board certified in one or more specialties?
8. How does a physician obtain board certification?
9. Are you presently practicing medicine?
10. How long have you been in practice?
11. During your _____ years of practice, have you had occasion to treat a good number of personal injury cases?

12. On or about _____ did you have occasion to see the patient on a professional basis?
13. Where?
14. Describe the patient's condition at the time.
15. What, if anything, did you do on that occasion?
16. Have you been the attending physician since that date?
17. Describe the nature of the examination that you made on the patient and any others from time to time since then.
18. Did you see the patient daily, several times a day at first?
19. Did you continue to see the patient?
20. How often?
21. Describe the treatment you rendered?
22. From your examination and treatment of the patient, did you determine what injuries were sustained?
23. As a result of your examination, did you find it necessary to seek consultation from another physician or specialist?
24. Did there come a time when you found it necessary to transfer the patient to another healthcare facility?

The credibility of a witness can be impeached if prior statements are inconsistent with later statements or if there is bias in favor of a party or prejudice against a party to a lawsuit. Either attorney to a lawsuit can ask the judge for permission to recall a witness.

After all the witnesses of the plaintiff have testified, the defense can call its witnesses, and the process of direct, cross, redirect, and recross-examination is repeated until the defense rests.

EVIDENCE

Evidence consists of the facts proved or disproved during a lawsuit. The law of evidence is a body of rules under which facts are proved. The rules of evidence govern the admission of items of proof in a lawsuit. A fact can be proven by either circumstantial or direct evidence. Evidence must be competent, relevant, and material to be admitted at trial. In a negligence case, there must be reasonable evidence that the resulting injury does not in the ordinary course of things happen if proper care is rendered and that there is *reasonable evidence*, in the absence of explanation by the defendants, that the accident arose from want of care.

Statutory Violation

Violation of a statute can constitute direct evidence of negligence, or it simply can voice a duty that is owed to a particular class of persons who are protected by the statute or regulation. For example, assume a regulation specifies a nurse–patient ratio of no less than one registered nurse for two patients on intensive care units. This regulation is an expression of the duty imposed on the facility to provide adequate nursing care to patients. Patients are, therefore, a class of people identified within the regulation who are to have the benefits of the protection to be gained by having a predetermined minimum standard nurse–patient care ratio.

Policy and Procedure Violations

Policies and procedures of a healthcare organization are established for day-to-day operations. If a violation of a facility's policy and procedures causes injury to one whom the policy or procedure is designed to protect, such violation can give rise to evidence for negligent conduct.

Direct Evidence

Direct evidence is proof offered through direct testimony. It is the jury's function to receive testimony presented by witnesses and to draw conclusions in the determination of the facts of a case.

Demonstrative Evidence

Demonstrative evidence is proof furnished by things themselves. It is considered to be the most trustworthy and preferred type of evidence. It consists of tangible objects to which testimony refers (e.g., medical supplies, instruments, equipment) that can be requested by a jury. Demonstrative evidence is admissible in court if it is relevant, has probative value, and serves the interest of justice. It is not admissible if it will prejudice, mislead, confuse, offend, inflame, or arouse the sympathy or passion of the jury. Other forms of demonstrative evidence include photographs, motion pictures, X-ray films, drawings, human bodies as exhibits, pathology slides, fetal monitoring strips, safety committee minutes, infection committee reports, medical staff bylaws, rules and regulations, nursing policy and procedure manuals, census data, and staffing patterns. The plaintiff's attorney uses all pertinent evidence to reconstruct chronologically the care and treatment rendered.

Photographs

When presenting photographs, as a form of evidence, the photographer or a reliable witness who is familiar with the object photographed must testify that the picture is an accurate representation and a fair likeness of the object portrayed. The photograph must not exaggerate the injury. Such exaggeration could unfairly prejudice a jury. Photographs can be valuable legal evidence when they illustrate graphically the nature and extent of a medical injury. Motion pictures also are valuable evidence. The same principles that apply to photographs apply to motion pictures. Motion pictures must be accurately portrayed. The cutting and/or splicing of videos are suspect and might have no probative value. Videotape is admissible in court, assuming the matter being taped, the time of the taping, and the manner in which such taping took place can be authenticated.

Imaging Studies

Imaging studies are considered to be pictures of the interior of the object portrayed and are admissible under the same requirements as photographs and motion pictures. Competent evidence must be offered to show that the films are those of the patient, the object, or body part under consideration; that the films were made in a recognized manner, taken by a competent technician; and, were interpreted by a competent physician trained to read the films. The value of films is that they illustrate fractures, foreign objects, and so forth.

Viewing Patient Injuries

Where an issue as to personal injuries is involved, an injured person may be permitted to exhibit to the jury the wound or injury, or the member or portion of his body upon which such wound or injury was inflicted, and if relevant, the exhibition is allowable at the discretion of the court where there is no reason to expect that the sympathy of the jury will be excited. The human body is considered to be the best evidence as to the nature and extent of the alleged injury/injuries. If there is no controversy about either the nature or the extent of an injury, presenting such evidence could be considered prejudicial, and an objection can be made as to its presentation to a jury.

Demonstrations are permitted in some instances to illustrate the extent of injuries. The resident in *Hendricks v. Sanford*[7] developed serious bedsores on her back. The defendant objected to the offer of the plaintiff to display her back to the jury. The court found that the plaintiff's injuries, which had healed, were completely relevant as evidence. Even though the injuries had healed and a skin graft had been performed, a declivity of about 3.5 inches in diameter and about the depth of a shallow ashtray was still discernible on the plaintiff's back.

Documentary Evidence

Documentary evidence is written information that is capable of making a truthful statement (e.g., drug manufacturer inserts, autopsy reports, e-mails, Facebook entries, birth certificates, and medical records). Documentary evidence must satisfy the jury as to authenticity. Proof of authenticity is not necessary if the opposing party accepts its genuineness. In some instances (e.g., wills), witnesses are necessary. In the case of documentation, the original of a document must be produced unless it can be demonstrated that the original has been lost or destroyed, in which case a properly authenticated copy may be substituted.

Facebook Entries and E-mails

A federal district court judge ruled in favor of the employer in *Lineberry v. Detroit Medical Center et al.*[8] The employer was found to have a reasonable belief that its employee was abusing her Family and Medical Leave Act leave when it concluded she was dishonest when she was confronted with questions about her Facebook postings of vacation pictures taken while on FMLA leave and was therefore entitled to terminate the employee. The Court granted summary judgment to the employer, dismissing the employee's suit accusing the hospital of interfering with her FMLA rights and retaliating against her for taking legally protected leave. The plaintiff had claimed that she had to use wheelchairs in all airports on her trip to Mexico. She was reminded that airports have cameras. Upon being showed her Facebook postings, she admitted that she had lied about the use of wheelchairs, as she had never used a wheelchair on her Mexico vacation. At her deposition, she testified:

Q. Is it not true that at the beginning of the [April 19, 2011] meeting, you told the group that you had used wheelchairs?

A. Yes.

Q. Then later on in the meeting, you admitted lying about that, correct?

A. Yes.

Q. Why did you initially lie to the group about using the wheelchair?

A. Because I had lied previously in an e-mail [the March 7, 2011, e-mail to Richards] and I wanted to remain consistent.

Entering Records into Evidence

A sampling of preliminary questions that a witness might be asked on entering a medical record into evidence includes the following:

1.   Please state your name.
2.   Where are you employed?

3. What is your position?

4. What is your official title?

5. Did you receive a subpoena for certain records?

6. Did you bring those records with you?

7. Can you identify these records?

8. Did you retrieve the records yourself?

9. Are these the complete records?

10. Are these the original records or copies of the originals?

11. How were these records prepared?

12. Are these records maintained under your care, custody, and control?

13. Were these records made in the regular course of business?

14. Was the record made at the time the act, condition, or event occurred or transpired?

15. Is this record regularly kept or maintained?

A manufacturer's drug insert or manual describing the proper use of medical equipment is generally admissible in court as evidence. In *Mueller v. Mueller,*[9] a physician was sued by a patient who charged that she had suffered a deterioration of bone structure and ultimately a collapsed hip as a result of the administration of cortisone over an extended period of time. The jury decided that the physician's prolonged use of cortisone was negligent, and the physician appealed. The appeals court held that the manufacturer's recommendations are not only admissible but also essential in determining a physician's possible lack of proper care.

Judicial Notice Rule

The *judicial notice* rule prescribes that well-known facts (e.g., that fractures need prompt attention and that two X-rays of the same patient might show different results) need not be proven, but rather are recognized by the court as fact. If a fact can be disputed, the rule does not apply.

The use of X-rays as a diagnostic aid in cases of fracture can be considered a matter of common knowledge to which a court, in the absence of expert testimony, can take judicial notice. Should a patient have a serious fall and a fracture is indicated, under the foregoing rule, it is a matter of common knowledge that the ordinary physician in good standing, in the exercise of ordinary care and diligence, would have ordered X-rays.

Hearsay Evidence

Hearsay evidence is based on what another has said or done and is not the result of the personal knowledge of the witness. Hearsay consists of written and oral statements. When a witness testifies to the utterance of a statement made outside court and the statement is offered in court for the truth of the facts that are contained in the statement, this is hearsay and therefore objectionable.

If a statement is offered not as proof of the facts asserted in the statement but rather only to show that the statement was made, the statement can come into evidence. For example, if it is relevant that a conversation took place, the testimony relating to the conversation may be entered as evidence. The purpose of that testimony would be to establish that a conversation took place and not to prove what was said during the course of the conversation. If testimony is based on personal knowledge, it would be admissible as evidence.

Because of the ability to challenge hearsay evidence successfully, which rests on the credibility of the witness as well as on the competency and veracity of other persons not before the court, it is admitted as evidence in a trial under very strict rules.

There are many exceptions to the hearsay rule that allow testimony that ordinarily would not be admitted. Included in the list of exceptions are admissions made by one of the parties to the action, threats made by a victim, dying declarations, statements to refresh a witness's recollection if he or she is unable to remember the facts known earlier, business records, medical records, and other official records (e.g., certified copies of birth and death records). If hearsay evidence is admitted without objection, its probative value is for the jury to determine.

Medical Books as Hearsay Evidence

Medical books are considered hearsay because the authors are not generally available for cross-examination. Although medical books are not admissible as evidence, a physician may testify as to how he or she formed an opinion and what part textbooks played in forming that opinion. During cross-examination, medical experts may be asked to comment on statements from medical books that contradict their testimony.

Expert Testimony

It is the jury's function to receive testimony presented by witnesses and draw conclusions in the determination of facts. The law recognizes that a jury is composed of ordinary men and women and that some fact-finding will involve subjects beyond their knowledge. When a jury cannot otherwise obtain sufficient facts from which to draw conclusions, an expert witness who has special knowledge, skill, experience, or training can be called on to submit an opinion. The expert witness assists the jury when the issues to be resolved in a case are outside the experience of the average juror.

Laypeople are quite able to render opinions about a great variety of general subjects, but for technical questions the opinion of an expert is necessary. At the time of testifying, each expert's training, experience, and special qualifications will be explained to the jury. The experts will be asked to give an opinion concerning hypothetical questions based on the facts of the case. Should the testimony of two experts conflict, the jury will determine which expert opinion provides the most reasonable and compelling evidence. Expert witnesses can be used to assist the plaintiff in proving the wrongful act of the defendant or to assist the defendant in refuting such evidence. In addition, expert testimony may be used to show the extent of the plaintiff's damages or to show the lack of such damages. To qualify as an expert witness in a specified area, that person must have the appropriate training, experience, and qualifications necessary to explain and/or answer questions based on the facts of a particular case.

Not all negligence cases require testimony from an expert witness. Citing *Donovan v. State*, "If a doctor operates on the wrong limb or amputates the wrong limb, a plaintiff would not have to introduce expert testimony to establish that the doctor was negligent. On the other hand, highly technical questions of diagnoses and causation which lie beyond the understanding of a layperson require introduction of expert testimony."[10]

Admissibility

Expert testimony concerning what a reasonable patient wanted to know and what doctors think patients wanted to know was found to be admissible in an informed consent case. Thus, where the patient sued the physician for medical malpractice, alleging information he had given her over the telephone, relating to her report of abdominal pain and nausea several months after stomach surgery, did not allow her to make an intelligent decision to seek emergency room treatment. Expert testimony by doctors who had extensive experience interacting with patients was found to be relevant concerning the amount and kinds of information that patients generally want in late night phone calls, and was relevant to establish whether the physician had given the patient as much information as a reasonable patient would want to know.[11]

▮ DEFENSES AGAINST PLAINTIFF'S CLAIMS

When a plaintiff's case has been established, the defendant may put forward a defense against the plaintiff's claim for damages. The defendant's case is presented to discredit the plaintiff's cause of action and prevent recovery of damages. This section reviews various legal defenses available to defendants in a negligence suit (**Figure 7–2**) that can relieve a defendant from liability.

Ignorance of Fact and Unintentional Wrongs

Ignorance of the law is not a defense; otherwise pleading ignorance would reward the defendant. Arguing that a negligent act is unintentional is no defense. If such a defense were acceptable, all defendants would use it.

Figure 7–2   Defenses Against Plaintiff's Claims

Assumption of a Risk

Assumption of a risk is knowing that a danger exists and voluntarily accepting the risk by exposing oneself to it, aware that harm might occur. Assumption of a risk can be implicitly assumed, as in alcohol consumption, or expressly assumed, as in relation to warnings found on cigarette packaging.

This defense provides that the plaintiff expressly has given consent in advance, relieving the defendant of an obligation of conduct toward the plaintiff and taking the chances of injury from a known risk arising from the defendant's conduct. For example, one who agrees to care for a patient with a communicable disease and then contracts the disease would not be entitled to recover from the patient for damages suffered. In taking the job, the individual agreed to assume the risk of infection, thereby releasing the patient and healthcare organization from all legal obligations.

The following two requirements must be established for a defendant to be successful in an assumption of a risk defense:

1. The plaintiff must know and understand the risk that is being incurred.
2. The choice to incur the risk must be free and voluntary.

The patient in *Faile v. Bycura*[12] was awarded $75,000 in damages on her allegations that a podiatrist used inappropriate techniques during an unsuccessful attempt to treat her heel spurs. On appeal, it was held that the trial court erred in striking the podiatrist's defense of assumption of a risk. Evidence established that the *patient signed consent forms* that indicated the risks of treatment as well as alternative treatment modalities.

Contributory Negligence

Contributory negligence occurs when a person does not exercise reasonable care for his or her own safety. As a general proposition, if a person has knowledge of a dangerous situation and disregards the danger, then that person is contributorily negligent. Actual knowledge of the danger of injury is not necessary for a person to be contributorily negligent. It is sufficient if a reasonable person should have been aware of the possibility of the danger.

In some jurisdictions, contributory negligence, no matter how slight, is sufficient to defeat a plaintiff's claim. Generally, the defense of contributory negligence has been recognized in a medical malpractice action when the patient has failed to follow a medical instruction, or refused or neglected prescribed treatment, or intentionally given erroneous, incomplete, or misleading information that led to the patient's injury.

The elements necessary to establish contributory negligence are that (1) the plaintiff's conduct fell below the required standard of personal care, and (2) there is a causal connection between the plaintiff's careless conduct and the plaintiff's injury. Under these circumstances the defendant contends that some, if not all, liability is attributable to the plaintiff's own actions.

The rationale for contributory negligence is based on the principle that all persons must be both careful and responsible for their acts. A plaintiff is required to conform to the broad standard of conduct of the reasonable person. The plaintiff's negligence will be determined and governed by the same tests and rules as the negligence of the defendant. A person incurs the risk of injury if he or she knew of a danger, understood the risk involved, and voluntarily exposed him- or herself to such danger.

Comparative Negligence

A defense of *comparative negligence* provides that the degree of negligence or carelessness of each party to a lawsuit must be established by the finder of fact and that each party then is responsible for his or her proportional share of any damages awarded. For example, when a plaintiff suffers injuries of $10,000 from an accident, and when the plaintiff is found 20% negligent and the defendant 80% negligent, the defendant would be required to pay $8,000 to the plaintiff. Thus, with comparative negligence, the plaintiff can collect for 80% of the injuries, whereas an application of contributory negligence would deprive the plaintiff of any monetary judgment. This doctrine relieves the plaintiff from the hardship of losing an entire claim when a defendant has been successful in establishing that the plaintiff contributed to his or her own injuries. A defense that provides that the plaintiff will forfeit an entire claim if he or she has been contributorily negligent is considered to be too harsh a result in jurisdictions that recognize comparative negligence.

Good Samaritan Statutes

Various states have enacted Good Samaritan laws, which relieve physicians, nurses, dentists, and other healthcare professionals, and, in some instances, laypersons, from liability in certain emergency situations. Good Samaritan legislation encourages healthcare professionals to render assistance at the scene of emergencies. The language that grants immunity also supports the conclusion that the physician, nurse, or layperson covered by the act will be protected from liability for ordinary negligence in rendering assistance in an emergency.

Under most statutes, immunity is granted only during an emergency or when rendering emergency care. The concept of emergency usually refers to a combination of unforeseen circumstances that require spontaneous action to avoid impending danger. Some states have sought to be more precise regarding what constitutes an emergency or accident. According to the Alaska statute 09.65.090(a), the emergency circumstances must suggest that the giving of aid is the only alternative to death or serious bodily injury.

Apparently, this provision was inserted to emphasize that the actions of a Good Samaritan must be voluntary. To be legally immune under the Good Samaritan laws, a physician or nurse must render help voluntarily and without expectation of later pay.

Statute Applicable: Due Care Rendered

The daughter of a deceased patient in *Dunlap v. Young*[13] had brought a wrongful death action against Emergency Medical Services (EMS) personnel for the death of her mother. The critically ill patient died after receiving care for respiratory distress in the ambulance while en route to the hospital. Under the Good Samaritan statute, an Illinois court found that EMS personnel were not negligent in their treatment of the decedent. They had acted promptly to get the patient to the hospital. Although EMS personnel had failed to intubate the patient, she had been provided with oxygen and assisted respiration.

Statute Not Applicable: Preexisting Duty to Care

The plaintiff, Kearney, suffered a life-threatening injury and was taken by ambulance to the emergency department of Kodiak Island Hospital (KIH), and was examined by the on-call emergency department physician, a family practitioner. It was determined that a surgical consultation was necessary, and Dr. Deal, a surgeon with staff privileges at the hospital, was called. After ordering certain tests, Deal was of the opinion that Kearney could not survive a transfer to Anchorage. Deal then performed emergency surgery that lasted over 9 hours, ending the following morning.

The plaintiff was eventually transferred to Anchorage. His condition worsened, and he suffered loss of circulation and tissue death in both legs. The plaintiff alleged that KIH was negligent in failing to properly evacuate him to Anchorage. Kearney reached a settlement totaling $510,000. He also brought an action against Deal for negligent acts. Deal moved for summary judgment claiming to be immune from suit under the Good Samaritan statute.

The trial court denied Deal's motion for summary judgment, ruling that the Good Samaritan statute was not applicable to Deal because he was acting under a preexisting duty to render emergency care to Kearney. Deal petitioned for review, and his petition was granted.

The superior court held that the immunity provided by the Good Samaritan statute is unavailable to physicians with a preexisting duty to respond to emergency situations. The court concluded that Deal was under a preexisting duty in the instant case by virtue of his contract with KIH, the duty being part of the consideration that Deal gave to KIH in exchange for staff privileges at the hospital. The court further found that the Good Samaritan statute did not apply to Deal in any event because the actions allegedly constituting malpractice occurred during the follow-up care and treatment given Kearney after surgery. By then, the court reasoned, Deal had become Kearney's treating physician and was no longer responding to an emergency situation. Deal appealed to the Alaska Supreme Court.

The Alaska Supreme Court held that the Good Samaritan statute does not extend immunity to physicians who have a preexisting duty to render emergency care. The legislature clearly intended this provision to encourage healthcare providers, including medical professionals, to administer emergency medical care, whether in a hospital or not, to persons who are not their patients, by immunizing them from civil liability. The clear inference of this recommendation is that the statute would not cover those with a preexisting duty to care.[14]

Borrowed Servant Doctrine

The *borrowed servant doctrine* is a special application of the doctrine of respondeat superior and applies when an employer lends an employee to another for a particular employment. Although an employee remains the servant of the employer, under the borrowed servant doctrine, the employer is not liable for injury negligently caused by the servant while in the special service of another. For example, in certain situations, a nurse employed by a hospital can be considered the employee of the physician. In these situations, the physician is the special or temporary employer and is liable for the negligence of the nurse. To determine whether a physician is liable for the negligence of a nurse, it must be established that the physician had the right to control and direct the nurse at the time of the negligent act. If the physician is found to be in exclusive control, and if the nurse is deemed to be the physician's temporary special employee, the hospital is not generally liable for the nurse's negligent acts.

Captain of the Ship Doctrine

In the context of the operating room, the application of the borrowed servant doctrine generally is referred to as the *"captain of the ship doctrine."* Historically, under this doctrine, the surgeon was viewed as being the one in command in the operating room. Today's courts, however, recognize that surgeons do not always have the right to control all persons within the operating room. An assignment of liability based on the theory of who had actual control over the patient more realistically reflects the actual relationship that exists in a modern operating room. For example, summary dismissal in *Thomas v. Raleigh*[15] was properly ordered for those portions of a patient's medical malpractice action that sought to hold a surgeon vicariously liable for throat injuries suffered by his patient because of the negligent manner in which an endotracheal tube was inserted during the administration of anesthesia. The patient's allegations that the surgeon exercised control over the administration of anesthesia were rebutted by evidence to the contrary. Liability of the surgeon could not be premised on the captain of the ship doctrine because that doctrine would not be recognized in West Virginia, where the surgery took place.

Statute of Limitations

The *statute of limitations* refers to legislatively imposed time constraints that restrict the period of time after the occurrence of an injury during which a legal action must be commenced. Should a cause of action be initiated later than the period of time prescribed, the case cannot proceed. Many technical rules are associated with statutes of limitations. Statutes in each state specify that malpractice suits and other personal injury suits must be brought within fixed periods of time. An injured person who is a minor or is otherwise under a legal disability may, in many states, extend the period within which an action for injury may be filed. Computation of the period when the statute begins to run in a particular state may vary based on any one or more of the following factors:

- the date that the physician terminated treatment,
- the time of the wrongful act,
- the time when the patient should have reasonably discovered the injury,
- the date that the injury was discovered, or
- the date when the contract between the patient and the physician ended.

The running of the statute will not begin if fraud (the deliberate concealment from a patient of facts that might present a cause of action for damages) is involved. The cause of action begins at the time fraud is discovered.

The statute of limitations does not generally begin to run in those cases where a patient is unaware that an act of malpractice has occurred. Such is the case when foreign objects are left in a patient during surgery.

 NEWSPAPER CLIPPINGS: What Surgeons Leave Behind

More than a dozen times a day, doctors sew up patients with sponges and other surgical objects mistakenly left inside. It's a deadly, yet easily avoidable phenomenon.

• • •

The consequences are enormous. Many patients carrying surgical sponges suffer for months or years before anyone determines the cause of the searing pain, digestive dysfunction and other typical ills.

—*Peter Eisler*, USA Today, *March 8–10, 2013*

A New Hampshire patient in *Shillady v. Elliot Community Hospital*[16] sued the hospital for negligence in treatment that was administered 31 years earlier. A needle had been left in the patient's spine after a spinal tap in 1940. In 1970, an X-ray showed the needle. The patient had suffered severe pain immediately after the spinal tap, which had decreased over the intervening years to about three "spells" a year. The court held that the 6-year statute of limitations does not begin "until the patient learns or in the exercise of reasonable care and diligence should have learned of its presence."[17] Therefore, the defendant's motion to dismiss the case on the grounds that the statute of limitations had run out was not granted.

Sovereign Immunity

Sovereign immunity refers to the common-law doctrine by which federal and state governments historically have been immune from liability for harm suffered from the tortious conduct of employees. For the most part, both federal and state governments have abolished sovereign immunity.

Action was brought on behalf of a minor in *Steele v. United States*,[18] who received treatment at a U.S. Army hospital and suffered injury because of the optometrist's failure to refer the child to an ophthalmologist for examination. The U.S. district court held that it was probable that an ophthalmologist would have diagnosed the child's problem and prevented the loss of his right eye. Recovery was permitted against the United States under the FTCA.

Intervening Cause

Intervening cause arises when the act of a third party, independent of the defendant's original negligent conduct, is the proximate cause of an injury. If the negligent act of a third party is extraordinary under the circumstances and unforeseeable as a normal and probable consequence of the defendant's negligence, then the third party's negligence supersedes that of the defendant and relieves the defendant of liability.

In *Cohran v. Harper,*[19] a patient sued a physician, charging him with malpractice for an alleged staphylococcus infection that she received from a hypodermic needle used by the physician's nurse. The grounds of negligence included an allegation that the physician failed to properly sterilize the hypodermic needle that was used to administer penicillin. Evidence showed that a prepackaged sterilized needle and syringe were used. There was inadequate proof that the physician or his nurse negligently contaminated the needle and syringe. The court found that even if there was evidence that the needle was contaminated and that the patient's ailment was caused thereby, there was no evidence that either the physician, his nurse, or anyone in his office knew, or by the exercise of ordinary care could have discovered, that the prepackaged needle and syringe were so contaminated. The defense of intervening cause would have been an adequate defense against recovery of damages if it had been established that the needle was contaminated when packaged by the manufacturer.

CLOSING STATEMENTS

After completion of the plaintiff's case and the defendant's defense, the judge calls for closing statements. Closing statements provide attorneys with an opportunity to summarize for the jury and the court what they have proven. They may point out faults in their opponent's case and emphasize points they want the jury to remember.

If there appears to be only a question of law at the end of a case, a motion can be made for a directed verdict. The court will grant the motion if there is no question of fact to be decided by the jury. A directed verdict also may, for example, be made on the grounds that the plaintiff has failed to present sufficient facts to prove his or her case or that the evidence fails to establish a legal basis for a verdict in the plaintiff's favor.

JUDGE'S CHARGE

After the attorneys' summations, the court charges the jury before the jurors recess to deliberate. Because the jury determines issues of fact, it is necessary for the court to instruct the jury with regard to applicable law. This is done by means of a charge. The charge defines the responsibility of the jury, describes the applicable law, and advises the

jury of the alternatives available to it. As an example, statements from the trial judge's oral charge to the jurors in *Estes Health Care Centers v. Bannerman,*[20] in which a nursing facility resident died after transfer to a hospital after suffering burns in a bath, included:

> The complaint alleges the defendant Jackson Hospital undertook to provide hospital and nursing care to the deceased, and that the defendant negligently failed to provide proper hospital and nursing care to the plaintiff's intestate.
>
> The defendants in response to these allegations . . . have each separately entered pleas of the general issue or general denial. Under the law, a plea of the general issue has the effect of placing the burden of proof on the plaintiffs to reasonably satisfy you from the evidence, the truth of those things claimed by them in the bill of the complaint. The defendants carry no burden of proof.
>
> As to the defendant Jackson Hospital, the duty arises in that in rendering services to a patient, a hospital must use that degree of care, skill, and diligence used by hospitals generally in the community under similar circumstances.
>
> Negligence is not actionable unless the negligence is the proximate cause of the injury. The law defines *proximate cause* as that cause which is the natural and probable sequence of events and without the intervention of any new or independent cause, produces the injury, and without which such injury would not have occurred. For an act to constitute actionable negligence, there must not only be some causal connection between the negligent act complained of and the injury suffered, but connection must be by natural and unbroken sequence, without intervening sufficient causes, so that "but for" the negligence of the defendant, the injury would not have occurred.
>
> If one is guilty of negligence, which concurs or combines with the negligence of another, and the two combine to produce injury, each negligent person is liable for the resulting injury. And the negligence of each will be deemed the proximate cause of the injury. *Concurrent causes* may be defined as two or more causes, which run together and act contemporaneously to produce a given result or to inflict an injury. This does not mean that the causes of the acts producing the injury must necessarily occur simultaneously, but they must be active simultaneously to efficiently and proximately produce a result.
>
> In an action against two or more defendants for injury allegedly caused by combined or concurring negligence of the defendants, it is not necessary to show negligence of all the defendants in order for recovery to be had against one or more to be negligent. If you are reasonably satisfied from the evidence in this case that all the defendants are negligent and

that their negligence concurred and combined to proximately cause the injury complained by the plaintiffs, then each defendant is liable to the plaintiffs.[21]

When a charge given by the court is not clear enough on a particular point, it is the obligation of the attorneys for both sides to request clarification of the charge. When the jury retires to deliberate, the members are reminded not to discuss the case except among themselves.

JURY DELIBERATION

After the judge's charge, the jury retires to the jury room to deliberate and determine the defendant's liability. The jury members return to the courtroom upon reaching a verdict, and their determinations are presented to the court.

If a verdict is against the weight of the evidence, a judge may dismiss the case, order a new trial, or set his or her own verdict. At the time judgment is rendered, the losing party has an opportunity to motion for a new trial.

AWARDING DAMAGES

Monetary damages generally are awarded to individuals in cases of personal injury and wrongful death. Damages generally are fixed by the jury and are nominal, compensatory, hedonic, or punitive.

1. *Nominal damages* are awarded as a mere token in recognition that wrong has been committed when the actual amount of compensation is insignificant.
2. *Compensatory damages* are estimated reparation in money for detriment or injury sustained (including loss of earnings, medical costs, and loss of financial support).
3. *Hedonic damages* are those damages awarded to compensate an individual for the loss of enjoyment of life. Such damages are awarded because of the failure of compensatory damages to compensate an individual adequately for the pain and suffering that he or she has endured as a result of a negligent wrong.
4. *Punitive damages* are additional money awards authorized when an injury is caused by gross carelessness or disregard for the safety of others.

Plaintiff's Schedule of Damages

Plaintiffs seek recovery for a great variety of damages. The following are typical: personal injuries; permanent physical disabilities; permanent mental disabilities; past and future physical and mental pain and suffering sustained and to be sustained; loss of enjoyment of life; loss of consortium where a spouse is injured in an accident; loss of child's services where a minor child is injured in the accident; medical and other health expenses reasonably paid or incurred or reasonably certain to be incurred in the future; past and future loss of earnings sustained and to be sustained; and permanent diminution in the plaintiff's earning capacity. The following cases illustrate a variety of damages sought by plaintiffs.

Future Pain and Suffering

In *Luecke v. Bitterman*,[22] an award of $490,000 for future pain and suffering was found reasonable with respect to a 20-year-old patient who, as a result of a physician's negligent application of liquid nitrogen to remove a wart, suffered a 12- by 4-inch third-degree burn. The burn resulted in a scar on the right buttock extending to the back of the thigh. The plaintiff suffered excruciating pain and post-traumatic stress disorder.

Punitive Damages

Punitive damages are awarded over and above that which is intended to compensate the plaintiff for economic losses resulting from the injury. Punitive damages cover such items as physical disability, mental anguish, loss of a spouse's services, physical suffering, injury to one's reputation, and loss of companionship. Punitive damages were referred to as that *mighty engine of deterrence* in *Johnson v. Terry*.[23]

The court in *Henry v. Deen*[24] held that allegations of gross and wanton negligence incidental to wrongful death in the plaintiff's complaint gave sufficient notice of a claim against the treating physician and physician's assistant for punitive damages. The original complaint, which alleged that the treating physician, the physician's assistant, and the consulting physician agreed to create and did create false and misleading entries in the patient's medical record, was sufficient to allege a civil conspiracy. The decision of the lower court was reversed, and the case was remanded for further proceedings.

In *Estes Health Care Centers v. Bannerman*, discussed earlier, the court stated:

While human life is incapable of translation into a compensatory measurement, the amount of an award of punitive damages may be measured by the gravity of the wrong done, the punishment called for by the act of the wrongdoer, and the need to deter similar wrongs in order to preserve human life.[25]

In *Payton Health Care Facilities, Inc. v. Estate of Campbell*,[26] a punitive damage award in the amount of $1.7 million for the wrongful death of a patient from infected decubitus ulcers was found to be justified. The treating physician had agreed to a settlement prior to trial in the amount of $50,000. The deceased, a stroke victim, had been admitted to the Lakeland Health Care Center for nursing and medical care. While at the center, the patient developed several severe skin ulcers that eventually necessitated hospitalization in Lakeland General Hospital. The patient's condition deteriorated to such a state that further treatment was inadequate to prolong his life. Expert testimony had been presented that indicated that the standard of care received by the patient while at the nursing facility was an outrageous deviation from acceptable standards of care. There was sufficient evidence of the willful and wanton disregard for rights of others to permit an award of punitive damages against the companies who owned and managed the nursing facility. The cause of death was determined to be bacteremia with sepsis, because of extensive infected necrotic decubitus ulcers, that the patient developed at the nursing facility.

Punitive Damages Not Awarded

Punitive damages in *Brooking v. Polito*[27] were determined to be inappropriate in an action alleging failure to timely diagnose pancreatic cancer. It was undisputed that the defendants performed various tests on the decedent, which included blood tests, CAT scans, an MRI, and ultrasound. The tests had been analyzed, and the patient was treated accordingly.

Damages for Surviving Spouse and Children

Damages may be awarded given evidence of a patient's pain and the mental anguish of the surviving husband and children. In *Jefferson Hospital Association v. Garrett*,[28] damages in the amount of $180,000 were found not to be excessive given evidence of the patient's pain and the mental suffering of the surviving spouse and children.

Damages for Emotional Distress

The court of appeals in *Haught v. Maceluch*[29] held that under Texas law the mother was entitled to recover for her emotional distress, even though she was not conscious at the time her child was born. The mother had brought a medical malpractice action, alleging that the physician was negligent in the delivery of her child, causing her daughter to suffer permanent brain injury. The district court entered judgment of $1,160,000 for the child's medical expenses and $175,000 for her lost future earnings. The court deleted a jury award of $118,000 for the mother's mental suffering over her daughter's impaired condition. On appeal, the court of appeals permitted recovery, under Texas law, for mental suffering. The mother was conscious for more than

11 hours of labor and was aware of the physician's negligent acts, his absence in a near-emergency situation, and the over-administration of the labor-inducing drug Pitocin.

Damages Not Excessive

In determining excessiveness, the courts often consider the severity of the injury, whether the injury is manifested by objective physical evidence or whether it is revealed only by the subjective testimony, whether the injury is permanent, whether the plaintiff can continue with his or her employment, and the size of out-of-pocket expenses.[30]

The plaintiff in *Burge v. Parke*[31] suffered a laceration of his right foot on April 2 and was taken to St. Margaret's Hospital. A physician in the emergency department cleaned and stitched the laceration and released the patient with instructions to keep the foot elevated. Even though reports prepared by the fire medic who arrived on the scene of the accident and by ambulance personnel indicated the chief complaint as being a fracture of the foot, no X-rays were ordered in the emergency department. The admitting clerk had typed a statement on the admission form indicating possible fracture of the right foot. However, a handwritten note stated the chief complaint as being a laceration of the right foot. The patient returned to the hospital later in the day with his mother, complaining of pain in the right foot. His mother asked if X-rays had been taken. The physician said that it was not necessary. The wound was redressed, and the patient was sent home again with instructions to keep the foot elevated. The pain continued to worsen, and the patient was taken to see another physician on April 5. X-rays were ordered, and an orthopedic surgeon called for a consultation diagnosed three fractures and compartment syndrome, a swelling of tissue in the muscle compartments. The swelling increased pressure on the blood vessels, thus decreasing circulation, which tends to cause muscles to die.

Approximately one-half pint of clotted blood was removed from the wound. By April 11, the big toe had to be surgically removed. It was alleged that the emergency department physician failed to obtain a full medical history, to order the necessary X-rays, and to diagnose and treat the fractures of the foot. As a result, the patient ultimately suffered loss of his big toe. The Macon County Circuit Court awarded damages totaling $450,000 for loss of a big toe, and the physician appealed. The Alabama Supreme Court found the damages not to have been excessive.

A medical malpractice action in *Callahan v. Cardinal Glennon Hosp.*[32] was brought against the employer of a physician, alleging that the physician's failure to properly treat an abscess some 3 weeks after an infant received a live polio vaccine resulted in suppression of the infant's immune system and the infant's contraction of paralytic polio. The jury in the circuit court returned a $16 million verdict in favor of the plaintiffs, and the defendant appealed. The case was transferred from the court of appeals to the state supreme court.

The Missouri Supreme Court held that there was no basis for a new trial on the grounds of excessiveness of the $16 million verdict. There is no formula for determining the excessiveness of a verdict. Each case must be decided on its own facts to determine what is fair and reasonable. A jury is in the best position to make such a determination. The trial judge could have set aside the verdict if a determination was made that passion and prejudice brought about an excessive verdict. The size of the verdict alone does not establish passion and prejudice. The appellant failed to establish that the verdict was: (1) glaringly unwarranted and (2) based on prejudice and passion. Compensation of a plaintiff is based on such factors as the age of the patient, the nature and extent of injury, diminished earnings capacity, economic condition, and awards in comparable cases. A jury is entitled to consider such intangibles that do not lend themselves to precise calculation, such as past and future pain, suffering, effect on lifestyle, embarrassment, humiliation, and economic loss.

Damages Excessive

A jury verdict totaling $12,393,130 was considered an excessive award in *Merrill v. Albany Medical Center*,[33] in which damages were sought with respect to the severe brain damage sustained by a 22-month-old infant as the result of oxygen deprivation. This occurred when the infant went into cardiac arrest during surgery for removal of a suspected malignant tumor from her right lung. Reduction of the amount to $6,143,130 was considered to be appropriate.

Damages Capped

The trial court in *Judd v. Drezga*[34] was found to have properly limited a brain-damaged infant's recovery of quality-of-life damages to $250,000. The Idaho cap on damages was designed to reduce healthcare costs, increase the availability of medical malpractice insurance, and secure the continued availability of healthcare resources—all legitimate legislative goals given the clear social and economic evil of rising healthcare costs and a shortage of qualified healthcare professionals. In attempting to meet its goals, the legislature had not unreasonably or arbitrarily limited recovery. Rather, it had chosen to place a limit on the recovery of noneconomic quality-of-life damages—one area where legislation had been shown to substantially further these goals. Applying each individual test, the open courts, uniform operation of laws, and due-process provisions of the constitution were not offended by the damage cap. Additionally, neither the right to a jury trial nor the constitutional guarantees of separation of powers were offended by the cap.

Joint and Several Liability

The doctrine of *joint and several liability* permits the plaintiff to bring suit against all persons (joint tort-feasors) who share responsibility for the plaintiff's injury. *Joint tort-feasors* are two or more persons who either act together in committing a wrong or whose independent acts cause the plaintiff's injury. The doctrine allows the plaintiff to recover monetary damages from any one or all the defendants. Any one defendant, even though partially responsible for the plaintiff's injury, can be required under this doctrine to pay the full judgment awarded. Awards have tended to fall in greater amounts on defendants with the ability to pay, often referred to as the *deep-pockets* theory; who has the most pays the most.

Hospital and Physician Jointly Liable

As noted above, *joint liability* is based on the concept that all joint or concurrent tort-feasors are actually independently at fault for their own wrongful acts. Both a hospital and its physicians can be held jointly liable for damages suffered by patients. In *Gonzales v. Nork & Mercy Hospital*,[35] the hospital was found negligent for failing to protect the patient, a 27-year-old man, from acts of malpractice by an independent, privately retained physician. The patient had been injured in an automobile accident and was operated on by Dr. Nork, an orthopedic surgeon. The plaintiff's life expectancy was reduced as a result of an unsuccessful and allegedly unnecessary laminectomy. It was found that the hospital knew or should have known of the surgeon's incompetence because the surgeon previously had performed many operations either unnecessarily or negligently. In such cases the defendant produced false and inadequate findings as well as false-positive myelograms. He deceived his patients with this information and caused them to undergo surgery. Evidence was presented showing that the surgeon had performed more than 3-dozen similar operations unnecessarily or in a negligent manner. Even if the hospital was not aware of the surgeon's acts of negligence, an effective monitoring system should have been in place for monitoring his abilities. Consequently, the surgeon and hospital were jointly liable for damages suffered.

Several Liability

Several liability should not be confused with *joint and several liability*. In *several liability*, each party to a lawsuit is liable only to the degree he or she has been determined to have contributed to the injury. In other words, when there are multiple defendants in a lawsuit, each defendant's responsibility for damages will not exceed the degree or percentage of his or her carelessness that contributed to the patient's injury. Whereas, under the doctrine of *joint and several liability* any one of the defendants to a lawsuit can be responsible to pay the full cost of damages awarded to the plaintiff/s.

APPEALS

An appellate court reviews a case on the basis of the trial record as well as written briefs and, if requested, concise oral arguments by the attorneys. A brief summarizes the facts of a case, testimony of the witnesses, laws affecting the case, and arguments of counsel. The party making the appeal is the appellant. The party answering the appeal is the appellee. After hearing oral arguments, the court takes the case under advisement until such time as the judges consider it and agree on a decision. An opinion then is prepared explaining the reasons for a decision.

Grounds for appeal can result from one or more of the following: the verdict was excessive or inadequate in the lower court; evidence was rejected that should have been accepted; inadmissible evidence was permitted; testimony that should have been admissible was excluded; the verdict was contrary to the weight of the evidence; the court improperly charged the jury; the jury was confused by jury instructions; and/or the jury verdict is the result of bias, prejudice, and/or passion.

Notice of appeal must be filed with the trial court, the appellate court, and the adverse party. The party wishing to prevent execution of an adverse judgment until such time as the case has been heard and decided by an appellate court also should file a stay of execution.

The appellate court may modify, affirm, or reverse the judgment or reorder a new trial on an appeal. The majority ruling of the judges in the appellate court is binding on the parties of a lawsuit. If the appellate court's decision is not unanimous, the minority may render a dissenting opinion. Further appeal may be made, as set by statute, to the highest court of appeals. If an appeal involves a constitutional question, it eventually might be appealed to the U.S. Supreme Court.

When the highest appellate court in a state decides a case, a final judgment results, and the matter is ended. The instances when one may appeal the ruling of a state court to the U.S. Supreme Court are rare. A federal question must be involved, and even then the Supreme Court must decide whether it will hear the case. A federal question is one involving the U.S. Constitution or a statute enacted by Congress, so it is unlikely that a negligence case arising in a state court would be reviewed and decided by the Supreme Court.

EXECUTION OF JUDGMENTS

When the amount of damages has been established and all the appeals have been heard, the defendant must comply with the judgment. If he or she fails to do so, a court order can be executed requiring the sheriff or other judicial officer to sell as much of the defendant's property as necessary, within statutory limitations, to satisfy the plaintiff's judgment.

Notes

1. *Collins v. Park*, 621 A.2d 996 (Pa. Super. Ct. 1993).
2. *Personal Representative, etc., Appellant, v. Osceola Mental Health, Inc., etc., et al. Appellee*, Court of Appeal of Florida, Fifth District (Opinion filed January 11, 2013).
3. 725 N.Y.S.2d 35 (2001).
4. 600 A.2d 1063 (D.C. 1991).
5. Steve Cohen, Malpractice, *New York Magazine*, Oct. 1, 1990, at 43, 47.
6. 720 N.E.2d 1175 (Ind. App. 1999).
7. 337 P.2d 974 (Or. 1959).
8. No. 11-13752 (E.D. Mich. Feb. 5, 2013).
9. 221 N.W.2d 39 (S.D. 1974).
10. 445 N.W.2d 763 (Iowa 1989).
11. *Marsingill v. O'Malley*, 128 P.3d 151 (Alas. 2006).
12. 346 S.E.2d 528 (S.C. 1986).
13. 187 SW.3d 828 (2006).
14. *Deal v. Kearney*, 851 P.2d 1353 (Alaska 1993).
15. 358 S.E.2d 222 (W. Va. 1987).
16. 320 A.2d 637 (N.H. 1974).
17. *Id.*
18. 463 F. Supp. 321 (D. Alaska 1978).
19. 154 S.E.2d 461 (Ga. Ct. App. 1967).
20. 411 So. 2d 109 (Ala. 1982).
21. 657 N.Y.S.2d 419 (N.Y. App. Div. 1997).
22. 658 N.Y.S.2d 34 (N.Y. App. Div. 1997).
23. No. 537-907 (Wis. Cir. Ct. Mar. 18, 1983).
24. 310 S.E.2d 326 (N.C. 1984).
25. 411 So. 2d 109, 113 (Ala. 1982).
26. 497 So. 2d 1233 (Fla. Dist. Ct. App. 1986).
27. 16 A.D.3d 898, 791 N.Y.S.2d 686 (N.Y. App. Div. 2005).
28. 804 S.W.2d 711 (Ark. 1991).
29. 681 F.2d 291 (5th Cir. 1982).
30. *Tesauro v. Perrige*, 650 A.2d 1079 (Pa. Super. 1994).
31. 510 So. 2d 538 (Ala. 1987).
32. *Callahan v. Cardinal Glennon Hosp.*, 863 S.W.2d 852 (Mo. 1993).
33. 512 N.Y.S.2d 519 (N.Y. App. Div. 1987).
34. 103 P.3d 135, 2004 UT 91 (Utah 2004).
35. No. 228566 (Cal. Super. Ct. Sacramento Co. 1976).

8
Corporate Structure and Legal Issues

Figure 8–1 The Corporate Board Room © iStockphoto.com/Photomorphic

Learning Objectives

The reader upon completion of this chapter will be able to:

- Explain express, implied, and corporate authority.
- Discuss corporate organization and committee structure.
- Describe the Sarbanes–Oxley Act.
- Explain the terms *respondeat superior* and *corporate negligence*.
- Describe "Darling—A Benchmark Case."
- Explain the concept joint liability.

- Describe the duties of healthcare organizations, the CEO, and medical staff.
- Explain the purpose of corporate reorganization.

This chapter introduces the healthcare professional to the responsibilities, as well as legal risks, of healthcare organizations and their governing bodies. Healthcare organizations are incorporated under state law as freestanding for-profit or not-for-profit corporations. Each corporation has a governing body (e.g., board of directors) that has ultimate responsibility for the operation of the organization. The existence of this authority creates certain duties and liabilities for governing boards and their individual members. The governing body is legally responsible for establishing and implementing policies regarding the management and operation of the organization. Responsibility for the day-to-day operations of an organization is generally accomplished by appointing a chief executive officer.

Not-for-profit healthcare organizations are usually exempt from federal taxation under Section 501(c)(3) of the Internal Revenue Code of 1986, as amended. Such federal exemption usually entitles the organization to an automatic exemption from state taxes as well. Such tax exemption not only relieves the organization from the payment of income taxes and sales taxes but also permits the organization to receive contributions from donors, who then may obtain charitable deductions on their personal income tax returns.

The tax-exempt status of healthcare corporations is coming under more scrutiny as they diversify their activities to generate higher revenues. The City of Pittsburgh initiated a challenge to the payroll tax exemption claimed by the University of Pittsburgh Medical Center ("UPMC"), which claims the exemption on the basis of its status as an "institution of purely public charity," or "IPPC," under Pennsylvania law. Questionable activities of UPMC's alleged offenses include: expanding business operations that include investment partnerships and more than 50 taxable corporations; not offering charitable services through many of its 400 doctors' offices and outpatient sites; closing facilities in locations with relatively high numbers of Medicare-eligible, Medicaid-eligible, or uninsured patients and opening or expanding facilities where there are proportionately more privately-insured patients; paying more than 20 officers, directors, and key employees compensation in excess of $1 million, with the CEO receiving significantly more, as well as a lavish office space, private chef and dining room, private chauffeur and private jet; turning over unpaid accounts to a collection agency or a law firm for further collections and legal action against its patients; and the list goes on. The outcome of this case could have far-reaching consequences for healthcare organizations expanding activities into questionable tax-exempt activities and could very likely be precedent setting for future cases challenging an organization's tax-exempt status.

Although healthcare organizations can operate as sole proprietorships or partnerships, most function as corporations. Thus, an important source of law applicable to governing boards and to the duties and responsibilities of their members is found in state incorporation laws. These duties include holding meetings, establishing policies, being financially scrupulous, providing adequate insurance, and paying taxes, as might be required.

AUTHORITY OF HEALTHCARE CORPORATIONS

Healthcare corporations—governmental, charitable, or proprietary—have certain powers expressly or implicitly granted to them by state statutes. Generally, the authority of a corporation is expressed in the law under which the corporation is chartered and in the corporation's articles of incorporation. The existence of this authority creates certain duties and liabilities for governing bodies and their individual members. Members of the governing body of an organization have both express and implied corporate authority.

Express Corporate Authority

Express corporate authority is the power specifically delegated by statute. A healthcare corporation derives its authority to act from the laws of the state in which it is incorporated. The articles of incorporation set forth the purpose(s) of the corporation's existence and the powers the corporation is authorized to exercise to carry out its purposes.

Implied Corporate Authority

Implied corporate authority is the right to perform any and all acts necessary to exercise a corporation's expressly conferred authority and to accomplish the purpose(s) for which it was created. Generally, implied corporate authority arises from situations in which such authority is required or suggested as a result of a need for corporate powers not specifically granted in the articles of incorporation. A governing body, at its own discretion, can enact new bylaws, rules, and regulations; purchase or mortgage property; borrow money; purchase equipment; select employees; adopt corporate resolutions that delineate decision-making responsibilities; and so forth. It should be noted that these powers can be enumerated in the articles of incorporation and, in such cases, would be categorized as express rather than implied corporate authority.

Duty to Appoint Competent Physicians

Hospitals have an implied duty to patients to select competent physicians who, although they are independent practitioners, would be providing in-hospital care to patients. Hospitals are in the best position to protect patients and consequently have an independent duty to select competent physicians seeking staff privileges.

The surgeon in *Purcell & Tucson General Hospital v. Zimbelman*[1] performed inappropriate surgery because of his misdiagnosis of the patient's ailment. Prior malpractice suits against the surgeon revealed that the hospital had reason to know or should have known that the surgeon apparently lacked the skill to treat the patient's condition. The court held that the hospital had a clear duty to select competent physicians; to regulate the privileges granted to staff physicians; to ensure that privileges are conferred only for those procedures for which the physician is trained and qualified; and to restrict, suspend, or require supervision when a physician has demonstrated an inability to perform certain procedures. The hospital assumed the duty of supervising the competence of its physicians through the department of surgery. The court noted that it is reasonable to conclude that if the hospital had taken some action against the surgeon, the patient would not have been injured.

Ultra Vires Acts

Ultra vires is a Latin term meaning "beyond the powers." *Ultra vires acts* are those acts conducted by an organization that lie beyond the scope of authority of a corporation to perform. A governing body can be held liable for acting beyond its scope of authority, which is either expressed (e.g., in its articles of incorporation) or implied in law. The governing body acts in and on behalf of the corporation. If any action is in violation of a statute or regulation, it is illegal. An example of an illegal act would be the "known" employment of an unlicensed person in a position that by law requires a license. The state, through its attorney general, has the power to prevent the performance of an ultra vires act by means of an injunction.

 REALITY CHECK: Ensuring Integrity

Jim, the administrator of East Campus Hospital, was reviewing his mail and reports placed in his inbox by Carol, his secretary. He noticed what appeared to be a copy of correspondence that had been forwarded to him from the Bishop. The letter, describing a donation that had been made, read:

> Dear Bishop John,
> Enclosed is a contribution from David and his wife. He originally heard about our fundraising activities through the co-chairman of the fund raising appeal. The care he received at the East Campus Hospital was outstanding and he would like to make a contribution on our behalf,
> Sincerely,

After reading his morning mail and reports, Jim placed the letter in his outbox for filing. Carol later picked up Jim's mail and other reports from his outbox. Later that afternoon, Carol walked back into Jim's office and inquired, "Did you read this letter forwarded to you from the corporate office?" Handing it to Jim, he replied, "Yes, I read it." Carol then asked, "Do you see anything that piqued your curiosity in this letter?" Jim replied that he had not. Carol, pointing at a strip of whiteout tape, urged Jim to look more closely. She then asked Jim to turn the letter over and read the words the tape was covering. He turned the letter over, noting what the letter had said. It appeared that only a copy had been meant for Jim, not the original correspondence. With the missing words inserted, the correspondence read:

> Dear Bishop John,
> Enclosed is a contribution from David and his wife. He originally heard about our fundraising activities through the co-chairman of the fund raising appeal. The care he received at the East Campus Hospital was outstanding and he would like to make a contribution on our behalf, earmarked for the East Campus Hospital.
> Sincerely,

Discussion

1. Discuss why the whiteout tape might have been placed over the words, "earmarked for the East Campus Hospital." Take into account the comma placed prior to the word "earmarked."
2. What action should Jim take? Remember that Jim could not absolutely determine who placed the whiteout tape on the correspondence, the letter's author or some other unknown person.

Corporate Organization and Committee Structure

Governing bodies should have their corporate charters reviewed periodically by legal counsel to ensure that their express powers are consistent with the organization's mission, operations, and development plans.

▌ CORPORATE COMMITTEE STRUCTURE

Ultimate responsibility for the functioning of a healthcare corporation rests with the governing body. Ideally, the governing body generally includes representation from both the community and the organization's medical staff. The business of the governing body is generally conducted through a variety of committees. Some of those committees are described here.

Executive Committee

The *executive committee* is a working group of the governing body that has delegated authority to act on behalf of the full board when it is not in session. The committee must act within the scope and authority assigned by the governing body. The duties and responsibilities of the committee should be delineated in the corporate bylaws. The functions of the executive committee generally include acting as a liaison between management and the full board, reviewing and making recommendations on management proposals, and performing special assignments as may be delegated by the full board from time to time. Business transacted and actions taken by the executive committee should be reported at regular sessions of the governing body and ratified. The executive committee generally has all the powers of the governing body, except such powers as the governing body may be prohibited from delegating in accordance with applicable laws.

Bylaws Committee

The bylaws committee reviews and recommends bylaw changes to the governing body. Bylaws generally are amended or rescinded by a majority vote of the governing body.

Finance Committee

The finance committee is responsible for overseeing the financial affairs of the organization and making recommendations to the governing body. This committee is responsible for directing and reviewing the preparation of financial statements, operating budgets, major capital requests, and so on. The governing body must approve actions of the finance committee.

Nominating Committee

The nominating committee is generally responsible for developing and recommending to the governing body criteria for governing body membership. The requirements for membership on a governing body generally include a willingness to devote the time and energy necessary to fulfill the commitment as a board member; residence in the community or an identifiable association with the community served; demonstration of knowledge of local healthcare issues; possession of the traits of good moral character and maturity; and professional, as well as appropriate, life

experiences necessary to make managerial decisions in the healthcare setting.

Planning Committee

The planning committee is responsible for recommending to the governing body the use and development of organizational resources as they relate to the mission and vision of the organization. Specifically, the planning committee oversees: the development of short-term and long-range goals; acquisition of major equipment; addition of new services based on identified community need; program development; and the preparation of progress reports for the full board.

Patient Care Committee

The patient care committee reviews the quality of patient care rendered in the organization and makes recommendations for the improvement for such care. The committee is generally responsible for developing a process to identify patient and family needs and expectations and to establish a process to continuously improve customer relations.

Audit and Regulatory Compliance Committee

The audit and regulatory compliance committee is responsible for the assessment of various functions and control systems and for providing management with analysis and recommendations regarding activities reviewed. Healthcare organizations must be vigilant in conducting their financial affairs. An effective audit committee can be helpful in uncovering and thwarting poor or inept financial decision-making. The committee should include members of the governing body and internal auditing staff. Responsibilities of the committee include: developing corporate auditing policies and procedures; recommending independent auditors to the governing body; reviewing the credentials of independent auditors and facilitating change in auditors as might be deemed appropriate; reviewing with independent auditors the proposed scope and general extent of their auditing duties and responsibilities; reviewing the scope and results of the annual audit with the independent auditors and the organization's management staff; setting, overseeing, reviewing, and acting on the recommendations of the internal audit staff; reviewing the internal accounting practices of the corporation, including policies and procedures; reviewing and evaluating financial statements (e.g., income statements, balance sheets, cash flow reports, investment accounts); promoting the prevention, detection, deterrence, and reporting of fraud; reviewing the means for safeguarding assets, and,

Figure 8–2 Corporate Ethics and Responsibilities   © Dusit/ShutterStock, Inc.

as appropriate, the existence of such assets; ensuring that financial reporting functions are in keeping with generally accepted accounting principles; and reviewing the reliability and integrity of financial and operating information.

ORGANIZATIONAL ETHICS

Organizational ethics describes the ethics of an organization and how it responds to internal or external circumstances affecting the organization's mission and values. Ethical behavior in an organization can be enhanced by providing staff members with a written code of ethics; providing training and education to improve each staff member's knowledge base, skills, and competencies; providing easy access to professional sources to assist in resolving ethical issues in the workplace; and providing systems for confidential reporting of breaches in unethical conduct both in and outside the organization.

Although most healthcare organizations have published their mission, vision, and values statements, policy and practice continue to be distant relatives. Commitment to organizational ethics must begin with the organization's leadership.

 REALITY CHECK: Allocating Scarce Funds from Operations to Capital Projects

At a time when many hospitals were on the brink of bankruptcy and struggling to survive, Brad, the administrator of a hospital in a multihospital system had a positive bottom line in the millions. The hospital was located in an upscale, affluent community. Unfortunately, the money was siphoned off to support the operations and capital projects of other hospitals in the system. Meanwhile, Brad's hospital was suffering from lack of supplies and funds for local capital projects. The physicians and many community members, aware of the positive bottom line, were disturbed that the hospital's funds from operations and donations were being earmarked to fund the day-to-day operations of the system's failing hospitals. In addition, at a time when these hospitals were losing money, funds from Brad's hospital were being earmarked for major building projects in these hospitals, as well as, corporate

(continued)

office projects. It was difficult to get people to donate to their own community hospital. The community had no trust their donations would stay in the community.

Corporate leadership was expanding its capital projects, expanding nonrevenue-producing projects, relocating corporate offices to a more expensive site, building lavish suites, adding staff with vague job descriptions that only served to burden and penalize the revenue-producing entities, and jeopardizing patient care with their pet projects by deluging hospital staff with paperwork so they could produce even more paperwork to justify their own existence. Hospital staff felt that corporate staff had become an obstacle to the provision of quality patient care. No relief from battlefield fatigue seemed to be on the horizon.

Brad was able to work with some local community leaders (e.g., banker, lawyer, physician, newspaper editor, real estate agent) to establish a fundraising board whose mission was to oversee the local fundraising process and assure the proper allocation of community funds to the local hospital. Although many of the hospital system's corporate leaders privately objected to the concept, the corporate board reluctantly recognized the community fundraising board's existence, hoping to make inroads into the pockets of the wealthy. With half-hearted support by the corporation's leadership, the death of many of the founding fathers of the community board, and the resignation of Brad, who had developed the trust and provided the leadership, the community board slowly faded out of existence under the leadership of administrators that followed him.

Discussion

1. Discuss the ethical issues related to Brad's dilemma regarding cash flow to other entities in the corporation. Do you consider this an isolated incident or an all too frequent occurrence with the rise of multihospital systems?
2. Discuss what steps you would take to resolve the resource allocation issues if you were in Brad's position.
3. Discuss the community's reluctance to donate to the local hospital. What would you do?

Sarbanes–Oxley Act

The *Sarbanes–Oxley Act of 2002*, commonly called SOX or SARBOX, was enacted as a response to the misconduct committed by executives in companies such as Enron, WorldCom, and Tyco, resulting in investor losses exceeding half a trillion dollars. To protect investors in public companies and improve the accuracy and reliability of corporate disclosures, SOX requires top executives of public corporations to vouch for the financial reports of their companies. The act encourages self-regulation and the need to promote due diligence; select a leader with morals and core values; examine incentives; constantly monitor the organization's culture; build a strong, knowledgeable governing body; continuously search for conflicts of interest in the organization; focus attention on processes and controls that support accurate financial reporting through documented policies and procedures; and establish strong standards of conduct and a code of ethics that encourages employees to report unethical or fraudulent behavior without fear of retribution.

The act covers issues such as establishing a public company accounting oversight board, auditor independence, corporate responsibility, and enhanced financial disclosure.

Major provisions of SOX include: certification of financial reports by CEOs and CFOs; ban on personal loans to any executive officer and director; accelerated reporting of trades by insiders; prohibition on insider trades during pension fund blackout periods; public reporting of CEO and CFO compensation and profits; inside audit board independence; criminal and civil penalties for securities violations; obligation to have an internal audit function, which will need to be certified by external auditors; significantly longer jail sentences and larger fines for corporate executives who knowingly misstate financial statements; and codes of ethics and standards of conduct for executive officers and board members.

Although not-for-profit organizations have been generally exempt from SOX, the accountability and financial reporting requirements have been adopted by many hospitals.

Two provisions of the Act that have universal application to both profit and not-for-profit corporations are:

- Section 802: prohibition from knowingly altering, destroying, mutilating, concealing, and impeding or covering up government investigations.
- Section 1107: Proscription of criminal penalties for retaliation against whistleblowers.

Corporate Compliance Program

NEWSPAPER CLIPPINGS: Texas Doctors Accused in Massive Home Healthcare Fraud

WASHINGTON—A Texas doctor, his office manager and five owners of home health agencies were arrested Tuesday in what law enforcement officials are calling "the largest alleged home health fraud scheme ever committed."

Jacques Roy, MD, 54, of Rockwell, Texas and the six others, have been accused of allegedly participating in a scam making $375 million in fraudulent claims for home health services. Among its accusations, the government claims that the accused recruited patients falsely, going even so far as to pay homeless people $50 per person to sign fake forms.

—*Stephanie Bouchard*, Healthcare Finance News, *February 29, 2012*

The federal government's initiative to investigate and prosecute healthcare organizations for criminal wrongdoing, coupled with strong sanctions imposed after conviction, has resulted in healthcare organizations establishing corporate compliance programs. These programs establish internal mechanisms for preventing, detecting, and reporting criminal conduct. Sentencing incentives are in place for organizations that establish such programs.

The following paragraphs describe the elements of an effective corporate compliance program.

An "effective program to prevent and detect violations of the law" means a program that has been reasonably designed, implemented, and enforced so that it generally will be effective in preventing and detecting criminal conduct. Failure to prevent or detect the instant offense, by itself, does not mean that the program was not effective. The hallmark of an effective program to prevent and detect violations of law is that the organization exercised due diligence in seeking to prevent and detect criminal conduct by its employees and other agents. Due diligence requires that an organization will, at the very least, have implemented the following:

1. The organization must have established compliance standards and procedures to be followed by its employees and other agents that are reasonably capable of reducing the prospect of criminal conduct.

2. Specific individual(s) within high-level personnel of the organization must have been assigned overall responsibility to oversee compliance with such standards and procedures.

3. The organization must have used due care not to delegate substantial discretionary authority to individuals whom the organization knew, or should have known through the exercise of due diligence, had a propensity to engage in illegal conduct.

4. The organization must have taken steps to communicate effectively its standards and procedures to all employees and other agents, for example, by requiring participation in training programs or by disseminating publications that explain in a practical manner what is required.

5. The organization must have taken reasonable steps to achieve compliance with its standards, for example, by utilizing monitoring and auditing systems reasonably designed to detect criminal conduct by its employees and other agents and by having in place and publicizing a reporting system whereby employees and other agents could report criminal conduct by others within the organization without fear of retribution.

6. The standards must have been consistently enforced through appropriate disciplinary mechanisms, including, as appropriate, discipline of individuals who are responsible for the failure to detect an offense. Adequate discipline of individuals who are responsible for an offense is a necessary component of enforcement; however, the discipline that will be appropriate will be case specific.

7. After an offense has been detected, the organization must have taken all reasonable steps to respond appropriately to the offense and to prevent similar offenses—including any necessary modifications to its program to prevent and detect violations of the law.[2]

 REALITY CHECK: Compliance Officer and Confidentiality

The employee who decides to place confidence and trust in a corporate compliance officer must understand the following points, among others, prior to filing a complaint against any organizational practice, individual, and/or department within or entity owned by the organization:

- The compliance officer is hired by and is responsible to the corporation by which he or she is hired.

(continued)

REALITY CHECK: Compliance Officer and Confidentiality (continued)

- Compliance officers often report directly to the organization's corporate counsel and/or chief executive officer and/or board of directors/trustees.
- The compliance officer is expected to abide by the laws of the land and follow the code(s) of ethics applicable to compliance officers in general and any ethical principles or codes of ethics that apply to his or her profession. For example, a compliance officer who is a lawyer is expected to adhere to those professional code(s) of ethics that apply to lawyers from both a professional and state licensing standpoint. Failure to do so can result in professional discipline and sanctions against the compliance officer.
- Compliance officers are expected to maintain confidentiality of the names of employees who file complaints.
- Organizations often have compliance hotlines to protect the identity of employees who file complaints.

The compliance officer has a difficult balancing act in maintaining the confidentiality of employees, working for the organization, adhering to standards of ethical conduct, and abiding by applicable federal and state laws. This is no easy task, as Phil was about to learn.

Phil, having exhausted all other appeals, called Beth, the compliance officer, to speak with her about a decision that the human resources department had made that he believed was out of compliance with the Federal Equal Pay Act. The office assistant, Mary, stated, "Beth will not be in the office until next week." Phil then scheduled a telephone conference with Beth for the following week. He asked Mary, "Will my telephone conference with Beth remain confidential?" Mary said, "Most certainly. Our office is here for you. Everything in our office remains confidential."

The following week Phil called Beth to discuss his concern that certain professionals were performing the same work as he was and were getting paid more. He described the specifics of his concern. Beth asked, "Is it OK for me to reveal your name to human resources so that I can obtain the necessary records that I would need from them to see if you are being paid equally to others for the same work?" Phil agreed to Beth's request. During his discussion with Beth, Phil discussed several other corporate leadership concerns with her and asked that his conversations with her remain confidential.

Beth replied, "If you wanted confidentiality, then you should have asked for it before speaking to me." Phil replied, "Confidentiality was promised prior to our discussion and am surprised at your response." Beth replied, "Well you are wrong."

Discussion

1. What lessons could employees learn from Phil's experience?
2. Discuss how this scenario could have ended with a win-win conclusion for both the employee and the compliance officer.

CORPORATE NEGLIGENCE

There are duties that the corporation itself owes to the general public and to its patients. These duties arise from statutes, regulations, principles of law developed by the courts, and the internal operating rules of the organization. A corporation is treated no differently than an individual. If a corporation has a duty and fails in the exercise of that duty, it has the same liability to the injured party as an individual would have.

> Corporate negligence is a doctrine under which the hospital is liable if it fails to uphold the proper standard of care owed the patient, which is to ensure the patient's safety and well-being while at the hospital. This theory of liability creates a nondelegable duty, which the hospital owes directly to a patient. Therefore, an injured party does not have to rely on and establish the negligence of a third party.[3]

Corporate negligence occurs when a healthcare corporation fails to perform those duties it owes directly to a patient or to anyone else to whom a duty may extend. If such a duty is breached and a patient is injured as a result of that breach, the organization can be held culpable under the theory of corporate negligence.

Hospitals once enjoyed complete tort immunity as charitable institutions. However, as hospitals evolved into more sophisticated corporate entities that expected fees for their services, their tort immunity receded. Courts first recognized that hospitals could be held liable for the negligence of their employees under the theory of respondeat superior. Liability later extended for nonemployees who acted as a hospital's ostensible agents. In *Thompson v. Nason Hospital*,[4] the evolution continued. The Pennsylvania court recognized that hospitals are more than mere conduits through which healthcare professionals are brought into contact with patients. Hospitals owe some nondelegable duties directly to their patients independent of the negligence of their employees or ostensible agents, such as a duty to:

- Use reasonable care in the maintenance of safe facilities and equipment
- Select and retain competent physicians
- Oversee all persons who practice medicine within their walls
- Formulate, adopt, and enforce rules and policies to ensure quality care

Darling—A Benchmark Case

The benchmark case in the healthcare field, which has had a major impact on the liability of healthcare organizations, was decided in 1965 in *Darling v. Charleston Community Memorial Hospital*.[5] The court enunciated a corporate negligence doctrine under which hospitals have a duty to provide an adequately trained medical and nursing staff. A hospital is responsible, in conjunction with its medical staff, for establishing policies and procedures for monitoring the quality of medicine practiced within the hospital.

The Darling case involved an 18-year-old college football player who was preparing for a career as a teacher and coach. The patient, a defensive halfback for his college football team, was injured during a play. He was rushed to the emergency department of a small, accredited community hospital where the only physician on emergency duty that day was Dr. Alexander, a general practitioner. Alexander had not treated a major leg fracture in 3 years.

The physician examined the patient and ordered an X-ray that revealed that the tibia and the fibula of the right leg had been fractured. The physician reduced the fracture and applied a plaster cast from a point 3 or 4 inches below the groin to the toes. Shortly after the cast had been applied, the patient began to complain continually of pain. The physician split the cast and continued to visit the patient frequently while the patient remained in the hospital. The emergency department physician did not call in any specialist for consultation.

After 2 weeks, the student was transferred to a larger hospital and placed under the care of an orthopedic surgeon. The specialist found a considerable amount of dead tissue in the fractured leg. During a period of 2 months, the specialist removed increasing amounts of tissue in a futile attempt to save the leg until it became necessary to amputate the leg 8 inches below the knee. The student's father did not agree to a settlement and filed suit against the emergency department physician and the hospital. Although the physician eventually settled out of court for $40,000, the case continued against the hospital.

The documentary evidence relied on to establish the standard of care included the rules and regulations of the Illinois Department of Public Health under the Hospital Licensing Act; the standards for hospital accreditation, today known as The Joint Commission; and the bylaws, rules, and regulations of Charleston Hospital. These documents were admitted into evidence without objection. No specific evidence was offered that the hospital failed to conform to the usual and customary practices of hospitals in the community.

The trial court instructed the jury to consider those documents, along with all other evidence, in determining the hospital's liability. Under the circumstances in which the case reached the Illinois Supreme Court, it was held that the verdict against the hospital should be sustained if the evidence supported the verdict on any one or more of the 20 allegations of negligence. Allegations asserted that the hospital was negligent in its failure to: (1) provide a sufficient number of trained nurses for bedside care—in this case, nurses who were capable of recognizing the progressive gangrenous condition of the plaintiff's right leg and (2) failure of its nurses to bring the patient's condition to the attention of the administration and staff so that adequate consultation could be secured.

Although these generalities provided the jury with no practical guidance for determining what constitutes reasonable care, they were considered to be relevant to aid the jury in deciding what was feasible and what the hospital knew or should have known concerning its responsibilities for patient care.

Evidence relating to the hospital's failure to review Alexander's work, to require consultation or examination by specialists, and to require proper nursing care was found to be sufficient to support a verdict for the patient. Judgment was eventually returned against the hospital in the amount of $100,000. The Illinois Supreme Court held that the hospital could not limit its liability as a charitable corporation to the amount of its liability insurance.

> [T]he doctrine of charitable immunity can no longer stand . . . a doctrine which limits the liability of charitable corporations to the amount of liability insurance that they see fit to carry permits them to determine whether or not they will be liable for their torts and the amount of that liability, if any.[6]

In effect, the hospital was liable as a corporate entity for the negligent acts of its employees and physicians. Among other things, the Darling case indicates the importance of instituting an effective credentialing and continuing medical evaluation and review program for all members of a professional staff.

Directors Not Liable for Contractor's Negligence

An officer or a director of a corporation is not personally liable for the torts of corporate employees. To incur liability, the officer or the director ordinarily must be shown to have in some way authorized, directed, or participated in a tortious act. The administrator of the estate of the deceased in *Hunt v. Rabon*[7] brought a malpractice action against hospital trustees and others for the wrongful death of the decedent during an operation at the hospital. A contractor had incorrectly crossed the oxygen and nitrous oxide lines of a newly installed medical gas system leading to the operating room. Trustees filed a pleading claiming that the facts of the case were not sufficient for an action against them individually as trustees. The South Carolina Supreme Court held that the allegations presented were insufficient to hold the trustees liable for the wrongs alleged.

▌ DOCTRINE OF RESPONDEAT SUPERIOR

Respondeat superior (let the master respond) is a legal doctrine holding employers liable, in certain cases, for the wrongful acts of their agents (employees). This doctrine has also been referred to as *vicarious liability*, whereby an employer is answerable for the torts committed by employees. In the healthcare setting, an organization, for example, is liable for the negligent acts of its employees, even though there has been no wrongful conduct on the part of the organization. For liability to be imputed to the employer:

1. A master–servant relationship must exist between the employer and the employee; and
2. The wrongful act of the employee must have occurred within the scope of his or her employment.

The question of liability frequently rests on whether persons treating a patient are independent agents (responsible for their own acts) or employees of the organization. The answer to this depends on whether the organization can exercise control over the particular act that was the proximate cause of the injury. The basic rationale for imposing liability on an employer developed because of the employer's right to control the physical acts of its employees. It is not necessary that the employer actually exercise control, only that it possesses the right, power, and authority to do so.

When filing a lawsuit, the plaintiff's attorney generally names both the employer and employee. This occurs because the employer is generally in a better financial condition to cover the judgment. The employer is not without remedy if liability has been imposed against the organization due to an employee's negligent act. The employer can seek indemnification from the employee. Although it would be highly unlikely for a hospital to seek recovery from an employee, the ever-increasing number of employed physicians could give rise to a hospital to seek indemnification from a physician who is the cause of a negligent injury and carries his own malpractice insurance policy.

Power to Control Not Established

Dr. Jan Cunningham was suffering from a physical ailment and was taken to the Thomas Hospital Emergency Department by his wife, Lynn. Upon arrival at the hospital, Jan was evaluated by a physician in the emergency department and then referred to Dr. Tarakji, hospitalist. Dr. Tarakji admitted Dr. Cunningham into the hospital, and provided care and treatment to Jan during his hospitalization. During a period when Dr. Tarakji was on vacation, Jan received treatment and care from another hospitalist associated with Dr. Tarakji, Dr. Rittinger, who arranged for a consultation with a surgeon, Dr. Fogle. Dr. Fogle performed exploratory surgery within a few days of Dr. Jan's admission to the hospital. Following surgery, Jan developed a serious infection that apparently resulted from the surgery. Jan ultimately required several follow-up surgeries and alleges that he has suffered permanent injury as a result of the infection.

Jan filed a medical malpractice action against Thomas Hospital, Dr. Tarakji, Dr. Rittinger, and Dr. Fogle, seeking to hold Thomas Hospital vicariously liable for the alleged negligence of the doctors on the theory that the doctors were employees or actual agents of the hospital, or that the doctors and corporate defendants Delphi and Hospitalist Medicine were engaged in a joint venture with the hospital.

The circuit court granted summary judgment in favor of Thomas Hospital, concluding the doctors were not actual agents or employees of Thomas Hospital at the time of the alleged negligence, and there was no joint venture. The Cunninghams appealed, seeking to hold Thomas Hospital vicariously liable for the allegedly negligent actions of the defendant doctors arguing they were actual agents or employees of the hospital and Thomas Hospital may, therefore, be held vicariously liable for their alleged negligence. In the alternative, the Cunninghams asserted that the doctors, along with Delphi and Hospitalist Medical, were involved in a joint venture with Thomas Hospital.

There are four general factors which bear upon whether a master–servant relationship exists for purposes of the doctrine of respondeat superior: (1) Selection and engagement of the servant; (2) Payment of compensation; (3) Power of dismissal; and (4) Power of control. The first three factors are not essential to the existence of the relationship; the fourth, the power of control, is determinative.

If the right to control or supervise the work in question is retained by the person for whom the work is being done, the person doing the work is an employee and not an independent contractor. The record showed no evidence to establish a question of fact with regard to the element of control exercised by the hospital over the doctors. The Supreme Court of Appeals agreed with the circuit court's conclusion that the doctors were not agents or employees of Thomas Hospital.[8]

INDEPENDENT CONTRACTOR

An *independent contractor* is responsible for his or her own negligent acts. The independent contractor relationship is established when the principal has no right of control over the manner in which the agent's work is to be performed. However, some cases indicate that an organization can be held liable for an independent contractor's negligence. For example, in *Mehlman v. Powell*,[9] the court held that a hospital could be found vicariously liable for the negligence of an emergency department physician who was not a hospital employee but who worked in the emergency department in the capacity of an independent contractor. The court reasoned that the hospital maintained control over billing procedures, maintained an emergency department in the main hospital, and represented to the patient that the members of the emergency department staff were its employees, which might have caused the patient to rely on the skill and competence of the staff.

DUTIES OF HEALTHCARE CORPORATIONS

Governing body members are considered by law to have the highest measure of accountability. They have a fiduciary duty that requires acting primarily for the benefit of the corporation. The general duties of a governing body are both implied and expressed. The duty to supervise and manage is applicable to the trustees just as it is to the managers of any other business corporation. In both instances, there is a duty to act as a reasonably prudent person would act under similar circumstances.

Appoint a CEO

The governing body is responsible for appointing a chief executive officer (CEO) to act as their agent in the management of the organization. The CEO is responsible for the day-to-day operations of the organization. The individual selected as CEO must possess the competence and the character necessary to maintain satisfactory standards of patient care within the organization.

The responsibilities and authority of the CEO should be expressed in an appropriate job description, as well as in any formal agreement or contract that the organization has with the CEO. Some state health codes describe the responsibilities of administrators in broad terms. They generally provide that the CEO/administrator shall be responsible for the overall management of the organization; enforcement of any applicable federal, state, and local regulations, as well as the organization's bylaws, policies, and procedures; appointment of, with the approval of the governing body, a qualified medical director; liaison between the governing body and staff (including both employed and appointed members of the professional staff); and appointment of an administrative person to act during the CEO's absence from the organization.

The general duty of a governing body is to exercise due care and diligence in supervising and managing the organization. This duty does not cease with the selection of a CEO. A governing body can be liable if the level of patient care becomes inadequate because of the governing body's failure to supervise properly the management of the organization. CEOs, as is the case with board members, can be personally liable for their own acts of negligence that injure others. An organization's board must take appropriate action when the CEO considers job security more important then the quality of patient care, as noted in the following Reality Check.

 REALITY CHECK: CEO Character Challenges Board

There is a story factually reported of a CEO who abruptly left a briefing being conducted by a group of consultants. The consultants had been hired by an organization's board of directors to review the quality of care being delivered at the hospital where he was employed. He was unhappy with the report. It apparently contained a listing of those things that needed to be addressed to improve the quality of patient care. As the CEO started to leave the room, he abruptly turned and said, "This is not just about the hospital! This is about my job!" His managers then rose up and followed the CEO out of the room, without looking back—no goodbyes, just stone cold faces.

(continued)

REALITY CHECK: CEO Character Challenges Board (continued)

Discussion

1. Using the Socratic method of dialogue, emphasizing discussion and debate, delve into the values described in this book, and apply them as you observe and believe how they were present or lacking in this case.
2. Discuss how you might present recommendations to your employer so as not to threaten or intimidate but to educate and bring about change for the better, remember that it is not necessarily what is said but how it is said.

Comply with Laws and Regulations

The governing body in general and its agents (assigned representatives) in particular are responsible for compliance with federal, state, and local laws regarding the operation of the organization. Depending on the scope of the wrong committed and the intent of the governing body, failure to comply could subject board members and/or their agents to civil liability and, in some instances, to criminal prosecution.

REALITY CHECK: Veterans Lack Insurance Benefits

Marc had a chat with some veterans about their healthcare benefits. Most seemed satisfied. Joe, one of the veterans, opening his mouth wide to show me, said, "Look at my teeth. [He had but a few teeth in his mouth.] They won't fix them because they are not considered a war-related injury." He turned his head sideways, and Marc noticed that an ear was missing. Joe continued, "Now this ear is gone. I lost it during the Viet Nam war. I was, however, able to get a prosthesis. It needs some work, so I didn't wear it. I guess they will provide me with a new one. I am able to get care for it because it is a war-related injury, but I really could use some teeth."

Marc queried the hospital about Joe's teeth. They said that because of policy and the fact that Joe's teeth were not related to a war injury, there was nothing that they could do for him. They did however suggest

Joe could go to the University Hospital and get a set of false teeth that should be relatively inexpensive. Marc asked to see the hospital's dental area. Following a tour of the dental suite, Marc commented, "This is the most modern dental facility I have ever seen." The staff was happy that Marc was pleased with the facility. After observing ample staff, work space, modern equipment, top of the line dental chairs, and unoccupied rooms, he asked, "Are you open? Where are the patients?" The staff in unison responded, "Oh yes, we are open but we don't have any patients at the moment. We should have a few later." The staff proceeded to discuss with enthusiasm the wide variety of dental procedures they could provide, including complicated extractions, implants, preparation of dentures, and so on.

Discussion

1. Would you consider this to be a form of political malpractice? Discuss your answer.
2. Since hospital staff was able to make suggestions to veterans for care outside the Veterans Administration healthcare system, how would you respond if you were the veteran?

Failure to comply with applicable statutory regulations can be costly. This was the case in *People v. Casa Blanca Convalescent Homes*,[10] in which there was evidence of numerous and prolonged deficiencies in resident care. The nursing home's practice of providing insufficient personnel constituted not only illegal practice but also unfair business practice. The trial court was found to have properly assessed a fine of $2,500 for each of 67 violations, totaling $167,500, where the evidence showed that the operator of the nursing home had the financial ability to pay that amount.

Regulatory Noncompliance Penalties

NEWSPAPER CLIPPINGS: CDPH Issues 12 Penalties to California Hospitals

The California Department of Public Health (CDPH) issued 12 penalties today to California hospitals along with fines totaling $785,000 after investigations found the facilities' noncompliance with licensing requirements caused, or was likely to cause, serious injury or death to patients.

—California Department of Health,
December 20, 2012

The penalties involved failure to: follow manufacturer's instructions for the use of a particular medical device; follow established policies and procedures for safe distribution and administration of medication; ensure the health and safety of a patient when it did not follow established maternity care policies and procedures; ensure the health and safety of a patient when it did not follow established policies and procedures related to patient assessment; ensure the health and safety of a patient when it did not follow surgical policies and procedures resulting in a patient having to undergo a second surgery to remove a retained foreign object; ensure the health and safety of a patient when it did not develop, maintain and implement a fire prevention policy and procedure; and follow established policies and procedures for safe distribution and administration of medication.[11]

Compliance with Joint Commission Requirements

NEWSPAPER CLIPPINGS: Cardiologists Flagging Woeful Patient Care Say They Paid with Their Jobs

San Jose, CA—When a California cardiologist and cardiac surgeon went to their superiors complaining of woeful patient care at their hospital, one had her job shifted to a satellite outpatient clinic, while the other's contract was terminated. Now, as their ensuing lawsuit—naming two additional cardiologists among the defendants—moves into its next phase, the plaintiffs have given an exclusive interview to heartwire detailing their experiences.

• • •

Some of their complaints have already been upheld. For example, the JC—a not-for-profit organization that accredits over 19,000 healthcare organizations in the U.S.—put the SCVMC on "conditional accreditation" for six months in 2010/2011.

—*Lisa Nainggolan*, theheart.org, *January 25, 2012*

The governing body, if accredited by the Joint Commission, is responsible for compliance with applicable accreditation requirements and standards promulgated by the Joint Commission. Noncompliance could cause an organization to be placed on conditional accreditation or even lose accreditation, which in turn would provide grounds for third-party reimbursement agencies (e.g., Medicare) to refuse payment for treatment rendered to patients.

NEWSPAPER CLIPPINGS: The Pain of Wrong Site Surgery

When the president of the Joint Commission, the Chicago-based group that accredits the nation's hospitals, unveiled mandatory rules to prevent operations on the wrong patient or body part, he did not mince words.

"This is not quite 'Dick and Jane,' but it's pretty close," surgeon Dennis O'Leary declared in a 2004 interview about the "universal protocol" to prevent wrong-site surgery. These rules require preoperative verification of important details, marking of the surgical site and a timeout to confirm everything just before the procedure starts.

—*Sandra G. Boodman*, Kaiser Health News/
The Washington Post, *June 20, 2011*

Provide Timely Treatment

Healthcare organizations can be held liable for delays in treatment that result in injuries to their patients. For example, the patient in *Heddinger v. Ashford Memorial Community Hospital*[12] filed a malpractice action against a hospital and its insurer, alleging that a delay in treating her left hand resulted in the loss of her little finger. Medical testimony presented at trial indicated that if proper and timely treatment had been rendered, the finger could have been saved. The U.S. District Court entered judgment on a jury verdict for the plaintiff in the amount of $175,000. The hospital appealed, and the U.S. Court of Appeals held that even if the physicians who attended the patient were not employees of the hospital but were independent contractors, the risk of negligent treatment was clearly foreseeable by the hospital.

REALITY CHECK: Waiting for a Neurological Consult

Speaking to Gary, his best friend from high school, Ryan related his first VA hospital experience. Ryan said, "I have to wait 6 months for a neurology consultation." Gary said to Ryan, "That's too long of a wait. If you need a neurological consultation, a lot could happen over 6 months." Ryan replied, "I know. They told me that if I needed to be seen sooner, they would take me to a local hospital. I discussed my concern with three

(continued)

Avoid Self-Dealing and Conflicts of Interest

Governing body members must refrain from self-dealing and avoid conflict of interest situations. Each board member should submit in writing all outstanding voting shares (where applicable) or any relationships or transactions in which the director might or could have a conflict of interest. Membership on the governing body or its committees should not be used for private gain. Board members are expected to disclose potential conflict of interest situations and withdraw from the boardroom at the time of voting on such issues. Board members who suspect a conflict of interest situation have a right and a duty to raise pertinent questions regarding any potential conflict. Conflict of interest is presumed to exist when a board member or a firm with which he or she is associated can benefit or lose from the passage of a proposed action.

Provide Adequate Staff

Staffing shortages for both hospitals and nursing homes continue to plague the healthcare industry. Because the quality of care provided by nursing homes is the subject of much scrutiny, American families face difficult decisions about whether to move a loved one into such a setting.

Under federal law, nursing facilities must have sufficient nursing staff to provide nursing and related services adequate to attain and maintain the highest practicable physical, mental, and psychosocial well-being of each resident, as determined by resident assessments and individual plans of care. As nursing facilities are increasingly filled with older, disabled residents with ever-increasing complex care needs, the demands for highly educated and trained nursing personnel continue to grow.

> Many medical and regulatory investigators who work in nursing homes every day characterize the number of wrongful deaths in terms such as "massive" and "pervasive," based on their daily experience. Most of the deaths can be traced to an inadequate number of nurses and aides to provide life-sustaining care. The U.S. Department of Health and Human Services reported to Congress in 2002 that 9 out of 10 nursing homes have staffing levels too low to provide adequate care.[13]

Lack of Nursing Care

The nursing facility in *Our Lady of the Woods v. Commonwealth of Kentucky Health Facilities*[14] was closed because of deficiencies found during an inspection of the facility, the most serious of which was the lack of continuous nursing care on all shifts. The court held that evidence that the nursing facility lacked continuous services required by regulation was sufficient to sustain an order to close the facility. The appellants in this case had been notified of the deficiencies and were ordered to correct them. Many witnesses testified concerning the deficiencies, and even the administrator admitted to the most serious violation—lack of continuous nursing services.

Timely Response to Patient Calls

The Court of Appeal in *Leavitt v. St. Tammany Parish Hospital*[15] held that the hospital owed a duty to respond promptly to patient calls for help. The hospital breached its duty by having less than adequate staff on hand and by failing to at least verbally answer an assistance light to inquire what the patient needed.

Postoperative Care

The patient in *Czubinsky v. Doctors Hospital,*[16] recovering from anesthesia, went into cardiac arrest and sustained permanent damages. The court of appeals held that the injuries sustained by the patient were the direct result of the hospital's failure to properly monitor and render aid when needed in the immediate postoperative period. The registered nurse assigned to the patient had a duty to remain with her until the patient was transferred to the recovery room. The nurse's absence was the proximate cause of the patient's injuries. Failure of the hospital to provide adequate staff to assist the patient in the immediate postoperative period was an act in dereliction of duty—a failure that resulted in readily foreseeable permanent damages.

Deficient Care Given

In *Montgomery Health Care Facility v. Ballard*,[17] three nurses testified that the nursing facility was understaffed. One nurse testified she had asked her supervisor for more help but did not get it. The estate of a nursing home resident (who had expired as the result of multiple infected bedsores) brought a malpractice action against the nursing home. First American Health Care, Inc., is the parent corporation of the Montgomery Health Care Facility. The trial court entered a judgment on a jury verdict against the home, and an appeal was taken. The Alabama Supreme Court held that reports compiled by the Alabama Department of Public Health concerning deficiencies found in the nursing home were admissible as evidence. Evidence showed that the care given to the deceased was deficient in the same ways as noted in the survey and complaint reports, which indicated that deficiencies in the home included:

> [I]nadequate documentation of treatment given for decubitus ulcers; 23 patients found with decubitus ulcers, 10 of whom developed those ulcers in the facility; dressings on the sores were not changed as ordered; nursing progress notes did not describe patients' ongoing conditions, particularly with respect to descriptions of decubitus ulcers; ineffective policies and procedures with respect to sterile dressing supplies; lack of nursing assessments; incomplete patient care plans; inadequate documentation of doctor's visits, orders or progress notes; A.M. care not consistently documented; inadequate documentation of turning of patients; incomplete "activities of daily living" sheets; "range of motion" exercises not documented; patients found wet and soiled with dried fecal matter; lack of bowel and bladder retaining programs; incomplete documentation of ordered force fluids. . . .[18]

From a corporate standpoint, the parent corporation of the nursing facility could be held liable for the nursing facility's negligence, where the parent company controlled or retained the right to control the day-to-day operations of the home. The defendants argued that the punitive damage award of $2 million against the home was greater than what was necessary to meet society's goal of punishing them. The Alabama Supreme Court, however, found the award not to be excessive. "The trial court also found that because of the large number of nursing home residents vulnerable to the type of neglect found in Mrs. Stovall's case, the verdict would further the goal of discouraging others from similar conduct in the future."[19]

Provide Adequate Insurance

The duty of the governing body is to purchase insurance against different risks. Organizations face as much risk of losing their tangible and intangible assets through judgments for negligence as they do through fires or other disasters. When this is true, the duty to insure against the risks of fire is as great as the duty to insure against the risks of negligent conduct.

Be Financially Scrupulous

Healthcare organizations searching for alternate sources of income must do so scrupulously and not find themselves in what could be construed as questionable corporate activities. Such was the case in *Smith v. van Gorkum*[20] where the board of directors authorized the sale of its company through a cash-out merger for a tendered price per share nearly 50% over the market price. Although that might sound like a good deal, the governing body did not make any inquiry to determine whether it was the best deal available. In fact, it made no decision during a hastily arranged, brief meeting in which it relied solely on the CEO's report regarding the desirability of the move. The Delaware Supreme Court held that the board's decision to approve a proposed cash-out merger was not a product of informed business judgment and that it acted in a grossly negligent manner in approving amendments to the merger proposal.

Require Competitive Bidding

Many states have developed regulations requiring competitive bidding for work or services commissioned by public organizations. The fundamental purpose of this requirement is to eliminate or at least reduce the possibility that such abuses as fraud, favoritism, improvidence, or extravagance will intrude into an organization's business practices. Contracts made in violation of a statute are considered to be illegal and could result in personal liability for board members, especially if the members become aware of a fraudulent activity and allow it to continue.

Provide Appropriate Supplies and Equipment

NEWSPAPER CLIPPINGS: What Surgeons Leave Behind

Solutions Ignored: The nation's hospitals have balked at using electronic technologies that sharply cut the risks of sponges being left in patients. Fewer than 15% of U.S. hospitals use sponges equipped with electronic tracking devices, based on a USA TODAY survey of the companies that make these products.

• • •

"In context of all the things we're worrying about and striving to improve so patients are experiencing better outcomes, this is a more rare event," says Nancy Foster, the American Hospital Association's vice president for quality and patient safety.

—*Peter Eisler*, USA Today, *March 8–10, 2013*

Forewarned is forearmed. Fortunately the technology for detecting items left behind during surgery has been on the market since the 1980's and has continuously been improved since then. Unfortunately, hospitals have been slow to adopt the necessary technology to prevent the horrendous injuries that result from sponges and other instrumentation left behind in patients during surgery. Articles abound in the news media and accrediting organizations are well aware of the problems. Emphasis for years has been to prevent falls from patient beds with insufficient attention being paid to the prevention of lost sponges and instrumentation in patients. Accrediting bodies most likely will be quick to admit that it would be difficult to find citations by their surveyors about procedures for preventing lost sponges during surgery as well as citations against hospitals for failing to institute best practices. Standards and regulations are useless without teeth. Too many Hospitals have historically balked at citations and at times disparaged surveyors for writing citations. Governing bodies need to be more aware of the potential for lawsuits that could be directed to them for failure to act in preventing patient injuries and failure to recognize the importance of the accreditation process in identifying problem areas and correcting them.

 A rare event becomes an all too common event when it personally affects one's own life.

—ANONYMOUS

Healthcare organizations are under a duty to exercise reasonable care to furnish appropriate supplies and equipment for use in the diagnosis and treatment of patients. Both supplies and equipment furnished by an organization should be fit for the purposes and uses intended. Failure to provide appropriate supplies and equipment can lead to patient injuries and legal actions.

REALITY CHECK: Diversion of Funds and a Challenge to Survive

It all began when Brad decided to leave his position at a local hospital to become the second-in-command at another hospital just minutes from where he lived. His boss coached him not to leave, but Brad saw opportunity at the relatively new hospital. Brad had no clue what he was about to face when he accepted the job—the head administrator resigned his position just 9 months after Brad's arrival. Following a long search for a new administrator, Brad was appointed the head administrator of the hospital, which was one entity of a multihospital system. At first Brad was managing a profitable hospital, but he quickly faced challenges on many fronts, including a continuing battle to obtain supplies from vendors due to the transfer of funds from his hospital by corporate leadership to prop up other failing entities in the system outside the state where his hospital was located. The following timeline documents his struggle to keep the hospital afloat:

July 2010—Director of Procurement

Proctor and Gamble has cut us off from all delivery of supplies. Johnson & Johnson has cut off all deliveries of supplies. Scott Labs and Anthony Medical have cut us off from all deliveries. If we don't soon get supplies, the lab will be forced to close.

August 2010—Lack of OR Sutures

Dr. Plastics entered Brad's office and said, "I can't perform surgery without the proper suture materials. I have a patient on the table and they don't have the sutures I prefer to close the surgical incision." He then turned to return to the OR, looking back and apologizing, "I know you don't control where the money goes."

August 2010—Lack of X-ray Film

One Friday at 5:00 P.M. a radiologist went to Brad's office to report, "I know you are under a lot of pressure, but we do not have sufficient X-ray film to get through the weekend!"

September 2010—Message from Secretary

"Dr. Wild stormed in. He is furious! The fetal monitor machine is out of commission. He was lied to and told it was working but it wasn't. This is a life-saving instrument and failure to have it fixed is intolerable (and a few more adjectives I couldn't get down in shorthand), inexcusable, and a legal matter—this is just the tip of the iceberg. If things don't start to improve he will pull his entire practice out of the hospital."

April 2011—Memo from the President of the Medical/Dental Staff

We have been reduced to using menstrual pads for abdominal dressings. On two occasions last week a major disaster was narrowly averted in the Operating Room only because of the proximity of ... City Hospital and their willingness to supply us with emergency equipment.

March 2012—Department of Supply Procurement

The director of supply procurement wrote a memo stating that the acute shortages of OR material and X-ray film were putting patients at risk. The memo recommended considering an orderly closing of the hospital.

June 2012—Message from Dr. Orthopedics

Dr. Orthopedics called at noon today (6/12). He said about a week ago he was here at night and there were no finger splints. Dr. Orthopedics said he had to resort to the use of Popsicle sticks that he obtained in the hospital coffee shop for splints.

September 2012—Memo from Dr. ER

Over the past 3 to 4 weeks the supply of orthopedic-related supplies in the emergency room has dwindled to a dangerous level. Something must be done soon.

October 2012—Dr. Peds

I was on call for the emergency room . . . on Friday, October 23, 2012. I was disappointed to note that important casting materials were not available. . . . I can repeat what others have said: if the hospital is to continue to provide high-quality care, a certain minimum level of supplies must be available.

January 2013—Board Minutes

The board requested that Brad and the president of the medical staff work together in locating the areas of greatest concern with regard to supply shortages. They were asked that this information be available at the next board meeting.

May 2013—Brad Speaks with the Corporate CEO

Brad called the corporate office to discuss the ongoing seriousness of the supply issues. The purchase, storage, and distribution of supplies had been centralized in a corporate location off site. At the same time, Accounts Payable was also centralized and was accused of paying vendors on the basis of who screamed the loudest rather than on patient need.

June 2013—Joint Memo to the Board from the Administrator and Medical Staff President

We sincerely believe that as a result of the supply shortages, the negative impact on morale of patients and employees during the past 5 years is substantial. The serious nature of these concerns are noted in the following paragraphs.

Major Vendors Requiring Advanced Payment

The system CEO was distressed that Brad had provided the above listed information to the board, complaining to him, "You're out to get me." Brad responded, "I am complying with the board's request, and it's in the board minutes. Besides, I gave you an advance copy of the memorandum."

Discussion

1. Discuss the ethical issues that this case raises.
2. Are there any circumstances in which CEOs should attempt to keep information from their boards?
3. Brad is in a multihospital system making major profits but cannot control the flow of funds out of the community hospital. The governing body is aware of the serious nature of the supply crisis. What should the board do?
4. If you were Brad or on the board, what action would you take?
5. What action should the community and government authorities take, considering there is a systemic problem throughout the state?

Healthcare organizations must be designed, constructed, equipped, and maintained to provide a safe, healthy, functional, sanitary, and comfortable environment for patients, employees, and the public. Buildings and equipment should be maintained and operated to prevent fire and other hazards to personal safety. Patient rooms should be designed and equipped for adequate nursing care, comfort, and privacy. Mechanical, electric, and patient care equipment should be maintained in a safe operating condition.

Driftwood Convalescent Hospital, operated by Western Medical Enterprises, Inc., in *Beach v. Western Medical Enterprises, Inc.,*[21] was fined $2,500 in civil penalties because of nonfunctioning hallway lights and the facility's failure to provide the required type and amount of decubitus preventive equipment necessary for resident care as required by the California Health and Safety Code. The regulations required equipment necessary for patient care be provided as ordered or indicated.

Provide a Safe Environment

Healthcare corporations are liable for injuries to both patients and employees rising from environmental hazards. For example, the license of a nursing facility operator was revoked in *Erie Care Center, Inc. v. Ackerman*[22] on findings of uncleanliness, disrepair, poor record keeping, and nursing shortages. The court held that although violation of a single public health regulation might have been insufficient in and of itself to justify revocation of the nursing home's operating license, multiple violations, taken together, established the facility's practice and justified revocation.

 REALITY CHECK: Perceptions are Deceiving

As the inspectors parked their cars and walked casually towards the hospital, they remarked as to how well the grounds were maintained. Upon entering the hospital they observed pristine hallways. This mindset soon changed as one of the inspectors began the review process. When walking down the hallway, he requested that one of the corridor doors be opened. The staff following the inspector seemed to fumble in their pockets looking for a key. No one seemed to have one. Finally the inspector said, "Does anyone have a master key?" There was momentary silence. Eventually one of the staff members was instructed by a superior to go find the key.

Behind the locked door, the inspector found a small closet with cardboard boxes sitting on the floor with water and wax seeping into the boxes. They appeared damp with black mold growing on the outside. The inspector asked what was in the boxes. The staff looked at each other for an answer but none was forthcoming. He then leaned down and opened one of the boxes. To his chagrin he found that the boxes contained the medical records of patients. They were damp with black mold slowly spreading over time and distorting the pages of the records, making it difficult to interpret the entries.

In another room the inspector found pieces of equipment stripped down with various components strewn on workbenches, as well as, on a soiled floor, that he would have preferred to label "filthy." The inspector looked at the staff and said, "This room looks like it needed some cleaning up."

The staff complained about every finding that the inspector had found, including several cinder blocks he discovered missing from the walls in one of the fire exit stairwells. The staff had replaced the blocks later that day, hoping that he would remove it from his report. He did not remove it, explaining that he had not checked every stairwell and smoke barrier and that this was something that they needed to do on a continuing basis as part of their safety rounds.

Yes, the inspector couched his closing words in a graceful manner at a summation conference in a kind but firm way to stress the significance of what he found.

The reader here should not be concerned as to whether this was a religious, civilian, or military hospital. The expectations for the safekeeping of patient records, equipment maintenance, and building safety applies to all healthcare facilities.

The point of an inspection is to show where improvements can be made and not to retaliate in some manner against the inspector, as occurred in this case, after the inspector left. When people hear things they do not like, there is a tendency to make things more personal and sometimes attack another's character. Inspectors are often seen as the enemy, seldom as the friend. Upon leaving, Carol, one of the inspectors, commented, "We were here to help you at your request. Don't kill the messenger." As Carol and her colleagues walked through the exit door, they heard someone mumble in a polite manner with a sad tone in her voice, "Sometimes we do kill the messenger."

Healthcare corporations are liable for injuries to both patients and employees rising from environmental hazards. For example, the license of a nursing facility operator was revoked in *Erie Care Center, Inc. v. Ackerman*[23] on findings of uncleanliness, disrepair, poor record keeping, and nursing shortages. The court held that although violation of a single public health regulation might have been insufficient in and of itself to justify revocation of the nursing home's operating license, multiple violations, taken together, established the facility's practice and justified revocation.

Fire Hazards

Hospitals have a duty to protect patients from fire hazards. As was the case, for example, in *Stacy v. Truman Medical Center*,[24] where the patients' families brought wrongful death actions against the medical center and one of its nurses. The wrongful death actions resulted from a fire in the decedents' room at the medical center. On the day of the fire, Ms. Stacy visited her brother, Stephen Stacy. When she arrived, Stephen, who suffered from head injuries and was not supposed to walk around, was sitting in a chair smoking a cigarette with the permission of one of the nurses. No one told Ms. Stacy not to allow her brother to smoke. Stacy also lit a cigarette and because she did not see an ashtray in the room, she used a juice cup and a plastic soup tray for her ashes. At approximately 5:00 P.M., a nurse came in and restrained Stephen in his chair with ties to prevent him from sliding out of the chair. Before Stacy left, she lit a cigarette, held it to Stephen's mouth, and extinguished it in the soup tray.

Shortly after 5:00 P.M., a fire started in a wastebasket in the room. There was no smoke detector in the room. Another patient, Wheeler, was in the bed next to the windows. When Ms. Schreiner, the nurse in charge, discovered the fire, she did not think Wheeler was in immediate danger. She unsuccessfully tried to untie Stephen from his restraints. Then she attempted to put out the fire by smothering it with a sheet. When her attempts to extinguish the fire failed, she ran to the door of the room and yelled for help, which alerted nurses Cominos and Rodriguez. After calling for help, Ms. Schreiner resumed her attempts to smother the flames with bed linens. Subsequently, she and others grabbed Stephen by the legs and pulled him and his chair toward the hallway. In the process, Stephen's restraints burned through, and he slid from the chair to the floor. Schreiner and her assistants pulled him the remaining few feet out of the room and into the hallway. Schreiner tried to get back into the room but was prevented by the intense smoke, flames, and heat.

After initially entering the room, both Rodriguez and Cominos returned to the nurse's station to sound alarms and to call security; neither attempted to remove Wheeler from the room. Both ran directly past a fire extinguisher, but neither grabbed it before returning to the room. After Stephen was removed from the room, Cominos entered the room with a fire extinguisher and tried to rescue Wheeler. Because of the intense smoke and heat, however, she was unable to reach Wheeler. Wheeler died in the room from smoke inhalation. Stephen survived for several weeks and then died as a result of complications from infections secondary to burns.

The medical center's policy in case of fire provided for the removal of patients from the room and out of immediate danger first. In its fire-training programs, the medical center used the acronym "RACE" to supply a chronology of steps to take in case of a fire.

R—Rescue or remove the patient first.

A—An alarm should be sounded second.

C—Contain the fire third.

E—Extinguish the fire last.

The medical center's written smoking policy at the time of the fire stated: "No smoking shall be permitted in the Truman Medical Center Health Care Facility except in those areas specifically designated and posted as smoking areas." The smoking policy further stated: "In the event violations of this policy are observed, the person violating the policy must be requested to discontinue such violation." Nurse Cominos admitted that she was a supervisor and that she violated this portion of the smoking policy on the date of the fire by observing smoking and the use of a juice cup for an ashtray.

The Missouri Supreme Court held that a causal connection between the medical center's negligence and the patients' deaths was sufficiently established. The medical center owed a duty of reasonable care to all of its patients. There was evidence that the fire started in the trash can from discarded smoking materials.

Prevent Falls

Falls are frequent occurrences in healthcare settings. They can occur anywhere from the time of arrival to the time of departure. Maintaining a safe environment and providing ongoing staff and patient education can reduce falls.

Safeguard Patient Valuables

A healthcare facility can be held liable for the negligent handling of a patient's valuables. Patients should be encouraged to have a trusted individual take their personal belongings and valuables home when such is feasible.

▌CEO/ADMINISTRATOR

The CEO is responsible for the supervision of the administrative staff and managers who assist in the daily operations of the organization. The CEO derives authority from the owner or governing body. CEOs, as is the case with governing body members, can be personally liable for their own acts of negligence that injure others.

CEO Code of Ethics

The following is the preamble to the Code of Ethics of the American College of Healthcare Executives (ACHE):[25]

> **American College of Healthcare Executives Code of Ethics: Preamble**
> The purpose of the Code of Ethics of the American College of Healthcare Executives is to serve as a standard of conduct for affiliates. It contains standards of ethical behavior for healthcare executives in their professional relationships. These relationships include colleagues, patients, or others served; members of the healthcare executive's organization and other organizations, the community, and society as a whole.
>
> The Code of Ethics also incorporates standards of ethical behavior governing personal behavior, particularly when that conduct directly relates to the role and identity of the healthcare executive.
>
> The fundamental objectives of the healthcare management profession are to maintain or enhance the overall quality of life, dignity, and well-being of every individual needing healthcare service; and to create a more equitable, accessible, effective, and efficient healthcare system.
>
> Healthcare executives have an obligation to act in ways that will merit the trust, confidence, and respect of healthcare professionals and the general public. Therefore, healthcare executives should lead lives that embody an exemplary system of values and ethics.
>
> In fulfilling their commitments and obligations to patients or others served, healthcare executives function as moral advocates and models. Since every

management decision affects the health and well-being of both individuals and communities, healthcare executives must carefully evaluate the possible outcomes of their decisions. In organizations that deliver healthcare services, they must work to safeguard and foster the rights, interests, and prerogatives of patients or others served.

The role of moral advocate requires that healthcare executives take actions necessary to promote such rights, interests, and prerogatives.

Being a model means that decisions and actions will reflect personal integrity and ethical leadership that others will seek to emulate.

 REALITY CHECK: CEO Warned Not to Appoint Jewish ED Director

It was a Monday morning. Jack remembers it well. As an administrator of one hospital in a multihospital system, Jack was settling in to his office when his secretary put through a call from Gerard, the CEO who was settling in to his plush office at corporate headquarters. He said, "I understand you are interviewing the final three candidates today for the emergency department director opening." Jack, replied, "Yes, I am." Gerard said, "He has to be a Christian." Jack interrupted with, "I don't understand what you are saying." Gerard responded, "This is what the board wants. There are too many Jewish medical directors." Jack, not pleased with his answer, said, "This is what the board wants?" Gerard, again quickly interrupting, said, "Well no, it's what I want." Jack, not believing that Gerard made this decision on his own, replied, "First of all, the selection of director is being conducted by a search committee that includes myself and the other medical directors as well as representatives from the general medical staff. The final decision is the consensus of that committee." Gerard replied, "You are the administrator, and you can pick who you want." Jack responded, "Who I want is the most qualified person for the position." Gerard replied, "You got my message," and he abruptly hung up the phone.

That afternoon after interviewing the final candidates, the entire search committee unanimously agreed to select the physician they considered most qualified, a person who happened to be Jewish.

Later that week, Jack decided to take a vacation day to see the Feast of San Gennaro in New York City. He received a call on his cell phone. Jack answered, and his secretary said, "Gerard wants to see you in his office on Monday morning." Jack said, "I can tell from your voice: it sounds ominous?" She said, "I think it is."

On Monday morning, Gerard said, "I am planning to move you to the corporate office. I need your skills here." The corporate office often was jokingly referred to as the deep dark hole. This was a place where people seemed to disappear from the face of the earth, never to be heard from again.

Jack said, "I really prefer to stay at the hospital as the administrator." Gerard replied, "That's not an option." Jack said, "Is this about the selection of the emergency department director? Because the doctor is Jewish?" Gerard said, "Now why would you think that?" Gerard, pausing for a moment, continued, "I really need your skills here." Jack replied, "As you probably remember, I have a recorder on my phone. Your conversation about the selection of an emergency room director was very clear."

Discussion

1. Discuss what you believe to be the ethical issues of this case. Do you think that such a scenario could occur in today's modern hospital?
2. What should Jack do, assuming he really did tape the conversation? If he had not done so, would that change your mind as to what he should do? Discuss your answer.

MEDICAL STAFF

The governing body is responsible for ensuring that medical staff bylaws, rules, and regulations include: application requirements for clinical privileges and admission to the medical staff; a process for granting emergency staff privileges; requirements for medical staff consultations; a peer-review process; a process for auditing medical records; a process for addressing disruptive physicians and substance abuse; and a process for instituting corrective action (disciplinary actions can take the form of a letter of reprimand, suspension, or termination of privileges).

Abusive Conduct Unacceptable

The health care industry has a long history of making excuses for allowing abusive behavior. Failure to effectively address such behavior can no longer be tolerated in a civil society.

 NEWSPAPER CLIPPINGS: Rage in the O.R.

For generations, bad behavior by doctors has been explained away as an inevitable product of stress or tacitly accepted by administrators . . . But that time–honored tolerance is waning . . . as a result of regulations imposed in 2009 by the Joint Commission, the group that accredits hospitals. These rules require hospitals to institute procedures for dealing with this drop of behavior, which can take passive forms such as refusing to answer pages or attend meetings. The commission has called for a "zero tolerance" approach.

—*Sandra G. Boodman*, The Washington Post, *March 5, 2013*

It is the responsibility of the CEO, medical board, and governing body to ensure that caregivers who engage in verbal or abusive behavior are appropriately disciplined. Accrediting bodies that claim a zero tolerance for such behavior must support surveyors who report inappropriate behavior. Further, to punish an individual for reporting such behavior and abuse is tantamount to being complicit with allowing inappropriate behavior to continue.

CORPORATE REORGANIZATION

Traditionally, hospitals have functioned as independent, freestanding corporate entities or as units or divisions of multihospital systems. Until recently, a freestanding hospital functioned as a single corporate entity with most programs and activities carried out within such entity to meet increasing competition.

Dependence on government funding and related programs (e.g., Medicare, Medicaid, and Blue Cross) and the continuous shrinkage occurring in such revenues have forced hospitals to seek alternative sources of revenue. Greater competition from nonhospital sources also has contributed to this need to seek alternative revenue sources. It has become apparent that traditional corporate structures are no longer appropriate to accommodate both normal hospital activities and those additional activities undertaken to provide alternative sources of revenue.

The typical hospital is incorporated under state law as a freestanding for-profit or not-for-profit corporation. The corporation has a governing body. Such a governing body has an overall responsibility for the operation and management of the hospital with a necessary delegation of appropriate responsibility to administrative employees and the medical staff.

Not-for-profit hospitals are usually exempt from federal taxation under Section 501(c)(3) of the U.S. Internal Revenue Code of 1986, as amended. Such federal exemption usually entitles the organization to an automatic exemption from state taxes as well. Such tax exemption not only relieves the hospital from the payment of income taxes, sales taxes, and the like, but also permits the hospital to receive contributions from donors who then can obtain charitable deductions on their personal tax returns.

Given the need to obtain income and to meet competition, hospitals often consider establishing business enterprises. They also might consider other nonbusiness operations, such as the establishment of additional nonexempt undertakings (e.g., ambulatory surgery centers, hospices, and long-term care facilities). Because hospitals have resources including the physical plant, administrative talent, and technical expertise in areas that are potentially profitable, the first option usually considered is direct participation by the hospital in health-related business enterprises. There are, however, regulatory and legal pressures that present substantial impediments, including: risk of loss of tax-exempt status if a substantial portion of the corporation's activities are related to nonexempt activities and costs not associated with patient care must be deducted from costs submitted to third-party payers for reimbursement. The "carving out" of these costs can be detrimental to the hospital unless alternative revenues are found.

Certificate of Need

Generally, hospitals may not add additional programs or services nor may they expend monies for the acquisition of capital in excess of specified threshold limits without first obtaining approval from appropriate state regulatory agencies. The process by which this approval is granted generally is referred to as the certificate of need (CON) process.

The National Health Planning and Resources Development Act of 1974, Public Law No. 93641, sought to encourage state review of all plans calling for the construction, expansion, or renovation of health facilities or services by conditioning receipt of certain federal funds on the establishment of an approved state CON program. Most states responded to this law by instituting state CON programs that complied with federal standards. Although the federal law is now history, CON programs remain in effect in a dwindling number of states. Some states continue to maintain control over Medicaid expenditures for hospital and nursing home care by controlling the number of beds through the CON process. This process can be lengthy and expensive. Further, it might not always result

in approval of the request to offer the new program or service or to make the capital expenditure.

Laws authorizing such programs are one mechanism by which state governments seek to reduce overall health and medical costs. Many "CON" laws initially were put into effect across the nation as part of the federal "Health Planning and Resources Development Act" of 1974. Despite numerous changes in the past 30 years, about 36 states retain some type of CON program, law or agency as of December 2011.[26]

Notes

1. 500 P.2d 335 (Ariz. Ct. App. 1972).
2. 56 Fed. Reg. 22,762 (May 16, 1991).
3. *Thompson v. Nason Hosp.*, 591 A.2d 703, 707 (Pa. 1991).
4. *Id.*
5. 211 N.E.2d 253 (Ill. 1965).
6. *Id.* at 260.
7. 272 S.E.2d 643 (S.C. 1980).
8. *Jan H. Cunningham and Lynn Cunningham, Plaintiffs, Petitioners v. Herbert J. Thomas Memorial Hospital Association, Defendant, Respondent*, No. 11-0398 (Supreme Court of Appeals of West Virginia, January 2012 Term).
9. 46 U.S.I.W. 2227 (Md. 1977).
10. 206 Cal. Rptr. 164 (Cal. Ct. App. 1984). 24. 734 F.2d 81 (1st Cir. 1984).
11. http://www.cdph.ca.gov/Pages/CDPHIssues12Penalties toCaliforniaHospitals.aspx.
12. 734 F.2d 81 (1st Cir. 1984).
13. Andrew Schneider and Phillip O'Connor, "Nation's Nursing Homes Are Quietly Killing Thousands," *St. Louis Post-Dispatch*, October 12, 2002.
14. 655 S.W.2d 14 (Ky. Ct. App. 1982).
15. 396 So.2d 406 (La. Ct. App. 1981).
16. 188 Cal. Rptr. 685 (Cal. Ct. App. 1983).
17. 565 So. 2d 221, 224 (Ala. 1990).
18. 28. Id. at 223–224.
19. *Id.* at 226.
20. 488 A.2d 858 (Del. 1985).
21. 171 Cal. Rptr. 846 (Cal. Ct. App. 1981).
22. 449 N.E.2d 486 (Ohio Ct. App. 1982).
23. 449 N.E.2d 486 (Ohio Ct. App. 1982).
24. 836 S.W.2d 911 (Mo. 1992).
25. ACHE, "ACHE Code of Ethics," http://www.ache.org/abt_ache/code.cfm.
26. NCSL, "Certificate of Need: State Health Laws and Programs," http://www.ncsl.org/issues-research/health/con-certificate-of-need-state-laws.aspx.

He is the best physician who is the most ingenious inspirer of hope.

—SAMUEL TAYLOR COLERIDGE

9
Medical Staff Organization and Physician Liability

Figure 9–1 The Complicated Case © ZurijetA/ShutterStock, Inc.

🔹 Learning Objectives

The reader upon completion of this chapter will be able to:

- Describe medical staff organization and committee structure.
- Describe the credentialing and privileging process.

- Discuss the purpose of physician supervision and monitoring.
- List and discuss common medical errors.
- Explain how the physician–patient relationship can be improved.

NEWSPAPER CLIPPINGS: Surgeons Still Make Preventable Mistakes

Using the National Practitioner Data Bank, an electronic warehouse of medical malpractice claims, researchers at John Hopkins University estimated the number of times that "never events" occurred within the past 20 years. They found that there were close to 10,000 reported instances when a foreign object was left in a patient, the wrong surgery was performed, or the surgery was performed on the wrong patient or wrong part of the body. These surgeries cost the healthcare industry an estimated $1.3 billion in malpractice payments over that same time period.

"It's a rare event but it's still an event that is entirely preventable," said Dr. Martin Makary, the lead investigator of the study published this week in the *Journal of Surgery*.

—*Reported by Dr. Lauren Browne,*
East Bound 11.com, *December 20, 2012*

This chapter provides an overview of medical staff organization, the credentialing process, and a review of common medical errors attributed to physicians and dentists. The cases presented highlight those areas in which physicians tend to be most vulnerable to lawsuits.

MEDICAL STAFF ETHICS

The Code of Medical Ethics for physicians emphasizes the importance of improving medical knowledge and skills, ultimately for the benefit of the patient. The structure of medical staff organization is accomplished through its bylaws, rules and regulations, application and credentialing process, and committee structure. This structure is important to improving the quality of patient care.

MEDICAL STAFF ORGANIZATION

The medical staff is an integral part of healthcare organizations with defined responsibilities under its bylaws. The medical staff is formally organized with officers, committees, bylaws, and laws. The responsibilities of a variety of medical staff committees include:

- *Executive committee*: The executive committee oversees the activities of the medical staff. It is responsible for recommending to the governing body such things as medical staff structure, a process for reviewing credentials and appointing members to the medical staff, a process for delineating clinical privileges, a process for peer review, a mechanism by which medical staff membership can be terminated, and a mechanism for fair hearings and appeals. The executive committee reviews and acts on the reports of the medical staff president, departmental chairpersons, and designated medical staff committees. Actions requiring approval of the governing body are forwarded to the governing body for approval.

- *Bylaws committee*: The functioning of the medical staff is described in its bylaws, rules, and regulations, which must be reviewed and approved by the organization's governing body. Bylaws must be kept current, and the governing body must approve recommended changes. The bylaws describe the various membership categories of the medical staff (e.g., active, courtesy, consultative, and allied professional staff) as well as the process for obtaining privileges.

- *Blood and transfusion committee*: The blood and transfusion committee develops blood usage policies and procedures. It is responsible for monitoring transfusion services and reviewing indications for transfusions, blood ordering practices, and transfusion reactions.

- *Credentials committee*: The credentials committee oversees the application process for medical staff applicants, requests for clinical privileges, and reappointments to the medical staff. The committee makes its recommendations to the medical executive committee.

- *Infection control committee*: The infection control committee is generally responsible for the development of policies and procedures for the investigation and prevention of infections.

- *Medical records committee*: The medical records committee develops policies and procedures as they pertain to the management of medical records. The committee reviews medical records for accuracy, completeness, legibility, and timely completion. The committee ensures that medical records reflect the condition and progress of the patient, including the results of tests and treatment rendered, and makes recommendations for disciplinary action as necessary for incomplete medical records.

- *Pharmacy and therapeutics committee*: The pharmacy and therapeutics committee is generally charged with developing policies and procedures relating to the selection, procurement, distribution, handling, use, and safe administration of medications and diagnostic testing material. The committee oversees: the development and maintenance of a drug formulary; the tracking of medication errors and adverse drug reactions; the management, control, effective and safe use of medications through monitoring and evaluation; the monitoring of problem-prone, high-risk, and high-volume medications utilizing parameters such as appropriateness, safety, effectiveness, medication errors, food–drug interactions, drug–drug interactions, drug–disease interactions, and adverse drug reactions.

- *Tissue committee*: The tissue committee reviews all surgical procedures involving the removal of body tissue and justification for doing so. Surgical case reviews address the presurgical diagnosis and postsurgical findings as born out by review and interpretation of pathology findings. The pathologist reviews any discrepancies between preoperative and postoperative findings with the operating surgeon. A determination is then made as to whether the clinical history provided on the pathology request is adequate to aid in rendering the correct diagnosis. Such reviews are necessary to help both pathologists and surgeons make more accurate diagnoses prior to surgery.

- *Utilization review committee*: The utilization review committee monitors and evaluates utilization issues such as medical necessity and appropriateness of admission and continued stay, as well as delay in the provision of diagnostic, therapeutic, and supportive services. The utilization review committee ensures that each patient is treated at an appropriate level of care. Objectives of the committee include timely transfer of patients requiring alternate levels of care and treatment; promotion of the efficient and effective use of the organization's resources; adherence to quality utilization standards of third-party payers; maintenance of high-quality, cost-effective care; and identification of opportunities for improvement.

Medical Director

The medical director serves as a liaison between the medical staff and the organization's governing body and management. The director provides guidance and leadership for an organization's medical staff and plays a major role in quality improvement activities. The responsibilities of a medical director include enforcing the bylaws of the governing body and medical staff and monitoring the quality of medical care in the organization. Because responsibilities can vary from organization to organization, the medical director should have a clearly written agreement with the organization, including duties, responsibilities, and compensation arrangements.

MEDICAL STAFF PRIVILEGES

Medical staff privileges are restricted to those professionals who fulfill the requirements as described in an organization's medical staff bylaws. Although cognizant of the importance of medical staff membership, both the medical staff and the governing body must meet their obligation to maintain standards of good medical practice in dealing with matters of staff appointment, credentialing, and the disciplining of physicians for such things as disruptive behavior, incompetence, psychological problems, criminal actions, and substance abuse.

Prior to appointment to the medical staff and the granting of the clinical privileges requested, there must be a thorough investigation of the applicant's qualifications and ability to perform the specific privileges requested. The delineation of clinical privileges should be discipline-specific and based on appropriate predetermined criteria including education, training, experience, and peer recommendations that adhere to national standards.

Credentialing and Privileging Process

 NEWSPAPER CLIPPINGS: Too Old to Practice?

New Hampshire healthcare consultant Jonathan Burrows, who has worked with hospitals seeking to implement testing policies for older physicians, estimates that roughly 5 to 10 percent of institutions have adopted them and that interest is growing.

"Colleagues have a code of silence," says Burroughs, who spent 30 years as an emergency department physician. During his career, Burroughs said he followed several elderly doctors around, quietly correcting their orders to prevent mistakes. Such experiences, he said, are nearly universal in medicine.

—*Sandra G. Boodman*, The Washington Post, *December 11, 2012*

The purpose of the credentialing process is to evaluate the competency of the applicant to determine whether he or she is qualified for appointment to the medical staff. The following sections describe the appointment process.

- *Application:* The medical staff application should provide pertinent information regarding the applicant's medical school; internship; residency; privileges requested; availability to provide on-call emergency department coverage; other hospital staff appointments; previous disciplinary actions against the applicant; unexplained breaks in work history; voluntary and/or involuntary limitations or relinquishment of staff privileges; and so on.
- *Medical staff bylaws:* Each member of the organization's medical staff should be required to sign a statement attesting to the fact that the medical staff bylaws have been read and that the physician agrees to abide by the bylaws and other policies and procedures that might be adopted from time to time.
- *Physical and mental status review*
- *Consent for release of information*
- *Certificate of insurance:* The applicant should provide evidence of professional liability insurance.
- *State licensure:* A physician's right to practice medicine is subject to the licensing laws contained in the statutes of the state in which the physician resides.
- *National Practitioner Data Bank:* The National Practitioner Data Bank (NPDB) was created by Congress as a national repository of information with the primary purpose of facilitating a comprehensive review of physicians' and other healthcare practitioners' professional credentials. The National Practitioner Data Bank must be queried as to information in its files that might pertain to medical staff applicants. Healthcare organizations must query the data bank every 2 years on the renewal of clinical privileges of healthcare practitioners.
- *References:* Both written and oral references should be obtained from previous organizations with which the applicant has been affiliated.
- *Applicant review process:* The applicant review process includes receipt and review of all documents prior to the interview; explanation of unaccounted for breaks or gaps in education or employment; review of any disciplinary action or misconduct investigation that has been initiated or is pending against the applicant by any licensing body; review of the applicant's license to practice medicine in any state, looking for any denials, limitations, suspensions, or revocations; determining if the applicant ever withdrew an application or resigned from any medical staff to avoid disciplinary action; determining if the applicant has ever been named as a defendant in a criminal proceeding; determining if the applicant has back-up coverage for his or her practice; determining if the applicant has reviewed and is willing to abide by the medical staff bylaws, rules, and regulations; and, where applicable,

departmental rules and regulations; and determining if the applicant has any physical or mental impairments that could affect his or her ability to practice medicine.
- *Delineation of clinical privileges:* The delineation of clinical privileges is the process by which the medical staff determines precisely what procedures a physician is authorized to perform. This determination is based on predetermined criteria as to what credentials are necessary to competently perform the privileges requested.
- *Governing body responsibility:* The governing body has ultimate responsibility for granting medical staff privileges.
- *Appeal process:* An appeal process should be described in the medical staff bylaws to cover issues such as the denial of professional staff privileges, grievances, and disciplinary actions. The governing body is the final arbitrator and has the right to hear any appeals and be the ultimate decision maker within the organization. A physician whose privileges are either suspended or terminated must exhaust all remedies provided in an organization's bylaws, rules, and regulations before commencing a court action.
- *Reappointments:* The medical staff must provide an effective mechanism for monitoring and evaluating the quality of patient care and the clinical performance of physicians. For problematic physicians, consideration should be given to privileges with supervision, a reduction in privileges, suspension of privileges with purpose (e.g., suspension pending further training), or termination of privileges.

Screening for Competency

Failure to properly screen a medical staff applicant's credentials can lead to liability for injuries suffered by patients as a result of that omission. This was the case in *Johnson v. Misericordia Community Hospital,*[1] where the patient brought a malpractice action against the hospital and its liability insurer for alleged negligence in granting orthopedic privileges to a physician who performed an operation to remove a pin fragment from the patient's hip. The Wisconsin Court of Appeals found the hospital negligent for failing to scrutinize the physician's credentials before approving his application for orthopedic privileges. The hospital failed to adhere to procedures established under both its own bylaws and state statute. The measure of quality and the degree of quality control exercised in a hospital are the direct responsibilities of the medical staff. Hospital supervision of the manner of appointment of physicians to its staff is mandatory, not optional. On appeal by the hospital, the Wisconsin Supreme Court affirmed the appellate court's decision, finding that if the hospital had exercised ordinary care, it "would not" have appointed the physician to the medical staff.

Physician Supervision and Monitoring

The medical staff is responsible to the governing body for the quality of care rendered by members of the medical staff. The landmark decision in this area occurred in *Darling v. Charleston Community Memorial Hospital*,[2] in which it was decided that the hospital's governing body has a duty to establish a mechanism for the medical staff to evaluate, counsel, and, when necessary, take action against an unreasonable risk of harm to a patient arising from the patient's treatment by a physician. Physician monitoring is best accomplished through a system of peer review. Most states provide statutory protection from liability for peer-review activities when they are conducted in a reasonable manner and without malice.

Practicing Outside Field of Competence

A physician must practice within his or her field of expertise or competence. The standard of care required in a malpractice case will be that of the specialty in which a physician is treating, whether or not he or she has been credentialed in that specialty.

In a California case, *Carrasco v. Bankoff*,[3] a small boy suffering third-degree burns over 18% of his body was admitted to a hospital. During his initial confinement, there was little done except to occasionally dress and redress the burned area. At the end of a 53-day confinement, the patient suffered hypergranulation of the burned area and muscular-skeletal dysfunction. The surgeon who treated him was not a board-certified plastic surgeon and apparently not properly trained in the management of burn cases. At trial, the patient's medical expert, a plastic surgeon who assumed responsibility for care after the first hospitalization, outlined the accepted medical practice in cases of this nature. The first surgeon acknowledged this accepted practice. The court held that there was substantial evidence to permit a finding of professional negligence because of the defendant surgeon's failure to perform to the accepted standard of care and that such failure resulted in the patient's injury.

Misrepresentation of Credentials

There was reliable, probative, and substantial evidence in *Graor v. State Medical Board* to support the Ohio State Medical Board's decision to permanently revoke a physician's license for misrepresenting his credentials by claiming that he was board certified in internal medicine, when he was not board certified.[4]

Limitations on Requested Privileges

A physician–pediatrician obtained associate staff privileges at a hospital in 1997. She later applied for full privileges through the hospital's credentials committee. Concern was raised about her alleged difficulty with the intubation of children. As a result, action on the pediatrician's request for full privileges was deferred. In May of 1998, the credentials committee recommended full privileges with the exception of neonatal resuscitation. The pediatrician filed a lawsuit after several in-hospital appeals. The court determined that there was substantial evidence to support the hospital's suspension of the pediatrician's resuscitation privileges.[5]

Disruptive Physicians

 NEWSPAPER CLIPPINGS: Rage in the O.R.

Experts say that doctor's bad behavior is not merely unpleasant; it also has a corrosive effect on morale and poses a significant threat to patient safety. A 2011 survey of 842 hospital administrators for the American College of physician executives found widespread concern: 71% said disruptive behavior occurs at least monthly at their hospital, while 11% said it was a daily occurrence. Ninety-nine percent said they believed such conduct negatively affected patient care, while nearly 21% link it to patient harm.

—*Sandra G. Boodman*, The Washington Post, *March 5, 2013*

Disruptive physicians can have a negative impact on an organization's staff and ultimately affect the quality of patient care. Having the right policies in place as they relate to conflict resolution is a must for an effective working environment. Criteria other than academic credentials (e.g., a physician's ability to work with others) should be considered before granting medical staff privileges.

The court in *Ladenheim v. Union County Hospital District*,[6] held that the physician's inability to work with other members of the staff was sufficient grounds to deny him staff privileges. The physician's record was replete with evidence of his inability to work effectively with other members of the hospital staff.

Most courts have found that the ability to work smoothly with others is reasonably related to the objective of ensuring patient welfare. A staff member in

Huffaker v. Bailey[7] was found incapable of getting along with others, which could severely hinder the effective treatment of patients.

REALITY CHECK: Disruptive Physician

Stephen, a hospital administrative consultant, selected a complex case on the 10th-floor orthopedic unit for review. Stephen reviewed the patient's record. Following several questions about the patient's care, a staff nurse asked, "Would you like Dr. Williams, the orthopedist, to discuss this case with you?" Stephen said, "Sure, that will be fine." Dr. Williams soon arrived and appeared a bit disturbed that he had been summoned. Stephen introduced himself and said that he just had a few questions he would like to ask. Stephen asked Dr. Williams which diagnoses the patient relayed to the organization at the time of admission and which diagnoses were made during the course of the patient's hospitalization. Dr. Williams said, "I am treating the patient for her orthopedic problems, not all of these other diagnoses." Following a few questions with the physician, Stephen asked to interview the patient. Dr. Williams agreed, "OK." Stephen asked, "Could you please ask the patient if I could speak with her?" Dr. Williams said, "That's not necessary." Dr. Williams and Stephen walked to the entrance of the patient's room. Stephen waited outside the patient's room. Dr. Williams walked into the patient's room, returned to the hallway, and said, "The patient was sleeping, but I woke her up."

Upon entry to the patient's room, realizing Dr. Williams had forgotten Stephen's name, Stephen introduced himself to the patient. Dr. Williams asked Stephen if he wanted him to leave the room. Stephen, politely, said, "You can stay if you would like."

The patient said, "Oh, I know what you do. My husband is a nurse." Stephen smiled and asked about her care. She said that it was excellent. She said the food could be better but she was pleased with her overall care. She talked about her hip fracture and back problems. Dr. Williams, interrupting the conversation, proceeded to tell the patient about her orthopedic issues. He described in explicit and frightening detail how the discs in her back were collapsing and how things could progress and how she could eventually be confined to a wheelchair.

Following his brief conversation with the patient, Stephen said, "You will be all right." The patient smiled and said, "Thank you." Upon leaving the room, Dr. Williams asked, "What kind of doctor are you?" Stephen replied, "I am not a doctor; I am an administrative consultant." Not having listened to Stephen's answer, Dr. Williams said in a threatening manner, just outside the patient's room, "Don't you ever tell one of my patients they are going to be OK!" Stephen said calmly, "I was not speaking clinically; I was relating a compassionate goodbye to the patient." Stephen then extended his hand to Dr. Williams, saying, "Thank you for your time." Dr. Williams shook Stephen's hand and then quickly walked away down the corridor.

Discussion

1. What action, if any, should the hospital consider taking to investigate the physician's behavior? Discuss your answer.
2. What information should Stephen share with the corporate leaders, if any? Discuss your answer.
3. Dr. Williams later apologized to Stephen for his conduct stating that he thought Stephen was a physician and believed him to be out of place for saying that his patient would be OK. Discuss how this affects how you would handle the conversation between Stephen and Dr. Williams.

Criminal History

The record in *Hoxie v. Ohio State Med. Bd.* indicated that the physician had made false statements concerning his criminal history when he stated in a deposition that he had never been arrested. There was sufficient evidence presented to support permanent revocation of his license to practice medicine. Certified records held by the state of California indicated that the physician had been arrested or detained by the Los Angeles Police Department multiple times in the 1970s and 1980s for possessing marijuana and PCP, for driving under the influence of alcohol and drugs, and for driving under a suspended license. Although the physician asserted that documentation of his criminal past had been fabricated by police and was not credible, law enforcement investigation reports were generally admissible. The physician himself added to the reliability of the records by verifying all significant identifying information contained within the documents and records.[8]

COMMON MEDICAL ERRORS

This section provides an overview of some of the more common medical errors. The reader should keep in mind when reading this section that "Ethical values and legal principles are usually closely related, but ethical obligations typically exceed legal duties . . . The fact that a physician charged with allegedly illegal conduct is acquitted or exonerated in civil or criminal proceedings does not necessarily mean that the physician acted ethically."[9]

Response to Emergency Department Calls

Physicians on call in an emergency department are expected to respond to requests for emergency assistance when such is considered necessary. Failure to respond is grounds for negligence should a patient suffer injury as a result of a physician's failure to respond.

Gynecologist's Refusal to Treat: Patient's Death

Issues of fact in *Dillon v. Silver*[10] precluded summary dismissal of an action charging that a woman's death from complications of an ectopic pregnancy occurred because of a gynecologist's refusal to treat her despite a request for aid by a hospital emergency department physician. Although the gynecologist contended that no physician–patient relationship had ever arisen, the hospital bylaws not only mandated that the physician accept all patients referred to him, but also stated that the emergency department physician had authority to decide which service physician should be called and required the on-call service physician to respond to such a call.

History and Physical Examination

The history and physical examination is the beginning point for preparing a patient's treatment plan. The often written note in a patient's medical record that, for example, references a patient's family history as "unremarkable" or "noncontributory" raises a red flag as to the thoroughness of the history and physical. Failure to conduct a thorough patient and family history and physical examination violates the appropriate standard of care required of the treating physician and can result in serious patient injury, as noted in the cases below.

Inadequate History and Physicals

There was a pattern of inadequate patient history and examinations in *Solomon v. Connecticut Medical Examining*

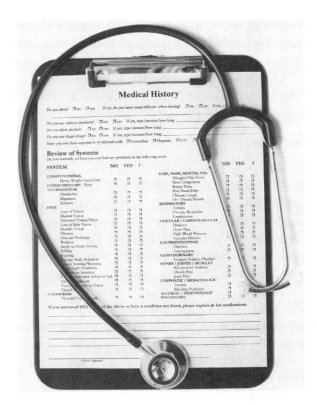

Figure 9–2 Medical History and Physical © Christopher Edwin Nuzzaco/ShutterStock, Inc.

Board,[11] where there was substantial evidence to support disciplinary action against a physician where the record indicated that the physician failed to: adequately document patient histories; perform adequate physical examinations; fully assess each patient's condition; or order appropriate laboratory tests or secure appropriate consultations.

The physician's practice of medicine was determined by the board to pose a threat to the health and safety of any person. The board concluded that there was a basis on which to subject the physician to disciplinary action.

Cursory Exam Fails to Reveal Head Injury

In *Ramberg v. Morgan*,[12] a police department physician, at the scene of an accident, examined an unconscious man who had been struck by an automobile. The physician concluded that the patient's insensibility was a result of alcohol intoxication, not the accident, and ordered the police to remove him to jail instead of the hospital. The patient subsequently died, and the autopsy revealed massive skull fractures. The court found that any physician should reasonably anticipate the presence of head injuries especially in those instances where a person is struck by a car. Although a physician does not ensure the correctness of the diagnosis or treatment, a patient is entitled to such thorough and careful examination as his or her condition and attending circumstances permit, with such diligence and methods of diagnosis as usually are approved and practiced by medical people of ordinary or average learning, judgment, and skill in the community or similar localities.

Delay in Treatment

A physician might be liable for failing to respond promptly if it can be established that such inaction caused a patient's injury. A patient afflicted with lung cancer was awarded damages in *Blackmon v. Langley* because of the failure of the examining physician to inform the patient in a timely manner that a chest X-ray showed a lesion in his lung.[13] The lesion eventually was diagnosed as cancerous. The physician contended that because the evidence showed the patient had less than a 50% chance of survival at the time of the alleged negligence, he could not be the proximate cause of injury. The Arkansas Supreme Court found that the jury was properly entitled to determine that the patient suffered and lost more than would have been the case had he been notified promptly of the lesion.

Medical Record Tool for Communications

The medical record is a tool for communicating between disciplines. The attending physician is responsible for reviewing entries entered into the record and coordinating the patient's overall plan of care. The physician is responsible for pulling the threads and making sense out of all the data collected regarding the patient's ongoing care. Someone must take the lead, and that lead must come from the physician.

It is imperative that patient records of treatment in the physician's office, as well as in the healthcare facility, be maintained. A jury could consider lack of documentation as sufficient evidence for finding a physician guilty of negligence.

Critical information that is gathered often gets lost in the record. Providers are responsible for assuring that the information critical to a patient's care is readily available to all caregivers in the opening pages of the record and not buried in the bowels of the record. Provider mistakes often occur because of the unwieldy, unorganized, and voluminous amount of information gathered on the patient. Caregivers, however, who fail to use the information collected when assessing patient needs could find themselves in a lawsuit.

Patients should be ever watchful and repeat information important to their care needs. Patients cannot assume that the information given will be both heard and recorded in the medical record and passed on to other caregivers in a timely fashion for action. Even if pertinent information is given, heard, and recorded accurately in the patient's medical record, there are no assurances that the information will be read by other caregivers and acted upon or used appropriately in his or her care.

Patient Allergy Communication Breakdown

The patient in *EHCA Dunwoody, L.L.C. v. Daniel*, advised her physician that she was allergic to latex and the hospital inserted a latex catheter into the patient. As a result, the patient developed interstitial cystitis (IC). Expert testimony was sufficient to establish to a reasonable degree of medical certainty that the catheter "caused" the patient's injury (chronic bladder disorder).[14]

Physician Fails to Read Nursing Notes

Physicians can breach their duty of care by failing to read nursing notes. In *Todd v. Sauls*,[15] Mr. Todd was admitted to Rapides General Hospital on October 3, 1988, and the next day, Dr. Sauls performed bypass surgery. Postoperatively, Todd sustained a heart attack. During the following days, Todd did not ambulate well and suffered a weight loss of 19.5 pounds.

On October 17, the medical record indicated that Todd's sternotomy wound and the mid-lower left leg incision were reddened, and his temperature was 99.6°F. Sauls did not commonly read the nurses' notes but instead preferred to rely on his own observations of the patient. In his October 18 notes, he indicated that there was no drainage. The nurses' notes, however, show that there was drainage at the chest tube site. Contrary to the medical records showing that Todd had a temperature of 101.2°F, Sauls noted that the patient was afebrile.

On October 19, Sauls noted that Todd's wounds were improving and he did not have a fever. Nurses' notes indicated redness at the surgical wounds and a temperature of 100°F. No white blood count had been ordered. Again on October 20, the nurses' notes indicated a wound, redness, and a temperature of 100.8°F. No wound culture had yet been ordered. Dr. Kamil, one of Todd's treating physicians, noted that Todd's nutritional status needed to be seriously confronted and suggested that Sauls consider supplemental feeding. Despite this, no follow-up to his recommendation appears, and the record is void of any action by Dr. Sauls to obtain a nutritional consult.

Todd was transferred to the intensive care unit on October 21 because he was gravely ill. The nurses' notes for the following day describe the chest tube site as draining foul-smelling bloody purulence. The patient's temperature was recorded to have reached 100.6°F. This is the first time that Sauls had the test tube site cultured. On October 23, the culture report from the laboratory indicated a staph infection, and Todd was started on antibiotics for treatment of the infection.

On October 25, at the request of family, Todd was transferred to St. Luke's Hospital. At St. Luke's, Dr. Leatherman, an internist and invasive cardiologist, treated Todd. Dr. Zeluff, an infectious disease specialist, examined Todd's surgical wounds and prescribed antibiotic treatment. Upon admission to St. Luke's, every one of Todd's surgical wounds was infected. Despite the care given at St. Luke's, Todd died on November 2, 1988. The family filed a malpractice suit against the surgeon. The district court entered judgment on a jury verdict for the defendant, and the plaintiff appealed claiming the surgeon breached his duty of care owed to the patient by failing to: (1) aggressively treat the surgical wound infections; (2) read the nurses' observations of infections; and (3) provide adequate nourishment, allowing the patient's body weight to rapidly waste away.

The Louisiana Court of Appeal held that Sauls committed medical malpractice when he breached the standard of care he owed to Todd. Sauls' testimony convinced the court that he failed to aggressively treat the surgical wound infections, that he chose "not" to take advantage of the nurses' observations of infection, and that he allowed Todd's body weight to waste away, knowing that extreme vigilance was required because of Todd's already severely impaired heart. Sauls' medical malpractice exacerbated an already critical condition and deprived Mr. Todd of a chance of survival.

Diagnostic Tests

NEWSPAPER CLIPPINGS: Doctors Often Don't Give Patients the Best Advice

Doctors often order tests and recommend drugs or procedures when they shouldn't—sometimes even when they know they shouldn't. The problem has become so serious that groups such as the American College of Physicians, the ABIM Foundation, The National Physicians Alliance, and a coalition of medical societies in a project called Choosing Wisely have compiled lists of tests and treatments that doctors themselves say are done too often.

—*Consumer reports insights,*
The Washington Post, *June 5, 2005*

The cases in this section describe some of the lawsuits that have resulted from medical failures as they relate to the ordering, delay in ordering, interpretation, review, relay, and failure to follow-up on test results. Although the following cases describe many of these issues, they are not exhaustive of the problems that can arise.

Failure to Order Diagnostic Tests

A plaintiff who claims that a physician failed to order proper diagnostic tests must show:

1. it is standard practice to use a certain diagnostic test under the circumstances of the case;
2. the physician failed to use the test, and therefore, failed to diagnose the patient's illness; and,
3. the patient suffered injury.

Failure to order diagnostic tests resulted in the misdiagnosis of appendicitis in *Steeves v. United States*.[16] In this case, physicians failed to order the appropriate diagnostic tests for a child who was referred to a Navy hospital with a diagnosis of possible appendicitis. Judgment in this case was entered against the United States, on behalf of the U.S. Navy, for medical expenses and for pain and suffering. The child had been referred to the hospital by an Air Force dispensary, where a lab test indicated a high white blood cell count. A consultation sheet had been given to the mother, indicating the possible diagnosis. The physician who examined the child at the Navy hospital performed no tests, failed to diagnose the patient's condition, and sent him home at 5:02 P.M., some 32 minutes after his arrival on July 21. The child was returned to the emergency department on July 22 at about 2:30 A.M. only to be sent home again by an intern who diagnosed the boy's condition as gastroenteritis. Once again, no diagnostic tests were ordered. The boy was returned to the Navy hospital on July 23, at which time diagnostic tests were performed. The patient was subsequently operated on and found to have a ruptured appendix. Holding the Navy hospital liable for the negligence of the physicians who acted as its agents, the court pointed out that a wrong diagnosis will not in and of itself support a verdict of liability in a lawsuit. However, a physician must use ordinary care in making a diagnosis. Only where a patient is examined adequately is there no liability for an erroneous diagnosis. In this instance, the physicians' failure to perform further laboratory tests the first two times the child was brought to the emergency department was found to be a breach of good medical practice.

Failure to Take Appropriate X-Rays

Failure to order a proper set of X-rays is as legally risky as the failure to order X-rays. In *Betenbaugh v. Princeton Hospital*,[17] the plaintiff had been taken to the hospital because she injured her lower back. One of the defendant–physicians directed that an X-ray be taken of her sacrum. No evidence of a fracture was found. When the patient's pain did not subside, the family physician was consulted. He found that the films taken at the hospital did not include the entire lower portion of the spine and sent her to a radiologist for further study. On the basis of additional X-rays, a diagnosis of a fracture was made, and the patient was advised to wear a lumbosacral support. Two months later, the fracture was healed. The radiologist who had taken X-ray films on the second occasion testified that it was customary to take both an anterior–posterior and a lateral view when making an X-ray examination of the sacrum. In his opinion, the failure at the hospital to include the lower area of the sacrum was a failure to meet the standard required. There was sufficient evidence to support findings that the physicians and the hospital were negligent by not having taken the appropriate X-rays and that such negligence was the proximate cause of the patient's additional pain and delay in recovery.

CT Misinterpretation Leads to Death

The deceased, Jane Fahr, in *Setterington v. Pontiac General Hospital*,[18] was concerned about a lump in her thigh. She had a CT scan taken at the hospital in August 1987. The radiologist, Dr. Mittner, did not mention that the lump could be cancerous. In reliance on the radiologist's report, Dr. Sanford, the plaintiff's treating physician, regarded the condition as a hematoma and believed that a biopsy was not warranted. In late January 1988, Fahr returned to the hospital for another CT scan because the lump seemed to be enlarging. The radiologist, Dr. Khalid, did not include the possibility of a malignant tumor in his report. As a result, Sanford continued to believe that Fahr had a hematoma. In early September 1988, Fahr returned to Sanford, who had another CT scan performed. Dr. Kayne, the radiologist, found an enlarged hematoma. In a follow-up discussion with Sanford, Kayne assured Sanford that the lump did not appear to be dangerous or invasive. As a result, Sanford concluded that Fahr had a hematoma with a leaking blood vessel. In October 1988, the tumor was biopsied and the cancer diagnosed. By December 1988, chest scans revealed metastasis. Fahr died on July 6, 1990, at the age of 32.

A malpractice action was filed against Sanford and the hospital, alleging that they failed to timely diagnose and treat Fahr. At trial, the jury found that the radiologists were agents of the defendant hospital and they breached the standard of care. The breach was a proximate cause of Fahr's death. The jury returned a verdict for the plaintiff.

Failure to Review Lab Tests

A physician's failure to review test results on a timely basis can be the proximate cause of a patient's injuries. As in *Smith v. U.S. Department of Veterans Affairs*,[19] the plaintiff, Smith, was taken to the VA hospital, where Dr. Rizk was assigned as Smith's attending physician. Smith developed an acute problem with his respiration and level of consciousness. During his stay, Smith began to complain of pain in his shoulders and neck. A rheumatology consultation was requested. Various tests were ordered, including an erythrocyte sedimentation rate (ESR).

A medical student noted that Smith was having difficulty breathing and called for a pulmonary consultation. Smith began complaining that his neck and back hurt and that he had no feeling in his legs and feet. A medical student noted that the result of Smith's ESR was 110 (more than twice the normal rate for a man his age). His white blood count was 18.1, also well above the normal rate. A staff member noted on the medical record that Smith had been unable to move his extremities for about 5 days. A psychiatric resident noted that Smith had been incontinent for 3 days and had a fever of 101.1°F.

Smith was taken to University Hospital for magnetic resonance imaging of his neck. Imaging revealed a mass subsequently identified as a spinal epidural abscess. By the time it was excised, it had been pressing on his spinal cord too long for any spinal function to remain below vertebrae four and five.

Smith filed a lawsuit alleging that the physicians' failure to promptly review his test results was the proximate cause of his paralysis. The U.S. District Court agreed.

An elevated ESR generally accounts for one of three problems: infection, cancer, or a connective tissue disorder. Most experts agreed that at the very least a repeat ESR should have been ordered. The VA's care of the plaintiff fell below the reasonable standard of care. The fact that the tests were ordered mandates the immediate review of the results. Although it cannot be known with certainty what would have occurred had the ESR been read and acted upon, it is certain that the plaintiff had a chance to fully recover from his infection.

Failure to review the results of the plaintiff's ESR constituted negligence that led to a failure to make an early diagnosis of the plaintiff's epidural abscess and was the *proximate cause* of the patient's eventual paralysis. Given that a high ESR can manifest in a very serious illness, it was *foreseeable* that ignoring a high ESR could lead to serious injury.

Surgeon Fails to Read X-ray Report

The patient in *Tams v. Lotz*[20] had to undergo a second surgical procedure to remove a laparotomy pad that had been left in the patient during a previous surgical procedure. The trial court was found to have properly directed a verdict with respect to the patient's assertion that the surgeon who performed the first operation failed to read a postoperative X-ray report, which allegedly would have put him on notice both that the pad was present and that there was a need for emergency surgery to remove the pad, therefore averting the need to remove a portion of the patient's intestine.

Failure to Consult with the Radiologist

The internist in *Lanzet v. Greenberg*[21] failed to consult with the radiologist after his conclusion that the patient suffered from congestive heart failure. This factor most likely contributed to the death of the patient while on the operating table.

Delay in Reporting Critical Tests

The patient's CT scan in *Gomez v. Tri City Community Hosp.*[22] revealed an aneurysm of the thoracic aorta. The deceased patient underwent emergency surgery, and the surgeons found a ruptured aneurysm of the thoracic aorta. The hospital had the responsibility of seeing to it that the findings of the grossly abnormal chest X-rays were conveyed to the attending physician on an emergent basis. There was evidence that the hospital's failure to ensure that the X-ray reading was promptly relayed to the attending physician was a proximate cause of the patient's death.

Failure to Communicate X-Ray Results

The court of appeals in *Washington Healthcare Corp. v. Barrow*[23] held that evidence was sufficient to sustain a finding that the hospital was negligent in failing to provide a radiology report demonstrating pathology on patient Barrow's lung in a timely manner. An X-ray of the patient taken on April 4, 1982, disclosed a small nodular density in her right lung. Within a year, the cancerous nodule had grown to the size of a softball.

A medical student who worked for Dr. Oweiss, the defendant, testified that she received no such report while working for the physician, thus accounting for 19 days after the X-ray was taken. Dr. Odenwald, who dictated the patient's report on April 4, 1982, stated that X-ray reports usually are dictated, typed, and mailed the same day. The jury could have determined that if the report did not reach Oweiss by April 23, then it did not reach him by May 3. The patient's record eventually was found; however, it was not in the patient's regular folder. One could infer that the record, therefore, was negligently filed.

Questions also arise as to why Oweiss did nothing to follow up on the matter in ensuing months. Oweiss testified that he did receive the report by May 3, 1982, and that he informed Mrs. Barrow of its contents. Barrow stated that although her folder was on the physician's desk at the time of her visit, he did not relay to her any information regarding an abnormal X-ray. Oweiss, however, was severely impeached at trial, and the jury chose not to believe him. Considering the entire record, there was reasonable probability that WHC was negligent and that Oweiss had not received the report.

Failure to Timely Diagnose

A medical malpractice action against a hospital through its interventional radiologists and other medical employees, in *Snyder v. George Washington Univ.*,[24] failed to timely diagnose and treat the patient's internal bleeding, which is alleged to have occurred during the performance of an angioplasty that resulted in a hematoma around the patient's spinal cord causing paralysis and subsequent loss of use of his limbs. The trial court was found to have erred in directing a verdict against the plaintiff where excluded expert testimony was sufficient to establish evidence of a national standard of care and breach of that standard. The expert had 40 years of experience as a board certified general surgeon.

Patient's Failure to Follow-Up

In a well-publicized case, actor John Ritter was allegedly misdiagnosed in a California hospital as suffering from a heart attack. It was later determined that he had a tear in his aorta, which led to his death. The plaintiffs, having reached a $14 million settlement with the hospital, continued with a $67 million suit against defendant–physicians, a radiologist and a cardiologist who treated Ritter in the hospital's emergency department. The plaintiffs alleged that a radiologist did not warn Ritter 2 years earlier that he had an enlarged aorta and that there was inadequate follow-up on this finding. It was also alleged that on the night of his death, an X-ray test was ordered but somehow not performed. It was alleged by the plaintiffs' experts that the X-ray would have been helpful in diagnosing Ritter's condition and have led to the correct treatment. Defense attorneys argued that, even if the order was performed, it is unlikely that Ritter's condition would have been diagnosed by an X-ray and that a CT scan or MRI would have been more helpful. However, the defendants argued that time was critical and the decision was made to treat Ritter for a heart attack. Further, the defendants argued that even if the correct diagnosis had been made in the emergency department, it is unlikely that he would have survived. The trial took on the classic battle of the plaintiffs' experts versus the defendants' experts. In the end, the plaintiffs failed to prove their case. It was determined that if Ritter had followed up with his family physician at the request of the radiologist, following a complete body scan in 2001, he would have at least increased his chances to be alive today.

Failure to Obtain Second Opinion

Dr. Goodwich, an obstetrician and gynecologist, in *Goodwich v. Sinai Hospital,*[25] had clinical practice patterns that were subject to question by his peers on a wide variety of medical matters. Dr. Goldstein (chairman of the department of obstetrics and gynecology) met with him on several occasions in 1988 regarding those concerns. It was suggested to Goodwich that he obtain second opinions from board certified OB/GYNs. He orally agreed to do so. This agreement was presented to Goodwich in writing on two occasions in 1988. Goodwich failed to comply with the agreement, and Goldstein held a second meeting with him and his attorney in February 1990.

Due to continued noncompliance, the Medical Executive Committee (MEC) met and suspended Goodwich's privileges for 3 months. The suspension of Goodwich's privileges was reported to the Maryland State Board of Physicians and the National Practitioner Data Bank.

Goodwich appealed the MEC decision to two different physician panels and the hospital's governing board. Both physician panels and the governing board affirmed the MEC's decision to abridge Goodwich's privileges. Goodwich then sued the hospital. The court of special appeals held that the record was replete with documentation of questionable patient management and continual failure to comply with second-opinion agreements.

Failure to Refer

A physician has a duty to refer his or her patient whom he or she knows or should know needs referral to a physician familiar with and clinically capable of treating the patient's ailments. To recover damages, the plaintiff must show that the physician deviated from the standard of care and that the failure to refer resulted in injury.

Untimely Referral

The California Court of Appeals found that expert testimony is not necessary where good medical practice would require a general physician to suggest a specialist's consultation.[26] The court ruled that because specialists were called in after the patient's condition grew worse, it is reasonable to assume that they could have been called in sooner. The jury was instructed by the court that a general practitioner has a duty to suggest calling in a specialist if a reasonably prudent general practitioner would do so under similar circumstances.

A physician is in a position of trust, and it is his or her duty to act in good faith. If a preferred treatment in a given situation is outside a physician's field of expertise, it is his or her duty to advise the patient.

Failure to Advise Patient's Need for a Specialist

In *Doan v. Griffith,*[27] an accident victim was admitted to the hospital with serious injuries, including multiple fractures of his facial bones. The patient contended that the physician was negligent in not advising him at the time of discharge that his facial bones needed to be realigned by a specialist before the bones became fused. As a result, his face became disfigured. Expert testimony demonstrated that the customary medical treatment for the patient's injuries would have been to realign his fractured bones surgically as soon as the swelling subsided and that such treatment would have restored the normal contour of his face. The appellate court held that the jury reasonably could have found that the physician failed to provide timely advice to the patient regarding his need for further medical treatment and that such failure was the proximate cause of the patient's condition.

Discounting Consulting Physicians' Advice

Failure of an attending physician to recognize recommendations by consulting physicians—who determine a different diagnosis and recommend a different course of treatment in a particular case—can result in liability for damages suffered by the patient. This was the case in *Martin v. East Jefferson General Hospital*[28] in which the attending physician continued to treat the patient for a viral infection despite three other physicians' diagnoses of lupus and their recommendations that the attending physician treat the patient for collagen vascular disease. The trial court found that lupus had been more probable than not as the cause of the patient's death and that her chances of recovery had been destroyed by the physician's failure to rule out that diagnosis.

If a consulting physician has suggested a diagnosis with which the treating physician does not agree, it would be prudent to consider obtaining the opinion of a second consultant who could either confirm or disprove the first consultant's diagnosis.

Diagnosis

Medical diagnosis is the process of determining a patient's disease. A physician can be liable for reducing a patient's chances for survival. Misdiagnosis is the most frequently cited injury event in malpractice suits against physicians. Although diagnosis is a medical art and not an exact science, early detection can be critical to a patient's recovery. Misdiagnosis can involve the diagnosis and treatment of a disease different from that which the patient actually suffers or the diagnosis and treatment of a disease the patient does not have. Misdiagnosis in and of itself will not necessarily impose liability on a physician, unless deviation from the accepted standard of care and injury can be established.

Pathologist Misdiagnoses Cancer

On July 1, 1988, the patient in *Anne Arundel Med. Ctr., Inc. v. Condon*[29] underwent a routine mammogram ordered by her gynecologist, which revealed suspicious findings in her right breast. Advised by her physician that her breast needed further examination, the patient selected a surgeon to perform a biopsy. The biopsy was ultimately performed on July 19, 1988. Based on the pathology report, the surgeon advised the patient that she did not have cancer but that she should undergo frequent mammograms. On February 7, 1990, the patient returned to her surgeon complaining of an inflammation of her right breast in the same area of her previous biopsy. The surgeon again recommended and performed a biopsy on February 15. Based on the second biopsy, the patient was advised that she was suffering from invasive carcinoma of the breast. On February 23, 1990, she underwent a bilateral modified radical mastectomy. The patient alleged the pathologist incorrectly interpreted the first biopsy specimen and that failure to interpret invasive carcinoma was a departure from the standard of care required and was the proximate cause of her injuries. On the eve of trial, December 9, 1992, counsel for the pathologist settled the claim against his client for $1 million.

Radiologist: Loss of Chance to Survive

In *Boudoin v. Nicholson, Baehr, Calhoun & Lanasa*,[30] expert testimony supported a finding of loss of chance to survive. A diagnostic radiologist's improper reading of a patient's X-ray resulted in a loss of chance to survive a chest-wall cancer. Boudoin had suffered a minor shoulder injury while lifting something at his job as a pipefitter. Because the pain did not subside after a few days, on May 19, he went to see Dr. Nicholson, the family practitioner who had treated him since he was 18. Based upon Boudoin's complaint of pain in the outer chest and a physical examination, Dr. Nicholson took a chest X-ray that, in his opinion, showed nothing remarkable and diagnosed Boudoin's injury as a muscle strain and prescribed accordingly. Nevertheless, he sent the X-ray to be evaluated by a diagnostic radiologist, Hendler. The radiology report returned to Nicholson read in part:

CHEST: Cardiac, hilar, and mediastinal shadows do not appear unusual. Both lung fields and angles appear clear. A 3.5-cm. broad-based benign osteomatous projection is noted at the level of the vertebral border of the inferior aspect of the left scapula. IMPRESSION: 1—No evidence of active pulmonary or cardiac pathology.

On April 18, 1989, Boudoin returned to Nicholson complaining of night sweats, weight loss, and pain in his left chest. A chest X-ray showed a large abnormal mass.

Dr. Rigby surgically removed the tumor. After recovering from his surgery, Boudoin underwent concurrent radiation and chemotherapy. Boudoin and his family were informed that even with chemotherapy, the prognosis was very poor. Further treatment was restricted to alleviating pain until Boudoin's death on December 18, 1990. Hendler appealed an award of $560,000 based upon a jury's finding that the physician's improper reading of Boudoin's X-ray resulted in a loss of chance to survive a chest-wall cancer. The appeals court affirmed the finding of liability and causation but reduced the amount of the award.

Physician Fails to Follow-Up: Lost Chance to Survive

The patient in *Downey v. University Internists of St. Louis, Inc.*[31] entered the hospital for heart-bypass surgery. Two chest X-rays were taken during this hospitalization. The X-rays were interpreted as showing a lesion in the patient's left lung and that a neoplasm could not be completely ruled out. If clinically warranted, CT scanning could be performed. No further tests or evaluations were ordered in response to these reports. A jury found that the now-deceased patient had a material chance of surviving his cancer and that his chance of survival was lost due to the physician's negligence. The jury, however, did not award damages to compensate for the harm suffered. The Missouri Court of Appeals found that the verdict of no-damage award was inconsistent with the evidence and remanded the case for a new trial.

Possibility of Survival Destroyed

On February 5, 1988, Mr. Griffett had been taken to the emergency department with a complaint of abdominal pain.[32] Two emergency department physicians evaluated him and ordered X-rays, including a chest X-ray. Dr. Bridges, a radiologist, reviewed the chest X-ray and noted in his written report that there was an abnormal density present in the upper lobe of Griffett's right lung. Griffett was referred to Dr. Ryan, a gastroenterologist, for follow-up care. Ryan admitted Griffett to the hospital for a 24-hour period and then discharged him without having reviewed the radiology report of the February 5 chest X-ray. On March 1, 1988, Griffett continued to experience intermittent pain. A nurse in Ryan's office suggested that Griffett go to the hospital emergency department if his pain became persistent.

In November 1989, Dr. Baker examined Griffett, who was complaining of pain in his right shoulder. Baker diagnosed Griffett's condition as being cancer of the upper lobe of his right lung. The abnormal density on the February 5, 1988, chest X-ray was a cancerous tumor that had doubled in size from the time it had been first observed. The tumor was surgically removed in February 1990; however, Griffett died in September 1990.

The Virginia Supreme Court held that the plaintiff had sufficiently identified Muller as an expert witness capable of testifying as to the question of causation. Evidence was sufficient to establish that the failure to diagnose lung cancer, in connection with the emergency department visit, was the proximate cause of the patient's death. The duty to review an X-ray contained in a patient's medical record should not vary between an internist and a gastroenterologist. Evidence showed that Ryan's negligence destroyed any substantial possibility of Griffett's survival.

Failure to Form a Differential Diagnosis

A case before the Mississippi Supreme Court, *Hill v. Stewart*,[33] involved a patient who became ill and was admitted to the hospital. The physician was advised of the patient's recent weight loss, frequent urination, thirst, loss of vision, nausea, and vomiting. Routine laboratory tests were ordered, including a urinalysis, but not a blood glucose test. On the following day, a consultant diagnosed the patient's condition as severe diabetic acidosis. Treatment was given, but the patient failed to respond to the therapy and died. The attending physician was sued for failing to test for diabetes and for failing to diagnose and treat the patient on the first day in the hospital. The attending physician said in court that he suspected diabetes and admitted that when diabetes is suspected, a urinalysis and a blood sugar test should be performed. An expert medical witness testified that failure to do so would be a departure from the skill and care required of a general practitioner. The expert also stated that the patient in this case probably would have had a good chance of survival if treated properly. The state supreme court determined that there was sufficient evidence presented to permit the case to go to the jury for decision.

When a physician concludes that a particular test is indicated, it should be performed and evaluated as soon as practicable. Delay might constitute negligence. The law imposes on a physician the same degree of responsibility in making a diagnosis as it does in prescribing and administering treatment.

Choice of Treatment: Differing Opinions

A physician will not be held liable for exercising his or her judgment in applying a course of treatment supported by a reputable and respected body of medical experts even if another body of expert medical opinion would favor a different course of treatment. The *two schools of thought doctrine* is only applicable in medical malpractice cases in which there is more than one method of accepted treatment for a patient's disease or injury. Under this doctrine, a physician will not be liable for medical malpractice if he or she follows a course of treatment supported by reputable, respected, and reasonable medical experts.

A physician's care and treatment does not constitute negligence simply because the outcome of a particular case is unsuccessful. A physician cannot be required to guarantee the results of his or her treatment. The mere fact that an adverse result might occur following treatment is not in and of itself evidence of professional negligence.

Medication Errors

 NEWSPAPER CLIPPINGS: Revealing Their Medical Errors: Why Three Doctors Went Public

In September 2010, Kimberly Hiatt made a medical error. The critical care nurse at Seattle Children's Hospital miscalculated and gave a fragile 8-month-old baby 1.4 grams of calcium chloride, 10 times the correct dose of 140 milligrams.

The mistake contributed to the death of the child and led to Hiatt's firing and an investigation by the state's nursing commission. In April 2011, devastated by the loss of her job and an infant patient, Hiatt committed suicide.

Hiatt, who had worked as a nurse for more than two decades, was another in a long line of "second victims" of medical error . . .

—*Kevin B. O'Reilly, amednews staff,* American Medical News, *August 15, 2011*

As noted in the following cases, medication errors by physicians include prescription of the wrong dosage, abuse in prescribing controlled substances, and prescribing controlled substances in excessive amounts.

Wrong Dosage

Expert testimony in *Leal v. Simon*[34] supported the jury's determination that the physician had been negligent when he reduced the dosage of a resident's psychotropic medication, Haldol. The resident, a 36-year-old individual who had been institutionalized his entire life, was a resident in an intermediate care facility. Expert medical testimony showed that the physician failed to familiarize himself with the resident's history, failed to secure the resident's complete medical records, and failed to wean the resident slowly off medication, thus causing the patient to suffer injury.

Abuse in Prescribing Medications

The board of regents in *Moyo v. Ambach*[35] determined that a physician prescribed methaqualone with gross negligence to 20 patients. The board of regents found that the physician did not prescribe methaqualone in good faith or for sound medical reasons. His abuse in prescribing controlled substances constituted the fraudulent practice of medicine. Expert testimony established that it was common knowledge in the medical community that methaqualone was a widely abused and addictive drug. Methaqualone should not have been used for insomnia without first trying other means of treatment. On appeal, the court found that there was sufficient evidence to support the board's finding.

Excessive Drug Dosage Leads to Death

Damages were awarded in *Argus v. Scheppegrell*[36] for the wrongful death of a teenage patient with a preexisting drug addiction. It was determined that the physician wrongfully supplied the patient with prescriptions for controlled substances in excessive amounts, with the result that the patient's preexisting drug addiction worsened, causing her death from a drug overdose. The Louisiana Court of Appeal held that the suffering of the patient caused by drug addiction and deterioration of her mental and physical condition warranted an award of $175,000. Damages of $120,000 were to be awarded for the wrongful death claims of the parents, who not only suffered during their daughter's drug addiction caused by the physician who wrongfully supplied the prescription, but also were forced to endure the torment of their daughter's slow death in the hospital.

Informed Consent

The doctrine of informed consent, as applied to physicians, refers to a physician's duty to disclose known risks, benefits, and alternatives associated with a proposed course of treatment. It is the physician's role to provide the necessary medical facts and the patient's role to make a subjective decision concerning treatment based on his or her understanding of those facts. Before subjecting a patient to a course of treatment, the physician has a duty to disclose information that will enable the patient to evaluate options available and the risks attendant to a specific procedure. A failure to disclose known and existing risks of proposed treatment when such risks might affect a patient's decision to forgo treatment constitutes a prima facie violation of a physician's duty to disclose. If a patient can establish that a physician withheld information concerning the inherent and potential hazards of a proposed treatment, consent is abrogated. Consent for a medical procedure may be withdrawn at any time before the act consented to is accomplished.

Failure to Advise the Patient of Treatment Alternatives

The patient in *Leggett v. Kumar*[37] was awarded $675,000 for pain and disfigurement resulting from a mastectomy procedure. The physician in this case failed to advise the patient of treatment alternatives. He also failed to perform the surgery properly.

Invasive Procedures

NEWSPAPER CLIPPINGS: Surgery Mix-Ups Surprisingly Common

Unthinkable errors by doctors and surgeons—such as amputating the wrong leg or removing organs from the wrong patient—occur more frequently than previously believed, a new study suggests.

Over a period of 6.5 years, doctors in Colorado alone operated on the wrong patient at least 25 times and on the wrong part of the body in another 107 patients, according to the study, which appears in the *Archives of Surgery*.

—*Amanda Gardner*, Health.com, *2011*

The frequency of surgical errors, such as the wrong patient, wrong site, and wrong surgery, continue to occur all to frequently. Guidelines as required by various regulatory and accreditation bodies help prevent such errors when performing invasive procedures.

Wrong Cervical Disc Removed

NEWSPAPER CLIPPINGS: Jury Awards 1.2 Million in Lawsuit

Chad Ooten, 33, suffered harm when Dr. Stephen Emery of Cody removed the wrong cervical disc during spinal surgery in the fall of 2000, Ooten's attorney, Todd Hambrick of Casper, argued successfully.

Hambrick said Emery acknowledged the mistake and wanted his insurance company, OHIC Insurance Co., to settle the case. But the company "would never make a reasonable offer," Hambrick said.

—*Chad Baldwin*, Casper Star Tribune, *May 13, 2005*

The following cases illustrate a variety of medical errors that have occurred during the course of surgery.

Catheter Fractured

The Plaintiff-Banks in *Banks v. Beckwith*,[38] filed a lawsuit alleging that Beckwith was negligent in improperly implanting the catheter in his vein. Banks presented expert testimony that a catheter does not fracture if properly placed in the subclavian vein and that the failure to do so is below the accepted standard of practice. It was later discovered that Banks' catheter had fractured, and a piece of it had migrated to Banks' heart. The manufacturer determined that the catheter was not defective, as the fractured catheter had a rough irregular edge that is "most commonly" the result of compressive forces associated with improper placement.

At the conclusion of the trial, Banks requested that the court instruct the jury on the doctrine of res ipsa loquitur. The trial court determined that the res ipsa loquitur instruction was not warranted stating "just because it's rare doesn't mean that we get to the point of the general negligence res ipsa instruction." The jury found the defendants were not at fault, and judgment was entered in favor of defendants. Banks appealed the trial court's ruling, alleging that the district court erred in failing to instruct the jury on the theory of res ipsa loquitur.

The Supreme Court held in summary that Banks introduced substantial evidence that a fracture of a catheter does not happen in the ordinary course of events without negligence and remanded the case for a new trial under the doctrine of res ipsa loquitur.

Wrong Patient

In *Southwestern Kentucky Baptist Hospital v. Bruce*,[39] a patient admitted for conization of the cervix was taken mistakenly to the operating room for a thyroidectomy. The physician was notified early during surgery that he had the wrong patient on the operating room table. The operation was terminated immediately. The thyroidectomy was not completed, and the incision was sutured. The patient had filed an action for malpractice and recovered $10,000 from the physician and $90,000 from the hospital.

The fact that the patient had mistakenly answered to the name of another patient who had been scheduled for a thyroidectomy did not excuse the failure of the surgeon, the anesthesiologist, and the surgical technician to determine the identity of the patient by examining her identification bracelet. The Kentucky Supreme Court held that the verdict was not excessive in view of the injuries, which consisted of a 4-inch incision along the patient's neck, which became infected and required cosmetic surgery.

Wrong Site: Colon

The patient in *Holdsworth v. Galler*[40] had a 2-cm cancerous tumor on the left side of his colon. Unfortunately, the surgeon erroneously performed right-sided colon surgery to remove the tumor. After the surgeon recognized the error, he performed the required left-sided abdominal surgery 3 days later. At the first surgery on the patient's right side, the surgeon removed the end of the patient's small intestine, his entire right colon, and the majority of his transverse colon; consequently, 40–45% of the colon was removed. Three days following the wrong-site surgery, the patient had to undergo left-sided surgery, after which he was left with approximately 20% of his colon. The patient developed complications and died 6 weeks thereafter.

Wrong Site: Herniated Disk

The plaintiff was diagnosed with a herniated disk at L4–L5. His surgeon performed a laminectomy. During a review of the plaintiff's postoperative X-rays, the surgeon noted that he had mistakenly removed the disk at L3–L4. The defendant's expert witness testified that removal of the healthy disk increased the likelihood the plaintiff would be more susceptible to future injuries.

The trial court directed a verdict against the defendant based on the defendant's own admission and that of his expert that he was negligent and that his negligence caused at least some injury to the patient. The defendant appealed. The Illinois Appellate Court held the evidence was sufficient to support a determination that the defendant's negligence caused the plaintiff's pain and suffering.[41]

Wrong Site Cover-Up: Kidney

The physician–petitioner in *In re Muncan*[42] did not review either the patient's CT scan or MRI films prior to surgery. In addition, he did not have the films with him in the operating room on the day of surgery. Had he done so, he would have discovered that the CT scan report erroneously indicated that there was a mass in the patient's left kidney when in fact such a mass was located in the patient's right kidney. During surgery, the physician did not observe any gross abnormalities or deformities in the left kidney and was unable to palpate any masses. Nonetheless, he removed the left kidney.

The physician was later advised that he had removed a healthy kidney and that he might have removed the wrong kidney. The physician discharged the patient with a postoperative diagnosis of left renal mass, failing to note that he had in fact removed a tumor-free kidney. In September 1999, another CT scan revealed the presence of a 6-cm by 7-cm mass in the patient's right kidney; the physician deemed this to be a new tumor that was not present on the CT scan conducted 4 months earlier. The diagnosis, however, appears highly suspect given the medical testimony that this new tumor was in the same location and had the same consistency and appearance as the tumor appearing in the prior CT study. The record also makes clear that it was highly unlikely that a tumor of this dimension could have achieved such size during the relatively brief period of time between the two CT studies.

The Supreme Court of New York, Appellate Division, Third Department held that the evidence was sufficient to support an inference of fraud. The physician knew he removed the wrong kidney and instead of taking steps to rectify the situation, intentionally concealed his mistake.

Needle Fragment Not Removed

On March 31, 1964, the patient–plaintiff was admitted to the medical center for treatment of metastatic malignant melanoma on her left groin.[43] On April 6, 1964, an unknown resident performed a bone marrow biopsy. The needle broke during the procedure, and a fragment lodged in the patient.

The patient was told that the needle would be removed the following day, when surgery was to be performed to remove a melanoma from her groin. The operating surgeons, Dr. Peede and Dr. Kilgore, were informed of the presence of the needle fragment prior to surgery. A notation by Peede stated that the needle fragment had been removed.

The needle fragment, however, had not been removed. The patient remained asymptomatic until she was hospitalized for back pain in September 1985. During her hospitalization, the patient learned that the needle fragment was still in her lower back. The needle fragment was finally removed in October 1985. The physician's discharge report suggested that there was a probable linkage between the needle fragment and recurrent strep infections that the patient had been experiencing. Although the patient's treating physicians had known as early as 1972 that the needle fragment had not been removed, there was no evidence that the patient was aware of this fact.

The defendant–physicians argued that the statute of limitations had tolled under Mississippi Code, thus barring the case from proceeding to trial. The circuit court entered a judgment for the physicians, and the plaintiff appealed.

The Mississippi Supreme Court held that the plaintiff's action was not time barred and was, therefore, remanded for trial. A patient's cause for action begins to accrue and the statute of limitations begins to run when the patient can reasonably be held to have knowledge of the disease or injury. In this instance, the patient began to experience infections and back pain in 1985. Moreover, this is the date she discovered that the needle was causing her problems, never having been informed previously that the needle from the 1964 biopsy procedure remained lodged within her.

Improper Performance of a Procedure

In *Ozment v. Wilkerson*,[44] Mrs. Wilkerson was suffering from Crohn's disease, a chronic ailment that affects the colon and small intestine. Part of the treatment for the disease is to allow the patient's GI system to rest, and this means that the patient cannot eat. The patient is given a concentrated caloric solution intravenously. To deliver the needed nutritional solution, Dr. Ozment needed to place a central venous catheter into Wilkerson's body. Wilkerson's pericardial sac was punctured during the procedure. As a result, a condition known as cardiac tamponade (accumulation of fluids in the pericardial sac) occurred. Wilkerson required emergency surgery to correct this condition and to repair the puncture.

The plaintiffs filed a lawsuit. Following trial, the jury rendered a verdict favorable to the plaintiffs and the defendants appealed.

The Alabama Supreme Court held expert testimony that supported the jury's finding that the catheter was inserted incorrectly. The plaintiff's expert, Dr. Moore, testified that the tip of the catheter should have been placed in the superior vena cava and should not have extended into the heart. Moore also stated that placing the tip of the catheter in the atrium, or against the wall of the atrium, was a deviation from the standard of care ordinarily exercised by a physician in the same line of practice under similar circumstances. Moore stated that the intravenous central line perforated the right atrium and caused the cardiac tamponade. Moore's testimony provided sufficient evidence from which the jury could determine that Ozment inserted the catheter incorrectly and, thereby, breached his duty of care to Wilkerson.

Anesthesia

NEWSPAPER CLIPPINGS: Longview Regional, Surgeon Part of $1.9 million Civil Lawsuit Verdict

The attorney representing the family of Roy Ross said Thursday that the jury agreed Ross' medical team concealed his death from his family until a neurologist told them Ross had no brain activity three days after surgery was halted.

Ross, 63, had undergone an endoscopy procedure to repair a Mallory-Weiss tear—a non-fatal open bleed in the stomach that develops from repeated vomiting.

Evidence before the jury showed a breathing tube was not inserted when Ross was put under anesthesia. When Ross began to retch during the procedure, his anesthetized body could not prevent the stomach contents from spilling into his lungs.

—*Glenn Evans, newa-journal.com, November 9, 2012*

Untimely Insertion of Breathing Tube

There are many acts or omissions committed by healthcare providers that give rise to lawsuits for wrongful death. In the case of Carol Ross, the suit was brought by the plaintiff on the basis that the hospital and physicians increased the family's pain and suffering by failure to properly inform them that Ross had suffered brain damage and was being kept alive artificially. The plaintiffs contended that the defendants' treatment was negligent and the hospital was vicariously liable for the acts of its employees. They

further asserted that Dr. Williams, anesthesiologist, and his assistant nurse anesthetist, Mr. Crane, were negligent for failing to manage and protect the decedent's airway during surgery. Expert testimony was presented that showed the intubation should have been performed prior to surgery.

Roy Ross, 63, had been admitted to Longview Regional Medical Center on May 28, 2009, with a nonfatal tear of the junction between the esophagus and the stomach. Since he was vomiting blood on May 29, the physicians performed an esophagogastroduodenoscopy (EGD). During the procedure he began to wretch and bleed into his lungs so Williams and Crane intubated him for 7 minutes before they could clear his airway. Ross's heart stopped after the procedure and he suffered brain damage due to a lack of oxygen. He was kept on life support until May 31.

Crane testified that not only had he not discussed the risks of the procedure beforehand with Williams, he was also not aware that Ross had a tear. Williams stated that there was a risk to intubate and that he weighed the risks for aspiration against the risk of intubation, and decided not to intubate.

The jury found in favor of Mrs. Ross and found the hospital and Dr. Williams each 50% liable for the death. The plaintiffs were awarded $1,920,22.24.[45]

Failure to Maintain Adequate Airway

The anesthesiologist in *Ward v. Epting*[46] failed to establish and maintain an adequate airway and properly resuscitate a 22-year-old postsurgical patient, which resulted in the patient's death from lack of oxygen. Expert testimony based on autopsy and blood gas tests showed that the endotracheal tube had been removed too soon after surgery and that the anesthesiologist, in an attempt to revive the patient, reinserted the tube into the esophagus. The record on appeal was found to have contained ample evidence that the anesthesiologist failed to conform to the standard of care and that such deviation was the proximate cause of the patient's death.

Improper Positioning of Arm

The plaintiff in *Wick v. Henderson*[47] experienced pain in her left arm upon awakening from surgery; an anesthesiologist told her that her arm was stressed during surgery. According to the plaintiff, she sustained an injury to the ulnar nerve in her left upper arm. A malpractice action was filed against the hospital and the anesthesiologist. The plaintiff sought recovery on theory of res ipsa loquitur. There was testimony that the main cause of the injury was the mechanical compression of the nerve by improper positioning of the arm during surgery. The trial court granted the defendants a directed verdict, resulting in dismissal of the case.

On appeal, the Iowa Supreme Court held that the res ipsa loquitur doctrine applied. The plaintiff must prove two foundational facts to invoke the doctrine of res ipsa loquitur. First, she must prove that the defendants had exclusive control and management of the instrument that caused her injury, and second, that it was the type of injury that ordinarily would not occur if reasonable care had been used. As to control, the plaintiff can show an injury resulting from an external force applied while she lay unconscious in the hospital. It is within common knowledge and experience of a layperson that an individual does not enter the hospital for gallbladder surgery and leave with ulnar nerve injury.

Aggravation of a Preexisting Condition

Aggravation of a preexisting condition through negligence might cause a physician to be liable for malpractice. If the original injury is aggravated, liability will be imposed only for the aggravation, rather than for both the original injury and its aggravation.

An 8-month-old girl in *Nguyen v. County of Los Angeles*[48] went to the hospital for tests on her hip. She had been injected with air for a hip study and suffered respiratory arrest. She later went into cardiac arrest and was resuscitated, but she suffered brain damage that was aggravated by further poor treatment. The Los Angeles Superior Court jury found evidence of medical malpractice, ordering payments for past and future pain and suffering as well as medical and total care costs that projected to the child's normal life expectancy.

Premature Discharge

The premature discharge of a patient is risky business. The intent of discharging patients more expeditiously is often due to a need to reduce costs. As pointed out by Dr. Nelson, an obstetrician and board member of the American Medical Association, such decisions "should be based on medical factors and ought not be relegated to bean counters."[49]

Failure to Follow-Up

In January or February 1974, the patient in *Truan v. Smith*[50] noticed a change in the size and firmness of her left breast, which she attributed to an implant. She later noticed discoloration and pain on pressure. While being examined by the defendant on March 25, 1974, for another ailment, the patient brought her symptoms to the physician's attention but received no significant response, and the physician made no examination of the breast at that time. The patient brought her symptoms to the attention of her physician for the second time on May 6, 1974. She had been advised by the defendant to observe her left breast for 30 days for a change in symptoms, which at the time of the examination included discomfort, discoloration, numbness, and sharp pain. She was given an appointment for 1 month later.

The patient, on the morning of her appointment, June 3, 1974, called the physician's office and informed the nurse that her symptoms had not changed and that she would like to know if she should keep her appointment. The nurse indicated that she would pass on her message to the physician. The patient assumed she would be called back if it was necessary to see the physician. By late June the symptoms became more acute, and the patient made an appointment to see the defendant–physician on July 8, 1974. The patient also was scheduled to see a specialist on July 10, 1974, at which time she was admitted to the hospital and was diagnosed as having a malignant mass and a radical mastectomy was performed.

Expert witnesses expressed the opinion that the mass had been palpable 7 months before the removal. When the defendant undertook to give the plaintiff a complete physical examination and embarked on a wait-and-see program as an aid in diagnosis, the physician should have followed up with his patient, who died before the conclusion of the trial.

The Tennessee Supreme Court entered judgment in favor of the plaintiffs, who had brought action against a treating physician for damages alleged to have been the result of malpractice by the physician in the examination, diagnosis, and treatment of breast cancer.

The state supreme court held that the evidence was sufficient to support a finding that the defendant was guilty of malpractice in failing to inform his patient that cancer was a possible cause of her complaints and in failing to make any effort to see his patient at the expiration of the observation period instituted by him.

Infections

Nosocomial (hospital-acquired) infections are a leading cause of injury and unnecessary deaths. Such infections have been linked to unsanitary conditions in the environment and poor practices (e.g., hand-washing technique). According to the Centers for Disease Control and Prevention, nearly 2 million patients annually get a hospital-acquired infection. There are estimates that as many as 90,000 of these patients die annually as a result of these infections.[51]

Infections a Recognized Risk

The mere fact that a patient contracted an infection after an operation will not, in and of itself, cause a surgeon to be liable for negligence. The reason for this, according to the Nebraska Supreme Court in *McCall v. St. Joseph Hospital*,[52] is as follows:

> Neither authority nor reason will sustain any proposition that negligence can reasonably be inferred from the fact that an infection originated at the site of a surgical wound. To permit a jury to infer negligence would be to expose every doctor and dentist to the charge of negligence every time an infection originated at the site of a wound. We note the complete absence of any expert testimony or any offer of proof in this record to the effect that a staphylococcus infection would automatically lead to an inference of negligence by the people in control of the operation or the treatment of the patient.[53]

Preventing Spread of Infection

A district court of appeals held in *Gill v. Hartford Accident & Indemnity Co.*[54] that the physician who performed surgery on a patient in the same room as the plaintiff should have known that the patient's infection was highly contagious. The failure of the physician to undertake steps to prevent the spread of the infection to the plaintiff and his failure to warn the plaintiff led the court to find that hospital authorities and the plaintiff's physician caused an unreasonable increase in the risk of injury. As a result, the plaintiff suffered injuries causally related to the negligence of the defendant.

Poor Infection-Control Technique

A jury verdict in the amount of $300,000 was awarded in *Langley v. Michael*[55] for damages arising from the amputation of the plaintiff's thumb. Evidence that the orthopedic surgeon failed to deeply cleanse, irrigate, and debride the injured area of the patient's thumb constituted proof of a departure from that degree of skill and learning ordinarily used by members of the medical profession, and that failure directly contributed to the patient's loss of the distal portion of his thumb.

Dentistry

Dental malpractice cases are generally related to patients who suffer from complications of a dental procedure. They can involve the improper treatment of dental infections or complications from the improper administration of anesthesia. Complications can also include damage to the nerves of the lower jaw, face, chin, lips, and tongue. Injuries can involve high-speed drills damaging the tongue and result in permanent loss of sensation or taste.

Practicing Outside the Scope of Practice

Practicing outside one's scope of practice involves both ethical and legal issues. For example, plaintiff Brown, in *Brown v. Belinfante*,[56] sued a dentist for performing several elective cosmetic procedures, including a facelift, eyelid revision, and facial laser resurfacing. The dentist was not a physician. He was licensed to practice dentistry in Georgia. Brown claims that after the cosmetic procedures, she could not close her eyes completely, developed chronic bilateral eye infections, and required remedial corrective surgery. Brown alleged that the dentist's performance of the cosmetic procedures constituted negligence because he exceeded the scope of the practice of dentistry.

The primary purposes of the Georgia Dental Act are to define and regulate the practice of dentistry. The statute limits the scope of the practice of dentistry. Such limitation protects the health and welfare of patients who submit themselves to the care of dentists by guarding against injuries caused by inadequate care or by unauthorized individuals. Brown falls within that class of persons the statute was intended to protect, and the harm complained of was of the type the statute was intended to guard against. In performing the elective cosmetic procedures, the dentist violated the Dental Practice Act by exceeding the statutory limits of the scope of dentistry.

Drill Bit Left in Tooth

The patient–plaintiff in *Mazor v. Isaacman*[57] visited the defendant–dentist in August 1997 for routine root canal surgery. After the surgery, the plaintiff began experiencing constant pain in the tooth in which the root canal was performed. The defendant told the plaintiff that such pain was ordinarily felt after root canal surgery. In February 1999, the plaintiff visited another dentist who discovered that a piece of a drill bit had been left inside the plaintiff's tooth during the previous root canal and the plaintiff filed a lawsuit against the defendant for dental malpractice. A motion was filed by the defendant to dismiss the lawsuit by arguing the plaintiff did not bring the claim within the 1-year statute of limitations. The Tennessee Court of Appeals held that the plaintiff had 1 year from the time she discovered or should have discovered the foreign object in which to file her lawsuit.

REALITY CHECK: Anesthesia Abuse and CEO Dilemma

Anytown Hospital has an outstanding reputation for surgical services. The operating room supervisor and a surgical nurse told Bob Wright, the CEO, that Dr. Flipton, an anesthesiologist, is abusing the use of anesthesia gases in the hospital's dental suite. He was reportedly seen by operating staff testing "laughing gas" by holding a mask against his face for short periods of time. This scene would be followed by a string of silly, seemingly meaningless jokes. Bob has repeatedly discussed this matter with the medical executive committee. The medical executive committee refuses to take any action without definitive action by the department chair. Bob suspects that if he pursues the matter further with the governing board, he could end up without a job. The governing body is generally unable to resolve disciplinary actions against a physician without support of the medical executive committee.

Discussion

1. What do you believe the ethical issues are for Bob? For Bob, doing the right thing and survival are competing concerns.
2. Which of the following would you do if you were in Bob's position, with two children in college and hefty mortgage payments?
   - Voluntarily leave my job
   - Aggressively pursue the problem
   - Secretly enlist the aid of the medical staff
   - Confront Dr. Flipton
   - Other options (explain)

Obstetrics

One of the most vulnerable medical specialties with significant risk exposure to malpractice suits is obstetrics. The following cases illustrate a variety of those risks.

C-Section Delay Causes Injury

The plaintiffs' experts in *Northern Trust Co. v. University of Chicago Hospitals and Clinics*[58] supported their contention that an obstetrical nurse's delay in placing a fetal monitor and an additional delay caused by the unavailability of a second operating room for a cesarean section caused an infant's mental retardation.

Failure to Perform C-Section

A medical malpractice action was brought against two obstetricians, a pediatrician, and the hospital in *Ledogar v. Giordano*[59] because of a newborn infant's prenatal and postnatal hypoxia, which allegedly caused brain damage resulting in autism. The record contained sufficient proof of causation to support a verdict in favor of the plaintiff when an expert obstetrician testified that both obstetricians were negligent in failing to perform a cesarean section at an earlier time, that the hospital staff departed from proper medical standards of care by not monitoring the fetal heartbeat at least every 15 minutes, and that, with a reasonable degree of medical certainty, it was probable that the fetus suffered hypoxia during labor.

Failure to Attend Delivery

The plaintiff in *Lucchesi v. Stimmell*[60] brought an action against a physician for intentional infliction of emotional distress, claiming that the physician failed to be present during unsuccessful attempts to deliver her premature fetus, and that he thereafter failed to disclose to her that the fetus was decapitated during attempts to achieve delivery by pulling on the hip area to free the head. The judge instructed the jury that it could conclude that the physician had been guilty of extreme and outrageous conduct for staying at home and leaving the delivery in the hands of a first-year intern and a third-year resident, neither of whom was experienced in breech deliveries.

The intentional infliction of emotional distress requires that the following four elements be proven: (1) the defendant's conduct was intentional or reckless; (2) the conduct was extreme and outrageous; (3) the conduct caused emotional distress to the plaintiff; and (4) the emotional distress was severe. All of these elements were present in *Lucchesi v. Stimmell*.

Failure to Perform Timely C-Section

The attending physician in *Jackson v. Huang*[61] was negligent in failing to perform a timely cesarean section. The attending physician applied too much traction when he was faced with shoulder dystocia, a situation in which a baby's shoulder hangs under the pubic bone, arresting the progress of the infant through the birth canal. As a result, the infant suffered permanent injury to the brachial plexus nerves of his right shoulder and arm. On appeal of this case, no error was found in the trial court's finding of fact when such finding was supported by testimony of the plaintiff's expert witness. The trial judge accepted the testimony of Dr. Forte, the expert witness, who testified that the defendant possessed the necessary skill and knowledge relevant to the practice of obstetrics and gynecology. The defendant, because of prolonged labor and weight of the baby, should have anticipated the possibility of shoulder dystocia and performed a timely cesarean section.

Wrongful Death of Unborn Fetus

A medical malpractice action was filed against the physician in *Modaber v. Kelley*[62] for personal injuries and mental anguish caused by the stillbirth of a child. The circuit court entered judgment on a jury verdict against the obstetrician, and an appeal was taken. The Virginia Supreme Court held that the evidence was sufficient to support a finding that the obstetrician's conduct during the patient's pregnancy caused direct injury to the patient. Evidence at trial showed that the physician failed to treat the mother's known condition of toxemia, including the development of high blood pressure and the premature separation of the placenta from the uterine wall, and that the physician thereafter failed to respond in a timely fashion when the mother went into premature labor. The court also held that injury to the unborn child constituted injury to the mother and that she could recover for the physical injury and mental anguish associated with the stillbirth. The court found that the award of $750,000 in compensatory damages was not excessive.

Psychiatry

The major risk areas of psychiatry include commitment, electroshock, duty to warn, and suicide. Matters relating to admission, consent, and discharge are governed by statute in most states.

Commitment

The recent emphasis on patient rights has had a major impact on the necessity to perform an appropriate assessment prior to commitment. The various state statutes often provide requirements granting an individual's rights to legal counsel and other procedural safeguards (e.g., patient hotline) governing the admission, retention, and discharge of psychiatric patients.

Most states have enacted administrative procedures that must be followed. The various statutes often require that two physicians certify the need for commitment. Physicians who participate in the commitment of a patient should do so only after first examining the patient and

reaching their own conclusions. Reliance on another's examination and recommendation for commitment could give rise to a lawsuit. Commitment is generally necessary in those situations in which a person might be in substantial danger of injuring himself or herself or third persons.

Commitment Upheld

Evidence was determined to be legally and factually sufficient to support a trial court's order committing a patient diagnosed with a psychotic disorder to a state hospital inpatient mental health services for a period to exceed 90 days. Two incidents in which the patient altered razors into weapons constituted recent overt acts that tended to confirm the likelihood of serious harm to a patient.[63]

Duty to Warn

NEWSPAPER CLIPPINGS: Shooting Suspect's Campus Had Threat-Assessment Team

Although psychiatrists have an ethical responsibility to offer confidential treatment, there are situations in which a doctor can, and legally must, breach the confidentiality and alert authorities to an imminent threat. Every state has its own laws and guidelines about this "duty to warn."

Colorado's law states that mental health professionals are protected from lawsuits if a patient turns violent "except where the patient has communicated to the mental health care provider a serious threat of imminent physical violence against a specific person or persons."

There are also laws protecting student privacy, which federal officials clarified after the Virginia Tech shooting. In general, a serious safety threat will trump privacy.

—*Jenna Johnson and Joel Achenbach,*
The Washington Post, *August 3, 2012*

In *Tarasoff v. Regents of the University of California*,[64] a former patient allegedly killed a third party after revealing his homicidal plans to his therapist. His therapist made no effort to inform the victim of the patient's intentions. The California Supreme Court held that when a therapist determines or reasonably should determine that a patient poses a serious danger of violence to others, there is a duty to exercise reasonable care to protect the foreseeable victims and to warn them of any impending danger. Discharge of this duty also can include notifying the police or taking whatever steps are reasonably necessary under the circumstances.

Under Nebraska law, the relationship between a psychotherapist and a patient gives rise to an affirmative duty to initiate whatever precautions are reasonably necessary to protect the potential victims of a patient. This duty develops when a therapist knows or should know that a patient's dangerous propensities present an unreasonable risk of harm to others.[65]

Exceptions to Duty to Warn

The Maryland Court of Special Appeals in *Shaw v. Glickman*[66] held that a plaintiff could not recover against a psychiatric team on the theory that they were negligent in failing to warn the plaintiff of the patient's unstable and violent condition. The court held that making such a disclosure would violate statutes pertaining to privilege against disclosure of communications relating to treatment of mental or emotional disorders. The court found that a psychiatrist might have a duty to warn the potential victim of a dangerous mental patient's intent to harm. However, the duty could be imposed only if the psychiatrist knew the identity of the prospective victim.

There was no duty on the part of the hospital or treating psychiatrists in *Sharpe v. South Carolina Department of Mental Health*[67] to warn the general public of the potential danger that might result from a psychiatric patient's release from a state hospital. There was no identifiable threat to a decedent who was shot by the patient approximately 2 months after the patient's release from voluntary commitment under a plan of outpatient care. In addition, there was nothing in the record indicating that the former patient and the decedent had known each other prior to the patient's release.

Suicidal Patients

Organizations have a duty to exercise reasonable care to protect suicidal patients from foreseeable harm. This duty exists whether the patient is voluntarily admitted or involuntarily committed. The district court in *Abille v. United States*[68] held that evidence supported a finding that the attending physician had not authorized a change in status of a suicidal patient to permit him to leave the ward without an escort. The nursing staff allowed him to leave the ward, and he found a window from which he jumped. This constituted a breach of the standard of due care under the law in Alaska, where the act or omission occurred.

The attendant in *Fernandez v. State*[69] left a patient alone in her room for 5 minutes when the patient appeared to be asleep. During the attendant's absence, the patient injured herself in a repeated suicide attempt. The court found that even if the hospital assumed a duty to observe the patient continually, such a 5-minute absence would not constitute negligence. Therefore, the hospital could not be held liable for the patient's injuries.

However, in a case in which a patient with a 14-year history of mental problems escaped from a hospital and committed suicide by jumping off a roof,[70] the record showed the patient was to be checked every 15 minutes. There was no evidence that such checks had been made.

The New York Supreme Court, Appellate Division, in *Eady v. Alter*,[71] held that an intern's notation on the hospital record that the patient tried to jump out the window was sufficient to establish a prima facie case against the hospital. The patient succeeded in committing suicide by jumping out the window approximately 10 minutes after having been seen by the intern. Testimony had been given that the patient was restrained inadequately after the reported attempted suicide.

Failure to Provide Appropriate Evaluation

John Doe was at his father's home seeking help in overcoming a heroin addiction. Doe was acting noticeably withdrawn and began vomiting. The plaintiff–father took his son to a local hospital. Doe tested negative for the presence of drugs in his blood and was discharged with instructions to attend a drug rehab program. The following day the father became aware that his son had attempted suicide. He called the office of a drug rehab program for help and was advised to take Doe to the hospital's crisis center.

The crisis center referred the father and his son to the hospital's emergency department. The father explained to the emergency department nurse that his son had attempted suicide by cutting his wrist. Doe's wrist was bandaged. The father and his son proceeded to the crisis center. Following an interview by a nurse and physician, the physician and nurse advised the father that his son was not suicidal but was "acting out" and looking for attention. Hospitalization was not offered, and the plaintiff was advised to follow up with a drug rehab program. Doe's medical records contain no information regarding voluntary hospitalization being recommended or offered, nor do the records reflect that the son refused any offer of voluntary hospitalization.

They returned home, and Doe went to bed. When the father checked Doe at about 6:00 A.M., he was gone. He telephoned the home of his ex-wife and was relieved to learn that his son was there. The father agreed to pick him up before the mother left for work. A few minutes later, the mother called and told the father that their son had left the house. The father immediately went to look for his son. While searching for his son, he noticed flashing lights on a nearby highway. When he went to see what was happening, he saw paramedics administering cardiopulmonary resuscitation (CPR) to his son. The father was told that his son jumped in front of a dump truck and was killed.

A lawsuit was filed against the defendants. The physician had testified at trial that the deceased declined voluntary admission to the hospital. However, in a deposition prior to trial, he testified that he could not recall whether Doe had declined voluntary admission or not. On cross-examination, the physician conceded that he had never specifically recommended hospitalization to Doe.

The nurse had testified that voluntary hospitalization was offered as an option to the plaintiff and his son but was not recommended. That option, if in fact offered, was not recorded in the hospital record.

The plaintiff's medical experts testified that: (1) because of Doe's two suicide attempts, he needed hospitalization; (2) additional steps should have been taken prior to ruling out major depression; (3) in all probability, Doe would not have killed himself had he been hospitalized earlier and put on medications; and (4) Doe's prior suicide attempts should have been taken more seriously. They opined that the failure to hospitalize Doe and keep him under close supervision was a deviation from accepted standards of medical practice. The defendants' expert testified to the contrary but conceded on cross-examination that Doe had at least three high-risk factors for suicide.

The trial largely turned to a contest between the experts. The jury, by its verdict, accepted the opinions of the plaintiff's experts. The court found, after a review of the record, no reason to disturb the jury's verdict. The plaintiff, as administrator of the estate of his late son, recovered a verdict of $425,000 against the defendants for their failure to provide appropriate evaluation and hospitalization of Doe.[72]

Abandonment

The relationship between a physician and a patient, when established, continues until it is ended by the mutual consent of the parties, the patient's dismissal of the physician, the physician's withdrawal from the case, or agreement that the physician's services are no longer required. A physician who decides to withdraw his or her services must provide the patient with reasonable notice so that the services of another physician can be obtained. Premature termination of treatment is often the subject of a legal action for abandonment; the unilateral termination of a physician–patient relationship by the physician without notice to the patient. The following elements should be established for a patient to recover damages for abandonment:

- Medical care was unreasonably discontinued.
- Discontinuance of medical care was against the patient's will.
- Termination of the physician–patient relationship must have been brought about by a unilateral act of the physician. There can be no issue of abandonment if the relationship is terminated by mutual consent or by dismissal of the physician by the patient.
- Physician failed to arrange for care by another physician.
- Foresight indicated that discontinuance might result in physical harm to the patient.
- Actual harm was suffered by the patient.

▌ PHYSICIAN–PATIENT RELATIONSHIP

The following suggestions can help to decrease the probability of malpractice suits:

- Personalized treatment. A patient is more inclined to sue an impersonal physician than one with whom he or she has developed a good relationship.
- Conduct a thorough assessment/history and physical examination that includes a review of all body systems.
- Develop a problems list and comprehensive treatment plan that addresses the patient's problems.
- Provide sufficient time and care to each patient. Take the time to explain treatment plans and follow-up care to the patient, his or her family, and other professionals who are caring for your patient.
- Request consultations when indicated and refer if necessary.
- Closely monitor the patient's progress and, as necessary, make adjustments to the treatment plan as the patient's condition warrants.
- Maintain timely, legible, complete, and accurate records.
- Do not make erasures.
- Do not guarantee treatment outcome.
- Provide for cross-coverage during days off.
- Do not overextend your practice.
- Avoid prescribing over the telephone.
- Do not become careless because you know the patient.
- Seek the advice of counsel should you suspect the possibility of a malpractice claim.

NOTES

1. 301 N.W.2d 156 (Wis. 1981).
2. 211 N.E.2d 253 (Ill. 1965).
3. 33 Cal. Rptr. 673 (Cal. Ct. App. 1963).
4. No. 04AP-72 (Ohio Ct. App. 2004).
5. *Warnick v. Natchez Community Hospital, Inc.*, No. 2003-CA-01513-SCT (Miss. 2004).
6. 394 N.E.2d 770 (Ill. App. Ct. 1979).
7. 540 P.2d 1398, 1400 (Or. 1975).
8. No. 05AP-681 (Ohio App. 2006).
9. AMA, "Opinion 1.02 - The Relation of Law and Ethics," http://www.ama-assn.org/ama/pub/physician-resources/medical-ethics/code-medical-ethics/opinion102.page?.
10. 520 N.Y.S.2d 751 (N.Y. App. Div. 1987).
11. 85 Conn. App. 854 (Conn. App. 2004).
12. 218 N.W.2d 492 (Iowa 1928).
13. 737 S.W.2d 455 (Ark. 1987).
14. 627 S.E.2d 830 (Ga. App. 2006).
15. 647 So. 2d 1366 (La. App. 3d Cir. 1994).
16. 294 F. Supp. 466 (D.S.C. 1968).
17. 235 A.2d 889 (N.J. 1967).
18. 568 N.W.2d 93 (Mich. App. 1997).
19. 865 F. Supp. 433 (N.D. Ohio 1994).
20. 530 A.2d 1217 (D.C. 1987).
21. 594 A.2d 1309 (N.J. 1991).
22. *Gomez v. Tri City Community Hosp.*, 4 S.W.3d 281 (Tex. App. 1999).
23. *Washington Healthcare Corp. v. Barrow*, 531 A.2d 226 (D.C. 1987).
24. 890 A.2d 237 (D.C. App. 2006).
25. 653 A.2d 541 (Md. App.1995).
26. *Valentine v. Kaiser Found. Hosps.*, 15 Cal. Rptr. 26 (Cal. Ct. App. 1961) (dictum).
27. 402 S.W.2d 855 (Ky. Ct. App. 1966).
28. 582 So. 2d 1272 (La. 1991).
29. 649 A.2d 1189 (1994).
30. 698 So. 2d 469 (La. App. 4 Cir. 1997).
31. No. ED83231 (Mo. App. 2004).
32. *Griffett v. Ryan*, 443 S.E.2d 149 (Va. 1994).
33. 209 So. 2d 809 (Miss. 1968).
34. *Leal v. Simon*, 542 N.Y.S.2d 328 (N.Y. App. Div. 1989).
35. 523 N.Y.S.2d 645 (N.Y. App. Div. 1988).
36. 489 So. 2d 392 (La. Ct. App. 1986).
37. *Leggett v. Kumar*, 570 N.E.2d 1249 (Ill. App. Ct. 1991).
38. No. 07-1278 (Iowa, February 27, 2009)
39. 539 S.W.2d 286 (Ky. 1976).
40. 785 A.2d 25 (2001).
41. *Bombagetti v. Amine*, 627 N.E.2d 230 (Ill. App. Ct. 1993).
42. 745 N.Y.S.2d 304 (N.Y. App. Div. 2002).
43. *Williams v. Kilgore*, 618 So. 2d 51 (Miss. 1992).
44. 646 So. 2d 4 (Ala. 1994).
45. *Roy Ross and the heirs of his estate, v. Mark J. Williams, M.D., Kenneth R. Crane, CRNA and Longview Regional Medical Center*, No. 2011-1266-B (TX 11-06-2012).
46. 351 S.E.2d 867 (S.C. Ct. App. 1987).
47. 485 N.W.2d 645 (Iowa 1992).
48. No. C538628 (L.A. Co. Cal. Super. Ct.).
49. Anita Manning, "AMA Calls Drive-Thru Birth Risky," *USA Today*, June 21, 1995.
50. *Truan v. Smith*, 578 S.W.2d 73 (Tenn. 1979).
51. JP Burke. "Infection Control-A Problem for Patient Safety." *New England Journal of Medicine 348* (2003): 651–656.
52. 165 N.W.2d 85 (Neb. 1969).
53. *Id.* at 89.
54. 337 So. 2d 420 (Fla. Dist. Ct. App. 1976).
55. 710 S.W.2d 373 (Mo. Ct. App. 1986).
56. 557 S.E.2d 339 (2001).
57. No. W2000-01485-COA-R3-CV (Tenn. App. 2002).
58. No. 1-02-3838 (Ill. App. Ct. Rpt. 2004).
59. 505 N.Y.S.2d 899 (N.Y. App. Div. 1986).
60. 716 P.2d 1013 (Ariz. 1986).
61. 514 So. 2d 727 (La. Ct. App. 1987).
62. 348 S.E.2d 233 (Va. 1986).
63. *In re States of Texas for the Best Interest and Protection of L.H.*, 183 S.W.3d 905 (Tex. App. 2006).
64. 551 P.2d 334 (Cal. 1976).
65. *Lipari v. Sears, Roebuck & Co.*, 497 F. Supp. 185 (D. Neb. 1980).
66. 415 A.2d 625 (Md. Ct. Spec. App. 1980).
67. 354 S.E.2d 778 (S.C. Ct. App. 1987).
68. 482 F. Supp. 703 (N.D. Cal. 1980).
69. 356 N.Y.S.2d 708 (N.Y. App. Div. 1974).
70. *Fatuck v. Hillside Hosp.*, 356 N.Y.S.2d 105 (N.Y. App. Div. 1974).
71. 380 N.Y.S.2d 737 (N.Y. App. Div. 1976).
72. *Vasilik v. Federbush*, 742 A.2d 591 (N.J. Super. Ct. App. Div. 1999).

- *In memory of all those patients that have enriched my life and blessed me with their spirit of living—while they are dying.*
- *Nursing is the honor and privilege of caring for the needs of individuals in their time of need. The responsibility is one of growth to develop the mind, soul, and physical well-being of oneself as well as the one cared for.*
- *There are many things I love about being an RN, but as a Recovery Room nurse, my favorite, by far, is being able to tell a groggy but anxious patient, "It was benign."*
- *Excellence is about who we are, what we believe in, what we do with every day of our lives. And in some ways we are a sum total of those who have loved us and those who we have given ourselves to.*
- *I have been with a number of people/patients when they die and have stood in awe.*
- *Nursing encompasses the sublime and the dreaded. We are regularly expected to do the impossible. I feel honored to be in this profession.*
- *To get well, I knew I had to accept the care and love that were given to me—when I did, healing washed over me like water.*
- *Through all of this I was never alone. Thank you!*
- *In the caring for one another, both are forever changed.*
- *A friend takes your hand and touches your heart.*

10
Nursing and the Law

- *To all of you whose names were blurred by the pain and the drugs.*
- *Don't ever underestimate your role in getting patients back on their feet.*
- *Will I lose my dignity? Will someone care? Will I wake tomorrow from this nightmare?*

—SWEDISH HOSPITAL, SEATTLE, WASHINGTON,
UNKNOWN AUTHORS

Figure 10–1   To Be a Nurse   © Tyler Olson/ShutterStock, Inc.

Learning Objectives

The reader upon completion of this chapter will be able to:

- Describe how the role of nursing practice continues to evolve.
- Explain the process of obtaining nurse licensure.
- Discuss the various categories of nursing staff and the legal risks of nurses.
- Describe the legal risks of advance practice nurses.

This chapter provides an overview of nursing practice, nurse licensure, various nursing specialties, as well as, a review of cases focused on the legal risks of nurses. The cases presented highlight those areas in which nurses tend to be most vulnerable to lawsuits.

SCOPE OF PRACTICE

NEWSPAPER CLIPPINGS: Nurses Pressing for More Autonomy

For years, nurses have been subordinate to doctors—both in the exam room and the political arena.

• • •

In 11 states, they are pushing legislation that would permit nurses with a masters degree or higher to order and interpret diagnostic tests, prescribe medications and administer treatments without physician oversight. Similar legislation is likely to be added soon in three other states.

—*N.C. Aizenman*, The Washington Post,
March 25, 2012

The role of the nurse continues to expand due to a shortage of primary care physicians in rural and inner-city areas, ever-increasing specialization, improved technology, public demand, and expectations within the profession itself. A nurse who exceeds his or her scope of practice as defined by applicable statutes (e.g., nurse practice acts) can be found to have violated licensure provisions and thus be subject to disciplinary action. Because of increasingly complex nursing and medical procedures, it is sometimes difficult to distinguish the tasks that are clearly reserved for the physician from those that can be performed by the professional nurse. Nurses, however, generally have not encountered lawsuits for exceeding their scope of practice unless negligent conduct is an issue.

NURSING DIAGNOSIS

Various states recognize that nurses can render a nursing diagnosis. As was the case in *Cignetti v. Camel*[1] where the defendant–physicians ignored a nurse's assessment of a patient's diagnosis, which contributed to a delay in treatment and injury to the patient. The nurse testified that she told the physician that the patient's signs and symptoms were not those associated with indigestion. The defendant–physician objected to this testimony, indicating that such a statement constituted a medical diagnosis by a nurse. The trial court permitted the testimony to be entered into evidence. Section 335.01(8) of the Missouri Revised Statutes (1975) authorizes an RN to make an assessment of persons who are ill and to render a nursing diagnosis. On appeal, the Missouri Court of Appeals affirmed the lower court's ruling, holding that evidence of negligence presented by a hospital employee, for which an obstetrician was not responsible, was admissible to show the events that occurred during the patient's hospital stay.

NURSE LICENSURE

The common organizational pattern of nurse licensing authority in each state is to establish a separate board, organized and operated within the guidelines of specific legislation, to license all professional and practical nurses. Each board is in turn responsible for the determination of eligibility for initial licensing and relicensing; for the enforcement of licensing statutes, including suspension, revocation, and restoration of licenses; and for the approval and supervision of educational institutions. Although a licensing board has the authority to suspend a license, it must do so within existing rules and regulations.

Requirements for Licensure

Formal professional training is necessary for nurse licensure in all states. The course requirements vary, but all courses must be completed at board-approved schools or institutions. Each state requires that an applicant pass a written examination, which is generally administered twice annually. A licensing board can draft examinations, or a professional examination service or national examining board can prepare them. Some states waive their written examination for applicants who present a certificate from a national nursing examination board. Graduate nurses are generally able to practice nursing under supervision while waiting for the results of their examination. The four basic methods by which boards license out-of-state nurses are (1) reciprocity, (2) endorsement, (3) waiver, and (4) examination.

Reciprocity

Reciprocity is a formal or informal agreement between states whereby a nurse licensing board in one state recognizes licensees of another state if the board of that state extends reciprocal recognition to licensees from the first state. To have reciprocity, the initial licensing requirements of the two states must be essentially equivalent.

Endorsement

Although some nurse licensing boards use the term "endorsement" interchangeably with "reciprocity," the two words have different meanings. In licensing by endorsement, boards determine whether out-of-state nurses' qualifications are equivalent to their own state requirements at the time of initial licensure. Many states make it a condition for endorsement that the qualifying examination taken in another state be comparable to their own. As with reciprocity, endorsement becomes much easier when uniform qualification standards are applied by the different states.

Waiver

Nurses can be licensed in some states by waiver and examination. When applicants do not meet all the requirements for licensure but have equivalent qualifications, the specific prerequisites of education, experience, or examination can be waived.

Examination

Some states will not recognize out-of state licensed nurses and make it mandatory that all applicants pass a licensing examination. Most states grant temporary licenses for nurses. These licenses may be issued pending a decision by a licensing board for permanent licensure or may be issued to out-of-state nurses who intend to be in a jurisdiction for a limited, specified time.

Graduates of schools in other countries are required to meet the same qualifications as are nurses trained in the United States. Many state boards have established special training, citizenship, and experience requirements for students who are educated abroad; others insist on additional training in the United States. Nurses who complete their studies in a foreign country are required to pass an English proficiency examination and/or a licensing examination administered in English. A few states have reciprocity or endorsement agreements with some foreign countries.

Suspension and Revocation of License

Nurse licensing boards have the authority to suspend or revoke the license of a nurse who is found to have violated specified norms of conduct. Such violations can include procurement of a license by fraud; unprofessional, dishonorable, immoral, or illegal conduct; performance of specific actions prohibited by statute; and malpractice.

Suspension and revocation procedures are most commonly contained in the licensing act; in some jurisdictions, however, the procedure is left to the discretion of the board or is contained in the general administrative procedure acts. For the most part, suspension and revocation proceedings are administrative, rather than judicial, and do not carry criminal sanctions.

Practicing Without a License

Healthcare organizations are required to verify that each nurse's license is current. The mere fact that an unlicensed practitioner is hired would not generally in and of itself impose additional liability unless a patient suffered harm as a result of the unlicensed nurse's negligence. However, a person posing as a nurse could face criminal charges.

CLASSIFICATION OF NURSE STAFF

The next several pages describe a variety of legal cases involving nursing care. Specific attention is given to nurse managers, registered nurses, licensed practical nurses, certified nursing assistants, float nurses, agency nurses, special-duty nurses, travel nurses, student nurses, and advance practice nurses.

Nurse Manager

The chief nursing officer (CNO) is a qualified RN who has administrative authority, responsibility, and accountability for the activities and training of the nursing staff. CNOs are generally responsible for maintaining standards of practice, maintaining current policy and procedure manuals, making recommendations for staffing levels based on need, coordinating and integrating nursing services with other patient care services, selecting nursing staff, and developing orientation and training programs.

A manager who knowingly fails to supervise an employee's performance or assigns a task to an individual whom he or she knows, or should know, is not competent to perform can be held personally liable if injury occurs. The employer will be liable under the doctrine of *respondeat superior* as the employer of both the manager and the individual who performed the task in a negligent manner. The manager is not relieved of personal liability even though the employer is liable under the doctrine of respondeat superior.

In determining whether a nurse with supervisory responsibilities has been negligent, the nurse is measured against the standard of care of a competent and prudent nurse in the performance of supervisory duties. Those duties include the setting of policies and procedures for the prevention of accidents in the care of patients.

Failure to Supervise

Nursing managers must properly supervise the care rendered to patients by their subordinates. Failure to do so can lead to disciplinary action by a state regulatory agency. This was the case in *Hicks v. New York State Department of Health*[2] in which the court held that evidence was sufficient to support a finding that a practical nurse was guilty of resident neglect for failing to ensure that the resident was properly cared for during her assigned shift. The record demonstrated that the petitioner was responsible for ensuring that the nursing aides' tasks were properly accomplished by conducting a visual check of each resident while making rounds at the end of her shift. The nurse's record indicated that a security guard found a resident lying in the dark, half in his bed and half still restrained in an overturned wheelchair. The nurse's record indicated that the resident was covered in urine and stool. The commissioner of health denied the petitioner's request to expunge the patient neglect report and assessed a penalty of $200, of which the petitioner was required to pay $50.

Registered Nurse

A registered nurse (RN) is a nurse who has graduated from an accredited nursing program and has passed a national licensing exam. Students are required to pass a national licensing examination, known as the NCLEX (National Council Licensure Examination)-RN, in order to obtain a registered nursing license. NCLEX examinations are developed and owned by the National Council of State Boards of Nursing, Inc. (NCSBN), which administers these examinations on behalf of its member boards. NCSBN is a not-for-profit organization whose membership comprises the boards of nursing in the 50 states, including the District of Columbia, and four U.S. territories. There are also nine associate members.

Nurses wishing to practice in a particular state should be sure to contact the state's nurse licensure body for information for specific registration and nurse licensing requirements.

Licensed Practical Nurse

Licensed practical nurses (LPNs), as well as licensed vocational nurses (LVNs), provide routine nursing care (e.g., vital signs, injections, assist patients with personal hygiene needs, and wound dressings) under the direction of a registered nurse or physician. To be licensed, they must graduate from a state approved program and pass a licensing exam approved by the state. Nurses wishing to practice in a particular state should be sure to contact the state's nurse licensure body for information for specific registration and nurse licensing requirements.

Certified Nurse Assistant

A certified nursing assistant (CNA) provides patient care, generally as they often involve activities of daily living. CNAs work under the supervision of an RN or LPN. The nursing assistant aids with positioning, turning, and lifting, and performs a variety of tests and treatments. The nursing assistant establishes and maintains interpersonal relationships with patients and other hospital personnel while ensuring confidentiality of patient information. Those who wish to become a CNA in a particular state should be sure to contact the state's nurse licensure body or a local healthcare facility for guidance and information for educational programs and certification requirements.

Failure to Follow Policy: Patient Scalded

Failure to follow hospital policy can result in a successful lawsuit for the plaintiff, as was the case in *Moon Lake Convalescent Center v. Margolis, Ovitz,*[3] where a 73-year-old resident of a convalescent center died after immersion in a tub of hot water that had been prepared by a nursing assistant. Ovitz had paralysis of his left side and could articulate only the words "yes" and "no." The nursing assistant checked the water with his hand and bathed the resident. Later in the day, a nurse noticed that the resident's leg was bleeding and his skin was sloughing off. The paramedics were contacted, and they transferred the resident to a hospital after determining that the patient had suffered third-degree burns. Dr. Drueck, the surgeon at the hospital, observed that Ovitz had suffered third-degree burns over 40% of his body, primarily on his back, buttocks, genitals, and lower legs.

Ovitz developed pneumonia during his hospitalization and died. There was testimony from Drueck that the cause of death was due to complications following the burns.

The center's daily temperature logs indicated that it knew that the water temperature in the system at times fluctuated above its bathing policy, sometimes exceeding 110°F, yet the center failed to take adequate measures to protect residents from exposure to excessive water temperatures. Moon Lake's own written policy was violated when the nursing assistant left the resident unattended in his bath. The appellate court held that revocation of the center's license was warranted in this case.

Float Nurse

A float nurse is a nurse who rotates from unit to unit based on staffing needs. "Floaters" can benefit an understaffed unit, but they also might present a liability as well if they are assigned to work in an area outside their expertise. If a patient is injured because of a floater's negligence, the standard of care required of the floater will be that required of a nurse on the assigned patient care unit.

Agency Nurse

Healthcare organizations are at risk for the negligent conduct of agency nurses. Because of this risk, it is important to be sure that agency staff have the necessary skills and competencies to carry out the duties and responsibilities assigned by the organization.

Resuscitation of Choking Child Fails

The plaintiffs' decedent, a 16-month-old child, was supervised by a visiting nurse who was employed by Sweet P Home Care Inc. Karishma suffered insufficiency of her lungs, so she received a continuous supply of oxygen that was provided via a tube that accessed her trachea. During the course of the day, the nurse provided a bottle of formula. The formula entered the child's tube and lungs. After several minutes had passed, the nurse observed that Karishma stopped breathing. The nurse attempted cardiopulmonary resuscitation, but she did not survive.

The plaintiffs sued Sweet P Home Care; an affiliated entity, Sweet Home Care Inc.; and the hospital that had provided Karishma's tracheal tube. The plaintiffs alleged that the nurse failed to perform proper resuscitative maneuvers and the hospital failed to provide a proper tracheal tube, that the failures constituted medical malpractice and that Sweet P Home Care was vicariously liable for the nurse's actions. The claim against the hospital was withdrawn and the lawsuit against Sweet P Home Care continued.

Karishma suffered asphyxiation caused by the ingestion of vomited material. Plaintiffs' counsel noted that the child choked and gagged throughout the nurse's resuscitative attempts. The jury found that the estate's damages totaled $4.5 million, all for Karishma's pain and suffering. Defense counsel moved to set aside the verdict.[4]

Special-Duty Nurse

A special-duty nurse is a healthcare professional employed by a patient or patient's family to perform nursing care for the patient. An organization is generally not liable for the negligence of a special-duty nurse unless a master–servant relationship can be determined to exist between the organization and the special-duty nurse. If a master–servant relationship exists between the organization and the special-duty nurse, the doctrine of respondeat superior may be applied to impose liability on the organization for the nurse's negligent acts.

A special-duty nurse might be required to observe certain rules and regulations as a precondition to working in the organization. The observance of organization rules is insufficient, however, to establish a master–servant relationship between the organization and the nurse. Under ordinary circumstances, the patient employs the special-duty nurse, and the organization has no authority to hire or fire the nurse. The organization does, however, have the responsibility to protect the patient from incompetent or unqualified special-duty nurses.

Traveling Nurse

A *traveling nurse* is one who travels to work in temporary nursing positions in different cities and states. There are a variety of traveling professionals such as physical therapists and physicians. The traveling professional often has opportunities that include higher wages, professional growth and development opportunities, and the adventure of traveling. Their skills are often enhanced due to their exposure to intriguing assignments in world-prominent medical centers. Travelers may work as independent contractors or elect to work with one or more recruitment agencies, which act as intermediaries between the traveler and healthcare provider.

Student Nurses

Student nurses are entrusted with the responsibility of providing nursing care to patients. They are personally liable for their own negligent acts, and the facility is liable for their acts on the basis of respondeat superior. A student nurse is held to the standard of a competent professional nurse when performing nursing duties. The courts, in several decisions, have taken the position that anyone who performs duties customarily performed by professional nurses is held to the standards of professional nurses. Every patient has the right to expect competent nursing services even if students provide the care as part of their clinical training. It would be unfair to deprive a patient of compensation for an injury simply because the nurse was a student.

ADVANCE PRACTICE NURSES

NEWSPAPER CLIPPINGS: The Role of Nurses Extends Beyond the Hospital Ward

A nurse is a doctor's best friend, according to Marvin M. Lipman, Consumers Union's chief medical adviser. This advice was given to him by a hospital ward's head nurse when he was a third-year medical student making contact with patients for the first time, along with the suggestion that he'd do well not to forget it.

Over the years, those words continued to echo in Lipman's mind. In part because hospital nurses work for the institution and many doctors work for themselves, occasional conflicts between the two are inevitable. When encountering such situations, he has generally tended to take the side of the nurses, sometimes to the chagrin of his fellow physicians. But he explains that his loyalty comes from the many times he has seen nurses go that extra step to make a patient more comfortable or more at ease.

—Consumers Union of United States Inc., The Washington Post, *May 30, 2011*

The practice of nursing continues to expand with an ever-increasing number of specialties, along with professional organizations and certifying boards. Discussed here are a variety of legal risks of advanced practice nurses, including nurse practitioners, clinical nurse specialists, certified nurse anesthetists, and certified nurse midwifes, who possess an advanced degree that allows them to treat patients in areas beyond those provided to registered nurses.

Nurse Practitioner

NEWSPAPER CLIPPINGS: The Role of Nurses Extends Beyond the Hospital Ward

Nurse practitioners . . . Studies have found that their ability to diagnose illnesses, order and interpret tests, and treat patients is equivalent to that of primary-care physicians. They also tend to spend more time with patients during routine office visits than physicians, and they are more likely to discuss preventative health measures. As of 2010, 140,000 NPs were working in the United States.

Nurse practitioners are poised to become even more visible with the passage last year of the Patient Protection and Affordable Care Act, which could add nearly 35 million people to the ranks of the insured.

—Consumers Union of United States Inc., The Washington Post, *May 30, 2011*

Nurse practitioners (NPs) are RNs who have completed the necessary education to engage in primary healthcare decision-making. The NP is trained in the delivery of primary health care and the assessment of psychosocial and physical health problems, such as the performance of routine examinations and the ordering of routine diagnostic tests. A physician may not delegate a task to an NP when regulations specify that the physician must perform it personally or when the delegation is prohibited under state law or by an organization's own policies.

The potential risks of liability for the NP are as real as the risks for any other nurse. The standard of care required most likely will be set by statute. If not, the courts will determine the standard based on the reasonable person doctrine, for example, "What would a reasonably prudent NP do under similar circumstances?" The standard would be established through the use of expert testimony of other NPs in the field. Because of potential liability problems and pressure from physicians, hospitals have been historically reluctant to use NPs to the full extent of their training. Such reluctance has been diminishing as the competency of NPs has been well demonstrated in practice.

Negligence Imputed to Physician

The negligence of a nurse practitioner can be imputed to a physician if the physician is the employer of the nurse. The plaintiff in *Adams v. Krueger*[5] went to her physician's office for diagnosis and treatment. An NP who was employed by the physician performed her assessment and diagnosed the plaintiff as having genital herpes. The physician prescribed an ointment to help relieve the patient's symptoms. The plaintiff eventually consulted with another physician who advised her that she had a yeast infection, not genital herpes.

The plaintiff and her husband filed an action against the initial treating physician and his NP for their failure to correctly diagnose and treat her condition. The action against the physician was based on his failure to review the NP's diagnosis and treatment plan.

The Idaho Supreme Court held that the negligence of the nurse was properly imputed to the physician. The Idaho Supreme Court held that the physician and NP stood in a master–servant relationship and that the nurse acted within the scope of her employment. Consequently, her negligence was properly attributed to her employer–physician.

Clinical Nurse Specialist

A clinical nurse specialist (CNS) is a professional RN with an advanced academic degree, experience, and expertise in a clinical specialty (e.g., obstetrics, pediatrics, psychiatry). Further, the CNS acts as a resource for the management of patients with complex needs and conditions. The CNS participates in staff development activities related to his or her clinical specialty and makes recommendations to establish standards of care for those patients. The CNS functions as a change agent by influencing attitudes, modifying behavior, and introducing new approaches to nursing practice. The CNS collaborates with other members of the healthcare team in developing and implementing a plan of care for patients.

Certified Nurse Anesthetist

Administration of anesthesia by a nurse anesthetist requires special training and certification. Nurse-administered anesthesia was the first-expanded role for nurses that required certification. Oversight and availability of an anesthesiologist is required by most organizations. The major risks for nurse anesthetists include improper placement of an airway, failure to recognize significant changes in a patient's condition, and the improper use of anesthetics (e.g., wrong anesthetic, wrong dose, wrong route).

Supervision of Nurse Anesthetist Required

Medical supervision of nurse anesthetists is required in some hospital settings. Failure to properly supervise a nurse anesthetist can lead to a lawsuit, as was the case in *Denton Reg'l Med. Ctr. v. LaCroix*,[6] where Mrs. LaCroix was admitted to the hospital's women's pavilion for the birth of her first child, Lawryn. She was admitted to the hospital under the care of Dr. Dulemba, her obstetrician. Prior to undergoing a cesarean section, LaCroix complained several times of breathing difficulty. When Dr. McGehee, the pediatrician, arrived, he noticed that LaCroix appeared to be in respiratory distress and heard her say, "I can't breathe." Dr. McGehee asked Nurse Blankenship, a certified registered nurse anesthetist (CRNA), if LaCroix was okay. She responded that LaCroix was just nervous. Mr. LaCroix claimed that his wife whispered to him that she could not breathe. Mr. LaCroix then shouted, "She can't breathe. Somebody please help my wife." Blankenship asked that Mr. LaCroix be removed from the operating room because his wife was having what appeared to her to be a seizure.

Blankenship could not establish an airway. She told one of the nurses: "Get one of the anesthesiologists here now!" Dr. Green, who was in his car, was paged. Upon receiving the page, he immediately drove to the women's pavilion, where Dulemba had already started the C-section. When Lawryn was delivered, she was not breathing, and Dr. McGehee had to resuscitate her. Meanwhile, Blankenship worked to establish an airway for LaCroix. The intubation was, however, an esophageal intubation. Dr. Dulemba stated that he thought that the intubation was esophageal. LaCroix's blood pressure and pulse dropped, and she went into cardiac arrest. A physician and nurse from the hospital's emergency department responded to a code for assistance. McGehee testified that the emergency department physician claimed he did not know how to resuscitate pregnant women and left without providing any medical care. Dr. Dulemba and a nurse began cardiopulmonary resuscitation on LaCroix. Dr. McGehee, having finished treating Lawryn, took control of the code. Unfortunately, LaCroix suffered irreversible brain damage.

Blankenship and Dr. Hafiz, the Denton Anesthesiology Associates (DAA), PA, anesthesiologist on call for the women's pavilion on the day of LaCroix's incident, settled with the LaCroixes by paying $500,000 and $750,000, respectively. The trial court entered a judgment against the hospital, awarding the LaCroixes approximately $8.8 million in damages.

The evidence established that the hospital owed a duty to the plaintiff to have an anesthesiologist provide or supervise all anesthesia care, including having an anesthesiologist personally present or immediately available in the operating suite. The hospital's breach of this duty proximately caused the patient's brain damage.

Certified Nurse Midwife

A certified nurse midwife provides comprehensive prenatal care including delivery for mothers who are at low risk for complications. For the most part, a nurse midwife manages normal prenatal, intrapartum, and postpartum care. Provided there are no complications, normal newborns are also cared for by a nurse midwife. Nurse midwives often provide primary care for women's issues from puberty to postmenopause.

LEGAL RISKS OF NURSES

This section provides an overview of some of the more common legal risks of nursing. As with many negligence cases, the reader should identify the ethical issues of the case, that if addressed, may help reduce the frequency of negligence suits.

Medication Errors

Nurses are required to handle and administer a vast variety of drugs that are prescribed by physicians and dispensed by an organization's pharmacy. Medications might range from aspirin to highly dangerous drugs (e.g., chemotherapy, potassium chloride) administered through IV solutions. Medications must be administered in the prescribed manner and dose to prevent serious harm to patients.

The practice of pharmacy includes the ordering, preparation, dispensing, and administration of medications. These activities can be carried out only by a licensed pharmacist or by a person exempted from the provisions of a state's pharmacy statutes. Nurses are exempted from the various pharmacy statutes when administering a medication on the oral or written order of a physician.

Failure to Administer Drugs

In *Kallenberg v. Beth Israel Hospital*,[7] a patient died after her third cerebral hemorrhage because of the failure of the physicians and staff to administer necessary medications. When the patient was admitted to the hospital, her physician determined that she should be given a specific drug to reduce her blood pressure and make her condition operable. For an unexplained reason, the drug was not administered. The patient's blood pressure rose, and after the final hemorrhage, she died. The jury found the hospital and physicians negligent by failing to administer the drug and ruled that the negligence caused the patient's death. On appeal, the appellate court found that the jury had

sufficient evidence to decide that the negligent treatment had been the cause of the patient's death.

Failure to Document Drug Wastage

The nurse in *Matthias v. Iowa Board of Nursing*[8] failed to conform to minimum standards of practice by neglecting to document the loss or wastage of controlled substances. The minimum standard of acceptable practice requires nurses to count controlled substances each shift, to document all loss or wastage of controlled substances, and to obtain the signature of a witness to the disposal of controlled substances. Iowa Code section 147 55(2) allows a professional license to be suspended or revoked when the licensee engages in professional incompetency. Iowa Administrative Code section 655 4. 19(2)(c), which regulates the actions of the board, defines professional incompetency as including "[w]illful or repeated departure from or failure to conform to the minimum standards of acceptable and prevailing practice of nursing in the state of Iowa."

Matthias argued that the board erred as a matter of law because it failed to find that she knowingly or willfully failed to conform to the minimum standards of practice regarding documentation of loss or wastage of controlled substances. The Iowa Court of Appeals found that there was substantial evidence supporting the board's finding that Matthias engaged in repeated departures from the minimum standards of nursing. The board, therefore, did not need to find that the departure was also willful.

Administering Drugs Without a Prescription

In *People v. Nygren*,[9] evidence was considered sufficient to establish probable cause for charging the director of nursing and a charge nurse with second-degree assault in the administration of Thorazine without a proper prescription to a resident at a time when the patient was incapable of providing consent. There was probable cause to believe that the defendants committed the offense charged and that it would have been established if the prosecution had been permitted to present its witnesses, two who would have testified that the nurses administered Thorazine without a prescription. The treating physician told the special investigator from the attorney general's office that Thorazine never had been prescribed for the resident while he was in the nursing facility. The resident was mentally retarded and incapable of consenting to administration of the drug. Medical evidence of the amount of Thorazine in the resident's blood was consistent with stupor and impairment of physical and mental functions.

Failure to Clarify Orders

A nurse is responsible for making an inquiry if there is uncertainty about the accuracy of a physician's medication order in a patient's record. In the Louisiana case of *Norton v. Argonaut Insurance Co.*,[10] the court focused attention on the responsibility of a nurse to obtain clarification of an apparently erroneous order from the patient's physician. The medication order, as entered in the medical record, was incomplete and subject to misinterpretation. Believing the order to be incorrect because of the dosage, the nurse asked two physicians present on the patient care unit whether the medication should be given as ordered. The two physicians did not interpret the order as the nurse did and therefore did not share the same concern. They advised the nurse that the attending physician's instructions did not appear out of line. The nurse did not contact the attending physician but instead administered the misinterpreted dosage of medication. As a result, the patient died from a fatal overdose of the medication.

The court upheld the jury's finding that the nurse had been negligent in failing to verify the order with the attending physician prior to administering the drug. The nurse was held liable, as was the physician who wrote the ambiguous order that led to the fatal dose. The court noted that it is the duty of a nurse to make absolutely certain what the physician intended regarding both dosage and route.

Administering the Wrong Dosage

The nurse in *Harrison v. Axelrod*[11] was charged with patient neglect because she administered the wrong dosage of the drug Haldol to a patient on seven occasions while she was employed at a nursing facility. The patient's physician had prescribed a 0.5 milligram dosage of Haldol. The patient's medication record indicated that the nurse had been administering dosages of 5.0 milligrams, the dosage sent to the patient care unit by the pharmacy. A department of health investigator testified that the nurse admitted that she administered the wrong dosage and that she was aware of the facility's medication administration policy, which she breached by failing to check the dosage supplied by the pharmacy against the dosage ordered by the patient's doctor. The nurse denied that she made these admissions to the investigator. The commissioner of the department of health made a determination that the administration of the wrong dosage of Haldol on seven occasions constituted patient neglect.

On appeal, the New York Supreme Court, Appellate Division, held that the evidence established that the nurse administered the wrong dosage of the prescribed drug Haldol to the patient. This was a breach of the facility's medication administration policy and was sufficient to support the determination of patient neglect.

Administering Drugs by the Wrong Route

The nurse in *Fleming v. Baptist General Convention*[12] negligently injected the patient with a solution of Talwin and Atarax subcutaneously rather than intramuscularly. The patient suffered tissue necrosis as a result of the improper injection. The suit against the hospital was successful. On appeal, the court held that the jury's verdict for the plaintiff found adequate support in the testimony of the plaintiff's expert witness on the issues of negligence and causation.

Failure to Discontinue a Drug

A healthcare organization will be held liable if a nurse continues to inject a solution into a patient after noticing its ill effects. In the Florida case of *Parrish v. Clark*,[13] the court held that a nurse's continued injection of saline solution into an unconscious patient's breast after the nurse noticed ill effects constituted negligence. After something was observed to be wrong with the administration of the solution, the nurse had a duty to discontinue its use.

Failure to Note an Order Change

In *Larrimore v. Homeopathic Hospital Association*,[14] the physician wrote an instruction on the patient's order sheet changing the method of administration from intramuscular to oral. When a nurse on the patient unit who had been off duty for several days was preparing to medicate the patient by injection, the patient objected and referred the nurse to the physician's new order. The nurse, however, told the patient she was mistaken and administered the medication intramuscularly. The court determined the jury could find the nurse negligent by applying ordinary common sense to establish the applicable standard of care.

Negligent Injection

In *Bernardi v. Community Hospital Association*,[15] a 7-year-old patient was in the hospital after surgery for the drainage of an abscessed appendix. The attending physician left a written postoperative order requiring an injection of tetracycline every 12 hours. During the evening of the first day after surgery, the nurse, employed by the hospital and acting under this order, injected the prescribed dosage of tetracycline in the patient's right gluteal region. It was claimed that the nurse negligently injected the tetracycline into or adjacent to the sciatic nerve, causing the patient to permanently lose the normal use of the right foot. The court did not hold the physician responsible. It concluded that if the plaintiff could prove the nurse's negligence, the hospital would be responsible for the nurse's act under the doctrine of respondeat superior. The physician did not know which nurse administered the injection because he was not present when the injection was given, and he had no opportunity to control its administration. The hospital was found liable under the doctrine of respondeat superior. The hospital was the employer of the nurse. Only it had the right to hire and fire her and it could assign the nurse to certain hours, designated areas, and specific patients.

Failure to Follow Physician Orders

The evidence in *Redel v. Capital Reg. Med. Ctr.*[16] noted that nurses failed to follow the treating doctor's orders and established that a case of medical negligence could be submitted against the hospital. It was established that, following bilateral knee replacement surgery, the action of nurses caused permanent drop foot to the patient. They failed to follow the doctor's verbal orders to watch the patient closely and to place him in one continuous passive motion machine at a time during physical therapy.

Failure to Record Patient's Care

The plaintiff in *Pellerin v. Humedicenters, Inc.*[17] went to the emergency department at Lakeland Medical Center complaining of chest pain. An emergency department physician, Dr. Gruner, examined her and ordered a nurse to give her an injection consisting of 50 mg of Demerol and 25 mg of Vistaril. Although the nurse testified that she did not recall giving the injection, she did not deny giving it, and her initials were present in the emergency department record as having administered the medication. The nurse admitted that she failed to record the site and mode of injection. She said she might have written this information in the nurse's notes, but no such notes were admitted into evidence.

The plaintiff testified she felt pain and a burning sensation in her hip during an injection. The burning persisted and progressively worsened over the next several weeks. The pain spread to an area approximately 10 inches in diameter around the injection site. She could not sleep on her right side, work, perform household chores, or participate in sports without experiencing pain.

The appeals court found that there was sufficient evidence to support a jury finding that the nurse had breached the applicable standard of care in administering an injection of Vistaril into Pellerin's hip. The jury awarded the plaintiff $90,304.68 in total damages. The nurse admitted that she failed to record the site and

mode of injection in the emergency department records. According to the testimony of two experts in nursing practice, failing to record this information is below the standard of care for nursing.

Failure to Identify Correct Patient

The plaintiff in *Meena v. Wilburn*[18] injured her leg and developed an ulcer because of poor blood circulation. Due to the plaintiff's diabetic condition, the ulcer did not heal. Dr. Maples, a vascular surgeon, performed surgery. Two days following surgery, Dr. Meena was at the hospital covering for one of his partners, Dr. Petro, who had asked him to remove the staples from one of his patients, 65-year-old Slaughter. Slaughter shared a semiprivate room with the plaintiff. Meena testified that he went and picked up Slaughter's chart at the nurse's desk and asked one of the nurses which bed Slaughter was in. Meena claimed that he was led to believe that she was in the bed next to the window. He picked up the chart and asked Greer, a nurse, to accompany him to the plaintiff's room. Shortly thereafter, Meena received an emergency call at the nursing station. He said that he asked Greer to take out the staples because he had to respond to an emergency call at another hospital. Greer conceded during her testimony that, before removing staples from a patient, a nurse should read the chart, be familiar with the chart, look at the patient's wristband, and compare the arm band to the chart—all of which she failed to do. Greer rationalized her failure: "When the doctor I work for is standing at the foot of a patient's bed, I would have no doubt—no reason to doubt what he tells me to do."

Greer began to remove the plaintiff's staples. The plaintiff's skin split open, revealing the layer of fat under the skin. Greer stopped the procedure and left the room to check the medical records maintained at the nursing station. She realized that she had removed staples from the wrong patient. At that point, she encountered Maples and explained to him what had happened. Maples immediately restapled the skin.

Following discharge, the plaintiff's health began to falter and she developed a fever of 101°F. The tissue where the staples had been removed became infected. The plaintiff was ultimately readmitted to the hospital; she remained there for approximately 22 days. Her condition gradually improved and, presumably, she had recovered completely with the exception of some scarring and skin indention.

A complaint was filed against Meena and Greer. After 4 days of trial, the jury returned a verdict against Meena and assessed damages in the amount of $125,000. The jury declined to hold the nurse liable for the plaintiff's injuries.

Meena appealed, claiming that the jury's exoneration of the nurse, who removed the surgical staples, was grounds for a new trial on the issue of the physician's liability. Further, Meena argued that the jury was bound to return a verdict against both defendants, inasmuch as the defendants were sued as joint tort-feasors. The Mississippi Supreme Court held that the jury's exoneration of Greer was not grounds for a new trial on the issue of the physician's liability.

This case was settled in 1992. In light of The Joint Commission's present day national patient safety goal requiring two forms of patient identification prior to rendering care or treatment, the patient's injury might have been avoided.

Infections

Failure to follow proper infection-control procedures (e.g., proper hand-washing techniques) can result in cross-contamination between patients, staff, and visitors. Staff members who administer to patients, moving from one patient to another, must wash their hands after changing dressings and carrying out routine procedures.

Cross-Contamination

The patient in *Helmann v. Sacred Heart Hospital*[19] was returned to his room following hip surgery. The patient's roommate complained of a boil under his right arm. A culture was taken of drainage from the wound and was identified as *Staphylococcus aureus*. The infected roommate was transferred immediately to an isolation room. Until this time, hospital employees administered to both patients regularly, moving from one patient to another without washing their hands as they changed dressings and carried out routine procedures. On the day the roommate was placed in isolation, the plaintiff's wound erupted, discharging a large amount of purulent drainage. A culture of the drainage showed it to have been caused by the presence of *Staphylococcus aureus*. The infection penetrated into the patient's hip socket, destroying tissue and requiring a second operation. The court ruled that there was sufficient circumstantial evidence from which the jury could have found that the patients were infected with the same *Staphylococcus aureus* strain and that the infection was caused by the hospital's employees' failure to follow sterile techniques in ministering to its two patients.

Failure to Notify Physician

The failure of nurses to follow adequate nursing procedures in treating decubitus ulcers was found to be a factor leading to the death of a nursing facility resident in *Montgomery Health Care v. Ballard*.[20] Two nurses testified they did not know that decubitus ulcers could be life threatening. One nurse testified she did not know that the patient's physician should be called if there were symptoms of infection. Such allegations would indicate that there was a lack of training and supervision of the nurses who were treating the patient. The seriousness of such failure was driven home when the court allowed $2 million in punitive damages.

Negligent Care Causes Laceration

The plaintiffs in *Morris v. Children's Hospital Medical Center*[21] alleged in their complaint that, while hospitalized at Children's Hospital Medical Center, the patient suffered a laceration to her arm as a result of treatment administered by the defendants and their agents that fell below the accepted standard of care. Morris alleged from personal observation that the laceration to her daughter's arm was caused by the jagged edges of a plastic cup that had been split and placed on her arm to guard an IV site. A nurse, in her affidavit, who stated her qualifications as an expert, expressed her opinion that the practice of placing a split plastic cup over an IV site as a guard constituted a breach of the standard of nursing care.

Failure to Follow Instructions

Failure of a staff nurse to follow the instructions of a supervising nurse to wait for her assistance before performing a procedure led to the revocation of the nurse's license in *Cafiero v. North Carolina Board of Nursing*.[22] The nurse had failed to heed instructions to wait for assistance before connecting a heart monitor to an infant. The heart monitor was connected incorrectly and resulted in an electrical shock to the infant. The board of nursing, under the nursing practice act, revoked the nurse's license. The board had the authority to revoke the nurse's license even though her work before and after the incident had been exemplary. The dangers of electric cords are within the realm of common knowledge. The record showed that the nurse failed to exercise ordinary care in connecting the infant to the monitor.

Failure to Report Physician Negligence

An organization can be liable for failure of nursing personnel to take appropriate action when a patient's personal physician is unavailable, unwilling, or unable to cope with a situation that threatens the life or health of the patient. In a California case, *Goff v. Doctors General Hospital*,[23] a patient was bleeding seriously after childbirth because the physician failed to suture her properly. Nurses testified they were aware of the patient's dangerous condition and that the physician was not present in the hospital. Both nurses knew the patient would die if nothing was done, but neither contacted anyone except the physician. The hospital was liable for the nurses' negligence in failing to notify their supervisors of the serious condition that caused the patient's death. Evidence was sufficient to sustain the finding that the nurses who attended to the patient and who were aware of the excessive bleeding were negligent and that their negligence was a contributing cause of the patient's death. The measure of duty of the hospital toward its patients is the exercise of that degree of care used by hospitals generally. The court held that nurses who knew that a woman they were attending was bleeding excessively were negligent in failing to report the circumstances so that prompt and adequate measures could be taken to safeguard her life.

Failure to Question Discharge

A nurse has a duty to question the discharge of a patient if he or she has reason to believe that such discharge could be injurious to the health of the patient. Jury issues were raised in *Koeniguer v. Eckrich*[24] by expert testimony that the nurses had a duty to attempt to delay the patient's discharge if her condition warranted continued hospitalization. By permissible inferences from the evidence, the delay in treatment that resulted from the premature discharge contributed to the patient's death. Summary dismissal of this case against the hospital by a trial court was found to have been improper.

Failure to Act: Swollen Beyond Recognition

Failure to take appropriate and timely action can lead to a lawsuit. As was the case in *NKC Hosps., Inc. v. Anthony*,[25] Mrs. Anthony was in her first pregnancy under the primary care of Dr. Hawkins, her personal physician. Mrs. Anthony was in good health, 26 years of age, employed, and about 30 weeks along in her pregnancy. On September 5, 1989, Mrs. Anthony's husband took her to the emergency department of Norton Hospital. She was experiencing nausea, vomiting, and abdominal pain. Because of her pregnancy, she was referred to the hospital's obstetrical unit. In the obstetrical unit, Mrs. Anthony came under the immediate care of Moore, a nurse, who performed an assessment.

Dr. Hawkins was called and she issued several orders, including an IV start, blood work, urinalysis, and a prescription to control her nausea. Later that night, a second call was made to Dr. Hawkins, giving her the test results and informing her that the patient was in extreme pain. Believing that Mrs. Anthony had a urinary tract infection, antibiotics were ordered along with an order for her discharge from the hospital.

That same night a third call was made to Dr. Hawkins because of the pain Mrs. Anthony was experiencing, as observed by Nurse Moore. Mr. Anthony also talked with Dr. Hawkins about his wife's pain. Nurse Moore became concerned about Hawkins's discharge order. Although aware of Nurse Moore's evaluation, Dr. Hawkins prescribed morphine sulfate but was unrelenting in her order of discharge.

Dr. Love, the resident physician on duty, did not see or examine the patient, although a prescription for morphine was ordered and administered pursuant to the telephoned directions of Dr. Hawkins. At approximately 2:00 A.M., morphine was administered to Mrs. Anthony. She rested comfortably for several hours but awakened in pain again. At 6:00 A.M., the patient was discharged in pain.

During trial testimony, Hale, a nursing supervisor, admitted that it was a deviation from the standard of nursing care to discharge a patient in significant pain. Nurse Moore, who was always concerned with the patient's pain, had grave reservations about her discharge. She suggested that Dr. Love examine Mrs. Anthony. She even consulted her supervisor, Nurse Hale.

At approximately 10:00 A.M., Mrs. Anthony was readmitted to the hospital. Upon readmission, Dr. Hawkins began personal supervision of her patient. It was determined that Mrs. Anthony had a serious respiratory problem. The next day the patient was transferred to the hospital's intensive care unit (ICU).

The following day, the baby was delivered by cesarean section. It was belatedly determined at that time that Mrs. Anthony's condition was caused by a perforation of the appendix at the large bowel, a condition not detected by anyone at the hospital during her first admission. Almost 3 weeks later, while still in Norton Hospital, Mrs. Anthony died of acute adult respiratory distress syndrome, a complication resulting from the delay in the diagnosis and treatment of her appendicitis.

Judgment was brought against the hospital. At trial, Dr. Fields, an expert witness for the estate of Mrs. Anthony, testified that the hospital deviated from the standard of care. Every patient who presents himself or herself to the labor and delivery area, the emergency department, or any area of the hospital should be seen by a physician and certainly before he or she is allowed to leave the institution. Further, to provide the patient with medication in the form of a prescription without the physician ever seeing the patient was below any standard of care with which Dr. Fields was acquainted. An award of more than $2 million was returned, with the apportionment of causation attributable to Dr. Hawkins as 65% and to the hospital as 35%. The hospital argued that the trial court erred in failing to grant its motions for directed verdict and for judgment notwithstanding the verdict because of the lack of substantial causation in linking the negligence of the hospital to Mrs. Anthony's death.

The Kentucky Court of Appeals found that the hospital failed to have Mrs. Anthony examined by a physician and by discharging her in pain. The hospital should have foreseen the injury to Mrs. Anthony because its own staff was questioning the judgments of Dr. Hawkins while at the same time failing to follow through with the standard of care required of it. The defense that the hospital's nurses were only following a "chain of command" by doing what Hawkins ordered is not persuasive. The nurses were not the agents of Dr. Hawkins. All involved had their independent duty to Anthony.

The evidence presented a woman conscious of her last days on earth, swollen beyond recognition, tubes exiting almost every orifice of her body, in severe pain, and who deteriorated to the point where she could not verbally communicate with loved ones. The trial court, when confronted with a motion for a new trial on excessive damages, must evaluate the award mirrored against the facts. No question, the award was monumental, but so was the injury.

Failure to Note Change in Patient's Condition

Nurses have the responsibility to observe the condition of patients under their care and report any pertinent findings to the attending physician. Failure to note changes in a patient's condition can lead to liability on the part of the nurse and the organization.

Failure to Recognize Patient Stopped Breathing

The recovery room nurse in *Eyoma v. Falco*,[26] who had been assigned to monitor a postsurgical patient, left the patient and failed to recognize that the patient stopped breathing. Nurse Falco had been assigned to monitor the patient in the recovery room. She delegated that duty to another nurse and failed to verify that the nurse accepted that responsibility.

Nurse Falco admitted she never got a verbal response from the other nurse, and when she returned there was no one near the decedent. She acknowledged that Dr. Brotherton told her to watch the decedent's breathing, but she claimed she was not told that decedent had been given narcotics. She maintained that upon her return she checked the decedent and observed his respirations to be 8 per minute.

Thereafter, Brotherton returned and inquired about the decedent's condition. Falco informed the doctor that the patient was fine. However, upon his personal observation,

Brotherton realized that the decedent had stopped breathing. The decedent, because of oxygen deprivation, entered a comatose state and remained unconscious for over a year until his death.[27]

The jury held the nurse to be 100% liable for the patient's injuries. The court held that there was sufficient evidence to support the verdict.

Failure to Report Deteriorating Condition

An organization's policies and procedures should prescribe guidelines for staff members to follow when confronted with a physician or other healthcare professional whose action or inaction jeopardizes the well-being of a patient. Guidelines in place but not followed are of no value, as was the case in *Utter v. United Hospital Center, Inc.*[28] where the patient suffered an amputation that the jury determined resulted from the failure of the nursing staff to properly report the patient's deteriorating condition. The nursing staff, according to written procedures in the nursing manual, was responsible for reporting such changes. It was determined that deviation from hospital policy constituted negligence.

Failure to Report Patient Symptoms

In *Citizens Hospital Association v. Schoulin*,[29] an accident victim sued the hospital and the attending physician for their negligence in failing to discover and properly treat his injuries. The court held that there was sufficient evidence to sustain a jury verdict that the hospital's nurse was negligent in failing to inform the physician of all the patient's symptoms, to conduct a proper examination of the plaintiff, and to follow the directions of the physician. Thus, because the nurse was the employee of the hospital, the hospital was liable under the doctrine of respondeat superior.

In another case arising from the death of a hospital patient following hernia surgery, evidence supported findings that both the patient's treating physician and the hospital deviated from applicable standards of care, and deviations were the cause of the patient's death. The applicable standard of care required the nurse to notify the physician if the patient complained of restlessness and had a heart rate fluctuating between 120 and 136. If the cardiologist had been called, it was probable that the patient could have been successfully treated. Hospital personnel had deviated from the standard of care when they observed bleeding from the patient and did not inform the physician, and that the physician deviated from the standard of care when he failed to call a cardiac consult for the patient. In addition, a nursing expert testified that the nurse had deviated from the standard of care when he failed to call the physician when the patient pulled off his oxygen mask and complained of difficulty breathing.[30]

Timely Reporting of Patient Symptoms

In *Hiatt v. Grace*,[31] on appeal by the hospital and the nurse, the Kansas Supreme Court held that there was sufficient evidence to authorize the jury to find that the nurse was negligent in failing to timely notify the physician that delivery of the plaintiff's child was imminent. This delay resulted in an unattended childbirth with consequent injuries. The trial court awarded the plaintiff $15,000.

Failure to Report Defective Equipment

Failure to report defective equipment can cause a nurse to be held liable for negligence if the failure to report is the proximate cause of a patient's injuries. The defect must be known and not hidden from sight.

Incorrect Transcription of Orders

Failure to take correct telephone orders can be just as serious as failure to follow, understand, and/or interpret a physician's order(s). Nurses must be alert in transcribing orders because there are periodic contradictions between what physicians claim they ordered and what nurses allege they ordered. Orders should be read back after they are transcribed for verification purposes. Verification of an order by another nurse on a second phone is helpful, especially if an order is questionable. Any questionable orders must be verified with the physician who initiated the order. Physicians must authenticate their verbal order(s) by signing the written order in the medical record. Nurses who disagree with a physician's order should not carry out an obvious erroneous order. In addition, they should confirm the order with the prescribing physician and report to the supervisor any concerns they might have with a particular order.

Misidentification of Infants

The inadvertent or negligent switching of infants can lead to liability for damages. Damages in the amount of $110,000 were awarded for the inadvertent switching of two babies born at the same time in *De Leon Lopez v. Corporacion Insular de Seguros*.[32]

Restraints

Standards for the application of both physical and chemical restraints have been evolving over the past decade, and they are becoming more stringent. Because of patient rights issues, injuries, and the improper and indiscreet use of restraints, organizations are attempting to develop restraint-free environments.

Failure to Follow Policy

The plaintiffs in *Estate of Hendrickson v. Genesis Health Venture, Inc.*[33] filed an action for negligence, breach of contract, and negligent infliction of emotional distress against Genesis ElderCare Network Services, Inc. (GENS), among others.

Hendrickson suffered a massive stroke while she was a patient at a hospital in the summer of 1996. The stroke left her totally dependent on others for her daily care. During one of her admissions to Salisbury Center, a nursing home, operated by the defendant GENS, Ferguson went into Hendrickson's room while making rounds and found Hendrickson dead, her head wedged between the mattress and the adjacent bed rail.

A jury found that Hendrickson's death was caused by negligence. On appeal, GENS argued that the plaintiff failed to show that it knew or should have known of the risk of injury to Hendrickson from the side rails. The North Carolina Court of Appeals disagreed, finding there was evidence tending to show that nursing assistants employed by GENS were aware that Hendrickson, on several occasions before her death on October 30, had slid to the edge of the bed and became caught between the edge of the mattress and the bed rail. Plaintiffs offered evidence showing that GENS had a restraint policy in effect that required a restraint assessment form for any resident for whom the use of restraints was required. The nursing staff was required to document the effectiveness of less restrictive measures. The assessment was required to be reviewed by a restraint alternative team/committee. Evidence was offered showing that no restraint assessment form had been completed for Hendrickson. In addition, her medical records contained no nursing notes documenting the use of less restrictive measures than the bed rails. The defendant argued that the bed rails were required for positioning and safety and were not restraints, so that no restraint assessment was required. While the evidence was conflicting as to whether the bed rails were used as a restraint or as a safety measure, evidence indicated that the rails should have been considered a restraint in connection with Hendrickson's care, as per organization policy.

The court of appeals concluded that the plaintiffs offered sufficient evidence to sustain a finding by the jury that defendant GENS was negligent in failing to conform to its own policies with respect to the use of physical restraints and that such negligence was the proximate cause of Hendrickson's death.

Failure to Take Vital Signs

Bradshaw, in *Brandon HMA, Inc. v. Bradshaw*,[34] had been admitted to Rankin Medical Center (RMC) under the care of Dr. Bobo for treatment of bacterial pneumonia. She was prescribed oxygen and various medications. A general surgeon inserted a chest tube in Bradshaw's left side to drain some fluid that accumulated. Due to the pain and discomfort associated with a chest tube, Extra Strength Tylenol and Lorcet Plus were prescribed for pain. Bobo also prescribed Ativan to relieve anxiety. During the afternoon and evening following insertion of the chest tube, two nurses periodically checked Bradshaw, took her vital signs, and noted that she exhibited "no distress." Around 11:00 P.M., Lewis, an LPN, was assigned by Nail, the floor's charge nurse, to provide care to Bradshaw. Before checking on Bradshaw, Lewis reviewed the notes and a tape left by the previous nurse that detailed Bradshaw's condition. Around midnight, Lewis made his first visit to Bradshaw's room, took her vital signs, and noted she was experiencing some pain on her left side. Some time before 1:00 A.M., a respiratory therapist checked on Bradshaw and did not notice any problems, but did note that Bradshaw was restless. Shortly after 1:00 A.M., Lewis made his second visit to Bradshaw's room. She continued to complain of pain in her chest. Lewis, however, did not take her vital signs. He gave her an Extra Strength Tylenol and made a note indicating that the patient was complaining of pain on the left side and appeared to be in distress. At 2:00 A.M. during Lewis's next visit, Bradshaw again complained that she could not sleep and that the pain had increased. Despite her complaints, Lewis again failed to take her vital signs. Instead, he consulted Nail and administered an injection of Ativan to relieve Bradshaw's anxiety and restlessness. Forty minutes later, Bradshaw again complained of increased pain. Lewis noticed that she was sitting up in bed and her respiration had become short and rapid. Feeling that the earlier Lorcet Plus was wearing off, Lewis administered another dose. Lewis again failed to check Bradshaw's vital signs.

Nail, while in Bradshaw's room at 3:00 A.M., did not note any problems. When Lewis returned to Bradshaw's room at 3:30 A.M., her condition had significantly worsened. She was nauseous, disoriented, covered in sweat, and did not follow verbal commands. Lewis checked her vital signs and found her temperature had fallen to 95.8°F. Realizing the seriousness of Bradshaw's condition, Lewis left the room to find Nail. At this point, testimony among RMC's employees varies. Lewis and Washington, a nurses' aide, testified that Lewis found Nail and Washington conversing in the hallway. According to the two testimonies, Nail and Lewis discussed Bradshaw's condition and returned to the room at 3:40 A.M.

When Lewis and Nail returned to the room, they found Bradshaw was cyanotic, had stopped breathing, and had no pulse. Nail called a "code" and started cardiopulmonary resuscitation (CPR). The code team arrived and revived Bradshaw by administering epinephrine. Bradshaw was transferred to ICU where she remained comatose for 2 weeks. She was eventually transferred to a rehabilitation center for treatment. While in treatment, MRIs of Bradshaw's brain were ordered and showed evidence of brain damage due to lack of oxygen. Bradshaw's present condition as a result of the cardiopulmonary arrest and hypoxic brain damage is permanent and severe. She has significant difficulty in moving due to rigidity in her muscles and is prone to bouts of spasms. Bradshaw cannot walk without assistance and often falls due to a lack of stability. She is unable to perform many daily activities without the aid of her mother or someone else, including dressing, brushing her teeth, driving a car, and going to the bathroom. As a result of the negligent nursing care, Bradshaw filed a lawsuit against Brandon HMA, Inc. Bradshaw alleged that nursing personnel failed to properly monitor her, report vital information to her physician, and allowed her condition to deteriorate to a critical stage before providing urgently needed care and implementing life support. The jury found in favor of Bradshaw and awarded $9 million in damages. The judge entered a final judgment on the jury verdict, and Brandon filed an appeal.

On appeal, the Supreme Court of Mississippi upheld the judgment of the circuit court. The court did not consider $9 million excessive. Bradshaw will have to live out her years with both emotional and physical pain. Her present existence will not remotely resemble her former life.

Foreign Objects Left in Patient

Romero v. Bellina[35] describes how both nurses and surgeons are responsible for sponge counts. Bellina performed laser surgery on Romero at the hospital. Markey and Toups, surgical nurses employed by the hospital, assisted Bellina during surgery. Before the final suturing of the incision, the nurses erroneously informed Bellina that all the lap pads had been accounted for.

The day after the procedure, Romero complained of severe abdominal pain. A few months later, she discovered a mass in her abdomen near the area where the surgery was performed. She visited her treating physician, Dr. Blue, who determined through an X-ray that the mass in her abdomen was a lap sponge from the surgery with Bellina.

Romero underwent corrective surgery with a different physician to remove the sponge.

The plaintiffs settled their claims with the hospital, and the case proceeded to trial against Bellina. After a bench trial, the trial court rendered judgment in favor of the plaintiffs for $170,966.41, and Bellina filed an appeal.

In ruling against Bellina, the trial court held that a surgeon's duty to remove foreign objects placed in a patient's body is an independent, nondelegable duty. The trial court found that Bellina was 70% at fault and the nurses employed by the hospital were 30% at fault. On appeal, Bellina argued that the trial judge erred in concluding that, in Louisiana, a surgeon cannot rely on surgical nurses to count sponges to make sure none are left inside a patient. Prevailing case law in Louisiana, however, holds that a surgeon has a nondelegable duty to remove all sponges placed in a patient's body.

The Louisiana Court of Appeals held that although nurses have an independent duty, apart from the surgeon's duty, to account for the sponges, and that they can be concurrently at fault with the surgeon for leaving a sponge in the patient's body, the nurses' count is a remedial measure that cannot relieve the surgeon of his or her nondelegable duty to remove the sponge in the first instance. Bellina had an independent, nondelegable duty to remove from the patient's body the foreign substance that he had placed into her.

Current jurisprudence more accurately reflects the modern team approach to surgery, whereby the nurses' count is a remedial measure that does not discharge the surgeon's independent duty to ensure that all sponges are removed before an incision is closed.

Negligent Amputation of Infant's Finger

A nurse employed by the defendant in *Ahmed v. Children's Hospital of Buffalo*[36] amputated nearly one-third of a 1-month-old infant's index finger while cutting an IV tube with a pair of scissors. Surgery to reattach the amputated portion of the finger was unsuccessful. The plaintiffs were awarded $87,000 for past pain and suffering and $50,000 for future damages. The defendant moved to set aside the verdict and sought a new trial, claiming that damages were excessive. The trial court rejected much of the testimony presented by the plaintiffs.

An appeals court determined that it was the jury's function to assess the credibility of witnesses and to evaluate the testimony regarding the child's pain, suffering, and disability. The trial court was found to have improperly invaded the jury's province to evaluate the nature and extent of the injury. The appellate court found that the jury's award of

damages did not deviate materially from what would be reasonable compensation. The jury's verdict was reinstated.

Monitor Alarm Discontinued

In *Odom v. State Department of Health and Hospitals*,[37] the appeals court held that the decedent's cause of death was directly related to the absence of being placed under the watch of a heart monitor. Jojo was born 12 weeks prematurely at the HPL Medical Center. Jojo remained in a premature infant's nursery and was eventually placed into two different foster homes prior to his admission to Pinecrest Foster Home. While Jojo was a Pinecrest resident, Mr. and Mrs. Odom adopted Jojo. He was unable to feed himself and was nourished via a gastrostomy tube. Because he suffered from obstructive apnea, he became dependent on a trach tube.

At Pinecrest, Jojo was assigned to Home 501. While making patient rounds, Ms. Means found Jojo with his trach out of the stoma. She called for help, and Ms. Wiley, amongst others, responded. Wiley immediately took the CPR efforts under her control. She noticed that Jojo was breathless and immediately reinserted the trach. She then noticed that Jojo was still hooked to a monitor.

No one had heard the heart monitor's alarm sound. Means asserts that the monitor was on because she saw that the monitor's red lights were blinking, indicating the heart rate and breathing rate. She stated that she took the monitor's leads off of Jojo to put the monitor out of the way, but the alarm did not sound. CPR efforts continued while Jojo was placed on a stretcher and sent by ambulance to HPL. Jojo was pronounced dead at HPL's emergency department at 7:02 P.M.

The Odoms filed a petition against Pinecrest, alleging that Jojo's death was caused by the negligence and fault of Pinecrest, its servants, and employees. Judgment was for the plaintiffs. The trial court's reason for judgment was enlightening because it stated that the monitor should have been on but was, however, disconnected by the staff and this was the cause, in fact, of Jojo's injury. The appeals court found that the record supported the trial court's findings. There was overwhelming evidence upon which the trial court relied to find that the monitor had been turned off, in breach of the various physicians' orders with which the nurses should have complied. The monitor was supposed to be on Jojo to warn the nurses of any respiratory distress episodes that he might experience. A forensic pathologist's report showed the cause of Jojo's death to be hypoxia, secondary to respiratory insufficiency, secondary to apnea episodes. Thus, Jojo's cause of death was directly related to the absence of being placed under the watch of a heart monitor.

Chance of Survival Diminished

Mr. Ard, in *Ard v. East Jefferson Gen. Hosp.*,[38] began feeling nauseous. He was in pain and had shortness of breath. Although his wife rang the call bell several times, it was not until sometime later that evening that someone responded and administered medication for his nausea. The nausea continued to worsen. Mrs. Ard then noticed that her husband was having difficulty breathing. Believing that her husband was dying, she continued to call for help. She estimated that she rang the call bell for 1.25 hours before anyone responded. A code was eventually called. Unfortunately, Mr. Ard did not survive the code. There was no documentation in the medical records between 5:30 P.M. and 6:45 P.M. that would indicate any nurse or physician checked on Ard's condition. This finding collaborated Mrs. Ard's testimony regarding this time period.

A wrongful death action was filed against the hospital, and the district court granted judgment for Mrs. Ard. The hospital appealed.

Ms. Krebs, an expert in general nursing, stated that it should have been obvious to the nurses from the physicians' progress notes that the patient was a high risk for aspiration. This problem was never addressed in the nurses' care plan or in the nurses' notes.

On May 20, Ard's assigned nurse was Ms. Florscheim. Krebs stated that Florscheim did not perform a full assessment of the patient's respiratory and lung status. There was nothing in the record indicating that she completed such an evaluation after he vomited. Krebs testified that a nurse had not conduct a swallowing assessment at any time. Although Florscheim testified that she checked on the patient around 6:00 P.M., there was no documentation in the medical record.

Ms. Farris, an expert in intensive care nursing, testified for the defense. She disagreed with Krebs that there was a breach of the standard of care. However, on cross-examination, she admitted that if a patient was in the type of distress described by Mrs. Ard and no nurse checked on him for 1.25 hours, this would fall below the expected standard of care. An appeals court concluded there was ample evidence to support the trial judge's conclusion that the nursing staff breached the standard of care. Ard would have had a much better chance of survival if he had been transferred to the intensive care unit. The court raised the general damages award from $50,000 to $150,000.

Notes

1. 692 S.W.2d 329 (Mo. Ct. App. 1985).
2. 570 N.Y.S.2d 395 (N.Y. App. Div. 1991).
3. 535 N.E.2d 956 (Ill. App. Ct. 1989).
4. *Deoraj Ramlochan, as Administrator of the Estate of Karishma Ramlochan, Deceased and Deoraj Ramlochan, Individually v. Sweet P Home Care Inc., Sweet Home Care, Inc. and North Shore University Hospital*, No. 24016/09, (Queens Supreme, NY, 11-30-2012.
5. 856 P.2d 864 (Idaho 1993).
6. 947 S.W.2d 941 (Tex. Ct. App. 1997).
7. 357 N.Y.S.2d 508 (N.Y. App. Div. 1974).
8. No. 2-153/01-1019 (Iowa Ct. of App. 2002).
9. 696 P.2d 270 (Colo. 1985).
10. 144 So. 2d 249 (La. Ct. App. 1962).
11. 599 N.Y.S.2d 96 (N.Y. App. Div. 1993).
12. 742 P.2d 1087 (Okla. 1987).
13. 145 So. 2d 848 (Fla. 1933).
14. 181 A.2d 573 (Del. 1962).
15. 443 P.2d 708 (Colo. 1968).
16. 165 S.W.3d 168 (Mo. App. 2005).
17. 696 So. 2d 590 (La. App. 1997).
18. 603 So.2d 866 (1992).
19. 381 P.2d 605 (Wash. 1963).
20. 565 So. 2d 221 (Ala. 1990).
21. 597 N.E.2d 1110 (Ohio Ct. App. 1991).
22. 403 S.E.2d 582 (N.C. Ct. App. 1991).
23. 333 P.2d 29 (Cal. Ct. App. 1958).
24. 422 N.W.2d 600 (S.D. 1988).
25. 849 S.W.2d 564 (Ky. Ct. App. 1993).
26. 589 A.2d 653 (N.J. Super. App. Div. 1991).
27. *Id.* at 655.
28. 236 S.E.2d 213 (W. Va. 1977).
29. 262 So. 2d 303 (Ala. 1972).
30. *Leblanc v. Walsh*, 922 So.2d 1248 (La. App. 2006).
31. 523 P.2d 320 (Kan. 1974).
32. 931 F.2d 116 (1st Cir. 1991).
33. 151 N.C. App. 139, 565 S.E.2d 254 (2002).
34. 809 So. 2d 611 (2001).
35. 798 So. 2d 279 (2001).
36. 661 N.Y.S.2d 164 (N.Y. App. Div. 1997).
37. 733 So. 2d 91 (La. App. 3 Cir. 1999).
38. 636 So. 2d 1042 (La. Ct. App. 1994).

My life is my message.

—Mahatma Gandhi

11

Hospital Departments and Allied Health Professionals

Learning Objectives

The reader upon completion of this chapter will be able to:

- Describe a variety of negligent errors by allied health professionals.
- Discuss the purpose of certification, licensure, and reasons for revocation of licenses.
- Describe helpful advice for caregivers.

 NEWSPAPER CLIPPINGS: Dying at the Hospital's Door: A Child Lost, Troubling Questions*

While communications were breaking down among a child's parent, a 9-1-1 dispatcher, and hospital personnel, the child's condition was quickly deteriorating. Twelve hours later, the 3-year-old girl was brain dead, and she expired 3 days later. Although there are several central issues involved in this story, the frustrating dialogue that took place is particularly important.

The 9-1-1 dispatcher answers the phone.

DISPATCHER: 9-1-1; is this an emergency?

PARENT: Yes, it's an emergency. I need an ambulance. I have a 3-year-old daughter that's passed out on me.

DISPATCHER: OK. Where do you need the ambulance?

PARENT: I'm right in front of the emergency exit in . . . Hospital.

DISPATCHER: You're right in front of the emergency exit?

PARENT: Yes, that's exactly where I am. And they won't do a . . . thing in this place. The dispatcher phones the hospital emergency department:

DISPATCHER: There's a guy that says he's right outside your emergency exit. And he needs an ambulance. He says his 3-year old daughter is passed out.

HOSPITAL: This is a guy who wants to be seen quicker. We're busy—so he figured if he called 9-1-1 he'd be seen quicker.

DISPATCHER: Well, he's saying he needs an ambulance right away. Is somebody going to go out there, or not?

HOSPITAL: There's nothing we can do.

The parents were offered an out-of-court settlement totaling $200,000. This tragedy might have been prevented if the patient had been screened and triaged by a person competent to determine the patient's need for immediate care. Failure to assign triage responsibility to a competent individual can lead to lawsuits that involve not only the hospital, but also the supervisor who assigns responsibilities to unqualified staff members.

*Miami Herald, April 16, 1995 by Ronnie Green. Copyright 1995 by Miami Herald. Reproduced with permission of Miami Herald in the format Textbook via Copyright Clearance Center.

This chapter presents an overview of professional ethics and lawsuits faced by a variety of healthcare professionals. Healthcare professionals are held to the prevailing standard of care required in their profession, which includes proper assessments, reassessments, diagnosis, treatment, and follow-up care. It should be noted that the following legal cases have application to all healthcare professionals.

PROFESSIONAL ETHICS

Professional ethics are standards or codes of conduct established by the membership of a specific profession. Codes of ethics are created in response to actual or anticipated ethical conflicts. It is only in the context of real life and real ethical ambiguity that the codes take on any meaning.

> Codes of ethics and case studies need each other. Without guiding principles, case studies are difficult to evaluate and analyze; without context, codes of ethics are incomprehensible. The best way to use these codes is to apply them to a variety of situations and see what results. It is from the back and forth evaluation of the codes and the cases that thoughtful moral judgments can best arise.[1]

The contents of codes of ethics vary depending on the risks associated with a particular profession. For example, ethical codes for psychologists define relationships with clients in greater depth because of the personal one-to-one relationship they have with their clients. Laboratory technicians and technologists, on the other hand, generally have minimal personal contact with patients but can have a significant impact on their care. In their ethical code, laboratory technologists pledge accuracy and reliability in the performance of tests. The importance of this pledge was borne out in a March 11, 2004, report by the *Baltimore Sun*, whereby state health officials discovered that a hospital's laboratory personnel overrode controls in testing equipment showing results that might be in error but mailed them to patients anyway.

The following cases illustrate some examples of ethical misconduct involving health professionals.

- The nurse's license in *Williams v. Bd. of Exam'rs for Prof. Nurses*[2] was suspended for falsifying patient records.
- The defendant–psychologist in *Gilmore v. Board of Psychologist Examiners*[3] had her license revoked by the board of psychologist examiners for sexual improprieties.
- A minister was paid by an attorney to attend a hospital chaplain's course in furtherance of a plan by which the minister could gain access to the emergency areas of a hospital to solicit patients and their families for the purpose of aiding the attorney in gaining legal cases based on negligence and malpractice. Disbarment was decided to be appropriate with respect to the attorney who had hired the minister as a paralegal.[4]

CHIROPRACTOR

A chiropractor is required to exercise the same degree of care, judgment, and skill exercised by other reasonable chiropractors under like or similar circumstances. Chiropractors have a duty to determine if a patient is treatable through chiropractic means and to refrain from chiropractic treatment when a reasonable chiropractor would or should be aware that a patient's condition would most likely not respond to chiropractic treatment. Failure to conform to the standard of care can result in liability for any injuries suffered.

EMERGENCY DEPARTMENT

NEWSPAPER CLIPPINGS: Jury Returns Largest Medical Malpractice Verdict, But Tort Reform Strikes Again!

A man arrived at the ER with severe neck pain and numbness in his arms and legs. A doctor diagnosed his condition as neck strain and released the man from the hospital. A few hours later, the man became completely paralyzed from the chest down. He returned to the hospital where he was left untreated for almost two more hours. He filed a medical malpractice lawsuit alleging negligence. According to evidence presented at trial, the man suffered from a herniated disk that was compressing his spinal cord and causing progressive neurologic injury. Now, he will spend the rest of his life in a wheelchair; he is unable to walk, run, ride a bike, or work. The jury awarded the plaintiff $15 million; $10 million of which was for non-economic damages.

—*Mark Bello*, The Legal Examiner, *December 30, 2012*[5]

Emergency departments are high-risk areas that tend to be a main source of lawsuits for hospitals. The courts recognize a general duty to care for all patients presenting themselves to hospital emergency departments.

Hospitals under the Emergency Medical Treatment and Active Labor Act (EMTALA) discussed in this text are required to provide either stabilizing treatment or appropriate transfer for patients with emergency medical conditions. Not only must hospitals accept, treat, and transfer emergency department patients if such is necessary for the patients' well-being, the hospital must adhere to the standards of care they have set for themselves, as well as to national standards.

Objectives of Emergency Care

The objectives of emergency care are the same regardless of severity. No matter how seemingly trivial the complaint, each patient must be examined. Treatment must begin as rapidly as possible, function to the extent possible must be maintained or restored, and scarring and deformity minimized. Every patient must be treated regardless of ability to pay.

> As the Sixth Circuit points out, there are many reasons other than indigence that might lead a hospital to give less than standard attention to a person who arrives at the emergency room doors. These might include: prejudice against the race, sex, or ethnic group of the patient; distaste for the patient's condition (e.g., acquired immune deficiency syndrome [AIDS] patients); personal dislike or antagonism between medical personnel and the patient; disapproval of the patient's occupation; or political or cultural opposition. If a hospital refuses treatment to persons for any of these reasons, or gives cursory treatment, the evil inflicted would be quite akin to that discussed by Congress in the legislative history, and the patient would fall squarely in the statutory language.[6]

No Duty to Patient Who Left

The patient and her sister became upset with the care offered, left the hospital, and went home without proper discharge. The patient died 2 days later at home. The county coroner's office initiated a postmortem examination and determined that the patient died from meningoencephalitis. The patient made a conscious decision to leave the hospital on her own accord without the knowledge or permission of the hospital. She did not tell the doctors, nurses, or anyone else that she was leaving the emergency room; she just left without informing anyone.

In a wrongful death medical malpractice action alleging negligence, the trial court properly granted the hospital summary judgment because under Ohio law, an emergency room nurse has no duty to interfere with a patient who refuses treatment and decides to leave the emergency department without notifying hospuitl staff.[7]

Failure to Admit

Roy went to the emergency department complaining of chest pains. The attending physician, Dr. Gupta, upon examination, performed an electrocardiogram that showed ischemic changes indicating a lack of oxygen to the heart tissue. He applied a transdermal nitroglycerin patch and gave Roy a prescription for nitroglycerin. After monitoring her progress, he sent her home. Several hours later, she returned to the emergency department, experiencing more chest pains. Three days later, Roy died of a massive myocardial infarction.

Gupta was found negligent in failing to hospitalize Roy. The trial court found that had Roy been hospitalized on her first visit, her chances of survival would have been greater. On appeal, the Louisiana Court of Appeal held that Gupta was negligent by failing to advise Roy that she should be hospitalized for chest pains. All of the medical expert witnesses, except Dr. Kilpatrick, a defense witness, testified that Roy should have been admitted. Kilpatrick testified that such a decision varied greatly among physicians. The trial court disregarded his testimony because of his hostile responses to questioning.

The trial judge was not convinced by Gupta's explanation of why Roy was not hospitalized. He focused on Gupta's failure to have X-rays taken during the first visit, which might have allowed him to determine whether the ischemic changes were due to her hypertension medication or indicated the beginning of a heart attack. The relative simplicity of the technique and its obvious availability gave credence to the trial judge's belief that the requisite attention was not paid to Roy's complaints. The law does not require proof that proper treatment would have been the difference between Roy's living or dying. It requires only proof that proper treatment would have improved her chances of survival.[8]

Documentation Sparse and Contradictory

An ambulance team found 26-year-old Feeney intoxicated, sitting on a street corner in South Boston. Feeney admitted to alcohol abuse but denied that he used drugs. His condition interfered with conducting an examination, and he was transported by ambulance to the hospital.

Documentation at the hospital between 10:45 P.M. and 11:30 P.M. was sparse and contradictory. The minimum standard for nursing care required monitoring the patient's respiratory rate every 15 minutes. It was doubtful that this occurred. This monitoring would have more likely permitted the nursing staff to observe changes in the patient's breathing patterns and/or the onset of respiratory arrest.

The emergency department physician failed to evaluate the patient and to initiate care within the first few minutes of Feeney's entry into the emergency facility. The emergency physician had an obligation to determine who was waiting for physician care and how critical was the need for care. Had the required standard of care been followed, respiratory arrest might have been averted. According to the autopsy report, respiratory arrest was the sole cause of death.

The failure to provide adequate care rationally could be attributed to the staff nurse assigned to the area in which the patient lay, as well as to the physicians in charge. The hospital was implicated on the basis of the acts or omission of its staff.[9]

Emergency Medical Treatment Under EMTALA

In 1986, Congress passed the Emergency Medical Treatment and Active Labor Act (EMTALA) that forbids Medicare-participating hospitals from "dumping" patients out of emergency departments. The act provides that:

> [i]n the case of a hospital that has a hospital emergency department, if any individual . . . comes to the emergency department and a request is made on the individual's behalf for examination or treatment for a medical condition, the hospital must provide for an appropriate medical screening examination within the capability of the hospital emergency department, including ancillary services routinely available to the emergency department, to determine whether or not an emergency medical condition . . . exists.[10]

Under EMTALA, hospital emergency rooms are subject to two principal obligations, commonly referred to as (1) the appropriate medical screening requirement and (2) the stabilization requirement. The appropriate medical screening requirement obligates hospital emergency rooms to provide an appropriate medical screening to any individual seeking treatment to determine whether the individual has an emergency medical condition. If an emergency medical condition exists, the hospital is required to provide stabilization treatment before transferring the individual.

Stabilizing the Patient

Patients can be transferred only after having been medically screened by a physician, stabilized, and cleared for transfer by the receiving institution. *Stabilized* means "with respect to an emergency medical condition . . . to provide such medical treatment of the condition as may be necessary to assure, within reasonable medical probability, that no material deterioration of the condition is likely to result from or to occur during the transfer of the individual from a facility."[11]

Transfer Prior to Stabilizing Patient

The plaintiff in *Huckaby v. East Ala. Med. Ctr.*[12] brought an action against the hospital alleging that the patient was transferred from the hospital's emergency department before her condition was stabilized. The patient went to the hospital, suffering from a stroke. The complaint alleged that the patient's condition was critical and materially deteriorating. The attending emergency department physician, Dr. Wheat, informed the patient's family that she needed the services of a neurosurgeon but that the hospital had problems in getting neurosurgeons to accept patients. Upon the recommendation of Wheat, the patient was transferred to another hospital where she expired soon after arrival. The plaintiff alleged that Wheat did not inform the family regarding the risks of transfer and that the transfer of the patient in an unstable condition was the proximate cause of her death. The U.S. District Court held that the plaintiff stated a cause of action under EMTALA for which monetary relief could be granted.

Inappropriate Transfer

In *Burditt v. U.S. Department of Health and Human Services*,[13] EMTALA was violated by Dr. Burditt, a physician, when he ordered a woman with dangerously high blood pressure (210/130) and in active labor with ruptured membranes to be transferred from the emergency department of one hospital to another hospital 170 miles away. The physician was assessed a penalty of $20,000. Dr. Louis Sullivan, secretary of the Department of Health and Human Services at that time, issued this statement:

> This decision sends a message to physicians everywhere that they need to provide quality care to everyone in need of emergency treatment who comes to a hospital. This is a significant opinion and we are pleased with the result.[14]

The American Public Health Association, in filing an amicus curiae, advised the appeals court that if Burditt wants to ensure that he will never be asked to treat a patient not of his choosing, then he ought to vote with his feet by affiliating only with hospitals that do not accept Medicare funds or do not have an emergency department.

Wrong Record—Fatal Mistake

> *Dr. McManus had not realized that he had made a grave and fatal mistake. Dr. McManus had looked at the wrong chart. . . .*

Terry Trahan, in *Trahan v. McManus*,[15] was taken to the hospital after being injured in an automobile accident. Terry's parents were informed about the accident and asked to come to the hospital. Mrs. Trahan drove to the hospital and consulted with Dr. McManus, the emergency department physician who treated Terry. Dr. McManus assured Mrs. Trahan that it would be all right to take her son home because there was nothing more that could be done for him at the hospital.

Upon ordering discharge, however, Dr. McManus had not realized that he had made a *grave and fatal mistake.* Dr. McManus had looked at the wrong chart in determining Terry's status. Dr. McManus had looked at a chart that indicated that the patient's vital signs were normal. In fact, the correct chart showed that Terry had three broken ribs as a result of the accident. His blood pressure was 90/60 when he was admitted to the emergency department. Forty-five minutes after being admitted, Terry's blood pressure had dropped to 80/50, and his respiration rate had doubled. Terry's vital signs clearly indicated that he was suffering from internal hemorrhaging.

In the 7 hours following his discharge, Terry's condition continued to worsen. Terry complained to his parents about severe pain. He could not turn from his back to his side without the aid of his father. Several hours after being brought home from the hospital, Mr. Trahan noticed that Terry's abdomen was swelling. Mrs. Trahan immediately called the hospital. Mr. Trahan asked Terry if he wanted to sit up. Terry replied, "Well, we can try." Those were Terry's final words. Terry slumped in his father's arms and his head fell forward. When Mr. Trahan attempted to lift Terry's head, Terry's face was white. Mr. Trahan immediately laid his son down on the bed, realizing for the first time that his son was not breathing and had no pulse. He attempted CPR as Mrs. Trahan called for an ambulance. Mr. Trahan continued CPR until the ambulance arrived a few minutes later. Terry was pronounced dead on arrival at the hospital.

Subsequently, during a medical review panel proceeding in which the Trahans participated, Dr. McManus admitted liability by tendering his $100,000 limit of liability, pursuant to the Medical Malpractice Act.

A jury returned a verdict absolving Dr. McManus of any liability, finding that Terry's injuries would have occurred despite the physician's failure to use reasonable care in his treatment of Terry. The Trahans appealed. On appeal, the jury's determination was found to be clearly erroneous when it concluded that the physician's actions were not the cause-in-fact of Terry's death. The record is replete with testimony, including Dr. McManus's own admissions, that

he acted negligently when he discharged Terry, that his actions led to Terry's death, and that there was treatment available that could have made a difference.

Duty to Contact On-Call Physician

Hospitals are expected to notify specialty on-call physicians when their particular skills are required in the emergency department. A physician who is on call and fails to respond to a request to attend a patient can be liable for injuries suffered by the patient because of his or her failure to respond.

Timely Response Required

Hospitals are not only required to care for emergency patients, but they also are required to do so in a timely fashion. In *Marks v. Mandel*,[16] a Florida trial court was found to have erred in directing a verdict against the plaintiff. It was decided that the relevant inquiry in this case was whether the hospital and the supervisor should bear ultimate responsibility for failure of the specialty on-call system to function properly. Jury issues had been raised by evidence that the standard for on-call systems was to have a specialist attending the patient within a reasonable time period of being called.

Failure to Contact On-Call Physician

In *Thomas v. Corso*,[17] a patient had been brought to the hospital emergency department after being struck by a car. A physician did not attend to him even though he had dangerously low blood pressure and was in shock. There was some telephone contact between the nurse in the emergency department and the physician who was providing on-call coverage. The physician did not act upon the hospital's call for assistance until the patient was close to death. Expert testimony was not necessary to establish what common sense made evident: the patient who was struck by a car may have suffered internal injuries and should have been evaluated and treated by a physician. Lack of attention in such cases is not reasonable care by any standard. The concurrent negligence of the nurse, who failed to contact the on-call physician after the patient's condition worsened, did not relieve the physician of liability for his failure to respond to his on-call duty. Because of the nurse's negligence, the hospital is liable under the doctrine of respondeat superior.

Failure to Respond to Call

Treatment rendered by hospitals is expected to be commensurate with that available in the same or similar communities or in hospitals generally. In *Fjerstad v. Knutson*,[18] the South Dakota Supreme Court found that a hospital could be held liable for the failure of an on-call physician to respond to a call from the emergency department. An intern who attempted to contact the on-call physician and was unable to do so for 3½ hours treated and discharged the patient. The hospital was responsible for assigning on-call physicians and ensuring that they would be available when called. The patient died during the night in a motel room as a result of asphyxia resulting from a swelling of the larynx, tonsils, and epiglottis that blocked the trachea. Testimony indicated that the emergency department's on-call physician was to be available for consultation and was assigned that duty by the hospital. Expert testimony also was offered that someone with the decedent's symptoms should have been hospitalized and that such care could have saved the decedent's life. The jury believed that an experienced physician would have taken the necessary steps to save the decedent's life.

Notice of Inability to Respond to Call

In *Millard v. Corrado*,[19] the Missouri Appellate Court found that on-call physicians owe a duty to provide reasonable notice when they will be unavailable to respond to calls. Physicians who cannot fulfill their on-call responsibilities must provide notice as soon as practicable when they learn of the circumstances that will render them unavailable. Imposing a duty requiring on-call physicians to notify hospital staff of their unavailability does not place an unreasonable burden on them. In this case, a mere telephone call would have significantly reduced the 4-hour time period between the accident and life-saving surgery. Whatever slight inconvenience may be associated with notifying the hospital of the on-call physician's availability is trivial when compared to the substantial risk to patients.

Telephone Medicine Costly

The diagnosis and treatment of patients by telephone can be costly. As noted in *Futch v. Attwood*,[20] the record shows that on the morning of February 28, 1990, Lauren, a 4-year-old diabetic child, awoke her mother, Wanda. She had vomited two or three times and her glucose reading was high. Wanda administered Lauren's morning insulin and intended to feed her a light breakfast before bringing her to see Dr. Attwood, a pediatrician, at about 9:45 A.M. According to the plaintiff, Dr. Attwood did not check Lauren's blood sugar level or her urine to determine whether ketones were present. If Dr. Attwood had done so, Lauren's condition could have been quickly corrected by the simple administration of insulin. Instead of administering insulin,

however, Dr. Attwood prescribed the use of Phenergan suppositories to address Lauren's nausea symptoms. Lauren's symptoms of nausea continued, and she was taken to the hospital emergency department. Hospital personnel contacted Dr. Attwood, who returned the call and again prescribed a Phenergan injection. Dr. Attwood did not go to the hospital and had not been given Lauren's vital signs when he suggested such an injection. Further, he failed to order any blood or urine tests.

Wanda returned home with Lauren at approximately 8:00 P.M. and put her to bed, waking her around midnight to administer the prescribed medication. Lauren woke but went back to sleep. Early the next morning, Wanda awoke and found Lauren with labored breathing. While attempting to wake up the 4-year-old, the only responses, according to plaintiff's brief, were "huh," followed by moaning. Wanda telephoned Dr. Attwood and informed him of her daughter's far-worsened condition. Dr. Attwood admitted Lauren to the hospital at 6:30 A.M. that morning.

Hospital records revealed that Lauren's glucose level was 507 at the time of admission with her blood acid revealing diabetic ketoacidosis. At approximately 9:13 A.M., Lauren went into respiratory arrest as a result of her brain swelling with rupturing into the opening at the base of her neck. Lauren was immediately transported by helicopter to Children's Hospital in New Orleans and diagnosed with ketoacidotic coma, cerebral edema, and bilateral pulmonary edema. She was pronounced dead at 5:07 P.M. on March 2, 1990.

The mother witnessed her daughter's decline in health, and her protracted wait was punctuated only by various traumatic episodes: Lauren's respiratory intubation; her respiratory failure and consequent code blue; numerous medical staff scurrying in and out to see Lauren behind doors closed to Wanda; and, finally, Wanda being asked to consider whether she would prefer to "pull the plug" on her daughter or to watch her linger indefinitely. Wanda decided to let her go and did. For Wanda, the period following Lauren's death has been marked by the inevitable sense of loss of a daughter and by the guilt of a mother whose unrelenting loss compels her to ask what she might have done differently to save her child's life.

Prevention of Lawsuits in the Emergency Department

Implementing and enforcing some fundamental common-sense policies, procedures, and programs can reduce emergency department lawsuits by:

- triaging and treating seriously ill patients first;
- treating each patient courteously and promptly;

- treating all patients regardless of ability to pay;
- establishing a mandatory on-call list for specialists;
- requiring consultations when determined necessary;
- communicating with the patient and the patient's family to ensure that a complete and accurate picture of the patient's symptoms and complaints is obtained;
- ensuring all caregivers are effectively communicating with one another;
- not taking lightly any patient's complaint (this may well be the single most fatal mistake in emergency departments);
- accepting the concept that all patients, regardless of ailment, must receive care;
- requiring that hospitals determine what types of patients and levels of care they can safely address;
- knowing when to admit or stabilize and transfer a patient;
- providing continuing emergency medicine education programs for all staff members; and
- requiring mandatory administrative rounds to the emergency department by the risk manager, medical director, chief nursing officer, and chief executive officer.

Emergency Rooms Vital to Public Safety

McBride, in *Simmons v. Tuomey Regional Medical Center*,[21] was involved in an accident while driving his moped. Upon learning of the accident, Simmons, McBride's daughter, rushed to the scene where she found emergency service personnel attending to an injury to the back of her father's head. McBride was taken to Tuomey where Simmons signed an admission form for her father. The admission form contained the following provision:

> The Physicians Practicing in this Emergency Room are not Employees of the Tuomey Regional Medical Center. They are Independent Physicians, as are All Physicians Practicing in this Hospital.

While in Tuomey's emergency department, Drs. Cooper and Anderson examined McBride. Despite McBride's confused state, the physicians decided to treat his contusions and release him from the hospital. The physicians, apparently attributing McBride's confusion to intoxication, did not treat his head injury.

The next day, McBride returned to Tuomey where his head injury was diagnosed as a subdural hematoma. Ultimately, McBride was transported to Richland Memorial Hospital. Approximately 6 weeks later, McBride died of complications from the hematoma.

When Simmons brought suit, Tuomey moved for summary judgment by alleging that it was not liable because the physicians were independent contractors. Tuomey relied on its June 1987 contract with Coastal Physicians Services, which set forth the procedures by which Coastal would provide emergency department physicians to Tuomey. The carefully worded contract referred numerous times to physicians as independent contractors and stated that Tuomey agreed not to exercise any control over the means, manner, or methods by which any physician supplied by Coastal carries out his duties. The trial court accorded great weight to the Coastal–Tuomey contract when it granted Tuomey's motion for summary judgment. Simmons appealed, arguing that the trial court erred in granting summary judgment on the issues of actual agency, apparent agency, and nondelegable duty.

Few things are more comforting in today's society than knowing that immediate medical care is available around the clock at any hospital. As the Texas Court of Appeals astutely observed:

> Emergency rooms are aptly named and vital to public safety. There exists no other place to find immediate medical care. The dynamics that drive paying patients to a hospital's emergency rooms are known well. Either a sudden injury occurs, a child breaks his arm or an individual suffers a heart attack, or an existing medical condition worsens, a diabetic lapses into a coma, demanding immediate medical attention at the nearest emergency room. The catch phrase in legal nomenclature, "time is of the essence," takes on real meaning. Generally, one cannot choose to pass by the nearest emergency room, and after arrival, it would be improvident to depart in hope of finding one that provides services through employees rather than independent contractors.[22]

The public not only relies on the medical care rendered by emergency departments, but it also considers the hospital as a single entity providing all of its medical services. A set of commentators observed:

> [T]he hospital itself has come to be perceived as the provider of medical services. According to this view, patients come to the hospital to be cured, and the doctors who practice there are the hospital's instrumentalities, regardless of the nature of the private arrangements between the hospital and the physician. Whether or not this perception is accurate seemingly matters little when weighed against the momentum of changing public perception and attendant public policy.[23]

Public reliance and public perceptions, as well as the regulations imposed on hospitals, have created an absolute duty for hospitals to provide competent medical care in their emergency departments. Hospitals contributed to the shift in public perception through commercial advertisements. By actively soliciting business, hospitals effectively removed themselves from the sterile world of altruistic agencies. The Alaska Supreme Court, the first American court to recognize a nondelegable duty in the hospital context, wrote:

> Not only is [finding a nondelegable duty] consonant with the public perception of the hospital as a multifaceted healthcare facility responsible for the quality of medical care and treatment rendered, it also treats tort liability in the medical arena in a manner that is consistent with the commercialization of American medicine.[24]

Given the cumulative public policies surrounding the operation of emergency departments and the legal requirement that hospitals provide emergency services, hospitals must be accountable in tort for the actions of caregivers who work in their emergency departments. The court in this case agreed with a New York court, which wrote:

> In this Court's opinion it is public policy, and not traditional rules of the law of agency or the law of torts, which should underlie the decision to hold hospitals liable for malpractice which occurs in their emergency rooms. In this regard the observation of former U.S. Supreme Court Justice Oliver Wendell Holmes is apt: "The true grounds of decision are consideration of policy and of social advantage, and it is vain to suppose that solutions can be attained merely by logic and the general propositions of law which nobody disputes. Propositions as to public policy rarely are unanimously accepted, and still more rarely, if ever, are capable of unanswerable proof."[25]

The appeals court in *Tuomey* held that hospitals have a nondelegable duty to render competent service to the patients of their emergency departments.

LABORATORY

An organization must provide for clinical laboratory services to meet the needs of its patients. Each healthcare organization is responsible for the quality and timeliness of the services provided. Because it is often necessary to contract out certain tests, the organization should be sure that it is contracting for services with a reputable licensed laboratory.

An organization's laboratory provides data that are vital to a patient's treatment. Among its many functions, the laboratory monitors therapeutic ranges, measures blood levels for toxicity, places and monitors instrumentation on patient units, provides education for the nursing staff (e.g., glucose

monitoring), provides valuable data utilized in research studies, provides data on the most effective and economical antibiotic for treating patients, serves in a consultation role, and provides valuable data as to the nutritional needs of patients.

Failure to Follow Recommended Transfusion Protocol

Fowler, in *Fowler v. Bossano*,[26] gave birth to twins on March 26, 1996. Due to premature birth, the twins were transferred to LCMH and were cared for by Bossano, a neonatologist. The infants experienced complications and problems associated with premature birth, including respiratory and feeding difficulties. The twins' treatment included blood transfusions. Bossano stated that the twins proceeded through these difficulties and began to make progress, but then Ryan (one of the twins) took a turn for the worse. According to Bossano, Ryan's condition generally continued to deteriorate until he died on May 25. Bossano stated that the most likely cause of death was a viral infection. At his urging, an autopsy was performed, and the pathologist found the presence of cytomegalovirus inclusion (CMV) disease. Bossano stated that he learned that the lab at the hospital did not, at that time, screen for the presence of the virus in the blood used for transfusions.

The Fowlers decided to file suit naming both Bossano and the hospital as defendants. They sought damages associated with a survival action and those for wrongful death. The jury found for the plaintiffs. LCMH breached the applicable standard of care by failing to test the blood used for this transfusion for CMV. The evidence presented was sufficient to support the jury's determination that the hospital's breach of the standard of care was the cause of Ryan's death.

Mismatched Blood

A laboratory technician in *Barnes Hospital v. Missouri Commission on Human Rights*[27] had been discharged because of inferior work performance. On three occasions, the employee allegedly mismatched blood. The employee then filed a complaint with the Commission on Human Rights, alleging racial discrimination as a reason for his discharge by the hospital. The hospital appealed, and the circuit court reversed the commission's order. The technician appealed to the Missouri Supreme Court, which held that the evidence did not support the ruling of racial discrimination by the Missouri Commission on Human Rights.

Failure to Detect Changes in Pap Smear

The patient had several gynecological examinations, including Pap smears, in 1977, 1978, 1980, 1984, 1986, and

1987. The patient's physician performed the examinations. Specimens for the Pap test were submitted to a laboratory for evaluation. The laboratory procedure included a clerk who assigned each specimen a number when it was received. A cytotechnologist would then screen the specimen. If the specimen was determined to be abnormal, a pathologist marked it for review. Out of the Pap tests that were determined to be normal, only 1 in 10 was actually viewed by a pathologist. The pathologist made recommendations based on the classification of the Pap tests. A biopsy would be recommended if a Pap test was determined to be Class IV.

Except for the Pap test in 1987, which showed premalignant cellular changes, all of the patient's other Pap tests were determined to be negative. In 1986, the laboratory made a notation to the patient's physician that "moderate inflammation" was present. The patient's physician, who was treating her with antibiotics for a foot inflammation, thought that the medication would also treat the other inflammation. In September 1987, the patient returned to her physician complaining of pain, erratic periods, and tiredness. After completing a physical, her physician took a Pap test, which he sent to the laboratory. He also referred her to a gynecologist. The pathologist recommended a biopsy. Biopsies and further physical examinations revealed squamous cell carcinoma that had spread to her pelvic bones. Her Pap tests were reexamined by the laboratory, which reported that the 1986 smear showed that malignancy was highly likely. The patient was referred to the University of Minnesota to determine whether she was a viable candidate for radiation treatment. The cancer, however, had spread, and the patient was not considered a candidate for radiation treatment because she had no chance of survival. When the university reviewed all of the available slides, they found cellular changes back to 1984.

The patient sued in 1988, alleging that the laboratory failed to detect and report cellular changes in her Pap tests in time to prevent the spread of the cancer. Before trial, the patient died. Her husband and sister were substituted as plaintiffs, and the complaint was amended to include a wrongful death action. After trial, a jury awarded $3.7 million in damages, which were reduced to $1 million by the circuit court. The jury found against the laboratory, and the laboratory appealed.

The South Dakota Supreme Court upheld the jury verdict and restored the $3.7 million damage award. The court determined that evidence relating to negligence claims pertaining to Pap tests taken more than 2 years before filing the action were admissible because the patient had a continuing relationship with the clinical laboratory as a result of her physician submitting her Pap tests to the laboratory over a period of time.[28]

MEDICAL ASSISTANT

A *medical assistant* is an unlicensed person who provides administrative, clerical, and/or technical support to a licensed practitioner. A licensed practitioner is generally required to be physically present in the treatment facility, medical office, or ambulatory facility when a medical assistant is performing procedures. Employment of medical assistants is expected to grow much faster than the average for all occupations as the health services industry expands. This growth is due in part to technological advances in medicine and a growing and aging population. Increasing use of medical assistants in the rapidly growing healthcare industry will most likely result in continuing employment growth for the occupation.

Medical assistants work in physicians' offices, clinics, nursing homes, and ambulatory care settings. The duties of medical assistants vary from office to office, depending on the location and size of the practice and the practitioner's specialty. In small practices, medical assistants usually are generalists, handling both administrative and clinical duties. Those in large practices tend to specialize in a particular area, under supervision. Administrative duties often include answering telephones, greeting patients, updating and filing patients' medical records, filling out insurance forms, handling correspondence, scheduling appointments, arranging for hospital admission and laboratory services, and handling billing and bookkeeping. Clinical duties vary according to state law and include assisting in taking medical histories, recording vital signs, explaining treatment procedures to patients, preparing patients for examination, and assisting the practitioner during examinations.

Poor Communications

In 1987, the patient Follett—plaintiff in *Follett v. Davis*[29] had her first office visit with Dr. Davis. In the spring of 1988, Follett discovered a lump in her right breast and made an appointment to see Davis; however, the clinic had no record of her appointment. The clinic's employees directed her to radiology for a mammogram. Davis or any other physician at the clinic did not offer Follett an examination nor was she scheduled for an examination as a follow-up to the mammogram. A technician examined Follett's breast and confirmed the presence of a lump in her right breast. After the mammogram, clinic employees told her that she would hear from Davis if there were any problems with her mammogram.

The radiologist explained in his deposition that the mammogram was not normal. Davis reviewed the mammogram report and considered it to be negative for malignancy. He was unaware about the lump in the patient's breast, and there was no evidence that clinic employees informed him about it. The clinic, including Davis, never contacted Follett about her lump or the mammogram. On April 6, 1990, Follett called the clinic and was told that there was nothing to worry about unless she heard from Davis. On September 24, 1990, Follett returned to the clinic after she had developed pain associated with the lump. A mammogram performed on that day gave results consistent with cancer. Three days later, Davis made an appointment for Follett with a clinic surgeon for a biopsy and treatment. Davis subsequently transferred her care to other physicians. Follett's biopsy had confirmed the diagnosis of cancer in October 1990.

Follett filed a lawsuit and the trial court granted summary judgment to Davis on the grounds that Follett failed to file her complaint within the applicable statute of limitations and she appealed.

The court of appeals determined that the evidence demonstrated that, had clinic procedures been properly followed, Davis or another physician at the clinic would have had made an accurate diagnosis. Follett timely filed her proposed complaint within 2 years of her last visits to Dr. Davis and the clinic. The trial court therefore improperly granted summary judgment.

NUTRITIONAL SERVICES

NEWSPAPER CLIPPINGS: Malnutrition: A Serious Concern for Hospitalized Patients

Today, malnutrition in hospitals remains a serious issue. It occurs worldwide and affects patients of all ages—from infants in the neonatal intensive care unit (ICU) to geriatric patients. 1-11 RDs have the ability to identify nutritional problems more readily than other healthcare professionals and are critical to the proper diagnosis, treatment, and prevention of malnutrition.

—*Theresa A. Fessler, MS, RD, CNSD,*
Today's Dietitian, *July 2008*

Healthcare organizations are expected to provide patients with diets that meet their individual needs. Failure to do so can lead to negligence suits.

Malnutrition

The daughter of the deceased in *Lambert v. Beverly Enterprises, Inc.*[30] filed an action claiming that her father had been mistreated. The deceased allegedly suffered malnutrition as a direct result of the acts or omissions of personnel, and that the plaintiff's father suffered actual damages that included substantial medical expenses and mental anguish due to the injuries he sustained. A motion to dismiss the case was denied.

PARAMEDIC

NEWSPAPER CLIPPINGS: Chicago City Council Approves $1.75M Settlement in Ambulance Case

The Chicago City Council today approved a $1.75 million settlement with the family of a 13-year-old girl who died a decade ago after city paramedics allegedly botched her care amid an asthma attack.

Paramedics in July 2002 incorrectly inserted a tube meant to help Arielle Starks breathe, said Jeffrey Levine, deputy corporation counsel.

—*Hal Dardick,* Chicago Tribune, *February 15, 2012*

Many states have enacted legislation that provides civil immunity to paramedics who render emergency lifesaving services. Immunity does not, however, extend to negligent acts.

Wrong Dosage Administered

In *Riffe v. Vereb Ambulance Service, Inc.*,[31] a wrongful death action was filed by appellants against Vereb Ambulance Service, St. Francis Hospital, and Custozzo. The complaint alleged that, while responding to an emergency call, defendant Custozzo, an emergency medical technician employed by Vereb, began administering lidocaine to Anderson as ordered over the telephone by the medical command physician at the defendant hospital. While in route to the hospital, Anderson was administered lidocaine 44 times the normal dosage. Consequently, normal heart function was not restored, and Anderson was pronounced dead at the hospital shortly thereafter.

The superior court held that the liability of medical technicians could not be imputed to the hospital. The court noted the practical impossibility of the hospital carrying ultimate responsibility for the quality of care and treatment given patients by emergency medical services (EMS).

Patient Refuses Transport and Expires

The deceased's parents in *Lemann v. Essen Lane Daiquiris*[32] filed a wrongful death action after paramedics failed to transport their son (Parker Lemann) to the hospital for evaluation after they had treated him following a fight in the parking lot of a bar. It was determined that the parents failed to establish that the paramedics breached their duty to care when they did not transport their son to the hospital. Police officers testified that Parker was intoxicated, had slurred speech, and erratic behavior. The paramedics had testified that they found Parker to be alert and oriented. In addition, he twice refused to be transported to the hospital and signed a waiver form that acknowledged his refusal to the paramedics to transport Parker to the hospital.

PHARMACY

NEWSPAPER CLIPPINGS: FD Finds Safety Problems at Specialized Pharmacies

Federal inspectors have found dozens of potentially dangerous safety problems at 30 specialized pharmacies, months after tainted steroid shots made by a Massachusetts pharmacy triggered the worst drug disaster in decades.

· · ·

FDA officials say the inspection show that compounders, in many cases, are failing to ensure the safety of their products, despite months of stepped-up scrutiny from state and federal regulators as well as consumer groups.

—*Lena H. Sun*, The Washington Post, *April 12, 2013*

Because of the immense variety and complexity of medications now available, it is practically impossible for nurses or doctors to keep up with the information required for safe medication use. The pharmacist has become an essential resource in modern hospital practice.[33] It is therefore mandatory that hospital pharmacies "have an adequate number of personnel to ensure quality pharmaceutical services, including emergencies."[34]

Medication errors are considered to be a leading cause of medical injury in the United States. Antibiotics, chemotherapeutic drugs, and anticoagulants are three categories of drugs responsible for many drug-related adverse events. The prevention of medication errors requires recognition of common causes and the development of practices to help reduce the incidence of errors. With thousands of drugs, many of which look alike and sound alike, it is understandable why medication errors are so common. The following listing describes some of the more common types of medication errors:

- prescription errors include: wrong patient; wrong drug; wrong dose; wrong route; wrong frequency; transcription errors (often due to illegible handwriting and improper use of abbreviations); and inadequate review of medication for appropriateness
- dispensing errors include: improper preparation of medication; failure to properly formulate medications; dispensing expired medications; mislabeling or failure to label drug containers; delivering the wrong dosages to floor stock; and misinterpretation of the physician's order
- administration errors include: wrong patient; wrong route; double dosing (drug administered more than once); failure to administer; wrong frequency; administering discontinued drugs; administering drugs without an authorized order; wrong dose (e.g., IV rate); documentation errors; transcription errors (often due to illegible handwriting and improper use of abbreviations); inaccurate transcription to *medication administration record* (MAR); charted but not administered; administered but not documented on the MAR; discontinued order not noted on the MAR; and medication wasted and not recorded

The practice of pharmacy has traditionally included the prepartion, compounding, and dispensing of drugs. These activities may be carried out only by a pharmacist with a state license or by a person who is exempted from the provisions of a state's pharmacy statutes. The entire stock of drugs in a pharmacy is subject to strict government regulation and control. The pharmacist is responsible for developing, coordinating, and supervising all pharmacy activities and reviewing the drug regimens of each patient.

The *Institute for Safe Medication Practices* (ISMP) is a nonprofit organization based in Philadelphia devoted entirely to medication error prevention and safe medication use. The organization's website (http://www.ismp.org/default.asp) should be visited on a regular basis to assist in the prevention of medication errors.

Controlled Substances Act

The Comprehensive Drug Abuse Prevention and Control Act of 1970, commonly known as the Controlled Substances Act (CSA), replaced virtually all preexisting federal laws dealing with narcotics, depressants, and stimulants.

The CSA places all substances that are regulated under existing federal law into one of five schedules. This placement is based upon the substance's medicinal value, harmfulness, and potential for abuse or addiction. Schedule I is reserved for the most dangerous drugs that have no recognized medical use, while Schedule V is the classification used for the least dangerous drugs. The act also provides a mechanism for substances to be controlled, added to a schedule, decontrolled, removed from control, rescheduled, or transferred from one schedule to another.[35]

Federal Food, Drug and Cosmetic Act

The Federal Food, Drug, and Cosmetic Act (FDCA) applies to drugs and devices carried in interstate commerce and to goods produced and distributed in federal territory. The act's requirements apply to almost every drug that would be dispensed from a pharmacy because nearly all drugs and devices, or their components, are eventually carried in interstate commerce.

Section 502 of the act sets forth the information that must appear on the labels or the labeling of drugs and devices. The label must contain, among other special information: (1) the name and place of business of the manufacturer, packer, or distributor; (2) the quantity of contents; (3) the name and quantity of any ingredient found to be habit forming, along with the statement "Warning—may be habit-forming"; (4) the established name of the drug or its ingredients; (5) adequate directions for use; (6) adequate warnings and cautions concerning conditions of use; and (7) special precautions for packaging.

The regulation implementing the labeling requirements of Section 502 exempts prescription drugs from the requirement that the label bear "adequate directions for use for laymen" if the drug is in the possession of a pharmacy or under the custody of a practitioner licensed by law to administer or prescribe legend drugs.[36] This particular exemption applies only to prescription drugs meeting the other requirements. Ordinary household remedies in the custody or possession of a practitioner or pharmacist would not fall under the labeling exemption.

If the drug container is too small to bear a label with all the required information, the label may contain only the quantity or proportion of each active ingredient and the lot or control number. The prescription legend may appear on the outer container of such drug units. The lot or control number may appear on the crimp of a dispensing tube, and the remainder of the required label information may appear on other labeling within the package.

Besides the label itself, each legend drug must be accompanied by labeling, on or within the sealed package from which the drug is to be dispensed, bearing full prescribing information including indications; dosage; routes, methods, and frequency of administration; contraindications; side effects; precautions; and any other information concerning the intended use of the drug necessary for the prescriber to use the drug safely. This information usually is contained in what is known in the trade as the package insert.

State Regulations

Besides federal laws affecting the manufacture, use, and handling of drugs, the different states have controlling legislation. All states regulate the practice of pharmacy, as well as the operation of pharmacies. State regulations generally provide that: (1) each healthcare organization must ensure the availability of pharmaceutical services to meet the needs of patients; (2) pharmaceutical services must be provided in accordance with all applicable federal and state laws and regulations; (3) pharmaceutical services must be provided under the supervision of a licensed pharmacist; (4) space and equipment must be provided within the organization for the proper storage, safeguarding, preparation, dispensing, and administration of drugs; (5) each organization must develop and implement written policies and procedures regarding accountability, distribution, and assurance of quality of all drugs; and (6) each organization must develop and follow current written procedures for the safe prescription and administration of drugs.

Storage of Drugs

Drugs must be stored in their original containers and must be labeled properly. The label should indicate the patient's full name, physician, prescription number, strength of the drug, expiration date of all time-dated drugs, and the address and telephone number of the pharmacy dispensing the drug. Medications must be stored in a locked cabinet in a secure location. Medications containing narcotics or other dangerous drugs must be stored under double lock (e.g., a locked box within the medicine cabinet). The keys to the medicine cabinet and narcotics box must be in the possession of authorized personnel. Medications for external use only must be marked clearly and kept separate from medications for internal use. Medications that are to be taken out of use must be disposed of according to federal and state laws and regulations.

Hospital Formulary

Healthcare organizations use a formulary system, whereby physicians and pharmacists create a formulary listing of drugs used in the institution. The formulary contains the brand names and generic names of drugs. Under the formulary system, a physician agrees that his or her prescription, which calls for a brand name drug, may be filled with the generic equivalent of that drug (i.e., a drug that contains the same active ingredients in the same proportions). If there is a medical contraindication to prescribing a generic drug for a particular patient, the physician may prescribe the brand name drug. Hospitals that dispense and administer a generic drug for financial reasons when a brand name drug is requested for medical reasons, the hospital will most likely be liable for any harm suffered by the patient as a result of being administered the generic equivalent of the brand name drug.

Expanding Role of the Pharmacist

Historically, the role of the pharmacist was centered on the management of the pharmacy and the accurate preparation and dispensing of drugs. The duties and responsibilities of pharmacists have moved well beyond the concept of filling prescriptions and dispensing drugs. Schools of pharmacy have recognized the ever-expanding role of the pharmacist into the clinical aspects of patient care—so much so that educational requirements are getting more stringent, with emphasis on patient safety, clinical education, and application.

Intravenous Admixture Service

NEWSPAPER CLIPPINGS: Error That Led to Baby's Death Slipped Through Many Hands

When a mistake goes through at least six staffers at Summerlin Hospital Medical Center, leading to the death of a premature baby, there's only one word to describe it, according to Dr. Florence Jameson, past president of the Clark County Medical Society:
"Sloppy."
The mistakes that led up to Alyssa Shinn's death on Nov. 9 started the night before when pharmacist Pamela Goff mishandled the entry of Alyssa's prescription into the pharmacy's computer. It ended with neonatal intensive care unit nurses hanging an IV bag containing zinc at 1,000 times the amount prescribed the preemie.

—*Annette Wells*, Las Vegas Review Journal, *August 5, 2007*

Intravenous fluids, with or without added medications, are generally prepared in an IV admixture room by highly skilled and trained pharmacists and technicians. Pharmacists are expected to oversee the work of pharmacy technicians. Medications prepared in admixture rooms include antibiotics, chemotherapy, and electrolytes, as well as intravenous nutrition solutions that are tailored for each patient's needs. Elements crucial to the process of preparing sterile products include stability of the mixtures, sterility, solubility of added ingredients, considerations of incompatibilities, storage, and proper labeling. Proper disposal is a key consideration for the protection of personnel and the environment.

A sterile compounding environment is maintained with the use of laminar flow hoods and aseptic techniques. Vertical and horizontal laminar flow hood cabinets are utilized in the preparation of intravenous fluids. The cabinets are designed for creation of a bacterial dust free air space. They are utilized for work with low-risk substances and materials, when protection of working material from the environment is required or work with an item requires a sterile working space. The hoods are maintained daily and periodically certified for proper functioning.

Aseptic technique is the key to producing a sterile product. The American Society of Health-System Pharmacists and the Occupational Safety and Health Administration, amongst others, provide guidelines and regulations in order to provide for a safe working environment.

An observational study of the accuracy in compounding IV admixtures at five hospitals showed that "Of every 100 errors, 2 were judged to be potentially clinically important. In five U.S. hospital pharmacies, the observed error rate for compounding i.v. admixtures was 9%."[37]

Dispensing and Administration of Drugs

NEWSPAPER CLIPPINGS: Inside a Pharmacy Where a Fatal Error Occurred

Lewis typed up a prescription label with erroneous dosage instructions. About 36 hours later, Smith died of what an autopsy found was an accidental methadone overdose.
It may be impossible to fix blame precisely for Smith's death, in part because Walgreens in December settled the lawsuit with his family in a confidential agreement that bars any discussion of the case. However, the depositions and interviews gathered before the settlement suggest that both a technician with limited experience and a pharmacist coping with a heavy workload figured in the tragedy.

—*Kevin McKoy*, USA Today, *February 12, 2008*

The *dispensing of medications* is the processing of a drug for delivery or for administration to a patient pursuant to the order of an appropriately licensed healthcare practitioner. It consists of checking the directions on the label with the directions on the prescription to determine accuracy; selecting the drug from stock to fill the order; counting, measuring, compounding, or preparing the drug; placing the drug in the proper container; and adding to a written prescription any required notations.

The administration of a medication is an act in which an authorized person in accordance with federal and state laws and regulations administers a single dose of a prescribed medication to a patient. The complete act of administration includes removing an individual dose from a previously dispensed, properly labeled container (including a unit-dose container), verifying it with the physician's order, giving the individual dose to the proper patient, and recording the time and dose given.

Each dose of a drug administered must be recorded in the patient's clinical records. A separate record of narcotic drugs must be maintained. In the event that an emergency arises requiring the immediate administration of a particular drug, the patient's record must be documented properly, showing the necessity for administration of the drug on an emergency basis. Procedures should be in place for handling emergency situations.

Duty to Monitor Patient's Medications

In *Baker v. Arbor Drugs, Inc.*,[38] a Michigan court imposed a duty on a pharmacist to monitor a patient's medications. The patient filled three different prescriptions by the same physician at the same pharmacy. The pharmacy maintained a computer system that detected drug–drug interactions. The pharmacy advertised to consumers that it could, through the use of a computer-monitoring system, provide a medication profile for its customers that would alert its pharmacists to potential drug–drug interactions. Because the pharmacy advertised and used the computer system to monitor the medications of its customers, the pharmacist voluntarily assumed a duty of care to detect the harmful drug–drug interaction that occurred in this case, where it was determined without question that decedent suffered injury when he suffered a stroke due to the adverse drug interaction between two drugs, Parnate and Tavist-D.

Warning Patients About Potential for Overdose

A Pennsylvania court held that a pharmacist failed to warn the patient about the maximum dosage of a drug the patient could take.[39] This failure resulted in an overdose, causing permanent injuries. Expert testimony focused on the fact that a pharmacist who receives inadequate instructions as to the maximum recommended dosage has a duty to ascertain whether the patient is aware of the limitations concerning the use of the drug. The pharmacist should have contacted the prescribing physician to clarify the prescription.

Questionable Prescription

In *Hooks v. McLaughlin*,[40] the Indiana Supreme Court held that a pharmacist had a duty to refuse to refill prescriptions at an unreasonably faster rate than prescribed pending directions from the prescribing physician. The Indiana code provides that a pharmacist is immune from civil prosecution or civil liability if he or she, in good faith, refuses to honor a prescription because, in his or her professional judgment, the honoring of the prescription would aid or abet an addiction or habit.[41]

Internet Pharmacy

 NEWSPAPER CLIPPINGS: Most On-Line Pharmacies Are Frauds, FDA Warns

The FDA is warning consumers that almost all Internet pharmacies are fraudulent and probably are selling counterfeit drugs that could harm them.

• • •

Instead, they're getting fake drugs that are contaminated, are past their expiration date or contain no active ingredient, the wrong amount of active ingredient or even toxic substances. These drugs could sicken people, cause them to develop a resistance to their real medicine, cause no side effects or trigger harmful interactions with other medications.

—*Associated Press*, The Washington Post, *October 2, 2012*

The use of Internet pharmacies has been on the rise due to the high cost of drugs. Not only are patients purchasing bogus medications but also they are obtaining questionable prescriptions from physicians through the Internet, as noted in *United States v. Nelson*,[42] where Fuchs operated an Internet pharmacy called NationPharmacy.com. Customers would obtain prescription and nonprescription drugs from the Internet pharmacy. In accord with federal law, all requests for prescription drugs had to be reviewed by a physician. Dr. Nelson, the defendant in this case, agreed to review the prescriptions, approving 90–95% of prescription requests without examining his purported patients. Customers who used Fuchs's Internet pharmacy would have their orders routed through a brick-and-mortar pharmacy called Main Street Pharmacy. Dr. Nelson would physically visit Main Street Pharmacy to sign the prescription requests, and customers would receive prescriptions by mail and pay Fuchs directly.

Dr. Nelson was charged and convicted of both conspiracy to distribute controlled prescription drugs outside the usual course of professional practice, in violation of 21 U.S.C. § 846, and conspiracy to launder money, in violation of 18 U.S.C. § 1956(h). Dr. Nelson appealed his conviction, arguing that there was insufficient evidence to support a conviction because there was no evidence of a conspiracy. On an appeal, the court determined that a reasonable jury could infer the existence of an agreement constituting a conspiracy to distribute prescription drugs outside the usual course of professional practice and to launder the proceeds of that distribution.

PHYSICAL THERAPY

Physical therapy is the art and science of preventing and treating neuromuscular or musculoskeletal disabilities through the evaluation of an individual's disability and rehabilitation potential; the use of physical agents (heat, cold, ultrasound, electricity, water, and light); and neuromuscular procedures that, through their physiologic effect, improve or maintain the patient's optimum functional level. Because of different physical disabilities brought on by various injuries and medical problems, physical therapy is an extremely important component of a patient's total health care. Physical therapists, therefore, have a legal duty as any other health professional to adhere to an accepted standard of care when providing care and treatment. Negligence occurs when the physical therapist fails to provide rehabilitation or treatment at the accepted standard of care that other physical therapists in similar circumstances would have provided.

Areas of liability concern for physical therapists include: failure to obtain a completed prescription from the prescribing physician; failure to follow physician's orders or to clarify such orders; aggressive treatment (e.g., use of heavy weights); and, treatment burns from hot packs. Adherence to the physician's treatment plan as prescribed and seeking clarification when necessary, review of patient's history and risk assessments, preparation of equipment to be used, as well as observation and feedback from the patient will go a long way in reducing the number of injuries suffered by physical therapy patients.

Incorrectly Interpreting Physician's Orders

Pontiff, in *Pontiff v. Pecot & Assoc.*,[43] filed a complaint for damages against Pecot and Associates and Morris for failing

to properly train, supervise, and monitor its employees, including Morris, and that Pecot and Associates was otherwise negligent. Pontiff alleged that employee Morris failed to exercise the degree of care and skill ordinarily exercised by physical therapists, failed to heed his protests that he could not perform the physical therapy treatments she was supervising, and failed to stop performing physical therapy treatments after he began to complain that he was in pain. Pontiff claimed he felt a muscle tear while he was exercising on the butterfly machine, a resistive exercise machine.

Pontiff's expert, Boulet, a licensed practicing physical therapist, testified that Pecot deviated from the standard of care of physical therapists by introducing a type of exercise that, according to her, was not prescribed by Dr. deAraujo, the treating physician. She stated that Pecot added resistive or strengthening exercises to Pontiff's therapy and these were not a part of the physician's prescription. Pecot argued that resistive exercises were implicitly part of the prescription, even if her interpretation of the prescription was not reasonable.

Legally, under Louisiana law, a physical therapist may not treat a patient without a written physical therapy prescription. Ethically, the Physical Therapists' Code of Ethics, Principle 3.4, states that any alteration of a program or extension of services beyond the program should be undertaken in consultation with the referring practitioner. Because resistive exercises were not set forth in the original prescription, Boulet stated that consultation with the physician was necessary before Pontiff could be advanced to that level. Only in the case where a physician has indicated on the prescription that the therapist is to evaluate and treat would the therapist have such discretion. There was no such indication on the prescription written by deAraujo.

Davis, a physical therapist in private practice and Pecot's expert witness, testified that the program that Pecot designed for Pontiff was consistent with how she interpreted the prescription for therapy that the physician wrote. Davis, however, did not at any time state that Pecot's interpretation was a reasonable one. In fact, Davis herself would not have interpreted the prescription in the manner that Pecot did. Davis testified only that Pecot's introduction of resistive exercises was reasonable based on her interpretation of the prescription.

It is clear that Pecot, as a licensed physical therapist, owed a duty to Pontiff, her client. Pecot's duty is defined by the standard of care of similar physical therapists and the Association of Physical Therapists of America. If Pecot found the prescription to be ambiguous, she had a duty to contact the prescribing physician for clarification. The appeals court found that the trial court was correct in its determination that Pontiff presented sufficient evidence to show that this duty was breached and that Pecot's care fell below the standard of other physical therapists.

PHYSICIAN ASSISTANT

NEWSPAPER CLIPPINGS: Jury Awards $3 Million in Malpractice Suit

Sinuses treated with steroids, not antibiotic

But Mr. Del Sole said that the doctors in the office failed to follow the protocol they laid out in employing a physician's assistant.

On paperwork submitted with the state, Drs. DeGiovanni and Dr. Montini said they would see every patient treated by Ms. Egidi [Physician's Assistant].

"The testimony was undisputed that that did not happen," Mr. Del Sole said. "Clearly, the doctor would have treated her differently."

—*Paula Reed Ward*, Pittsburgh Post-Gazette, *November 24, 2007*

A physician assistant (PA) is a medical professional who is a graduate of an accredited PA educational training program and is nationally certified and state-licensed to practice medicine with the supervision of a physician. One of the solutions to the shortage of physicians has been to train PAs, as well as nurse practitioners, to perform the more routine and repetitive medical procedures. PAs are generally licensed to administer injections, perform routine history and physical examinations, order and interpret tests, diagnose and treat patient ailments (e.g., assist in surgery, suture minor lacerations), prescribe medications, and provide patient education and counseling. A physician may not delegate a task to a PA in those instances where regulations specify that the physician must perform the task or when delegation of a task is prohibited under state law or by an organization's policies by whom the PA may be employed.

PAs are responsible for their own negligent acts. The employer of a PA can be held liable for the PA's negligent acts on the basis of respondeat superior. Guidelines and procedures should be established, as with any professional, to provide a standard mechanism for reviewing a PA's skills and performance. The reader is encouraged to review applicable laws that regulate a physician's assistant scope of practice, which may vary from state to state (e.g., Title 16 California Code of Regulations Section 1399.541). Due to the ever-increasing shortage of physicians, the educational requirements and scope of practice for physician's assistants will most likely continue to expand.

PODIATRIST

Podiatry is that branch of medicine involving the study of, diagnosis, and medical treatment of disorders of the feet, ankles, and lower extremities. Although the scope of practice is based on a state's licensing laws, podiatrists generally provide the following services: perform complete medical histories and physical examinations; order and interpret imaging studies; prescribe medications; perform minor surgery and set fractures; prescribe and fit orthotics; and, prescribe physical therapy as required. The legal concerns of podiatrists, similar to those of surgeons, include misdiagnosis and negligent surgery.

Failure to Adhere to Standard of Care

The podiatrist, for example, in *Strauss v. Biggs*[44] was found to have failed to meet the standard of care required of a podiatrist and that failure resulted in injury to the patient. The podiatrist, by his own admission, stated that his initial incision in the patient's foot had been misplaced. The trial court was found not to have erred in permitting the jury to consider additional claims that the podiatrist acted improperly by failing to refer the patient, stop the procedure after the first incision, inform the patient of possible nerve injury, and provide proper postoperative treatment. Testimony of the patient's experts was adequate to show that such alleged omissions violated the standard of care required of podiatrists.

RESPIRATORY THERAPIST

Respiratory therapy is the allied health profession responsible for the treatment, management, diagnostic testing, and control of patients with cardiopulmonary deficits. A respiratory therapist is a person employed in the practice of respiratory care who has the knowledge and skill necessary to administer respiratory care. Respiratory therapists are responsible for their negligent acts. A respiratory therapist's employer is responsible for the negligent acts of the therapist under the legal doctrine of respondeat superior.

Failure to Remove Endotracheal Tube

The court in *Poor Sisters of St. Francis v. Catron*[45] held that the failure of nurses and a respiratory therapist to report to the supervisor that an endotracheal tube had been left in the plaintiff longer than the customary period of 3 or 4 days was sufficient to allow the jury to reach a finding of negligence. The patient experienced difficulty speaking and underwent several operations to remove scar tissue and open her voice box. At the time of trial, she could not speak above a whisper and breathed partially through a hole in her throat created by a tracheotomy. The hospital was found liable for the negligent acts of its employees and the resulting injuries to the plaintiff.

Multiple Use of Same Syringe

The respiratory therapist in *State University v. Young*[46] was suspended for using the same syringe for drawing blood from a number of critically ill patients. The therapist had been warned several times of the dangers of that practice and that it violated the state's policy of providing quality patient care.

Restocking the Code Cart

Dixon had been admitted to the hospital and was diagnosed with pneumonia in her right lung. Dixon's condition began to deteriorate and she was moved to the intensive care unit (ICU). A code blue was eventually called signifying that her cardiac and respiratory functions were believed to have ceased. During the code, a decision was made to intubate, which is to insert an endotracheal tube into Dixon so that she could be given respiratory support by a mechanical ventilator. As Dixon's condition stabilized, Dr. Taylor, Dixon's physician at that time, ordered that she gradually be weaned from the respirator. Blackham, a respiratory therapist employed by the hospital, extubated Dixon at 10:15 p.m. Dr. Taylor then left the room to advise the family that she had been extubated. Blackham decided an oxygen mask would provide better oxygen to Dixon but could not locate a mask in the ICU, so he left ICU and went across the hall to the critical care unit (CCU). When Blackham returned to Dixon's room with the oxygen mask and placed it on Dixon, he realized that she was not breathing properly. Blackham realized that she would have to be reintubated as quickly as possible.

A second code was called and Shackleford, a nurse from the cardiac CCU, responded to the code. Shackleford recorded on the code sheet that she arrived in Dixon's room at 10:30 p.m. She testified that Blackham said he needed a medium Number 4 MacIntosh laryngoscope blade, which was not on the code cart. The code cart is a cart that is equipped with all the medicines, supplies, and instruments needed for a code emergency. The code cart in the ICU had not been restocked after the first code that morning, so Shackleford was sent to obtain the needed blade from the CCU across the hall. When Shackleford returned to the ICU, the blade was passed to Taylor, who had responded to the code and was attempting to reintubate Dixon. Upon receiving the blade, Dr. Taylor was able to quickly intubate Dixon, after which she was placed on a ventilator, but she never regained consciousness. After the family was informed there was no hope that Dixon would recover the use of her brain, the family requested that no extraordinary measure be taken to prolong her life.

A medical negligence claim was filed against Dr. Taylor and the hospital. The jury found that Dr. Taylor was not negligent. Evidence presented at trial established that the hospital's breach of duty in not having the code cart properly restocked resulted in a 3-minute delay in the intubation of Dixon. Reasonable minds could accept from the testimony at trial that the hospital's breach of duty was a cause of Dixon's brain death, without which the injury would not have occurred. Foreseeability on the part of the hospital could be established from the evidence introduced by the plaintiff that the written standards for the hospital require every code cart be stocked with a Number 4 MacIntosh blade. This evidence permits a reasonable inference that the hospital should have foreseen that the failure to have the code cart stocked with the blade could lead to critical delays in intubating a patient. Accordingly, there was substantial evidence that failure to have the code cart stocked with the proper blade was a proximate cause of Dixon's injuries.[47]

▌ CERTIFICATION OF HEALTH PROFESSIONALS

The *certification* of healthcare professionals is the recognition by a governmental or professional association that an individual's expertise meets the standards of that group. Some professional groups establish their own minimum standards for certification in those professions that are not licensed by a particular state. Certification by an association or group is a self-regulation credentialing process.

▌ LICENSING HEALTH PROFESSIONALS

Licensure can be defined as the process by which some competent authority grants permission to a qualified individual or entity to perform certain specified activities that would be illegal without a license. As it applies to healthcare personnel, licensure refers to the process by which licensing boards, agencies, or departments of the several states grant to individuals who meet certain predetermined standards the legal right to practice in a healthcare profession and to use a specified healthcare practitioner's title. The commonly stated objectives of licensing laws are to limit and control admission to the different healthcare occupations and to protect the public from unqualified practitioners by promulgating and enforcing standards of practice within the professions.

The authority of states to license healthcare practitioners are explicit in their regulatory powers. Implicit in the power to license is the authority to collect license fees, establish standards of practice, require certain minimum qualifications and competency levels of applicants, and impose on applicants other requirements necessary to protect the general public welfare. This authority, which is vested in the legislature, may be delegated to political subdivisions or to state boards, agencies, and departments. In some instances, the scope of the delegated power is made specific in the legislation; in others, the licensing authority may have wide discretion in performing its functions. In either case, however, the authority granted by the legislature may not be exceeded.

Suspension and Revocation of License

Licensing boards have the authority to suspend or revoke the license of a healthcare professional found to have violated specified norms of conduct. Such violations may include procurement of a license by fraud; unprofessional, dishonorable, immoral, or illegal conduct; performance of specific actions prohibited by statute; and malpractice. Suspension and revocation procedures are most commonly contained in a state's licensing act.

PROFESSIONAL MISCONDUCT

Some states require the reporting of professionals found liable for medical misconduct. Medical misconduct generally includes obtaining a license fraudulently; practicing a profession fraudulently, beyond its authorized scope, with gross incompetence; practicing a profession while the ability to practice is impaired by alcohol, drugs, physical disability, or mental disability; refusing to provide professional service to a person because of the person's race, creed, color, or national origin; permitting, aiding, or abetting an unlicensed person to perform activities requiring a license; and being convicted of committing an act constituting a crime.

The penalties that may be imposed on a licensee found guilty of medical misconduct include suspension of the license to practice, revocation of the license to practice, limitation on registration or issuance of any further licenses, and imposition of a fine.

Sexual Improprieties

A significant number of cases address healthcare professionals who have been involved in sexual relationships with their patients. Such cases are being litigated, in many instances, in both civil and criminal arenas. Healthcare professionals finding themselves in such unprofessional relationships must seek help for themselves as well as refer their patients to other appropriate professionals. Besides being subject to civil and criminal litigation, healthcare professionals also are subject to having their licenses revoked for sexual improprieties.

Dentist

Revocation of a dentist's license on charges of professional misconduct was properly ordered in *Melone v. State Education Department*[48] on the basis of substantial evidence that while acting in his professional capacity, the dentist engaged in physical and sexual contact with 5 different male patients within a 3-year period. Considering the dentist's responsible position, the extended time period during which the sexual contacts occurred, the age and impressionable nature of the victims (7–15 years of age), and the possibility of lasting effects on the victims, the penalty was not shocking to the court's sense of fairness.

Physician

A hospital technologist in *Copithorne v. Framingham Union Hospital*[49] alleged that a staff physician raped her during the course of a house call. The technologist's claim against the hospital was summarily dismissed for lack of proximate causation. On appeal, the dismissal was found to be improper when the record indicated that the hospital had received notice of allegations that the physician assaulted patients on and off the hospital's premises. The hospital had instructed the physician to have another individual present when visiting female patients and had instructed nurses to keep an eye on him. The physician's sexual assault was foreseeable. There was evidentiary support for the proposition that failure to withdraw the physician's privileges caused the rape when the technologist asserted that it was the physician's good reputation in the hospital that led her to seek his services.

Psychiatrist

The sexual relationship a psychiatrist had with the spouse of a patient was found to be improper in *Richard v. Larry*.[50] California Civil Code Section 43.5, abolishing causes of action for alienation of affection, criminal conversation, and seduction of a patient over the age of consent, did not bar damages for emotional distress caused by the alleged professional negligence of the psychiatrist who had sexual relations with the plaintiff's wife. The psychiatrist owed a special duty to use due care for his patient's health. The statute was not intended to lower the standard of care that psychiatrists owed their patients. Besides an action against the psychiatrist, allegations that the psychiatrist was an agent of the hospital stated a cause of action against the hospital.

HELPFUL ADVICE FOR CAREGIVERS

- Abide by the ethical code of one's profession.
- Do not criticize the professional skills of others.
- Maintain complete and adequate medical records.
- Seek the aid of professional medical consultants when indicated.
- Inform the patient of the risks, benefits, and alternatives to proposed procedures.
- Practice the specialty in which you have been trained.
- Participate in continuing education programs.
- Keep patient information confidential.
- Check patient equipment regularly, and monitor it for safe use.
- When terminating a professional relationship with a patient, provide adequate notice to the patient.
- Authenticate all telephone orders.
- Obtain a qualified substitute when you will be absent from your practice.
- Be a good listener, and allow each patient sufficient time to express fears and anxieties.
- Safely administer patient medications.
- Closely monitor each patient's response to treatment.
- Provide education and teaching to patients.
- Foster a sense of trust and feeling of significance.
- Communicate with the patient and other caregivers.

Notes

1. Illinois Institute of Technology. Center for the Study of Ethics in the Professions, http://www.iit.edu/departments/csep/PublicWWW/codes/coe/Users_Guide.html (accessed October 13, 2010).
2. No. 31328 (W. Va. 2004).
3. 725 P.2d 400 (Or. Ct. App. 1986).
4. *Florida Bar v. Barrett*, No. SC03-375 (Fla. 2005).
5. http://farmingtonhills.legalexaminer.com/medical-malpractice/jury-returns-largest-medical-malpractice-verdict-but-tort-reform-strikes-again.aspx?googleid=306214.
6. *Cleland v. Bronson Health Care Group*, 917 F.2d 266, 272 (6th Cir. 1990).
7. *Griffith v. University Hospitals of Cleveland*, No. 84314 (Ohio Ct. of App. 2004).
8. *Roy v. Gupta*, 606 So.2d 940 (La. Ct. App. 1992).
9. *Feeney v. New England Medical Center, Inc.*, 615 N.E.2d 585 (Mass. App. Ct. 1993).
10. 42 U.S.C.A. § 1395dd(a) (1992).
11. 42 U.S.C.A. § 1395dd(3)(A) (1992).
12. 830 F. Supp. 1399 (M.D. Ala. 1993).
13. 934 F.2d 1362 (5th Cir. Tex. 1991).
14. "Courts Uphold Law, Regulations against Patient Dumping." *Nation's Health.* (August 1991): 1.
15. 689 So. 2d 696 (La. App. 1997).
16. 477 So. 2d 1036 (Fla. Dist. Ct. App. 1985).
17. 288 A.2d 379 (Md. 1972).
18. 271 N.W.2d 8 (S.D. 1978).
19. 14 S.W.3d 42 (Mo. App. 1999).
20. 698 So. 2d 958 (La. App. 1997).
21. 498 S.E.2d 408 (1998).
22. *Baptist Mem'l Hosp. Sys. v. Sampson*, 969 S.W.2d 945, 947 (Tex. 1998).
23. Martin C. McWilliams, Jr. & Hamilton E. Russell, III, Hospital Liability for Torts of Independent Contractor.
24. *Jackson v. Powei*, 743 P.2d 1376, 1385 (Alaska 1987).
25. *Martell v. St. Charles Hosp.*, 523 N.Y.S.2d 342, 352 (N.Y. Sup. Ct. 1987).
26. 797 So. 2d 160 (2001).
27. 661 S.W.2d 534 (Mo. 1983).
28. *Sander v. Geib, Elston, Frost Prof'l Ass'n*, 506 N.W.2d 107 (S.D. 1993).
29. 636 N.E.2d 1282 (Ind. Ct. App. 1994).
30. 753 F. Supp. 267 (W.D. Ark. 1990).
31. 650 A.2d 1076 (Pa. Super. 1994).
32. 933 S.2d 627 (La. 2006).
33. Institute of Medicine. To Err Is Human: Building a Safer Health System, supra note 1, at 194.
34. C.F.R., Title 42, Subpart C § 482.25, 2011.
35. www.usdoj.gov/dea/agency/csa.htm.
36. 21 C.F.R. § 1.106.
37. EA Flynn, RE Pearson, and K Barker. "Observational study of accuracy in compounding i.v. admixtures at five hospitals." *Am J Health-Syst Pharm* 54, no. 8 (1997): 904–12. http://www.ncbi.nlm.nih.gov/pubmed/9114922.
38. 544 N.W.2d 727 (Mich. Ct. App. 1996).
39. *Riff v. Morgan Pharmacy*, 508 A.2d 1247 (Pa. Super. Ct.1986).
40. 642 N.E.2d 514 (Ind. 1994).
41. IND. CODE § 25-26-13-16(b)(3) (1993).
42. No. 02-6183 (C.A. 10, Okla. 2004).
43. 780 So.2d 478 (2001).
44. 525 A.2d 992 (Del. 1987).
45. 435 N.E.2d 305 (Ind. Ct. App. 1982).
46. 566 N.Y.S.2d 79 (N.Y. App. Div. 1991).
47. *Dixon v. Taylor*, No. 9224SC760 (Filed 20 July 1993).
48. 495 N.Y.S.2d 808 (N.Y. App. Div. 1985).
49. 520 N.E.2d 139 (Mass. 1988).
50. 243 Cal. Rptr. 807 (Cal. Ct. App. 1988).

12

Patient Rights
and Responsibilities

Learning Objectives

The reader upon completion of this chapter will be able to:

- Discuss the importance of understanding patient rights.
- Discuss the importance of understanding patient responsibilities.
- Describe the Advisory Commission on Consumer Protection and Quality in the Health Care Industry's listing of patient responsibilities.

 NEWSPAPER CLIPPINGS: Think Preventive Medicine Will Save Money? Think Again

"Preventive care is more about the right thing to do" because it spares people the misery of illness, said economist Austin Frakt of Boston University. "But it's not plausible to think you can cut health-care spending through preventive care. This is widely misunderstood."

A 2010 study in the journal Health Affairs, for instance, calculated that if 90 percent of the U.S. population used proven preventive services, more than do now, it would save only 0.2 percent of healthcare spending.

— *Sharon Begley*, Reuters, *January 29, 2013*

This chapter provides a brief overview of both the rights and responsibilities of patients. Every person possesses certain rights guaranteed by the Constitution of the United States and its amendments, including freedom of speech, religion, and association, and the right not to be discriminated against on the grounds of race, creed, color, or national origin. The Supreme Court has interpreted the Constitution as also guaranteeing certain other rights, such as the right to privacy and self determination, and the right to accept or reject medical treatment.

The news article quoted above is placed here as a reminder that all of us have *both a right and responsibility* to maintain our health as best we can, thus limiting many of the terrible tragedies described herein. The law and ethics meet here. It is about doing the right thing for one's health, even if the cost savings is but minimal. There can be no price tag to save humanity from its destructive ways and free us from the ravages of pain and suffering.

PATIENT RIGHTS

Patients of the various states have certain rights and protections guaranteed by state and federal laws and regulations. Patient rights include the right to participate in healthcare decisions and to understand treatment options. Patients have a right to receive a clear explanation of tests, diagnoses, prognosis, and treatment options.[1]

The continuing trend of consumer awareness, coupled with increased governmental regulations, makes it advisable for caregivers to understand the scope of patient rights.

The Patient Self-Determination Act of 1990 (PSDA),[2] describes the rights of patients to make their own health-care decisions. Healthcare organizations may no longer passively permit patients to exercise their rights but must educate patients as to their rights. The PSDA provides that each individual has a right under state law (whether statutory or as recognized by the courts of the state) to make decisions concerning his or her medical care, including the right to accept or refuse medical or surgical treatment and the right to formulate advance directives.

Patient rights may be classified as either legal, those emanating from law, or human statements of desirable ethical principles, such as the right to health care or the right to be treated with human dignity. A variety of patient rights are presented in this chapter.

Right to Examination and Treatment

 NEWSPAPER CLIPPINGS: Is Your Doctor Missing the Mark?

"It took almost my whole life to get the right diagnosis because no one person had asked me enough questions."

—*Karen Asp*, Shape magazine, *March 2013*

Patients have a right to expect the physician will conduct an appropriate history and physical examination based on the patient's presenting complaints. The assessment is the process by which a physician investigates the patient's state of health, looking for signs of trauma and disease. It sets the stage for accurately diagnosing the patient's medical problems that leads to an agreed upon treatment plan. A cursory assessment can lead to a misdiagnosis and inappropriate treatment plan.

Right to Ask Questions

Attributed to Socrates the Classical Greek philosopher is the *socratic method of teaching and learning* by asking and answering questions as depicted in **Figure 12–1**. Patients have the right to ask questions regarding their care from entry to the hospital through the time of departure. Question regarding care should include, for example, "I saw blood in my IV tubing. Is this okay? Is it infiltrating?" or "My wound dressing seems wet. Is this okay? Should the dressing be changed?" Patients should not hesitate to ask for:

- clarification of a caregiver's instructions
- interpretation of a caregiver's handwriting
- instructions for medication usage (e.g., frequency, dosing, drug–drug or drug–food interactions, contraindications, side effects)
- clarification of a physician's diet orders
- explanation of treatment plans
- a copy of the organization's hand-washing policy
- a description of the hospital's procedures to prevent wrong-site surgery
- consultations and second opinions
- accurate and complete discharge instructions

This listing is but a sampling of the many questions that patients have a right to ask during the course of their care in any healthcare setting.

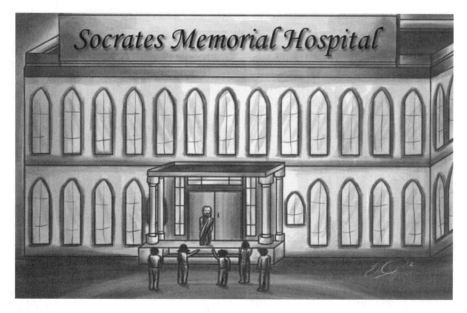

Figure 12–1   Socrates Says Ask Questions   Courtesy of Brittany Salzone, Forest, VA

REALITY CHECK: Standards Pertaining to a Patient Right to Ask Questions

Hillary was the lead consultant assigned to speak at a state-sponsored conference. The purpose of the conference was to review new and revised standards designed to encourage patients to ask questions about their care. They were scheduled to be effective on January 1. Hillary scheduled four junior consultants to speak with her on a variety of topics. Rebecca, one of the more junior of the consultants, addressed the right of patients to ask questions. She spoke about the newly designed program that would require healthcare providers to encourage patients to speak up and ask questions about any concerns they may have regarding their care. Following her presentation, Rebecca asked for questions from the audience. One participant said, "I really don't understand the need for this regulation. Patients don't seem to have a problem complaining." Rebecca began to flounder as she attempted to continue answering the questions of what was to be a generally disgruntled person. Hillary listened intently but said nothing.

Jerome jumped to rescue Rebecca from the constant interruptions of that day's apparently self-appointed antagonist in the audience. Jerome raised his hand, and after being recognized by Rebecca, he responded, "Many patients are not afraid to ask questions and complain when they believe things are not going right. These often are ambulatory patients who can leave a particular provider if they become dissatisfied. Other, more seriously ill in-patients may fear some sort of retaliation if they complain. This is often the case in long-term care facilities." A caregiver in the audience strongly disagreed. Jerome said, "I realize this is not the case with all patients. This fear can often arise, however, with an elderly person or extremely ill individual who is weak and feels vulnerable to upsetting someone, believing that his or her care could be compromised if he or she asks too many questions or complains. Seniors have sometimes been abused at home or care setting and are often not willing to risk further confrontation."

Figuring a picture is worth 1,000 words, Jerome had asked for an overhead projector and proceeded to show some newspaper clippings illustrating why some patients have developed a fear to ask questions. After the session was over, the audience member who had raised the issue approached Jerome and said, "All caregivers are not like the ones you displayed." Jerome said, "I agree. I tried to illustrate for you why some patients are fearful." Jerome looked for Rebecca but learned that she had left the conference following her presentation.

Discussion

1. Do you agree with Jerome's attempt to help Rebecca by responding to the concern of the antagonist?
2. What approach would you have taken in responding to a persistent antagonist? Explain your answer.

Right to Know Your Rights

Organization policy should provide each patient upon admission with a written statement of his or her rights and responsibilities. Patients have a right to receive "Notice of Privacy Standards," a requirement under the Health Insurance Portability and Accountability Act.

The written statement provided to patients at the time of admission is generally referred to as "The Patient's Bill of Rights."

Access to a copy of a patient rights and responsibilities should be available to the general public when so requested. A limited random sample of three hospitals in two states revealed that staff was reluctant and suspicious as to why a copy of the patient's bill of rights was being requested. Neither of the three hospitals would provide a copy on site.

Right to an Explanation of Your Rights

Patients have a right to receive an explanation of their rights and responsibilities. The rights of patients must be respected at all times. Each patient is an individual with unique healthcare needs. The patient has a right to make decisions regarding his or her medical care, including the decision to discontinue treatment, to the extent permitted by law.

Right to Admission

Civil rights are rights ensured by the U.S. Constitution and by the acts of Congress and the state legislatures. Generally, the term includes all the rights of each individual in a free society. Most federal, state, and local programs specifically require, as a condition for receiving funds under such programs, an affirmative statement on the part of the organization that it will not discriminate. For example, the

Medicare and Medicaid programs specifically require affirmative assurances prohibiting discrimination.

Discrimination Prohibited

Discrimination in the admission of patients and segregation of patients on racial grounds are prohibited in any organization receiving federal financial assistance. Pursuant to Title VI of the Civil Rights Act of 1964, the guidelines of the Department of Health and Human Services (DHHS) prohibit the practice of racial discrimination by any organization or agency receiving money under any program supported by DHHS. This includes all providers of service receiving federal funds under Medicare legislation.

According to the Fourteenth Amendment to the Constitution, a state cannot act to deny any person equal protection of the laws. If a state or a political subdivision of a state, whether through its executive, judicial, or legislative branch, acts in such a way as to deny unfairly to any person the rights accorded to another, the amendment has been violated.

Government Facilities

Whether a person is entitled to admission to a particular governmental facility depends on the statute establishing that organization. Governmental hospitals, for example, are by definition creatures of some unit of government; their primary concern is service to the population within the jurisdiction of that unit. Military hospitals, for example, have been established to care for those persons who are active members of the military.

Although persons who are not within the statutory classes have no right of admission, hospitals and their employees owe a duty to extend reasonable care to those who present themselves for assistance and are in need of immediate attention. With respect to such persons, governmental hospitals are subject to the same rules that apply to private hospitals. For example, the patient–plaintiff in *Stoick v. Caro Community Hospital*[3] brought a medical malpractice action against a government physician in which she alleged that the physician determined that she was having a stroke and required hospitalization but that he refused to hospitalize her. The plaintiff's daughter-in-law called the defendant, Caro Family Physicians, P.C., where the patient had a 1:30 P.M. appointment. She was told to take the patient to the hospital. On arriving at the hospital, there was no physician available to see the patient, and a nurse directed her to Dr. Loo's clinic in the hospital. On examination, Loo found right-sided facial paralysis, weakness, dizziness, and an inability to talk. He told the patient that she was having a stroke and that

immediate hospitalization was necessary. Loo refused to admit her because of a hospital policy, which stated that only the patient's family physician or treating physician could admit her. The plaintiff went to see her physician, Dr. Quines, who instructed her to go to the hospital immediately. He did not accompany her to the hospital. At the hospital she waited approximately 1 hour before another physician from the Caro Family Physicians arrived and admitted her. Loo claimed that he did not diagnose a stroke and that there was no bad faith on his part.

The court of appeals reversed, holding that the plaintiff did plead sufficient facts constituting bad faith on the part of Loo. His failure to admit or otherwise treat the patient is a ministerial act for which governmental immunity does not apply and may be found by a jury to be negligence.

Right to Have Special Needs Addressed

Patients have a right to an interpreter whenever possible. Patients who have physical or mental disabilities or are hearing or vision impaired have a right to special help, such as an interpreter.

Right to Know Caregivers

Patients have a right to be informed of the names, qualifications, and positions of the caregivers who will be in charge of their care in the hospital. Patients have a right to know the functions of any hospital staff involved in their care and to refuse examination or treatment.

Right to Appoint Decision Makers

Patients' have a right to appoint a surrogate decision maker should they become incapacitated or unable to make decisions on his or her behalf. Because patients are often helpless and unable to speak for themselves, all caregivers, whether they are volunteers or paid staff, should consider themselves patient advocates.

Right to Execute Advance Directives

Patients must be informed of their right to execute advance directives. The advance directives must be honored within the limits of the law.

Right to Compassionate Care

Patients have a right to be free from harassment, including verbal and physical abuse. They should receive considerate and respectful care given from competent caregivers who respect the patient's personal belief systems.

Right to Quality Care

Healthcare professionals are expected to monitor the quality of each patient's care beginning with the history and physical and followed by the development of the treatment plan and, ultimately, the delivery of care to the patient. The patient has a right to expect that the quality of care rendered will be based best practices recognized in the healthcare industry.

Right to Dignity and Respect

The right to dignity and respect is a common right to be enjoyed by patients, families, and caregivers.

Right to a Timely Response to Care Needs

Patients have a right to have their care needs responded to within a reasonable time frame. Delay in responding to a patient's needs can put a patient's life at risk and the organization at legal risk for injuries the patient must suffer as a result of a delay in treatment.

Right to Participate in Care Decisions

Patients have a right to participate in all aspects of their care and should be encouraged to do so. They have a right to know their treatment options and to accept or refuse care.

Right to Informed Consent

Patients have a right to receive all the information necessary to make an informed decision prior to consenting to a proposed procedure or treatment. This information should include the possible risks, benefits, and alternatives to each procedure or treatment. The right to receive information from the physician includes information about the illness, the suggested course of treatment, and the prospects of recovery in terms that can be understood.

Right to Privacy and Confidentiality

Patients have a right to expect that information regarding their care and treatment will be kept confidential. Confidentiality requires that the caregiver safeguard a patient's confidences within the constraints of law. Caregivers must be careful not to discuss any aspect of a patient's case with others not involved in the case.

Patient Privacy Breached

The phlebotomist in *Bagent v. Blessing Care Corp.*[4] revealed the results of a patient's pregnancy test to the patient's sister at a public tavern. Although there was an attempt by the hospital to have the case dismissed for the phlebotomist's breach of confidentiality, invasion of privacy, and the negligent infliction of emotional distress, the appeals court determined that there were legal issues of fact precluding dismissal of the case. It was asserted that the phlebotomist had been trained to maintain the confidentiality of patient information and that she knew that she had violated the patient's rights.

Written permission must be obtained before a patient's medical record can be made available to anyone not associated with the patient's care.

The limitations of space and financial restraints make it difficult to continuously preserve a patient's right to privacy in many hospital settings (e.g., emergency departments). Nevertheless, healthcare organizations have a responsibility to provide for a reasonable amount of privacy for patients.

The issues of confidentiality and privacy are both ethical and legal. Caregivers must safeguard each patient's right to privacy and the right to have information pertaining to his or her care to be kept confidential.

Disclosures Permitted

Patient information (e.g., diagnoses, anesthesia history, surgical and other invasive procedures, drug allergies, medication usage, lab test results, and imaging studies) may be disclosed to other providers who may be caring for the patient to provide safe healthcare treatment. The following list describes some of the ways a healthcare provider may disclose medical information about a patient without his or her written consent.

- Disclosure of information to third-party payers so the providers of care bill for services rendered.
- Disclosure of information necessary to render care and treatment.
- Disclosure of information as may be required by a law enforcement agency.
- Disclosure of information as may be required to avert a serious threat to public health or safety.
- Disclosure of information as required by military command authorities for their medical records.
- Disclosure of information to worker's compensation or similar programs for processing of claims.
- Disclosure of information in response to a subpoena for a legal proceeding.
- Disclosure of information to a coroner or medical examiner for purposes of identification.

Limitations on Disclosures

Some of the individual rights a patient has regarding disclosure of access to his or her medical information are as follows:

- Right to request restrictions or limitations regarding information used or disclosed about one's treatment.
- Right to an accounting of nonstandard disclosures: The patient has a right to request a list of the disclosures made of information released regarding his or her care.
- Right to amend: If a patient believes that medical information regarding his or her care is incorrect or incomplete, he or she has a right to request that the information be corrected.
- Right to inspect and copy medical information that may be used to make decisions about one's care.
- Right to file a complaint with the provider, or the Secretary of the Department of Health and Human Services in Washington, DC, if a patient believes his or her privacy rights have been violated.
- Right to a paper copy of a notice pertaining to patient.
- Right to know of restrictions on rights.

Any restrictions on a patient's visitors, mail, telephone, or other communications must be evaluated for their therapeutic effectiveness and fully explained to and agreed upon by the patient or patient representative.

Right to Refuse Treatment

Patients have a right to refuse treatment and be told what effect such a decision could have on their health. The responsibility of caregivers requires balancing risks and benefits. This balancing can lead to situations where healthcare professionals view their obligations to a patient as different from the patient's own assessment.

Right to Discharge

Patients have a right to be discharged. An unauthorized detention could subject the offending organization to charges of false imprisonment. Although patients have a right not to be held against their will, there are circumstances where reasonable detainment can be justified (e.g., a minor's release only to a parent or authorized guardian).

Discharge Orders

When discharging a patient, a physician should issue and sign all discharge orders. If there is no need for immediate care, the patient should be advised to seek follow-up care with his or her family physician.

Release from Hospital Contraindicated

The plaintiff in *Somoza v. St. Vincent's Hospital*[5] was admitted to the hospital during the 29th week of her pregnancy. She was admitted under the care of her private attending physician, defendant Dr. Svesko. She presented herself to the hospital with complaints of severe abdominal pain. Upon the plaintiff's admission to the hospital, Dr. Gutwein (a resident physician at the hospital) examined her. According to the notations she made on the plaintiff's chart, Dr. Gutwein independently formed the impression that the plaintiff might be suffering from left pyelonephritis, premature labor, or polyhydramnios. Dr. Gutwein recorded a written plan and orders requiring that the plaintiff be hooked up to a fetal monitor. The plaintiff also was to undergo a number of diagnostic tests, including a renal pelvic sonogram. The results of the sonogram were abnormal, and the radiologist recommended a follow-up sonogram. However, the attending physician did not order a follow-up. Despite the abnormal sonogram and various findings on the physical examinations, Dr. Svesko decided to release the plaintiff from the hospital because her pain had subsided. He orally conveyed this order to Dr. Gutwein. According to Dr, Gutwein, she did not formulate an opinion as to the correctness of the decision to discharge because she was of the opinion that it was not her place to make such a decision. Instead, pursuant to Dr. Svesko's instruction, on her early morning rounds, Dr. Gutwein simply signed an order discharging the plaintiff from the hospital. Four days later, the plaintiff returned to the hospital suffering severe pain and soon thereafter delivered twin girls. The twins were diagnosed as suffering from cerebral palsy resulting from their premature birth. The plaintiff brought a medical malpractice action against the hospital and Dr. Svesko arising out of the premature birth of the twins. The defendants filed a motion for summary judgment, and it was denied. The defendants appealed.

The New York State Supreme Court, Appellate Division, held that there were material issues of fact as to whether the mother's symptoms exhibited during her physical assessment contraindicated her release from the hospital and that ordinary prudence required further inquiry by the resident physician, Dr. Gutwein.

The plaintiffs presented an affidavit by expert witness Dr. Sherman, who stated "the failure of the hospital staff to discharge without another physical examination, in my opinion, with a reasonable degree of medical certainty, is a departure from good and accepted medical practice. The resident clearly had an obligation to examine even a private patient in the face of a changing cervix and not just to discharge her pursuant to some attending physician's order."[6] A hospital whose staff carries out a physician's order may be held responsible where the hospital staff knows, or should know, that the orders are so clearly contraindicated by normal practice that ordinary prudence requires inquiry into the correctness of the orders. In this case, the plaintiff's release from the hospital was so clearly contraindicated by normal practice that ordinary prudence required further inquiry by Dr. Gutwein into the appropriateness of the discharge order.

Right to Stabilization and Transfer

Patients have a right to be diverted or transferred to an alternate facility when the admitting facility is unable to meet a patient's particular care needs. This will at times necessitate the stabilization and transfer of the patient to an alternate healthcare organization that has the special services the patient requires. For this reason, it is helpful for each organization to cooperate with one another by executing transfer agreements.

Patients also have a right to choose a receiving facility, whenever possible. The Medicaid patient in *Macleod v. Miller*[7] was entitled to an injunction preventing his involuntary transfer from the nursing home. The patient had not been accorded a pretransfer hearing as was required by applicable regulations. In addition, it was determined that the trauma of transfer might result in irreparable harm to the patient. The appeals court remanded the case to the trial court with directions to enter an order prohibiting the defendants from transferring the plaintiff pending exhaustion of his administrative remedies.

Healthcare organizations should have a written transfer agreement in effect with other organizations to help ensure the smooth transfer of patients from one facility to another when such is determined appropriate by the attending physician(s). Generally speaking, a *transfer agreement* is a written document that sets forth the terms and conditions under which a patient may be transferred to a facility that more appropriately provides the kind of care required by the patient. It also establishes procedures to admit patients of one facility to another when their condition warrants a transfer.

Transfer agreements should be written in compliance with and reflect the provisions of federal and state laws, regulations, and standards affecting healthcare organizations. The parties to a transfer agreement should be particularly aware of applicable federal and state regulations.

Right to Access Records

The courts have taken the view that patients have a legally enforceable interest in the information contained in their medical records and, therefore, have a right to access their records in a timely manner upon request. Legislation enacted by the various states permit patients access to their records. Patients may also have access to review and/or obtain copies of their imaging studies (e.g., CT, MRI, and PET scans), laboratory and other diagnostic test results. Access to information includes that maintained or possessed by a healthcare organization and/or a healthcare practitioner who has treated or is treating a patient. Organizations and physicians can withhold records if it is determined that the information could reasonably be expected to cause substantial and identifiable harm to the patient (e.g., patients in psychiatric hospitals, institutions for the mentally disabled, or alcohol- and drug-treatment programs).

Hospital Peer-Review Materials Discoverable: Patient's Right to Know

Florida voters, in November 2004, adopted the "Patients' Right to Know About Adverse Medical Incidents" amendment to Florida's constitution ("Amendment 7"). In a medical malpractice action in which the plaintiffs sought the production of documents relating to the investigation of the plaintiffs' decedent's death and any medical incidents of negligence, neglect, or default of any healthcare provider who rendered services to the decedent, the trial court properly held that the Patient's Right to Know Amendment to the state constitution allowed for discovery, during the course of litigation by a patient against a healthcare provider, of information and documents that emanate from the self-policing processes of healthcare providers.[8]

Right to Know Third-Party Care Relationships

Patients have a right to know the hospital's relationships with outside parties that may influence their care and treatment. These relationships may be with educational institutions, insurers, and other healthcare caregivers.

Right to Pain Management

> *I am locked in a prison of pain,*
> *Where doctors hold the key,*
> *Why can't they think beyond the box,*
> *And develop a cure for me?*
>
> —Nina

Pain is the body's way of alerting the patient that something is not quite right. *Pain management* is the process whereby caregivers work with the patient to develop a pain control treatment plan. The process involves educating the patient as to the importance of pain management in the healing process. With current treatments, pain can often be prevented or at least be controlled.

Patients have a right to have a pain assessment and management of any pain identified. A *pain rating scale* is a visual tool often used to help patients describe their pain level. It helps the caregiver know how well treatment is working and whether change in the treatment plan is necessary. The pain assessment scale is a tool often used because of its ease of use in performing a task. Just as important as the severity of pain are its locations and type (e.g., burning sensation, throbbing, dull, stabbing, numbing, sharp, shooting). A diagram of the body should be used so that the patient can more accurately identify various locations of his or her pain. The severity of pain can be described to the physician to assist in diagnosing and treating the patient.

A patient has the right to the following with regard to pain management:

- A pain control treatment plan developed with the caregiver.
- Alternative and/or complementary strategies should be included in the pain management treatment plan that might help improve the efficacy of traditional treatment options (e.g., pain medications), for example, acupuncture.
- Inclusion of family and caregivers in the decision-making process.
- An explanation of the medications or other treatments planned.
- An explanation of the risks, benefits, and alternatives (e.g., acupuncture) to suggested treatment(s).
- Request changes in treatment if pain persists.
- Refuse pain treatment(s) recommended.
- Receive pain medication in a timely manner.

Right to Know Restrictions on Rights

Any restrictions on a patient's visitors, mail, telephone, or other communications must be evaluated for their therapeutic effectiveness and fully explained to and agreed upon by the patient or patient representative.

REALITY CHECK: The Patient Merry-Go-Round

The following is a letter that a frustrated patient with complex medical issues wrote to her consulting physician.

When I went to your office, it was with great hopes that someone was finally going to piece together all of the bizarre symptoms I have been experiencing over the last several months and get to the cause of my pain.

I was quite frankly shocked by how I was treated as a patient—especially one experiencing a health crisis.

I was examined by a medical student. He wrote my history and current health problems on a small "yellow

sticky pad." You were not in the room when he examined me, and then I saw you for approximately 10 minutes.

You took the card of my New York doctor and said you were going to call him, and then call me regarding what you thought the next steps should be.

I called you on Friday because my local doctor said that you had not called, and I was told you were on vacation until yesterday. I had asked that you call me. You never did. I called you yesterday again, but you did not answer nor did you return my call.

On Monday, I received a letter from a medical student, I assume. Although I empathize with the demands on your time, I have never seen a handwritten letter, which I received, informing me of test results I provided to you prior to my appointment with you. You never mentioned the liver enzyme elevations or my February test from New York. Moreover, no mention was made regarding any plan to help me alleviate immediate problems.

Doctor, I am not a complainer or a person with a low pain tolerance. Since moving here, I've had fainting episodes, severe chest pain and pressure, leg and arm pain and stiffness, congestion on the left side when the pain kicks in, and by 3 o'clock I have to go home and lie down because I'm so weak and tired. I cannot continue to exist like this. It is not normal. If you're too busy and don't want to take me as a patient, you will not offend me. Frankly, I need attention now to get these things resolved. Testing my cholesterol in a month will not address the problem. I've been treated for that for 3 years.

Please call or write to me so I can get another doctor if I have to.

—Nina

The physician never responded.

Discussion

1. Describe the legal and ethical and issues that appear in the correspondence.
2. The patient continues on her merry-go-round, discuss what you would advise her to do?

Transparency and Hospital Charges

Patients have a right to transparency when requesting information about hospital emergency room, outpatient and inpatient treatment charges. The North Carolina Senate is considering a bill entitled the Health Care Cost Reduction and Transparency Act to be effective January 1, 2014, which is intended to allow patients to compare treatment costs among different providers. Hospitals and ambulatory surgical facilities would be required to annually provide financial information for their 50 most common episodes of care to the North Carolina Health Information Exchange (Exchange), which allows free public access to its most current information. The Act is intended to allow patients to compare treatment costs among different providers.

REALITY CHECK: Transparency Not So Transparent

I traveled to . . . for a continuing education program on patient care in my specialty. I unfortunately forgot my asthma inhaler. When I got off the plane after landing and not knowing where to go, as I was new to the area and it was late evening, I decided to go to a local hospital emergency department for a prescription. I was in no distress but was concerned that I had forgotten my inhaler. I unfortunately made the mistake of believing that an emergency room was an appropriate place to go for help and advice when traveling. I sat in a hallway, had my temperature and blood pressure taken, and inhaled some albuterol. My visit from beginning to end was about 20 minutes.

Upon returning home, I received an emergency room bill in excess of $3,000, so now I was distressed. Although I have an insurance policy, there is a $2,000 deductible that I was responsible to pay. I decided to request more detail on my bill. After a less then pleasant experience with the billing department I decided also to request a copy of my medical record. For a hospital that claimed transparency on its website, it took me six weeks and several annoying phone conversations with hospital staff to obtain the billing information and a copy of what turned out to be an 18 page barely readable computerized medical record that listed yes and no answers to questions I was never specifically asked. I couldn't believe it and said to my husband, "Wow, the bill says $27.00 for the medication and I have to pay $2,973 to inhale it."

In summary, I discovered there was a lack of transparency publicized on the hospital's website. Lucky for me I have a friend who helped me resolve my billing concerns. For me, I totally understand the U.S. citizen's frustration with the healthcare system.

—Anonymous

PATIENT RESPONSIBILITIES

Patients have responsibilities as well as rights. Both rights and responsibilities are dependent on one another. One cannot exist without the other in an orderly society. Various patient responsibilities are described below.

Practice a Healthy Lifestyle

Recognize the effect of lifestyle on one's health and make the necessary changes to practice a healthy lifestyle for a longer and healthy future.

Maintain Medication Records

Maintain a record of medications, including dosages and frequency. Drug allergies should be included on the list. Medication records should be reviewed periodically to be sure the listing is current. A copy should be provided to treating physicians and treating facility.

Keep Appointments

Be sure to keep your appointments. When necessary to cancel an appointment, be sure to notify caregivers of a cancellation. Failure to notify the caregiver results in longer delays for other patients who may already be finding it difficult to schedule appointments.

Provide Full Disclosure of Medical History

Provide full disclosure of all information relevant to one's medical condition, medical complaints, symptoms, location and severity of pain, previous pain control concerns, past illnesses, treatments, surgical or other invasive procedures, hospitalizations, medications, and allergies. Information provided must be accurate, timely, and complete. (The court of appeal in *Fall v. White*[9] affirmed the superior court's ruling that the patient had a duty to provide the physician with accurate and complete information and to follow the physician's instructions for further care or tests.)

Inpatient Care Responsibilities

Report unexpected changes in your condition to caregivers. Make it known whether you clearly understand the plan of care. Ask questions to seek clarification of concerns when in doubt about the plan of care. Such questions include: "What is this medication for?" "What diet am I on?" "Since you are going to change my dressing, did you wash your hands?"

Be sure to follow the treatment plan agreed upon. Accept responsibility for the consequences of refusing treatment. Refrain from self-administration of medications not prescribed by the physician, as well as those you may have brought to the hospital with you. Be considerate of the rights of others (e.g., noise control, no-smoking, respect for the rights and property of others).

When in doubt, seek a second opinion. Participate in marking the site of a surgical or other invasive procedure. Communicate to staff your care preferences, including who you have selected as a decision maker in the event you become incapacitated and unable to make decisions for yourself.

Stay Informed

Understand caregiver instructions. Consider the following case where a patient had been sedated during the performance of a colonoscopy at an endoscopy center. He decided to drive himself home against medical advice. Claims against the clinic and a nurse were dismissed with respect to fatal injuries that the patient received during a one-car collision. The trial court correctly ruled that the nurse had no duty to prevent the patient from leaving its premises once she repeatedly warned the patient not to drive. The nurse was justified in relying upon the patient's false representations that he had a friend available to drive him home. She was not required to keep the patient in a gown in the recovery room once she learned the truth, and she was not required to use other options to prevent him from driving, such as putting him in a taxi cab, putting him in a hotel, calling the police, admitting him to the hospital, personally driving him home, taking his keys away from him, or physically restraining him. The center and the nurse owed no legal duty to the patient to do more than warn him that he should not drive. The center is not an insurer of the patients' safety. The patient acted recklessly in ignoring the advice he was given and suffered the consequences. The circuit court correctly found no duty to ensure that no patient drives after the procedure.[10]

Comply with Rules and Regulations

Adhere to rules and regulations in patient handbooks and posted instructive materials. Limit the number of visitors as requested by hospital policy and to protect the privacy of other patients.

Advisory Commission Describes Patient Responsibilities

A 1997 report to the president by the Advisory Commission on Consumer Protection and Quality in the Health Care Industry clearly describes patient responsibilities:[11]

- In a healthcare system that protects consumers' rights, it is reasonable to expect and encourage consumers to assume reasonable responsibilities. Greater individual involvement by consumers in their care increases the likelihood of achieving the best outcomes and helps support a quality improvement, cost-conscious environment. Such responsibilities include:

- Take responsibility for maximizing healthy habits, such as exercising, not smoking, and eating a healthy diet.
- Become involved in specific healthcare decisions.
- Work collaboratively with healthcare providers in developing and carrying out agreed upon treatment plans.
- Disclose relevant information and clearly communicate wants and needs.
- Use the health plan's internal complaint and appeal processes to address concerns that may arise.
- Avoid knowingly spreading disease.
- Recognize the reality of risks and limits of the science of medical care and the human fallibility of the healthcare professional.
- Be aware of a healthcare provider's obligation to be reasonably efficient and equitable in providing care to other patients and the community.
- Become knowledgeable about his or her health plan coverage and health plan options (when available) including all covered benefits, limitations and exclusions, rules regarding use of network providers, coverage and referral rules, appropriate processes to secure additional information, and the process to appeal coverage decisions.
- Show respect for other patients and health workers.
- Make a good-faith effort to meet financial obligations.
- Abide by administrative and operational procedures of health plans, healthcare providers, and government health benefit-programs.
- Report wrongdoing and fraud to appropriate resources or legal authorities.

◆ Notes

1. State of New York, Department of Health. Your Rights as a Hospital Patient in New York State.
2. 42 U.S.C. 1395cc(a)(1).
3. 421 N.W.2d 611 (Mich. Ct. App. 1988).
4. 844 N.E.2d 649 (Ill. App. 2006).
5. 596 N.Y.S.2d 789 (N.Y. App. Div. 1993).
6. *Id.* at 791.
7. 612 P.2d 1158 (Colo. Ct. App. 1980).
8. *Florida Hosp. Waterman, Inc. v. Buster*, 932 So.2d 344 (Fla. App. 2006).
9. 449 N.E.2d 628 (Ind. Ct. App. 1983).
10. *Young v. Gastro-Intestinal Center, Inc.*, No. 04-595 (Ark. 2005).
11. President's Advisory Commission on Consumer Protection and Quality in the Health Care Industry. "Chapter 8: Consumer Bill of Rights and Responsibilities," in *Consumer Responsibilities*, (July 17, 1998). http://www.hcqualitycommission.gov/cborr/chap8.html (accessed October 12, 2010).

. . . no right is held more sacred, or is more carefully guarded, by the common law, than the right of every individual to the possession and control of his own person.

—*Union Pacific Ry. Co. v. Botsford*[1]

13
Patient Consent

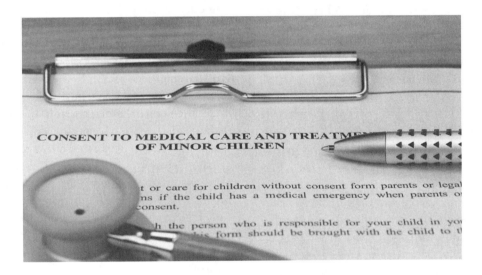

Figure 13–1 Consent for Minor   © Keith A Frith/ShutterStock, Inc.

Learning Objectives

The reader upon completion of this chapter will be able to:

- Explain the concept of informed consent.
- Discuss the difference between verbal, written, and implied consent.
- Describe the role of the patient, physician, nurse, and hospital in informed consent.
- Explain how consent differs between competent patients, minors, guardians, and incompetent patients.
- Discuss under what circumstances a patient might refuse treatment.
- Explain the available defenses for defendants as it relates to informed consent.

Consent, in the healthcare setting, is the voluntary agreement by a person who possesses sufficient mental capacity to make an intelligent choice to allow a medical procedure and/or treatment proposed by another to be performed on himself or herself. Consent changes a touching that otherwise would be nonconsensual to one that is consensual. Consent can be either express or implied.

Express consent can take the form of a (1) *verbal agreement*, or it can be accomplished through the execution of a (2) *written document* authorizing medical care.

Implied consent is determined by some act or silence, which raises a presumption that consent has been authorized.

Consent must be obtained from the patient, or from a person authorized to consent on the patient's behalf before any medical procedure can be performed. Every individual has a right to refuse to authorize a touching. Touching of another without authorization to do so could be considered a battery. Consent is not required for the normal, routine, everyday touching and bumping that occurs in life. In the process of caring for patients, it is inevitable that they will be touched and handled. Most touching in the healthcare setting is considered to be routine. Typical routine touching includes bathing, administering medications, dressing changes, and so forth.

This chapter reviews the many issues surrounding consent in the healthcare setting.

INFORMED CONSENT

Informed consent is a legal doctrine that provides that a patient has the right to know the potential risks, benefits, and alternatives of a proposed procedure. Where there are two or more medically acceptable treatment options, the patient has the absolute right to know about and select from the available treatment options after being informed of the alternatives, risks, and benefits of each.

NEWSPAPER CLIPPINGS: After He Fell Off a Ladder, One Medical Error Led to Another

If you're considering buying your eighth $30,000 car, you can refer to the government-required manufacturers sticker containing information about such things as the price, gas mileage, crash tests and the car's rollover rating. If you're considering a $30,000 medical procedure, you often have to make a choice based solely on what a doctor does—and doesn't—tell you.

—*Kerry O'Connell*, The Washington Post,
August 25, 2012

Informed consent is predicated on the duty of the physician to disclose to the patient sufficient information to enable the patient to evaluate a proposed medical or surgical procedure before submitting to it. Informed consent requires that a patient have a full understanding of that to which he or she has consented. The informed consent doctrine provides that a physician has a legal, ethical, and moral duty to respect patient autonomy and to provide only such medical care as authorized by the patient. An authorization from a patient who does not understand to what he or she is consenting is not effective consent.

The right to be free from unwanted medical treatment has long been recognized by the courts. The right to control the integrity of one's own body spawned the doctrine of informed consent.[2] The U.S. Supreme Court, in *Cruzan v. Director, Missouri Dep't of Health*,[3] held that a competent adult patient has the right to decline any and all forms of medical intervention, including lifesaving or life-prolonging treatment.

Physicians and Informed Consent

It is the treating physician who has the education, expertise, skill, and training necessary to treat a patient and determine what information a patient should have to give informed consent.

Therefore, the physician is expected to disclose to the patient the risks, benefits, and alternatives of a procedure. The duty to inform rests with the physician and requires the exercise of delicate medical judgment.

A physician is not under a duty to elucidate all the possible risks but only those of a serious nature. Expert testimony is often required to establish whether a reasonable physician in the community would make the pertinent disclosures under the same or similar circumstances. Disclosure should include what a reasonable person would consider material to his or her decision of whether or not to undergo treatment.

The Pennsylvania Superior Court held in *Stover v. Surgeons*[4] that the physicians had to discuss alternative prostheses with the patient, where it represented medically recognized alternatives. Evidence that the heart valve actually implanted was no longer in general use at the time of operation was relevant and material to the issue of informed consent.

Although the physicians argued that the choice of the valve should belong to them, the court held that if there are other recognized, medically sound alternatives, the patient must be informed about the risks and benefits of them to make a sound judgment regarding treatment, including the desire to execute a waiver of consent. The agreement between the physician and the patient is contractual. Therefore, for valid consent to occur, there must be a finding that both parties understood the nature of the procedure, including what any possible, as well as expected, results would be. The consent is not valid if the patient did not understand the operation to be performed, its seriousness, the disease or incapacity, and possible results. In the instant case, the physicians failed to inform the patient about the recognized risks of the valve that was implanted.

Finally, the court reasoned that there were alternative valves available that were never discussed with the patient.

To arrive at an informed decision concerning treatment, it was material for the patient to have been told about the alternatives, risks, and benefits of the different valves available for use.

REALITY CHECK: Physician Ignores Patient Instructions

Travis had been sent to a radiologist by his cardiologist to determine his calcium scores. The radiologist found that Travis had a high calcium score. The radiologist suggested CT angiography, which was reluctantly agreed to by Travis' cardiologist. Although the radiologist did find heart disease on the scan, he explained to Travis that in his opinion a cardiac catheterization was a risky procedure and not necessary due to the minimal level of blockage he had. The cardiologist insisted that a cardiac catheterization was necessary to determine the extent of the disease. Travis reluctantly consented to a cardiac catheterization. Although he consented to the procedure for diagnostic purposes, he did not, however, consent to extend the procedure to include the insertion of stents into his coronary arteries. His consent form specifically stated that he did not agree to the insertion of stents. An interventional cardiologist inserted them despite Travis' instructions verbally and in writing on his consent form, provided by the hospital, not to insert stents. Travis reported the incident to the hospital's medical director, who then referred the complaint to the CEO. Travis eventually heard through a cardiac nurse that the hospital did take action to prevent the reoccurrence of such incidents. Travis decided not to file a lawsuit.

Discussion

1. Discuss what legal action the patient can take.
2. Describe actions healthcare organizations should take to prevent such occurrences.

Nurses and Informed Consent

Nurses in most cases have no duty to advise a patient as to a particular procedure to be employed; advise the patient as to the risks, benefits, and alternatives to the recommended procedure; or obtain a patient's informed consent. The physician is in the best position to know the patient's medical history and to evaluate and explain the risks of a particular operation in light of the particular medical history.[5] In instances where a procedure is routine, a nurse

could be liable for failing to inform the patient as to the risks of a CT scan with contrast. The hospital, as employer, would be liable for the nurse's negligence under the doctrine of respondeat superior.

Hospitals and Informed Consent

Although hospitals are not generally responsible for informing patients as to the risks, benefits, and alternatives to specific procedures, there are some cases in which hospitals have a duty to provide patients with informed consent. The patient–plaintiff, in *Keel v. St. Elizabeth Medical Center, Ky.*,[6] filed a medical malpractice action alleging that the hospital failed to provide him with informed consent when he went there for a CT scan. The scan involved the injection of a contrast dye material. Prior to the test, Keel was given no information concerning any risks attendant to the procedure. The dye was injected, and the scan was conducted. However, the plaintiff developed a thrombophlebitis at the site of the injection.

The plaintiff argued that expert medical testimony was not required to prove the absence of informed consent. The hospital argued that the question of informed consent, like the question of negligence, must be determined against the standard of practice among members of the medical profession.

The Kentucky Supreme Court held that expert testimony was not required to establish lack of informed consent and that the hospital had a duty to inform the patient of the risks associated with the procedure. Responsibility did not lie solely with the patient's personal physician.

In view of the special circumstances of this case, the court found it significant that the hospital offered the plaintiff no information whatsoever concerning any possible hazards of this particular procedure, while at the same time the hospital admits that it routinely questions every patient about to undergo a dye injection as to whether he or she has had any previous reactions to contrast materials. Failure to adequately inform the patient need not be established by expert testimony if the failure is so apparent that laypersons may easily recognize it or infer it from evidence within the realm of common knowledge. The hospital's questions to patients regarding reactions to the CT scan procedure demonstrated that the hospital recognized the substantial possibility of complications.

Patients and Informed Consent

At the end of the day and as recognized by the courts, it is the patient's right to accept or refuse treatment based on the alternatives available. Each patient must be "informed" by his or her treating "physician" as to what the alternatives are. The operation, for example, one gets often depends on where you live. Some patients undergo a mastectomy only to learn that a less-destructive alternative procedure is available. The procedure, a lumpectomy, is argued to have the same survival rate as a mastectomy. In one case a patient claimed the surgeon never "informed" her as to the alternative. In the final analysis, the patient decides.

The plaintiff–patient in *Matthies v. Mastromonaco*,[7] an elderly woman living alone in a senior citizens' residence, fell and fractured her hip and was taken to the hospital. An orthopedic surgeon, the defendant, reviewed the patient's history, condition, and X-rays, and decided that, rather than utilizing a pinning procedure for her hip involving the insertion of four steel screws, it would be better to adopt a conservative course of treatment, bed rest.

Prior to her injury, the plaintiff maintained an independent style of living. She did her own grocery shopping and other household duties and had been able to climb steps unassisted.

Expert testimony at trial indicated that bed rest was an inappropriate treatment. The defendant was of the opinion that given the frail condition of the patient and her age, she would be best treated in a nursing home and, therefore, opted for a more conservative treatment. At the heart of the informed consent issue was the plaintiff's assertion that she would not have consented to bed rest if she had been informed of the probable effect on the quality of her life.

The New Jersey Supreme Court held that it is necessary to advise a patient when considering alternative courses of treatment. The physician should have explained medically reasonable invasive and noninvasive alternatives, including the risks and likely outcomes of those alternatives, even when the chosen course is noninvasive.

If the patient's choice is not consistent with the physician's recommendation, the physician has the option of withdrawing from the case. The patient then has the option to seek another physician who is comfortable with the alternative treatment preferred by the patient.

Why Did You Let Them Do That to Me?

Four children, in *Riser v. American Medical Intern, Inc.*,[8] brought a medical malpractice action against Dr. Lang, a physician who performed a femoral arteriogram on their 69-year-old mother. Her physician, Dr. Sottiurai, ordered bilateral arteriograms to determine the cause of the patient's impaired circulation. Because De La Ronde Hospital could not accommodate Dr. Sottiurai's request, Riser was transferred to Dr. Lang, a radiologist at St. Jude Hospital. Dr. Lang performed a femoral arteriogram, not

the bilateral brachial arteriogram ordered by Dr. Sottiurai. The procedure seemed to go well, and the patient was prepared for transfer back to De La Ronde Hospital. However, shortly after the ambulance departed the hospital, the patient suffered a seizure in the ambulance and was returned to St. Jude. Riser's condition deteriorated, and she died 11 days later. The plaintiffs claimed in their lawsuit that Riser was a poor risk for the procedure.

The district court ruled for the plaintiffs, awarding damages in the amount of $50,000 for Riser's pain and suffering and $100,000 to each child and Dr. Lang appealed the decision.

The Louisiana Court of Appeal held that Dr. Lang breached the standard of care by subjecting the patient to a procedure that would have no practical benefit to the patient. Further, Dr. Lang failed to obtain informed consent from the patient. Dr. Sottiurai ordered a brachial arteriogram, not a femoral arteriogram. Riser was under the impression that she was about to undergo a brachial arteriogram, not a femoral arteriogram. O'Neil, one of Riser's daughters, claimed that her mother said following the arteriogram, "Why did you let them do that to me?"[9]

▌ INFORMATION TO BE DISCLOSED

A physician should provide as much information about treatment options as is necessary based on a patient's personal understanding of the physician's explanation of the risks of treatment and the probable consequences of the treatment. The needs of each patient can vary depending on age, maturity, and mental status.

Some courts have recognized that the condition of the patient may be taken into account to determine whether the patient has received sufficient information to give consent. The individual responsible for obtaining consent must weigh the importance of giving full disclosure to the patient against the likelihood that such disclosure will seriously and adversely affect the condition of the patient.

The courts generally utilize an "objective test" or "subjective test" to determine whether a patient would have refused treatment if the physician had provided adequate information as to the risks, benefits, and alternatives of the procedure. In the *objective test*, the plaintiff must prove that a "reasonable person" would not have undergone the procedure if he or she had been properly informed. Under the *subjective test* theory, the court examines whether the "individual patient" would have chosen the procedure if he or she had been fully informed. As described in the following cases, the courts favor the objective test.

Objective Standard

When applying the objective standard, the finder of fact may take into account the characteristics of the plaintiff, including the plaintiff's idiosyncrasies, fears, age, medical condition, and religious beliefs. Accordingly, the objective standard affords the ease of applying a uniform standard and yet maintains the flexibility of allowing the finder of fact to make appropriate adjustments to accommodate the individual characteristics and idiosyncrasies of an individual patient. The standard to be applied in informed consent cases is whether a reasonable person in the patient's position would have consented to the procedure or treatment in question if adequately informed of all significant perils. Under the *objective analysis*, the plaintiff's testimony is only one factor when determining the issue of informed consent. The issue is not whether a particular patient would have chosen a different course of treatment. The issue is whether a reasonable patient would have chosen a different course of treatment.

Subjective Standard

The *subjective standard* relies solely on the credibility of the patient's testimony. Patients must testify and prove that they would not have consented to the procedure(s) had they been advised of the particular risk in question. Proponents of the subjective standard argue that a patient should have the right to make medical decisions regarding his or her care regardless of whether the determination is rational or reasonable. The subjective standard, however, potentially places the physician in jeopardy of the patient's hindsight and bitterness.

▌ ASSESSING DECISION-MAKING CAPACITY

A patient is considered to be competent to make medical decisions regarding his or her care, unless a court determines otherwise. The clinical assessment of decision-making capacity should include the patient's ability to:

- understand the risks, benefits, and alternatives of a proposed test or procedure
- evaluate the information provided by the physician
- express his or her treatment preferences
- voluntarily make decisions regarding his or her treatment plan without undue influence by family, friends, or medical personnel

▌ ADEQUACY OF CONSENT

When questions arise as to whether adequate consent has been given, some courts take into consideration the information that is ordinarily provided by other physicians. A physician must reveal to his or her patient information a skilled practitioner of good standing would provide under similar circumstances. A physician must disclose to the patient the potential of death, serious harm, and other complications associated with a proposed procedure. The scope of a physician's duty to disclose, as noted in *Wooley v. Henderson*,[10] is to be measured by those communications that a reasonable medical practitioner in that branch of medicine would make under the same or similar circumstances.

The plaintiff in *Ramos v. Pyati*[11] brought a medical malpractice action, alleging that the physician performed surgery on his hand outside the scope of surgery to which he consented. The plaintiff had injured his thumb while at work. He was referred to the defendant after seeing three other physicians. The plaintiff was diagnosed as having a ruptured thumb tendon. The plaintiff consented to a surgical repair of the thumb. During surgery, the defendant discovered that scar tissue had formed, causing the ends of the tendons in the thumb to retract. As a result, the surgeon decided to use a donor tendon to make the necessary repairs to the thumb. He chose a tendon from the ring finger. On discovering additional disability from the surgery, the plaintiff filed a suit alleging that his hand was rendered unusable for his employment as a mechanic. The plaintiff testified although he signed a written consent form authorizing surgery on his thumb, he did not consent to a graft of his ring finger tendon or any other tendon. The plaintiff's expert testified the ring finger is the last choice of four other tendons that could have been selected for the surgery. The circuit court entered a judgment for the plaintiff, and the defendant appealed. The appellate court upheld the judgment for the plaintiff, finding that the plaintiff had not consented to use of the ring finger tendon for repair of the thumb tendon.

▌ VERBAL CONSENT

Verbal consent, if proved, is as binding as written consent, for there is, in general, no legal requirement that a patient's consent be in writing. However, oral consent is more difficult to corroborate.

Verbal Consent to Surgery Sufficient

The plaintiff in *Siliezar v. East Jefferson General Hospital*[12] argued that the defendants breached the standard of care by failing to obtain written consent for a surgical procedure. The trial judge found that the plaintiff failed to sustain her burden of proof that the defendants were liable to her for damages. On appeal, the appellees admitted that they breached hospital policy by failing to obtain written consent prior to surgery. The physician, however, testified he explained the surgical procedure, as well as the risks of the procedure. He testified that after he explained the procedure and its risks, he left a written consent for the patient to sign. He explained that while it is the policy of the clinic to obtain a written consent prior to performing surgery, the patient did not sign the consent form. The surgeon testified that he did not know why the form was not signed, but that the patient did not refuse to sign the form.

At trial, a nurse testified that she placed the patient in an operating room and prepared her for surgery. Although she was not in the room when the surgeon discussed the surgical procedure with the plaintiff, she testified that she was in the next room and was able to hear the physician explain the procedure to the plaintiff. The nurse also had no explanation as to why the consent was not signed. She did state that the patient never said she did not want surgery nor did she ask the physician to stop the procedure. The nurse testified that as the physician performed the surgery, he explained to the patient what he was doing.

Louisiana statutes do not require that a patient's consent be written. Verbal consent was sufficient. The verbal consent included the information required by statute, and the patient was given an opportunity to ask questions and those questions were answered. The plaintiff claimed that she was told that surgery would not be performed. The trial judge did not find her testimony to be credible. The appellate court found that the defendants did not commit malpractice by failing to obtain written consent prior to surgery.

WRITTEN CONSENT

Written consent is preferred over oral consent. It provides evidence of a patient's wishes. Because the function of a written consent form is to preserve evidence of informed consent, the nature of the treatment, the risks, the benefits, and the consequences involved should be incorporated into the consent form. States have taken the view that consent, to be effective, must be informed consent. An informed consent form should include the following elements:

- the nature of the patient's illness or injury
- the procedure or treatment consented to
- the purpose of the proposed treatment

- the risks and probable consequences of the proposed treatment
- the probability that the proposed treatment will be successful
- any alternative methods of treatment and their associated risks and benefits
- the risks and prognosis if no treatment is rendered
- an indication that the patient understands the nature of any proposed treatment, the alternatives, the risks involved, and the probable consequences of the proposed treatment
- the signatures of the patient, physician, and witnesses
- the date the consent is signed

Healthcare professionals have an important role in the realm of informed consent. They can be instrumental in averting lawsuits by being observant as to a patient's doubts, changes of mind, confusion, or misunderstandings expressed regarding any proposed procedures he or she is about to undergo.

CONSENT FOR ROUTINE PROCEDURES

Many physicians and healthcare organizations have relied on consent forms worded in such general terms that they permit the physician to perform almost any medical or surgical procedure believed to be in the patient's best interests. There is little difference between a surgical patient who signs no authorization and one who signs a form consenting to whatever procedure the physician deems advisable.

Consent forms signed at the time of admission generally record the patient's consent to routine services, general diagnostic procedures, medical treatment, and everyday routine touchings of the patient. The danger from its use arises from the potential of unwarranted reliance on it for specific, potentially high-risk procedures or treatments.

CONSENT FOR SPECIFIC PROCEDURES

There are a variety of consent forms found in the healthcare setting designed to more specifically describe the risks, benefits, and alternatives of particular invasive and noninvasive procedures. Such forms include consent for anesthesia, cardiac catheterization, surgery, radiation therapy, administration of blood and blood byproducts, chemotherapy, CT and MRI scans, endoscopies, and colonoscopies.

IMPLIED CONSENT

Although the law requires consent for the intentional touching that stems from medical or surgical procedures, exceptions do exist with respect to emergency situations. *Implied consent* will generally be presumed when immediate action is required to prevent death or permanent impairment of a patient's health. If it is impossible in an emergency to obtain the consent of the patient or someone legally authorized to consent, the required procedure may be undertaken without liability for failure to procure consent.

Unconscious patients are presumed under law to approve treatment that appears to be necessary. It is assumed that such patients would have consented if they were conscious and competent. However, if a conscious patient expressly refuses to consent to certain treatment, such treatment may not be instituted after the patient becomes unconscious. Similarly, conscious patients suffering from emergency conditions retain the right to refuse consent.

If a procedure is necessary to protect one's life or health, every effort must be made to document the medical necessity for proceeding with medical treatment without consent. It must be shown that the emergency situation constituted an immediate threat to life or health.

In *Luka v. Lowrie*,[13] a case involving a 15-year-old boy whose left foot had been run over and crushed by a train, consultation by the treating physician with other physicians was an important factor in determining the outcome of the case. On the boy's arrival at the hospital, the defending physician and four house surgeons decided it was necessary to amputate the foot. The court said it was inconceivable that, had the parents been present, they would have refused consent in the face of a determination by five physicians that amputation would save the boy's life. Thus, despite testimony at the trial that the amputation might not have been necessary, professional consultation before the operation supported the assertion that a genuine emergency existed and could be implied consent.

STATUTORY CONSENT

Many states have adopted legislation concerning emergency care. An emergency in most states eliminates the need for consent. When a patient is clinically unable to give consent to a lifesaving emergency treatment, the law implies consent on the presumption that a reasonable person would consent to lifesaving medical intervention.

When an emergency situation does arise, there may be little opportunity to contact the attending physician, much less a consultant. The patient's records, therefore, must be complete with respect to the description of his or her illness and condition, the attempts made to contact the physician as well as relatives, and the emergency measures taken and procedures performed. If time does not permit a court order to be obtained, a second medical opinion, when practicable, is advisable.

JUDICIAL CONSENT

Judicial consent may be necessary in those instances where there is concern as to the absence or legality of consent. Judicial intervention is periodically necessary to grant consent on an emergency basis when a court is not in session. A judge should be contacted only after alternative methods have been exhausted and the matter cannot wait for a determination during the normal working hours of the court. Some courts (e.g., Massachusetts trial courts) require an attorney to initiate the call to the justice and to certify that there are no alternatives, other than a judicial response, available in the matter.

WHO MAY CONSENT

Consent of the patient ordinarily is required before treatment. However, when the patient is either physically unable or legally incompetent to consent and no emergency exists, consent must be obtained from a person who is empowered to consent on the patient's behalf. The person who authorizes treatment of another must have sufficient information to make an intelligent judgment on behalf of the patient.

Competent Patients

A competent adult patient's wishes concerning his or her person may not be disregarded. The court in *In re Melideo*[14] held that every human being of adult years has a right to determine what shall be done with his or her own body and cannot be subjected to medical treatment without his or her consent. When there is no compelling state interest that justifies overriding an adult patient's decision, that decision should be respected.

In *Fosmire v. Nicoleau*,[15] the New York Court of Appeals, New York's highest court, stated that the citizens of the state have long had the right to make their own medical care choices without regard to their medical condition or status as parents. The court of appeals held that a competent adult has both a common law and statutory right under public health law to refuse lifesaving treatment. Citing the state's authority to compel vaccination to protect the public from the spread of disease, to order treatment for persons who are incapable of making medical decisions, and to prohibit medical procedures that pose a substantial risk to the patient alone, the court of appeals did note that the right to choose is not absolute. However, if there is no compelling state interest to justify overriding a patient's refusal to consent to a medical procedure because of religious beliefs, states are reluctant to override such a decision.

Guardianship

A *guardian* is an individual who by law is vested with the power and charged with the duty of taking care of a patient by protecting the patient's rights and managing the patient's estate. Guardianship is often necessary in those instances in which a patient is incapable of managing or administering his or her private affairs because of physical and/or mental disabilities or because he or she is under the age of majority.

Temporary guardianship can be granted by the courts if it is determined that such is necessary for the well-being of the patient. Temporary guardianship was granted by the court in *In re Estate of Dorone*,[16] where the physician and administrator petitioned the court on two occasions for authority to administer blood to a 22-year-old male patient brought to the hospital center by helicopter after an automobile accident was diagnosed as suffering from an acute subdural hematoma. It was determined that the patient would die unless he underwent a cranial operation. The operation required the administration of blood to which the parents would not consent because of their religious beliefs. After a hearing by telephone, the court of common pleas appointed the hospital's administrator as temporary guardian, authorizing him to consent to the performance of blood transfusions during emergency surgery. A more formal hearing did not take place because of the emergency situation that existed. Surgery was required a second time to remove a blood clot, and the court once again granted the administrator authority to authorize administration of blood. The superior court affirmed the orders, and the parents appealed.

The Pennsylvania Supreme Court held that the judge's failure to obtain direct testimony from the patient's parents and others concerning the patient's religious beliefs were not in error when death was likely to result from withholding blood. The judge's decisions granting guardianship and the authority to consent to the administration of blood were considered absolutely necessary in the light of the facts of this case. Nothing less than a fully conscious contemporary decision by the patient himself would have been sufficient to override the evidence of medical necessity.

Consent for Minors

When a medical or surgical procedure is to be performed on a minor, the question arises as to whether the minor's consent alone is sufficient and, if not, who should provide the necessary consent. The courts have held, as a general proposition, that the consent of a minor to medical or surgical treatment is ineffective and that the physician must secure the consent of the minor's parent or someone standing in loco parentis; otherwise, he or she will risk liability. Although parental consent should be obtained before treating a minor, treatment should not be delayed to the detriment of the child.

Parental consent is not necessary when the minor is married or otherwise emancipated. Most states have enacted statutes making it valid for married and emancipated minors to provide effective consent. Several courts have held the consent of a minor to be sufficient authorization for treatment in certain situations. In any specific case, a court's determination that the consent of a minor is effective and that parental consent is unnecessary will depend on such factors as the minor's age, maturity, mental status, and emancipation and the procedure involved, as well as public policy considerations.

In *Carter v. Cangello*,[17] the California Court of Appeals held that a 17-year-old girl who was living away from home, in the home of a woman who gave her free room and board in exchange for household chores, and who made her own financial decisions, legally could consent to medical procedures performed on her. The court made this decision knowing that the girl's parents provided part of her income by paying for her private schooling and certain medical care. The physician was privileged under statute to act on the minor's consent to surgery, and such privilege insulated him from liability to the parents for treating their daughter without their consent.

Many states have recognized by legislation that treatment for conditions as pregnancy, venereal disease, and drug dependency does not require parental consent. State legislatures have reasoned that a minor is not likely to seek medical assistance when parental consent is demanded. Insisting on parental consent for the treatment of these conditions would increase the likelihood that a minor would delay or do without treatment to avoid explanation to the parents.

State's Interests on Behalf of Minor

The Nevada Supreme Court in *Soto v. Valley Medical Center Nevada*, (2004), determined that

> 'Substantive due process guarantees that no person shall be deprived of life, liberty or property for arbitrary reasons.' The due process clause of the Fourteenth

Amendment protects those liberty interests that are deemed fundamental and are deeply rooted in this nation's history and tradition. Certain family privacy rights, including the parent–child relationship, had therefore been recognized as fundamental rights. We have adopted a 'reasonable test' to address family privacy cases involving competing interests within the family. This test "implicitly calibrates the level of scrutiny in each case to match the particular degree of intrusion upon the parents' interest."

While a parent has a fundamental liberty interest in the 'care, custody, and management' of his child, that interest is not absolute. 'The state also has an interest in the welfare of children and may limit parental authority,' even permanently depriving parents of their children. Therefore, while Jason and Rebecca have a parental interest in the care of their son, both the state and H. S. have an interest in preserving the child's life. As H. S. is unable to make decisions for himself, the State's interest is heightened. Jason and Rebecca's liberty interest in practicing their religion must also give way to the child's welfare. Here the District Court found that Jason and Rebecca's refusal to consent to treatment put H. S.'s life at substantial risk. Additionally, the State has an interest in protecting the 'ethical integrity' of the medical profession and in allowing hospitals the full opportunity to care for patients under their control, especially when medical science is available to save that patient's life.

'Here, the child's interest in self–preservation and the State's interest in protecting the welfare of children and the integrity of medical care outweigh the parents' interest in the care, custody and management of their children, and their religious freedom. The combined weight of the interest of the child and the State are great and, therefore, mandate interference with Jason and Rebecca's parental rights.'[18]

The Right to Choose: A Minor's Consent

Abraham Cherrix was 16-years old when he was diagnosed with Hodgkin's disease. He was treated with chemotherapy. He later learned that chemotherapy had not cured his disease. Doctors recommended a higher dosage of chemotherapy combined with radiation and culminating in stem cell therapy. The treatment program offered Abraham less than a 50% chance of survival. Abraham and his family chose to pursue alternative treatment in Mexico. Cherrix's oncologist reported the family's decision to the Department of Social Services (DSS). Cherrix's parents were accused of medical neglect by DSS. A judge granted the DSS temporary joint custody with the Cherrixes. The parents faced charges in the juvenile and domestic court

for parental neglect. The family obtained a stay from the circuit court.[19] The Accomack Virginia Circuit Court judge cleared Abraham's parents of all charges of medical neglect and allowed Abraham to pursue alternative treatment under a doctor of the family's choice. The family will provide the court updates on Abraham's care every 3 months until he's cured or turns 18. The questions to be asked in this case include: Whose body is it, anyway? Did the state go too far? The judge must have thought so: "The judge agreed to allow me to see an oncologist of my choice! My alternative treatments WILL continue. He also ruled that my parents were not guilty of medical neglect, and social services no longer had any jurisdiction over my case! Free, happy, and ready to live, that's me!"[20]

Incompetent Patients

The ability to consent to treatment is a question of fact. The attending physician, who is in the best position to make the determination, should become familiar with his or her state's definition of legal incompetence. In any case in which a physician doubts a patient's capacity to consent, the consent of the legal guardian or next of kin should be obtained. If there are no relatives to consult, application should be made for a court order that would allow the procedure. It may be the duty of the court to assume responsibility of guardianship for a patient who is non compos mentis. The most frequently cited conditions indicative of incompetence are mental illness, mental retardation, senility, physical incapacity, and chronic alcohol or drug abuse.

A person who is mentally incompetent cannot legally consent to treatment. Therefore, consent of the patient's legal guardian must be obtained. When no legal guardian is available, a court that handles such matters must be petitioned to permit treatment.

Subject to applicable statutory provisions, when a physician doubts a patient's capacity to consent, even though the patient has not been judged legally incompetent, the consent of the nearest relative should be obtained. If a patient is conscious and mentally capable of giving consent for treatment, the consent of a relative without the consent of the competent patient would not protect the physician from liability.

Limited Power of Attorney

A limited power of attorney authorizes, for example, school officials, teachers, and camp counselors to act on the parent's/parents' or legal guardian's behalf when seeking emergency care for injured students or campers. Such consent for treatment provides limited protection in the care of a particular child.

RIGHT TO REFUSE TREATMENT

[T]he individual's right to make decisions vitally affecting his private life according to his own conscience . . . is difficult to overstate . . . because it is, without exaggeration, the very bed rock on which this country was founded.

—*WONS V. PUBLIC HEALTH TRUST* [21]

Adult patients who are conscious and mentally competent have the right to refuse medical care to the extent permitted by law, even when the best medical opinion deems it essential to life. If a patient rejects treatment, the hospital should take all reasonable steps to inform the patient of the risks of refusing treatment. Such a refusal must be honored whether it is grounded in religious belief or mere whim. Every person has the legal right to refuse to permit a touching of his or her body. Failure to respect this right can result in a legal action for assault and battery. Coercion through threat, duress, or intimidation must be avoided.

A patient's right to make decisions regarding his own health care is addressed in the Patient Self-Determination Act of 1990.[22] The act provides that each person has a right under state law (whether statutory or as recognized by the courts of the state) to make decisions concerning his or her medical care, including the right to accept or refuse medical or surgical treatment.

A competent patient's refusal to consent to a medical or surgical procedure must be adhered to, whether the refusal is grounded on lack of confidence in the physician, fear of the procedure, doubt as to the value of a particular procedure, or mere whim. The U.S. Supreme Court stated that the "notion of bodily integrity has been embodied in the requirement that informed consent is generally required for medical treatment" and the "logical corollary of the doctrine of informed consent is that the patient generally possesses the right not to consent, that is, to refuse treatment."[23]

The question of liability for performing a medical or surgical procedure without consent is separate and distinct from any question of negligence or malpractice in performing a procedure. Liability can be imposed for a nonconsensual touching of a patient, even if the procedure improved the patient's health. The eminent Justice Cardozo, in *Schloendorff v. Society of New York Hospital*, stated:

> Every human being of adult years and sound mind has a right to determine what shall be done with his own body and a surgeon who performs an operation without his patient's consent commits an assault, for

which he is liable in damages, except in cases of emergency where the patient is unconscious and where it is necessary to operate before consent can be obtained.[24]

The courts perform a balancing test to determine whether to override a competent adult's decision to refuse medical treatment. The courts balance state interests, such as preservation of life, protection of third parties, prevention of suicide, and the integrity of the medical profession against a patient's rights of bodily integrity and religious freedom.

The most frequently used state right to intervene in a patient's decision-making process is for the protection of third parties. In *In re Fetus Brown*,[25] the state of Illinois asserted that its interest in the well-being of a viable fetus outweighed the patient's rights to refuse medical treatment. The state argued that a balancing test should be used to weigh state interests against patient rights. The appellate court held that it could not impose a legal obligation upon a pregnant woman to consent to an invasive medical procedure for the benefit of her viable fetus.

Religious Beliefs

As part of their religious beliefs, Jehovah's Witnesses generally have refused the administration of blood, even in emergency situations. Case law over the past several decades has developed to a point where any person, regardless of religious beliefs, has the right to refuse medical treatment.

The plaintiff, Bonita Perkins, in *Perkins v. Lavin*,[26] was a Jehovah's Witness. She gave birth at the defendant–hospital on September 26, 1991, and was discharged 2 or 3 days later. After going home, she began hemorrhaging and returned to the hospital. She specifically informed the defendant's employees that she was not to be provided any blood or blood derivatives and completed and signed a form to that effect:

> I request that no blood or blood derivatives be administered to (plaintiff) during this hospitalization, notwithstanding that such treatment may be deemed necessary in the opinion of the attending physician or his assistants to preserve life or promote recovery. I release the attending physician, his assistants, the hospital and its personnel from any responsibility whatever for any untoward results due to my refusal to permit the use of blood or its derivatives.[27]

Due to the plaintiff's condition, it became necessary to perform an emergency dilation and curettage on her. She continued to bleed, and her condition deteriorated dramatically. Her blood count dropped, necessitating administration of blood products as a lifesaving measure. Her husband, who was not a Jehovah's Witness, consented to a blood transfusion, which was administered. The plaintiff recovered and filed an action against the defendant for assault and battery and intentional infliction of emotional distress. The plaintiff's claim as to assault and battery was sustained. The claim as to the intentional infliction of emotional distress was overruled.

Good People: Bad Choices

Both the provider and the patient can make bad choices. Although in the following case the hospital was exonerated from wrongdoing, an argument could be made that the hospital should have been more alert to the patient's needs. The patient, however, unwilling to wait, left the hospital without care and thus suffered harm.

The Long Wait

On August 10, 1988, Matthews had gone unassisted to the emergency department (ED) of the hospital complaining of a burning pain in her upper chest that had radiated down her right side that evening. Upon arriving at the hospital at about 11:25 P.M., Matthews was triaged by a nurse who took her vital signs, recorded her medical history, and made an assessment of her immediate medical needs. Although slightly elevated, Matthews's vital signs were within normal limits. Matthews was classified by a triage nurse as a category-2 patient, which refers to a determination by the nurse that the patient was in a nonthreatening condition. It was explained to her that she would have a long wait because the ED was busy. A social services representative (SSR) testified that he spoke to Matthews six or eight times during her wait in the ED, stating she was in no apparent distress during those times that he spoke to her. Following a 4½-hour wait, Matthews decided to leave the ED without being treated. The SSR stated that he told Matthews that a treatment room was ready for her and that she would be attended to shortly. Matthews said that she had already waited long enough and she was leaving. The SSR stated that he pleaded with her to stay but she refused, claiming that she would see her own physician in the morning. Matthews went to work the following day without having seen her physician. She died on August 12, 1988. A malpractice action was brought against the hospital arising out of the death of Matthews. The DeKalb Superior Court granted the hospital's motion for summary judgment, and an appeal was taken.

Matthews voluntarily terminated her relationship with the emergency department personnel, severing any "causal" relationship that might have existed between the hospital's act of classifying Matthews as a category-2 patient and her death. Accordingly, the hospital was held not liable for her death.[28]

Release from Liability

A patient's refusal to consent to treatment, for any reason, religious or otherwise, should be noted in the medical record, and a release form should be executed. The completed release provides documented evidence of a patient's refusal to consent to a recommended treatment. A release will help protect the organization and physicians from liability should a suit arise as a result of a failure to treat. The best possible care must be rendered to the patient at all times within the limits imposed by the patient's refusal. Should a patient refuse to sign the release, documentation of the refusal should be placed on the form, and the form should be included as part of the patient's permanent medical record.

Advice of legal counsel should be sought in those cases where a parent or guardian's refusal of treatment for a minor poses a serious risk to a minor's health. With the advice of legal counsel, the organization should formulate a policy regarding treatment when consent has been refused. A procedure should be developed to facilitate application for a court order when one is necessary and there is sufficient time to obtain one.

DEFENSES FOR FAILURE TO PROVIDE CONSENT

Several defenses are available to provider–defendants who have been sued on the basis of failure to provide their patients with sufficient information to make an informed decision. Some of the defenses include:

- the risk not disclosed is too commonly known to warrant disclosure
- the patient assured the medical practitioner that he or she would undergo the treatment or procedure regardless of the risk involved, or the patient assured the medical practitioner that he or she did not want to be informed of the matters to which he or she would be entitled to be informed
- consent by or on behalf of a patient was not reasonably possible
- the medical practitioner, after considering all of the attendant facts and circumstances, used reasonable discretion as to the manner and extent to which such alternatives

or risks were disclosed to the patient because the practitioner reasonably believed that the manner and extent of such disclosure could reasonably be expected to adversely and substantially affect the patient's condition.

A patient's condition during surgery may be recognized as different from that which had been expected and explained, requiring a different procedure than the one to which the patient initially consented. The surgeon may proceed to treat the new condition; however, the patient should be aware of the possibility of extending the procedure.

The patient in *Winfrey v. Citizens & Southern National Bank*[29] brought a suit against the deceased surgeon's estate, alleging that during exploratory surgery, the surgeon performed a complete hysterectomy without the patient's consent. The superior court granted summary judgment for the surgeon's estate, and the patient appealed. The court of appeals held that even though the patient may not have read the consent document, when no legally sufficient excuse appeared, she was bound by the terms of the consent document that she voluntarily executed. The plain wording of the binding consent authorized the surgeon to perform additional or different operations or procedures that he might consider necessary or advisable in the course of the operation. Relevant sections of the consent signed by the patient included the following:

1. I authorize the performance on (patient's name) of the following operation/laparoscopy, possible laparotomy. . . .
2. I consent to the performance of operations and procedures in addition to or different from those now contemplated, which the above named doctor or his associates or assistants may consider necessary or advisable in the course of the operation. . . .

• • •

7. I acknowledge that the nature and purpose of the operation, possible alternative methods of treatment, the risks involved, and the possibility of complications have been fully explained to me.[30]

ETHICS AND INFORMED CONSENT

The ethical rationale underlying the doctrine of informed consent is firmly rooted in the notions of liberty and individual autonomy. Informed consent protects the basic right of the patient to make the ultimate informed decision regarding the course of treatment to which he or she consents. The focus of informed consent must involve the patient receiving informed consent as a result of active personal interaction with the physician. Consent forms should be used as a supplement to the oral disclosure of risks, benefits, and alternatives to the proposed procedure that a physician normally gives. Ideally, consent should be the result of an active process of dialogue between the patient and physician.

Notes

1. 141 U.S. 250, 21 (1891).
2. *In re Duran*, 769 A.2d 497 (Pa. 2001).
3. 497 U.S. 261 (1990).
4. 635 A.2d 1047 (Pa. Super. Ct. 1993).
5. *Mathias v. St. Catherine's Hosp., Inc.*, 569 N.W.2d 330 (Wis. App. 1997).
6. 842 S.W.2d 860 (Ky. 1992).
7. *Matthies v. Mastromonaco*, 733 A.2d 456 (1999).
8. 620 So. 2d 372 (La. Ct. App. 1993).
9. *Id.* at 380.
10. 418 A.2d 1123 (Me. 1980).
11. 534 N.E.2d 472 (Ill. App. Ct. 1989).
12. No. 04-CA-939 (La. Ct. App. 5 Cir. 1/11/05).
13. 136 N.W. 1106 (Mich. 1912).
14. 390 N.Y.S.2d 523 (N.Y. Sup. Ct. 1976).
15. 536 N.Y.S.2d 492 (N.Y. App. Div. 1989).
16. 534 A.2d 452 (Pa. 1987).
17. 164 Cal. Rptr. 361 (Cal. Ct. App. 1980).
18. Jwdivorces.bravehost.com/blood.html.
19. My Journey. Abraham Cherrix's Page. www.abrahamsjourney.com/theHOMEpage.html.
20. *Id.*
21. 500 So. 2d 679, 687 (Fla. Dist. Ct. App. 1987), aff'd 541 So. 2d 96 (Fla. 1989).
22. Public Law 101-508, November 5, 1990, sections 4206 and 4751 of the Omnibus Budget Reconciliation Act.
23. *Cruzan v. Director, Missouri Dep't of Health*, 497 U.S. 261, 269 (1990).
24. 105 N.E. 92, 93 (N.Y. 1914).
25. 689 N.E.2d 397 (Ill. App. Ct. 1997).
26. 648 N.E.2d 839 (Ohio App. 9 Dist. 1994).
27. *Id.* at 840.
28. *Matthews v. DeKalb County Hosp. Auth.*, 440 S.E.2d 743 (Ga. Ct. App. 1994).
29. 254 S.E.2d 725 (Ga. Ct. App. 1979).
30. *Id.* at 727.

14

Procreation and Ethical Dilemmas

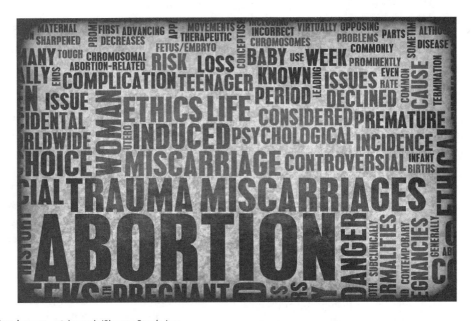

Figure 14–1 Abortion Issues © kentoh/ShutterStock, Inc.

Learning Objectives

The reader upon completion of this chapter will be able to:

- Discuss the 1973 Supreme Court ruling in *Roe v. Wade* and the continuing controversy over abortion.

- Describe the flow of abortion cases beginning with *Roe v. Wade*, concentrating on counseling, consent, partial birth abortion, and funding.

- Explain the legal issues of sterilization, artificial insemination, and surrogacy.

- Describe the legal and moral issues of wrongful birth, wrongful life, and wrongful conception.

There are numerous ethical questions involving the entire life span, from the right to be born to the right to die. This chapter reviews a variety of issues of procreation. Primary emphasis is placed on abortion. Discussed to a lesser extent are issues relating to sterilization, artificial insemination, wrongful birth, wrongful life, and wrongful conception.

Ethical dilemmas arise that often require a choice that must be made between unpleasant alternatives. It can occur whenever a choice involves giving up something good and suffering something bad, no matter what course of action is taken. Ethical dilemmas often require caregivers to make decisions that may break some ethical norm or contradict some ethical value. For example, should I choose life knowing that an unborn child will be born with severe disabilities, or should I choose abortion and thus, possibly, preventing pain for both parent and child? Should I adhere to my spouse's wishes not to be placed on a respirator, or should I choose life over death, disregarding her wishes and right to self-determination? Should I encourage the abortion of my pregnant daughter, the victim of a gang rape, or should I choose life and "do no harm" to the unborn child? Such dilemmas give rise to conflicting answers.

Both this chapter and the chapter on end-of-life issues focus on some of the more common daunting questions facing healthcare providers where both ethics and the law intersect. When reviewing these chapters, the reader should apply the ethical theories, principles, and values discussed in the ethics chapter.

ABORTION

 We shall have to fight the politician, who remembers only that the unborn have no votes and that since posterity has done nothing for us we need do nothing for posterity.

—WILLIAM RALPH INGE (1860–1954)[1]

Abortion is the premature termination of pregnancy. It can be classified as spontaneous or induced. It may occur as an incidental result of a medical procedure or it may be an elective decision on the part of the patient. In addition to having substantial ethical, moral, and religious implications, abortion has proven to be a major legal issue and will continue as such in the future. More laws will be proposed, more laws will be passed, and more lawsuits, as noted in the following cases, will wind their way up to the U.S. Supreme Court.

A consensus as to when life begins has not been reached. There has been no final determination as to the proper interplay among a mother's liberty, the interests of an unborn child, and the state's interests in protecting life. In abortion cases, the law presupposes a theory of ethics and morality, which, in turn, presupposes deeply personal ideas about being and existence. Answers to such questions as to when life begins define ethical and religious beliefs, and these beliefs often determine how we govern ourselves. Abortion in this context is less a question about constitutional law and more about who we are as a people. This is a decision

the Supreme Court cannot make. Taking these issues out of the public discourse threatens to foment hostility, stifle the search for answers, distance people from their Constitution, and undermine the credibility of that document.[2]

With more than 1 million abortions performed annually in the United States, it is certain that the conflict between "pro-choice" and "pro-life" advocates will continue to pervade America's landscape. The issues are numerous, and emotions run high.

These are but a few of the many questions yet to be fully resolved. As the following pages point out, for each new issue decided in the courts, numerous new issues arise, all of which seem to involve both legal and moral questions as to what is acceptable behavior in American society. The following cases were decided by the U.S. Supreme Court and have the effect of law.

Right to Abortion

1973: In *Roe v. Wade* in 1973, the Supreme Court gave strength to a woman's right to privacy in the context of matters relating to her own body, including how a pregnancy would end.[3] However, the Supreme Court also has recognized the interest of the states in protecting potential life and has attempted to spell out the extent to which the states may regulate and even prohibit abortions.

In *Roe v. Wade*, the U.S. Supreme Court held the Texas penal abortion law unconstitutional, stating: "State criminal abortion statutes . . . that except from criminality only a lifesaving procedure on behalf of the mother, without regard to the stage of her pregnancy and other interests involved, is violating the Due Process Clause of the Fourteenth Amendment."[4]

First Trimester

During the first trimester of pregnancy, the decision to undergo an abortion procedure is between the woman and her physician. A state may require that abortions be performed by a licensed physician pursuant to law; however, a woman's right to an abortion is not unqualified because the decision to perform the procedure must be left to the medical judgment of her attending physician. "For the stage prior to approximately the end of the first trimester, the abortion decision and its effectuation must be left to the medical judgment of the pregnant woman's attending physician."[5]

Second Trimester

In *Roe v. Wade*, the Supreme Court stated, "[f]or the stage subsequent to approximately the end of the first trimester, the State, in promoting its interest in the health of the mother, may, if it chooses, regulate the abortion procedure in ways that are reasonably related to maternal health."[6] Thus, during approximately the fourth to sixth months of pregnancy, the state may regulate the medical conditions under which the procedure is performed. The constitutional test of any legislation concerning abortion during this period would be its relevance to the objective of protecting maternal health.

Third Trimester

The Supreme Court reasoned that by the time the final stage of pregnancy has been reached, the state has acquired a compelling interest in the product of conception, which would override the woman's right to privacy and justify stringent regulation even to the extent of prohibiting abortions. In the *Roe* case, the Supreme Court formulated its ruling as to the last trimester in the following words: "For the stage subsequent to viability, the State in promoting its interest in the potentiality of human life, may, if it chooses, regulate, and even proscribe, abortion except where it is necessary, in appropriate medical judgment for the preservation of the life or health of the mother."[7]

Thus, during the final stage of pregnancy, a state may prohibit all abortions except those deemed necessary to protect maternal life or health. The state's legislative powers over the performance of abortions increase as the pregnancy progresses toward term. For example, the cutoff for legal abortions in Pennsylvania is the 24th week. As noted in the following news report and grand jury hearing, without enforcement of abortion laws, abuses of the system will continue to occur due to financial greed and the blatant disrespect for human life.

NEWSPAPER CLIPPINGS: Why Dr. Kermit Gosnell's Trial Should Be a Major News Story

There is, finally, the fact that abortion, one of the most hotly contested, polarizing debates in the country, is at the center of this case. It arguably informs the abortion debate in any number of ways, and has numerous plausible implications for abortion policy, including the oversight and regulation of clinics, the appropriateness of late-term abortions, the penalties for failing to report abuses, the statute of limitations for killings like those with which Gosnell is charged, whether staff should be legally culpable for the bad behavior of doctors under whom they work . . .

—*Conor Friedersdorf*, The Atlantic | National Journal,
April 12, 2013

IN THE COURT OF COMMON PLEAS
FIRST JUDICIAL DISTRICT OF PENNSYLVANIA
CRIMINAL TRIAL DIVISION

IN RE	: MISC. NO. 0009901-2008
COUNTY INVESTIGATING	:
GRAND JURY XXIII	: C-17

This case is about a doctor who killed babies and endangered women. What we mean is that he regularly and illegally delivered live, viable, babies in the third trimester of pregnancy—and then murdered these newborns by severing their spinal cords with scissors. The medical practice by which he carried out this business was a filthy fraud in which he overdosed his patients with dangerous drugs, spread venereal disease among them with infected instruments, perforated their wombs and bowels – and, on at least two occasions, caused their deaths. Over the years, many people came to know that something was going on here. But no one put a stop to it.

• • •

There remained, however, a final difficulty. When you perform late-term "abortions" by inducing labor, you get babies. Live, breathing, squirming babies. By 24 weeks, most babies born prematurely will survive if they receive appropriate medical care. But that was not what the Women's Medical Society was about. Gosnell had a simple solution for the unwanted babies he delivered: he killed them. He didn't call it that. He called it "ensuring fetal demise." The way he ensured fetal demise was by sticking scissors into the back of the baby's neck and cutting the spinal cord. He called that "snipping."[8]

Abortion Review Committee Too Restrictive

1973: The Supreme Court went on to delineate what regulatory measures a state lawfully may enact during the three stages of pregnancy. In the companion decision, *Doe v. Bolton*,[9] where the Court considered a constitutional attack on the Georgia abortion statute, further restrictions were placed on state regulation of the procedure. The provisions of the Georgia statute establishing residency requirements for women seeking abortions and requiring that the procedure be performed in a hospital accredited by the Joint Commission were declared constitutionally invalid. In considering legislative provisions establishing medical staff approval as a prerequisite to the abortion procedure, the Court decided that "interposition of the hospital abortion committee is unduly restrictive of the patient's rights and needs that . . . have already been medically delineated and substantiated by her personal physician. To ask more serves neither the hospital nor the State."[10]

The Court was unable to find any constitutionally justifiable rationale for a statutory requirement of advance approval by the abortion committee of the hospital's medical staff. Insofar as statutory consultation requirements are concerned, the Court reasoned that the acquiescence of two copractitioners has no rational connection with a patient's needs and, further, unduly infringes on the physician's right to practice.

Thus, by using a test related to patient needs, the Court, in *Doe v. Bolton*, struck down four preabortion procedural requirements commonly imposed by state statutes: (1) residency, (2) performance of the abortion in a hospital accredited by The Joint Commission, (3) approval by an appropriate committee of the medical staff, and (4) consultations.

Funding

Some states have placed an indirect restriction on abortion through the elimination of funding. Under the 1997 Hyde Amendment, the U.S. Congress, through appropriations legislation, has limited the types of medically necessary abortions for which federal funds may be spent under the Medicaid program. Although the Hyde Amendment does not prohibit states from funding nontherapeutic abortions, this action by the federal government opened the door to state statutory provisions limiting the funding of abortions.

Not Required for Elective Abortions

1977: In *Beal v. Doe*,[11] the Pennsylvania Medicaid plan was challenged based on denial of financial assistance for nontherapeutic abortions. The Supreme Court held that Title XIX of the Social Security Act (the Medicaid program) does not require the funding of nontherapeutic abortions as a condition of state participation in the program.[12] The state has a strong interest in encouraging normal childbirth, and nothing in Title XIX suggests that it is unreasonable for the state to further that interest. The Court ruled that it is not inconsistent with the Medicaid portion of the Social Security Act to refuse to fund unnecessary (although perhaps desirable) medical services.

1977: In *Maher v. Roe*,[13] the Supreme Court considered the Connecticut statute that denied Medicaid benefits for first-trimester abortions that were not medically necessary. The Court rejected the argument that the state's subsidy of medical expenses incident to pregnancy and childbirth created an obligation on the part of the state to subsidize the expenses

incident to nontherapeutic abortions. The Supreme Court voted six to three that the states may refuse to spend public funds to provide nontherapeutic abortions for women.

Not Required for Therapeutic Abortions

1980: The Supreme Court, in *Harris v. McRae*,[14] upheld five to four the Hyde Amendment, which restricts the use of federal funds for Medicaid abortions. Under this case, the different states are not compelled to fund Medicaid recipients' medically necessary abortions for which federal reimbursement is unavailable, but may choose to do so. Mr. Justice Marshall, dissenting, stated that the Court's decision marked a retreat from *Roe v. Wade* and represented a cruel blow to the most powerless members of our society.

Funding Bans Unconstitutional in California

The California Supreme Court held that funding bans were unconstitutional; the court asked rhetorically:

> If the state cannot directly prohibit a woman's right to obtain an abortion, may the state by discriminatory financing indirectly nullify that constitutional right? Can the state tell an indigent person that the state will provide him with welfare benefits only upon the condition that he join a designated political party or subscribe to a particular newspaper that is favored by the government? Can the state tell a poor woman that it will pay for her needed medical care but only if she gives up her constitutional right to choose whether or not to have a child?[15]

Funding Discrimination Prohibited in Arizona

2002: The Arizona Supreme Court, in *Simat Corp. v. Arizona Health Care Cost Containment Sys.*,[16] found that the state's constitution does not permit the state and the Arizona Health Care Cost Containment System (AHCCCS) to refuse to fund medically necessary abortion procedures for pregnant women suffering from serious illness while funding such procedures for victims of rape or incest or when the abortion was necessary to save the woman's life (A.R.S. § 35-196.02. AHCCCS). After the state has chosen to fund abortions for one group of indigent, pregnant women for whom abortions are medically necessary to save their lives, the state may not deny the same option to another group of women for whom the procedure is also medically necessary to save their health. An example is cancer, for which chemotherapy or radiation therapy ordinarily cannot be provided if the patient is pregnant, making an abortion necessary before proceeding with the recognized medical treatment. Other therapy regimens that must at times be suspended during pregnancy include those for heart disease, diabetes, kidney disease, liver disease, chronic renal failure, inflammatory bowel disease, and lupus. In many of the women suffering from these diseases, suspension of recognized therapy during pregnancy will have serious and permanent adverse effects on their health and lessen their life span. In such a situation, the state is not simply influencing a woman's choice but is actually conferring the privilege of treatment on one class and withholding it from another.

A woman's right to choose preservation and protection of her health and, therefore, in many cases, her life is at least as compelling as the state's interest in promoting childbirth. The court's protection of the fetus and promotion of childbirth cannot be considered so compelling as to outweigh a woman's fundamental right to choose and the state's obligation to be evenhanded in the design and application of its healthcare policies. The majority of states that have examined similar Medicaid funding restrictions have determined that their state statutes or constitutions offer broader protection of individual rights than does the U.S. Constitution, and they have found that medically necessary abortions should be funded if the state also funds medically necessary expenses related to childbirth. The case was remanded to the trial court for further proceedings consistent with this opinion.

States May Protect Viable Fetus

1979: The Supreme Court, in *Colautti v. Franklin,*[17] voted six to three that the states may seek to protect a fetus that a physician has determined could survive outside the womb. Determination of whether a particular fetus is viable is, and must be, a matter for judgment of the responsible attending physician. State abortion regulations that impinge on this determination, if they are to be constitutional, must allow the attending physician the room that he or she needs to make the best medical judgment.

Consent

Missouri: Parental Consent Statute Ruled Unconstitutional

1976: The Supreme Court ruled in *Danforth v. Planned Parenthood*[18] that a Missouri statute requiring all women under age 18 to obtain written consent of a parent or person in loco parentis prior to an abortion is unconstitutional. The Court, however, failed to provide any definitive guidelines as to when and how parental consent may be required if the minor is too immature to fully comprehend the nature of the procedure.

Massachusetts: Parental Consent Statute Ruled Unconstitutional

1979: The Supreme Court, in *Bellotti v. Baird,*[19] ruled eight to one that a Massachusetts statute requiring parental consent before an abortion could be performed on an unmarried woman under age 18 was unconstitutional. Justice Stevens, joined by Justices Brennan, Marshall, and Blackmun, concluded that the Massachusetts statute was unconstitutional, because under that statute as written and construed by the Massachusetts Supreme Judicial Court, no minor, no matter how mature and capable of informed decision making, could receive an abortion without the consent of either both parents or a superior court judge, thus making the minor's abortion subject in every instance to an absolute third-party veto.

Utah: Notifying Parent for Immature Minor Constitutional

1981: The Supreme Court, in *H. L. v. Matheson,*[20] by a six to three vote, upheld a Utah statute that required a physician to "notify, if possible" the parents or guardian of a minor on whom an abortion was to be performed. In this case, the physician advised the patient that an abortion would be in her best medical interest but, because of the statute, refused to perform the abortion without first notifying her parents. The Supreme Court ruled that although a state may not constitutionally legislate a blanket, unreviewable power of parents to veto their daughter's abortion, a statute setting out a mere requirement of parental notice when possible, does not violate the constitutional rights of an immature, dependent minor.

Consent Not Required for Emancipated Minor

1987: The trial court in *In re Anonymous*[21] was found to have abused its discretion when it refused a minor's request for waiver of parental consent to obtain an abortion. The record indicated that the minor lived alone, was within 1 month of her 18th birthday, lived by herself most of the time, and was employed full time.

Parental Notification Not Required

2000: The issue in *Planned Parenthood v. Owens*[22] was whether the Colorado Parental Notification Act (Colorado Revised Statute §§ 12-37.5-101, et seq. [1998]), which requires a physician to notify the parents of a minor prior to performing an abortion upon her, violates the minor's rights protected by the U.S. Constitution. The act, a citizen-initiated measure, was approved at Colorado's general election. The act generally prohibits physicians from performing abortions on a minor who is not emancipated until at least 48 hours after written notice has been delivered to the minor's parent, guardian, or foster parent.

The U.S. District Court decided that the act violated the rights of minor women protected by the Fourteenth Amendment. The Supreme Court, for more than a quarter of a century, has recognized the right to an abortion based on medical necessity for the preservation of the mother's health. The act failed to provide such a health exception.

Minor's Decision to Abort Found Sufficient

2006: In another case, the minor in *In re Doe*[23] was determined to be sufficiently mature to decide whether to terminate her pregnancy, thus precluding notification of her pregnancy to a parent or guardian, which placed her less than 1 year from being outside the scope of notification law. The minor was a good student, was employed part time, and had formulated a plan for her future. Although she admitted that her pregnancy was the result of an immature decision, her acknowledgment supported her belief that she had sufficient maturity concerning whether or not to terminate pregnancy.

Abortion Case Returned to Lower Court

2006: The U.S. Supreme Court, in a unanimous ruling, determined that the U.S. Court of Appeals for the First Circuit erred when it declared unconstitutional a state law requiring that a minor notify her parents before obtaining an abortion. The Court sent the case, *Ayotte v. Planned Parenthood of Northern New England*,[24] back to the appeals court and told it to find a way to include an exception to the law for a medical emergency. Justice Sandra Day O'Connor wrote the majority opinion, her last as an associate justice.

Minor's Decision to Abort Not Sufficient

2008: Proceedings were brought in *In re petition of Doe*,[25] in which the juvenile sought judicial waiver of a statutory requirement that the physician notify her parent or guardian prior to terminating her pregnancy. The juvenile failed to prove by clear and convincing evidence that she was mature enough to warrant waving the requirement for parental notification of the abortion. A U.S. District Judge in Tallahassee upheld a Florida law requiring abortion providers to notify a minor's parent or legal guardian prior to performing an abortion. The law requires doctors to notify in person or by phone the parents or legal guardians of minors seeking an abortion at least 48 hours

in advance of performing the procedure or 72 hours in advance by certified mail if the parents or guardians cannot be reached. The law allows for exceptions in cases of medical emergency, if the minor is married or has children, if a judge determines the minor is mature enough to make her own decision, if the juvenile is a victim of abuse, or if notification is not in the juvenile's best interests. The juvenile in this case failed to demonstrate any knowledge regarding specific immediate or long-term physical, emotional, or psychological risks of having an abortion. Furthermore, there was no evidence that the juvenile had sought advice or emotional support from any adults or that she had considered what she would do should any physical or emotional complications arise from abortion. The juvenile's concerns that her parents would not understand and would be upset about her pregnancy amounted to nothing more than generalized fear of telling her parents and did not establish that notification would not be in her best interests.

State Interest Not Compelling

1975: A provision of the Florida Therapeutic Abortion Act that required a married woman to obtain the husband's consent before abortion was found to be unconstitutional. The state's interest was found not to be sufficiently compelling to limit a woman's right to abortion. The husband's interest in the baby was held to be insufficient to force his wife to face the mental and physical risks of pregnancy and childbirth.[26]

Spousal Consent Requirement Unconstitutional

1975: In *Doe v. Zimmerman*,[27] the court declared unconstitutional the provisions of the Pennsylvania Abortion Control Act, which required that the written consent of the husband of a married woman be secured before performing an abortion. The court found that these provisions impermissibly permitted the husband to withhold his consent either because of his interest in the potential life of the fetus or for capricious reasons.

Father of Unborn Fetus Could Not Stop Abortion

1988: The natural father of an unborn fetus in *Doe v. Smith*[28] was found not entitled to an injunction to prevent the mother from submitting to an abortion. Although the father's interest in the fetus was legitimate, it did not outweigh the mother's constitutionally protected right to an abortion, particularly in the light of the evidence that the mother and father had never married. The father had demonstrated substantial instability in his marital and romantic life. The father was able to beget other children and, in fact, did produce other children.

Spousal Consent Undue Burden

1992: In the 1992 decision of *Planned Parenthood v. Casey*,[29] the Supreme Court ruled that spousal consent would be an undue burden on the woman.

Restricting Right to Abortion Affirmed

1992: In *Planned Parenthood v. Casey*, the Supreme Court affirmed Pennsylvania law restricting a woman's right to abortion. The Court was one vote shy of overturning *Roe v. Wade*. The Supreme Court ruling, as enunciated in *Roe v. Wade*, reaffirmed:

- the constitutional right of women to have an abortion before viability of the fetus, as first enunciated in *Roe v. Wade*;
- the state's power to restrict abortions after fetal viability, as long as the law contains exceptions for pregnancies that endanger a woman's life or health; and
- the principle that the state has legitimate interests from the outset of the pregnancy in protecting the health of the woman and the life of the fetus.

The Supreme Court rejected the trimester approach in *Roe v. Wade*, which limited the regulations states could issue on abortion depending on the development stage of the fetus. In place of the trimester approach, the Court will evaluate the permissibility of state abortion rules based on whether they unduly burden a woman's ability to obtain an abortion. A rule is an undue burden if its purpose or effect is to place a substantial obstacle in the path of a woman seeking an abortion before the fetus attains viability. The Supreme Court ruled that it is not an undue burden to require that:

- a woman be informed of the nature of the abortion procedure and the risks involved;
- a woman be offered information on the fetus and on the alternatives to abortion;
- a woman give her informed consent before the abortion procedure;
- parental consent be given for a minor seeking an abortion, providing for a judicial bypass option if the minor does not wish or cannot obtain parental consent; and
- there be a 24-hour waiting period before any abortion can be performed.

Abortion Counseling

Physician Counseling of Patient Upheld

1983: The Supreme Court, in *City of Akron v. Akron Center for Reproductive Health*,[30] voted six to three that the different states cannot (1) mandate what information physicians give abortion patients or (2) require that abortions for women more than 3 months pregnant be performed in a hospital.

With respect to a requirement that the attending physician must inform the woman of specified information concerning her proposed abortion, it is unreasonable for a state to insist that only a physician is competent to provide the information and counseling relative to informed consent. A state may not adopt regulations to influence a woman's informed choice between abortion and childbirth. With regard to a second-trimester hospital requirement, this could significantly limit a woman's ability to obtain an abortion. This is especially so in view of the evidence that a second-trimester abortion may cost more than twice as much in a hospital as in a clinic.

Prohibition of Abortion Counseling Not Unconstitutional

1991: Federal regulations that prohibit abortion counseling and referral by family planning clinics that receive funds under Title X of the Public Health Service Act were found not to violate the constitutional rights of pregnant women or Title X grantees in a five to four decision by the Supreme Court in *Rust v. Sullivan*.[31] Proponents of abortion counseling argued (1) that the regulations impermissibly burden a woman's privacy right to abortion and (2) that by prohibiting the delivery of abortion information, even as to where such information could be obtained, the regulations deny a woman her constitutionally protected right to choose under the First Amendment. The question arises: How can a woman make an informed choice between two options when she cannot obtain information as to one of them? In *Sullivan*, however, the Supreme Court found that there was no violation of a woman's or provider's First Amendment rights to freedom of speech. The Court extended the doctrine that government need not subsidize the exercise of the fundamental rights to free speech. The plaintiff had argued that the government may not condition receipt of a benefit on the relinquishment of constitutional rights.

24-Hour Waiting Period Not Burdensome

1992: The Supreme Court, in *Planned Parenthood of Southeastern Pennsylvania v. Casey*,[32] determined that in asserting an interest in protecting fetal life, a state may place some restrictions on previability abortions, as long as those restrictions do not impose an "undue burden" on the woman's right to an abortion. The Court determined that the 24-hour waiting period, the informed consent requirement, and the medical emergency definitions did not unduly burden the right to an abortion and were therefore constitutional.

1993: The Utah Abortion Act Revision, Senate Bill 60, provides for informed consent by requiring that certain information be given to the pregnant woman at least 24 hours prior to the performance of an abortion. The law allows for exceptions to this requirement in the event of a medical emergency.

The Utah Women's Clinic, in *Utah Women's Clinic, Inc. v. Leavitt*,[33] filed a 106-page complaint challenging the constitutionality of the new Utah law. It was determined that the 24-hour waiting period did not impose an undue burden on the right to an abortion. On appeal, a U.S. District Court held that the Utah abortion statute's 24-hour waiting period and informed consent requirements do not render the statute unconstitutionally vague. Because Senate Bill 60 is less restrictive than the Pennsylvania abortion statute, the plaintiffs may not prevail unless they can show material differences between the circumstances of Utah and Pennsylvania.

It would be extremely difficult in light of the *Casey* decision to bring a good faith facial challenge to the constitutionality of Utah's 24-hour waiting period and informed consent requirements. In an emergency situation, there is no requirement of informed consent or a 24-hour waiting period. The plaintiffs' contention that Senate Bill 60, when read together with provisions from Utah's 1991 abortion law, does not clearly provide that a woman can obtain an abortion in a medical emergency, is without merit.

> The abortion issue is obviously one that invokes strong feelings on both sides. Individuals are free to urge support for their cause through debate, advocacy, and participation in the political process. The subject also might be addressed in the courts so long as there are valid legal issues in dispute. Where, however, a case presents no legitimate legal arguments, the courthouse is not the proper forum. Litigation, or the threat of litigation, should not be used as economic blackmail to strengthen one's hand in the political battle. Unfortunately, the court sees little evidence that this case was filed for any other purpose.[34]
>
> Senate Bill 60, the duly enacted law of the people of Utah, has not been enforced for nearly nine months. That will change today. The court hereby adopts the report and recommendation of the magistrate judge, lifts the injunction, and dismisses plaintiffs' case in its entirety with prejudice.[35]

Incompetent Persons

1987: An abortion was found to have been proper by a family court in *In re Doe*[36] for a profoundly retarded woman. She became pregnant during her residence in a group home as a result of a sexual attack by an unknown person. The record supported a finding that if the woman had been able to do so, she would have requested the abortion. The court properly chose welfare agencies and the woman's guardian ad litem (a guardian appointed to prosecute or defend a suit on behalf of a party incapacitated by infancy, mental incompetence, etc.) as the surrogate decision makers, rather than the woman's mother. The mother apparently had little contact with her daughter over the years.

Viability Test Required

1989: *Webster v. Reproductive Health Services*[37] began the U.S. Supreme Court's narrowing of abortion rights by upholding a Missouri statute providing that no public facilities or employees should be used to perform abortions and that physicians should conduct viability tests before performing abortions.

Partial-Birth Abortion

D&E Ban Constitutionally Vague

1998: The Supreme Court in *Women's Medical Professional Corp. v. Voinovich*[38] denied certiorari for the first partial-birth case to reach the federal appellate courts. This case involved an Ohio statute that banned the use of the intact dilation and extraction (D&E) procedure in the performance of any—previability or postviability—abortion. The Sixth Circuit Court of Appeals held that the statute banning any use of the D&E procedure was unconstitutionally vague. It is likely that a properly drafted statute will eventually be judged constitutionally sound.

Partial-Birth Abortion Ban Act Unconstitutional

1999: The defendants in *Little Rock Family Planning Services v. Jegley*[39] appealed a district court decision holding Arkansas's Partial-Birth Abortion Ban Act of 1997 unconstitutional. The act prohibited knowingly performing a partial-birth abortion. Arkansas code defines *partial-birth abortion* as an abortion in which the person performing the abortion partially vaginally delivers a living fetus before taking the life of the fetus and completing the delivery. Under this definition, any physician who knowingly partially vaginally delivers a living fetus and then takes the life of the fetus and completes delivery would violate the act. Because both the D&E procedure and the suction curettage procedure used in second-trimester abortions often include what the act prohibits, physicians performing those procedures would have violated the act. The act provided that, in addition to committing a felony, a physician who knowingly performed a partial-birth abortion would be subject to disciplinary action by the state medical board. The federal district court held the act unconstitutional because it was unconstitutionally vague, imposed an undue burden on women seeking abortions, and did not adequately protect the health and lives of pregnant women. The circuit court agreed, holding the act unconstitutional.

Partial-Birth Abortion Statute Vague

2000: New Jersey's partial-birth abortion statute was void for vagueness, in that it did not define the proscribed conduct with certainty and could be easily construed to ban the safest, most common, and most readily available conventional abortion procedures. The statute also was unconstitutional because it created an undue burden on a woman's right to obtain an abortion, in that its broad language covered many conventional, constitutionally permissible methods of abortion, and it failed to contain a health exception.[40]

Partial-Birth Abortion: Ban Unconstitutional

2002: The U.S. Supreme Court, in *Stenberg v. Carhart*,[41] struck down a Nebraska ban on partial-birth abortion, finding it an unconstitutional violation of *Roe v. Wade*. The court found these types of bans to be extreme descriptive attempts to outlaw abortion—even early in pregnancy—that jeopardizes women's health. Following *Stenberg v. Carhart*, a Virginia statute that attempted to criminalize partial-birth abortion was also held to be unconstitutional under the Fourteenth Amendment because it lacked an exception to protect a woman's health.[42]

Partial-Birth Abortion Act: First Federal Restrictions

2003: President George W. Bush, on November 6, signed the first federal restrictions banning late-term partial-birth abortions. The partial-birth abortion, also referred to as the D&E procedure, is a late-term abortion involving partial delivery of the baby before it is aborted. The ban is referred to as the Partial-Birth Abortion Act of 2003. Both houses of Congress passed the ban. The ban permits no exceptions when a woman's health is at risk or the fetus has life-threatening disabilities. A U.S. District Court in Nebraska issued a restraining order on the ban.

Partial-Birth Abortion Act: Supreme Court Asked to Review

2005: On September 26, 2005, the Bush administration asked the Supreme Court to review an appellate court's decision holding the Partial-Birth Abortion Act of 2003 unconstitutional.

Partial-Birth Abortion Unconstitutional

2006: The Partial-Birth Abortion Ban Act, 18 U.S.C. Section 1531, in *National Abortion Fed'n v. Gonzages*,[43] was found to be unconstitutional because it lacked any exception to preserve the health of the mother, where such exception was constitutionally required. Also, the act was unconstitutional because it imposed an undue burden on a woman's right to choose previability abortion and was constitutionally vague.

Physician Concern: Abortion Controversy

1991: Physicians are feeling the heat and are concerned about the ongoing abortion controversy. In *Beverly v. Choices Women's Medical Center*,[44] a physician, whose picture was published in an abortion calendar without her consent, brought a civil rights action against the for-profit medical center for publication of her picture. The calendar was disseminated to the public by the center. The plaintiff was awarded $50,000 in compensatory damages and $25,000 in punitive damages. The physician testified that the publication of her picture caused her to suffer physical and mental injury. She also testified as to the effect of the publication on her lifestyle and career decisions.

Antiabortion Demonstrations

1994: In March 1989, the San Diego police became aware that Operation Rescue planned to stage several antiabortion demonstrations in the city.[45] The purpose of the demonstrations was to disrupt operations at the target clinics and ultimately to cause the clinics to cease operations. In each of the three demonstrations at issue, protesters converged on a medical building, blocking entrances, filling stairwells and corridors, and preventing employees and patients from entering.

For each arrest, the officers warned the demonstrators that they would be subjected to pain-compliance measures if they did not move, that such measures would hurt, and that they could reduce the pain by standing up, eliminating the tension on their wrists and arms. The officers then forcibly moved the arrestees by tightening two sticks of wood connected at one end by a cord used to grip a demonstrator's wrist around their wrists until they stood up and walked. All arrestees complained of varying degrees of injury to their hands and arms. Several subsequently filed suit, claiming that the police violated the Fourth Amendment by using excessive force in executing the arrests. The judge allowed the case to proceed to the jury to determine whether any particular uses of force were unconstitutional. After viewing a videotape of the arrests, the jury concluded that none involved excessive force and returned a verdict for the city. An appeal was taken.

The U.S. Court of Appeals for the Ninth Circuit held that the police did not use excessive force. The videotape created an extensive evidentiary record: "Thanks to videotaped records of the actual events, plus the testimony of witnesses on both sides, the jury had more than a sufficient amount of evidence presented to them from which they could formulate their verdicts. The extensive use of video scenes of exactly what took place removed much argument and interpretation of the facts themselves."[46] The city clearly had a legitimate interest in quickly dispersing and removing the lawbreakers with the least risk of injury to police and others. The arrestees were part of a group of more than 100 protesters operating in an organized and concerted effort to invade private property, obstruct business, and hinder law enforcement.

Obstructing Access to Abortion Clinics

1993: Abortion clinics and others sought enforcement of an injunction precluding antiabortion groups from blockading or obstructing access to abortion clinics. The order required the defendants to appear before the court to show cause why each of them should not be cited for contempt for violating and inducing others to violate an injunction order. The defendants, Tucci, Terry, and Mahoney, spoke at a rally. Tucci was introduced as a leader of Operation Rescue National and spoke about how the group successfully had closed down clinics. He also solicited funds for his organization. Terry said that they needed contributions to keep their work going. The defendants appeared before the court at two hearings to show cause why they should not be cited in contempt for violating the court's injunction.[47] The questions posed are: (1) Can antiabortion leaders and groups be fined for violating an injunction barring them from blockading or obstructing access to abortion clinics? and (2) Can antiabortion groups be ordered to pay damages to compensate an abortion clinic for property damage resulting from an abortion clinic blockage that violated an injunction?

The U.S. District Court for the District of Columbia held that leaders and groups would be fined for violating the injunction. In addition, antiabortion groups are liable to abortion clinics for property damages resulting from blockades. The defendants violated provisions of the injunction "barring all defendants and those acting in concert with them 'from inducing, encouraging, directing, aiding, or abetting others' to trespass on, blockade, or obstruct access to or egress from facilities at which abortions are performed and other medical services are rendered."[48] In blockading the clinics, the defendants violated District of Columbia trespass law, which states, "Any person who,

without lawful authority, shall enter, or attempt to enter, any public or private dwelling . . . against the will of the lawful occupant or of the person lawfully in charge thereof . . . shall be guilty of a misdemeanor" (D.C. Code § 22-3102).

The participants in the blockades were under court order not to trespass on the clinics and were ordered by clinic personnel and the police at the time of the blockades to leave the property. Their presence on the property clearly constituted trespass.

Continuing Controversy

NEWSPAPER CLIPPINGS: Kan. House Passes Sweeping Anti-Abortion Bill

TOPEKA, Kan. (AP)—A sweeping anti-abortion bill is headed to Kansas Gov. Sam Brownback.

The House gave final approval Friday to the measure, which blocks tax breaks for abortion providers and outlaws abortions performed solely because of the baby's sex.

The measure also declares that life begins "at fertilization," language that abortion opponents call a statement of principle and not an outright ban on abortion, though the bill's opponents are skeptical.

Brownback is likely to sign the bill into law.

—*John Hanna*, Associated Press, *April 6, 2013*

NEWSPAPER CLIPPINGS: Abortion Laws In Arkansas, North Dakota Set Stage For Legal Battle

Rival legal teams, well-financed and highly motivated, are girding for court battles over the coming months on laws enacted in Arkansas and North Dakota that would impose the nation's toughest bans on abortion.

. . .

The Arkansas law, approved March 6 when legislators overrode a veto by Democratic Gov. Mike Beebe, would ban most abortions from the 12th week of pregnancy onward. On March 26, North Dakota went further, with Republican Gov. Jack Dalrymple signing a measure that would ban abortions as early as six weeks into a pregnancy, when a fetal heartbeat can first be detected and before some women even know they're pregnant.

—*David Crary*, The Huffington Post, *March 31, 2013*

Right-to-life advocates argue that life comes from God and that no one has a right to deny the right to life. *Pro-choice advocates* argue that a woman has a right to choose preservation and protection of her health and, therefore, in many cases, her life is at least as compelling as the state's interest in promoting childbirth. The protection of a fetus and promotion of childbirth cannot be considered so compelling as to outweigh a woman's fundamental right to choose and the state's obligation to be evenhanded in the design and application of its healthcare policies.

Although pro-choice advocates are arguing the rights of women to choose, they are also pointing out the fact that legalized abortions are safer. In 1972, for example, the year before *Roe v. Wade* was upheld, the number of deaths from abortions in the United States is estimated to have reached the thousands; by 1985, the figure was six.[49] In addition, pro-choice advocates argue that women who have a right to an abortion when pregnancy threatens the life of the mother also have the right to an abortion when pregnancy is the result of incest or rape.

There will most likely be a continuing stream of court decisions, as well as political and legislative battles, well into the 21st century. Given the emotional, religious, and ethical concerns, as well as those of women's rights groups, it is certain that the controversies and ethical dilemmas surrounding abortion will continue for many years to come.

State Abortion Statutes

As noted in the previously mentioned cases, the effect of the Supreme Court's 1973 decisions in *Roe* and *Doe* was to invalidate all or part of almost every state abortion statute then in force. The responses of state legislatures to these decisions were varied, but it is clear that many state laws had been enacted to restrict the performance of abortions as much as possible. Although *Planned Parenthood v. Casey* was expected to clear up some issues, it is evident that the states have been given more power to regulate the performance of abortions.

Abortion and Conflicting Beliefs

Two or more ethical principles in conflict with one another are considered "ethical dilemmas," such as in the case of abortion. Further complication of ethical dilemmas occurs when laws and regulations affect the decision-making process and, further, when the courts enter the melting pot by interpreting laws and regulations while recognizing the rights of individuals as provided under the Constitution.

To help us make choices in the resolution of ethical dilemmas, it is often necessary to value one ethical principle more than another. The difficulty in the abortion dilemma arises because beliefs, religion, culture, education, and life experiences can differ from person to person. Good people cannot be considered bad people merely because their beliefs differ from another's beliefs. Values differ, and therefore, determinations of morality may differ.

Morality of Abortion

The morality of abortion is not a legal or constitutional issue; it is a matter of philosophy, ethics, and theology. It is a subject where reasonable people can, and do, adhere to vastly divergent convictions and principles. Our obligation is to define the liberty of all, not to dictate our own moral code.[50]

STERILIZATION

Sterilization is the termination of the ability to produce offspring. Sterilization often is accomplished by a vasectomy for men and tubal ligation for women. A *vasectomy* is a surgical procedure in which the vas deferens is severed and tied to prevent the flow of the seminal fluid into the urinary canal. A *tubal ligation* is a surgical procedure in which the fallopian tubes are cut and tied, preventing passage of the ovum from the ovary to the uterus. Sterilizations are often sought because of: (1) economic necessity to avoid the additional expense of raising a child; (2) therapeutic purposes to prevent harm to a woman's health (e.g., to remove a diseased reproductive organ); and (3) genetic reasons to prevent the birth of a defective child.

Elective Sterilization

Voluntary or elective sterilizations on competent individuals present few legal problems, as long as proper consent has been obtained from the patient and the procedure is performed properly. Civil liability for performing a sterilization of convenience may be imposed if the procedure is performed in a negligent manner.

Blood Vessel Mistakenly Cut

The physician in *McLaughlin v. Cooke*[51] was found negligent for mistakenly cutting a blood vessel in the patient's scrotum while he was performing a vasectomy. Excessive bleeding at the site of the incision was found to have occurred because of the physician's negligent postsurgical care. On appeal, the jury's finding of negligence was supported by testimony that the physician's failure to intervene sooner and to remove a hematoma had been the proximate cause of tissue necrosis.

Regulation of Sterilization for Convenience

Like abortion, voluntary sterilization is the subject of many debates over its moral and ethical propriety. Some health-care institutions have adopted policies restricting the performance of such operations at their facilities. The U.S. Court of Appeals for the First Circuit ruled in *Hathaway v. Worcester City Hospital*[52] that a governmental hospital cannot impose greater restrictions on sterilization procedures than on other procedures that are medically indistinguishable from sterilization with regard to the risk to the patient or the demand on staff or facilities. The court relied on the Supreme Court decisions in *Roe v. Wade*[53] and *Doe v. Bolton*,[54] which accorded considerable recognition to the patient's right to privacy in the context of obtaining medical services.

Therapeutic Sterilization

A *therapeutic sterilization* is performed to protect the life or health of a woman whose health could be jeopardized due to a pregnancy. The medical necessity for sterilization renders the procedure therapeutic.

Involuntary/Eugenic Sterilization

 NEWSPAPER CLIPPINGS: Chemical and Surgical Castration

> Both the California and Florida statutes provide for mandatory injections for repeat sex offenders, as well as discretionary injections for first-time offenders. Despite the mandatory language in the Florida law, the law has apparently been invoked only a few times since its passage in 1997.
>
> The ACLU contends that chemical castration violates an offender's implied right to privacy under the Fourteenth Amendment, rights of due process and equal protection, and the Eighth Amendment's ban of cruel and unusual punishment.
>
> Pursuant to a 1997 law, Texas permits surgical castration of offenders. By May 2005, three men had undergone the voluntary procedure.
>
> —*FindLaw.com*[55]

The term eugenic sterilization refers to the involuntary sterilization of certain categories of persons described in statutes, without the need for consent by, or on behalf of, those subject to the procedures. Those who are classified as mentally deficient, feeble minded, and, in some instances, epileptic, are generally within the scope of applicable statutes.

 NEWSPAPER CLIPPINGS: Governor Signs Chemical Castration Bill, Authorizing the Castration of Sex Offenders in Louisiana

> BATON ROUGE—Governor Bobby Jindal today signed the Sex Offender Chemical Castration Bill, SB 144, authorizing the castration of convicted sex offenders.
>
> Governor Bobby Jindal said, "The Sex Offender Chemical Castration Bill is a good bill, and I am especially glad to sign it into Louisiana law today, on the same day the Supreme Court has made an atrocious ruling against our state's ability to sentence those who sexually assault our children to the fullest extent. Those who prey on our children are among the very worst criminals imaginable."
>
> —*Press Release*, The Governor's Office, *June 25, 2008*[56]

Several states also have included certain sexual deviates and persons classified as habitual criminals. Such statutes ordinarily are designed to prevent the transmission of hereditary defects to succeeding generations, but several statutes also have recognized the purpose of preventing procreation by individuals who would not be able to care for their offspring.

▌ ARTIFICIAL INSEMINATION

Generally, *artificial insemination* is the injection of seminal fluid into a woman to induce pregnancy. The term also may include insemination that takes place outside of the woman's body, as with so-called test-tube babies. *Homologous artificial insemination* is a medical procedure where the semen of the woman's husband is used to impregnate her. *Heterologous artificial insemination* is a medical procedure where the semen of a nonspousal donor is used to impregnate a woman.

The absence of answers to many questions concerning heterologous artificial insemination may have discouraged couples from seeking to use this procedure and physicians from performing it. Some of the questions concern the procedure itself; others concern the status of the offspring and the effect of the procedure on the marital relationship.

Consent

The Oklahoma heterologous artificial insemination statute specifies both husband and wife must consent to the procedure.[57] The husband's consent helps to ensure against liability accruing if a court adopted the view that without the consent of the spouse, heterologous artificial insemination was a wrong to the husband's interest for which he could sustain a suit for damages. The spouses and donor prior to insemination should execute written consent.

Confidentiality

Another problem that directly concerns medical personnel involved in heterologous artificial insemination birth is preserving confidentiality. This problem is met in the Oklahoma heterologous artificial insemination statute, which requires that the original copy of the consent be filed pursuant to the rules for the filing of adoption papers and is not to be made a matter of public record.[58]

SURROGACY

Surrogacy is a method of reproduction whereby a woman agrees to give birth to a child she will not raise but hand over to a contracted party, who is often unable to conceive a natural child of her own.

A surrogate "may be the child's genetic mother (the more traditional form of surrogacy), or she may, as a gestational carrier, carry the pregnancy to delivery after having been implanted with an embryo. In some cases surrogacy is the only available option for parents who wish to have a child that is biologically related to them."[59]

Surrogacy raises many ethical and legal issues to consider before searching for a surrogate mother. For example, is it ethical to enter a contract with a woman by offering her money in exchange for bearing a child and then transferring all parental rights and physical custody of the child to the "commissioning couple?" Although the long-term effects of surrogacy contracts are not known, the adverse psychological impact could be detrimental to the child who learns that he or she is the offspring of someone who gave birth only to obtain money. Would the child want to search for his or her gestational mother? Should records be kept, and should the child have access to those? After the child is taken, the surrogate mother may be negatively impacted as her feeling of isolation is felt along with the reality of the sale of her body.

Although there are arguments offered for and against surrogacy contracts, there are many parents who have experienced the joy of raising happy, psychologically well-balanced, and career-successful surrogate children. Those who have done their research and understand the issues live as happy together as those in any other family relationship.

WRONGFUL BIRTH, LIFE, AND CONCEPTION

There have been many cases in recent years involving actions for wrongful birth, wrongful life, and wrongful conception. Such litigation originated with the California case in which a court found that a genetic testing laboratory can be held liable for damages from incorrectly reporting genetic tests, leading to the birth of a child with defects.[60] Injury caused by birth had not been previously actionable by law. The court of appeals held that medical laboratories engaged in genetic testing owe a duty to parents and their unborn child to use ordinary care in administering available tests for the purpose of providing information concerning potential genetic defects in the unborn. Damages in this case were awarded on the basis of the child's shortened life span.

Wrongful Birth

In a wrongful birth action, the plaintiffs claim that but for a breach of duty by the defendant(s) (e.g., improper sterilization), the child would not have been born. A wrongful birth claim can be brought by the parent(s) of a child born with genetic defects against a physician who or a laboratory that negligently fails to inform them, in a timely fashion, of an increased possibility that the mother will give birth to such a child, therefore precluding an informed decision as to whether to have the child.

Recovery for damages was permitted for wrongful birth but not wrongful life in *Smith v. Cote.*[61] The physician in this case was negligent because he failed to test in a timely fashion for the mother's exposure to rubella and to advise her of the potential for birth defects. She therefore was entitled to maintain a cause of action for wrongful birth. However, for compelling reasons of public policy, the mother would not be permitted to assert on the child's behalf a claim for damages on the basis of wrongful life.

Recovery for damages was permitted for wrongful birth in *Keel v. Banach*[62] where the Alabama Supreme Court held that a cause of action for wrongful birth is recognized in Alabama, and compensable losses are any medical and hospital expenses incurred as a result of the physician's negligence, physical pain suffered by the mother, loss of consortium, and mental and emotional anguish suffered by the parents. The basic rule of tort compensation is that the plaintiffs should be placed in the position where they would have been without the defendant's negligence. A jury could conclude that the defendants, in failing to inform the mother of the possibility of giving birth to a child with multiple congenital deformities, directly deprived her and her husband of the option to accept or reject a parental relationship with the child and thus caused them to experience mental distress.

Wrongful Life

Wrongful life claims are initiated by the parent(s) or child based on harm suffered as a result of being born. Plaintiffs generally contend that the physician or laboratory negligently failed to inform the child's parents of the risk of bearing a genetically defective infant and hence prevented the parents' right to choose to avoid the birth.[63] Because there is no recognized legal right not to be born, wrongful life cases are generally not successful.

> [L]egal recognition that a disabled life is an injury would harm the interests of those most directly concerned, the handicapped. Disabled persons face obvious physical difficulties in conducting their lives. They also face subtle yet equally devastating handicaps in the attitudes and behavior of society, the law, and their own families and friends. Furthermore, society often views disabled persons as burdensome misfits. Recent legislation concerning employment, education, and building access reflects a slow change in these attitudes. This change evidences a growing public awareness that the handicapped can be valuable and productive members of society. To characterize the life of a disabled person as an injury would denigrate both this new awareness and the handicapped themselves.[64]

In *Kassama v. Magat*,[65] Kassama alleged that Dr. Magat failed to advise her of the results of an alpha-fetoprotein blood test that indicated a heightened possibility that her child might be afflicted with Down syndrome. Had she received that information, Kassama contends, she would have undergone an amniocentesis, which would have confirmed that prospect. Kassama claims, if that occurred, she would have chosen to terminate the pregnancy through an abortion.

The Supreme Court of Maryland decided that for purposes of tort law, an impaired life was not worse than nonlife, and, for that reason, life itself was not, and could not, be considered an injury. There was no evidence that the child was not deeply loved and cared for by her parents or that she did not return that love.

Wrongful birth is based on the premise that being born, and having to live, with the affliction is a disadvantage and thus a cognizable injury. The injury sued upon is the fact that the child was born; she bears the disability and will bear the expenses only because, but for the alleged negligence of Dr. Magat, her mother was unable to terminate the pregnancy and avert her birth. The issue here is whether Maryland law is prepared to recognize that kind of injury—the injury of life itself.

The child has not suffered any damage cognizable at law by being brought into existence. One of the most deeply held beliefs of society is that life, whether experienced with or without a major physical handicap, is more precious than nonlife. No one is perfect, and each person suffers from some ailments or defects, whether major or minor, which make impossible participation in all the activities life has to offer. Our lives are not thereby rendered less precious than those of others whose defects are less pervasive or less severe. Despite their handicaps, the Down syndrome child is able to love and be loved and to experience happiness and pleasure—emotions that are truly the essence of life and that are far more valuable than the suffering that may be endured.

The right to life and the principle that all are equal under the law are basic to our constitutional order. To presume to decide that a child's life is not worth living would be to forsake these ideals. To characterize the life of a disabled person as an injury would denigrate the handicapped themselves. Measuring the value of an impaired life as compared to nonexistence is a task that is beyond mortals.

Unless a judgment can be made on the basis of reason, rather than the emotion of any given case, that nonlife is preferable to impaired life—that the child–plaintiff would, in fact, have been better off had he or she never been born—there can be no injury, and, if there can be no injury, whether damages can or cannot be calculated becomes irrelevant.

The crucial question, a value judgment about life itself, is too deeply immersed in each person's own individual philosophy or theology to be subject to a reasoned and consistent community response in the form of a jury verdict.

In another case, the mother, in her capacity as guardian for her minor son, brought a wrongful life action on behalf of the child against a physician. It was alleged, that because the physician failed to adequately and timely diagnose the child's condition, the mother was denied the opportunity to decide whether to terminate the pregnancy while she was legally allowed to do so. The court, in deciding whether to render a verdict in the child's favor or what damages, if any, should be awarded, a jury would be faced with an imponderable question: Is a severely impaired life so much worse than no life at all that the child is entitled to damages? The civil justice system places inestimable faith in the ability of jurors to reach a fair and just result under the law, but even a jury collectively imbued with the wisdom of Solomon would be unable to weigh the fact of being born with a defective condition against the fact of not being born at all; in other words, nonexistence. It is simply beyond the human experience to analyze this position. The court declined to recognize a cause of action for wrongful life brought by or on behalf of a child born with a congenital defect. It was untenable to argue that a child who already had been born should have the chance to prove it would have been better if he had never have been born at all.[66]

Wrongful Conception

Wrongful conception refers to a claim for damages sustained by the parents of an unexpected child based on an allegation that conception of the child resulted from negligent sterilization procedures or a defective contraceptive device.[67]

Damages sought for a negligently performed sterilization might include: pain and suffering associated with pregnancy and birth; expenses of delivery; lost wages; father's loss of consortium; damages for emotional or psychological pain; suffering resulting from the presence of an additional family member in the household; the cost and pain and suffering of a subsequent sterilization; and damages suffered by a child born with genetic defects.

The most controversial item of damages claimed is that of raising a normal healthy child to adulthood. The mother in *Hartke v. McKelway*[68] had undergone sterilization for therapeutic reasons to avoid endangering her health from pregnancy. The woman became pregnant as a result of a failed sterilization. She delivered a healthy child without injury to herself. It was determined that "the jury could not rationally have found that the birth of this child was an injury to this plaintiff. Awarding child rearing expense would only give Hartke a windfall."[69]

However, the costs of raising a normal healthy child in *Jones v. Malinowski*[70] were recoverable. The plaintiff had three previous pregnancies. The first pregnancy resulted in a breech birth; the second child suffered brain damage; and the third child suffered from heart disease. For economic reasons, the plaintiff had undergone a bipolar tubal laparoscopy, which is a procedure that blocks both fallopian tubes by cauterization. The operating physician misidentified the left tube and cauterized the wrong structure, leaving the left tube intact. As a result of the negligent sterilization, Mrs. Malinowski became pregnant. The court of appeals held that the costs of raising a healthy child are recoverable and that the jury could offset these costs by the benefits derived by the parents from the child's aid, comfort, and society during the parents' life expectancy. The jury was instructed not to consider that the plaintiffs "might have aborted the child or placed the child out for adoption [since] . . . as a matter of personal conscience and choice parents may wish to keep an unplanned child."[71]

The cost of raising a healthy newborn child to adulthood was recoverable by the parents of the child conceived as a result of an unsuccessful sterilization by a physician employee at Lovelace Medical Center. The physician in *Lovelace Medical Center v. Mendez*[72] found and ligated only one of the patient's two fallopian tubes and then failed to inform the patient of the unsuccessful operation. The court held that:

> The Mendezes' interest in the financial security of their family was a legally protected interest which was invaded by Lovelace's negligent failure properly to perform Maria's sterilization operation (if proved at trial), and that this invasion was an injury entitling them to recover damages in the form of the reasonable expenses to raise Joseph to majority.[73]

Some states bar damage claims for emotional distress and the costs associated with the raising of healthy children but will permit recovery for damages related to negligent sterilizations. In *Butler v. Rolling Hills Hospital*,[74] the Pennsylvania Superior Court held that the patient stated a cause of action for the negligent performance of a laparoscopic tubal ligation. The patient was not, however, entitled to compensation for the costs of raising a normal healthy child. "In light of this Commonwealth's public policy, which recognizes the paramount importance of the family to society, we conclude that the benefits of joy, companionship, and affection which a normal, healthy child can provide must be deemed as a matter of law to outweigh the costs of raising that child."[75]

As the Court of Common Pleas of Lycoming County, Pennsylvania, in *Shaheen v. Knight*, stated:

> Many people would be willing to support this child were they given the right of custody and adoption, but according to plaintiff's statement, plaintiff does not want such. He wants to have the child and wants the doctor to support it. In our opinion, to allow such damages would be against public policy.[76]

Prevention of Wrongful Birth, Life, and Conception Suits

The occurrence of an unplanned pregnancy is not necessarily the result of negligence on the part of a physician. Although slight, there is known to be a given failure rate of sterilizations. Physicians can prevent lawsuits by informing each patient both orally and through written consent as to the likelihood of an unsuccessful sterilization, as well as the inherent risks in the procedure.

Notes

1. English Clergy, Dean of Westminster.
2. *Causeway Medical Suite v. Ieyoub*, 109 F.3d 1096 (1997).
3. 410 U.S. 113 (1973).
4. *Id*. at 164.
5. *Id*.
6. *Id*.
7. *Id*.
8. http://www.phila.gov/districtattorney/pdfs/grandjurywomensmedical.pdf.
9. 410 U.S. 179 (1973).
10. *Id*. at 198.
11. 432 U.S. 438 (1977).
12. *Id*.
13. 432 U.S. 464 (1977).
14. 448 U.S. 297 (1980).
15. *Committee to Defend Reproductive Rights v. Myers*, 625 P.2d 779, 798 (Cal. 1981).
16. 56 P.3d 28 (Ariz. 2002).
17. 99 S. Ct. 675 (1979).
18. 428 U.S. 52 (1976).
19. 443 U.S. 622 (1979).
20. 101 S. Ct. 1164 (1981).
21. 515 So. 2d 1254 (Ala. Civ. App. 1987).
22. 107 F. Supp. 2d 1271 (2000).
23. 921 So. 2d 753 (Fla. App. 2006).
24. 546 U.S. 320 (2006).
25. 973 So. 2d 548 (Fla. App. 2008).
26. *Poe v. Gerstein*, 517 F.2d 787 (5th Cir. 1975).
27. 405 F. Supp. 534 (M.D. Pa. 1975).
28. 486 U.S. 1308 (1988).
29. *Planned Parenthood v. Casey*, 112 S. Ct. 2792 (1992).
30. 103 S. Ct. 2481 (1983).
31. 111 S. Ct. 1759 (1991).
32. 112 S. Ct. 2791 (1992).
33. 844 F. Supp. 1482 (D. Utah 1994).
34. 844 F. Supp. 1482 (D. Utah 1994) at 1494.
35. *Id*. at 1495.
36. 533 A.2d 523 (R.I. 1987).
37. 492 U.S. 490 (1989).
38. 118 S. Ct. 1347 (1998).
39. 192 F.3d 794 (8th Cir. 1999).
40. *Planned Parenthood of Cent. N.J. v. Farmer*, 220 F.3d 127 (3rd Cir. 2000).
41. 192 F.3d 1142 (8th Cir. 1999), 120 S. Ct. 2597 (2000).
42. *Richmond Med. Ctr. for Women v. Hicks*, 409 F.3d 619 (C.A. 4, Va. 2005).
43. 437 F.3d 278 (C.A. 2, N.Y. 2006).
44. 565 N.Y.S.2d 833 (N.Y. App. Div. 1991).
45. *Forrester v. City of San Diego*, 25 F.3d 804 (9th Cir. 1994).
46. *Id*. at 807.
47. *NOW v. Operation Rescue*, 816 F. Supp. 729 (D. D.C. 1993).
48. *Id*. at 734.
49. Lawrence Terenzi, "Abortion: A World View," *Self*, November 1992, at 54.
50. *American Acad. of Pediatrics v. Lungren*, 940 P.2d 797 (1997).
51. 774 P.2d 1171 (Wash. 1989).
52. 475 F.2d 701 (1st Cir. 1973).
53. 410 U.S. 113 (1973).
54. 410 U.S. 179 (1973).
55. http://criminal.findlaw.com/criminal-charges/chemical-and-surgical-castration.html.
56. http://gov.louisiana.gov/index.cfm?md=newsroom&tmp=detail&articleID=270.
57. Okla. Stat. Ann. 10, §§ 551–553.
58. Okla. Stat. Ann. 10, §§ 551–553.
59. "Surrogacy and Child Rights," http://surrogacyqicac.blogspot.com/2009/04/surrogacy-and-its-consequences-on-right.html (accessed October 14, 2010).
60. 165 Cal. Rptr. 477 (Cal. Ct. App. 1980).
61. 513 A.2d 341 (N.H. 1986).
62. 624 So. 2d 1022 (Ala. 1993).
63. *Smith v. Cote*, 513 A.2d 344 (N.H. 1986).
64. *Id*. at 353.
65. 136 Md. App. 38 (2002).
66. *Willis v. Wu*, No. 25915 (S.C. 2004).
67. *Cowe v. Forum Group, Inc.*, 575 N.E.2d 630, 631 (Ind. 1991).
68. 707 F.2d 1544 (D.C. Cir. 1983).
69. *Id*. at 1557.
70. 473 A.2d 429 (Md. 1984).
71. *Id*. at 431.
72. 805 P.2d 603 (N.M. 1991).
73. *Id*. at 612.
74. 582 A.2d 1384 (Pa. Super. Ct. 1990).
75. *Id*. at 1385.
76. 11 Pa. D. & C.2d 41, 46 (Lycoming Co. Ct. Com. Pl. 1957).

When we finally know we are dying, and all other sentient beings are dying with us, we start to have a burning, almost heart breaking sense of the fragility and preciousness of each moment and each being, and from this can grow a deep, clear, limitless compassion for all beings.

—SOGYAL RINPOCHE

15
End-of-Life Issues

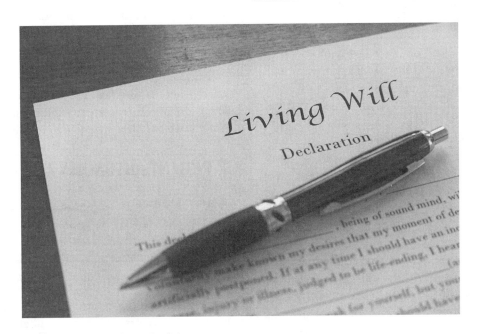

Figure 15–1   The Living Will   © zimmytws/ShutterStock, Inc.

✚ Learning Objectives

The reader upon completion of this chapter will be able to:

- Discuss the human struggle to survive and the right to autonomous decision-making.

- Describe how patient autonomy has been impacted by case law and legislative enactments.

- Discuss the following concepts: preservation of life with limits, euthanasia, advance directives, futility of treatment, withholding and withdrawal of treatment, and do-not-resuscitate orders.

- Discuss the purpose of an ethics committee and its consultative role in the delivery of patient care.

- Explain end-of-life issues as they relate to autopsy, organ donations, research experimentation, and clinical trials.

- Describe how human genetics and stem cell research can have an impact on end-of-life issues.

The human struggle to survive and dreams of immortality have long been instrumental in inspiring medicine to develop the means to prevent and cure illness. Advances in medical technology have resulted in the power to *prolong a productive life*, as well as *delay inevitable death*. Although our bodies may physically decline over time, our treasure trove of life experiences and wisdom accrues over time. As we age, we become a source of comfort and joy to those we love and who love us.

End-of-life issues continue to cause the most controversy and debate facing healthcare providers. Although it is well settled that competent terminally ill patients may refuse life-sustaining treatment, physician-assisted suicide remains a major point of contention. The competing concerns of privacy, morality, patient autonomy, legislation, and states' interests swirl around those involved in the decision-making process. The scope of healthcare ethics is not limited to philosophical issues but embraces economic, political, and medical dilemmas.

REALITY CHECK: End of Life or Beginning of Life?

My mother is 92 years old, and she is more active and is enjoying life more than when she was much younger. Her advanced age has actually proven to be something of an advantage, as it has given her the time and freedom to do some of the things she couldn't do while she was raising a family. It has been a joy to me, as her son, and to the rest of the family to witness her joy and vigor. Even strangers have found her stamina to be an inspiration as to the value of the end years of life. Three years ago, however, it wasn't so. Mother was critically ill, comatose on a respirator in an intensive care unit. Survival was not considered likely. I am embarrassed to say that I was making arrangements for a funeral. I am even more embarrassed because I am a physician and did not see how she could survive for long except as a vegetable. Then the unlikely occurred. She recovered! Her condition rapidly and surprisingly improved dramatically including both physical and mental status, and she promptly resumed a life even more active than before. It would have been a tragedy to deprive her of these joyous years of her life after she worked and sacrificed so much for others most of her life. I had thought it would be an act of mercy to disconnect the respirator when her condition had looked so hopeless. I was so wrong. I learned that we must not make life and death decisions casually. Life is a beautiful mystery with many wonderful surprises if we will let them happen.

Advances in medical technology have made it possible to survive to an older age. Although our bodies may physically decline over time, our treasure trove of life experiences accrues over time. Our knowledge and judgment may often be better than when we were younger. Furthermore, the aged may be a source of comfort and joy to their children, grandchildren, and even great-grandchildren. As long as we are alive, we have value.

Discussion

1. That longer survival inevitably involves considerable cost and can therefore be a substantial financial burden to the family and the government; is it worth it?
2. How do we make a judgment about quality of life?
3. What is the financial value of another day, week, or year of life?
4. Should we assume that younger years are better than older years?

Although the emphasis of this chapter is end-of-life issues, there is to a lesser extent an overview of autopsy, organ donations, research, experimentation, and clinical trials as well as human genetics and stem cell research.

PATIENT AUTONOMY AND CASE LAW

 No right is held more sacred, or is more carefully guarded, by the common law, than the right of every individual to the possession and control of his own person, free from all restraint or interference of others, unless by clear and unquestioned authority of law.[1]

To analyze the important questions regarding whether life-support treatment can be withheld or withdrawn, it is necessary to consider first what rights a patient possesses. Courts, in addition to statutory law, often point to the common law case of *Schloendorff v. Society of New York Hospital*[2] wherein the eminent Justice Cardozo stated:

 Every human being of adult years and sound mind has a right to determine what shall be done with his own body and a surgeon who performs an operation without his patient's consent commits an assault, for which he is liable in damages, except in cases of emergency where the patient is unconscious and where it is necessary to operate before consent can be obtained.[3]

This right of self-determination was emphasized in *In re Storar*[4] when the court announced that every human being of adult years and sound mind has the right to determine what shall be done with his or her own body. The *Storar* case was a departure from the New Jersey Supreme Court's rationale in the case of *In re Quinlan.*

The *Quinlan* court, relying on *Roe v. Wade*,[5] announced that the constitutional right to privacy protects a patient's right to self-determination. The court noted that the right to privacy "is broad enough to encompass a patient's decision to decline medical treatment under certain circumstances, in much the same way as it is broad enough to encompass a woman's decision to terminate pregnancy under certain conditions."[6]

The *Quinlan* court, in reaching its decision, applied a test balancing the state's interest in preserving and maintaining the sanctity of human life against Karen's privacy interest. It decided that, especially in light of the prognosis (physicians determined that Karen Quinlan was in an irreversible coma), the state's interest did not justify interference with her right to refuse treatment. Thus, Karen Quinlan's father was appointed her legal guardian, and the respirator was shut off. Despite intense criticism by legal and religious scholars, the *Quinlan* decision paved the way for courts to consider extending the right to decline treatment to incompetents as well.

In the same year as the *Quinlan* decision, the case of *Superintendent of Belchertown State School v. Saikewicz*[7] was decided. There, the court, using the balancing test enunciated in *Quinlan*, approved the recommendation of a court-appointed guardian that it would be in Saikewicz's best interests to end chemotherapy treatment. Saikewicz was a mentally retarded, 67-year-old patient suffering from leukemia. The court found from the evidence that the prognosis was grim, and even though a "normal person" would probably have chosen chemotherapy, it allowed Saikewicz to die without treatment to spare him the suffering.

The *Saikewicz* court asserted that even though a judge might find the opinions of physicians, medical experts, or hospital ethics committees helpful in reaching a decision, there should be no requirement to seek out their advice. The court decided that questions of life and death with regard to an incompetent should be the responsibility of the courts, which would conduct detached but passionate investigations. The court took a "dim view of any attempt to shift the ultimate decision-making responsibility away from duly established courts of proper jurisdiction to any committee, panel, or group, ad hoc or permanent."[8]

Six months after *Saikewicz*, the Massachusetts Appeals Court narrowed the need for court intervention in *In re Dinnerstein*[9] by finding that no-code orders are valid to prevent the use of artificial resuscitative measures on incompetent, terminally ill patients. The court was faced with the case of a 67-year-old woman who was suffering from Alzheimer's disease. It was determined that she was permanently comatose at the time of trial. Further, the court decided that *Saikewicz*-type judicial proceedings should take place only when medical treatment could offer a reasonable expectation of affecting a permanent or temporary cure of or relief from the illness.

The Massachusetts Supreme Judicial Court attempted to clarify its *Saikewicz* opinion with regard to court orders in *In re Spring*.[10] It held that such different factors as the patient's mental impairment and his or her medical prognosis with or without treatment must be considered before judicial approval is necessary to withdraw or withhold treatment from an incompetent patient. The problem in all three cases is that there was still no clear guidance as to exactly when the court's approval of the removal of life-support systems would be necessary. *Saikewicz* seemed to demand judicial approval in every case. *Spring*, however, in partially retreating from that view, stated that it did not have to articulate what combination of the factors it discussed, thus making prior court approval necessary.

The inconsistencies presented by the Massachusetts cases led many courts to follow the parameters set by *Quinlan*, requiring judicial intervention. In cases where physicians have certified the irreversible nature of a patient's loss of consciousness, a neurological team could certify the patient's hopeless neurological condition. Then a guardian would be free to take the legal steps necessary to remove life-support systems. The main reason for the appointment of a guardian is to ensure that incompetents, like all other patients, maintain their right to refuse treatment. Most holdings indicate that because a patient has the constitutional right of self-determination, those acting on the patient's behalf can exercise that right when rendering their best judgment concerning how the patient would assert the right. The guardian's decision is sound if based on the known desires of a patient who was competent immediately before becoming comatose.

Courts adhering to the *Quinlan* rationale have recognized that fact, and in 1984 the highest state court of Florida took the lead and accepted the living will as persuasive evidence of an incompetent's wishes. In *John F. Kennedy Memorial Hospital v. Bludworth*,[11] the Florida Supreme Court allowed an incompetent patient's wife to act as his guardian, and, in accordance with the terms of a living will he executed in 1975, she was told to substitute her judgment for that of her husband. She asked to have a respirator removed. The court declined the necessity of prior court approval, finding that the constitutional right to refuse treatment had been decided in *Satz v. Perlmutter*.[12] The court required the attending physician to certify that the patient was in a permanent vegetative state, with no reasonable chance for recovery, before a family member or guardian could request termination of extraordinary means of medical treatment.

In keeping with *Saikewicz*, the decision maker would attempt to ascertain the incompetent patient's actual interests and preferences. Court involvement would be mandated only to appoint a guardian when: family members disagree as to the incompetent's wishes; physicians disagree on the prognosis; the patient's wishes cannot be known because he or she always has been incompetent; evidence exists of wrongful motives or malpractice; and/or no family member can serve as a guardian.

The decision in *John F. Kennedy Memorial Hospital v. Bludworth* increased the desire of the public, courts, and religious groups to know when a patient is considered to be legally dead and what type of treatment can be withheld or withdrawn. Most cases dealing with euthanasia speak of the necessity that a physician diagnose a patient as being either in a persistent vegetative state or terminally ill.

The courts have recognized that the irreversible cessation of brain function constitutes death. The American Medical Association in 1974 accepted that death occurs when there is "irreversible cessation of all brain functions including the brain stem."[13] Most states recognize brain death by statute or judicial decision.

In *In re Westchester County Medical Center ex rel. O'Connor*[14] the court determined that artificial nutrition could be withheld from O'Connor, a stroke victim who was unable to converse or feed herself. The court held that nothing less than proof of a patient's wishes will suffice when the decision to terminate life support is at issue.[15] The factors outlined by the court in determining the existence of clear and convincing evidence of a patient's intention to reject the prolongation of life by artificial means were the persistence of statements regarding an individual's beliefs; desirability of the commitment to those beliefs; seriousness with which such statements were made; and inferences that may be drawn from the surrounding circumstances.

The Missouri Supreme Court applied the *Westchester* ruling and held that the family of Nancy Cruzan, who was in a persistent vegetative state since 1983, could not order physicians to remove artificial nutrition.[16] In 1983, Nancy sustained injuries in a car accident, in which her car overturned, after which she was found face down in a ditch without respiratory or cardiac function. In December of 1990, Nancy was determined to be in an irreversible vegetative state. Because

of the prognosis, Nancy's parents asked the hospital staff to cease all artificial nutrition and hydration procedures. The staff refused to comply with their wishes without court approval. The state trial court granted authorization for termination, finding that Nancy had a fundamental right—grounded in both the state and federal constitutions—to refuse or direct the withdrawal of death-prolonging procedures. Testimony at trial from a former roommate of Nancy indicated to the court that she had stated that if she were ever sick or injured, she would not want to live unless she could live halfway normally. The court interpreted that conversation, which had taken place when Nancy was 25 years old, as meaning that she would not want to be forced to take nutrition and hydration while in a persistent vegetative state.

The case was appealed to the Missouri Supreme Court, which reversed the lower court decision. The court held that Nancy's parents were not entitled to order the termination of her treatment. The court found that Nancy's statements to her roommate did not rise to the level of clear and convincing evidence of her desire to end nutrition and hydration.

In June 1990, the U.S. Supreme Court heard oral arguments and held that:

- The U.S. Constitution does not forbid Missouri from requiring that there be clear and convincing evidence of an incompetent's wishes as to the withdrawal of life-sustaining treatment.
- The Missouri Supreme Court did not commit constitutional error in concluding that evidence adduced at trial did not amount to clear and convincing evidence of Cruzan's desire to cease hydration and nutrition.
- Due process did not require the state to accept the substituted judgment of close family members, absent substantial proof their views reflected those of the patient.[17]

The Supreme Court held that right-to-die should be decided pursuant to state law, subject to a due-process liberty interest, and in keeping with state constitutional law. After the Supreme Court rendered its decision, the Cruzans returned to Missouri probate court, where on November 14, 1990, Judge Charles Teel authorized physicians to remove the feeding tubes from Nancy. The judge determined that testimony presented to him early in November demonstrated clear and convincing evidence that Nancy would not have wanted to live in a persistent vegetative state. Several of her coworkers testified she told them before her accident she would not want to live like a vegetable. On December 26, 1990, 2 weeks after her feeding tubes were removed, Nancy died.

The integrity of medicine in its promise to do no harm is not threatened by allowing competent patients to decide for themselves whether a particular medical treatment is in their best interests. If the doctrines of informed consent and right of privacy have as their foundations the right to bodily integrity and control of one's own fate, then those rights are superior to the institutional considerations of hospitals and their medical staffs.

LEGISLATIVE RESPONSE

After the *Cruzan* decision, states began to rethink existing legislation and draft new legislation in the areas of living wills, durable powers of attorney, healthcare proxies, and surrogate decision-making. Pennsylvania and Florida were two of the first states to react to the *Cruzan* decision. The Pennsylvania statute is applied to terminally ill or permanently unconscious patients. The statute, the *Advance Directive for Health Care Act*,[18] deals mainly with individuals who have prepared living wills. It includes in its definition of life-sustaining treatment the administration of hydration and nutrition by any means if it is stated in the individual's living will. The statute mandates that a copy of the living will be given to the physician to be effective. Further, the patient must be incompetent or permanently unconscious. If there is no evidence of the presence of a living will, the Pennsylvania probate codes allow an attorney-in-fact who was designated in a properly executed durable power of attorney document to give permission for "medical and surgical procedures to be utilized on an incompetent patient."[19]

Patient Self-Determination Act

The Patient Self-Determination Act of 1990 (PSDA) requires healthcare organizations to explain to patients their legal right to direct their own medical and nursing care as it corresponds to existing state law. A person's right to refuse medical treatment is not lost when the person's mental or physical status changes. When a person is no longer competent to exercise his or her right of self-determination, the right still exists, but the decision must be legally delegated to a surrogate decision maker. The PSDA provides that patients have a right to formulate advance directives (e.g., living wills) and to make decisions regarding their health care. Self-determination includes the right to accept or refuse medical treatment. Healthcare providers (including hospitals, nursing homes, home health agencies, health maintenance organizations, and hospices) that receive federal funds under Medicare are required to comply with the regulations.

Providers are not entitled to reimbursement under the Medicare program if they fail to meet PSDA requirements.

PRESERVATION OF LIFE WITH LIMITS

Medical ethics do not require that a patient's life be preserved at all costs and in all circumstances. The ethical integrity of the profession is not threatened by allowing competent patients to decide for themselves whether a particular medical treatment is in their best interests. If the doctrines of informed consent and right of privacy have as their foundations the right to bodily integrity and control of one's own fate, then those rights are superior to the institutional considerations of hospitals and their medical staffs. A state's interest in maintaining the ethical integrity of a profession does not outweigh, for example, a patient's right to refuse blood transfusions.

EUTHANASIA

 There is nothing more sacred than life and there is nothing more natural in life to wish to cling on to it for those you love! And nothing more cruel than to play god by artificially holding onto that which God wants to bring home.

—*Author Unknown*

Originating from the Greek word euthanatos, euthanasia, meaning "good death" or "easy death," was accepted in situations in which people had what were considered to be incurable diseases. Euthanasia is defined broadly as "the mercy killing of the hopelessly ill, injured, or incapacitated." Any discussion of euthanasia obliges a person to confront humanity's greatest fear—death. The courts and legislatures have faced it and have made advances in setting forth guidelines to assist decision makers in this arena. The legal system must ensure that the constitutional rights of the patient are maintained, while at the same time protect society's interests in preserving life, preventing suicide, and maintaining the integrity of the medical profession. In the final analysis, the boundaries of patient rights remain uncertain.

Active euthanasia is commonly understood to be the intentional commission of an act, such as giving a patient a lethal drug that results in death. The act, if committed by the patient, is thought of as suicide. Moreover, because the patient cannot take his or her own life, any person who assists in the causing of the death could be subject to criminal sanction for aiding and abetting suicide.

Passive euthanasia occurs when life-saving treatment (such as a respirator) is withheld, allowing the patient diagnosed as terminal to die a natural death. Passive euthanasia is generally accepted pursuant to legislative acts and judicial decisions. These decisions, however, generally are based on the facts of a particular case.

From its inception, euthanasia has evolved into an issue with competing legal, medical, and moral implications that continues to generate debate, confusion, and conflict. Currently, there is a strong movement advocating death with dignity, which excludes machines, monitors, and tubes. **Figure 15–2** and **Figure 15–3** illustrate and summarize the numerous ramifications of euthanasia discussed in this chapter.

Figure 15–2 Euthanasia Questioned

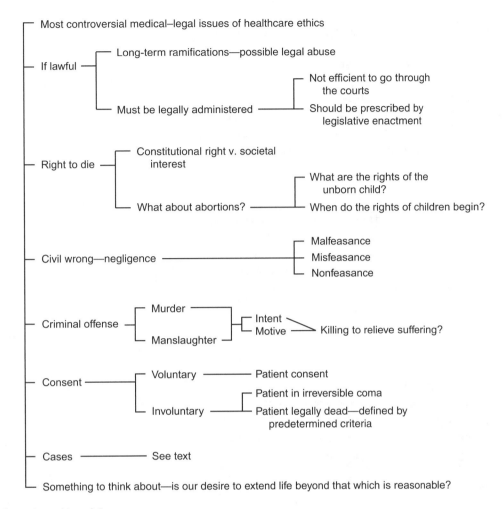

Figure 15–3   Euthanasia and Legal Concerns

Physician-Assisted Suicide

The issue of assisted suicide presents profound questions of medicine and medical ethics, theology and sociology, and numerous other far-reaching public policy issues. States have been confronted with the question of whether it is ever right for a physician to provide a patient with aid in dying. Dr. Jack Kevorkian, of Michigan, for example, announced in October 1989 that he had developed a device that would end one's life quickly, painlessly, and humanely. As a result, Dr. Kevorkian assisted patients in committing suicide. He was charged with first-degree murder, but the charge was later dismissed because Michigan had no law against assisted suicide.

The Michigan House approved legislation placing a temporary ban on assisted suicide, which became effective on April 1, 1993, and made assisting suicide a felony punishable by up to 4 years in prison and a $2,000 fine. Under the new law, assisted suicide was banned for 15 months. During this time period, a special commission studied assisted suicide and submitted its recommendations to the Michigan legislature for review and action.

Dr. Kevorkian faced prosecution for murder and for assisting in suicide. As a result, he appealed a Michigan Supreme Court ruling that found there is no right to assisted suicide.[20] The U.S. Supreme Court rejected Dr. Kevorkian's argument that assisted suicide is a constitutional right. The high court's decision allowed the state of Michigan to move forward and prosecute Kevorkian on pending charges. In 1999, Dr. Kevorkian was convicted of second-degree murder and for performing and assisting in patient suicide. He was released on parole in 2007 and passed away in June 2011. Dr. Kevorkian claimed that he assisted in the death of 130 patients.

Oregon's Death with Dignity Act

Ironically, while Dr. Kevorkian served time in a Michigan prison, physician-assisted suicide became a legal medical option for the terminally ill residents of Oregon on October 27,

---

Request for Medication to End My Life in a Humane and Dignified Manner

I, _____, am an adult of sound mind.

I am suffering from _____, which my attending physician has determined is a terminal disease and which has been medically confirmed by a consulting physician.

I have been fully informed of my diagnosis, prognosis, the nature of medication to be prescribed and potential associated risks, the expected result, and the feasible alternatives, including comfort care, hospice care, and pain control.

I request that my attending physician prescribe medication that will end my life in a humane and dignified manner.

Initial One:

_____ I have informed my family of my decision and taken their opinions into consideration.

_____ I have decided not to inform my family of my decision.

_____ I have no family to inform of my decision.

I understand that I have the right to rescind this request at any time.

I understand the full import of this request and I expect to die when I take the medication to be prescribed.

I make this request voluntarily and without reservation, and I accept full moral responsibility for my actions.

Signed: _____

Date: _____

Declaration of Witnesses

We declare that the person signing this request:

(a) Is personally known to us or has provided proof of identity;

(b) Signed the request in our presence;

(c) Appears to be of sound mind and not under duress, fraud or undue influence;

(d) Is not a patient for whom either of us is the attending physician.

Figure 15–4 Oregon Request Form to End Life

1997. The Oregon Death with Dignity Act[21] allows physicians to prescribe but not administer lethal drugs to the requester who must be terminally ill with fewer than 6 months to live. The patient must convince doctors that the decision is voluntary, sincere, and not based on depression. The waiting period is 15 days. The medication can only be given orally. Two physicians must examine the patient to confirm the diagnosis and prognosis. The patient must have made a witnessed request both orally and in writing. All prescriptions must be reported to the state health department. A request for a medication for ending one's life under Oregon law must be substantially in the format shown in **Figure 15–4**.

Criminalizing Assisted Suicide

The U.S. Supreme Court in June 1997 ruled in two unanimous and separate decisions that the laws in Washington and New York prohibiting assisted suicide are constitutional—yet the U.S. Supreme Court also ruled states can allow physicians to assist in the suicide of their terminally ill patients.

The U.S. Supreme Court determined that New York's prohibition on assisted suicide does not violate the equal protection clause of the Fourteenth Amendment. The assisted suicide ban and the law permitting patients to refuse medical treatment do not conflict. There is a distinction between letting a patient die and making one die. In its decision, the Supreme Court determined that New York had valid reasons for distinguishing between refusing treatments and assisting suicide. Those reasons included prohibiting intentional killing and preserving life; preventing suicide; maintaining the physician's role as his or her patient's healer; and protecting vulnerable people from indifference, prejudice, and psychological and financial pressure to end their lives.[22]

In *Washington v. Glucksberg*,[23] the Supreme Court held that assisted suicide is not a liberty protected by the Constitution's due-process clause. Although a majority of states now ban assisted suicide, these rulings do not affect the right of patients to refuse treatment. It is clear that this emotionally charged issue is not settled.

■ ADVANCE DIRECTIVES

Advance directives for health care are instructions given by individuals specifying what actions they want taken for their health in the event that they are no longer able to make healthcare decisions as a result of illness or incapacity. Patients can appoint an agent to make those decisions on his or her behalf. Patients should be asked at the time of admission to a healthcare facility if they have an advance directive. If a patient does not have an advance directive, the organization should provide the patient with information as to what an advance directive is and given the opportunity to execute an advance directive. The patient should clearly understand that an advance directive is a guideline for caregivers as to his or her wishes for what medical care he or she would and would not want to receive in the event he or she becomes incapacitated and unable to make decisions. This interaction should be documented in the patient's medical record. If the patient has an advance directive, a copy should be requested for insertion into the patient's record. If the patient does not have a copy of the advance directive with him or her, documentation in the medical record should include the location of the advance directive, the name and telephone number of the designated healthcare agent, and any information that might be helpful in the immediate care situation (e.g., patient's desire for food and hydration).

Making Preferences Known

Patients have an obligation to make medical preferences known to the treating physician. Any glimmer of uncertainty as to a patient's desires in an emergency situation should be resolved in favor of preserving life. The court in the *Matter of Hughes*[24] emphasized that in the context of elective surgery, patients have an obligation to make medical preferences known to the treating physician, including the course to follow, if life-threatening complications should arise. This protects the patient's right to freedom of religion and self-determination.

Living Will

A *living will* is the instrument or legal document that describes those treatments an individual wishes or does not wish to receive should he or she become incapacitated and unable to communicate treatment decisions. Typically, a *living will* allows a person, when competent, to inform caregivers in writing of his or her wishes with regard to withholding and withdrawing life-supporting treatment, including nutrition and hydration.

The living will should be signed and dated by two witnesses who are not blood relatives or beneficiaries of property. A living will should be discussed with the patient's physician, and a signed copy should be placed in the patient's medical record. A copy also should be given to the individual designated to make decisions in the event the patient is unable to do so. A person who executes a living will when healthy and mentally competent cannot predict how he or she will feel at the time of a terminal illness. Therefore, it should be updated as necessary to accurately reflect a patient's wishes. The written instructions become effective when a patient is either in a terminal condition, permanently unconscious, or suffering irreversible brain damage. An example of a living will is illustrated in **Figure 15–5**.

Healthcare Proxy

A *healthcare proxy* is a legal document that allows a person to appoint a healthcare agent to make treatment decisions in the event he or she becomes incapacitated and unable to make decisions. The agent must be made aware of the patient's wishes regarding nutrition and hydration to be allowed to make a decision concerning withholding or withdrawing treatment. In contrast to a living will, a healthcare proxy does not require a person to know about and consider in advance all situations and decisions that could arise. Rather, the appointed agent would know about and interpret the expressed wishes of the patient and then make decisions about the medical care and treatment to be administered or refused. The *Cruzan* decision indicates that the Supreme Court views advance directives as clear and convincing evidence of a patient's wishes regarding life-sustaining treatment.

Before exercising an incompetent patient's right to forgo medical treatment, the surrogate decision maker must satisfy the following conditions:

- The surrogate must be satisfied that the patient executed a document (e.g., Durable Power of Attorney for Health Care and Health Care Proxy) knowingly, willingly, and without undue influence, and that the evidence of the patient's oral declaration is reliable.
- The patient must not have reasonable probability of recovering competency so that the patient could exercise the right.
- The surrogate must take care to ensure that any limitations or conditions expressed either orally or in written declarations have been considered carefully and satisfied.

Determining Incapacity

Before declaring an individual incapacitated, the attending physician must find with a reasonable degree of medical

My Living Will

To my Family, Doctors, and All Those Concerned with My Care:

I, _____, being of sound mind, make this statement as a directive to be followed if for any reason I become incapacitated and unable to participate in decisions regarding my medical care.

If I should be in an incurable or irreversible mental or physical condition with no reasonable expectation of recovery, I direct my attending physician to withhold or withdraw treatment that merely prolongs my dying. I direct that my treatment in this instance be limited to comfort care and the control of and relief from pain.

Care I Want:

_____

_____

_____

_____

_____

_____

To live as long as possible regardless of the quality of life that I may experience:

- I direct that all appropriate medical/surgical measures be provided to sustain my life regardless of my mental or physical condition.
- Upon my death, I want to donate any parts of my body that may be of benefit to others.

Care I Do Not Want:

_____

_____

_____

_____

_____

- I am permanently unconscious with and permanently connected to a ventilator.
- I am permanently unconscious with a feeding tube and/or intravenous hydration.
- I am on a ventilator when there is little or no chance of recovery.
- I am conscious but unable to communicate, being fed with a feeding tube and/or hydrated.
- I am in the end stage of a fatal irreversible mental or physical illness, disease, or condition.
- I do not want: _____ Mechanical ventilation _____ CPR _____ Dialysis _____ Feeding tubes
- Other exceptions and/or comments:

_____

_____

_____

Additional Comments or Exceptions:

This living will describes my express wishes and legal right to accept or refuse treatment. As I am of sound mind, I expect my family, physician/s, and all those concerned with my care to regard themselves as legally and morally bound to act in accord with my wishes.

Signed: _____

Date: _____

Witness (Cannot be designated healthcare agent). I declare that the person who signed the document or asked another to sign this document on his/her behalf did so in my presence and that he/she appears to be of sound mind and free of duress or undue influence.

Signed: _____

Date: _____

Signed: _____

Date: _____

Note: A copy of the executed living will should be provided to the patient's physician and healthcare agent.

Figure 15–5   Living Will

certainty that the patient lacks capacity. A notation should be placed in the patient's medical record describing the cause, nature, extent, and probable duration of incapacity. Before withholding or withdrawing life-sustaining treatment, the incapacity determination must be confirmed by a second physician making an appropriate entry in the medical record before honoring decisions by a healthcare agent.

Agent's Rights

A healthcare agent's rights are no greater than those of a competent patient. However, the agent's rights are limited to any specific instructions included in the proxy document. The agent has the right to consent or refuse to consent to any service or treatment, routine or otherwise; to refuse life-sustaining treatment; and to access all of the patient's medical information to make informed decisions. The agent must make decisions based on the patient's moral and religious beliefs. If a patient's wishes are not known, decisions must be based on a good-faith judgment of what the patient would have wanted.

Durable Power of Attorney

Power of attorney is a legal device that permits one individual, known as the "principal," to give to another person, called the "attorney-in-fact," the authority to act on the principal's behalf. The attorney-in-fact is generally authorized to handle banking and real estate affairs, incur expenses, pay bills, and handle a wide variety of legal affairs for a specified period of time. The power of attorney may continue indefinitely during the lifetime of the principal as long as that person is competent and capable of granting power of attorney. Because a power of attorney is limited by the competency of the principal, some states have authorized a special legal device for the principal to express intent concerning the durability of the power of attorney, to allow it to survive disability or incompetency. A durable power of attorney is more general in scope, and the patient does not have to be in imminent danger of death as is necessary in a living will situation. Although it need not delineate desired medical treatment specifically, it must indicate the principal has communicated his or her healthcare wishes to the attorney-in-fact. Although laws vary from state to state, all 50 states and the District of Columbia have durable power of attorney statutes. An example of a *durable power of attorney for health care* is illustrated in **Figure 15–6**.

Guardianship

Guardianship is a legal mechanism by which the court declares a person incompetent and appoints a guardian. The court transfers the responsibility for managing financial affairs, living arrangements, and medical care decisions to the guardian.

When a person has been declared incompetent as a result of being in a persistent vegetative state and has left no advance directive, life-sustaining decisions become more complex. Since 1990, Terri Schiavo from Clearwater, Florida, had been in a persistent vegetative state after a heart attack cut off the supply of oxygen to her brain. Her husband, Michael, became her legal guardian and fought to have her feeding tube removed, which was against her parents' wishes. Michael argued that Terri had articulated her desire not to be kept alive by artificial means.

In an unprecedented move, on October 21, 2003, Governor Jeb Bush signed an order based on a hastily passed law called Terri's Law, mandating the reinsertion of Ms. Schiavo's feeding tube, which had been removed 6 days earlier. Mr. Schiavo filed an appeal based upon a violation of his wife's right to privacy under the Florida Constitution, asserting that the law intruded upon the separation of powers. This case is the first time a governor and legislative branch of government have usurped not only the authority of the judiciary, but the rights of legal guardians to make decisions.

The law was narrowly tailored to fit Terri Schiavo's circumstances in which a patient has not left a living will, is in a persistent vegetative state, has had feeding tubes removed, and a family member challenges the removal. Florida law Chapter 2003-418 was passed by the Florida legislature, which provided that the governor shall have authority to issue a one-time stay to prevent the withholding of nutrition and hydration from the patient. The act was determined to be unconstitutional as applied in the Schiavo case. The Supreme Court of Florida in *Schiavo* concluded:

> As the Second District noted in one of the multiple appeals in this case, we "are called upon to make a collective, objective decision concerning a question of law. Each of us, however, has our own family, our own loved ones, our own children. . . . But in the end, this case is not about the aspirations that loving parents have for their children. . . ." Schiavo IV, 851 So.2d at 186. Rather, as our decision today makes clear, this case is about maintaining the integrity of a constitutional system of government with three independent and coequal branches, none of which can either encroach upon the powers of another branch or improperly delegate its own responsibilities.
>
> The trial court's decision regarding Theresa Schiavo was made in accordance with the procedures and protections set forth by the judicial branch and in accordance with the statutes passed by the Legislature in effect at that time. That decision is final and the Legislature's attempt to alter that final adjudication is unconstitutional as applied to Theresa Schiavo. Further, even if there had been no final judgment in

Durable Power of Attorney for Health Care

I, _____, appoint:

1. Name: _____   Phone #: _____

Address: _____

as my attorney-in-fact or agent to make my health and personal care decisions for me if I become unable to make my own decisions. If the person I have named above is unable to act as my agent, I hereby designate the following person to serve as my agent:

2. Name: _____   Phone #: _____

Address: _____

This *durable power of attorney* shall become effective upon my incapacity to make health or personal care decisions. (Please initial the statement/s below that best expresses your wishes.)

_____ I authorize my admission to or discharge from any medical, nursing, residential, or similar facility and to enter into agreements for my care.

_____ I authorize my agent to refuse or withdraw consent to any and all types of treatment, including, but not limited to, nutrition and hydration administered by artificial or invasive means.

I have discussed with my agent my wishes for health care. If my agent is not able to determine what I would want, I trust my agent to make his/her decision based on what he/she believes would be my wishes. This durable power of attorney is meant to replace all others.

Signed: _____   Date: _____

Witness (Cannot be the principal's designated healthcare agent). I declare that the person who signed this document or asked another to sign this document on his/her behalf did so in my presence and that he/she appears to be of sound mind and free of duress or undue influence.

Signed: _____   Date: _____

Signed: _____   Date: _____

Primary Agent

I, _____, have read the above durable power of attorney and am the person identified as the agent for _____. My signature below indicates that I acknowledge and accept responsibility to act as the agent and will exercise the powers herein granted in the best interest of the principal.

Signed: _____   Date: _____

Substitute Agent

I, _____, have read the above durable power of attorney and am the person identified as the agent for _____. My signature below indicates that I acknowledge and accept responsibility to act as the agent and will exercise the powers herein granted in the best interest of the principal.

Signed: _____   Date: _____

State of _____

County of _____

On this date, the _____ day of _____, 201 _____, before me, the undersigned officer, personally appeared _____, known to me (satisfactorily proven) to be the person whose name is subscribed to the foregoing instrument, and acknowledged that he/she executed it for the purposes therein contained.

Witness my hand and official seal the day and year aforesaid _____.

Notary Public

Note: A copy of the executed durable power of attorney should be provided to the patient's physician and healthcare agent.

Figure 15–6 Durable Power of Attorney for Health Care

this case, the Legislature provided the Governor constitutionally inadequate standards for the application of the legislative authority delegated in chapter 2003-418. Because chapter 2003-418 runs afoul of article II, section 3 of the Florida Constitution in both respects, we affirm the circuit court's final summary judgment.[25]

The U.S. Supreme Court, on January 24, 2005, denied an appeal by Florida Governor Jeb Bush to overturn the decision by the Florida Supreme Court, which ruled Terri's Law unconstitutional.

Substituted Judgment

Substituted judgment is a form of surrogate decision-making where the surrogate attempts to establish what decision the patient would have made if that patient were competent to make a decision. This conclusion can be based on the patient's preference expressed in previous statements or the surrogate's knowledge of the patient's beliefs (e.g., religious) and values.[26]

FUTILITY OF TREATMENT

Futility of treatment, as it relates to medical care, occurs when the physician recognizes that the effect of treatment will be of no benefit to the patient. Morally, a physician has a duty to inform the patient when there is little likelihood of success. The determination as to futility of medical care is a scientific decision.

After a diagnosis has been made that a person is terminally ill with no hope of recovery and is in a chronic vegetative state with no possibility of attaining cognitive function, a state generally has no compelling interest in maintaining life. The decision to forgo or terminate life-support measures is, at this point, simply a decision that the dying process will not be artificially extended. Although the state has an interest in the prolongation of life, it has no interest in the prolongation of dying, and although there is a moral and ethical decision to be made to end the process, that decision can be made only by the surrogate. The decision whether to end the dying process is a personal decision for family members or those who bear a legal responsibility for the patient.

A determination as to the futility of medical care is a decision that must be made by a physician. Even if death is not imminent but a patient's coma is irreversible beyond doubt and there are adequate safeguards to confirm the accuracy of the diagnosis with the concurrence of those responsible for the patient's care, it is not unethical to discontinue all means of life-prolonging medical treatment.

WITHHOLDING AND WITHDRAWAL OF TREATMENT

Withholding of treatment is a decision not to initiate treatment or medical intervention for the patient. This is a decision often made when death is imminent and there is no hope of recovery. *Withdrawal of treatment* is a decision to discontinue treatment or medical interventions for the patient, when death is imminent and cannot be prevented by available treatment. Withholding or withdrawing treatment should be considered when:

- the patient is in a terminal condition and there is a reasonable expectation of imminent death of the patient;
- the patient is in a noncognitive state with no reasonable possibility of regaining cognitive function; and/or
- restoration of cardiac function will last for a brief period.

Theologians and ethicists have long recognized a distinction between ordinary and extraordinary medical care. The theological distinction is based on the belief that life is a gift from God that should not be destroyed deliberately by humans. Therefore, extraordinary therapies that extend life by imposing grave burdens on the patient and family are not required. Although the courts have accepted decisions to withhold or withdraw extraordinary care, especially the respirator, from those who are comatose or in a persistent vegetative state with no possibility of emerging, they have been unwilling until now to discontinue feeding, which they have considered to be ordinary care.

The American Medical Association, on March 17, 1986, changed its code of ethics on comas,[27] allowing physicians to withhold food, water, and medical treatment from patients in irreversible comas or persistent vegetative states with no hope of recovery—even if death is not imminent. Although physicians can consider the wishes of the patient and family or the legal representatives, they cannot cause death intentionally. The wording is permissive, so those physicians who feel uncomfortable withdrawing food and water may refrain from doing so.

The Illinois Supreme Court, in *In re Estate of Longeway*,[28] found that the authorized guardian of a terminally ill patient in an irreversible coma or persistent vegetative state has a common-law right to refuse artificial nutrition and hydration. The court found that there must be clear and convincing evidence that the refusal is consistent with the patient's interest. The court also required the concurrence of the patient's attending physician and two other physicians. Court intervention is also necessary to guard against the possibility that greed may taint the judgment of the surrogate decision maker. Although there may be a duty to provide life-sustaining equipment in the immediate aftermath of cardiopulmonary arrest, there is no duty to continue its use when it has become futile and ineffective to do so in the opinion of qualified medical personnel.

Physicians Charged for Removal of Life Support

Although there might be a duty to provide life-sustaining equipment in the immediate aftermath of cardiopulmonary arrest, there is no duty to continue its use when it has become futile and ineffective to do so in the opinion of qualified medical personnel. Two physicians in *Barber v. Superior Court*[29] were charged with the crimes of murder and conspiracy to commit murder. The charges were based on their acceding to requests of the patient's family to discontinue life-support equipment and intravenous tubes. The patient suffered a cardiopulmonary arrest in the recovery room after surgery. A team of physicians and nurses revived the patient and placed him on life-support equipment. The patient suffered severe brain damage, which placed him in a comatose and vegetative state from which, according to tests and examinations by other specialists, he was unlikely to recover. On the written request of the family, the patient was taken off life-support equipment. The family, his wife and eight children, made the decision together after consultation with the physicians. Evidence had been presented that the patient, before his incapacitation, had expressed to his wife that he would not want to be kept alive by a machine. There was no evidence indicating that the family was motivated in their decision by anything other than love and concern for the dignity of their loved one. The patient continued to breathe on his own. Showing no signs of improvement, the physicians again discussed the patient's poor prognosis with the family. The intravenous lines were removed, and the patient died sometime thereafter.

A complaint then was filed against the two physicians. The magistrate who heard the evidence determined that the physicians did not kill the deceased because their conduct was not the proximate cause of the patient's death. On motion of the prosecution, the superior court determined as a matter of law that the evidence required the magistrate to hold the physicians to answer and ordered the complaint reinstated. The court of appeals held that the physicians' omission to continue treatment, although intentional and with knowledge that the patient would die, was not an unlawful failure to perform a legal duty. The evidence amply supported the magistrate's decision. The court of appeals determined that the superior court erred in determining that the evidence required the magistrate to hold the physicians to answer.

DO-NOT-RESUSCITATE ORDERS

Do-not-resuscitate (DNR) orders, given by a physician, indicate that in the event of a cardiac or respiratory arrest, no resuscitative measures should be used to revive the patient. A DNR order is an extremely difficult decision to make for both the patient and family. It is generally made when one's quality of life has been so diminished that heroic rescue methods are no longer in the patient's best interests. DNR orders must be in writing, signed, and dated by the physician. Appropriate consents must be obtained from the patient or his or her healthcare agent. Many states have acknowledged the validity of DNR orders in cases involving terminally ill patients in which the patients' families make no objections to such orders.

DNR orders must comply with statutory requirements, be of short duration, and be reviewed periodically to determine whether the patient's condition or other circumstances (e.g., change of mind by the patient or family) surrounding the no-code[30] orders have changed. Presently, it is generally accepted that if a patient is competent, a DNR order is considered to be the same as other medical decisions in which a patient may choose to reject life-sustaining treatment. In the case of an incompetent, absent any advance written directives, the best interests of the patient must be considered.

ETHICS COMMITTEE

The numerous ethical questions facing health professionals involve the entire life span, from the right to be born to the right to die. Ethics committees concern themselves with issues of morality, patient autonomy, legislation, and states' interests. Healthcare ethics committees address legal–ethical issues that arise during the course of a patient's care and treatment. They serve as a resource for patients, families, and staff. They offer objective counsel when dealing with difficult healthcare issues. Ethics committees generally provide both educational and consultative services to patients, families, and caregivers. They enhance but do not replace important patient/family–physician relationships; nevertheless, they afford support for decisions made within those relationships.

Although ethics committees first emerged in the 1960s, attention was focused on them in the 1976 landmark *Quinlan* case,[31] where the parents of Karen Ann Quinlan were granted permission by the New Jersey Supreme Court to remove Karen from a ventilator after she had been in a coma for a year. She died 10 years later at the age of 31, having been in a persistent vegetative state the entire time. The *Quinlan* court looked to a prognosis committee to verify Karen's medical condition. It then factored in the committee's opinion with all other evidence to reach the decision to allow withdrawing her life-support equipment. Although ethics committees do not have sole surrogate decision-making authority, they play an ever-expanding role in the development of policy and procedural guidelines to assist in resolving ethical dilemmas. Most organizations describe the functioning of the ethics committee and how to access the committee at the time of admission in patient handbooks and informational brochures.

Always mindful of its basic orientation toward the patient's best interests, the ethics committee provides options and suggestions for resolution of ethical conflict in actual cases. Consultation with an ethics committee is not mandatory, but it is conducted at the request of a physician, patient, family member, or other healthcare professional.

The ethics committee strives to provide viable alternatives that will lead to the optimal resolution of ethical dilemmas involving the continuing care of the patient. It is important to remember that an ethics committee functions in an advisory capacity and should not be considered a substitute proxy for the patient. The Ethics Consultation in **Figure 15–7** presents a suggested form for documenting an ethics committee consultation.

Ethics Consultation

Date: _____ Time: _____ Caller: _____

Reason for call: _____

Action taken: _____

Patient: _____ Age: _____

Record #: _____ Consultation requested by: _____

Relationship (e.g., caregiver, spouse): _____

Attending physician: _____

Other physicians: _____

Will the patient participate in the consultation?   ☐ Yes ☐ No

Does the patient have decision-making capacity?   ☐ Yes ☐ No Explain _____

Surrogate decision maker?   ☐ Yes ☐ No If yes, name: _____

Phone #: _____ Advance directives (e.g., living will)? _____

Availability of advance directive: _____

Consultation participants:

☐ Family/relationship _____

☐ Physicians _____

☐ Nurses _____

☐ Ethics committee members (e.g., Chaplain, social worker, community representative) _____

_____

_____

_____

Medical Treatment/Care Information

Diagnoses: _____ Prognosis: _____

Course of illness: _____

Treatment options appropriate: _____

Treatment options medically beneficial: _____

Treatment options available: _____

Would the patient have wanted the treatment? _____

Ethical issues: _____

Legal issues: _____

Other persons to contact for input, if any. _____

Consultative guidance: _____

Guidance communicated?   ☐ Yes ☐ No If yes, to whom? _____

Consultation noted on the medical record   ☐ Yes ☐ No

Disposition: _____

_____

Form completed by: _____ Date/Time: _____

Figure 15–7   Ethics Consultation

Requests for an ethics committee consultation often involve: clarification of issues regarding decision-making capacity, informed consent, and advance directives; do-not-resuscitate orders; withdrawal of treatment; and assistance in conflict resolution.

AUTOPSY

Autopsies, or postmortem examinations, are conducted to ascertain the cause of a person's death, which, in turn, may resolve several legal issues. An autopsy may reveal whether death was the result of criminal activity, whether the cause of death was one for which payment must be made in accordance with an insurance contract, whether the death is compensable under workers' compensation and occupational disease acts, or whether death was the result of a specific act or a culmination of several acts. Aside from providing answers to these specific questions, the information gained from autopsies adds to medical knowledge. As such, medical schools have an interest in autopsies for educational purposes.

In those instances when the death of a patient is the result of criminal activity or unusual or suspicious circumstances, the patient's death must be reported to the medical examiner. Deaths resulting from natural causes within 24 hours of admission to a hospital do not need to be reported as long as the patient was in the hospital at the time of death and as long as an appropriate physician signs the death certificate and records the cause of death.

Deaths that occur during a surgical procedure are generally reportable events to the medical examiner. If an autopsy for medical evaluation is desired by the hospital, consent must be obtained from the next of kin. An unauthorized autopsy may disturb persons whose religious beliefs prohibit such a procedure as well as those persons who have a general aversion to the procedure. When autopsies are performed without statutory authorization and without the consent of the decedent, the surviving spouse, or an appropriate relative, liability may be imposed.

ORGAN DONATION

Federal regulations require hospitals have, and implement, written protocols regarding the organization's organ procurement responsibilities. The regulations impose specific notification duties, as well as other requirements concerning informing families of potential donors. They encourage

discretion and sensitivity in dealing with the families and in educating hospital staff on a variety of issues involved with donation matters in order to facilitate timely donation and transplantation.

NEWSPAPER CLIPPINGS: The Meat Market

Harvesting human organs for sale! The idea suggests the lurid world of horror movies and 19th-century graverobbers. Yet right now, Singapore is preparing to pay donors as much as 50,000 Singapore dollars (almost US$36,000) for their organs....

Millions of people suffer from kidney disease, but in 2007 there were just 64,606 kidney-transplant operations in the entire world. In the U.S. alone, 83,000 people wait on the official kidney-transplant list. But just 16,500 people received a kidney transplant in 2008, while almost 5,000 died waiting for one.

—*Alex Tabarrok*, The Wall Street Journal, *January 8, 2010*

Success in organ transplantation has created the problem of obtaining a sufficient supply of replacement body parts. Fear that people would buy and sell organs led to enactment of the National Organ Procurement Act in 1984, making it illegal to buy or sell organs. Throughout the country, there are tissue banks and other facilities for the storage and preservation of organs and tissue that can be used for transplantation and for other therapeutic services.

NEWSPAPER CLIPPINGS: Nurse Discarded Donated Kidney

A nurse accidentally disposed of a kidney from a living donor this month at an Ohio hospital, and doctors tried unsuccessfully for at least two hours to resuscitate the organ and what medical experts describe as a rare accident, health officials said. "Human air rendered the kidney unusable," University of Toledo medical Center spokesman Toby Clinger said Saturday.

—*The Associated Press*, The Washington Post, *August 26, 2012*

The ever-increasing success of organ transplantations and demand for organ tissue require close scrutiny of each case, making sure that established procedures have been followed in the care and disposal of all body parts. Section 1138, Title XI, of the Omnibus Budget Reconciliation Act of 1986 requires hospitals to establish organ procurement protocols or face a loss of Medicare and Medicaid funding.

Uniform Anatomical Gift Act

The American Bar Association has endorsed a Uniform Anatomical Gift Act drafted by the Commission on Uniform State Laws. The Uniform Anatomical Gift Act drafted by the Commission on Uniform State Laws has been enacted by all 50 states and has many detailed provisions that apply to a wide variety of issues raised in connection with the making, acceptance, and use of anatomic gifts. The act allows a person to make a decision to donate organs at the time of death and allows potential donors to carry an anatomical donor card. State statutes regarding donation usually permit the donor to execute the gift during his or her lifetime.

Virtually all states have based their enactments on the Uniform Anatomical Gift Act, but it should be recognized that in some states there are deviations from this act or laws dealing with donation.

Individuals who are of sound mind and 18 years of age or older are permitted to dispose of their own bodies or body parts by will or other written instrument for medical or dental education, research, advancement of medical or dental science, therapy, or transplantation. Among those eligible to receive such donations are any licensed, accredited, or approved hospitals; accredited medical or dental schools; surgeons or physicians; tissue banks; or specified individuals who need the donation for therapy or transplantation. The statute provides that when only a part of the body is donated, custody of the remaining parts of the body shall be transferred to the next of kin promptly after removal of the donated part.

A donation by will becomes effective immediately on the death of the testator, without probate, and the gift is valid and effective to the extent that it has been acted on in good faith. This is true even if the will is not probated or is declared invalid for testimonial purposes.

RESEARCH, EXPERIMENTATION, AND CLINICAL TRIALS

Research studies are designed to answer specific questions, sometimes about a drug or device's safety and its effectiveness. Ethical considerations, to name but a few, that should be addressed when conducting research on human subjects include: autonomy; self-determination; the Hippocratic maxim of *do no harm*; the application of justice and how to fairly distribute organs fairly; blind trial studies; honesty; and integrity.

REALITY CHECK: Failed Research?

Was it the failures of research that we saw or was it cruelty inflected by the helpless? As students in healthcare administration, we toured several psychiatric facilities in the . . . area. At one facility we were taken to a below-ground dark dingy corridor where we observed iron barred cells with patients that appeared to lack the attributes that reflect a human being. There seemed to be no dignity related to their care. They were caged in like animals behind bars. As we walked in the corridor we were told not to go to near the caged cells. Each cage seemed to have a distinct species of a being totally different than what we would expect to see above ground. What cruelties were inflicted on these people? It was unsettling to see and unnerving to describe. We just thought to ourselves, how ghastly, there are people like this in the world. Were they born this way and if they were, why were they hidden away in a dungeon? Were these the results of lobectomies and failed experiments? Where are such people today? Do they still exist?

Discussion

1. Discuss what legal and ethical values you believe were violated.
2. Discuss what action state government could take to prevent such inhumanity.

Both federal and state regulations provide guidelines for experimentation involving human subjects. Federal regulations control federal grants that apply to experiments involving new drugs, new medical devices, stem cell research and human cloning, as well as, new medical procedures.

Office of Research Integrity

The *Office of Research Integrity* (ORI) oversees and directs Public Health Service (PHS) research integrity activities on behalf of the Secretary of Health and Human Services with the exception of the research integrity activities of the

Food and Drug Administration. The ORI carries out its responsibility by developing policies, procedures and regulations related to the detection, investigation, and prevention of research misconduct and the responsible conduct of research. The ORI is responsible for implementing activities and programs to teach the responsible conduct of research, promote research integrity, prevent research misconduct, and improve the handling of allegations of research misconduct. The ORI administers programs for: maintaining institutional assurances, responding to allegations of retaliation against whistleblowers, approving intramural and extramural policies and procedures, and responding to Freedom of Information Act and Privacy Act requests.

Institutional Review Board

Federal regulations require hospital-based researchers to obtain the approval of an *Institutional Review Board* (IRB) prior to conducting clinical trials. The IRB should include community representation. The IRB is responsible for reviewing, monitoring, and approving clinical protocols for investigations of drugs and medical devices involving human subjects. The IRB is responsible for ensuring that the rights of each individual are protected and that all research is conducted within appropriate state and federal guidelines.

Informed Consent

Physicians have a clear duty to warn patients as to the risks and benefits of an experimental procedure, as well as the alternatives to a proposed experimental procedure. Written consent should be obtained from each patient who participates in a clinical trial. Consent should include the risks, benefits, and alternatives to the proposed treatment protocol. The consent form must not contain any coercive language through which the patient is forced to waive his or her legal rights, including the release of the investigator, sponsor, or organization from liability for negligent conduct.

Federal and state regulations require organizations conducting clinical trials on human subjects to: fully disclose to the patient the inherent risks, benefits, and treatment alternatives to the proposed research protocol(s); determine the competency of the patient to consent; obtain written consent from the patient; educate the staff as to the potential side effects, implementation of, and ongoing monitoring of protocols; require financial disclosure issues associated with the protocols; promote awareness of ethical issues; promote education in regard to ethical decision making; increase nurse participation in ethical decision making; and monitoring of approved protocols.

Failure to Obtain Informed Consent

Federal regulations require that the nature of experimental drugs and possible adverse consequences must be explained to the patient. Failure to obtain consent for the administration of experimental drugs can give rise to a lawsuit. The district court, in *Blanton v. United States*,[32] held that when a new drug of unknown effectiveness was administered to a patient at a Navy medical center, despite the availability of other drugs of known effectiveness, the hospital violated the accepted medical standards and its duty of due care, so that in the absence of the patient's consent to the experiment, the United States was liable for the resulting injury.

Patents Delay Research

NEWSPAPER CLIPPINGS: Where Are the Cures? How Patent Gridlock Is Blocking the Development of Lifesaving Drugs

While investment in biotech research and development has increased over the last three decades, new drugs that improve human health have not been forthcoming at the same rate.

What explains this drug discovery gap? Patent gridlock plays a large role. Since a 1980 Supreme Court decision allowing patents on living organisms, 40,000 DNA-related patents have been granted. Now picture a drug developer walking into an auditorium filled with dozens of owners of the biotech patents needed to create a potential lifesaving cure. Unless the drug maker can strike a deal with every person in the room, the new drug won't be developed.

Peter Ringrose, former chief science officer at Bristol Myers Squibb, told *The New York Times* that the company would not investigate some 50 proteins that could be cancer-causing, because patent holders would either decline to cooperate or demand big royalties.

—*Michael Heller,* Forbes, *August 11, 2008*

The legal system—caught up in the rights of patent holders—has resulted in delayed cures. What happens to the rights of those who would have benefited from the cures? The rights of the few, those who could be viewed as seeing money as the ultimate good, hold the rights of the many hostage—that is, until they need the cure. Ethical concerns seem to be ignored by the courts. The legal system is so ruled by rules that it cannot get out of its own harmful way.

Food and Drug Administration

The FDA, under enormous criticism over the years because of the red tape involved in the approval of new drugs, issued rules to speed up the approval process. The rules permit the use of experimental drugs outside a controlled clinical trial if the drugs are used to treat a life-threatening condition. In *Abigail Alliance for Better Access to Developmental Drugs v. Eschenbach*,[33] the U.S. Court of Appeals for the District of Columbia ruled that terminally ill patients have a "fundamental right" protected by the U.S. Constitution to access to experimental drugs that have not yet been fully approved by the FDA. The appeals court ruled that once the FDA has determined, after Phase I trials, that a potentially lifesaving new drug is sufficiently safe for expanded human trials, terminally ill patients have a constitutional right to seek treatment with the drug if no other FDA-approved drugs are available. The court said that if FDA wishes to prevent such patients from gaining access to investigational drugs that have completed Phase I trials, it bears the burden of demonstrating that its restrictions are "narrowly tailored" to serve a compelling governmental interest.

▍ HUMAN GENETICS

 NEWSPAPER CLIPPINGS: A Decade Later, Gene Map Yields Few New Cures

Ten years after President Bill Clinton announced that the first draft of the human genome was complete, medicine has yet to see any large part of the promised benefits.

—*Nicholas Wade*, The New York Times, *June 12, 2010*

Human genetics describes the study of inheritance as it occurs in human beings. It includes such areas as stem cell research, clinical genetics (e.g., genetic disease markers), and molecular genetics.

Genetic Markers

Genetic markers are genes or DNA sequences with a known location on a chromosome that can be used to identify specific cells and diseases, as well as individuals and species. They are often used to study the relationship between an inherited disease and its genetic cause in order to determine an individual's predisposition/proclivity to a specific disease. Genetic markers show observable information in DNA sequence variation, which may arise as a result of mutation of a specific gene. There are companies that will evaluate a person's DNA for these markers and provide a person with a report of his or her potential health risks. Health insurers, life insurers, employers, and others could potentially use this information to determine one's insurance premiums and even one's job future and so forth. There are going to be ethical issues that will arise. For instance, suppose a woman has a family history of breast cancer and has a genetic marker for it, but she is young (e.g., 30 years old) and free of any evidence of cancer. If a physician recommends prophylactic mastectomies or if the patient wants prophylactic mastectomies, should this be covered by insurance?

Genetic Information Nondiscrimination Act of 2008

President Bush signed into law the *Genetic Information Nondiscrimination Act* (GINA) on May 21, 2008, which resulted largely from the efforts of Senator Ted Kennedy. The law prohibits discrimination on the basis of genetic information with respect to the availability of health insurance and employment. GINA prohibits group health plans and insurers from denying coverage to a healthy individual or charging that person higher premiums based solely on a genetic predisposition to developing a specific disease (e.g., cancer or heart disease) at some future time. GINA also prohibits employers from using an individual's genetic information when making hiring, firing, job placement, or promotion decisions.

The relatively recent mapping of the human genome and the likelihood of increasing clinical application of advances in genetic disease markers make this an issue of potential increasing importance in the practice of medicine. Most of the states also have legislation that addresses this issue.

▍ STEM CELL RESEARCH

Stem cell research involves the use of embryonic stem cells to create organs and various body tissues. It continues to be a highly controversial issue generally involving religious beliefs and fears as to how far scientists might go in their attempt to create, for example, another human being. After all, a sheep named Dolly was already cloned and born in 1996.

The search for a cure for cancer, autoimmune diseases, and heart disease is often slowed by political, religious, and personal beliefs and conflicts. The moral issues surrounding embryonic stem cell research, for example, slowed the wheels of progress for many years.

NEWSPAPER CLIPPINGS: Obama Reversing Stem Cell Limits Imposed by Bush

"By removing politics from science," said Peter T. Wilderotter, the organization's president and chief executive [Christopher and Dana Reeve Foundation], "President Obama has freed researchers to explore these remarkable stem cells, learn from them and possibly develop effective therapies using them."

—*David Stout*, The New York Times, *March 6, 2009*

Some opponents of stem cell research argue that this practice is a slippery slope to reproductive cloning and fundamentally devalues the worth of a human being. Contrarily, some medical researchers in the field argue that it is necessary to pursue embryonic stem cell research because the resultant technologies could have significant medical potential and that excess embryos created for in vitro fertilization could be donated with consent and used for the research. This, in turn, conflicts with opponents in the pro-life movement, who advocate for the protection of human embryos. The ensuing debate has prompted authorities around the world to seek regulatory frameworks and highlighted the fact that embryonic stem cell research represents a social and ethical challenge that includes concern to the natural order of the ecosystem and, ultimately, the survival of the human race.

✛ Notes

1. *Union Pac. Ry. Co. v. Botsford*, 141 U.S. 250, 251 (1891).
2. 105 N.E. 92, 93 (N.Y. 1914).
3. *Id.*
4. 438 N.Y.S.2d 266, 272 (N.Y. 1981).
5. 410 U.S. 113 (1973).
6. Supra note 6.
7. 370 N.E.2d 417 (Mass. 1977).
8. *Id.* at 434.
9. 380 N.E.2d 134 (Mass. 1978).
10. 405 N.E.2d 115 (Mass. 1980).
11. 452 So.2d 925 (Fla. 1984).
12. 362 So.2d 160 (Fla. Dist. Ct. App. 1978).
13. Statement of Medical Opinion Re: "Brain Death," A.M.A. House of Delegates Res. (June 1974).
14. 534 N.E.2d 886 (N.Y. 1988).
15. *Id.* at 891.
16. *Cruzan v. Harman*, 760 S.W.2d 408 (Mo. 1988).
17. *Cruzan v. Director of the Mo. Dep't of Health*, 497 U.S. 261 (1990).
18. Pa. S.646, Amendment A3506, Printer's No. 689, Oct. 1, 1990.
19. 20 PA. Cons. Stat. Ann. § 5602(a)(9) (1988).
20. *Hobbins v. Attorney Gen. of Mich.*, No. 941473 (Mich. 1994); *Kevorkian v. Michigan*, No. 94-1490 (Mich. 1994).
21. Or. Rev. Stat. Sects. 127.800-897.
22. *Quill v. Vacco*, 117 S. Ct. 2293 (1997).
23. 117 S. Ct. 2258 (1997).
24. 611 A.2d 1148 (N.J. Super. Ct. 1992).
25. *Bush v. Schiavo*, No. SC04-925 (Fla. App. 2004).
26. Ascension Health. "Issues and Concepts," http://www.ascensionhealth.org/ethics/public/issues/substituted.asp (accessed October 14, 2010).
27. "AMA Changes Code of Ethics on Comas," *Newsday*, Mar. 17, 1986, p. 2.
28. 549 N.E.2d 292 (Ill. 1989).
29. 195 Cal. Rptr. 484 (Cal. Ct. App. 1983).
30. *John F. Kennedy Mem'l Hosp. v. Bludworth*, 452 So.2d 921, 925 (Fla. 1984) (citing *In re Welfare of Colyer*, 660 P.2d 738 (Wash. 1983), in which the court found prior court approval to be "unresponsive and cumbersome").
31. *In re Quinlan*, 70 N.J. 10, 355 A.2d 647 (1976).
32. 428 F. Supp. 360 (D.D.C. 1977).
33. Washington Legal Foundation, "Abigail Alliance for Better Access to Developmental Drugs v. Eschenbach," http://www.wlf.org/litigating/case_detail.asp?id=266 (accessed October 14, 2010).

16
AIDS

Figure 16–1 AIDS Awareness © Shamleen/ShutterStock, Inc.

Learning Objectives

The reader upon completion of this chapter will be able to:

- Describe what AIDS is and how it is spread.
- Discuss confidentiality concerns for AIDS patients.
- Describe how AIDS patients are discriminated against.
- Explain the importance of AIDS-related education.

 NEWSPAPER CLIPPINGS: Gilead's 4-in-1 Stribild HIV Pill Wins U.S. FDA Approval

Gilead Sciences Inc., (GILD) the world's biggest maker of AIDS drugs, won U.S. approval to sell a pill for new HIV patients that combines four of the company's drugs into one.

The therapy, called Stribild, was cleared as a medicine that will help simplify patients' treatment regimens . . . Stribild contains two new drugs and two previously approved compounds that make up Foster City, California-based Gilead's Truvada HIV medicine.

—*Anna Edney*, Bloomberg Businessweek, *August 28, 2012*

The *Acquired Immune Deficiency Syndrome* (AIDS), caused by the *Human Immunodeficiency Virus* (HIV), a highly contagious blood-borne virus, is the most severe form of the HIV infection. HIV destroys the body's immune system and thus its capacity to ward off infections and viruses that ordinarily would be fought off by a properly functioning immune system. AIDS, generally, is accepted as a syndrome—a collection of specific, life-threatening opportunistic infections and manifestations that are the result of an underlying immune deficiency.

The AIDS epidemic is considered to be the deadliest epidemic in human history with the first case appearing in the literature in 1981. Internationally, AIDS continues to pose serious social, ethical, economic, and health problems. Although there is no cure for AIDS, indications are that proper management of the disease can improve the quality of life and delay progression of the disease.

SPREAD OF AIDS

NEWSPAPER CLIPPINGS: Global HIV/AIDS Response—Epidemic Update and Health Sector Progress Towards Universal Access—Progress Report 2011*

HIV has proven to be a formidable challenge, but the tide is turning. The tools to achieve an AIDS-free generation are in our hands. Let us move forward together on the ambitious goals set for 2015 and bring us closer to realizing our collective vision of zero new HIV infections, zero discrimination and zero AIDS-related deaths.[1]

AIDS is spread by direct contact with infected blood or body fluids, such as vaginal secretions, semen, and breast milk. There is no evidence that the virus can be transmitted through food, water, or casual body contact. The HIV does not survive well outside the body. Although there is presently no cure for AIDS, early diagnosis and treatment with new medications can help HIV-infected persons remain relatively healthy. High-risk groups for AIDS include homosexuals, heterosexuals, intravenous drug users, and those who require blood transfusions.

Blood Transmission

Suits often arise as a result of a person with AIDS claiming that he or she contracted the disease as a result of a transfusion of contaminated blood or blood products. In blood transfusion cases, the most commonly identified issues concern donor screening for HIV. An injured party generally must prove that a standard of care existed, that the defendant's conduct fell below the standard, and that this conduct was the proximate cause of the plaintiff's injury.

The risk of HIV infection and AIDS through a blood transfusion has been reduced through health history screening and blood donation testing. All blood donated in the United States has been tested for HIV antibodies since May 1985.

Historically: Transfusion Before Testing

Dismissal of a case against a hospital and the American Red Cross was ordered in *Kozup v. Georgetown University*,[2] in which it was alleged that the death of a premature infant was due to causes related to AIDS contracted through a blood transfusion administered in January 1983, without the parent's informed consent. The case was dismissed on the basis that the possibility of contracting AIDS from a blood transfusion in 1983 was not a material risk. Dismissal also was justified on the basis that the transfusion was the only method of treating the child for a life-threatening condition.

Today: Negligence in Collecting Blood

In January 1983, a blood center knew that blood should not be drawn from homosexual or bisexual males. On April 22, 1983, Kraus, a cardiologist, discovered that Mr. B received seven units of blood. In May 1987, B had chest pain and trouble breathing. On June 5, 1987, B was hospitalized. Kraus consulted with two specialists in pulmonary medicine about the unusual pneumonia evident in X-rays of B's lungs. Because there was a possibility that the lung infection was secondary to AIDS, B was tested for HIV. Although B had not yet been formally diagnosed, physicians started him on therapy for AIDS.

B was formally diagnosed as HIV positive. His wife was then tested for HIV, and she learned that she was also HIV positive. On July 2, 1987, B expired. On April 21, 1989, the plaintiffs, Mrs. B and her son, filed suit against the blood center, alleging that her husband contracted HIV from the transfusion of a unit of blood donated at the blood center on April 19, 1983, by a donor identified at trial as Doe. The parties stipulated at trial that Doe was a sexually active homosexual male with multiple sex partners.

The plaintiffs contend that the blood center's negligence in testing and screening blood donors caused Mrs. B's contraction of HIV. At trial, the jury awarded the plaintiffs $800,000 in damages. The blood center filed an appeal arguing the evidence of causation was legally insufficient to support the jury verdict.

The Texas Court of Appeals held that evidence supported a finding that the blood center's negligence in the collection of blood was the proximate cause of B's HIV infection. The blood center, despite its knowledge about the dangers of HIV-contaminated blood, failed to reject gay men; the blood center's donor screening was inadequate; and these omissions were substantial factors in causing Mr. and Mrs. B's HIV infections. A technical director at the blood center admitted that there was "strong evidence" that the blood accepted from Doe was contaminated with HIV. Another recipient of components of Doe's blood was diagnosed as HIV positive less than 6 months within Mr. B having been diagnosed as HIV positive.[3]

Sexual Transmission

Heterosexual relations are becoming a main conduit for the spread of AIDS. Heterosexual transmission is one of the predominant modes of infection and is increasing. "It is a myth that AIDS is a gay disease. The fact is 32% of Americans who were diagnosed with HIV/AIDS in 2007 were heterosexual."[4]

Partner's Right to Know

A person has a right to know when his or her partner has tested positive for HIV. Physicians are expected to counsel an HIV-positive patient to notify his or her sexual or needle-sharing partners or to seek help in doing so from public health officials. If a patient refuses to do so, a physician may, without the patient's consent, notify public health officials of a patient's sexual partner known to be at risk of HIV infection. Some states have developed informational brochures and consent, release, and partner notification forms.

Healthcare Workers Transmission

Guidelines drafted by the Centers for Disease Control and Prevention (CDC) call on healthcare workers who perform "exposure-prone" procedures to undergo tests voluntarily to determine whether they are infected. The guidelines also recommend that patients be informed. Both healthcare workers and patients claim that mandatory HIV testing violates their Fourth Amendment right to privacy. The dilemma is how to balance these rights against the rights of the public in general to be protected from a deadly disease.

Although transmission of HIV from an infected physician to his or her patient during invasive surgery may be unlikely, it is possible and therefore foreseeable. Because of the potentially deadly consequence of such transmission, infected physicians should not engage in activity that creates a risk of transmission.

The ever-increasing likelihood that healthcare workers will come into contact with persons carrying the AIDS virus demands that healthcare workers comply with approved safety procedures. This is especially important for those who come into contact with blood and body fluids of HIV-infected persons.

An AIDS-infected surgeon in New Jersey was unable to recover on a discrimination claim when the hospital restricted his surgical privileges. In *Estate of Behringer v. Medical Center at Princeton*,[5] the New Jersey Superior Court held that the hospital acted properly in initially suspending a surgeon's surgical privileges, thereafter imposing a requirement of informed consent and ultimately barring the surgeon from performing surgery. The court held that in the context of informed consent, the risk of a surgical accident involving an AIDS-positive surgeon and implications thereof would be a legitimate concern to a surgical patient that would warrant disclosure of the risk.[6] The risk of transmission of HIV from the surgeon to the patient can be exacerbated during surgery if the surgeon, for example, cuts himself with a scalpel and his blood contaminates the patient as a result of that cut, which may subject the patient to postsurgery HIV testing.[7]

CONFIDENTIALITY

The unauthorized disclosure of confidential HIV-related information can subject an individual to civil and/or criminal penalties. Information regarding a patient's diagnosis as being HIV positive must be kept confidential and should be shared with other healthcare professionals only on a need-to-know basis. Each person has a right to privacy as to his or her personal affairs.

The plaintiff–surgeon, in the *Estate of Behringer v. Medical Center at Princeton*,[8] was entitled to recover damages from the hospital and its laboratory director for the unauthorized disclosure of his condition during his stay at the hospital. The hospital and the director breached their duty to maintain confidentiality of the surgeon's medical records by allowing placement of the patient's test results in his medical chart without limiting access to the chart, which they knew was available to the entire hospital community. "The medical center breached its duty of confidentiality to the plaintiff, as a patient, when it failed to take reasonable precautions regarding the plaintiff's medical records to prevent the patient's AIDS diagnosis from becoming a matter of public knowledge."[9]

The hospital in *Tarrant County Hospital District v. Hughes*[10] was found to have properly disclosed the names and addresses of blood donors in a wrongful death action alleging that a patient contracted AIDS from a blood transfusion administered in the hospital. The physician–patient privilege expressed in the Texas Rules of Evidence did not apply to preclude such disclosure because the record did not reflect that any such relationship had been established. The disclosure was not an impermissible violation of the donors' right of privacy. The societal interest in maintaining an effective blood donor program did not override the plaintiff's right to receive such information. The order prohibited disclosure of the donors' names to third parties.

Duty and the Right to Confidentiality

Healthcare professionals and others working with AIDS patients have a right to know when they are caring for patients with highly contagious diseases. There are times when the duty to disclose outweighs the rights of confidentiality. The U.S. Court of Appeals for the Tenth Circuit in *Dunn v. White*[11] declared there is no Fourth Amendment impediment to a state prison's policy of testing the blood of all inmates for HIV. Under the U.S. Supreme Court's drug-testing decisions, the proper analysis is to balance the prisoner's interest in being free from bodily intrusion inherent in a blood test against the prison's institutional rights in combating the disease. The U.S. Court of Appeals held that in or out of prison, a person has a limited privacy interest in not having his or her blood tested. The court cited *Schmerber v. California*,[12] which rejected a Fourth Amendment challenge to the blood testing of a suspected drunken driver. Against the prisoner's minimal interest, prison authorities have a strong interest in controlling the spread of HIV.

Mandatory Testing

The U.S. District Court found that routine testing of firefighters and paramedics for the AIDS virus does not violate an individual's Fourth Amendment or constitutional privacy rights.[13] Because the tested employees are a high-risk group for contracting and transmitting HIV to the public, the city has a compelling interest and legal duty to protect the public from contracting the virus. Firefighters and paramedics are in a higher-risk category than hospital personnel because they work in a noncontrolled setting. *Skinner v. Railway Executives Association* confirmed "society's judgment that blood tests do not constitute an unduly extensive imposition on an individual's privacy and bodily integrity."[14] However, "mandatory testing by a governmental agency for the sole purpose of obtaining a baseline to determine whether an employee contracted AIDS on the job, and thereby to determine the validity of any future worker's compensation claim, is not valid. Mandatory AIDS testing of employees can be valid only if the group of employees involved is at risk of contracting or transmitting AIDS to the public."[15]

Delicate Balance

Guidelines drafted by the CDC call for healthcare workers who perform exposure-prone procedures to undergo tests voluntarily to determine whether they are infected. The guidelines also recommend that patients be informed. Both healthcare workers and patients claim mandatory HIV testing violates their Fourth Amendment right to privacy. The dilemma is how to balance these rights against the rights of the public in general to be protected from a deadly disease.

▌ DISCRIMINATION

Discrimination against persons who have contracted AIDS is found to be in violation of their constitutional rights. The sufferings and hardships of those who have contracted the disease extend to family as well as friends. The infringements of those infected with HIV include discrimination in access to health care, education, employment, housing, insurance benefits, and military service. Those who believe that they have been discriminated against can contact their state's human rights commission.

Access to Health Care

The need for health care for AIDS patients continues to grow, particularly for those who are homeless or have no family support system. In response to the need for nursing home care, some health departments are encouraging the development of specialized HIV/AIDS nursing homes that will combine medical services and drug treatment for AIDS patients who have become infected through drug abuse.

With millions of people around the world infected with AIDS, the greatest challenge involves the nearly 90% of AIDS patients who live in resource-poor countries. As a result of poor access to health care, former President Bill Clinton made the battle against HIV/AIDS a focal point of his foundation's activities in global health security to reach the underserved populations.[16]

Right to Treatment

Some healthcare organizations are expressing in their ethics statements that HIV-infected patients have a right not to be discriminated against in the provision of treatment. The ethics committee of the American Academy of Dermatology, for example states, "it is unethical for a physician to discriminate against a class or category of patients and to refuse the management of a patient because of medical risk, real or imagined."[17] Patients with HIV infection, therefore, should receive the same compassionate and competent care given to other patients.

Education

A school's refusal to admit students with HIV generally is considered an unnecessary restriction on an individual's liberty. However, there are circumstances where it would be unreasonable to infer that Congress intended to force institutions to accept or readmit persons who pose a significant risk of harm to themselves or others. For example, in *Doe v. Washington University*,[18] the university disenrolled a dental student based on his positive HIV status: "the circumstance surrounding plaintiff's HIV status presented little alternative to those charged with evaluating plaintiff's ability to qualify as a dental student."[19]

Employment

AIDS-related employment issues are a two-sided coin: employment discrimination on one side and the refusal of employees to care for AIDS patients on the other. The growing consensus of case law indicates employment-related discrimination is unlawful. The California Court of Appeals, Second District, in *Raytheon v. Fair Employment & Housing Commission*,[20] determined an employee with AIDS who was admitted to and treated in a hospital was unlawfully denied his right to return to work after treatment. The court held that AIDS is a protected physical handicap under California's Fair Employment and Housing Act and that the employer failed to prove its defense of protecting the health and safety of its other workers. The employer ignored the advice of county health officials and communicable disease authorities that there was no risk to other employees at the plant.

Employees who have contracted the AIDS virus and whose symptoms warrant should not be placed in positions that threaten the health and safety of patients and employees. The court in *School Board of Nassau County v. Airline* noted "a person who poses a significant risk of communicating an infectious disease will not be otherwise qualified for his or her job if reasonable accommodations will not eliminate the risk."[21]

In the final analysis, many competing issues (e.g., humanitarian, legal, moral, ethical, and religious) pertain to the rights of patients and caregivers who have contracted the AIDS virus, as well as those who have not, and employers.

Insurance Benefits

In *Weaver v. Reagan*,[22] Medicaid recipients who were denied benefits for AZT (zidovudine, trade name Retrovir) treatments were found entitled to summary judgment in their class action suit to require Missouri's authorities to provide Medicaid coverage for the cost of AZT treatments. In this case, the U.S. Court of Appeals for the Eighth Circuit decided that states must provide Medicaid coverage for the drug AZT to HIV-infected individuals who are eligible for Medicaid and whose physicians had certified that AZT was a medically necessary treatment.

NEGLIGENCE

NEWSPAPER CLIPPINGS: VA Hospital May Have Infected 1,800 Veterans with HIV

A Missouri VA hospital is under fire because it may have exposed more than 1,800 veterans to life-threatening diseases such as hepatitis and HIV. . . .

The issue stems from a failure to clean dental instruments properly, the hospital told CNN affiliate KSDK.

—*CNN Wire Staff*, CNN U.S., *June 30, 2010*

As noted in this section, there have been a variety of HIV- and AIDS-related lawsuits. Such suits, as described here, have involved the administration of blood and untimely diagnosis of AIDS.

Administration of Wrong Blood

The plaintiff, Mrs. Bordelon, in *Bordelon v. St. Francis Cabrini Hospital*,[23] was admitted to the hospital to undergo a hysterectomy. Prior to surgery, she provided the hospital with her own blood in case it was needed during surgery. During surgery, Bordelon did indeed need blood but was administered donor blood other than her own. Bordelon filed a lawsuit claiming that the hospital's failure to provide her with her own blood resulted in her suffering mental distress. The hospital filed a peremptory exception claiming that there was no cause of action. The Ninth Judicial District Court dismissed the suit because the plaintiff did not allege that she suffered any physical injury.

On appeal by the plaintiff, the court of appeal held that the plaintiff did in fact state a cause of action for mental distress. It is well established in law that a claim for negligent infliction of emotional distress unaccompanied by physical injury is a viable claim of action. Bordelon's fear was easily associated with receiving someone else's blood and, therefore, a conceivable consequence of the defendant's negligent act.[24] It is undisputed that the hospital had a duty to administer the plaintiff's own blood. The hospital breached that duty by administering the wrong blood.

Failure to Make a Timely Diagnosis

The plaintiff, Jane Doe, had been exposed to HIV as the result of sexual contact. The plaintiff consulted her defendant–physicians, but they failed to diagnose her condition as being positive for either HIV or AIDS. The disease weakened her immune system, and she developed pneumonia and was admitted to a hospital. The patient was eventually diagnosed with AIDS. The patient's infectious disease expert, Dr. Hill, claimed that proper diagnosis prior to her acute episode would have provided greater opportunity for improved long-term treatment. The defendants admitted that they negligently failed to timely diagnose the patient's condition.

The Louisiana Court of Appeal held that the evidence supported the jury's finding that the defendant failed to timely diagnose the plaintiff's condition. The medical defendants agreed that they negligently failed to timely diagnose the patient's condition. The plaintiff's expert witness testified that within the "reasonable medical probability" standard and the "more-likely-than-not" standard, if the plaintiff had been properly diagnosed she would have worked, as well as lived, for another year.[25]

Patient Wrongly Notified She Had AIDS

A service member brought an action under the Federal Tort Claims Act in *Johnson v. United States*,[26] alleging that on or about October 8, 1986, Army physicians and medical personnel negligently and wrongly advised her that she had AIDS after she had donated blood to a public blood drive sponsored by the Walter Reed Hospital, which resulted in her having an unnecessary and unwanted abortion. In November 1986, prior to being notified of this error, the plaintiff discovered that she was pregnant. On November 21, 1986, physicians at Walter Reed Hospital advised the plaintiff that her child would most certainly be born with AIDS and would not live beyond 5 years. The physicians indicated that under these circumstances it would be better for the plaintiff to have an abortion than to carry the child to term. As a result of this counseling, and for no other reason, the plaintiff had an abortion on December 4, 1986. It was not until February 3, 1987, nearly 4 months later, that a physician at Walter Reed Hospital told the plaintiff that there had been an error in the paperwork, and she did not have AIDS.

The United States moved to have the case dismissed on the grounds that the action was barred by the *Feres doctrine*. Under this doctrine, the United States is not liable under the Federal Tort Claims Act for injuries that arise out of or are in the course of activity incident to service. The district court held that the donation of blood was not incident to service, and, therefore, the doctrine did not bar the action.

In another case, the *Feres doctrine* did not bar a serviceman's claim in *C.R.S. v. United States*.[27] The serviceman had been infected with the AIDS virus during surgery performed on him while he was on active duty. He allegedly spread the virus to both his wife and daughter. The policy rationale for the doctrine was not appropriate for barring the claims made in this case.

Insurance Company Fails to Disclose HIV Status

Unbeknown to a husband and wife, Mr. and Mrs. P, they were infected with HIV at the time they applied for life insurance from the Farm Bureau Life Insurance Company in 1999. At the time of the application, Farm Bureau collected the initial premium and arranged for blood tests from the husband and wife in furtherance of the application. Blood samples were forwarded for analysis to an independent laboratory, LabOne, which in turn reported the HIV status to the insurance company. On receipt of the information, Farm Bureau sent a notice of rejection to Mr. and Mrs. P and advised them that it would disclose the reason for their rejection to their physician if they so wished. Mr. and Mrs. P took no action. Two years later, R. P. was diagnosed with AIDS, and on inquiry she and her husband learned that Farm Bureau records showed the HIV infection at the time of the life insurance rejection. Mr. and Mrs. P sued, alleging that the defendants were negligent in failing to tell them they were HIV positive. A federal court, balancing all the interests involved as Wyoming law requires, concluded that if an insurance company, through independent investigation by it or a third party for purposes of determining policy eligibility, discovers that an applicant is infected with HIV, the company has a duty to disclose to the applicant information sufficient to cause a reasonable applicant to inquire further.[28]

REPORTING REQUIREMENTS

AIDS is a reportable communicable disease in every state. Physicians and hospitals must report every case of AIDS—with the patient's name—to government public health authorities. Cases reported to local health authorities are also reported to the CDC, with the patients' names encoded by a system known as Soundex. CDC records

come under the general confidentiality protections of the Federal Privacy Act of 1974. However, the statute permits disclosures to other federal agencies under certain circumstances.

AIDS EMERGENCY ACT

AIDS has been reported in all 50 states. Because the incidence of HIV affects different localities of the United States disproportionately, the Senate and House of Representatives enacted the Ryan White Comprehensive AIDS Resources Emergency Act of 1990.[29] The purpose of the act is to:

> provide emergency assistance to localities that are disproportionately affected by the human immunodeficiency virus epidemic and to make financial assistance available to States and other public or private nonprofit entities to provide for the development, organization, coordination and operation of more effective and cost efficient systems for the delivery of essential services to individuals and families with the HIV disease.[30]

Under the HIV Care Grants section of the act, a state may use grant funds to: (1) establish and operate HIV-care consortia within areas most affected by HIV disease; (2) provide a comprehensive continuum of care to individuals and families with HIV disease; (3) provide home- and community-based care services for individuals with HIV disease; (4) provide assistance to ensure the continuity of health insurance coverage for individuals with HIV disease; and, (5) provide treatments that have been determined to prolong life or prevent serious deterioration of health to individuals with HIV disease.[31]

Congress extended the Ryan White HIV/AIDS Treatment Extension Act for an additional 4 years, signed by President Obama on October 30, 2009.

OCCUPATIONAL SAFETY AND HEALTH ACT

The Occupational Safety and Health Act (OSHA) requires that healthcare organizations implement strict procedures to protect employees against HIV that causes AIDS. OSHA requires strict adherence to guidelines developed by the CDC. Complaints investigated by OSHA can result in the issuance of fines for failure to comply with regulatory requirements.

AIDS EDUCATION

NEWSPAPER CLIPPINGS: FDA Approves First Drug for HIV Prevention

Truvada Approved for HIV-Negative People at High Risk of Infection

The FDA has approved use of the HIV drug Truvada to help people at high risk avoid infection with the AIDS virus.

Truvada is already approved as part of treatment regimens for people with HIV infection. But this is the first time the FDA has approved any drug for "pre-exposure prophylaxis" or PrEP—that is, for protecting uninfected people against HIV.

—*Daniel J. DeNoon*, WebMD Health News,
July 16, 2012

The ever-increasing likelihood that healthcare workers will come into contact with persons carrying HIV demands continuing development of and compliance with approved safety precautions. This is especially important for those who come into contact with blood and body fluids of HIV-infected persons. The CDC expanded its infection control guidelines and has urged hospitals to adopt universal precautions to protect their workers from exposure to patients' blood and other body fluids. Hospitals are following universal precautions in the handling of body fluids, which is the accepted standard for employee protection.

A wide variety of HIV–AIDS-related educational materials are available on the market. One of the most important sources of AIDS information is the CDC. The process of staff education in preparing to care for patients with AIDS is extremely important and must include a training program on prevention and transmission in the work setting. Educational requirements specified by OSHA for healthcare employees include epidemiology, modes of transmission, preventive practices, and universal precautions. See the Center for AIDS Prevention Studies website for some helpful information: http://caps.ucsf.edu.

Notes

1. http://www.who.int/hiv/pub/progress_report2011/summary_en.pdf.
2. 663 F. Supp. 1048 (D.D.C. 1987).
3. *J. K. & Susie L. Wadley Research Inst. v. Beeson*, 835 S.W.2d 689 (Tex. Ct. App. 1992).
4. HIV Vaccine Trials Network, "How HIV Is Increasing Among Heterosexuals," http://www.hvtn.org/community/straight.html (accessed October 13, 2010).
5. 592 A.2d 1251 (N.J. Super. Ct. Law Div. 1991).
6. *Id.* at 1255.
7. *Id.* at 1255.
8. 592 A.2d 1251 (N.J. Super. Ct. Law Div. 1991).
9. *Id.* at 1255.
10. 734 S.W.2d 675 (Tex. Ct. App. 1987).
11. No. 88-2194 (10th Cir. Aug. 1, 1989) (unpublished).
12. 384 U.S. 757 (1966).
13. *Anonymous Fireman v. Willoughby*, No. C881182 (D.C. N. Ohio Dec. 31, 1991) (unpublished).
14. 489 U.S. 602, 625 (1989).
15. *Anonymous Fireman*, No. C88-1182.
16. HIV/AIDS Initiatives, Clinton Foundation. www.clintonfoundation.org/aids-initiative2.htm.
17. Ethics Committee of the American Academy of Dermatology, *Ethics in Medical Practice* (Washington, DC: American Academy of Dermatology, 1992), 6.
18. 780 F. Supp. 628 (E.D. Mo. 1991).
19. *Id.* at 628.
20. No. B035809 (Cal. Ct. App. Aug. 7, 1989) (unpublished).
21. 107 S. Ct. 1131 (1987).
22. 886 F.2d 194 (8th Cir. 1989).
23. 640 So. 2d 476 (La. App. 3d Cir. 1994).
24. *Id.* at 479.
25. *Doe v. McNulty*, 630 So. 2d 825 (La. Ct. App. 1993).
26. 735 F. Supp. 1 (D.D.C. 1990).
27. 761 F. Supp. 665 (D.C. Minn. 1991).
28. The plaintiffs in *Pehle v. Farm Bureau Life Insurance Company, Inc.*
29. HIV/AIDS, Rep. Henry Waxman. http://www.waxman.house.gov/issues/health/issues_health_HIV_legislation_sum_82_91.htm.
30. PUB. L. NO. 101-381, 1990 U.S. CODE CONG. & AD. NEWS (104 Stat.) 576.
31. *Id.* at 586.

17

Legal Reporting Requirements

�+ Learning Objectives

The reader upon completion of this chapter will be able to:

- Describe various forms of child abuse, how to recognize it, and reporting requirements.
- Describe various forms of elder abuse, how to recognize it, and reporting requirements.
- Discuss the importance of reporting births and deaths.
- Explain why it is important to report communicable diseases, adverse drug reactions, and infectious diseases.
- Explain how and why physician incompetency is reported.
- Understand the importance of incident reporting, sentinel events and the purpose of "root cause analyses."
- Describe the variety of patient events that are reportable under state law.

This chapter provides an overview of a variety of healthcare reporting requirements mandated by both federal and state regulatory agencies. Most states have legislated a variety of mandatory reporting requirements including child abuse, elder abuse, adverse drug reactions, hospital-acquired infections, financial fraud, communicable diseases, births and deaths, physician incompetency, and incident reporting.

▌CHILD ABUSE

Child abuse is intentional serious mental, emotional, sexual, and/or physical injury inflicted by a family member or other person who is responsible for the child's care. Some states extend the definition to include a child who suffers from starvation. Other states include moral neglect in the definition of abuse. Others mention immoral associations; endangering a child's morals; and the location of a child in a disreputable place or in association with vagrant, vicious, or immoral persons. Sexual abuse also is enumerated as an element of neglect in the statutes of some states.

The *Child Abuse Prevention and Treatment Act* defines the term "child abuse and neglect" as, "Any recent act or failure to act on the part of a parent or caretaker, which results in death, serious physical or emotional harm, sexual abuse or exploitation, or an act or failure to act that presents an imminent risk of serious harm."[1]

Reporting Child Abuse

Presently, all states have enacted laws to protect abused children. Most states protect the persons required to report cases of child abuse. In some states, certain identified individuals who are not required to report instances of child abuse, but who do so, are protected. Persons in the healthcare setting who are required to report, or cause a report to be made, when they have reasonable cause to suspect that a child has been abused include administrators, physicians, interns, registered nurses, chiropractors, social service workers, psychologists, dentists, osteopaths, optometrists, podiatrists, mental health professionals, and volunteers in residential facilities.

Detecting Abuse

The physically abused or neglected child presents a medical, social, and legal problem. What constitutes an abused child is difficult to determine because it is often impossible to ascertain whether a child was injured intentionally or accidentally.

An individual who reports child abuse should be aware of the physical and behavioral indicators of abuse and maltreatment that appear to be part of a pattern (e.g., bruises, burns, and broken bones). In reviewing the indicators of abuse and maltreatment, the reporter does not have to be absolutely certain that abuse or maltreatment exists before reporting. Rather, abuse and maltreatment should be reported whenever they are suspected, based on the existence of the signs of abuse and maltreatment and in light of the reporter's training and experience. Behavioral indicators include, but are not limited to, substantially diminished psychological or intellectual functioning, failure to thrive, no control of aggression, self-destructive impulses, decreased ability to think and reason, acting out and misbehavior, or habitual truancy. Such impairment must be clearly attributable to the unwillingness or inability of the person responsible for the child's care to exercise a minimum degree of care toward the child.

Good-Faith Reporting

Any report of suspected child abuse must be made with a good-faith belief that the facts reported are true. The definition of good faith as used in a child abuse statute may vary from state to state. However, when a healthcare practitioner's medical evaluation indicates reasonable cause to believe a child's injuries were not accidental and when the healthcare practitioner is not acting from his or her desire to harass, injure, or embarrass the child's parents, making the report will not result in liability. Statutes generally require that when a person covered by a statute is attending a child and suspects abuse, the staff member must report such concerns. Typical statutes provide that an oral report be made immediately, followed by a written report. Most states require the report to contain the following information: the child's name and address; the person(s) responsible for the child's care; the child's age; the nature and extent of the child's injuries (including any evidence of previous injuries); and any other information that might be helpful in establishing the cause of the injuries, such as photographs of the injured child and the identity of the alleged abuser.

Psychologist Immune from Liability

The psychologist in *E.S. by D.S. v. Seitz*[2] was immune from liability in a suit charging her with negligence in formulating and reporting her professional opinion to a social worker that a father sexually abused his 3-year-old daughter. The psychologist made the report in compliance with the Wisconsin statute after having examined the child in the course of her professional duties as a mental health professional.

The patient in *Marks v. Tenbrunsel*[3] had been assured that anything he disclosed during his treatment sessions would remain confidential. During the treatment sessions, the patient disclosed that he had fondled two children under the age of 12. As a result of that disclosure, two psychologists made a good-faith report to Child Protective Services. The report caused the patient to be prosecuted for his admitted sexual misconduct. Because the patient admitted to the abuse of two children, the psychologists had reasonable cause to believe that the children currently were being abused. The psychologists were found immune from both civil and criminal liability as a result of their good-faith report.

Failure to Report Child Abuse

The criminal and civil risks for healthcare professionals do not lie in good faith reporting of suspected incidents of child abuse, but in failing to report such incidents. Most states have legislated a variety of civil and criminal penalties for failure to report suspected child abuse incidents.

Psychologist: Failure to Report Past Abuse

The Minnesota Board of Psychology was found to have acted properly when it placed the license of a psychologist on conditional status.[4] The psychologist argued that he was not required to report past abuse that was not ongoing, that a report made 5 weeks after the incident was not untimely, and that the reporting laws were unconstitutional because they violated the privacy rights of clients and the privilege against self-incrimination. The psychologist had failed to report incidents of sexual child abuse. The court held that there was no merit to the psychologist's contentions that the child abuse reporting laws were unclear and that they did not apply to one patient who was a grandfather responsible for the child's care at the time of the incident in question.

Nurse: Failure to Document and Report

In *State v. Brown*,[5] rescue personnel who were summoned to the scene of an emergency found a 2-year-old foster child unconscious, not breathing, and "posturing," which is an abnormal rigidity of the body and a sign of brain damage. While performing emergency medical treatment, rescue personnel discovered a series of small, round, dime- to quarter-sized bruises running parallel along the child's spine. They also noticed a red bruise under his eye. This information was relayed to the flight crew, who airlifted the child to the hospital. The flight crew then reported the information to a nurse employed at the hospital. The child recovered after treatment and was released from the hospital on August 14, 2002. Four days later, on August 18, the child was returned to the hospital where he died of abusive head trauma.

The nurse did not document the bruises or call the state's child abuse hotline because the boy's foster mother said the bruises were the result of the boy leaning back in a booster seat. In February 2003, the prosecutor alleged that the nurse had reasonable cause to suspect that the child had been abused or neglected. She was charged with failure to report child abuse to the division of family services and to a physician. The nurse sought to dismiss the charges, alleging that Missouri statutes were unconstitutionally vague. The appellate court determined that the statutes were not vague. The test for determining whether a law is void for vagueness is whether its language conveys to a person of ordinary intelligence a sufficiently definite warning as to the proscribed conduct when measured by common understanding and practices. The statute criminalizing a health professional's failure to report child abuse upon "reasonable cause to suspect" abuse was not unconstitutionally vague.

Physician Entitled to Immunity

A physician who was not the initial reporter of suspected child abuse, but who performed a medical examination of a child at the request of the department of children and families to determine whether reasonable cause existed to suspect child abuse, was entitled to the immunity from liability provided by statutory law. It was clear that the physician, a mandated reporter under the law, examined the child in the ordinary course of his employment in the emergency department. He complied with applicable statutes when he relayed his findings that there was a reasonable suspicion of child abuse to the department. Inasmuch as the plaintiffs did not allege that the physician acted in bad faith during the examination and reporting process, his actions constituted a report of suspected child abuse protected by statutory law.[6]

ELDER ABUSE AND NEGLECT

Elder abuse is any form of mistreatment that results in harm or loss to an older person. It can involve physical abuse (that results in bodily injury, pain, or impairment and includes assault, battery, and inappropriate restraint); sexual abuse (nonconsensual sexual contact of any kind with an older person); domestic violence (an escalating pattern of violence by an intimate partner where the violence is used to exercise power and control); psychological abuse (the willful infliction of mental or emotional anguish by threat, humiliation, or other verbal or nonverbal conduct); or financial abuse (the illegal or improper use of an older person's funds, property, or resources).[7] Elder abuse can involve neglect of caregivers for failing to provide the care necessary to avoid physical harm (e.g., the failure of staff to turn a patient periodically to prevent pressure sores) or mental anguish.

Most states have enacted statutes mandating the reporting of elder abuse. In general, elder abuse is less likely to be reported than child abuse. Physical and emotional neglect, as well as verbal and financial abuse, is perceived as the most prevalent form of elder abuse. Seniors often fail to report incidents of abuse because they fear retaliation and not being believed or threats of placement in a nursing home. In addition, proving such charges is often difficult. Signs of abuse or neglect include: unexplained or unexpected death; development of pressure sores; heavy medication and sedation used in place of adequate nursing staff; occurrence of broken bones; sudden and unexpected emotional outbursts, agitation, or withdrawal; bruises, welts, discoloration, burns; absence of hair and/or hemorrhaging below the scalp; dehydration and/or malnourishment without illness-related cause; hesitation to talk openly; implausible stories; unusual or inappropriate activity in bank accounts; signatures on checks and other written materials that do not resemble the patient's signature; power of attorney given or recent changes or creation of a will when the person is incapable of making such decisions; missing personal belongings such as silverware or jewelry; an untreated medical condition; and the patient is unable to speak for himself or herself, or see others, without the presence of the caregiver who could be suspected as an abuser.

Documentation

Caregivers who suspect abuse are expected to report their findings. Symptoms and conditions of suspected abuse should be defined clearly and objectively.

- Witnesses: Reporters of abuse must describe statements made by others as accurately as possible. Information should include information as to how witnesses can be contacted.
- Photographs: It may be necessary to photograph wounds or injuries. A hospital emergency room or the police department can be asked to photograph in emergency situations.

BIRTHS AND DEATHS

All births and deaths are reportable by statute. Births occurring outside of a healthcare facility should be reported by the legally qualified physician in attendance at a delivery or, in the event of the absence of a physician, by the registered nurse or other attendant. The physician who pronounces death must sign the death certificate. Statutes requiring the reporting of births and deaths are necessary to maintain accurate census records.

Suspicious Deaths

Greater than a state's interest in the recording of all births and deaths is the state's desire to review suspicious deaths that may be the result of some form of criminal activity. Unnatural deaths must be referred to the medical examiner for review. Such cases include violent deaths, deaths caused by unlawful acts or criminal neglect, and deaths that may be considered suspicious or unusual. The medical examiner may conduct an investigation as to the cause of death through an autopsy and report his findings to the police department or prosecutor who may have been assigned to the case. The purpose of a medical examiner's investigation is to determine the actual cause of death and thereby provide assistance for any further criminal investigation that may be considered necessary. If the medical examiner determines the death was due to an intentional act, he would be subject to be called as a witness to testify as to his findings if a trial ensues.

COMMUNICABLE DISEASES

Most states have enacted laws that require the reporting of actual or suspected cases of communicable diseases. The need for statutes requiring the reporting of communicable diseases is clear. If a state is to protect its citizens' health through its power to quarantine, it must ensure the prompt reporting of infection or disease.

ADVERSE DRUG REACTIONS

Adverse drug reactions (ADR) are unwanted or harmful reactions that occur as a result of administration of a drug or combination of drugs that is thought to be related to use of the drug. Pharmacies must maintain and report adverse drug reactions to the Food and Drug Administration (FDA). MedWatch is the FDA's "program for reporting serious reactions, product quality problems, therapeutic inequivalence/failure, and product use errors with human medical products, including drugs, biologic products, medical devices, dietary supplements, infant formula, and cosmetics."[8]

ADRs can also be reported through online reporting by consumers, printing a form located on the FDA website (https://www.accessdata.fda.gov) and faxing or mailing it to the U.S. Food and Drug Administration, 10903 New Hampshire Avenue, Silver Spring, MD 20993, or by calling the FDA (800-332-1088 or 888-463-6332).

HOSPITAL-ACQUIRED INFECTIONS

In 2006, the Archives of Internal Medicine reported that up to 98,000 deaths and hundreds of thousands of injuries occur annually in the United States because of medical errors and infections. Just two conditions caused by hospital acquired infections (sepsis and pneumonia) were responsible for nearly 50,000 deaths and cost more than $8 billion to treat, according to the February report.[9]

Approximately 30 states have requirements to report hospital-acquired infections. In spite of that, there have been federal regulations put into place to deal with this increasing problem. In 2006, the Deficit Reduction Act signed by President George W. Bush, as amended in 2008, cited four hospital-acquired infections that Medicaid and Medicare will not reimburse hospitals for if the patient was not admitted with the infection. Those are: catheter associated urinary tract infections, surgical site infections following bariatric surgery, surgical site infections following certain elective surgery, and surgical site infections.

Further, the 2010 Patient Prevention and Affordable Health Care Act requires acute care hospitals paid by Medicare to report hospital-acquired infections or be subjected to a reduction in Medicare reimbursement. On the other hand, hospitals that show improvement, will receive more money. Tying monetary incentives to this reporting is a move in the right direction for patients. In a move toward transparency, the Consumers' Union, which publishes *Consumer Reports* magazine, found that beginning in 2014, the U.S. Health and Human Services Department will report on its hospital website each hospital's record for medical errors and infections involving Medicare patients.

PHYSICIAN COMPETENCY

 NEWSPAPER CLIPPINGS: After He Fell Off a Ladder, One Medical Error Led to Another

. . . I left the medical system damaged and broke.

I believe that if I had access to some solid, physician-specific outcome data and better information on the risks and benefits of the medical devices my doctors were proposing, even I could have made healthcare decisions that wouldn't have resulted in my having to type this essay with one hand.

—*Kerry O'Connell*, The Washington Post, *August 25, 2012*

Congress enacted the *Health Care Quality Improvement Act* (HCQIA)[10] of 1986 to improve the quality of medical care by encouraging physicians to participate in peer review and by restricting incompetent physicians' ability to move from state to state without disclosure or discovery of their previous substandard performance or unprofessional conduct. The HCQIA was enacted in part to provide those persons giving information to professional review bodies and those assisting in review activities limited immunity from damages that may arise as a result of adverse decisions that affect a physician's medical staff privileges. Prior to enacting the HCQIA, Congress found that "[t]he increasing occurrence of medical malpractice and the need to improve the quality of medical care . . . [had] become nationwide problems," especially in light of "the ability of incompetent physicians to move from State to State without disclosure or discovery of the physician's previous damaging or incompetent performance."[11] HCQIA was enacted to facilitate the frank exchange of information among professionals who conduct peer review inquiries without the fear of reprisals in civil lawsuits. The statute attempts to balance the chilling effect of litigation on peer review with concerns for protecting physicians who are improperly subjected to disciplinary action.

National Practitioner Data Bank

The *National Practitioner Data Bank* (NPDB)[12] was created by Congress as a national repository of information with the primary purpose of facilitating a comprehensive review of physicians' and other healthcare practitioners' professional credentials. Hospitals are required to report to the NPDB professional review actions that are related to a physician's competence or conduct and that adversely affect clinical privileges for more than 30 days, and a physician's voluntary surrender or restriction of clinical privileges.

Responsibility for data bank implementation resides in the Bureau of Health Professions, Health Resources and Services Administration of the DHHS. The act authorizes the data bank to be used to collect and release information on the professional competence and conduct of physicians, dentists, and other healthcare practitioners. The regulations are intended to encourage good-faith professional review activities.

The NPDB presents a number of challenges to healthcare institutions. A major one is to educate the medical staff so that the data bank will not erode medical staff participation in risk management. The purpose of the data bank is not punishment; rather, it is prevention and deterrence.

Reporting Requirements

The regulations establish reporting requirements applicable to hospitals; healthcare entities; boards of medical examiners; professional societies of physicians, dentists, or other healthcare practitioners that take adverse licensure or professional review actions (e.g., reduction, restriction, suspension, revocation, or denial of clinical privileges or membership in a healthcare entity of 30 days or longer); and individuals and entities (including insurance companies) who make payments as a result of medical malpractice actions or claims. A medical malpractice action (or claim) has been defined as a written complaint or claim demanding payment based on a healthcare practitioner's provision of or failure to provide healthcare services, including the filing of a cause of action based on tort law, brought in any state or federal court or other adjudicative body.

Required Queries and Medical Staff Privileges

Healthcare organizations must query the data bank every 2 years on the renewal of staff privileges of physicians and dentists. The data bank serves as a flagging system whose principal purpose is to facilitate a more comprehensive review of professional credentials. As a nationwide flagging system, it provides another resource to assist state licensing boards, hospitals, and other healthcare entities in conducting extensive independent reviews of the qualifications of healthcare practitioners they seek to license or hire or to whom they wish to grant clinical privileges.

Who Should Report?

For those healthcare providers who question whether they are covered under this law, DHHS defines the term "entity" broadly, rather than attempting to focus on the myriad healthcare organizations, practice arrangements, and professional societies, to ensure that the regulations include all entities within the scope of the statute. A healthcare entity is an entity that provides healthcare services and engages in professional review activity through a formal peer-review process for the purpose of furthering quality health care or a committee of that entity. Healthcare practitioners include all healthcare practitioners authorized by a state to provide healthcare services by whatever formal mechanism the state uses (e.g., certification, registration, and licensure).

Data Bank Queries

Data bank queries can be made by state licensing boards, hospitals, other healthcare entities, and professional societies that have entered or may be entering employment or affiliation relationships with a physician, dentist, or other healthcare practitioner who has applied for clinical privileges or appointment to a medical staff. A plaintiff's attorney is permitted to obtain information from the data bank when a malpractice action has been filed and the practitioner on whom information has been sought is named in the suit.

Confidentiality of Data Bank Information

Information reported to the data bank is considered to be strictly confidential and cannot be disclosed except as specified in the NPDB regulations. Individuals and entities that knowingly and willfully report to or query the data bank under false pretenses or fraudulently access the data bank computer directly are subject to civil penalties.

The Privacy Act of 1974 protects the contents of federal systems of records such as those contained in the NPDB from disclosure, unless the disclosure is for a routine use of the system of records as published annually in the Federal Register. The published routine uses of NPDB information do not allow for disclosure of information to the general public.

∎ INCIDENT REPORTING

State health codes, regulatory bodies, and accreditation agencies often provide that healthcare facilities investigate and report specifically defined incidents regarding patient care in a manner prescribed by regulation. Reportable incidents often include such things as those events that have resulted in a patient's serious injury or death, an event such as fire or loss of emergency power, certain infection outbreaks, and strikes by employees.

Incident Reports

Incident reports should not be placed in the medical record. They should be directed to counsel for legal advice. This will help prevent discovery on the basis of attorney–client privilege. There is conflicting case law in that some courts will not permit incident reports to be discovered whereas others will allow discovery.

State Reportable Incidents

State reportable events include the reporting of communicable diseases, infections, and unusual or an unexpected cluster of patients with symptoms/diseases or exposures suggestive of a health emergency or terrorism event.

Many states have enacted legislation requiring hospitals to report incidents that result in patient injury. The Pennsylvania Medical Care Availability and Reduction of Error Act reporting requirements, for example, are intended to help reduce and eliminate medical errors by identifying problems and implementing solutions to improve patient safety. The act requires healthcare facilities to report serious events and incidents to a newly established patient safety authority. The act defines a serious event as an event, occurrence, or situation involving the clinical care of a patient in a medical facility that results in death or compromises patient safety and results in an unanticipated injury requiring the delivery of additional healthcare services to the patient.

Hospital procedures for reporting patient care incidents must comply with state regulations. As with Joint Commission requirements, the Pennsylvania law prohibits retaliatory action against the healthcare worker for reporting patient care incidents and provides for written notification to patients.

Failure to Report

Individuals designated to report incidents must do so if required by state statute. The director of nursing at a nursing facility in *Choe v. Axelrod* [13] was fined $150 for failure to report an instance of patient neglect. An anonymous telephone call had been placed with the department of health regarding two incidents of alleged patient neglect. In one incident, a patient had been left unattended in a shower by an orderly, and the patient sprayed himself with hot water, which resulted in second-degree burns on his forehead. On a second occasion, a similar incident occurred, but no one was injured. On investigation by the department of health, a determination was made that both incidents constituted patient neglect and that failure to report these incidents was a violation of New York public health law. After a hearing by an administrative law judge, the charge in the first incident was sustained and in the second incident was dismissed. The director of nurses petitioned to annul the administrative determination. She contended that the department of health failed to establish a prima facie case of patient neglect, that the incident was an unavoidable accident, and that the department of health's proof was based on hearsay evidence. The court held that evidence supported a finding that the director of nurses failed to report the incident of patient neglect as required by statute.

Although it may not always be clear as to when an incident report should be filed, appropriate procedures should be in place to address how questionable events should be handled.

Sentinel Events

The Joint Commission encourages healthcare organizations to self-report sentinel events. The Joint Commission defines a *sentinel event* as "an unexpected occurrence involving death or serious physical or psychological injury, or the risk thereof. Serious injury specifically includes loss of limb or function. The phrase, 'or the risk thereof,' includes any process variation for which a recurrence would carry a significant chance of a serious adverse outcome."[14] Frequently reported sentinel events include patient suicides, medication errors, death due to delays in treatment, operative/postoperative complications, and surgical procedures on the wrong site. Although The Joint Commission encourages but does not require the reporting of sentinel events, it does expect organizations to conduct a root cause analysis when sentinel events occur.

Root Cause Analysis

A *root cause analysis* (RCA) is a process for identifying the basic or causal factors that underlie variation in performance, including the occurrence or possible occurrence of a sentinel event. A root cause analysis focuses primarily on systems and processes, not on individual performance. It progresses from special causes in clinical processes to common causes in organizational processes and systems and identifies potential improvements in processes or systems that would tend to decrease the likelihood of such events in the future or determines, after analysis, that no such opportunities exist.[15]

The basic purpose of an RCA is to improve organizational performance outcomes. Organizations are often concerned with the possibility that RCAs could be subject to discovery by a plaintiff's attorney and could then be used against them in civil trials. To address this concern and minimize the risks of additional liability exposure, The Joint Commission continues to work on ways to prevent the disclosure of the substance of RCAs.

The RCA process involves thoroughly investigating an unwanted event to determine the root cause of the event (e.g., human error, staffing issues, equipment malfunction). Once the root cause of a sentinel event has been determined, a search for best practices is conducted. This is accomplished by a thorough review of pertinent literature, an online web search, and consultation with organizations that have had similar incidences. Once the search for best practices has been accomplished, appropriate staff review the information gathered and determine the best option to prevent the likelihood future occurrences of the sentinel event.

Reporting sentinel events, conducting root cause analyses, and sharing that information with The Joint Commission is helpful to all organizations in improving patient care. For helpful information on sentinel events and root cause analyses, visit the Joint Commission's website (http://jointcommission.org/).

Notes

1. 42 U.S.C., § 5106g.
2. 413 N.W.2d 670 (Wis. Ct. App. 1987).
3. No. 1031515 (Ala. 2005).
4. 415 N.W.2d 436 (Minn. Ct. App. 1987).
5. 140 S.W.3d 51 (Mo. banc).
6. *Manifold v. Ragaglia*, No. SC 17150 (Conn. 2004).
7. What is Elder Abuse? National Committee for the Prevention of Elder Abuse, www.preventelderabuse.org/elderabuse.
8. http://www.fda.gov/Safety/MedWatch/HowToReport/ucm053074.htm.
9. www.newmexicoindependent.com/60795/nm-2-start-reporting-hospital-acquired-infections-publicly.
10. PUB. L. No. 99-660, tit. IV (1986).
11. 42 U.S.C. § 11101[0].
12. http://www.npdb-hipdb.hrsa.gov/.
13. 534 N.Y.S.2d 739 (N.Y. App. Div. 1988).
14. *2012 Comprehensive Manual for Hospitals: The Official Handbook*, The Joint Commission on Accreditation of Healthcare Organizations, at SE-1.
15. *Id.* at SE-2.

18
Medical Records

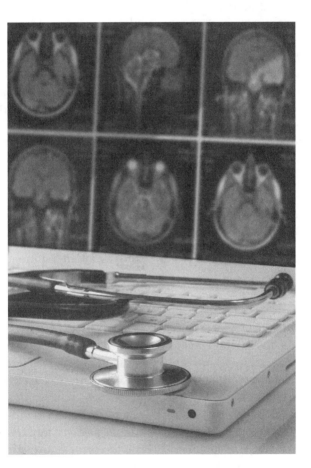

Figure 18–1 Electronic Records   © lenetstan/ShutterStock, Inc.

Learning Objectives

The reader upon completion of this chapter will be able to:

- Describe the contents of medical records.
- Explain the ownership and who can access a patient's medical record.
- Explain the importance of maintaining complete and accurate records.
- Describe the advantages and disadvantages of computerized records.
- Explain what is meant by the medical record battleground.
- Describe why the medical record is important in legal proceedings.

NEWSPAPER CLIPPINGS: Reducing Medical Errors

To significantly reduce the tens of thousands of deaths and injuries caused by medical errors every year, health care organizations must adopt information technology systems that are capable of collecting and sharing essential health information on patients and their care. . . . These systems should operate seamlessly as part of a national network of health information that is accessible by all health care organizations and that includes electronic records of patients' care, secure platforms for the exchange of information among providers and patients, and data standards that will make health information uniform and understandable to all. . . .

—News: Institute of Medicine, *November 20, 2003*

The effective and efficient delivery of patient care requires that an organization determine its information needs. Organizations that do not centralize their information needs will often suffer scattered databases, which may result in such problems as duplication of data gathering, inconsistent reports, and inefficiencies in the use of economic resources.

The medical record is the principal means of communication between healthcare professionals in matters relating to patient care. The medical record: provides documentation of a patient's illness, symptoms, diagnosis, and treatment; serves as a planning tool for patient care; protects the legal interests of patients, healthcare organizations, and caregivers; provides a database for use in statistical reporting, continuing education, and research; and provides information necessary for third-party billing and regulatory agencies. Healthcare organizations are required to maintain a medical record for each patient in accordance with accepted professional standards and practices.

Nurses tend to access the medical record more often than other healthcare professionals, simply because of the amount of time they spend caring for patients. The nurse monitors the patient's illness, response to medication, display of pain and discomfort, and general condition. The patient's care, as well as the nurse's observations, should be recorded on a regular basis. A nurse who has doubt as to the appropriateness of a written order should verify with the prescribing physician the intent of the order.

Licensure rules and regulations contained in state statutes generally describe the requirements and standards for the maintenance, handling, signing, filing, and retention of medical records. Failure to maintain a complete and accurate medical record reflecting the treatment rendered may affect the ability of an organization and/or physician to obtain third-party reimbursement (e.g., from Medicare, Medicaid, or private insurance carriers). Under federal and state laws, the medical record must reflect accurately the treatment for which the organization or physician seeks payment. Thus, the medical record is important to the organization for medical, legal, and financial reasons.

MANAGING INFORMATION

All organizations, regardless of mission or size, develop and maintain information management systems, which often include financial, medical, and human resource data. Information management is a process intended to facilitate the flow of information within and between departments and caregivers. An information management plan must address: the *information necessary* in the care of each patient; how *information flows* logically to provide quality patient care; *third-party payer* needs; set *goals* and establish *priorities*; improve *accuracy* of data *collection* and medical record *entries*; provide *uniformity* of data collection and *definitions*; limit *duplication* of entries; deliver *timely* and *accurate* information; provide *easy access* to information; provide *security* and *confidentiality* of information; improve *collaboration* across disciplines and the organization through information sharing; establish *disaster plans* for the *recovery* of information; *orientation* and *training* of staff on the information management system; and provide an *annual review* of the plan; and *managing change*.

CONTENTS OF THE MEDICAL RECORD

Because the medical record fulfills many crucial roles within a healthcare organization, practitioners must strive to maintain the integrity and accuracy of records. The inpatient medical record includes, for example: the admission record, which describes pertinent demographic information; consent and authorization for treatment forms; advance directives; history and physical examination, including a preliminary/working diagnosis and findings that support the diagnosis; patient screenings and assessments (e.g., nursing, functional, nutritional, social, and discharge planning); treatment plans; physicians' orders; progress notes; nursing notes; diagnostic reports; consultation reports; vital signs charts; anesthesia assessments; operative reports; medication administration records; discharge planning documentation; patient education; and discharge summaries.

OWNERSHIP AND RELEASE OF RECORDS

Healthcare providers who handle medical records must fully understand the related issues of ownership and privacy. Medical records are the property of the provider of care and are maintained for the benefit of the patient. Ownership resides with the organization or professional who renders treatment. Although medical records typically have been protected from public scrutiny by a general practice of nondisclosure, this practice has been waived under a limited number of specifically controlled situations. Jurisdictions generally recognize that individuals have a right to privacy and to be protected from the mass dissemination of information pertaining to their personal or private affairs. The right of privacy generally includes the right to be kept out of the public spotlight. The Privacy Act of 1974 was enacted to safeguard individual privacy from the misuse of federal records and to give individuals access to records concerning themselves that are maintained by federal agencies.

Requests by Patients

Patients have a legally enforceable interest in the information contained in their medical records and, therefore, have a right to access their records. Patients may have access to review and obtain copies of their records, including diagnostic tests. Access to information includes that maintained or possessed by healthcare organizations or healthcare practitioners who have treated or is treating a patient. Organizations and physicians can withhold records if the information could reasonably be expected to cause substantial and identifiable harm to the patient (e.g., patients in psychiatric hospitals, institutions for the mentally disabled, and substance abuse treatment programs).

Changes to the Health Insurance Portability and Accountability Act (HIPAA) released by the U.S. Department of Health and Human Services (HHS) 45 CFR Parts 160 and 164 adopts rules on individuals' right of access to protected health information that include in part the following:

- Expand individuals' rights to receive electronic copies of their health information and to restrict disclosures to a health plan concerning treatment for which the individual has paid out of pocket in full.
- Require modifications to, and redistribution of, a covered entity's notice of privacy practices.[1]

Failure to release a patient's record can lead to legal action. The patient in *Pierce v. Penman*[2] brought a lawsuit seeking damages for severe emotional distress when physicians repeatedly refused to turn over her medical records. The defendants had rendered different professional services to the plaintiff for approximately 11 years. The patient moved and found a new physician, Dr. Hochman. She signed a release authorizing Hochman to obtain her records from the defendant–physicians. Dr. Hochman wrote a letter for her records but never received a response. The defendants claimed that they never received the request. The patient changed physicians again and continued in her efforts to obtain a copy of the records. Eventually the defendants' offices were burglarized, and the plaintiff's records were allegedly taken. The detective in charge of investigating the burglary stated that he was never notified that any records were taken. The patient was awarded $250 compensatory damages and $10,000 in punitive damages.

Requests by Third Parties

The medical record is a peculiar type of property because there is a variety of third-party interest in the information contained in medical records. Healthcare organizations may not generally disclose information without patient consent. Policies regarding the release of information should be formulated to address the rights of third parties, such as insurance carriers processing claims, physicians, medical researchers, educators, and governmental agencies.

Criminal Investigations

A restriction on disclosing information obtained in a confidential relationship may occur when a patient is the victim of a crime. The hospital in *In re Brink*[3] sought to quash a grand jury request for the medical records pertaining to blood tests administered to a person under investigation. The court of common pleas held that physician–patient privilege did not extend to medical records subpoenaed pursuant to a grand jury investigation. A proceeding before a grand jury is considered secret in nature, inherently preserving the confidentiality of a patient's records.

Patient records may also be obtained during investigations into such alleged criminal actions as Medicaid fraud. The grand jury in *People v. Ekong*[4] was permitted to obtain certain patient files and records that were in the possession of the physician who was under investigation for Medicaid fraud.

DOCUMENTATION OF TREATMENT

Pertinent findings during the course of a patient's treatment must be well documented. In one such case, *Tulier-Pastewski v. State Board for Professional Medical Conduct*,[5] two hospital administrators testified and showed undisputed proof that the physician had recorded a patient was alert during the purported examination when the patient was actually sedated and asleep. Evidence also indicated the physician failed to properly document medical histories and current physical status. Although the physician asserted that evidence of failure to document did not support findings of negligence because there was no expert testimony that her omissions actually caused or created a risk of harm to a patient, an expert witness testified that the missing information as to certain patients was needed for proper assessment of the patient's condition and choice of treatment. This testimony, together with the obvious importance of cardiac information when treating patients with chest pain, provided a rational basis for the conclusion by the administrative review board for professional medical conduct that the physician's deficient medical record keeping could have affected patient care. The physician was found to be practicing medicine negligently on more than one occasion.

RETENTION OF RECORDS

The length of time medical records must be retained varies from state to state. Failure to preserve a patient's records, including X-rays and other imaging studies can lead to lawsuits. For example, the plaintiff in *Rodgers v. St. Mary's Hosp. of Decatur*[6] filed a complaint for damages against a hospital, alleging that the hospital breached its statutory duty to preserve for 5 years all of the X-rays taken of his wife. He alleged that the hospital's failure to preserve one of the X-rays was a breach of its duty arising from the state's X-ray retention act and from the hospital's internal

regulations. The plaintiff asserted that because the hospital failed to preserve the X-ray, he was unable to prove his case in a lawsuit. The circuit court entered judgment in favor of the hospital, and the plaintiff appealed.

The Illinois Supreme Court held that a private cause of action existed under the X-ray retention act and that the plaintiff stated a claim under the act. The act provides that hospitals must retain X-rays and other such photographs or films as part of regularly maintained records for a period of 5 years.

The hospital also argued that the loss of one X-ray out of a series of six should not be considered a violation of the statute. The court disagreed, finding that the statute requires that all X-rays be preserved, not just some of them.

ELECTRONIC RECORDS

NEWSPAPER CLIPPINGS: Health Systems at Risk of Hacking

Security researchers warn that intruders could exploit known gaps to steal patient's records for use in identity theft schemes and even launch disruptive attacks that could shut down critical hospital systems.

A year–long examination of cyber security by *The Washington Post* has found that healthcare is among the most vulnerable industries in the country, in part because it lags behind in addressing known problems.

. . .

In February 2009, Congress mandated the widespread adoption of electronic health records (EHR) computer systems as part of the stimulus legislation known as the American Recovery and Reinvestment Act.

—*Robert O'Harrow Jr.*, The Washington Post, *December 26, 2012*

The Health Information Technology for Economic and Clinical Health Act (HITECH) is designed to promote the widespread adoption and interoperability of health information technology. HITECH was enacted under Title XIII of the American Recovery and Investment Act of 2009 (Public Law 111-5). Under the act, the Department of Health and Human Services is promoting the expansion and adoption of health information technology through program funding. For more detailed information see the government website http://www.healthit.gov.

Healthcare organizations undergoing computerization must determine user needs, design an effective system, select appropriate hardware and software, develop user training programs, develop a disaster recovery plan (e.g., provide for emergency power systems and backup files), and provide for data security. A reliable electronic information system requires knowledge based planning and design.

Advantages

Computers have become an economic necessity and play an important role in the delivery of healthcare by assisting healthcare providers in improving the quality of care. Electronic medical records provide timely access to patient information that includes: demographics; problems lists; history and physical exams; vital signs; diagnostic test results (e.g., laboratory and radiology); and consultant reports. Other of many advantages of electronic records include: order entries for medications and diagnostic tests; generation of critical alerts (e.g., out-of-range test values and drug–drug and food–drug interactions; computer-assisted diagnosis and treatment; generation of reminders for follow-up testing; assistance in standardizing treatment protocols; improving the ability to timely share information with treating providers; improved productivity and quality; reduced charting costs; support for clinical education and research; generation and transmission of electronic prescriptions; and storage of medical records indefinitely.

Disadvantages

With the advent of electronic medical records, organizations, for the most part, have failed to achieve a paperless electronic system. Instead, organizations find themselves with a hybrid system with various elements of a patient's care recorded in both paper and electronic format. Although computerization is costly, the road to progress is reaping rewards by improving patient care and treatment.

MEDICAL RECORD BATTLEGROUND

The contents of a medical record must not be tampered with after an entry has been made; therefore, it should be used wisely. Although the record should be complete and accurate, it should not be used as an instrument for registering complaints about another individual or the organization. Its purpose is to record the patient's course of care. Those individuals who choose to make derogatory remarks in a patient's record about others could find themselves in a courtroom trying to defend such notations in the record. Inappropriate comments written during a time of anger may have been based on inaccurate information, which, in turn, could be damaging to one's credibility and future statements.

LEGAL IMPORTANCE OF RECORDS

The ever-increasing frequency of personal injury suits mandates that healthcare organizations maintain complete, accurate, and timely medical records. The integrity and completeness of the medical record are important in reconstructing the events surrounding alleged negligence in the care of a patient. Medical records aid police investigations, provide information for determining the cause of death, and indicate the extent of injury in workers' compensation or personal injury proceedings.

When healthcare professionals are called as witnesses in a proceeding, they are permitted to refresh their recollections of the facts and circumstances of a particular case by referring to the medical record. Courts recognize that it is impossible for a medical witness to remember the details of every patient's treatment. The record therefore may be used as an aid in relating the facts of a patient's course of treatment.

If a medical record is admitted into evidence in a legal proceeding, the court must be assured the information is accurate, was recorded at the time the event took place, and was not recorded in anticipation of a specific legal proceeding. When a medical record is introduced into evidence, its custodian must testify as to the manner in which the record was produced and the way in which it is protected from unauthorized handling and change. If a record can be shown to be inaccurate or incomplete or that it was made long after the event it purports to record, its credibility as evidence will be diminished.

Alteration of Records

 NEWSPAPER CLIPPINGS: Falsified Patient Records Are Untold Story of California Nursing Home Care

A supervisor at a Carmichael nursing home admitted under oath that she was ordered to alter the medical records of a 92-year-old patient, who died after developing massive, rotting bedsores at the facility.

In Santa Monica, a nursing home was fined $2,500 by the state for falsifying a resident's medical chart, which claimed that the patient was given physical therapy 5 days a week. The catch? At least 28 of those sessions were documented by nurse assistants who were not at work on those days.

—*Marjie Lundstrom*, The Sacramento Bee,
September 18, 2011

In criminal law, falsification of records with the intent to deceive another for personal gain is considered fraud. When handling medical records, professionals must recognize that intentional alteration, falsification, or destruction to avoid liability for medical negligence is generally sufficient to show actual malice. Punitive damages may be awarded whether or not the act of altering, falsifying, or destroying records directly causes compensable harm. The evidence in *Dimora v. Cleveland Clinic Foundation*[7] showed that the patient had fallen and broken five or six ribs; yet, upon examination, the physician stated in the progress notes that the patient was smiling and laughing pleasantly, exhibiting no pain upon deep palpation of the area. Other testimony indicated that she was in pain and crying. The discrepancy between the written progress notes and the testimony of the witnesses who observed the patient was sufficient to raise a question of fact. The court then considered the possible falsification of documents by the physician in an effort to hide the possible negligence of hospital personnel. The testimony of the witnesses, if believed, would have been sufficient to show that the physician falsified the record or intentionally reported the incident inaccurately to avoid liability for the negligent care of the patient.

The intentional alteration or destruction of medical records to avoid liability for medical negligence is sufficient to show actual malice, and punitive damages may be awarded whether the act of altering, falsifying, or destroying records directly causes compensable harm.[8]

Fraud can also be considered an intentional tort. For example, writing a post procedure note before actually beginning the procedure is in reality falsifying a patient's record even though it might be considered normal practice for the physician. A physician who claims that notes are revised following the procedure, if necessary, is placing the patient in jeopardy if he fails to do so and that failure leads to injury during post-procedure follow-up care.

Objection to Record Notations

As noted in *Dodds v. Johnstone*,[9] during a physical exam the appellee indicated in her progress notes that she believed the appellant had been using cocaine prior to her last office visit. Appellee's notes read: "I believe by physical exam the patient was using cocaine on Friday before her office visit." The appellant filed a complaint in which she alleged that the appellee was negligent in her diagnosis of the appellant and that as a result she incurred a loss of compensation for her automobile accident claim and suffered severe emotional distress. The court reviewed the record of proceedings before the trial court and found that there was no genuine issue of material fact as to negligent infliction of severe emotional distress, loss of employment opportunities, or a decreased insurance settlement as a result of the notation in the patient's medical records.

Tampering with Records

Tampering with records sends the wrong signal to jurors and can shatter one's credibility. Altered records can create a presumption of negligence. The court in *Matter of Jascalevich*[10] held:

> We are persuaded that a physician's duty to a patient cannot but encompass his affirmative obligation to maintain the integrity, accuracy, truth and reliability of the patient's medical record. His obligation in this regard is no less compelling than his duties respecting diagnosis and treatment of the patient since the medical community must, of necessity, be able to rely on those records in the continuing and future care of that patient. Obviously, the rendering of that care is prejudiced by anything in those records, which is false, misleading or inaccurate. We hold, therefore, that a deliberate falsification by a physician of his patient's medical record, particularly when the reason therefore is to protect his own interests at the expense of his patient's, must be regarded as gross malpractice endangering the health or life of his patient.[11]

Dr. McCroskey faced a lawsuit for tampering with documents. The state board of medical examiners, in a disciplinary hearing in *State Board of Medical Examiners v. Mc-Croskey*,[12] issued a letter of admonition to Dr. McCroskey based upon a series of incidents arising out of the care of a patient's stab wound. Although the patient's condition was initially thought to be stable, he bled to death several hours after his admission to the hospital. McCroskey was the attending surgeon on the date of the incident and, therefore, responsible for the accurate completion of the patient's medical record. McCroskey declined to accept the letter of admonition and a formal disciplinary hearing was held.

McCroskey erased and wrote over a preoperative note made by another physician concerning the patient's estimated blood loss. Specifically, the original record entry was completed by a surgical resident on the date of the patient's death and stated that the patient's blood loss just prior to surgery was "now greater than 3,000 cc." Sometime after the autopsy, McCroskey changed the record to read that the patient's blood loss was "now greater than 2,000 cc."[13]

The Colorado Supreme Court held that the findings of the board were supported by substantial evidence. Because of the expertise of the board, it was in a position to determine the seriousness of the physician's conduct by placing the events in their proper factual context.

All three of the inquiry panel's witnesses testified the generally accepted standard of practice requires that a medical record entry be dated with the date it is made. Even one of McCroskey's witnesses acknowledged that misdating the medical record was "certainly something that should not have been done." McCroskey did not simply backdate a trivial note in a patient's medical record. Instead McCroskey's actions took place in the context of a patient's death, which resulted in a coroner's autopsy, peer review activities, publicity, and several legal actions. McCroskey was the attending physician responsible for the accuracy of the patient's medical record, and yet he engaged in conduct that cast doubt upon the medical record's integrity. Under these circumstances, the Board was justified in considering McCroskey's conduct to violate the standard of care.[14]

Rewriting and Replacing Notes

Another temptation of healthcare professionals is the desire to clarify and explain one's activities in the care of a patient. In a well-publicized case that involved the death of a child, the nurse replaced her original notes with a second set of notes that were much more detailed and indicated that she had seen the patient more frequently than was reported in her original notes.[15] Rewriting one's notes in a patient's medical record casts doubt as to the accuracy of other entries in the record. It is easier to explain why one did not chart all activities than it is to explain why a new entry was recorded and an original note replaced.

In another case, two hospital administrators in *Tulier-Pastewski v. State Board for Professional Medical Conduct*,[16] testified and showed undisputed proof that the physician had recorded a patient was alert during the purported examination when the patient was actually sedated and asleep. Evidence also indicated the physician failed to properly document medical histories and current physical status. Although the physician asserted that evidence of failure to document did not support findings of negligence because there was no expert testimony that her omissions actually caused or created a risk of harm to a patient, an expert witness testified that the missing information as to certain patients was needed for proper assessment of the patient's condition and choice of treatment. This testimony, together with the obvious importance of cardiac information when treating patients with chest pain, provided a rational basis for the conclusion by the administrative review board for professional medical conduct that

the physician's deficient medical record keeping could have affected patient care. The physician was found to be practicing medicine negligently on more than one occasion.

ILLEGIBLE HANDWRITING

Illegible handwriting is as ancient as the first stylus. Unfortunately, poor penmanship can cause injury to patients. Medical errors because of poor handwriting can lead to extended length of hospital stays and, in some cases, the death of patients.

Fatal Handwriting Mix-Up

Forty-two-year-old Vasquez died as a result of a handwriting mix-up on the medication prescribed for his heart. Vasquez had been given a prescription for 20 mg of Isordil to be taken four times per day. The pharmacist misread the physician's handwriting and filled the prescription with Plendil, a drug for high blood pressure, which is usually taken at no more than 10 mg per day. As a result, Vasquez was given the wrong medication at eight times the recommended dosage. He died 2 weeks later from an apparent heart attack and the family filed a lawsuit. A West Texas jury ordered the physician, drugstore, and pharmacist to pay $225,000 to the family. The likelihood of similar occurrences is a growing danger as the number and variety of medications increase with similar names and look-alikes.[17]

TIMELY COMPLETION OF RECORDS

Not only must the chart be accurate but also healthcare professionals must promptly complete records after patients are discharged. Persistent failure to conform to a medical staff rule requiring physicians to complete records promptly can be the basis for suspension of medical staff privileges, as was the case in the *Board of Trustees Memorial Hospital v. Pratt*.[18]

CONFIDENTIAL AND PRIVILEGED COMMUNICATIONS

The duty of an organization's employees and staff to maintain confidentiality encompasses both verbal and written communications and applies to consultants, contracted individuals, students, and volunteers. Information about a patient, regardless of the method in which it is acquired, is confidential and should not be disclosed without the patient's permission. All healthcare professionals who have access to medical records have a legal, ethical, and moral obligation to protect the confidentiality of the information in the records, as well as verbal communications between physicians and patients.

Breach of Physician–Patient Confidentiality

Patients enter the physician–patient relationship assuming that information acquired by physicians will not be disclosed, unless the patient consents or the law requires disclosure. Mutual trust and confidence are essential to the physician–patient relationship. A breach of physician–patient confidentiality is analogous to invasion of privacy, and plaintiffs are entitled to recover damages, including emotional damages, for the harm caused by the physician's unauthorized disclosure.

Ordinary Business Documents

Privileged communications statutes do not protect from discovery the records maintained in the ordinary course of doing business and rendering inpatient care. Such documents often can be subpoenaed after showing cause.

Attorney–Client Privilege

Attorney–client privilege generally will preclude discovery of memorandums written to an organization's general counsel by the organization's risk management director. In *Mlynarski v. Rush Presbyterian–St. Luke's Medical Center*,[19] a memorandum written by the risk management coordinator to the hospital's general counsel was barred from discovery. There was undisputed evidence that the risk management coordinator had consulted with and assisted counsel in determining the legal action to pursue and the advisability of settling a claim that she had been assigned to investigate. Information contained in the memorandum was available from witnesses whose names and addresses were made available to the plaintiff. If the hospital later at trial decided to attempt to impeach those witnesses based on the coordinator's testimony, privilege would be waived, and the hospital would be required to produce the relevant reports.

HIPAA

Congress enacted the Health Insurance Portability and Accountability Act (HIPAA) in 1996.

> The HIPAA Privacy Rule provides federal protections for personal health information held by covered entities and gives patients an array of rights with respect to that information. At the same time, the Privacy Rule is balanced so that it permits the disclosure of personal health information needed for patient care and other important purposes.
>
> The Security Rule specifies a series of administrative, physical, and technical safeguards for covered entities to use to assure the confidentiality, integrity, and availability of electronic protected health information.[20]

According to the Centers for Medicare and Medicaid Services, Title I of HIPAA protects health insurance information for workers and their families when they change or lose their jobs. Title II of HIPAA, the administrative simplification (AS) provisions, requires the establishment of national standards for electronic healthcare transactions and national identifiers for providers, health insurance plans, and employers. The AS provisions also address the security and privacy of health information. The standards are meant to improve the efficiency and effectiveness of the nation's healthcare system by encouraging the widespread use of electronic data interchange in health care.

The key privacy provisions of HIPAA include: patients must be able to access their record and request correction of errors; patients must be informed of how their personal information will be used; patient information cannot be used for marketing purposes without the explicit consent of the involved patients; patients can ask their health insurers and providers to take reasonable steps to ensure that their communications with the patient are confidential (e.g., a patient can ask to be called at his or her work phone number instead of home or cell phone number); patients can file formal privacy-related complaints with the U.S. Department of Health and Human Services (DHHS) Office for Civil Rights; health insurers or providers must document their privacy procedures, but they have discretion on what to include in their privacy procedure; health insurers or providers must designate a privacy officer and train their employees; providers may use patient information without patient consent for the purposes of providing treatment, obtaining payment for services, and performing the nontreatment operational tasks of the provider's business.

CHARTING—SOME HELPFUL ADVICE

The medical record is the most important document in providing quality patient care. In a malpractice action, both the plaintiff and defendant use it as a basis for their actions and defense in a lawsuit. The following suggestions on documentation should prove to be helpful when charting in a patient's record.

- The medical record describes the care rendered to a patient. It should provide a clear timeline of patient care needs and how they were addressed from the time of admission to the time of discharge. It should include a complete and accurate medical history and physical, medications at the time of admission, allergies, over-the-counter drugs, vitamins, differential diagnoses, treatment plan, care rendered, and follow-up instructions.
- Medical record entries should be timely, legible, clear, and meaningful to a patient's course of treatment. Illegible medical records not only damage one's ability to defend oneself in a court action, but also can have an adverse effect on the credibility of other healthcare professionals who read the record and act on what they read.
- Progress notes should describe the symptom/s or condition/s being addressed, the treatment rendered, the patient's response, and status at the time inpatient care is discontinued. All notes must be dated and signed in order to provide an accurate history of the patient's care and treatment during the hospital stay. Follow-up on other caregiver notes should be described in the progress notes (e.g., observations of consultants, dietitians, nurses, pharmacists, physical therapists, and respiratory therapists).
- Long, defensive, or derogatory notes should not be written. Only the facts should be related. Criticism, complaints, emotional comments, and extraneous remarks have no place in the medical record. Such remarks can precipitate a malpractice suit.
- Erasures and correction fluid should not be used to cover up entries. Do not tamper with the chart in any form. A single line should be drawn through a mistaken entry, the correct information entered, and the correction signed and dated.
- Charts related to pending legal action should be placed in a separate file under lock and key. Legal counsel should be notified immediately of any potential lawsuit.

- A medical record has many authors. Entries made by others must not be ignored. Good patient care is a collaborative interdisciplinary team effort. Entries made by healthcare professionals provide valuable information in treating the patient.
- Reasoning for not following the advice of a consultant should be noted in the medical record, not so as to discredit the consultant, but to show the reasoning why a consultant's advice was not followed.

Notes

1. "Rules and Regulations," *Federal Register* 78, no. 17 (Friday, January 25, 2013). http://www.gpo.gov/fdsys/pkg/FR-2013-01-25/pdf/2013-01073.pdf.
2. 515 A.2d 948 (Pa. Super. Ct. 1986).
3. 536 N.E.2d 1202 (Ohio Com. Pl. 1988).
4. 582 N.E.2d 233 (Ill. App. Ct. 1991).
5. No. 94969 (Supreme Court of N.Y. App. Div. 2004).
6. 597 N.E.2d 616 (Ill. 1992).
7. 683 N.E.2d 1175 (Ohio App. 1996).
8. *Moskovitz v. Mount Sinai Med. Ctr.*, 635 N.E.2d 331 (Ohio 1994).
9. No. L-03-1303 (Ohio App. 2004).
10. 442 A.2d 635 (N.J. Super. Ct. 1982).
11. *In re Jascalevich*, 182 N.J. Super. 445, 442 A.2d 635, 644–45 (1982).
12. 880 P.2d 1188 (Colo. 1994).
13. *Id.* at 1192.
14. *Id.* at 1196.
15. Ronnie Greene, "Examiner: Treatment 'Appropriate,'" *The Miami Herald*, April 16, 1995, 14A.
16. No. 94969 (Supreme Court of N.Y. App. Div. 2004).
17. "Doctor Held Liable for Fatal Handwriting Mixup," *USA Today*, Oct. 21, 1999.
18. 262 P.2d 682 (Wyo. 1953).
19. 572 N.E.2d 1025 (Ill. App. Ct. 1991). 1995, at 14A.
20. http://www.hhs.gov/ocr/privacy/hipaa/understanding/index.html.

19

National Health Insurance and Managed Care

Learning Objectives

The reader upon completion of this chapter will be able to:

- Discuss the purpose and various titles of the *Patient Protection and Affordable Care Act of 2010 (PPACA)*.

- Discuss the Supreme Court's ruling on the constitutionality of the PPACA.

- Describe the common models of managed care organizations.

- Explain what can happen if a state fails to comply with the PPACA.

Health care has come a long way from the days when, answering a knock at the front door, you were met by a genuine, black leather bag-carrying, independent practicing family physician. The physician knew you and every member of your family and, most likely, delivered you, as well as your mother and father. The only charge for a home visit may have been your mother's home-baked apple pie. This scene has changed dramatically over the years. The healthcare setting is being bombarded by mergers, buyouts, up-sizing and down-sizing, managed care organizations (MCOs), cost controls, regulations, regulators monitoring regulators, and now national health insurance. The emphasis here is on national health insurance and managed care organizations.

NATIONAL HEALTH INSURANCE

The declining trust in the nation's ability to deliver quality health care is evidenced by a system caught up in the morass of managed care companies, which have in some instances inappropriately devised ways to deny healthcare benefits to their constituency. That, coupled with the increased cost of insurance premiums and health care itself, have lead to a lack of insurance and proper health care, and has led to an outcry for changes in the system.

Congress, after months of contentious debate, by a slim margin enacted the *Patient Protection and Affordable Care Act* (the Act). Its dual purpose was to increase by approximately 30 million people, the number of Americans covered by health insurance, while decreasing the cost of the insurance. Moreover, the purpose of the Act was to transform U.S. health insurance and make it more affordable through *shared responsibility*, and to eliminate discriminatory acts such as exclusion because of preexisting conditions, health status, and gender.

Upon being signed into law, of the 10 titles that the Act contains in 900 pages, some of the reforms were put into place immediately. Bulleted below are those reforms.

- Eliminate lifetime and unreasonable annual limits on benefits.
- Prohibit recessions of health insurance policies.

- Provide assistance for those who are uninsured because of preexisting conditions.
- Require coverage of preventative services and immunzations.
- Extend dependent coverage up to age 26.
- Develop uniform coverage documents so consumers can make equal comparisons when shopping for health insurance.
- Cap insurance company nonmedical, administrative expenditures.
- Ensure consumers have access to an effective appeals process and provide a place to turn for help navigating the appeals process and assessing their coverage.
- Create a temporary reinsurance program to support coverage for early retirees.
- Establish an Internet portal to assist Americans in identifying coverage options.
- Facilitate administrative simplification to lower health system costs.

Some of the Act's remaining provisions began in 2012, some are scheduled for 2013, and the remainder will begin to take effect in 2014.

Supreme Court Ruling

Before summarizing the major points within the titles, it is first necessary to review what the Supreme Court determined after it heard oral arguments concerning the case in its 2012 term since that decision altered the terms of some of the major provisions in the Act.

Almost immediately after the president signed the Act into law, the legal battles began. First, nationwide there were a number of lawsuits brought challenging it. These challenges were originally viewed as essentially harmless, but as more states joined the fray, a central theme emerged that Congress was assuming that if it had the power to require its citizens to follow this law and its mandates, then it could basically require Americans to buy foods, for example, deemed healthy for them.

Finally, the Supreme Court accepted a suit brought by Florida and 25 other states in addition to a challenge by the National Federation of Independent Business. On June 28, 2012, (to the shock of conservatives) Chief Justice John G. Roberts Jr. aligned himself with the Court's liberals in a 5-4 ruling upholding the major portions of the Act. The decision agreed that the requirement for nearly all Americans to buy health insurance is permissible under Congress's taxing authority, and not the commerce clause as the Government had argued. The decision creates state run insurance exchanges where Americans can buy private insurance at a more affordable price, and eliminates some of the most unpopular insurance practices, such as removing barriers to gaining access to clinical preventative services, and new refundable tax credits for those with incomes between 100 and 400% of the *federal poverty level* (FPL).

The high court did excise one major portion of the law, which required states to expand their Medicaid coverage in a joint federal–state effort, to families with incomes up to 133% of the FPL, and are not entitled to Medicare, who would then have become eligible for Medicaid. The Court held that the law's requirement that states rapidly extend coverage or lose existing federal payments was unduly coercive. Most state governors have reservations about expansions, in spite of the federal government's promise of covering 100% of the cost of covering new eligible beneficiaries between 2014 and 2017. Their major concerns center around questions to which they have not yet received answers such as:

- What if a state decides to opt in and then cut back in later years?
- Can a state partially participate by raising the income cutoff to a level lower than the law's 133%?
- What if a state opts out and then wants to opt in later? Will the federal government continue to pay its costs?

If many states opt out, the cost of the health law would decrease, as would the amount of new beneficiaries. This would defeat two of the goals of the Act: expanding access to insurance coverage and controlling the growth of costs for health care.

In response to the Supreme Court decision, the House voted on July 11, 2012 (for the 33rd time) to repeal the law in its entirety. This was viewed as a symbolic gesture however, although judges may begin to hear new cases depending upon how each state interprets the law.

Act Titles

Most of the Act's provisions contained in the titles will go into effect starting in 2014 since those provisions will take some time to implement.

Title I. Quality Affordable Health Care for All Americans

This Act puts individuals, families and small business owners in control of their health care. It reduces premium costs for millions of working families and small businesses by providing hundreds of billions of dollars in tax relief—the largest middle class tax cut for health care in history. It also reduces what families will have to pay for health care by capping out-of-pocket expenses and requiring preventive care to be fully covered without any out-of-pocket expense. For Americans with insurance coverage who like what they have, they can keep it. Nothing in this act or anywhere in the bill forces anyone to change the insurance they have, period.

Americans without insurance coverage will be able to choose the insurance coverage that works best for them in a new open, competitive insurance market—the same insurance market that every member of Congress will be required to use for their insurance. The insurance exchange will pool buying power and give Americans new affordable choices of private insurance plans that have to compete for their business based on cost and quality. Small business owners will not only be able to choose insurance coverage through this exchange, but will receive a new tax credit to help offset the cost of covering their employees.

It keeps insurance companies honest by setting clear rules that rein in the worst insurance industry abuses. And it bans insurance companies from denying insurance coverage because of a person's pre-existing medical conditions while giving consumers new power to appeal insurance company decisions that deny doctor ordered treatments covered by insurance.

The Secretary has the authority to implement many of these new provisions to help families and small business owners have the information they need to make the choices that work best for them.

Title II. The Role of Public Programs

The Act extends Medicaid while treating all States equally. It preserves CHIP, the successful children's insurance plan, and simplifies enrollment for individuals and families.

It enhances community-based care for Americans with disabilities and provides States with opportunities to expand home care services to people with long-term care needs.

The Act gives flexibility to States to adopt innovative strategies to improve care and the coordination of services for Medicare and Medicaid beneficiaries. And it saves taxpayer money by reducing prescription drug costs and payments to subsidize care for uninsured Americans, as more Americans gain insurance under reform.

The Secretary has the authority to work with states and other partners to strengthen key public programs.

Title III. Improving the Quality and Efficiency of Health Care

The Act will protect and preserve Medicare as a commitment to America's seniors. It will save thousands of dollars in drug costs for Medicare beneficiaries by closing the coverage gap called the "donut hole." Doctors, nurses and hospitals will be incentivized to improve care and reduce unnecessary errors that harm patients. And beneficiaries in rural America will benefit as the Act enhances access to healthcare services in underserved areas.

The Act takes important steps to make sure that we can keep the commitment of Medicare for the next generation of seniors by ending massive overpayments to insurance companies that cost American taxpayers tens of billions of dollars per year. As the numbers of Americans without insurance falls, the Act saves taxpayer dollars by keeping people healthier before they join the program and reducing Medicare's need to pay hospitals to care for the uninsured. And to make sure that the quality of care for seniors drives all of our decisions, a group of doctors and healthcare experts, not Members of Congress, will be tasked with coming up with their best ideas to improve quality and reduce costs for Medicare beneficiaries.

The Secretary has the authority to take steps to strengthen the Medicare program and implement reforms to improve the quality and efficiency of health care.

Title IV. Prevention of Chronic Disease and Improving Public Health

The Act will promote prevention, wellness, and the public health and provides an unprecedented funding commitment to these areas. It directs the creation of a national prevention and health promotion strategy that incorporates the most effective and achievable methods to improve the health status of Americans and reduce the incidence of preventable illness and disability in the United States.

The Act empowers families by giving them tools to find the best science-based nutrition information, and it makes prevention and screenings a priority by waiving co-payments for America's seniors on Medicare.

The Secretary has the authority to coordinate with other Departments, develop and implement a prevention and health promotion strategy, and work to ensure more Americans have access to critical preventive health services.

Title V. Health Care Workforce

The Act funds scholarships and loan repayment programs to increase the number of primary care physicians, nurses, physician assistants, mental health providers, and dentists in the areas of the country that need them most. With a comprehensive approach focusing on retention and enhanced educational opportunities, the Act combats the critical nursing shortage. And through new incentives and recruitment, the Act increases the supply of public health professionals so that the United States is prepared for health emergencies.

The Act provides state and local governments flexibility and resources to develop health workforce recruitment strategies. And it helps to expand critical and timely access to care by funding the expansion, construction, and operation of community health centers throughout the United States.

The Secretary has the authority to take action to strengthen many existing programs that help support the primary care workforce.

Title VI. Transparency and Program Integrity

The Act helps patients take more control of their health care decisions by providing more information to help them make decisions that work for them. And it strengthens the doctor–patient relationship by providing doctors access to cutting edge medical research to help them and their patients make the decisions that work best for them.

It brings greater transparency to nursing homes to help families find the right place for their loved ones and enhances training for nursing home staff so that the quality of care continuously improves. The Act promotes nursing home safety by encouraging self corrections of errors, requiring background checks for employees who provide direct care and by encouraging innovative programs that prevent and eliminate elder abuse.

Finally, the Act reins in waste, fraud and abuse by imposing tough new disclosure requirements to identify high-risk providers who have defrauded the American taxpayer. It gives states new authority to prevent providers who have been penalized in one state from setting up in another. And it gives states flexibility to propose and test tort reforms that address several criteria, including reducing health care errors, enhancing patient safety, encouraging efficient resolution of disputes, and improving access to liability insurance.

The Secretary has new and improved authority to promote transparency and ensure that every dollar in the Act and in existing programs is spent wisely and well.

Title VII. Improving Access to Innovative Medical Therapies

The Act promotes innovation and saves consumers money. It extends drug discounts to hospitals and communities that serve low-income patients. And it creates a pathway for the creation of generic versions of biological drugs so that doctors and patients have access to effective and lower cost alternatives.

The Secretary of Health and Human Services has the authority to implement these provisions to help make medications more affordable.

Title VIII. CLASS Act

The Act provides Americans with a new option to finance long-term services and care in the event of a disability.

It is a self-funded and voluntary long-term care insurance choice. Workers will pay in premiums in order to receive a daily cash benefit if they develop a disability. Need will be based on difficulty in performing basic activities such as bathing or dressing. The benefit is flexible: it could be used for a range of community support services, from respite care to home care.

No taxpayer funds will be used to pay benefits under this provision. The program will actually reduce Medicaid spending, as people are able to continue working and living in their homes and not enter nursing homes. Safeguards will be put in place to ensure its premiums are enough to cover its costs.

The Secretary has the authority to establish the CLASS Program.

Title IX. Revenue Provisions

The Act makes health care more affordable for families and small business owners by providing the largest middle class tax cuts for health care in American history. Tens of millions of families will benefit from new tax credits which will help them reduce their premium costs and purchase insurance. Families making less than $250,000 will see their taxes cut by hundreds of billions of dollars.

When enacted, health reform is completely paid for and will reduce the deficit by more than one hundred billion dollars in the next ten years.

This title will be implemented by the U.S. Department of the Treasury.

Title X. Strengthening Quality

The Act reauthorizes the Indian Health Care Improvement Act (IHCIA) which provides health care services to American Indians and Alaskan Natives. It will modernize the Indian health care system and improve health care for 1.9 million American Indians and Alaska Natives.

The Secretary, in consultation with the Indian Health Service, has the authority to implement the Indian Health Care Improvement Act.[1]
—Reproduced from http://www.healthcare.gov/law/full/index.html

As more Americans are becoming aware of the law's provisions and what they can gain from it, the support for it is growing.

MANAGED CARE

Managed care is the process of structuring or restructuring the healthcare system in terms of financing, purchasing, delivering, measuring, and documenting a broad range of healthcare services and products. Managed care is nothing new to the U.S. healthcare delivery system; it has been around in some form for decades. *Managed care organizations* (MCOs) represent a major shift away from the domination of the fee-for-service system toward networks of providers supplying a full range of services. Historically, one of the major objected-to constraints of MCOs has been their requirement for prior authorization to obtain services. There are, however, a wide variety of managed care models that integrate financing and management with the delivery of healthcare services to an enrolled population. The following sections describe selected models of MCOs.

Health Maintenance Organizations

Health maintenance organizations (HMOs) are organized healthcare systems that are responsible for both the financing and the delivery of a broad range of comprehensive health services to an enrolled population. They are the most highly regulated form of MCOs. HMOs act both as insurer and provider of healthcare services. They charge employers a fixed premium for each subscriber. An independent practice association (IPA)-model HMO provides medical care to its subscribers through contracts it establishes with independent physicians. In a staff-model HMO, the physicians would normally be full-time employees of the HMO. Individuals who subscribe to an HMO are often limited to the panel of physicians who have contracted with the HMO to provide services to its subscribers.

Preferred Provider Organizations

Preferred provider organizations (PPOs) are entities through which employer health benefit plans and health insurance carriers contract to purchase healthcare services for covered beneficiaries from a selected group of participating providers. Most states have specific PPO laws that directly regulate such entities. Common characteristics of PPOs include:

- select provider panel
- negotiated payment rates
- rapid payment terms
- utilization management (programs to control utilization and cost)
- consumer choice (allow covered beneficiaries to use non-PPO providers for an additional out-of-pocket charge [point-of-service option])

In PPOs, a payer, such as an insurance company, provides incentives to its enrollees to obtain medical care from a panel of providers with whom the payer has contracted a discounted rate.

Exclusive Provider Organizations

Exclusive provider organizations (EPOs) limit their beneficiaries to participating providers for any healthcare services. EPOs use a gatekeeper approach to authorize nonprimary care services. The primary difference between an HMO and an EPO is that the former is regulated under HMO laws and regulations, whereas the latter is regulated under insurance laws and regulations. Characteristics of EPOs include:

- Primary care physicians are reimbursed through capitation payments or other performance-based reimbursement methods.
- Primary care physicians act as the gatekeepers.

Point-of-Service Plans

Point-of-service (POS) plans use primary care physicians as gatekeepers to coordinate and control medical care. Subscribers covered under POS plans may decide whether to use HMO benefits or indemnity-style benefits for each instance of care. In other words, the member is allowed to make a coverage choice at the POS. A patient who chooses a provider outside the plan is responsible for higher copayments.

Experience-Rated HMOs

Under *experience-rated* benefit options, an HMO receives monthly premium payments much as it would under traditional premium-based plans. Typically, to arrive at a final premium rate, there is a settlement process in which the employer is credited with some portion or all of the actual utilization and cost of its group. Then refunds or additional payments are calculated and made to the appropriate party.

Specialty HMOs

Specialty HMOs provide limited components of healthcare coverage. Dental HMOs, for example, have become more common as an option to indemnity dental insurance coverage.

Independent Practice Associations

An *independent practice association* (IPA) is a legal entity composed of physicians organized for the purpose of negotiating contracts to provide physician services. For example, an IPA might contract with an HMO or a physician–hospital organization (PHO). The physicians maintain their own practices and do not share services, such as claims, billing, scheduling, accounting, and so forth.

Physician Group Practice

A *physician group practice* that has only one or a small number of service delivery locations is a group practice. It is completely integrated economically, sharing costs and revenues. Group practices often are either specialty or primary care dominated.

Group Practice Without Walls

A *group practice without walls* is a physician organization formed for the purpose of sharing some administrative and management costs while physicians continue to practice at their own locations rather than at a centralized location.

Physician–Hospital Organizations

A *physician–hospital organization* (PHO) is a legal entity consisting of a joint venture of physicians and a hospital. It is formed to facilitate managed care contracting, to improve cost management and services, and to create new healthcare resources in the community.

Medical Foundations

In a *medical foundation*, the foundation employs or contracts with physicians to provide care to the foundation's patients.

Management Service Organizations

A *management service organization* (MSO) is an entity that provides administrative and management services to physicians. The organization performs services, such as practice management, marketing, managed care contracting, accounting, billing, and personnel management. The MSO can be hospital affiliated, a hospital–physician joint venture, physician owned, or investor owned.

Vertically Integrated Delivery System

A *vertically integrated delivery system* (IDS) is any organization or group of affiliated organizations that provides physician and hospital services to patients. The goal of hospital–physician integration is to provide a full range of services to patients. A vertical IDS achieves this goal, providing services ranging from primary outpatient care to tertiary inpatient care. More elaborate systems provide additional services, such as home health care, long-term care, rehabilitation, and mental health care.

Horizontal Consolidations

A *horizontal merger* involves similar or identical businesses at the same level of the market. There is no single qualitative or quantitative factor from which it can be determined whether such a group merger is permissible. Recognizing a congressional intent to preserve competition by preventing undue market concentration, the courts have focused primarily on the possibility that consolidation will substantially lessen competition.

Federally Qualified HMOs

Many HMOs are federally qualified. Federal qualification, which is entirely voluntary, requires HMOs to meet federal standards for legal and organizational status, financial viability, marketing, and health service delivery systems, as delineated in the federal HMO act and its implementing regulations. The disadvantage of federal qualification—beyond the fees involved—is that a federally qualified HMO has less flexibility in its benefits package and in developing premium rates.

Federally qualified HMOs must provide or arrange for basic health services for their members as needed and without limitation as to time, cost, frequency, extent, or kind of services actually provided. Basic health services include:

- physician services, including consultant and referral services by a physician
- inpatient and outpatient services, including short-term rehabilitation services and physical therapy
- medically necessary emergency health services
- 20 outpatient visits per member per year for short-term, evaluative, or crisis intervention mental health services
- medical treatment and referral services
- diagnostic laboratory and diagnostic and therapeutic radiology services
- home health services
- preventive health services, including immunizations and well-child care from birth

State HMO Laws

Most states have enacted comprehensive HMO laws that are often based on the National Association of Insurance Commissioners' Model HMO Act. State laws generally specify what type of entities can apply for a certificate of authority to operate an HMO. Typically, the state insurance department is the primary regulatory body.

Generally, state HMO laws require that an application for a certificate of authority be accompanied by a description of the proposed marketing plan that the regulator must approve. HMO laws generally specify that a schedule of charges and amendments must be filed and approved by the commissioner.

The majority of state HMO laws require that the provision of basic health services include emergency care, inpatient care, physician care, and outpatient care. State HMO laws contain several provisions designed to protect enrollees in the event that the HMO becomes insolvent. These include deposit, capital, reserve, and net worth requirements. State laws pertaining to HMOs generally require that:

- The HMO cannot cancel or refuse to renew an enrollee solely because of the individual's health.
- If an individual terminates employment or membership in a group, that person must be permitted to convert to a direct payment basis.
- Grievance procedures must be in place.

Case Management Firms

Case management firms assist employers and insurers in managing catastrophic cases. They identify cases that will become catastrophic, negotiate services and reimbursement with providers who can treat the patient's condition, develop a treatment protocol for the patient, and monitor the treatment.

Third-Party Administrators

A *third-party administrator* (TPA) is a firm that provides services for employers and associations that have group insurance policies. The TPA acts as a liaison between the employer and the insurer. The TPA performs administrative activities, such as claims processing, certifying eligibility, and a preparation of reports required by the staff.

Utilization Review

Utilization review (UR) is a process whereby a third-party payer evaluates the medical necessity of a course of treatment. Managed care organizations use a utilization review process to compare a patient's request for care with what treatment doctors commonly practice in similar medical circumstances. Medical care is considered to be necessary when it is needed to prevent, diagnose, and treat a patient's medical condition. Generally, UR is performed prospectively, concurrently, or retrospectively.

- *Prospective review*: The payer determines whether to pay for treatment before the treatment is initiated. If the review reveals that the treatment is not medically necessary, the payer then indicates its decision not to pay for the medical care.
- *Concurrent review*: This review is performed during the course of treatment. Concurrent review entails monitoring whether medical care continues to be appropriate and necessary. If it is not, the payer will discontinue payment for additional care.
- *Retrospective review*: This type of review is performed after treatment has been completed. If the review indicates that medical care was not necessary, the insurer can deny the claim.

Most insurance companies and MCOs rely on prospective and concurrent UR to determine if care is necessary, as well as what level of care is appropriate. Utilization review has become an accepted and essential part of cost containment.

Case management is an important aspect of utilization management. It involves identifying at an early stage those patients who can be treated more cost effectively in an alternative setting or at a lower level of care without negatively affecting the quality of care. Case management usually is employed in catastrophic or high-cost cases.

Utilization Management Firms

Utilization management firms perform utilization management activities for managed care entities, insurers, or employers. Mental health and dental care are two common types of such firms. In recent years, the regulation of utilization by private review agents or utilization review organizations (UROs) has increased dramatically.

Just as healthcare entities have a corporate duty to select and monitor physicians carefully, they also have a duty to carefully select the URO with which they contract. That duty entails investigating the URO before contracting with it to ensure that its procedures are adequate and its personnel are qualified to perform UR activities.

Negligent UR Decisions

MCOs that perform UR may be found liable for undesirable patient outcomes because of defects or failures in the UR process or because of a negligent UR decision. The first reported case involving liability for UR was *Wickline v. State of California*.[2] In that case, the court stated that a third-party payer of healthcare services might be held legally accountable when medically inappropriate decisions result from defects in the design or implementation of cost-containment mechanisms. Liability in the UR process can arise from several sources, including failure to gather information adequately before making a decision as to medical necessity, failure to initiate a meaningful dialogue between UR personnel and the treating physician, failure to inform members of their right to appeal an adverse UR decision, and failure to issue a timely UR decision.

Liability for Nonparticipating Physicians

MCOs may be liable for the medical malpractice of nonemployee participating physicians under an *ostensible or apparent agency theory* if (1) the patient reasonably views the entity (e.g., hospital) rather than the individual physician as the source of care and (2) the entity engages in conduct that leads the patient reasonably to believe that the source of care is the entity or that the physician is an employee of the entity.

The *doctrine of corporate negligence* clearly applies to staff-model HMOs in which the HMO employs the physicians and provides the facility within which they offer care. If an HMO employs physicians, such as in a staff-model HMO, the HMO can be held liable for the negligence of its employees under the doctrine of respondeat superior.

Employee Retirement Income Security Act

Congress enacted the *Employee Retirement Income Security Act of 1974* (ERISA). It was designed to ensure that employee welfare and benefit plans conform to a uniform body of benefits law. ERISA sets minimum standards for most voluntarily established pension and health plans in private industry to provide protection for individuals in these plans. ERISA requires plans to provide participants with plan information including important information about plan features and funding; provides fiduciary responsibilities for those who manage and control plan assets; requires plans to establish a grievance and appeals process for participants to get benefits from their plans; and gives participants the right to sue for benefits and breaches of fiduciary duty.

The law does not, however, regulate the contents of the welfare benefit plans. For example, it does not mandate that specific benefits be provided to beneficiaries. To qualify as an employee benefit plan, the plan must be maintained by an employer or employee organization for the benefit of its employees. ERISA requires that every plan (1) describe procedures for the allocation of responsibilities for its operation and administration and (2) specify the basis on which payments are made to and from the plan.

The *Consolidated Omnibus Budget Reconciliation Act* (COBRA) included an amendment that expanded benefits, providing some workers and their families with the right to continue their health coverage for a limited time under certain circumstances, such as the loss of a job. Another amendment to ERISA is contained in the Health Insurance Portability and Accountability Act (HIPAA), which provides protection for employees and their families who have preexisting medical conditions or might otherwise suffer discrimination in health coverage based on factors that relate to an individual's health. In general, ERISA does not cover group health plans established or maintained by governmental entities, churches for their employees, or plans that are maintained solely to comply with applicable workers' compensation, unemployment, or disability laws.

Health Care Quality Improvement Act of 1986

The *Health Care Quality Improvement Act of 1986* (HCQIA) was enacted in part as a response to numerous antitrust suits against participants in peer-review and credentialing activities. Congress passed the act to encourage continued participation in these activities. The purpose of the HCQIA is to provide those persons giving information to professional review bodies and those assisting in review activities limited immunity from damages that may arise as a result of adverse decisions that affect a physician's medical staff privileges. The immunity does not extend to civil rights litigation or suits filed by the United States or an attorney general of a state.

Open Enrollment

Federal HMO regulations require federally qualified HMOs to hold an open enrollment period of not less than 30 days per year during which the HMO must accept individual applicants for coverage regardless of their health status. Not all state HMO laws require open enrollment periods.

Emergency Care

HMOs can refuse benefit coverage to patients if they determine retrospectively that a patient's condition did not require emergency care. Of course, hindsight is 20/20. Determining whether one's chest pains are because of diet or a coronary condition requires expensive testing. To refuse a patient care before determining the etiology of a patient's condition could be financially disastrous to an organization. In addition, federal law prohibits hospital emergency departments from turning away patients seeking emergency care. Unfortunately, retrospective denial places the burden on the provider to seek reimbursement from the patient if the insurer denies the charges.

Market Power

Whenever an MCO possesses significant market power or deals with a group that has significant market power, antitrust implications should be considered. To determine market power, it is necessary first to identify the market in which the entity exercises power. For antitrust purposes, the relevant market has two components: (1) a product component and (2) a geographic component.

Product Market

The relevant product market involves the product or service at issue and all substantially acceptable substitutes for it. The relevant product market for MCOs is the market for healthcare financing. Broadly defined, this market includes traditional insurers, HMOs, PPOs, IPAs, and so on, and their subscriber members.

Market power results from the ability to cut back the market's total supply and then raise prices because of consumer demand for the product. Generally, the market in healthcare financing is competitive because the customers can switch companies readily, new suppliers can enter the market quickly, and existing suppliers can expand their sales rapidly.

Geographic Market

The relevant geographic market is the market area in which the seller operates and to which the purchaser can practically turn for supplies. The primary factors that courts have examined to determine the geographic scope of the market for hospital services are: patient flow statistics; location of physicians who admit patients; determinations of health planners; and public perception.

Ethics and the Denial of Services

In 1996, Dr. Linda Peeno, featured in Michael Moore's 2007 film *Sicko*, testified before Congress to discuss her prior work as a medical reviewer for Humana. Her testimony included the following remarks after which she embarked on a journey to become one of the best-known whistle-blowers about HMOs and the healthcare industry.

> I am here primarily today to make a public confession. In the spring of 1987, as a physician, I denied a man a necessary operation that would have saved his life and thus caused his death. No person and no group has held me accountable for this, because in fact, what I did was I saved a company a half a million dollars for this.

The public has the right to expect expert physicians to be accurate and truthful when giving testimony. If the profession cannot police itself, then the states will be forced to intervene to protect the public.

> Health care is a special category of business in that every decision, whether clinical or economic, has an ethical component. The ethical issues for "managed care" fall into four major categories of concern: professional, medical, business, and social. Some of the more important areas for attention include: the lack of professional code of ethics for physician executives; interference with the principles of informed consent and patient autonomy; violation of consumer rights; and social maleficence in obstruction to access and delivery.
>
> I contend that "managed care," as we currently know it, is inherently unethical in its organization and operation. Furthermore, I maintain that we have an industry, which can exist only through flagrant ethical violations against individuals and the public. Based on my experience, a health plan's resistance to ethical correctives will be proportionate to its reliance on ethical transgressions for its "success." We must not sanction their unethical practices at the expense of individual rights and public good will.[3]

PPACA AND STATE LAW

The ultimate effect of national health insurance in the day-to-day operation of managed-care organizations remains in a state of flux as the various States determine how to ensure their laws will be compliant with the *Patient Protection and Affordable Care Act* for reimbursement purposes. If a state elects to opt out of the extension and expansion of Medicaid as set forth in the Act, the program will be implemented by the Department of Health and Human Services, and the federal government will cover the additional expenditures. The Act's provision that states that opted out of the Medicaid extension would not be reimbursed by Medicaid or Medicare funding was not upheld since it was punitive in the U.S. Supreme Court's opinion.

Notes

1. Reproduced from http://www.healthcare.gov/law/full/index.html.
2. 239 Cal. Rptr. 810 (Cal. Ct. App. 1986).
3. http://www.thenationalcoalition.org/DrPeenotestimony.html.

I never was ruined but twice—once when I gained a lawsuit, and once when I lost one.
—Francois Marie de Voltaire (1694–1778)

20
Professional Liability Insurance

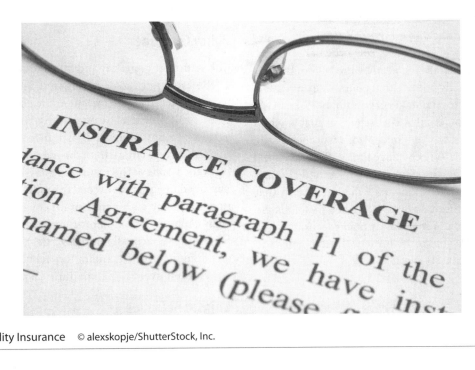

Figure 20–1   Liability Insurance   © alexskopje/ShutterStock, Inc.

Learning Objectives

The reader upon completion of this chapter will be able to:

- Describe the purpose of an insurance policy including risk categories and the importance of professionals to carry professional liability insurance.
- Explain the elements and conditions of an insurance policy.
- Describe the investigation and settlement of claims.

This chapter introduces the reader to some of the basic concepts related to professional liability insurance. The purpose of liability insurance is to spread the risk of economic loss among members of a group who share common risks. For example, an obstetrician would share risk with other obstetricians. As risks increase, premiums increase to cover associated risks. The premiums are placed in a shared risk fund from which funds are drawn to cover the costs of lawsuits. Because of skyrocketing malpractice premiums, some physicians limit their practice to less costly procedures, restrict their practices by not accepting new patients, decide to close their practice, or accept a position as an employee, for example, in a hospital setting.

Medical malpractice insurance is subject to the cyclical nature of the insurance market. Problems intrinsic in malpractice insurance include the uncertainty of the U.S. legal system, inflation, damages awarded, emerging technology, and high-risk procedures.

INSURANCE POLICY

Insurance is a contract that creates legal obligations on the part of both the insured and the insurer. It is a contract in which the insurer agrees to assume certain risks of the insured for consideration or payment of a premium. Under the terms of the contract, also known as the insurance policy, the insurer promises to pay a specific amount of money if a specified event takes place. An insurance policy contains three necessary elements: (1) identification of the risk covered; (2) specific amount payable; and (3) specified occurrence.

Insurance companies are required by the laws of the different states to issue only policies that contain certain mandated provisions and to maintain certain financial reserves to guarantee policyholders that coverage is available when needed. The basic underlying concept of insurance is the spreading of risk. By writing coverage for a sufficiently large pool of individuals, the company has determined actuarially that a certain number of claims will arise within that pool, and if the premium structure has been established correctly and the prediction of claims made accurately, the company ought to be able to both meet those claims and return a profit to its shareholders.

Risk Categories

A *risk* is the possibility that a financial loss might occur, for example, as a result of a negligent act by the insured. The main function of insurance is to provide financial security for the insured against this loss by providing compensation for damages.

An insured individual may be exposed to three categories of risk: (1) property loss or damage; (2) personal injury; and, (3) liability. *Property risk* is the possibility that an insured's property may be damaged or destroyed by fire, flood, tornado, hurricane, or other catastrophe. *Personal risk* is the possibility that the insured may be injured in an accident or may become ill; the possibility of death is a personal risk covered in the typical life insurance plan. *Liability* risk is the possibility that the insured may become

legally liable to pay monetary damages to another and includes accident and professional liability insurance.

Policy Period Reporting Requirements

The period of the policy is stated in the insurance contract. Under an *occurrence policy*, the contract provides protection only for claims that occur during the time frame within which the policy is stated to be in effect. Any incident that occurs before or after the policy period would not be covered under the insuring agreement.

A *claims-made policy* provides coverage for only those claims instituted during the policy period. Notice of a claim is required during the policy period.

Tail coverage policies provide for an uninterrupted extension of an insurance policy period.

Umbrella policies cover awards over the amount provided in the basic policy coverage. The dollar amount of coverage is specified in the policy.

Policy Coverage

The insurance company and the injured party may negotiate a settlement prior to or during trial. Some states have provisions mandating that consent of the court must be obtained prior to the settlement of a negligence claim on behalf of a minor. In any event, the insurance company will pay the injured party no more than the maximum limit stated in the insurance policy. The insured professional must personally pay any damages that exceed the policy limits. For example, under a policy with a maximum coverage of $1 million for each claim and $3 million for aggregate claims (the total amount payable to all injured parties), the insured must pay any amount over $1 million on each individual claim and any amount over $3 million during a policy period.

Uninsured Claims

An insurer has no duty to defend or provide coverage for intentional torts. Contracts insuring against loss from intentional wrongs are generally void as being against public policy.

Criminal Acts: Sexual Assault

Sexual assault does not constitute rendering professional services within the coverage provisions of insurance policies. As a result, malpractice insurers are not required to indemnify the insured for sexual assault. For example, the Medical Protective Company, in *R.W. v. Schrein*,[1] a physician's professional liability insurer, sought a judgment determining that it had no duty to defend or indemnify the physician with respect to five former patients who claimed that they were sexually abused during examination and treatment. The Supreme Court of Nebraska held the physician's acts did not fall within the coverage provided in the insurance policy.

Insurance Policy Conditions

Insurance policies, as noted below, contain a number of important conditions. Failure to comply with conditions of a policy could result in nonpayment of claims against it.

- *Notice of Occurrence* [*more expensive*]—provides that the insured is notified when an injury has occurred as a result of acts covered under the contract. The insured must notify the insurance company promptly. The form of notice may be either oral or written, as specified in the policy.

- *Notice of Claim*—provides that, whenever the insured receives notice of a claim or lawsuit, prompt notice will be provided by the insured to the insurance company. The mere failure to advise in a timely manner may be in and of itself a breach of the insurance policy, entitling the insurer to decline coverage. If the insurer refuses to honor a claim because of late notice and the insured wishes to challenge such refusal, an action can be brought, asking a court to determine the reasonableness of the insurer's position.

- *Cooperation of the insured*—provides that the insured must cooperate with the insurance company by rendering any assistance necessary to reach a settlement.

- *Co-insurance*—policies provide that the insured with multiple policies covering the same event must notify each insurer and that any settlement reached, depending on the language of the various policies, may be divided equally between the various insurers.

- *Assignment*—is the protections contracted for by the insured may not be transferred to another unless the insurance company grants permission.

- *Subrogation*—is the right of a person who pays another's debt to be substituted for all rights in relation to the debt. When an insurance company makes a payment for the insured under the terms of the policy, the company becomes the beneficiary of all the rights of recovery the insured has against any other persons who also may have been negligent. For example, if several nurses were found liable for negligence arising from the same occurrence and the insurance company for one nurse pays the entire claim, the company will be entitled to the rights of that nurse and may collect a proportionate share of the claim from the other nurses.

- *Changes*—cannot be made in the policy without the written consent of the insurance company. Thus, an agent of the insurance company ordinarily cannot modify or remove any condition of the liability contract. Only the insurance company, by written authorization, may permit a condition to be altered or removed.

- *Cancellation*—clauses spell out the conditions and procedures necessary for the insured or the insurer to cancel a policy. The insured person's failure to comply with any terms of the policy can result in cancellation and possible nonpayment of a claim by the insurance company.

LIABILITY OF THE PROFESSIONAL

An individual who provides professional services to another person may be legally responsible for any harm the person suffers as a result of negligence. Many professionals protect themselves from their exposure to a legal loss by acquiring a professional liability insurance policy.

Need for Liability Insurance

NEWSPAPER CLIPPINGS: $44M Paid in Nurse Practitioner Liability Claims Over Past 5 Years: Report

According to the Nurse Practitioner 2012 Liability Update: A Three-part Approach, the average malpractice indemnity payment (judgments and settlements) for the five-year study period has increased 19 percent since the 2009 NSO/CNA nurse practitioner claims analysis, rising from $186,282 to $221,852. The average cost to defend a lawsuit also rose to $63,792.

—Claims Journal, *November 27, 2012*[2]

All healthcare professionals should carry liability insurance. Even though a hospital, for example, as an employer can be held liable for the acts of its employees under the *doctrine of respondeat superior*, employees can be financially liable to the employer for his or her own negligent acts. From a cost–benefit standpoint, the answer to the question "Do I really need insurance?" is yes. Although individual personal insurance premiums for employed professionals are relatively reasonable, this could change if employers began to seek indemnification from the wrongdoer. Malpractice insurance coverage is especially important if a caregiver is working as, for example, a volunteer at a clinic not sponsored by his or her employer; an independent contractor providing a service to a patient; or, an independent agency or registry.

The following highlights of the "Nurse Practitioner 2012 Liability Update: A Three-part Approach" illustrates the importance of having professional liability insurance:

- More than $44 million was paid in indemnity and expenses for professional liability claims on behalf of nurse practitioners during the five-year study period.
- Sixty-one percent of licensing board actions against nurse practitioners resulted in 'no action,' while 3.1 percent of licensing complaints resulted in the end of the nurse practitioner's career.
- Nearly 73 percent of survey respondents involved in professional liability claims have worked for more than 11 years, confirming findings that the longer a nurse practitioner is in practice, the risk of experiencing a claim increases.[3]

MEDICAL LIABILITY INSURANCE

Professional liability policies vary in coverage, exclusions from coverage, and interpretations a company places on the language of the contract. Insurance policy clauses generally provide for payment on behalf of the insured if an injury arises from malpractice, error, or mistake in rendering or failing to render professional services during the policy period. The most common risks covered by medical professional liability insurance include, for example, negligence and failure to obtain "informed" consent to a medical or surgical procedure.

SELF-INSURANCE

Exorbitant malpractice insurance premiums often have produced situations in which the premium cost of insurance has approached and, on occasion, reached the face amount of the policy. Because of the extremely high cost of maintaining such insurance, some institutions have sought alternatives to this conventional means of protecting against medical malpractice. One alternative is *self-insurance*. When a healthcare facility self-insures its malpractice risks, it no longer purchases a policy of malpractice insurance but instead periodically sets aside funds to cover losses that may occur due to negligent acts. An institution that self-insures generally retains the services of

a self-insurance consulting firm and actuary to determine the proper level of funding that the organization should maintain.

A self-insurance program need not involve the elimination of insurance coverage in its entirety. A healthcare organization may find it prudent to purchase excess coverage whereby the organization self-insures the first agreed on dollar amount of risk and the insurance carrier insures the balance. For example, in a typical program the organization may self-insure the first $1 million of professional liability risk per year. Because claims are often disposed of within such limitation, the cost of excess insurance is often reasonable.

Before an organization makes a decision to self-insure, not only must it determine the economic aspects of such a decision and the necessary funding levels to maintain an adequate reserve for future claims, but it must determine whether there are any legal impediments to such a program. A corporation that has obtained funding from governmental sources or has issued bonds or other obligations containing certain covenants may find itself unable to self-insure because of these prior commitments. Healthcare organizations should consult legal counsel to review appropriate and applicable documentation before making the self-insurance decision.

TRUSTEE COVERAGE

Board members should be covered by liability insurance just as physicians and other healthcare professionals. The corporation generally provides liability insurance coverage for board members. Such coverage is helpful in attracting qualified board members. Before an insurer responds to defend or pay a claim on behalf of a trustee, it must be shown that the trustee acted in good faith and within the scope of his or her responsibilities. Ordinarily, coverage would not be afforded when a trustee is accused of acting improperly in his or her relationship with the corporation, for example, failure to obtain other necessary insurance, such as fire insurance.

MANDATED MEDICAL STAFF INSURANCE COVERAGE

Physicians are often required by healthcare organizations to carry their own malpractice insurance. Physicians who fail to maintain malpractice insurance can be suspended from a hospital's medical staff. A federal district court in

Pollack v. Methodist Hospital[4] ruled that a hospital has the legal right to suspend a staff physician for failing to comply with its requirement that physicians carry medical malpractice insurance coverage. The decision resulted from a suit brought against a hospital by a physician whose staff privileges were suspended because he failed to comply with a hospital requirement that all staff physicians provide proof of malpractice coverage of at least $1 million. The court rejected the physician's charges that the requirement violated his civil rights and antitrust laws.

As held in *Wilkinson v. Madera Community Hospital*,[5] a healthcare organization can require its medical staff to show evidence of professional liability insurance. The physician in this case was refused reappointment because he failed to maintain malpractice insurance with a recognized insurance company as required by the hospital.

INVESTIGATION AND SETTLEMENT OF CLAIMS

As a first step toward settlement of a claim, the insurance carrier may have an investigator interview a claimant regarding the details of the alleged occurrence that led to an injury. After an investigation, the insurance company may agree to a settlement if liability is questionable and the risks of proceeding to trial are too great. The company's only obligation is to act reasonably and not to the detriment of the insured. Should settlement negotiations fail, an attorney may be employed by the injured party to negotiate a settlement. If the attorney fails to obtain a settlement, either the claim can be dropped or legal action commenced.

Plaintiff/s sign a general release surrendering right of action against the defendant/s when a settlement is reached. If the claimant is married, a general release also should be obtained from the spouse because there may be a cause of action due to loss of the injured spouse's services (e.g., companionship). A parent's release surrenders only a parental claim. Approval of a court may be necessary to release a child's claim. A release by a minor could possibly be repudiated by a minor upon reaching majority.

Notes

1. 263 Neb. 708, 642 N.W.2d 505 (2002).
2. http://www.claimsjournal.com/news/national/2012/11/27/218080.htm.
3. http://www.nso.com/nursing-resources/claim-studies.jsp?refID=npclaimreport2012.
4. 392 F. Supp. 393 (E.D. La. 1975).
5. 192 Cal. Rptr. 593 (Cal. Ct. App. 1983).

21
Labor Relations

Learning Objectives

The reader upon completion of this chapter will be able to:

- Explain the various federal and state labor acts.
- Discuss the rights and responsibilities of unions and management.
- Describe the purpose of an "Affirmative Action Plan."
- Describe a patient's rights during labor disputes.
- Discuss the types of discrimination that occur in the workplace.

Federal and state regulations generally pervade all areas of employer–employee relationships. The most significant piece of federal legislation dealing with labor relations is the National Labor Relations Act. Although federal laws generally take precedence over state laws, when there is a conflict between the state and the federal laws, state laws are applied when state regulations are more rigid than federal legislation. This chapter provides an overview of those laws affecting the healthcare industry.

U.S. DEPARTMENT OF LABOR

The *U.S. Department of Labor (DOL)* is a cabinet level department within the executive branch of government. The secretary of labor advises the president on labor policies and issues. The functions of the DOL are to foster, promote, and develop the welfare of wage earners, to improve working conditions, and advance opportunities

for profitable employment. The DOL administers a variety of federal labor laws guaranteeing workers' rights to safe working conditions, a minimum hourly wage and overtime pay, freedom from employment discrimination, unemployment insurance, and workers' compensation. There are various agencies within the DOL responsible for carrying out the purpose of the department (e.g., Occupational Safety and Health Administration).

REALITY CHECK: Equal Pay for Equal Work

The annual Health Systems Consulting conference was held at the New York City Hilton. During the closing session on Friday, the company's leadership sat onstage summarizing the week's training and conducting a question-and-answer period. Prior to the session, Frank, an administrator consultant, had asked his manager, "The grapevine is telling me that nurses have been placed at a higher pay rate than administrators. Is that true?" His manager replied, "You asked a direct question, so I will answer it, even though per company policy we don't generally share such information. The answer is yes. It was implemented several weeks ago. The consulting process is more and more clinical and therefore nurses are getting a higher starting salary." Frank answered, "That is true, but we still all do the same work." His manager replied, "That's the way it is," and walked away.

NATIONAL LABOR RELATIONS ACT

Congress enacted the *National Labor Relations Act (NLRA)*[1] in July 1935 to govern the labor–management relations of business firms engaged in interstate commerce. The act is generally known as the Wagner Act, after Senator Robert R. Wagner of New York. The act defines certain conduct of employers and employees as unfair labor practices and provides for hearings on complaints that such practices have occurred. The NLRA was modified by the Taft-Hartley amendments of 1947 and the Landrum-Griffin amendments of 1959.

National Labor Relations Board

The *National Labor Relations Board (NLRB)*, which enforces and administers the NLRA, has jurisdiction over labor issues pertaining to healthcare organizations. The NLRB is an agency, independent of the DOL, that is responsible for preventing and remedying unfair labor practices by employers and labor organizations or their agents. The NLRB conducts secret ballot elections among employees in appropriate collective bargaining units to determine whether they desire to be represented by a labor organization and among employees under union–shop agreements to determine whether they wish to revoke their union's authority. The general counsel of the NLRB has final authority to investigate charges of unfair labor practices, issue complaints, and prosecute such complaints before the NLRB. There are regional directors, under the direction of the general counsel, who are responsible for processing representation and addressing unfair labor practices and jurisdictional dispute cases.

Unions and Healthcare Organizations

An exemption for governmental institutions was included in the 1935 enactment of the NLRA, and charitable healthcare institutions were exempted in 1947 by the Taft-Hartley Act amendments to the NLRA. However, a July 1974 amendment to the NLRA extended coverage to employees of nonprofit healthcare organizations that previously had been exempted from its provisions. In the words of the amendment, a healthcare facility is "any hospital, convalescent hospital, health maintenance organization, health clinic, nursing home, extended care facility, or other institution devoted to the care of the sick, infirm or aged."[2]

The amendment also enacted unique, special provisions for employees of healthcare organizations who oppose unionization on legitimate religious grounds. These provisions allow a member of such an organization to make periodic contributions to one of three nonreligious charitable funds selected jointly by the labor organization and the employing institution rather than paying periodic union dues and initiation fees. If the collective bargaining agreement does not specify an acceptable fund, the employee may select a tax-exempt charity.

Many labor organizations attempt to become the recognized collective bargaining representative for employees in healthcare settings. Craft unions devote their primary organizing efforts to skilled employees, such as carpenters and electricians, and industrial unions and unions of governmental employees seek to represent large groups of unskilled or semiskilled employees. Professional and occupational associations, such as state nurses' associations, historically known for their social and academic efforts, often participate in collective bargaining for their professions. To the extent that professional organizations seek goals directly concerned with wages, hours, and other employment conditions and engage in bargaining on behalf of employees, they often perform the functions of labor unions.

Elections

The NLRA sets out the procedures by which employees may select a union as their collective bargaining representative to negotiate with healthcare organizations over employment and contract matters. A healthcare organization may choose to recognize and deal with the union without resorting to the formal NLRA procedure. If the formal process is adhered to, employees may vote on union representation in an election held under NLRB supervision.

The NLRA provides that the representative, having been selected by a majority of employees in a bargaining unit, is the exclusive bargaining agent for all employees in the unit. The scope of the bargaining unit is often the subject of dispute, for its boundaries may determine the outcome of the election, the employee representative's bargaining power, and the level of labor stability.

Unfair Labor Practices

The NLRA prohibits healthcare organizations from engaging in certain conduct classified as unfair labor practices. For example, discriminating against an employee for holding union membership is not permitted. The NLRA stipulates that the employer must bargain in good faith with representatives of the employees; failure to do so constitutes an unfair labor practice.

The NLRA places duties on labor organizations and prohibits certain employee activities that are considered to be unfair labor practices. Coercion of employees by a union constitutes an unfair labor practice; such activities as mass picketing, assaulting nonstrikers, and following groups of nonstrikers away from the immediate area of the facility plainly constitute coercion and can be prohibited by the NLRB.

Unlawful Interrogation

Ms. Welton attended a union organization meeting on July 5. At a hearing before an administrative law judge (ALJ), she testified that the day after the meeting her supervisor asked whether she or anyone from the dietary department attended the meeting. Mr. Hopkins worked as a janitor for the nursing facility. He also attended the meeting on July 5 and he testified that his supervisor questioned him as to whether any of the nurses or aides harassed him about the union.

On July 18, the facility circulated a memorandum to all employees that stated: "This is to advise that the NLRB has tentatively set a hearing on Wednesday, July 25, to decide who can vote in a union election. Our position is that supervisors, RNs, and LPNs cannot vote. We will keep you advised." On July 19, the facility held a mandatory meeting for all nurses and supervisors. The facility's administrator, Mr. Wimer; the facility's attorney, Mr. Yocum; and the chief executive officer, Mr. Colby, told the nurses that, in the facility's opinion, nurses could not vote in the upcoming election but must remain loyal to the facility.

The NLRB determined that the facility, through Yocum, violated the National Labor Relations Act by telling nurses present at the meeting that they could not vote in the upcoming union election or participate in union activities. The U.S. Court of Appeals for the Seventh Circuit found that the employer's interrogation of nursing facility employees about a union meeting constituted an unfair labor practice.[3]

Failure to Discharge Non-Dues Paying Nurses

The NLRB in *St. John's Mercy Health Systems v. National Labor Relations Board*[4] was found to have properly upheld a union's unfair labor practice charge against a hospital that had refused to discharge registered nurses who had not paid union dues, as required by the applicable collective bargaining agreement (CBA). There was no public policy of Missouri that prevented enforcement of the union-security provision of the CBA, notwithstanding statistical evidence of a regional or national nursing shortage that would make it difficult to replace nurses. In addition, the hospital was not exempt from the NLRA union-security provisions.

NORRIS-LAGUARDIA ACT

Congress enacted the *Norris-LaGuardia Act*[5] to limit the power of federal courts to issue injunctions in cases involving or growing out of labor disputes. The act's strict standards must be met before such injunctions can be issued. Essentially, a federal court may not apply restraints in a labor dispute until after the case is heard in open court and the finding is that unlawful acts will be committed unless restrained and that substantial and irreparable injury to the complainant's property will follow.[6]

The Norris-LaGuardia Act is aimed at reducing the number of injunctions granted to restrain strikes and picketing. An additional piece of legislation designating procedures limiting strikes in healthcare institutions is the 1974 amendment to the NLRA. This amendment sets out special procedures for handling labor disputes that develop from collective bargaining at the termination of an existing agreement or during negotiations for an initial contract between a healthcare institution and its employees. The procedures were designed to ensure that the needs of patients would be met during any work stoppage (strike) or labor dispute in such an institution.

More significantly, 10 days' notice is required in advance of any strike, picketing, or other concerted refusal to work, regardless of the source of the dispute. This allows the NLRB to determine the legality of a strike before it occurs and also gives healthcare institutions ample time to ensure the continuity of patient care. In summary, the amendment's provisions are designed to ensure that every possible approach to a peaceful settlement is explored fully before a strike is called.

LABOR-MANAGEMENT REPORTING AND DISCLOSURE ACT

The *Labor-Management Reporting and Disclosure Act of 1959*[7] was enacted to place controls on labor unions and the relationships between unions and their members. The act requires that employers report payments and loans made to officials or other representatives of labor organizations or any promises to make such payments or loans. Expenditures made to influence or restrict the way employees exercise their rights to organize and bargain collectively are illegal unless the employer discloses them. Agreements with labor consultants, under which such persons undertake to interfere with certain employee rights, also must be disclosed.

FAIR LABOR STANDARDS ACT

The *Fair Labor Standards Act (FLSA)*[8] of 1938 established, for example, a national minimum wage, guaranteed overtime pay, and prohibited most employment for minors. The *Wage and Hour Division* of the U.S. Department of Labor conducts audits and workplace inspections, and administers the FLSA. Employees of all governmental, charitable, and proprietary healthcare organizations are covered by the FLSA. Employers must conform to minimum wage and overtime pay provisions. However, bona fide executive, administrative, and professional employees are exempted from the wage and hour provisions.

The law permits employers to enter into agreements with employees, establishing a work period of 14 consecutive days as an alternative to the usual 7-day work week. If the alternative period is chosen, the employer must pay the overtime rate only for hours worked in excess of 80 hours during the 14-day period. The alternative 14-day work period does not relieve a facility from paying overtime for hours worked in excess of 8 hours in any one day even if no more than 80 hours are worked during the period.

CIVIL RIGHTS ACT

Title VII of the Civil Rights Act of 1964, as amended by the *Equal Employment Opportunity Act of 1972*,[9] prohibits private employers and state and local governments from discrimination in employment in any business on the basis of race, color, religion, sex, or national origin. The act prohibits harassment based on one's affiliation (e.g., religion), physical and cultural traits and clothing (e.g., headscarf), perception (e.g., due to national origin), and association (e.g., discrimination based on association with an individual or organization). The federal antidiscrimination law provides that it is unlawful for most public and private employers to discriminate against, fail or refuse to hire, or to discharge any individual, with respect to his or her compensation, terms, conditions, or privileges of employment because of such individual's race, color, religion, sex, pregnancy status, or national origin.

Title VII also prohibits retaliation against employees who oppose such unlawful discrimination. The *Equal Employment Opportunity Commission* (EEOC) enforces Title VII. The EEOC investigates, mediates, and sometimes files lawsuits on behalf of employees. Title VII also provides that an individual can bring a private lawsuit.

An exception to prohibited employment practices may be permitted when religion, sex, or national origin is a bona fide occupational qualification necessary to the operation of a particular business or enterprise.

OCCUPATIONAL SAFETY AND HEALTH ACT

Congress enacted the *Occupational Safety and Health Act of 1970 (OSHA)*[10] to establish administrative machinery for the development and enforcement of standards for occupational health and safety. The legislation was enacted based on congressional findings that personal injuries and illnesses arising out of work situations impose a substantial burden on and are substantial hindrances to interstate commerce in terms of lost production, wage loss, medical expenses, and disability compensation payments. Congress declared that its purpose and policy were to ensure, so far as possible, every working man and woman in the nation safe and healthful working conditions and to preserve human resources by, for example, encouraging employers and employees in their efforts to reduce the number of occupational safety and health hazards at their places of employment, and stimulating employers and employees to institute new and to perfect existing programs for providing safe and healthful working conditions.[11]

Promulgation and Enforcement of OSHA Standards

OSHA develops and promulgates occupational safety and health standards for the workplace. It develops and issues regulations, conducts investigations and inspections to determine the status of compliance, and issues citations and proposes penalties for noncompliance. Inspections are conducted without advance notice.

Employers are responsible for becoming familiar with standards applicable to their businesses and for ensuring that employees have and use personal protective equipment when required for safety. Employees must comply with all rules and regulations that are applicable to their work environment. Where OSHA has not promulgated specific standards, the employer is responsible for following the act's general-duty clause. The *general-duty clause* states that each employer must furnish a place of employment that is free from recognized hazards that are causing or likely to cause death or serious physical harm.

Recordkeeping

Employers of 11 or more employees are required to maintain records of occupational injuries and illnesses. The purpose of maintaining records is to permit the Bureau of Labor Statistics to help define high-hazard industries and to inform employees of the status of their employer's record.

Education

Employers are responsible for keeping employees informed about OSHA and about the various safety and health matters with which they are involved. OSHA requires that employers post certain material at a prominent location in the workplace (e.g., a job safety and health protection workplace poster informing employees of their rights and responsibilities under the act).

Infectious Body Fluids

OSHA issued standards on December 2, 1991, that are to be followed by employers to protect employees from blood-borne infections. Universal precautions are mandatory, and employees who are likely to be exposed to body fluids must be provided with protective clothing (e.g., masks, gowns, and gloves). In addition, post exposure testing must be available to employees who have been exposed to body fluids.

Employee Complaints

Employees should inform their supervisors if they suspect or detect a dangerous situation in the workplace. Employers are expected to address reported hazards in the workplace. Employees or their representatives have the right to file complaints with an OSHA office and request a survey when they believe that conditions in the workplace are unsafe or unhealthy. If a violation of the act is found at the time of a survey, the employer may receive a citation stating a time frame within which the violation must be corrected.

State Regulation

The states have statutes charging employers with the duty to furnish employees with a safe working environment. The city and county in which a healthcare facility is located also may prescribe rules regarding the health and safety of employees. Many communities have enacted sanitary and health codes that require certain standards.

Legal Liability

From a liability point of view, an employer can be held legally liable for damages suffered by employees through exposure to dangerous conditions that are in violation of OSHA standards. Proof of an employee's exposure to noncompliant conditions is generally necessary to find an employer liable.

REHABILITATION ACT

The essential purpose of the *Rehabilitation Act of 1973*[12] provides protection to handicapped people from discrimination. The law basically is administered by the Department of Health and Human Services (DHHS), which derives its jurisdiction from the fact that healthcare organizations participate in such federal programs as Medicare and Medicaid. The law therefore is applied to both public and private organizations because both participate in these programs.

Since July 1977, all institutions receiving federal financial assistance from DHHS have been required to file assurances of compliance forms. Each employer must designate an individual to coordinate compliance efforts. A grievance procedure should be in place to address employee complaints alleging violation of the regulation. All employment decisions must be made without regard to physical or mental handicaps that are not disqualifying (e.g., an employer is not obligated to employ a person with a highly contagious disease that can be easily transmitted to others).

Jobs should not be purposely designed to eliminate the hiring of disabled persons. Employers, however, are not required to change the essential elements of a job to create a position for a disabled person. The Iowa Supreme Court, in *Schlitzer v. U of I Hosp. and Clinics*,[13] decided that an employer is not required to create a vacancy or a job for a disabled person. The court found that a nurse's 20-pound lifting restriction, due to a car accident, limited her ability to lift, thus making the demands of her job incompatible with her physical disability. The law does not require that an employer change the essential elements of a job to meet a claimant's disability. In this case, the job required that the nurse be able to work with severely disabled persons. The 20-pound limitation, in this case, was an impossible hurdle to overcome.

FAMILY AND MEDICAL LEAVE ACT

The *Family and Medical Leave Act of 1993 (FMLA)* was enacted to grant temporary medical leave to employees under certain circumstances. The act provides that covered employers must grant an eligible employee up to a total of 12 workweeks of unpaid leave during any 12-month period for one or more of the following reasons: the birth and care of an employee's child; placement of an adopted or foster child with the employee; for the care of an immediate family member (spouse, child, or parent) with a serious health condition; or inability to work because of a serious health condition. It is illegal to terminate health insurance coverage for an employee on FMLA leave. Following an FMLA leave, the employee's job—or an equivalent job with equivalent pay, benefits, and other terms and conditions of employment—must be restored.

STATE LABOR LAWS

The federal labor enactments serve as a pattern for many state labor laws that comprise the second labor regulation system touching healthcare organizations. State labor acts vary from state to state. Therefore, it is important that each institution familiarize itself not only with federal regulations but also with state regulations affecting labor relations within the institution.

Because the NLRA excludes from coverage healthcare organizations operated by the state or its political subdivisions, regulation of labor–management relations in these organizations is left to state law. Unless the constitution in such a state guarantees the right of employees to organize and imposes the duty of collective bargaining on the employer, healthcare organizations do not have to bargain collectively with their employees. However, in states that do have labor relations acts, the obligation of an organization to bargain collectively with its employees is determined by applicable statute. State laws vary considerably in their coverage, and often employees of state and local governmental organizations are covered by separate public employee legislation. Some states have labor relations acts granting employees the right to organize, join unions, and bargain collectively. Strikes and lockouts generally require compulsory arbitration whenever a collective bargaining contract cannot otherwise be executed amicably.

Union Security Contracts and Right-to-Work Laws

Labor organizations frequently seek to enter union–security contracts with employers. Such contracts are of two types: (1) the *closed-shop contract*, which provides that only members of a particular union may be hired, and (2) the *union-shop contract*, which makes continued employment dependent on membership in the union, although the employee need not have been a union member when applying for the job.

Various states have made such contracts unlawful. Statutes forbidding such agreements generally are called right-to-work laws on the theory that they protect everyone's right to work even if a person refuses to join a union. Several state statutes and court decisions purport to restrict union–security contracts or specify procedures to be completed before such agreements may be made.

Wage and Hour Laws

State and federal labor minimum wages can vary. When state minimum wage standards are higher than federal standards, the state's standards are applicable.

Child Labor Acts

Many states prohibit the employment of minors younger than a specified age and restrict the employment of other minors. Child labor legislation commonly requires that working papers be secured before a child may be hired, forbids the employment of minors at night, and prohibits minors from operating certain types of dangerous machinery.

Workers' Compensation

Workers' compensation is a program by which an employee can receive certain wage benefits because of work-related injuries. An employee who is injured while performing job-related duties is generally eligible for workers' compensation. Workers' compensation programs are administered by the states.

State legislatures have recognized that it is difficult and expensive for employees to recover from their employers and therefore have enacted workers' compensation laws. Employers are required to provide workers' compensation as a benefit. Workers' compensation laws give the employee a legal way to receive compensation for injuries on the job. The acts do not require the employee to prove that the injury was the result of the employer's negligence. Workers' compensation laws are based on the employer–employee relationship and not on the theory of negligence.

Job Stress

Workers' compensation has been awarded for depression related to job stress. In *Elwood v. SAIF*,[14] a registered nurse filed a workers' compensation claim for an occupational disease based on depression. The referee and the workers' compensation board affirmed the insurer's denial of the claim, and the claimant sought judicial review. Questions that needed to be answered to determine job stress included:

- What were the "real" events and conditions of plaintiff's employment?
- Were the real stressful events and conditions the major contributing cause of plaintiff's mental disorder?

The record established that many events and conditions of her employment, including her termination, were real and capable of producing stress when viewed objectively. The claimant's treating physician advised her that she was suffering from anxiety, depression, and stress and advised her to seek a psychiatric evaluation. The court held that the claimant established that her condition was compensable.

LABOR RIGHTS

Rights and responsibilities run concurrently. Employee rights include the following:

- The right to organize and bargain collectively
- The right to solicit and distribute union information during nonworking hours (i.e., mealtimes and coffee breaks)
- The right to picket (Picketing is the act of patrolling, by one or more persons, a place related to a labor dispute. It varies in purpose and form. It may be conducted by employees or nonemployees, and like strikes, some picketing may be legislatively or judicially disapproved and subject to regulation.)
- The right to strike (A strike may be defined as the collective quitting of work by employees as a means of inducing the employer to assent to employee demands. Employees possess the right to strike, although this right is not absolute and is subject to limited exercise. The 1974 amendments to the NLRA have added requirements with respect to strikes and picketing in an attempt to reduce the interruption of healthcare services. The NLRB is urged to give top priority to settling labor–management disputes resulting in the loss of healthcare personnel or medical services.)

Employees granted these rights have the concomitant responsibility to perform their work duties properly. A nursing home housekeeper, for example, was terminated properly after repeated oral and written reprimands concerning her improper cleaning of rooms in *Ford v. Patin*.[15] Her substandard performance, despite repeated warnings, evidenced willful and wanton disregard of her employer's interest and constituted misconduct within purview of Section 23:1601(2) of the Louisiana Revised Statutes Annotated.

MANAGEMENT RIGHTS

As with labor, management also has certain rights and responsibilities. Specific management rights are reviewed here.

Receive Strike Notice

Management has a right to a 10-day advance notice of a bargaining unit's intent to strike.

Hire Replacement Workers

Although management may not discharge employees in retaliation for union activity, concomitant with the employees' right to strike is management's right to hire replacement workers in the event of a strike. The nursing home in *Charlesgate Nursing Center v. State of Rhode Island*[16] brought an action against the state, seeking a determination that a state statute prohibiting strike-affected employers from using the services of a third party to recruit replacement workers during a strike was unconstitutional. Employees of the nursing home went on strike on June 2, 1988, and Charlesgate hired temporary replacement workers to provide continued services for its patients. The temporary employees were hired through employment agencies. The actions of Charlesgate and the agencies violated Sections 28-10-10 and 28-10-12 of the General Laws of Rhode Island (1956) (1986 Reenactment), which read:

> 28-10-10. Recruitment prohibited—It shall be unlawful for any person, partnership, agency, firm or corporation, or officer or agent thereof, to knowingly recruit, procure, supply or refer any person who offers him or herself for employment in the place of an employee involved in a labor strike or lockout in which such person, partnership, agency, firm, or corporation is not directly interested.
>
> 28-10-12. Agency for procurement—It shall be unlawful for any person, partnership, firm or corporation, or officer or agent thereof, involved in a labor strike or lockout to contract or arrange with any other person, partnership, agency, firm or corporation to recruit, procure, supply, or refer persons who offer themselves

for employment in the place of employees involved in a labor strike or lockout for employment in place of employees involved in such labor strike or lockout.

Citing these statutes, the labor unions involved in the strike notified nursing pools throughout the state that it was unlawful to provide Charlesgate with replacement workers. At the same time, the unions urged the city of Providence and the Rhode Island attorney general to prosecute Charlesgate, at which time Charlesgate filed its suit claiming that the Rhode Island statutes were unconstitutional. Although the strike was settled, the federal district court held that the statute was unconstitutional because it prohibited activity that Congress had intended to leave open to strike-affected employers as a peaceful weapon of economic self-help.

Restrict Union Activity to Prescribed Areas

Management has the right to reasonably restrict union organizers to certain locations in the healthcare facility and to certain time periods to avoid interference with facility operations.

Prohibit Union Activity During Working Hours

Management has the right to prohibit union activities during employee working hours.

Prohibit Supervisors from Participating in Union Activity

Management has the right to prohibit supervisors from engaging in union organizational activity. Congress excluded supervisors from participating in union activity to assure management the loyalty of its supervisory personnel by making sure that no employer would have to retain as its agent one who is obligated to a union. The certification of 17 RNs as an employee-bargaining unit in *NLRB v. American Medical Services*[17] was shown to be improper because there was substantial evidence that had been presented to the court showing that the nurses exercised substantial supervisory powers, including the authority to issue work assignments and discipline employees. The Taft-Hartley Act as applied in this case illustrates the importance of balancing the rights of both employees and employers.

> Taft-Hartley applied some brakes, so that the balance of power between companies and unions would not shift wholly to the union side. The exclusion of supervisors is one of the brakes. If supervisors were free to join or form unions and enjoy the broad protection

of the Act for concerted activity, see Sec. 7, 29 U.S.C. Sec. 157, the impact of a strike would be greatly amplified because the company would not be able to use its supervisory personnel to replace strikers. More important, the company with or without a strike could lose control of its work force to the unions because the very people in the company who controlled hiring, discipline, assignments, and other dimensions of the employment relationship might be subject to control by the same union as the employees they were supposed to be controlling on the employer's behalf.[18]

PATIENT RIGHTS DURING LABOR DISPUTES

Patient rights take precedence over employee and management rights during labor disputes when a patient's right to privacy or wellbeing is in jeopardy. Both the union and management must work together in good faith to assure the health and safety of patients.

AFFIRMATIVE ACTION PLAN

An affirmative action plan refers to equal opportunity employment measures that federal contractors and subcontractors are legally required to adopt. These measures are intended to prevent discrimination against employees or applicants for employment. Healthcare organizations are required to comply with all applicable DHHS regulations "including but not limited to those pertaining to nondiscrimination on the basis of race, color, or national origin (45 C.F.R. part 80), nondiscrimination on the basis of handicap (45 C.F.R. part 84), nondiscrimination on the basis of age (45 C.F.R. part 91), protection of human subjects of research (45 C.F.R. part 46), and fraud and abuse (42 C.F.R. part 455). Although these regulations are not in themselves considered requirements under this part, their violation may result in the termination or suspension of or the refusal to grant or continue payment with federal funds."[19] To comply with the spirit of these regulations and Executive Order 11246, healthcare organizations should have an equal employment opportunity or affirmative action plan in place.

The purpose of an affirmative action is to redress the disadvantages associated with discrimination. An affirmative action plan includes such things as the collection and analysis of data on the race and sex of all applicants for employment, as well as a statement in the personnel policy/procedure manuals and employee handbooks that would read, for example, "Health Care Facility, Inc., is an equal opportunity/affirmative action employer and does not discriminate on the basis of race, color, religion, sex, national origin, age, handicap, or veteran status."

INJUNCTIONS

An injunction is an order by a court directing that a certain act be performed or not performed. Persons who fail to comply with court orders are said to be in contempt of court. The earliest use of injunctions in labor relations was by employers to stop strikes or picketing by employees. Today, the general rule limits the availability of injunctive relief to halt work stoppages. The federal government and many states have enacted anti-injunction acts. These acts restrict the power of the courts to limit injunctions in labor disputes by setting strictly defined standards that must be met before injunctions can be granted to restrain activities such as strikes and picketing.

ADMINISTERING A COLLECTIVE BARGAINING AGREEMENT

When a collective bargaining agreement has been negotiated in good faith, it should be administered with care and good faith as well. Supervisors are responsible for administering the agreement at the grassroots level. They should familiarize themselves with the provisions of the agreement. Educational programs should be provided by the organization. Special emphasis should be placed on the use of corrective discipline, as provided under the contract, and on how to respond to grievances. The organization's management, through its human relations department, maintains the ultimate responsibility in the facility for the fair and effective administration of its union contract(s).

Maintaining propitious records of all grievances, grievance meetings, and grievance resolutions is the responsibility of supervisors and management. Regardless of whether a grievance is meritorious and settled by management or whether it is spurious and therefore denied, clear and complete records should be maintained. The ability to document resolutions of particular problems, as well as management's approach to grievances is especially important if arbitration is required to settle a grievance.

Arbitration procedures are set in motion when the union files a demand for arbitration either with the employer or with the arbitration agency named in the contract. The arbitration hearing is a relatively informal proceeding at which labor and management frequently choose to be represented by counsel. The arbitrator's decision is binding on both parties.

The arbitrator's decision can be upset by showing any of the following: the arbitrator has clearly exceeded his or her authority under the collective bargaining agreement; the decision is the product of fraud or duress; the arbitrator has been guilty of impropriety; and/or, the award violates the law or requires a violation of the law.

DISCRIMINATION IN THE WORKPLACE

Discrimination in the workplace comes in many forms and in numerous ways, and each has its own little twist of facts: You are either too old or too young for the job; you are either overqualified or under-qualified. There are laws prohibiting discrimination against any individual because of his or her race, color, religion, sex, or national origin, or to classify or refer for employment any individual on the basis of his or her race, color, religion, sex, or national origin. Unfortunately, prohibition and practice do not always match up. A variety of cases are presented in this section that describe but a few of the various forms of discrimination prohibited by law.

Age Discrimination

The *Age Discrimination in Employment Act of 1967 (ADEA)*[20] prohibits age-based employment discrimination against persons 40 years of age or older. The purpose of this law is to promote employment of older persons on the basis of their ability without regard to their age. The law prohibits arbitrary age discrimination in hiring, discharge, pay, term, conditions, or privileges of employment. The ADEA covers private employers with 20 or more employees, state and local governments, employment agencies, and most labor unions. The Age Discrimination and Claims Assistance Amendment of 1990 extends the suit filing period for ADEA charges that meet certain criteria. There are strict time frames in which charges of age discrimination must be filed.

According to the U.S. Supreme Court, in *Texas Department of Community Affairs v. Burdine,* a prima facie case of age discrimination requires that evidence sufficient to support a finding for the complainant must establish all of the following:

- The complainant is in a protected age group.
- The complainant is qualified for his or her job.
- The complainant was discharged.
- The discharge occurred in circumstances that give rise to the inference of age discrimination.[21]

Disability

The *Americans with Disabilities Act of 1990 (ADA)* was enacted by Congress to prohibit employers from discriminating against job applicants and employees on the basis of disability.[22] It applies to employers with 15 or more employees working for 20 or more weeks during a calendar year. The ADA protects employees who are qualified individuals with disabilities capable of performing the essential functions of the job in question with or without reasonable accommodation, from discrimination by the employer.

Census data, national polls, and other studies have documented that people with disabilities, as a group, occupy an inferior status in society. The nation's proper goals regarding individuals with disabilities are to ensure equality of opportunity, full participation, independent living, and economic self-sufficiency for such individuals.

The ADA prohibits job discrimination in hiring, promotion, or other provisions of employment against qualified individuals with disabilities by private employers, state and local governments, employment agencies, and labor unions. On July 26, 1991, the EEOC issued final regulations implementing Title I of the ADA. The purpose of the ADA is to:

- Provide a clear and comprehensive national mandate for the elimination of discrimination against individuals with disabilities.
- Provide clear, strong, consistent, enforceable standards addressing discrimination against individuals with disabilities.
- Ensure that the federal government plays a central role in enforcing the standards established in the act on behalf of individuals with disabilities.
- Invoke the sweep of congressional authority, including the power to enforce the 14th Amendment and to regulate commerce to address the main areas of discrimination faced day to day by people with disabilities.[23]

The general rule of discrimination under Title I of the act provides that "no covered entity shall discriminate against a qualified individual with a disability because of the disability of such individual in regard to job application procedures, the hiring, advancement, or discharge of employees, employee compensation, job training, and other terms, conditions, and privileges of employment."[24]

Disability Requires Reasonable Accommodation

The appellee Alley in *Alley v. Charleston Area Med. Ctr., Inc.*[25] worked for CAMC for over 17 years and suffered from epilepsy and asthma, with the asthma becoming increasingly aggravated by on-the-job exposure to certain chemicals. Alley requested a 12-week family medical leave of absence, which the hospital approved, with the agreement that the leave could be taken intermittently as needed.

Alley's physician wrote a letter explaining her physical conditions and requested that Alley be allowed to work in an outpatient setting and not be exposed to people with multiple infections. Although Alley presented her request for accommodation to various CAMC supervisory personnel and to employee health services at the hospital, she was told that no accommodation would be made. The employee health services physician, Dr. Ranadive, met with Alley for 5 minutes. He did not perform any tests. Ranadive called the physician who had written the request and summarily concluded that there was no medical reason why Alley could not continue her employment and that CAMC would not accommodate her.

Alley was eventually terminated, and she filed suit against CAMC in the circuit court alleging that she had been subjected to retaliatory discharge based on physical and mental impairment. Alley claimed that CAMC refused to make reasonable accommodations for her known impairments and that this was a violation of the West Virginia Human Rights Act, and CAMC, with knowledge of Alley's asthma, exposed her to substances that exacerbated her condition.

The jury returned a verdict in favor of Alley, awarding $325,000 in damages. On appeal, the court determined that the evidence was sufficient for a jury to find that Alley was a qualified person with a disability and that CAMC was aware of her disability and that a reasonable accommodation could have been made.

National Origin

The *Immigration Reform and Control Act of 1986, 1990, and 1996 (IRCA)* prohibits most employers from discriminating against employees or applicants because of national origin or U.S. citizenship status, with respect to hiring, referral, or discharge. The act establishes penalties for employers who knowingly hire illegal aliens. Determining the legality of the employee's status is the employer's responsibility.

Pay Discrimination

The Equal Pay Act (1963)[26] is an amendment to the Fair Labor Standards Act that prohibits any discrimination in the payment of wages for men and women performing substantially equal work under similar conditions. The EPA is applicable everywhere that the minimum wage law is applicable and is enforced by the EEOC. The EPA, simply stated, requires that employees who perform equal work receive equal pay. There are situations in which wages may be unequal as long as they are based on factors other than sex, such as in the case of a formalized seniority system or a system that objectively measures earnings by the quantity or quality of production.

Pregnancy Discrimination

The *Pregnancy Discrimination Act* is an amendment to Title VII of the Civil Rights Act of 1964. Discrimination on the basis of pregnancy, childbirth, or related medical conditions constitutes unlawful sex discrimination under Title VII. Women affected by pregnancy or related conditions must be treated in the same manner as other applicants or employees with similar abilities or limitations by, for example, providing modified tasks, alternative assignments, disability leave, or leave without pay.

Race Discrimination

Discharge of an employee on the basis of racial bias is actionable under state and federal laws. Title VII of the Civil Rights Act of 1964 "requires the elimination of artificial, arbitrary, and unnecessary barriers to employment that operate invidiously to discriminate on the basis of race."[27] An at-will employee's claim of racially motivated retaliatory discharge for filing a discrimination complaint can be actionable in tort as a violation of public policy.

In *Buckley Nursing Home v. Massachusetts Commission against Discrimination*,[28] Young, a black applicant for a nurse's aide position, filed a complaint alleging racial discrimination. Young responded to a newspaper advertisement for a nurse's aide position, filed her application, and was interviewed by the acting supervisor of nursing. The applicant called to inquire about the position on several occasions and eventually was told that the position had been filled. The advertisement ran again in the newspaper, and the applicant again called in response to the advertisement. Young was told that her application was on file and that she would be called as needed. The facility had hired four full-time and one-part-time nurse's aides for the evening shifts between March 1, 1974, and July 1, 1974.

On the upper right hand corner of Young's application, there is a handwritten notation "no openings," even though during the relevant time periods there were openings and other persons were hired for the evening shift. That notation does not appear on any other application, and none of Buckley's witnesses could identify who wrote it or when it appeared.

Despite testimony to the contrary, the commission found that Buckley had entered discussion about Young's race and had decided not to hire her on that basis. The commission thus concluded that Buckley's reason for not hiring Young (that she was not the best qualified applicant for the job) was a pretext and that she would have been hired but for her race.

The commission awarded Young $6,986 plus interest for lost wages and $2,000 for emotional distress. Besides the monetary award to Young, the nursing facility had been instructed by the commission to develop a minority recruitment program. On appeal by the facility, the trial court upheld the commission's decision. On further appeal, the appeals court held that the evidence was sufficient to support a reasonable inference that the nursing facility's rejection of the applicant occurred after consideration of her race.

Religious Discrimination

Discrimination based on religion is valuing a person or group lower because of their religion, or treating someone differently because of what they do or do not believe. While many religious and secular authorities tend to stress that religion is something personal, the highly social nature of most religions makes conflicts between religious groups, and thus discrimination, still very probable. Reasonable accommodations should be made for an employee's religious beliefs.

Sex Discrimination

In *Jones v. Hinds General Hospital*,[29] a prima facie case of sex discrimination was established by evidence showing that a hospital terminated female nursing assistants while retaining male orderlies who performed the necessary functions. The court, however, held that Title VII of the Civil Rights Act was not violated by the hospital's use of gender as a basis for terminating employees. Gender was a bona fide occupational qualification for orderlies because a substantial number of male patients objected to the performance of catheterizations and surgical preparation by female assistants.

Sexual Harassment

Section 703 of Title VII and the EEOC defines sexual harassment in employment as unwelcome sexual advances, requests for sexual favors, and other verbal or physical conduct of a sexual nature when this conduct explicitly or implicitly affects an individual's employment; unreasonably interferes with an individual's work performance; or creates an intimidating, hostile, or offensive work environment.

Sexual conduct becomes unlawful only when it is unwelcome by the victim. The victim must not have solicited or invited the actions and must have considered the conduct undesirable or offensive. To determine if the victim may have solicited or encouraged the claimed sexual harassment, a court may assess the victim's sexual aggressiveness or consistent use of sexually oriented language in the work environment. Of course, indications of an employee's sexually aggressive nature will not necessarily negate a claim of sexual harassment, just as voluntary participation in sexual conduct by the victim will not necessarily negate the claim. An employee may participate in sexual conduct for fear of repercussions, thus each claim must be examined individually to determine whether the particular conduct complained of was unwelcome.

Unwelcome sexual conduct becomes harassment when it creates a working environment that is unreasonably intimidating or offensive. A reasonable person must find the work environment offensive, and the complaining employee must have perceived the conduct as offensive.

When sexual conduct is determined to be unwelcome, the court must evaluate its level of interference with the employee's job, and whether the harassment created a hostile work environment. The court will consider the type of harassment (verbal, physical, or both), as well as the frequency of the harassment. A hostile work environment usually requires a pattern of conduct that has a repetitive effect. An isolated incident of physical advance is more likely to constitute a hostile environment (such as unwanted touching of the intimate body parts) than would a single case of verbal advance. In the same respect, sexual flirtation or vulgar language will not often constitute a hostile work environment as readily as would pervasive and continuous proliferation of pornography and demeaning comments.

An employer may be held liable for harassment inflicted by a supervisor, which results in a tangible employment action, or a significant change in the victim's employment status. Such tangible employment action may fall under categories such as: hiring, firing, promotion, demotion, undesirable reassignment, decision causing a significant change in benefits, compensation decisions, and work assignment. The victim of sexual harassment as well as the harasser may be a man or woman. The harasser can be the victim's supervisor, an agent of the employer, a supervisor in another area, a coworker, or a nonemployee. The victim does not have to be the person harassed but could be anyone affected by the offensive conduct. Unlawful sexual harassment may occur without economic injury.

An employee who claims harassment based upon a hostile work environment must demonstrate that the conduct complained of was sufficiently severe and/or pervasive to alter the conditions of employment and create a work environment

that would qualify as hostile or abusive to employees because of their sex. An employer, however, will not always be held liable for sexual harassment that occurs in the workplace if the employer can prove: (1) it had in place an anti-harassment policy with an effective complaint procedure; (2) it promptly took action to prevent and correct any harassment; and (3) that the employee unreasonably failed to avoid further harm by complaining to management. If a nonsupervisor commits harassment, the lower courts have held that the employer will only be liable if it knew or should have known about the conduct and failed to take appropriate corrective action.

Notes

1. 29 U.S.C. § 151.
2. NLRA § 2 (14) (1974).
3. *NLRB v. Shelby Mem'l Hosp. Ass'n*, 1 F.3d 550 (7th Cir. 1993).
4. 436 F.3d 843 (C.A. 8, Mo. 2006).
5. *Norris-LaGuardia Act*, 29 U.S.C. ch. 6 (1932).
6. *United States v. Hutcheson*, 312 U.S. 219 (1941).
7. *Labor-Management Reporting and Disclosure Act of 1959*, Pub. L. No. 86-257 (29 U.S.C. ch. 11).
8. *Fair Labor Standards Act of 1938*, 29 U.S.C. ch. 8.
9. *Equal Employment Opportunity Act of 1972*, 42 U.S.C. § 2000e et seq.
10. *Occupational Safety and Health Act of 1970*, 29 U.S.C. § 651.
11. PUB. L. NO. 91-596, § 2, 84 Stat. 1590 (Dec. 29, 1970); see also 29 U.S.C.A. § 651 (1990).
12. *Rehabilitation Act of 1973*, 29 U.S.C. ch. 14.
13. 641 N.W.2d 525 (Iowa 2002).
14. 676 P.2d 922 (Or. Ct. App. 1984).
15. 534 So. 2d 1003 (La. Ct. App. 1988).
16. 723 F. Supp. 859 (D.R.I. 1989).
17. 705 F.2d 1472, 1474–75 (7th Cir. 1983).
18. *NLRB v. Res-Care, Inc.*, 705 F.2d 1461, 1465 (7th Cir. 1983).
19. 42 C.F.R. § 483.75 (1989).
20. *Age Discrimination in Employment Act of 1967*, 29 U.S.C. ch. 14, as amended.
21. 450 U.S. 248, 253 (1981).
22. *Americans with Disabilities Act of 1990*, PUB. L. NO. 101-336, 104 Stat. 327 (July 26, 1990).
23. *Id.* at 329.
24. *Id.* at 331–332.
25. No. 31591 (W.Va. 2004).
26. *Equal Pay Act of 1963*, 29 U.S.C. ch. 8.
27. *Griggs v. Duke Power Co.*, 401 U.S. 424 (1971).
28. 478 N.E.2d 1292 (Mass. App. Ct. 1985).
29. 666 F. Supp. 933 (D. Miss. 1987).

22
Employment at Will and Discharge

Learning Objectives

The reader upon completion of this chapter will be able to:

- Discuss the "Employment at Will" doctrine.
- Explain public policies that protect employees from unlawful discharge.
- Describe what is meant by retaliatory discharge and how to defend a claim for unfair discharge.
- Describe under what circumstances employers often discharge an employee.
- Describe effective hiring practices and the importance of clear communications.

Fairly balancing the rights of the employee and the needs of the organization is an extremely complex objective. This chapter provides some understanding of this balancing act. For the healthcare worker, an unexpected termination may mean a significant setback in career progression, financial hardship, and loss of self-esteem. For the organization and its community, a termination can foster ill will and lead to possible disruption and realignment of services. A growing consensus is that high turnover rates are unhealthy and provide a disservice to an industry plagued with financial and staffing hardships. The high cost of human errors and greed that lead to so many patient injuries and deaths often result in negative news coverage, thus exacerbating the poor image many have of the healthcare industry.

Wrongful discharge claims are difficult, time consuming, and expensive lawsuits to defend. Employers who experience favorable court decisions in wrongful discharge claims often have unfavorable repercussions because of bad press and the negative effects a discharge can have on employee morale.

Leadership is responsible for leading, and that includes accepting responsibility for missing the mark as noted in the following reality check.

REALITY CHECK: Leadership Skills Affects Image

Nathan, the hospital's CEO, recently returning from a golf outing, attended an exit conference conducted by a group of auditors in the hospital's boardroom. The auditors had been hired by the governing body to review the quality of care being delivered at the hospital. Nathan was unhappy with the report because it contained a list of items that needed to be addressed to improve the quality of patient care. Nathan, as he listened to the report which was not harsh but more insightful and helpful in nature, stood up at the conference table, hesitated for a moment, and said, "This is not just about the hospital. This is about my job!" Nathan, somewhat angry, turned and proceeded to leave the conference room. His leadership staff, appearing confused, rose and followed him out of the conference room, without looking back—no good-byes, just stone-cold faces.

Upon board members learning about Nathan's response to the auditors, they realized Nathan was disengaged and not supportive of their desire to continue to improve the quality of care provided at the hospital. Nathan's personal career objectives and his responsibility to the hospital and community were not in harmony.

Discussion

1. Describe how the CEO's conduct could affect his staff.
2. Discuss what disciplinary action, if any, should be taken.

EMPLOYMENT AT WILL

An at will prerogative without limits could be suffered only in an anarchy, and there not for long; it certainly cannot be suffered in a society such as ours without weakening the bond of counter balancing rights and obligations that holds such societies together.

—*SIDES V. DUKE HOSPITAL*[1]

The common-law *employment-at-will* doctrine provides that employment is at the will of the employer or the employee; where the employer or employee may terminate employment at any time for any or no reason, unless there is a contract in place that specifies the terms and duration of employment. Historically, termination of employees for any reason was widely accepted. However, contemporary thinking does not support this concept.

In recent years the rule that employment for an indefinite term is terminable by the employer whenever and for whatever cause he chooses without incurring liability has been the subject of considerable scholarly debate and judicial and legislative modification. Consequently, there has been a growing trend toward a restricted application of the at-will employment rule whereby the right of an employer to discharge an at-will employee without cause is limited by either public policy considerations or an implied covenant of good faith and fair dealing.[2]

In *Sides v. Duke Hospital*, the North Carolina Court of Appeals found it to be an

obvious and indisputable fact that in a civilized state where reciprocal legal rights and duties abound, the words "at will" can never mean "without limit or qualification," as so much of the discussion and the briefs of the defendants imply; for in such a state the rights of each person are necessarily and inherently limited by the rights of others and the interests of the public.

• • •

If we are to have law, those who so act against the public interest must be held accountable for the harm inflicted thereby; to accord them civil immunity would incongruously reward their lawlessness at the unjust expense of their innocent victims.[3]

The concept of the employment-at-will doctrine is embroiled in a combination of legislative enactments and judicial decisions. Some states have a tendency to be more employer oriented, such as New York, whereas others, such as California, emerge as being much more forward thinking and in harmony with the constitutional rights of the employee.

The employment-at-will common law doctrine is not truly applicable in today's society, and many courts have recognized this fact. In the last century, the common law developed in a laissez-faire climate that encouraged industrial growth and improved the right of an employer to control his own business, including the right to fire without cause an employee at will. . . . The twentieth century has witnessed significant changes in socioeconomic values that have led to reassessment of the common law rule. Businesses have evolved from small- and medium-size firms to gigantic corporations in which ownership is separate from management. Formerly there was a clear delineation between employers, who frequently were owners of their own businesses, and employees. The employer in the old sense has been replaced by a superior in the corporate hierarchy who is himself an employee.[4]

As discussed here, exceptions to the employment-at-will doctrine involve contractual relationships, public policy issues, defamation, retaliatory discharge, and fairness. It would seem that the doctrine has diminished applicability in modern society.

PUBLIC POLICY ISSUES

 NEWSPAPER CLIPPINGS: Ex-'Price is Right' Model Gets $8.5M in Damages

LOS ANGELES (AP)—The producers of "The Price is Right" owe a former model on the show more than $7.7 million in punitive damages for discriminating against her after a pregnancy, a jury determined Wednesday.

The judgment came one day after the panel determined the game show's producers discriminated against Brandi Cochran. They awarded her nearly $777,000 in actual damages.

• • •

FremantleMedia said it was standing by its previous statement, which said it expected to be "fully vindicated" after an appeal.

—*Anthony McCartney*, Associated Press, *November 21, 2012*

The public policy exception to the employment-at-will doctrine provides that employees may not be terminated for reasons that are contrary to public policy. Public policy originates with legislative enactments that prohibit, for example, the discharge of employees on the basis of disability, age, race, color, religion, sex, national origin, pregnancy, union membership, and/or filing of safety violation with various governmental agencies. Any attempt to limit, segregate, or classify employees in any way that would tend to deprive any individual of employment opportunities on these bases is contrary to public policy.

Public policy also can arise as a result of judicial decisions that address those issues not covered by statutes, rules, and regulations. "[I]t can be said that public policy concerns what is right and just and what affects the citizens of the state collectively. It is to be found in the state's constitution and statutes and, when they are silent, in its judicial decisions."[5]

In those instances in which state and federal laws are silent, not all courts concur with the use of judicial decisions as a means for determining public policy. A California court determined that a public policy exception to the at-will employment doctrine must be based on constitutional or statutory provisions rather than judicial policy making.[6]

Reporting Patient Abuse

An employer may not discharge an employee for fulfilling societal obligations or in those instances in which the employer acts with a socially undesirable motive.[7] A tort claim for wrongful discharge was stated in *McQuary v. Air Convalescent Home*[8] by allegations that the plaintiff was discharged wrongfully from her position at the nursing facility in retaliation for threatening to report to state authorities instances of alleged patient mistreatment. Such mistreatment purportedly involved violation of a patient's rights under the Nursing Home Patient's Bill of Rights. To prevail, the discharged employee was not required to prove that patient abuse actually had occurred but only that she acted in good faith.

> This conclusion is consistent with established Oregon law. Statutes which protect employees against retaliation do not require that the alleged violation which the employee claims be ultimately proved. See, e.g., ORS 652.355 (protects an employee who merely consults an attorney or agency about a wage claim); ORS 654.062(5) (protects any employee who makes a complaint under the Oregon Safe Employment Act); ORS 659.030(1)(f) (prohibits discrimination against an employee who filed a civil rights complaint); ORS 633.120(3) (prohibits discrimination against an employee for filing an unfair labor practices complaint). We have, in fact, upheld awards for retaliation despite holding that the original complaint did not show discrimination.

• • •

> Similar considerations of public policy lead to our conclusion that an employee who reports a violation of a nursing home patient's statutory rights in good faith should be protected from discharge for that action.[9]

This case, which had been dismissed in the lower court, was reversed and remanded for trial.

Whistleblowing

According to the public policy exception, an employer may not rely on the at-will doctrine as a basis for escaping liability for discharging an employee because of the doing of, or the refusing to do, such an act. Moreover, statutes in several jurisdictions protect an employee from an employer's retaliation for engaging in certain types of protected activities, such as whistleblowing.[10]

A *whistleblower* is a person who reports corruption, management, criminal and unethical business practices in the workplace to appropriate government authorities. A whistleblower reveals wrongdoing in the organization to a public entity or someone in authority. This often occurs when one believes that the public interest overrides the interest of the organization and can involve illegal or fraudulent activities. A whistleblower provides information he or she reasonably believes evidences violation of any law, rule, or regulation; gross mismanagement; a gross waste of funds; an abuse of authority; a substantial and specific danger to public health; and/or a substantial and specific danger to public safety.[11]

The False Claims Act of 1863 was enacted to prevent scams against the federal government in response to frauds that were costing the U.S. Treasury millions of dollars. Under the 1986 amendments to the False Claims Act, financial rewards to whistleblowers were expanded (see, 31 U.S.C.A. § 3729). The purpose of the False Claims Act is to discourage fraud against the federal government in areas such as billing for: services not rendered; unnecessary procedures, such as knowingly placing cardiac stents into patients; and billing for homecare visits that never took place.

The SmithKline Beecham Settlement as in 1998 was reported by the Department of Justice to be the largest healthcare settlement that involved whistleblowers.

> In this settlement . . . three whistleblowers will share $52 million for their part in tipping off the government in the Medicare fraud investigation of SmithKline Beecham Clinical Laboratories. In its settlement with the government, SmithKline Beecham agreed to pay more than $325 million to resolve allegations of billing fraud initially brought by the lab's former billing supervisor in a qui tam action.[12]

Cases such as this serve as a reminder to healthcare practitioners and organizations that reporting of criminal activity within one's medical practice or healthcare organization will reap rewards for the whistleblower. Thus, encouraging the reporting of illegal activity.

Paving Her Way to Heaven

The nurse–plaintiff in this case was employed as a charge nurse with supervisory duties. A short time after one of her patients had been admitted to the hospital, the charge nurse determined the patient was suffering from toxic shock syndrome. Knowing that death would result if left untreated, the charge nurse assumed that the physician would order antibiotics. After a period of time passed without having received such orders, the charge nurse discussed the patient's condition with the nursing director. The charge nurse was told by the nursing director to document, report the facts, and stay out of the matter.

The charge nurse decided to discuss the patient's condition and lack of orders with the chief of staff. Although the chief of staff took appropriate steps to treat the patient, the patient died. A member of the patient's family informed the nursing director that the charge nurse offered to obtain the medical records and was later told that the charge nurse was heard to say that the physician was paving the patient's way to heaven. As a result, the charge nurse was terminated.

The trial court entered a summary judgment for the defendant–hospital, stating that there were no triable issues of fact, and there was no public policy exception to the charge nurse's at-will termination. The court could not find any law or regulation prohibiting the hospital from discharging her as a nurse.

The Missouri Court of Appeals reversed the decision and remanded the case for trial, holding that the Nursing Practice Act (NPA) provided a clear mandate of public policy that nurses had a duty to provide the best possible care to patients. Therefore, if the plaintiff refused to follow her supervisor's orders to stay out of a case where the patient was dying from a lack of proper medical treatment, there would be no grounds for her discharge under the public policy exception to the employment-at-will doctrine. Her persistence in attempting to get the proper treatment for the patient was her absolute duty. The hospital could not lawfully require the nurse to stay out of a case that would have obvious injurious consequences to the patient.[13] The hospital here violated both the rights and responsibilities of the nurse.

RETALIATORY DISCHARGE

There is a tendency for some people in positions of power to abuse that power through threats, abuse, intimidation, and retaliatory discharge, all of which are cause for legal action. Employees who become the targets of a vindictive supervisor often have difficulty proving a bad-faith motive. In an effort to reduce the probability of wrongful discharge, some states have enacted legislation that protects employees from terminations found to be arbitrary and capricious.

The burden of proof for establishing some hidden motive for discharge from employment rests on discharged employees.

> The National Labor Relations Act and other labor legislation illustrate the governmental policy of preventing employers from using the right of discharge as a means of oppression. . . . Consistent with this policy, many states have recognized the need to protect employees who are not parties to a collective bargaining agreement or other contract from abusive practices by the employer. . . . Those states have recognized

a common law cause of action for employees-at-will who were discharged for reasons that were in some way "wrongful." The courts in those jurisdictions have taken various approaches: some recognizing the action in tort, some in contract.[14]

The court in *Khanna v. Microdata Corp.*[15] held that substantial evidence supported a finding that the employer fired the employee in bad-faith retaliation for bringing a lawsuit against the employer, thus violating an implied covenant of good faith and fair dealing.

Under the traditional common-law rule, codified in section 2922 of the [California] Labor Code, an employment contract of indefinite duration is in general terminable at the will of either party. During the past several decades, however, judicial authorities in California and throughout the United States have established the rule that, under both common law and the statute, an employer does not enjoy an absolute or totally unfettered right to discharge even an at-will employee.[16]

FAIRNESS: THE ULTIMATE TEST

"Is it fair?" is the ultimate question that a supervisor must ask when considering a termination. In general, bad-faith and inexplicable terminations are subject to the scrutiny of the courts. Some courts and legislative enactments have overturned the view that employers have total discretion to terminate workers who are not otherwise protected by collective bargaining agreements or civil service regulations. Montana legislation grants every employee the right to sue the employer for wrongful discharge. The mere fact that an employment contract is terminable at will does not give the employer an absolute right to terminate it in all cases.

There is an implied covenant of good faith and fair dealing in every contract that neither party will do anything that will injure the right of the other to receive benefits from the agreement. An employee in *Pugh v. See's Candies*[17] was found to have shown a prima facie case of wrongful termination in violation of an implied promise that the employer would not act arbitrarily in dealing with the employee. The employer's right to terminate an employee is not absolute. It is limited by fundamental principles of public policy and by expressed or implied terms of agreement between the employer and the employee.

Procedural issues are as important as issues of discrimination. In *Renny v. Port Huron Hospital*,[18] the Michigan Supreme Court found, as did the jury, that the employee's discharge hearing was not final and binding because it did not comport with elementary fairness. The Court found that there was sufficient evidence for the jury to find that the employee had not been discharged for just cause. The existence of a just-cause contract is a question of fact for the jury when the employer establishes written policies and procedures and does not expressly retain the right to terminate an employee at will. That the hospital followed the grievance procedure with the plaintiff is evidence that a just-cause contract existed on which the plaintiff relied.

The employee handbook provided for a grievance board as a fair way to resolve work-related complaints and problems. This was not a mandatory procedure to which the hospital's employees had to submit. The employee was not bound by the grievance board's determination that her discharge was proper because evidence supported a finding that she was not given adequate notice of who the witnesses against her would be. In addition, she was not permitted to be present when witness's testified, and she was not given the right to present certain evidence.

There was sufficient evidence for the jury to conclude that the plaintiff had suffered damages. Evidence presented indicated that her subsequent professional employment did not equal her earnings before discharge and that she experienced increased expenses because of the loss of her health insurance as well as other financial losses that she suffered as a result of her discharge.

Defending a Claim of Unfair Discharge

An employee who believes that he or she has been unfairly discharged will most likely seek access to the following information in defense of his or her claim: minutes of pertinent meetings; written reports, typed or handwritten; personnel file; tapes; letters, cards, and handwritten notes written on the employee's behalf from the public; personnel handbook; personnel and departmental policies and procedures books; and, oral testimony from fellow employees and supervisors.

Employers must document carefully and fairly any disciplinary proceedings that might be subject to discovery by a disgruntled employee; failure to do so could place the organization or supervisor at a disadvantage should a complaint reach the courts.

TERMINATION

A decision to terminate an employee should be reviewed carefully by a member of management who is familiar with the issues of wrongful discharge. Oral counseling, written counseling, written counseling with suspension, and written counseling with termination are the textbook responses to disciplinary action and discharge. Whatever form of discipline is used, it should be designed to produce a more effective and productive employee.

The employer's right to terminate an employee is not absolute. It is limited by fundamental principles of public policy and by express or implied terms of agreement between the employer and the employee.

> Formulating a standard for substantive fairness in employee dismissal law requires accommodating a number of different interests already afforded legal recognition. The legal interest of employees to be protected against certain types of unfair and injurious action . . . are at the core of any employee dismissal proposal. Arrayed against these interests are employer and societal interests in effective management of organizations, which require that employees not be shielded from the consequences of their poor performance or misconduct and that supervisors not be deterred from exercising their managerial responsibilities by the inconvenience of litigating employees' claims.[19]

Before termination of an employee, the employer should ask: was the termination: a violation of public policy; a violation of any policy or procedure outlined in an administrative manual, the employee handbook, the human resource department's policies and procedures, or any other health care facility policies and procedures or regulations; retaliatory in nature (e.g., refusal to perform an illegal act or a questioning of a management practice); arbitrary and capricious; discriminatory on the basis of age, disability, race, creed, color, religion, gender, national origin, or marital status; a violation of any contract, oral or written; consistent with the reasons for discharge; discriminatory against the employee for filing a lawsuit; fixed before any appeal actions can be taken; and/or, an interference with an employee's rights as secured by the laws or Constitution of the United States (e.g., right to freedom of speech).

Employment Disclaimers

A *disclaimer* is the denial of a right that is imputed to a person or that is alleged to belong to him or her. Although a disclaimer is often a successful defense for employers in wrongful discharge cases, it should not be considered a license to discharge at will and at the whim of the supervisor in an arbitrary and capricious manner.

Employers can help prevent successful lawsuits for wrongful discharge that are based on the premise that an employee handbook or departmental policy and procedure manual is an implied contract by incorporating disclaimers in published manuals, such as that described in *Battaglia v. Sisters of Charity Hospital*,[20] in which a personnel manual could not be interpreted to limit the hospital's power to terminate an at-will employee. Language in the manual indicated that the personnel manual was not a contract; that it could be modified, amended, or supplemented; and that the hospital retained the right to make all necessary management decisions for the delivery of patient care services and the selection, direction, compensation, and retention of employees.

Handbooks that do not contain disclaimers can alter an employee's at-will status. An appeals court in *Trusty v. Big Sandy Health Care Center*[21] noted that the handbook did not contain any disclaimer or any other language that employment was at will. The court held that there was sufficient evidence to establish that the handbook had altered the employee's at-will status and determined that the employee could bring a wrongful discharge suit.

The employer's disclaimers were considered to be clear in *Simonson v. Meader Distribution Co.*,[22] in which an employee filed a breach of contract suit alleging that a dismissal was outside company-adopted disciplinary guidelines. The court held that the company could and did reserve the discretion to discipline employees outside adopted guidelines. The policy manual contained the following three specific reservations of management discretion: (1) management reserves the right to make any changes at any time by adding to, deleting, or changing any existing policy; (2) the rules set out below are as complete as we can reasonably make them, however, they are not necessarily all-inclusive because circumstances that we have not anticipated may arise; and (3) management may vary from the above policies if, in its opinion, the circumstances require it.[23]

Healthcare organizations can be successful when confronted with wrongful discharge suits based on breach of contract by placing similar language in their personnel manuals.

Termination for Cause

A termination-for-cause-only clause in an employment contract is binding. The employment contract in *Eales v. Tanana*[24] provided an employee hired up to retirement age could be terminated only for cause and was upheld by the court.

Termination and Financial Necessity

No breach of employment contract occurred in *Wilde v. Houlton Regional Hospital*[25] when, because of financial difficulties, a hospital terminated the employment of two nurses, a ward clerk, and a dietary supervisor. Even if the employees were correct in contending that their indefinite contracts of employment had been modified by virtue of a dismissal for cause provision in the employee's handbook and by management's oral assurances that they were permanent, full-time employees whose jobs were secure so long as they performed satisfactorily, the employees' discharge for financial or other legitimate business reasons did not offend the employment contracts as thus modified. A private employer had an essential business prerogative to adjust its workforce as market forces and business necessity required, and the layoffs in question violated no compelling public policy.

Hostile Attitude

The chief X-ray technician in *Paros v. Hoemako Hospital*[26] was dismissed because of a chronic argumentative and hostile attitude inconsistent with the performance of supervisory duties. The trial court entered a summary judgment in favor of the hospital and the administrator. On appeal, the appeals court held that the discharge was properly based on good cause and precluded recovery for breach of contract and wrongful discharge.

Poor Work Performance

In *Yerry v. Ulster County*,[27] a nurse's aide had been terminated from a county infirmary for misconduct. Among other things, she failed to report, in a timely manner, bumping and injuring a resident's leg, failed to feed a resident properly as ordered by the resident's physician, and, on another occasion, fed a resident food that burned the resident's mouth. The court held that eyewitness testimony and believable hearsay were sufficient to sustain the findings of the hearings officer who recommended her termination. The court found that the penalty imposed was not disproportionate to the offenses of the nurse's aide.[28]

The plaintiff in *Silinzy v. Visiting Nurse Association*[29] brought an action claiming racial discrimination and retaliatory discharge. The court granted a motion for summary judgment by the defendant–employer. The district court held that the plaintiff failed to establish a prima facie case of racial discrimination and retaliatory discharge. The plaintiff's poor job performance was the reason for her discharge. The defendant was found to have produced ample evidence that the plaintiff was not performing her job adequately. Numerous complaints regarding her negative attitude and poor job performance, from a variety of sources, were documented.

Alcoholism

Discharge of an employee because of alcoholism is not necessarily a discriminatory practice. The hospital's discharge of a staff physician for alcoholism in *Soentgen v. Quain & Ramstad Clinic*[30] was found not to be a discriminatory practice. The physician had been discharged on a bona fide occupational qualification reasonably necessary for a physician.

Insubordinate Behavior

Substantial evidence supported a finding that the claimant's employment as a certified nurse's aide in a residential healthcare facility was terminated due to misconduct where the record indicated that the nurse's aide had been terminated after she refused to attend a meeting to discuss her job performance. She did this despite the request of her supervisor, who had warned her that she would be discharged if she did not attend the meeting. Although the nurse's aide asserted that her refusal was because she was upset and feared she might say something prompting her termination, her insubordinate conduct in failing to comply with her employer's reasonable request constituted disqualifying misconduct.[31]

▌ CONSTRUCTIVE DISCHARGE

The term *constructive discharge* describes a work environment where an employee is pushed to quit a job because the employer has made working conditions intolerable. For example, an employee: is discriminated against based on race creed, color or disability; is sexually harassed; and/or has a negative change in job responsibilities, pay, and benefits for reasons not associated with the employee's performance. Employers who make workers' jobs so unbearable that they would rather resign than to agonize over continuing abuse cannot be tolerated in a free society. Although employers can disapprove of an employees' job performance and deny benefits for reasons that are business related, improper disciplinary actions can lead to a complaint for constructive discharge. An employee may be successful in a constructive discharge lawsuit even though the employee does not sever employment, where an employer intentionally allowed such an intolerable workplace situation to exist that the employee ends up on permanent unpaid medical leave.

In a constructive discharge action, an employee must prove: (1) working conditions were constructively made intolerable and were directly aimed at the employee by the employer; (2) there was a continuous pattern of employer misconduct; and (3) conditions were so egregious and intolerable that any reasonable person would or did resign.

Damages for constructive discharge can be awarded for: wages the employee would have been paid; wages while the employee searches for a comparable job; legal fees; compensatory damages for pain and suffering or mental distress; and punitive damages.

Sexual Harassment and Constructive Discharge

Rivera, the plaintiff in *Rivera Maldonado v. Hospital Alejandro Otero Lopez*, filed a lawsuit for *constructive discharge* alleging her supervisor subjected her to sexual harassment. According to Rivera, the defendant offered her unsolicited gifts, made unsolicited comments about her physical appearance, stalked her, touched her, intimidated her, and requested sexual favors. The plaintiff also alleged to the extent she rejected the defendant's advances that he threatened her with unjust disciplinary actions including suspension without pay. Rivera claims that she began to suffer both physically and emotionally as a result of the defendant's sexual harassment. Puerto Rico's Law 80 defines constructive discharge as follows:

> . . . the resignation of the employee caused by the actions of the employer directed to induce or compel him to resign, such as imposing or trying to impose on him more onerous working conditions, reducing his salary, lowering his category or submitting him to derogatory criticisms or humiliations by deed or word.
> —P.R. LAWS ANN., TIT. 29 § 185E.

The basic elements for a constructive discharge claim [under Law No. 80] are: (1) considerably serious actions by the employer that create an intimidating, hostile, and offensive work environment; and (2) for the employee to have no other available alternative but to resign.[32]

The United District Court found that issues of fact remain as to whether or not Rivera was informed that the defendant had been terminated following the investigation of her complaint. Accordingly, the court is unable to make the necessary inferences to determine whether or not, judging from Rivera's state of mind, she was unable to return to work because her working conditions were going to continue to be so intolerable that the only reasonable alternative for her was to not return to work. The defendant's motion for summary judgment on the Law No. 80 claim was, therefore, denied.[33]

EFFECTIVE HIRING PRACTICES

NEWSPAPER CLIPPINGS: Job Applicants Not Always Screened

Despite the danger of hiring an employee who might jeopardize assisted living residents, some facilities neglect background screening of new workers.

More than 1 in 10 facilities inspected by state regulators in seven states during a two-year period within 2000–2002 picked up at least one citation for neglecting background checks on prospective caregivers . . .

—*Kevin McCoy,* USA Today, *May 26, 2004*

The best way to prevent negligent hiring is to become familiar with the risks and avoid hiring workers who are likely to become problematic employees. The organization should:

- Develop clear policies and procedures on hiring, disciplining, and terminating employees.
- Include appropriate language in the organization's policies and procedures reserving the right to add, delete, and/or revise the same.
- Develop an application that realistically determines an applicant's qualifications before hiring.
- Take appropriate precautions to prevent the hiring of those who might be a hazard to others.
- Review each applicant's background and past work behavior.
- Become familiar with any state laws that might be applicable when hiring an individual with a past criminal record.
- Develop an effective interview system for screening applicants. (The interviews should be conducted first by an appropriately trained member of the human resources department and then by the supervisor of the service to which the applicant is applying.)
- Solicit references with the applicant's permission using a release form, and follow up with a telephone call for further information.
- Provide an employee handbook and present a job description to each new employee. (Signed documentation should be maintained in the employee's personnel folder indicating that the employee received, read, and understood the employee handbook and job description.)

- Develop constructive performance evaluations that reinforce good behavior, and provide instruction in those areas needing improvement. (The performance evaluation should include a written statement regarding the employee's performance.)
- Develop a progressive disciplinary action policy.
- Provide in-service education programs for supervisors on such subjects as interviewing techniques, evaluations, and discipline. (Various colleges, universities, and consultants provide in-service education programs for employers.)
- Be mindful of the importance of developing appropriate employment contract language.

CLEAR COMMUNICATIONS

Employers must communicate clearly to prospective employees that their employment is at will and can be terminated at any time by either the employer or the employee. During the course of employment, handbooks and personnel manuals must provide fair and unambiguous standards for employee discipline and termination.

Notes

1. 328 S.E.2d 818 (N.C. Ct. App. 1985).
2. 44 A.L.R. 4th 1136 (1986).
3. Supra Note 1.
4. *Pierce v. Ortho Pharm. Corp.*, 417 A.2d 505, 509 (N.J. 1980).
5. *Palmateer v. International Harvester Co.*, 421 N.E.2d 876, 878 (Ill. 1981).
6. *Gantt v. Sentry Ins.*, 824 P.2d 680, 687–688 (Cal. 1992).
7. *Delaney v. Taco Time Int'l*, 681 P.2d 114 (Or. 1984). This case involved an employer found liable by the Oregon Supreme Court for the wrongful discharge of an at-will employee who was discharged for fulfilling a societal obligation because he refused to sign a false and arguably tortious statement that cast aspersions on the work habits and moral behavior of a former employee.
8. 684 P.2d 21 (Or. Ct. App. 1984).
9. *Id.* at 24.
10. Annotation, 99 A.L.R. Fed. 775.
11. U.S. Office of Special Counsel, "Whistleblowing," http://www.osc.gov/documents/pubs/post_wb.htm.
12. http://www.medicalpracticecme.com/qui_tam_actions .htm.
13. *Kirk v. Mercy Hosp. Tri-County*, 851 S.W.2d 617 (Mo. Ct. App. 1993).
14. *Pierce v. Ortho Pharm. Corp.*, 417 A.2d 505, 509 (N.J. 1980).
15. 215 Cal. Rptr. 860 (Cal. Ct. App. 1985).
16. *Id.* at 865.
17. 171 Cal. Rptr. 917 (Cal. Ct. App. 1981).
18. 398 N.W.2d 327 (Mich. 1986).
19. H. H. Perritt, "Employee Dismissal," *Law and Practice* 354 (1984).
20. 508 N.Y.S.2d 802 (N.Y. App. Div. 1986).
21. No. 89-CA-2272-MR (Ky. Ct. App. Mar. 22, 1991).
22. 413 N.W.2d 146 (Minn. Ct. App. 1987).
23. *Id.* at 147.
24. 663 P.2d 958 (Alaska 1983).
25. 537 A.2d 1137 (Me. 1987).
26. 681 P.2d 918 (Ariz. Ct. App. 1984).
27. 512 N.Y.S.2d 592 (N.Y. App. Div. 1987).
28. *Id.* at 593.
29. 777 F. Supp. 1484 (E.D. Mo. 1991).
30. 467 N.W.2d 73 (N.D. 1991).
31. *Daniul v. Commissioner of Labor*, 807 N.Y.S.2d 477 (N.Y. App. Div. 2006).
32. *Rivera Maldonado v. Hospital Alejandro Otero Lopez*, 614 F. Supp. 2d 181 (Dist. Court, D. Puerto, 2009).
33. *Id.*

Man never fastened one end of a chain around the neck of his brother that God did not fasten the other end round the neck of the oppressor.

—LAMARTINE (1790–1869)

23
Employee Rights and Responsibilities

Learning Objectives

The reader upon completion of this chapter will be able to:

- Describe and understand the rights of employees.
- Describe and understand the responsibilities of employees.
- Explain what professionals can do to improve professional relationships between one another, as well as between caregivers and patients.

This chapter presents an overview of the rights and responsibilities of employees in the healthcare setting, many of which are expressed in both federal and state laws. Healthcare organizations are not exempt from the impact of these laws and are required to take into account employment practices, such as, wages, hours, working conditions, union activity, workers' compensation laws, occupational safety and health laws, and employment discrimination laws. As this chapter reveals, fairly balancing the rights and responsibilities of the employee and employer is not always an easy task.

EMPLOYEE RIGHTS

Employment-at-will does not abrogate employee rights. Employees have faced discrimination involving age, race, creed, color, gender, wages, benefits, wrongful termination, as well as a host of other common labor issues. A variety of federal and state laws protect employee rights to be treated fairly in the workplace. The following listing describes but a few of the rights of employees in the workplace.

Equal Pay for Equal Work

The *Equal Pay Act* (EPA) of 1963 prohibits gender discrimination in the payment of wages for women and men performing substantially equal work in the same establishment and requires that employees who perform equal work receive equal pay. There are situations in which wages may be unequal as long as they are based on factors other than gender, such as in the case of a formalized seniority system or a system that objectively measures earnings by the quantity or quality of production.

Refuse to Participate in Patient Care

Caregivers have a right to refuse to participate in certain aspects of patient care and treatment. This can occur when there is conflict with one's cultural, ethical, and/or religious beliefs, such as the administration of blood or blood products, participation in elective abortions, and end-of-life issues such as disconnecting a respirator. In the attempt to honor staff rights, a patient's health must not be compromised. Questionable requests not to participate in certain aspects of a patient's care should be referred to an organization's ethics committee for review and consultative advice.

Refusal to Participate in Care vs. Patient Rights

Caregivers have a right to refuse to participate in abortions and can abstain from involvement in abortions as a matter of conscience, religious beliefs, or moral conviction. In a Missouri case, *Doe v. Poelker*,[1] the city was ordered to obtain the services of physicians and personnel who had no moral objections to participating in abortions. The city also was required to pay the plaintiff's attorneys' fees because of the wanton disregard of the indigent woman's rights and the continuation of a policy to disregard and/or circumvent the U.S. Supreme Court's rulings on abortion.

Refusal to Participate in Care vs. Patient Rights

In the attempt to honor staff rights, a patient's health must not be compromised. The New York Supreme Court, Appellate Division in *Larson v. Albany Medical Center*[2] held that although a nurse has the right to refuse to participate in an elective termination of pregnancy on grounds of freedom from religious discrimination in employment, the case at issue did not involve an elective procedure. The mother was in need of emergency care and the nurses were asked by their nursing supervisor to assist in an "emergency" evacuation of a dead fetus. The nurses launched an argument about elective abortions and the court ruled their action as insubordinate behavior.

Pharmacists Refusal to Fill Prescriptions

Some pharmacists' religious beliefs prohibit abortion or the use of birth control. They believe that dispensing such medications to others is an infringement on their freedom of religion. There are others who believe that pharmacists have an obligation to fill all prescriptions, and that refusing to fill them violates the patients' freedom of conscience. The First Amendment protects individual free exercise of religion. The question here, "Does requiring pharmacists to fill prescriptions conflict with religious beliefs and violate their rights under the First Amendment?" Some say yes, because people whose religious beliefs prohibit birth control or abortion cannot freely exercise their religion if they are forced to dispense these medications. Others say no, because the patients' need to obtain their medication outweighs the pharmacists' rights.[3]

> Some states have subsequently proposed legislation and passed laws designed to allow doctors and other direct providers of health care to refuse to perform or assist in an abortion, and hospitals to refuse to allow abortion on their premises. Now, the issue is expanding as pharmacists are refusing to fill emergency contraception and contraception prescriptions.[4]

As each state often has different rulings on this issue, the reader should review applicable state statutes.

Question Physician Care

A caregiver has the right to question the care being rendered to a patient by another caregiver if there is reason to believe that the care is likely to be detrimental to the well-being of the patient. If, for example, a caregiver believes

that a particular order appears to be questionable, the caregiver has the responsibility to seek verification from the prescribing physician. If the prescribing physician believes the order to be correct and the caregiver still questions the order, the concern must be relayed to the employee's supervisor for verification and further follow-up if necessary.

Suggest Changing Physicians

There are circumstances in which a caregiver may have a right to suggest that a patient change to a different more responsive physician. In one case, a patient began losing weight and having hallucinations. A nurse documented the patient's difficulties and attempted on several occasions to call the patient's physician. The physician failed to return the nurse's calls. Because of the patient's deteriorating condition, the family contacted the nurse. After the nurse advised the patient's family about her concerns, a member of the patient's family asked her what they should do. The nurse advised that she would reconsider their "choice of physicians." The nurse was terminated because she had advised the patient's family to consider changing physicians.

The nurse brought a lawsuit for wrongful discharge in violation of public policy. The language in the Nursing Practice Act of North Carolina and regulations of the Board of Nursing describe the practice of nursing as assessing a patient's health, which entails a responsibility to communicate, counsel, and provide accurate guidance to clients and their families. The nurse's comments that resulted in her termination were made in fulfillment of these responsibilities.

The North Carolina Court of Appeals held that the nurse stated a claim for wrongful discharge in violation of public policy. The nurse's termination for fulfilling her responsibilities as a nurse violated public policy and was a factual question for jury determination. There can be no right to terminate employment for an unlawful reason or purpose that contravenes public policy.[5]

Freedom from Sexual Harassment

Employees and staff have a right to be free from sexual harassment. Sexual harassment can be verbal or physical, and it includes a request for a sexual favor, sexual advances made as a condition of employment and unreasonably interfering with an employee's work performance, and creating an intimidating or offensive work environment. In 1980, the EEOC issued landmark sexual harassment guidelines that prohibit unwelcome sexual advances or requests that are made as a condition of employment. The U.S. Supreme Court held that a hostile work environment refers not only to conduct that is psychologically injurious, but also to conduct that is perceived as abusive.

Treated with Respect and Dignity

 One's dignity may be assaulted, vandalized, and cruelly mocked, but it cannot be taken away unless it is surrendered.

—Author Unknown

Each employee has the right to be treated with dignity and respect in a fair and consistent manner by their employer. Employers have a responsibility to address employee complaints, and concerns regarding their rights and entitlements. Furthermore, employers should respond promptly to employees' questions, especially when they are working in geographic areas distant from corporate offices.

REALITY CHECK: Call for Additional Help—No Response

Three consultants were assigned by their employer, International Consulting (IC) to review the quality of care being delivered at Newtown Medical Center. Newtown was larger and more complex than the consultants were expecting. In addition, it was located in a different state than IC's headquarters. On the first day of the consulting assignment, the consultants called the IC corporate office to discuss the need for additional help. The manager responsible for addressing field requests did not respond. Despite the lack of a follow-up call from the corporate manager, the team covered the assigned task. Newtown's leadership expressed their appreciation to the consultants for a job well done.

Discussion

1. IC policy required a team of nine, and three reviewed the quality of care being delivered. Describe what actions could be taken to improve scheduling.
2. Discuss the training opportunities for corporate managers responsible for providing support for field consultants.

Privacy and Confidentiality

Employees have a right to privacy and confidentiality, such as information that the employer may become aware of as

to an employee's health status. Modern technology enables employers to monitor their employees' activities through their computer site visits, electronic e-mails, voicemail, and video monitoring (video monitoring is not permissible in bathrooms and locker rooms). Such monitoring is generally unregulated, and unless an organization's policy specifically states otherwise, the employer may listen, watch, and read an employee's workplace communications. Such information must be used wisely and discreetly without malice.

Whistleblowing

NEWSPAPER CLIPPINGS: The Price Whistle-Blowers Pay for Secrets

"It's a life-changing experience," said John R. Phillips, founder of the law firm Phillips & Cohen and the man credited with devising the amendments that strengthened the government antifraud law, the False Claims Act, in 1986. "If you look at the field of whistle-blowers, you see a high degree of bankruptcies. You may find yourself unemployable. Home foreclosures, divorce, suicide and depression all go with this territory."

—*Paul Sullivan*, The New York Times, *September 21, 2012*

NEWSPAPER CLIPPINGS: Physician Whistle-Blowers Can Sue Hospitals Without Delay, Appeals Court Rules

Judges say a law enables California doctors to take immediate legal action against health centers suspected of retaliation.

A 2007 amendment to California's whistle-blower protection law allows physicians lodging complaints about hospitals to sue the facilities for retaliating against them without the doctors first having to exhaust lengthy administrative remedies, a federal appeals court has ruled.

The ruling encourages more doctors to speak up about patient care concerns in health facilities, said Long X. Do, legal counsel for the California Medical Assn. The CMA wrote a friend-of-the-court brief in support of the doctor who is the plaintiff in the case.

—*Alicia Gallegos*, American Medical News, *September 3, 2012*[6]

NEWSPAPER CLIPPINGS: Whistleblower Lawsuit Alleges Florida Hospital Filed Millions in False Claims

A whistle-blower lawsuit based on insider information from a former Florida Hospital Orlando billing employee and a staff physician alleges that seven Adventist Health hospitals in Central Florida have overbilled the federal government for tens of millions of dollars in false or padded medical claims.

The suit claims Florida Hospital used improper coding for more than a decade to overbill Medicare, Medicaid and Tricare, all federal government payers. In addition, it alleges, the hospital commonly overbilled for a drug used, for example, in MRI scans and billed for computer analyses that were never performed.

—*Marni Jameson,* Orlando Sentinel, *August 8, 2012*

NEWSPAPER CLIPPINGS: Lawsuit Claims Poor Care at Catholic Charities' Clinics in MD, District

The whistleblower lawsuit, filed Thursday in D.C. Superior Court, identifies the plaintiff, Charles Briggs, as the sole staff doctor at the clinic from March 2008 until October 1, 2010, when he was fired.

Briggs, 66, says in the suit that he was fired in retaliation for raising concerns about patient care with supervisors who did little to address them. . . .

For those patients, "Catholic Charities was the place they trusted to go for quality health care," said Alexis Ronickher, a lawyer with Katz, Marshall & Banks, which is representing Briggs. ". . . Instead of addressing the problems, Catholic Charities took the all too common approach of shooting the messenger."

—*Lena H. Sun,* The Washington Post, *April 7, 2011*

Employees have both a right and responsibility to report unethical conduct. Whistleblowing has been defined as an act of someone "who, believing that the public interest overrides the interest of the organization he serves, publicly blows the whistle if the organization is involved in corrupt, illegal, fraudulent, or harmful activity."[7]

Given the concern of the public about ethical behavior in government, the strong policy statement of the legislature in enacting the whistle-blower statute and the explicit inclusion of the state within its reach,

the Whistleblower Act operates as an implied waiver of the statutory immunity provision of Minn. Stat. A4 3.736. A decision to shield potential government wrongdoing, as urged by the state, would exacerbate public cynicism about the ethics of public officials, and this we do not choose to do.[8]

Healthcare organizations often describe their whistleblower policy in their compliance manuals. Compliance officers are responsible for providing information to employees regarding the organization's compliance program. The policies provide reporting procedures that ensure anonymity for employees through, for example, the use of phone hotlines answered by third parties not affiliated with the organization. Organizations must not retaliate against employees for disclosing activities that he or she reasonably believes is in violation of public policy, such as, fraudulent billing practices. OSHA's Whistleblower Protection program, for example,

enforces the whistleblower provisions of more than twenty whistleblower statutes protecting employees who report violations of various workplace safety, airline, commercial motor carrier, consumer product, environmental, financial reform, food safety, health insurance reform, motor vehicle safety, nuclear, pipeline, public transportation agency, railroad, maritime, and securities laws. Rights afforded by these whistleblower acts include, but are not limited to, worker participation in safety and health activities, reporting a work related injury, illness or fatality, or reporting a violation of the statutes.[9]

Freedom from Intimidation

NEWSPAPER CLIPPINGS: Hospitals Crack Down On Tirades By Angry Doctors

At a critical point in a complex abdominal operation, a surgeon was handed a device that didn't work because it had been loaded incorrectly . . . the surgeon slammed it down, accidentally breaking the technician's finger . . .

The 2011 incident illuminates a long–festering problem that many hospitals have been reluctant to address: disruptive and often angry behavior by doctors. Experts estimate that 3 to 5 percent of physicians engage in such behavior, berating nurses who call them in the middle of the night about a patient . . . demeaning co-workers they consider incompetent or cutting off patients who ask a lot of questions.

—*Sandra G. Boodman,* The Huffington Post, *March 5, 2013*

Employees have a right to be free from intimidation by angry individuals and veiled threats by managers in the workplace. Employees have a right to be protected from the abuse of others whether they are managers, coworkers, or independent contractors such as physicians.

Privacy Rights

Employees have historically had the right to privacy in the workplace. It is possible for employers to monitor employee activities through both written and electronic communications, unless an organization's policies and procedures provide otherwise. Company policy should provide information to employees as to monitoring rights. State laws may vary as to telephone monitoring and may require that both parties to a conversation be informed when they are being monitored. Employee rights often ride a fine line as related to privacy. As the following reality check illustrates, it is sometimes difficult to know where to draw the line between corporate integrity and the rights of employees in the workplace.

REALITY CHECK: Your Mail Was Opened

The XYZ Corporation has decided to open all mail sent to employees who work in the field. A memorandum was sent to the field staff saying, "Sorry, your mail will be either opened or returned to the sender if it is delivered to your workplace. If the sender is from a healthcare organization, it will be opened to determine if its contents relate to XYZ's business. If the mail is from any other person or place, it will be returned unopened to the sender. This action is necessary from a cost-savings standpoint. XYZ cannot afford to forward the on average 60 pieces of mail that it receives each month addressed to field staff." What happens to opened mail that is not XYZ's business remains a mystery. What is it that drives an organization to make such decisions? Is it fear of competition, paranoia, distrust, or some other hidden issue? The answer remains elusive. Although it is legal for an organization to open all mail before sorting and delivering it, employees should be told that they should have no expectation of privacy and that they should not have anything personal sent to work that they don't want others to see. Managers should not open an employee's mail indiscriminately, such invasion of privacy will undermine employee morale.

Discussion

1. Discuss under what circumstances an organization should open an employee's mail.

2. Discuss any legal and ethical concerns (e.g., right to privacy).

3. What should happen to the mail of an employee that is opened but is not intended for the organization? What if that information is confidential in nature and is shared with others?

4. What safeguards should organizations put into place to safeguard personal information?

EMPLOYEE RESPONSIBILITIES

I believe that every right implies a responsibility; every opportunity, an obligation; every profession, a duty.
—JOHN D. ROCKEFELLER, JR.

Employees are expected to comply with their job-related duties and responsibilities as defined in their job description and the organization's policies and procedures. Rights and responsibilities run parallel to one another. With every right, there is a corresponding duty, for example, although there is a right to expect respect from others, there is a corresponding duty and responsibility to respect the rights of other. The following sections describe but a few of the many responsibilities required of healthcare employees.

Compassion

How far you go in life depends on you being tender with the young, compassionate with the aged, sympathetic with the striving and tolerant of the weak and strong. Because someday in your life you will have been all of these.

—GEORGE WASHINGTON CARVER

The ability to show strength of character through compassion leads this list of employee responsibilities. Caregivers hold in their hands the gift to be instruments of God in the healing process. It is the compassionate caregiver who guides the patient as he or she struggles through illness, pain, and suffering. It is the compassionate caregiver who provides hope when there appears to be no hope.

REALITY CHECK: Compassion for the Patient and Caregiver

Recently I started to show a healthcare worker a short video of a man who most likely weighed over 500 pounds. As a popular singer, he performed his last

(continued)

REALITY CHECK: Compassion for the Patient and Caregiver (continued)

concert and maybe his last song, the caregiver noticed in the video that there was an oxygen tank beside his wheelchair with tubing leading from the tank into his nostrils. The caregiver abruptly turned away from the computer screen and ranted about how heavy people are so exasperating to work with. The caregiver proceeded to criticize the man saying that he was responsible for his own obesity, making it difficult for caregivers to lift and move. The singer had acknowledged in his public life that he knew he was addicted to food, which led to his early death. His message before singing a heartbreaking song was the purpose of showing the video. The message now, goes further then this, the needs of the patient must be met with compassion and the provider must provide the caregiver with sufficient assistance to move such patients in order to prevent the caregiver from also becoming a patient.

Discussion

1. Discuss the various ethical issues affecting patients, caregivers, and hospitals.
2. Describe what actions you could take to make this a win-win scenario for the patients, caregivers, and healthcare facilities.

Patient Advocacy

Caregivers have a responsibility to advocate for their patients. Because patients are often helpless and unable to speak for themselves, all employees should consider themselves to be patient advocates. Various states have mandated by legislation the establishment of ombudsman programs.

REALITY CHECK: Staff Affects Physician Practice Image

Mark was waiting to be seen by his physician in a multispecialty physician office practice. As Mark was waiting to see his physician, he observed a woman, most likely in her late 70s, limping into the office. She had a large leg brace that ran from her thigh to the calf of her leg. She struggled to push her husband in a wheelchair into the office. She carefully parked the wheelchair and approached the check-in counter. She apologized for being late for her appointment as she was late getting out of another physician's office. The patient was

told, "You are late for your appointment. The office has a 15-minute late arrival rule. You will have to reschedule your appointment." She apologized for being late but said that she did tell the office staff she would be late. She was then told, "You can wait, and I will try to squeeze you into the schedule, but I don't know how long you will have to wait." The lady said, "I don't want to bother anyone. I will reschedule my appointment." She was directed around the corner to another desk to reschedule her appointment. Mark got up out of his chair, walked over to the scheduler, and said, "I don't believe this. Her husband is sitting in a wheelchair, and she is having difficulty walking. She can have my appointment, and I can reschedule." The lady suddenly turned to Mark and gave him a big hug. The scheduler asked, "Who is your physician?" Mark told her, and she said, "I am sorry, but this lady has a different physician." The lady, now a bit teary eyed, continued to make her appointment.

Discussion

1. Mark saw what he perceived to be a wrong and tried to make a right. Discuss his actions.
2. Discuss why healthcare workers, patients, and visitors should consider themselves, when appropriate, patient advocates.

Honor Patient Wishes

Caregivers have a responsibility to honor a patient's right to participate in decisions regarding his or her care, including the right to formulate advance directives and have those directives honored.

Maintain Confidentiality

The duty to maintain confidentiality encompasses both verbal and written communications. This requirement also applies to consultants, contracted individuals, students, and volunteers. Information about a patient, regardless of the method in which it is acquired, is confidential and should not be disclosed without the patient's permission. Those who come into possession of the most intimate personal information about patients have both a legal and an ethical duty not to reveal confidential communications.

Adhere to Safe Practice

Caregivers have a responsibility to adhere to safe practices in order to minimize patient injuries. This responsibility requires employees to adhere to national patient safety goals (e.g., hand washing, patient identification, verification of operative site), the purpose of which is to protect the health of the patient.

Comply with Sterile Technique Protocols

The Centers for Disease Control and Prevention has estimated that "nosocomial [hospital-acquired] bloodstream infections are a leading cause of death in the United States. If we assume a nosocomial infection rate of 5%, of which 10% are bloodstream infections, and an attributable mortality rate of 15%, bloodstream infections would represent the eighth leading cause of death in the United States."[10] It is believed that such infections have resulted in as many as 100,000 deaths and billions of dollars in additional healthcare costs. These numbers do not reflect nonhospital-acquired infections that have occurred in physicians' offices.

The seriousness of these numbers should awaken all caregivers as to the importance of complying with sterile practice techniques through recommended hand-washing and maintaining a sterile environment for patients.

Adhere to Professional Standards

Caregivers have a responsibility to be professional in the performance of their work. The operation of a hospital requires the coordination of numerous employees and departments, each with different responsibilities that depend on each other. Thus, staff cooperation and communication are essential for ensuring professionalism in the provision of high quality patient care.

Protect Patients from Harm

Caregivers have an ethical and legal responsibility to protect patients from harm. The rules of ethics applicable to nurses, for example, specifically recognize a nurse's obligation to safeguard not only patients' health but also their safety as well.

Maintain Professional Relationships

Employees are responsible for maintaining an appropriate professional relationship with patients, families, coworkers, and others who they may come into contact in the organization (e.g., consultants).

REALITY CHECK: Shoot the Consultant

Justin, a new consultant, was assigned to review an organization's human resources department and provide recommendations on how to improve processes and systems. As Justin was new to the job, Mel, a more seasoned consultant, was assigned to work with him. Justin was working on a preliminary report to be presented to the organization later that day. Judy, the organization's coordinator assigned to work with Justin, was asked to provide additional information on its staffing process. Justin believed that the organization's staffing processes were well done. Mel, whispering in Justin's ear, out of Judy's eyesight, said, "I disagree. These processes are not what we would expect to see in place, but then, this is your assignment. I am just here to evaluate you." Justin understood his message. Justin described to Judy his concerns about human resources staffing processes as Mel stood in the back of the room watching their interaction. Judy turned to Mel and said, "Don't you think Justin is wrong?" Mel quickly replied, "I am just an observer." Judy left the room as Justin completed his report.

Later that afternoon Justin presented his report to the organization's leadership. Justin made his suggestions for improvement. After his report, the CEO asked whether there were any questions regarding Justin's report. Mel was sitting to the immediate left of Justin, and Judy was to the left of Mel. Judy, leaning over to look at Justin, pointing at him, said, "I could just shoot him." After a few moments of silence, followed by a thank you and goodbye, Justin handed his report to the CEO. He, along with Mel, got up to leave the room. Judy, ignoring Justin, shook Mel's hand and hugged him goodbye as she looked at Justin with disdain.

Discussion

1. Assuming that Mel adequately explained his recommendations, discuss what other actions, if any, Justin might have taken to defuse Judy's discontent.
2. What action should the CEO take regarding Judy's reaction to the consultant? Explain your answer.

Report Unethical Behavior

Caregivers have both a right and responsibility to report impaired, incompetent, and unethical colleagues in accordance with the legal requirements of each state. Unethical behavior includes conduct that threatens patient care or welfare, behavior that violates state licensing provisions, and conduct that violates criminal statutes.

Work with Team Spirit

Employees have a responsibility to work together as a team in the delivery of quality patient care, as noted, for example, in the following reality check.

REALITY CHECK: Multidisciplinary Approach to Patient Care

Bill recently visited a pain center where Dr. Jones, the medical director, had recently included a physical therapist on his pain management team. After several visits to the pain management program, Bill complimented the staff as to their multidisciplinary approach to his care. Dr. Jones discussed with Bill how patient outcomes had improved over time, as treatment plans became more multidisciplinary focused. He went to explain how patients are encouraged to ask questions of the caregiver.

- Have you reviewed my medical records?
- Have you discussed my treatment plan with my physician?
- What were my physician's specific orders?
- May I see them?
- What precautions have you been asked to follow with me?
- Have you seen my imaging studies?
- Has anyone discussed them with you?

Bill, before leaving, said to Dr. Jones, "I truly am getting individualized care and treatment in your pain center in a style worthy of the words, quality care is alive and well here."

Discussion

1. If you are a practicing professional, discuss how the multidisciplinary approach to patient care might be improved in your organization.
2. Consider and discuss what questions you might ask if you were the patient undergoing treatment.

Participate in Continuing Education

It is expected that each professional have current understanding of one's area of specialization and practice. Education has value and is a legal necessity in order to be in conformity with the national standard of care of one's profession. Every professional is responsible to be current in his or her knowledge and skills. This comes by reading one's professional literature, attending continuing education programs, and mentoring.

HELPFUL ADVICE

- Do not blame others for your mistakes.
- Take responsibility for caring and communicating.
- Include the patient in the decision-making process. Encourage—do not discourage—the patient to participate in his or her healthcare decisions.
- Take the time to explain to patients the risks, benefits, and alternatives to each course of treatment.
- Avoid the paternalistic approach to medical care.
- Show respect and sensitivity to a patient's needs.
- Listen to what the patient is saying without interruption. Remember that your wishes and those of the family may be different than those of the patient. It is, however, the patient who faces the consequences of his or her decisions. You are, therefore, responsible for considering the patient's wishes sacred and protecting the patient from those who would disregard them.
- Refrain from demeaning and criticizing a patient's wishes because of his or her frail condition.

CAREGIVER'S PLEDGE

- I will be compassionate.
- I will not neglect my duties and responsibilities.
- I will read instructions and follow protocols.
- I will seek verification of questionable orders.
- I will report concerns for patient safety (e.g., staffing concerns).
- I will not assume responsibilities beyond my capabilities.
- I will call for help when a patient's medical needs suddenly change.
- I will continuously seek to improve my skills and participate in continuing education.

Notes

1. 515 F.2d 541 (8th Cir. 1975).
2. 676 N.Y.S. 2d 293 (N.Y. App., 1998).
3. National Constitutional Center, "Laws Protecting Pharmacist's Refusal," http://www.constitutioncenter.org/education/ForEducators/DiscussionStarters/PharmacistConscienceLaws.shtml.
4. http://www.ncsl.org/issues-research/health/pharmacist-conscience-clauses-laws-and-information.aspx.
5. *Deerman v. Beverly Cal. Corp.*, 518 S.E.2d 804 (N.C. App. 1999).
6. Alicia Gallegos, "Physician Whistle-Blowers Can Sue Hospitals Without Delay, Appeals Court Rules," *American MedicalNews,* September 3, 2012. http://www.amednews.com/article/20120903/government/309039959/6/
7. R. Nader, K. Blackwell, and P. J. Petkas, *Whistle Blowing: The Report of the Conference on Professional Responsibility,* (New York: Grossman, 1972).
8. *Gambee v. State Bd. of Med. Exam'rs,* 923 P.2d 679 (1996).
9. http://www.whistleblowers.gov.
10. http://wwwnc.cdc.gov/eid/article/7/2/70-0174_article.htm.

24
Tort Reform

Learning Objectives

The reader upon completion of this chapter will be able to:

- Describe the meaning of defensive medicine.
- Describe various programs designed to lower the cost of malpractice insurance.
- Describe the various ways to manage and reduce the number of negligence claims.

The tort system has proven to be inadequate in the prevention of medical malpractice. Damage awards as a deterrent to malpractice have failed to reduce the number of claims. Exorbitant jury awards and malpractice insurance premiums are costing the healthcare industry billions of dollars annually. Given the difficulties in the present tort system, we often become victims of the failures of medicine as opposed to beneficiaries of its many successes. Physicians have lost in that they have changed, limited, or closed their practices after having spent the most productive years of their lives training for such work. Patients have lost in that the physicians of their choice, with whom they have developed trusting relationships, are no longer available to care for them. Frivolous and unscrupulous malpractice actions have caused physicians to place limitations on their scope of practice. Many obstetricians/gynecologists, for example, have dropped the high-risk obstetrics portion of their practices to reduce their malpractice premiums. There is also an ever-increasing reluctance by physicians to perform heroic measures on accident victims because of the high risks of malpractice exposure.

Physicians who wish to practice medicine and remain financially independent have accepted the concept of practicing defensive medicine. *Defensive medicine* is believed to be one of the most harmful effects produced by the threat of malpractice litigation. Such medicine is practiced to forestall potential litigation and provide an advantageous legal defense should a lawsuit be instituted. Defensive medicine often results in under-treatment, perhaps by avoiding high-risk tests and procedures, or *over-treatment*, such as the excessive use of diagnostic tests. "The message the tort system is sending to doctors is not so much deterrence, in terms of practicing good medicine, but more just 'drive defensively,' because any patient you may see may be a litigant."[1]

The various states have not ignored the need for tort reform and have and continue to legislate tort reform. This chapter reviews selected programs designed to help reduce exorbitant malpractice awards.

ARBITRATION AND MEDIATION

Among the many factors contributing to the malpractice crisis is the high cost of litigation. Trial by jury is lengthy and expensive. If case disputes can be handled out of court, the process and expense of a lawsuit can be significantly reduced. Arbitration and mediation are basically mechanisms for simplifying and expediting the settlement of claims.

Arbitration is the process by which parties to a dispute voluntarily agree to submit their differences to the judgment of an impartial mediation panel for resolution. It is used as a means to evaluate, screen, and resolve medical malpractice disputes before they reach the courts. Arbitration can be accomplished by mutual consent of the parties or statutory provisions. A decision made at arbitration may or may not be binding, depending on prior agreement between the parties or statutory requirements.

Mediation is the process whereby a third party, the mediator, attempts to bring about a settlement between the parties of a complaint. The mediator cannot force a settlement.

STRUCTURED AWARDS

Structured awards are set up for the periodic payment of judgments by establishing a reversible trust fund for specified risks of malpractice parts of awards due plaintiffs. The purpose of a structured award is to provide compensation during a plaintiff's lifetime. It would eliminate an unwarranted windfall to the plaintiff's beneficiaries in the event of death. Some states have sought to deal with award limitations by mandating so-called structured recoveries when awards exceed a certain dollar amount.

Structured recoveries provide that money awarded to the plaintiff be placed in a trust fund and invested appropriately so that those funds will be available to the plaintiff over a long period of time. The rationale behind such legislation is that an immediate award of a large sum of money is not necessary for a plaintiff to be well taken care of after suffering injuries. The prudent investment of a smaller amount of money can produce a recovery commensurate with the needs and the rights of the plaintiff. This, in turn, requires a smaller cash outlay by the defendant or the defendant's insurance company, thereby holding down the costs of malpractice insurance and the ultimate cost of medical care to the consumer.

PRETRIAL SCREENING PANELS

Pretrial screening panels are designed to evaluate the merits of medical injury claims to encourage the settlement of claims outside the courtroom. "Panels render an opinion on provider liability and, in some cases, on damages. In most states, the panel's decision on the merit of the claim is admissible in court."[2] Unlike binding arbitration, the decision of a screening panel is not binding and is imposed as a condition precedent to trial, whereas arbitration is conducted in lieu of a trial. Mandatory screenings of alleged negligence cases are useful in discouraging frivolous lawsuits from proceeding to trial.

COLLATERAL SOURCE RULE

The *collateral source rule* is a common-law principle that prohibits a court or jury from taking into account when setting an award that part of the plaintiff's damages covered by other sources of payment (e.g., health insurance and disability). Several states have modified the collateral source rule so that evidence regarding other sources of payment to the plaintiff may be introduced for purposes of reducing the amount of the ultimate award to the plaintiff. The jury then would be permitted to assign the evidence such weight as it chooses. The award could be reduced to the extent that the plaintiff received compensation from other sources.

Imposition of the collateral source rule can result in recoveries to plaintiffs far in excess of their economic loss. Such excessive payments contribute significantly to the high cost of malpractice insurance and the high cost of health care to the public. When evidence regarding collateral sources of payment are allowed to be introduced to mitigate the damages payable to a plaintiff, excessive recoveries may be discouraged.

CONTINGENCY FEE LIMITATIONS

A *contingency fee* is payment for services rendered by an attorney predicated on the favorable outcome of a case. Payment is based on a preestablished percentage of the total award. Some states set this percentage by statute. Under a contingency agreement, if there is no award to the plaintiff, then the attorney receives no payment for services rendered.

Physicians argue that the contingency fee arrangement serves to encourage an inordinate number of lawsuits. Attorneys reason that if they or their clients must bear the initial cost of a lawsuit, only those with obvious merit will be brought forward. The contingency fee structure allows those unable to bear the cost of litigation to initiate a suit for damages. Limiting contingency fees on a sliding scale basis, with the percentage decreasing as the award to the plaintiff increases, and/or providing for a lesser fee if a claim is settled prior to trial, seems to have some merit.

COUNTERSUITS AND FRIVOLOUS CLAIMS

Healthcare providers, in some instances, have filed countersuits after being named in what they believe to be malicious, libelous, slanderous, frivolous, and nonmeritorious medical malpractice suits. The threat of countersuits, however, has not been helpful in reducing the number of malpractice claims. Remedies for such actions vary from one jurisdiction to the next. For a physician to prevail in a suit against a plaintiff or plaintiff's attorney, the physician must show that the:

- suit was frivolous
- motivation of the plaintiff was not to recover for a legitimate injury
- physician suffered damages as a result of the suit

The courts, however, have not generally looked favorably on countersuits in negligence actions.

JOINT AND SEVERAL LIABILITY

The *doctrine of joint and several liability* provides that a person causing an injury concurrently with another person can be held equally liable for the entire judgment awarded by a court. It is proposed by some that each defendant in a multidefendant action should be limited to payment for the percentage of fault ascribed to him or her. Some states have taken action to modify the doctrine. A Wyoming statute, for example, provides that each defendant to a lawsuit is liable only for that proportion of the total dollar amount of damages according to the percentage of the amount of fault attributed to him or her.[3] A Minnesota statute provides that a defendant whose fault is 15% or less may be jointly liable for a percentage of the whole award not greater than four times his or her percentage of fault.[4]

Fair Share Act

Governor Tom Corbett of Pennsylvania signed the *Fair Share Act* (42 Pa. Cons. Stat. § 7102) into law on June 28, 2011. The *Act* provides for a proportionate share of liability among joint tort-feasors and eliminates the common law doctrine of joint and several liability. Under the law, with few exceptions, each defendant is liable for "that proportion of the total dollar amount awarded as damages in the ratio of the amount of that defendant's liability to the amount of liability attributed to all defendants and other persons to whom liability is apportioned under subsection (a.2)." [42 Pa. Cons. Stat. § 7102(a.1)(1)].

MALPRACTICE CAPS

The impetus for malpractice liability caps is due, in part, because jury awards often vary substantially from one jurisdiction to the next within the same state. As a result, negligence attorneys often attempt to try personal injury cases in those jurisdictions in which a jury is likely to grant a higher award. Different states are attempting to stem the tide of rising malpractice costs by passing laws that impose restrictions on limiting the total dollar damages allowable in malpractice actions. Although there have been challenges to statutes limiting awards, it would appear that limitations on malpractice recoveries are constitutional. The battle continues as to just how effective malpractice liability caps really are. States that have them in place are finding that the caps are far from resolving the high malpractice insurance premiums paid by physicians.

NO-FAULT SYSTEM

A *no-fault system* compensates injured parties for economic losses regardless of fault. It is intended to compensate more claimants with smaller awards. A no-fault system compensates victims of medical injury whether or not they can prove medical negligence. Proponents of the no-fault approach cite as its advantages swifter and less-expensive resolution of claims and more equitable compensation for patients.

A no-fault system of compensation has its drawbacks. Opponents of the no-fault system are concerned about the loss of whatever deterrence effect the present tort system exerts on healthcare providers. The system's lower administrative costs can be an incentive to file lawsuits and, therefore, may not produce the desired outcome of reducing the incidence of malpractice claims.

REGULATION OF INSURANCE PRACTICES

Many believe that the regulation of insurance practices is necessary to prevent windfall profits. Both the medical profession and the legal profession believe that insurance carriers have raised premiums disproportionately to their losses and that, despite their claims of substantial losses, they have reaped substantial profits.

PHYSICIAN PARTICIPATION IN TORT REFORM

Physicians who are on the front lines of medicine often have been excluded from the decision-making processes that threaten their autonomy and financial security. A concerted effort must be made to include them in the process of tort reform. The present system of punishment for all because of the inadequacies of the few has proven to be costly and far from productive. The key to improving quality and controlling costs is cooperation, not alienation. Policy makers have failed in this arena and must return to a commonsense approach to policy development by including those who are on the front lines of medicine.

The medical malpractice crisis continues to be a major dilemma for the healthcare industry. Although there have been many approaches to resolving the crisis, there appears to be no one magic formula. The solution most likely will require a variety of efforts, including tort reform, as reviewed in this chapter.

Notes

1. The Robert Wood Johnson Foundation, "The Tort System for Medical Malpractice: How Well Does It Work, What Are the Alternatives?" *Abridge*, Spring 1991, 2.
2. The Robert Wood Johnson Foundation, "Legal Reform," *Abridge*, Spring 1991, 3.
3. Wyo. Stat. § 1-1-109 (1986).
4. Minn. Stat. § 604.02 (1988).

25
Culture of Safety

Figure 25-1 Patient Safety Score © IdeaStepConceptStock/ShutterStock, Inc.

Learning Objectives

The reader upon completion of this chapter will be able to:

- Discuss a process for developing a culture of safety in healthcare organizations.
- Describe a variety of organizations that are dedicated to improving patient care and safety.
- Explain the process of communications and why different people often have different views on various discussion topics.

- Explain how the checklist tool can be used for evaluating the quality of patient care.
- Discuss how performance improvement processes, adoption of best practices, risk management programs, failure mode effects analysis, and addressing sentinel events can be effectual in developing a culture of safety.

NEWSPAPER CLIPPINGS: Thousands of Mistakes Made in Surgery Every Year

More than 4,000 preventable mistakes occur in surgery every year at a cost of more than $1.3 billion in medical malpractice payouts, according to a new study.

How preventable? Well, researchers call them "never events" because they are the kind of surgical mistakes that should never happen, like performing the wrong procedure or leaving a sponge inside a patient's body after surgery.

. . .

"Even with marking the surgical site there are reports of the wrong site still being operated on, and you have to say it's a lack of attention to detail when it happens," he says.

—*Jennifer Warner, Rev. by Laura J. Martin, MD,*
WebMD Health News, December 26, 2012

The Institute of Medicine (IOM) in its often quoted November 1999 report entitled, "To Err Is Human: Building a Safer Health System," found that at least 44,000 and perhaps as many as 98,000 people die in hospitals each year as a result of preventable medical errors. Such figures rank medical errors as the eighth leading cause of death in the United States, ahead of deaths from motor vehicle accidents, breast cancer, or AIDS.

We become so comfortable in the routine,
because nobody got hurt.
Yesterday, I cut a corner and everything was fine.
No one got hurt.
Today, I took a chance and texted you while driving.
I did it for so many years and promised myself I would stop.
Today, again I survived.
My friends did not and the other car . . .
Today I skipped a routine step at work.
I did it a thousand times and nothing happened
Today I was not so lucky.
And yes, someone died.
It is certain we all take risks.
Like Russian Roulette,
Luck runs out.

—Anonymous

Healthcare organizations and accrediting bodies are adopting a zero-tolerance policy for poor judgment and careless mistakes. Strides are being made to ensure that desired outcomes are more closely aligned with predictability. More focus on how to do things right the first time will lessen the likelihood of having to ask why things went wrong after a medical error occurs.

This chapter focuses on the development of a corporate *culture of safety* with emphasis on national patient safety goals. A self-evaluation process, including a variety of safe practices, is also presented on the following pages, as well as how performance improvement processes, adoption of best practices, risk management programs, failure mode effects analysis, and addressing sentinel events can be effectual in developing a culture of safety.

DEVELOPING A CULTURE OF SAFETY

Organizations are encouraged to create and maintain a *culture of safety* to reduce the risks of patient injuries and deaths due to common mistakes. Patients expect hospitals to provide a safe environment for medical care. Although healthcare organizations are aware of where systems often break down, evidence suggests that they have been ineffective in preventing patient injuries that are often the result of human error or just plain carelessness. Implementation of the following suggestions will help hospitals move toward a culture of safety:

- Ensure that accountability and responsibility has been assigned for monitoring an organization's safety initiatives.
- Involve the medical staff in the development and implementation of systems that are designed to create a culture of safety.
- Educate all staff as to their individual roles in establishing and maintaining a safe environment for patients.
- Encourage patients to question their care. Provide guidelines in patient handbooks as to the kinds of questions that patients should be asking caregivers (e.g., Is this a new medication? I don't recognize it. What is this medication for? Did you wash your hands before changing my surgical dressing?).
- Appoint a patient safety officer.
- Establish a patient safety committee with responsibility for oversight of the organization's patient safety program. The patient safety committee is a multidisciplinary committee that includes representation from administration, various hospital departments, and medical staff.

- Set up a 24-hour-a-day dedicated safety hotline.
- Establish a voluntary event reporting system. Educate employees and patients as to reporting options (e.g., telephone, e-mail). Assure employees that there will be no retaliation for reporting patient safety concerns.
- Implement lifesaving initiatives that include: establishing rapid response teams for stroke and heart patients; preventing medication errors; reducing the number of hospital-acquired infections; developing programs for suicide prevention; preventing infant abduction and patient falls.
- Use the online tools released by Agency for Healthcare Research and Quality (AHRQ) to assist in evaluating and improving safe care.

Agency for Healthcare Research and Quality

The Agency for Healthcare Research and Quality (AHRQ) is the health services research arm of the U.S. Department of Health and Human Services (HHS), complementing the biomedical research mission of its sister agency, the National Institutes of Health. AHRQ is a home to research centers that specialize in major areas of healthcare research such as quality improvement and patient safety, outcomes and effectiveness of care, clinical practice and technology assessment, and healthcare organization and delivery systems. It is also a major source of funding and technical assistance for health services research and research training at leading U.S. universities and other institutions, as well as a science partner, working with the public and private sectors to build the knowledge base for what works—and does not work—in health and health care and to translate this knowledge into everyday practice and policymaking.[1]

For more information, go to the AHRQ website (http://www.ahrq.gov) and the Mission and Budget page (http://www.ahrq.gov/about/budgtix.htm).

National Patient Safety Goals

The Joint Commission is striving to improve patient safety by identifying national patient safety goals in its accreditation process. Some of these goals have included improving the accuracy of patient identification (e.g., using two patient identifiers when administering medications); eliminating transfusion errors; improving the effectiveness of communication among caregivers; timely reporting of critical tests and critical results; improving the safety of using medications (e.g., labeling medications); reducing harm from anticoagulation therapy; reducing the risk of healthcare associated infections (e.g., meeting hand hygiene guidelines, preventing multidrug-resistant organism infections,

preventing central line-associated blood stream infections); accurately and completely reconciling medications wherever patient care is rendered (e.g., comparing current and newly ordered medications); communicating medications to the next provider; providing a reconciled medication list to each patient; reducing the risk of patient harm resulting from falls; preventing healthcare-associated pressure ulcers (decubitus ulcers); identifying safety risks inherent in patient populations served; identifying individuals at risk for suicide; reducing the risks of falls and injury; and developing a *Universal Protocol for Preventing Wrong Site, Wrong Procedure, and Wrong Person Surgery* that applies to all surgical and nonsurgical invasive procedures. The protocol requires implementation of a preprocedure verification process verifying the correct procedure, for the correct patient, at the correct site and includes *marking of the procedure site* and *conducting a time-out* before the procedure is performed.

Periodically, the Joint Commission introduces national patient safety goals into the survey process. Joint Commission surveyors evaluate organizations at the time of an organization's accreditation survey, determining compliance with patient safety goals. The goals are designed to encourage compliance with safe practices and reduce the likelihood of medical errors. The Joint Commission website (http://www.jointcommission.org) should be referenced for current information.

Joint Commission Patient Complaint Process

The Joint Commission has implemented a patient complaint process that requires healthcare organizations it accredits to educate employers and employees as to their right to report safety or quality concerns to the Joint Commission. The Joint Commission policy forbids accredited organizations from taking retaliatory actions against employees for having reported quality of care concerns to the Joint Commission. Patient complaints may be reported by:

- Online: http://www.jointcommission.org/report_a_complaint.aspx
- Fax: Office of Quality Monitoring at (630) 792-5636
- Written correspondence: Office of Quality Monitoring, The Joint Commission, One Renaissance Boulevard, Oakbrook Terrace, IL 60181
- Telephone: (800) 994-6610 for questions about how to file a complaint

National Quality Forum

The *National Quality Forum* (NQF) is a private, non-profit public-benefit corporation created for the purpose of developing and implementing a national strategy for healthcare quality. Its purpose is to improve the quality of health care for all Americans through fulfillment of its three-part mission:

- Setting national priorities and goals for performance improvement;
- Endorsing national consensus standards for measuring and publicly reporting on performance; and
- Promoting the attainment of national goals through education and outreach programs.

NQF's membership includes a wide variety of healthcare stakeholders, including consumer organizations, public and private purchasers, physicians, nurses, hospitals, accrediting and certifying bodies, supporting industries, and healthcare research and quality improvement organizations. The breadth and diversity of its membership allows NQF to be well positioned to maintain a constant drumbeat for healthcare quality. NQF's unique structure enables private and public sector stakeholders to work together to craft and implement cross-cutting solutions to drive continuous quality improvement in the American healthcare system.[2] For more in-depth information on the activities and functioning of the NQF, the reader should visit the organization's website (http://www.qualityforum.org/).

Institute for Healthcare Improvement

The Institute for Healthcare Improvement (IHI) is a not-for-profit organization whose mission is to improve health care throughout the world. The IHI was founded in 1991 and is based in Cambridge, Massachusetts. The IHI offers a wide range of resources and teaching tools to help healthcare professionals lead effective improvement efforts, enhance clinical outcomes, reduce costs, and describes various ways to measure the success of new programs. For complete information on the activities and functioning of the IHI, visit the corporation's website at www.IHI.org/.

The Leapfrog Group for Patient Safety

The Leapfrog Group and its members work together to reduce preventable medical mistakes and improve the quality and affordability of health care. The Leapfrog Group promotes improvements in the safe delivery of health care by collecting and providing the necessary information for healthcare consumers to make informed healthcare decisions. For complete information on the activities and functioning of The Leapfrog Group, visit its website at www.leapfroggroup.org/.

Emergency Care Research Institute

Emergency Care Research Institute (ECRI) is a nonprofit health services research agency and a collaborating center of the World Health Organization (WHO). It is designated as an evidence-based practice center by the AHRQ. ECRI is widely recognized as one of the world's leading independent organizations committed to advancing the quality of health care. ECRI's mission is to promote the highest standards of safety, quality, and cost effectiveness in health care to benefit patient care through research, publishing, education, and consulting. For complete information on the activities and functioning of ECRI, the reader should visit the ECRI website (http://www.ecri.org/).

IMPROVE COMMUNICATIONS

 Think all you speak, but speak not all you think. Thoughts are your own; your words are so no more.
—Patrick Delany

The materials presented in this text challenge the reader to better understand the communications process, human conflict, and the world of relationships. The cases presented throughout this text are engaging in that they arise out of communications and the complexity of human affairs. **Figure 25–2** is helpful in understanding the communications process.

Communications is the exchange of thoughts and information through speech, the written word, or behavior. Words are the tools of thought, therefore, the more expansive one's vocabulary, the more effectively one can articulate thoughts and ideas to others. In addition to the spoken word, messages are often transmitted through body language, posture, gestures, facial expressions, and eye contact. Nonverbal communication has been called the *silent language*, which plays a key role in the day-to-day communications process.

Communications are influenced by diverse religious beliefs, regional traditions, cultures, gender, and race, all of which influence our virtues and values. The *Pillars of Moral Strength* (in Figure 2–2) describe various virtues and values that make up each individual's moral character. It is what sets each individual apart from the crowd. In the final analysis, it is the degree and worth a person assigns to each virtue and value that affects the rest of his or her life. There are literally thousands of events in one's life that affect one's behavior and ability to communicate effectively. Biases that spring up from environmental influences need to be challenged to validate one has not been unreasonably *conditioned* to believe what others wish him or her to believe.

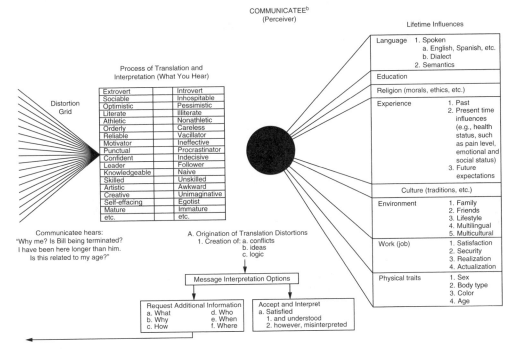

Figure 25–2 The Process of Communications

My words fly up, my thoughts remain below: Words without thoughts never to heaven go.

—WILLIAM SHAKESPEARE

The damage that can result from unskilled communications is incalculable, and the manager may find that poor communications experienced with one employee is compounded by its effect on other employees. If a message is not clear, the message should be rephrased. The rephrased message may provide clarity and perhaps convey a different meaning than what the unclear original message seemed to imply. To ensure a message is clearly understood, it should be repeated back to the messenger for clarity.

Stress factors in any given conversation often result in a disproportional rise in the distortion of the intent of a message. If a message is emotional, take time to clear the air. One's ability to communicate is much easier in a respectful setting than in one that is antagonistic. Both managers and employees tend to perceive each new communication as reinforcing their ideas and biases and, at the same time, screen out those things that do not strengthen their beliefs or individual opinions. There is a tendency to make value judgments from one's own perspective and to evaluate all new knowledge according to its positive or negative impact on one's partisan beliefs. A better understanding of the communications process described here serves as a catapult to improved communications.

EVALUATING SAFE PATIENT CARE

A checklist tool for evaluating the safe delivery of patient care is presented below. Each statement is meant to assist the practicing professional in evaluating a healthcare organization. This tool has been developed to apply to a variety of healthcare organizations. Each bulleted statement is meant to encourage the reader to ask more—who, how, what, why, when, and where.

Leadership

- The organization's mission, vision, and values have been identified.
- There is a strategy that charts the direction of the organization in response to community need.
- The planning process identifies the organization's strengths and opportunities for improvement.
- Patient input is solicited to improve services through, for example, patient satisfaction surveys and focus groups.
- A process for setting priorities has been established.
- The governing body has adopted a conflict-of-interest policy.
- Care is not based on ability to pay.
- A corporate compliance program has been developed and implemented.
- The governing body monitors the effectiveness of the organization's leadership.

Credentialing Licensed Practitioners

- There is a process for credentialing licensed healthcare practitioners.

- The National Practitioner Data Bank is utilized in the credentialing process.
- There is ongoing evaluation of each professional.
- Delineation of clinical privileges includes: a description of the privileges requested; relevant education, training, and experience; limitations on privileges requested; evidence of competency in performing requested privileges; verification of current licensure; relevant references; and evaluation of current competency.

Human Resources Process

- Job descriptions reflect each staff member's duties and responsibilities.
- The technical skills of each position have been determined.
- The organization has the appropriate competencies, mix, and numbers of employees.
- Recruitment, retention, development, and recognition programs have been implemented.
- There is a department-specific orientation program for employees, agency, and contracted staff, and volunteers.
- The education and training needs of staff are assessed.

Patient Education

- The patient's first contact with a staff member involves the establishment of trust, which emanates from patient recognition that the caregiver is knowledgeable and competent.
- Greetings, gestures, manner of taking information, and attitude are important ingredients in establishing a good relationship with the patient.
- There is evidence of patient/family education in the patient's record.
- An assessment of the patient's readiness/willingness, ability, and need to learn is conducted.
- Education is conducted in all settings (e.g., inpatient, ambulatory, emergency department, home care) on a collaborative basis.
- Education includes medication safety; nutrition; medical equipment use; access to community resources; how to obtain further care if necessary; and responsibilities of the patient and family.
- The patient understands the care instructions.

Communications

- The organization has implemented effective communicative processes throughout the organization.
- Abbreviations are discouraged. Where abbreviations are permitted, they have one meaning.
- A process is in place for validating the correct interpretation of illegible medication orders.

Critical Tests

- Critical test results and values are reported on a timely basis.
- Data are collected to measure and assess the success of timely reporting.
- Action is taken, when necessary, to improve the reporting process.

Emergency Services

- Adequate staff is available to care for patients.
- Medical records are maintained for each patient treated.
- Patients are triaged, assessed, and treated within a reasonable period of time.
- Criteria for admission and discharge have been established.
- Response time by on-call physicians is timely.
- The organization has a mechanism for obtaining consultations.
- All patients are assessed and treated by a physician prior to discharge.
- The records of patients treated in other settings within the organization (e.g., ambulatory care settings) are readily available.
- Patient education is provided in the emergency department (ED) prior to discharge.
- Documentation is complete.
- There is a procedure in place for reading X-rays and other imaging studies when there is no radiologist readily available.

Security

- Security issues have been addressed throughout the organization.
- Sensitive areas have been identified.
- Newborns are foot-printed.
- An organization-approved identification band is attached to mothers and infants.
- Identification badges for mother and infant match.
- All staff members have current color photo identification badges.
- Staff and parents are educated as to security procedures.
- Infant abduction drills are conducted.
- An electronic security alarm system has been installed.
- Security cameras and monitors have been installed.

Emergency Preparedness

- The organization has an emergency preparedness plan for both internal and external disasters.
- The plan has been developed in cooperation with local and national emergency preparedness programs.
- The organization identifies its vulnerabilities (e.g., equipment, supplies, staff, communications) and implements improvements.
- The plan is periodically practiced to determine the organization's readiness for a variety of disasters (e.g., earthquake, hurricane, act of terrorism).

Patient Identification

- The patient's wristband is checked for identification prior to rendering treatment.
- Two identifiers are noted prior to treatment (patient's name, birth date, medical record number, etc.) and match the information on the wristband to the patient's medical chart.
- A patient's room number or bed location within a room is never used as a patient identifier.

Infection Control

- Hand hygiene protocols have been developed.
  - Use recommended soaps.
  - Use alcohol-based hand rubs.
- Recommended temperature and humidity levels are maintained.
- Patients at risk for developing pressure ulcers are assessed.
  - Protocols to prevent development of pressure ulcers are followed.
- Food products are labeled as to contents and expiration dates.
- Infection-control policies and procedures include gowning, masks, and glove changes between patients.
- Furniture, equipment, and toys are disinfected with appropriate germicidal solutions.

Laboratory Services

- Critical lab values are reported promptly.
- Therapeutic ranges are closely monitored.
- Blood levels for toxicity are closely followed.
- Test results that do not fit a patient's clinical picture or expected outcomes are addressed by the patient's physician(s).

Nephrology

- Nursing standards are current.
- History and physical are complete.
- Physician orders for dialysis are current.

- Medication lists are current.
- Allergies are recorded.
- Laboratory test results are available.
- Staff competency is evaluated.
- There is a certified nephrology nurse.
- Space and storage are adequate.
- Dialysis orders are current.
- Equipment is properly cleaned.
- Infection control risks are addressed.

Surgical Specimens

- Second reads of specimen are conducted as considered necessary.
- Procedures are implemented to reduce the risk of surgical specimen mix-ups.
- Specimens are properly jarred and labeled at the surgical table.
- All specimens, including blood, do not leave one's possession until labeled.
- A strict chain of custody for each specimen is maintained.
- Pre- and postoperative pathology report discrepancies are addressed.

Medication Safety

- Drugs are safely stored, ordered, and distributed.
- Potentially dangerous look-alike, sound-alike drugs are separated in the pharmacy to prevent mix-ups.
- All medications are labeled including the drug, dosage, and expiration date.
- A process is implemented for obtaining and documenting a complete listing of a patient's current medications upon admission to the organization.
- Medications to be continued during a patient's stay are made by the physician.
- Upon discharge, the attending physician instructs the patient as to which drugs should be continued or discontinued.
- A complete list of drugs is made available to the next provider when the patient is transferred to another setting, service, practitioner, or level of care within or outside the organization.
- Risk-reduction activities are in place to reduce the likelihood of adverse drug reactions and medication errors.
- There is a mechanism for monitoring the effect of medications on patients.
- Responsibility for ensuring the integrity of crash carts has been assigned.

- The organization maintains the appropriate medications and equipment on crash carts for treating both children and adults.
- Staff members are appropriately trained in the testing and use of equipment contained in or on the crash cart.
- Staff members who participate in codes are periodically tested for competency.
- High-risk drugs are easily identified and standardized when feasible.
- There is a mechanism in place for approving and overseeing the use of investigational drugs.
- Investigational drug protocols and criteria have been developed and approved.
- Look-alike medications are repackaged or relabeled, as necessary, in the pharmacy.
- Causes and trends of medication errors are tracked.
- Educational processes have been implemented to reduce the likelihood of medication errors.

Patient Assessments

- Thorough history and physicals are conducted.
- There is a process for assessing patient care needs.
- The organization has a policy for conducting screenings and assessments.
- Nutritional screens and assessments are performed.
- Functional screens and assessments are performed.

Surgery and Invasive Procedures

- Patients are informed of the risks, benefits, and alternatives to anesthesia, surgical procedures, and the administration of blood or blood products.
- Consent forms are executed and placed in the patient's record.
- Responsibility has been assigned for ensuring that appropriate equipment, supplies, and staffing are available prior to the administration of anesthesia.
- A pertinent and thorough history and physical have been completed and reviewed prior to surgery.
- A process exists by which there is a correlation of pathology and diagnostic findings.
- A preanesthesia assessment has been conducted.
- The surgeon has been credentialed to perform the surgical procedure that he or she is about to perform.
- Vital signs, airway, and surgical site assessments are continuously monitored.
- A procedure for instrument and sponge counts prior to closing the surgical site has been implemented.
- Surgical equipment is properly cleaned and stored following each procedure.

Universal Precautions

- A process has been implemented to clearly mark the correct surgical site.
- If the actual site cannot be marked, a mark is placed in close proximity of the surgical site.
- Both the operating physician and patient are involved in the preoperative marking process.
- The patient's medical record is available to help determine the correct site prior to the start of surgery.
- Imaging studies are available for review prior to surgery to help determine the correct surgical site.
- Observation confirms that the correct site has been marked, with the patient's participation.
- The surgical team (all disciplines) conducts a documented "time out" prior to the start of surgery to confirm the correct patient, correct site, and correct procedure.

Spiritual Care Services

- The spiritual needs of patients are addressed.
- Patients know such services are available and how to access them.
- Organizational policies and procedures address the psychosocial, spiritual, and cultural variables that influence one's understanding and perception of illness.
- Referrals are made for spiritual assessment, reassessment, and follow-up.
- Documentation is placed in the patient's medical record to indicate that the patient's spiritual needs have been addressed.

CQI APPROACH TO PERFORMANCE IMPROVEMENT

Continuous quality improvement (CQI) is an approach to improving quality on a continuing basis. CQI involves improving performance at every functional level of an organization's operation, using available resources (human and capital). It combines fundamental management techniques, innovative improvement efforts, and specialized technical skills in a structure focused on continuously improving processes. CQI relies on people and involves everyone. CQI is concerned with providing a quality product, getting to market on time, providing the best service, reducing costs, broadening market share, and organizational growth. The benefits of CQI are well documented and include reduced customer complaints and turnover;

increased ability to attract new customers; and improved productivity, services, and quality.

The ultimate successes of CQI require commitment by the organization's leadership. In the healthcare setting, leadership includes the administration, governing body, medical staff, and nursing staff. From the leadership, involvement must be expanded to include the entire organization.

The organization's plan should be designed to provide a systematic and ongoing process for monitoring and evaluating patient care, identifying opportunities for improvement, and identifying high-risk areas having the potential for adverse outcomes and increased exposure to litigation.

CQI Data Collection

Data collection for improving quality performance in an organization is often categorized and based on: volume indicators, occurrence screens, focused reviews, and clinical pertinence reviews of medical records. It should be remembered that it is not just data collection that is important but the aggregation of the data in a meaningful format, such as graphs and charts. This information is then analyzed to show trends and to determine if there is a need for improving performance.

Volume Indicators

Volume indicators provide data that demonstrate the scope and frequency of services provided over time (e.g., admission/discharge data, number of procedures, and outpatient visits). Volume indicators also provide valuable information for monitoring the incidence of adverse outcomes (e.g., infection rates following surgical procedures, adverse drug reactions, and medication errors). The information and data gathered by an organization are of significant importance as they relate to budgeting, resource allocation, and strategic planning.

Clinical Indicators

Clinical indicators are used to screen the care provided to patients by clinical specialty. The screens are generally confined to those related to high-volume or high-risk problems that may be unique to the clinical specialty. Each specialty uses such indicators to aid in the identification of opportunities for improving care practices. These opportunities are identified when collected data elements cross a preestablished threshold set by the clinical department or service. When the threshold has been crossed, those cases are then examined and the reason for variation is determined.

Occurrence Screens

Occurrence screens are predetermined indicators used to signal the need for evaluation of some aspect of patient care. Screens may describe the processes in the delivery of care, clinical events, complications, or outcomes for which data can be collected to compare actual results with criteria related to the screen. Events such as unexpected deaths, returns to the surgical suite, or adverse drug reactions should prompt an investigation to determine whether the events could be traced to structural problems (e.g., availability of resources) or process problems (e.g., timeliness and skills in the delivery of health care).

Focused Reviews

Focused reviews are concentrated reviews of key areas in a department or clinical specialty determined by their high risk, high volume, or history of identified problems. Focused reviews might target a representative sample of high-volume diagnoses or procedures over a finite time period or a review of all cases of low-volume but high-risk care.

Clinical Pertinence Review of Medical Records

The clinical pertinence review of medical records is a CQI process that monitors and evaluates the clinical pertinence, completeness, accuracy, timeliness, and legibility of documentation as reflected in the medical record. The purpose of such a review is to identify opportunities for improvement in the record documentation process.

Successful CQI Programs

Listed here are a few of the many areas in which healthcare organizations have successfully implemented the CQI process:

- reducing the likelihood of medication errors
- minimizing the risks of hospital acquired infections
- improving response time for thrombolytic therapy
- recognizing abnormal vital signs and changes in patient's condition
- improving response time (e.g., cardiopulmonary arrest)
- improving charting (charting objectively, descriptively, and clinically)
- providing patient–family education
- improving safety
- improving patient satisfaction

- designing and implementing clinical pathways
- providing security and confidentiality of computer-generated information
- using antibiotics effectively and efficiently
- improving pain management

The implementation of CQI in healthcare organizations will improve the quality of patient care and reduce the number of human errors that result in patient injuries and lawsuits. Success will come with true commitment by each organization's leadership. Such commitment requires the full participation of all caregivers. The evolution of a truly successful CQI program involves the transition from CQI as a plan to CQI as a process, and ultimately to CQI as an organizational culture.

Paradigm Shift

Most healthcare organizations have recognized the need for a paradigm shift from the autocratic style of management to a more humanistic participative style of management. The hierarchical autocratic organization is not appropriate for modern society's highly competitive marketplace. The fruits of the autocratic style of management, which include high staff turnover, low morale, resistance to change, limited creativity, lack of excitement and challenge, rigidity, entrenchment in the status quo, low ownership and accountability, and a passive following, have served only to slow the wheels of progress.

IMPLEMENTATION OF BEST PRACTICES

The implementation of best practices can help improve patient outcomes. "Many of the specialty societies either have drafted or are drafting practice guidelines for their medical area of expertise. For example, the American Society of Anesthesiologists developed guidelines for intraoperative monitoring in 1986. During the following year, no lawsuits were brought for hypoxic injuries; in previous years hypoxic injury suits averaged six per year."[3]

RISK MANAGEMENT

The purpose of a risk-management program is to reduce the number of patient injuries and minimize the exposure of an organization to lawsuits. An effective risk-management program includes a monitoring system that identifies potential risks to patients and staff. Information gathered is used to improve patient care and treatment practices. In risk management, steps are taken on a team-effort basis to improve the quality of care and eliminate or minimize the number of accidents that become potential lawsuits. Liability insurers have been strong proponents of risk management; in many cases, insurers have cut premiums for physicians and healthcare organizations that adopt risk-management practices.

Risk management must include a heightened sensitivity to providing a safe environment and addressing the emotional needs of patients. The input of the provider–patient relationship cannot be overemphasized when the provider–patient relationship is intense and inescapable. Individuals, not incidents, bring lawsuits. Good relationships with patients are very important in preventing malpractice suits. Public relations for healthcare professionals are a challenge. It is not only good medical practice, but it is also at the very core of the problem of medical malpractice.

Increasing insurance costs and general financial constraints have pressured hospitals to assume leadership in the prevention of medically related injuries. Risk-management programs should include the following components:

- a grievance or complaint mechanism designed to process and resolve as promptly and effectively as possible grievances by patients or their representatives
- a collection of data with respect to negative healthcare outcomes (whether they give rise to claims)
- medical care evaluation mechanisms, which shall include a tissue committee or medical audit committee to periodically assess the quality of medical care being provided
- education programs for staff personnel engaged in patient care activities dealing with patient safety, medical injury prevention, the legal aspects of patient care, problems of communication and rapport with patients, and other relevant factors known to influence malpractice claims and suits

FAILURE MODE EFFECTS ANALYSIS

Failure mode effects analysis is a method used for identifying and preventing product and process problems before they occur. The healthcare industry is continuously focusing on identifying and reducing medical errors. This approach is proactive in nature. The Joint Commission adopted this concept as a standard in its accreditation process and is surveying organizational compliance with this standard. Organizations are cooperating to reduce the number of medical errors in the nation and, in some instances, the world.

SENTINEL EVENTS

A *sentinel event* is an unexpected occurrence involving death or serious injury or risk thereof. In the healthcare setting, a sentinel event is an unanticipated death or major permanent loss of function not related to the natural course of the patient's illness or underlying condition(s). Sentinel events include such things as a blood transfusion reaction, surgery on the wrong patient or body part, and leaving an unintended foreign object in a patient's body during surgery. They are sentinel because they signal the need for immediate response for investigation and systems improvement in order to prevent reoccurrence of the event.

The Joint Commission requires that a *root cause analysis* (RCA) of a sentinel event be conducted to review an event to identify what, how, why, when, and where an unwanted event occurred in order to help prevent reoccurrence of the same or similar events.

Notes

1. Agency for Healthcare Research and Quality, Frequently Asked Questions, https://info.ahrq.gov/cgi-bin/ahrq.cfg/php/enduser/std_adp.php?p_faqid=2.
2. National Quality Forum, About NQF, http://www.qualityforum.org/About_NQF/About_NQF.aspx.
3. The Robert Wood Johnson Foundation, "Preventing Negligence," *Abridge*, Spring 1991, 8.

26
World Wide Search

Figure 26–1 World Wide Web Search © ra2 studio/ShutterStock, Inc.

✚ Learning Objectives

The reader upon completion of this chapter will be able to:

- Describe how the Internet is an invaluable tool for improving patient care.
- Explain the use of search engines, browsers, and search tips.
- Determine the trustworthiness of healthcare websites.
- Identify a variety of legal, ethics, and government-related websites.

This chapter is designed to provide the reader with a variety of helpful websites when searching for information related to healthcare, ethics, and law-related topics. "The World Wide Web (WWW) is the universe of network-accessible information, an embodiment of human knowledge," according to the organization that Web inventor Tim Berners-Lee helped found, the World Wide Web Consortium. Although a search for information can be challenging, the following information presents the reader with a solid foundation for searching the Web.

SEARCHING THE WEB

Hope is the last thing that dies in man; and though it be exceedingly deceitful, yet it is of this good use to us, that while we are traveling through life, it conducts us in an easier and more pleasant way to our journey's end.

—FRANCOIS DE LA ROCHEFOUCAULD

Begin your search by first taking an enlightening journey to the National Library of Medicine's website at (www .nlm.nih.gov/). The library, located on the grounds of the National Institutes of Health in Bethesda, Maryland, is the world's largest medical library. There are more than 6 million items, including books, journals, photographs, and images, in its collection. The library coordinates a 6,000-member National Network of Libraries of Medicine that promotes and provides access to health information in communities across the United States.

Evaluating Websites

When evaluating healthcare websites on the Internet, look for the symbol of the Health on the Net Foundation (HON) code of conduct for health care at the bottom of webpages. HON is the leading organization promoting and guiding the deployment of useful and reliable online medical and health information and its appropriate and efficient use. Created in 1995, HON is a nonprofit, nongovernmental organization, accredited to the Economic and Social Council of the United Nations. For more information, visit the HON website (www.hon.ch).

Search Engines

A *search engine* is a program that searches the World Wide Web for websites and creates a catalog of information about those sites. The search engine that one chooses to use will search its catalogue for the occurrences of the text being searched. A majority of search engines are subject and keyword engines. Not all search engines access all possible Internet websites; therefore, it may be necessary to use different search engines to conduct a successful search. Listed here are some of the more popular search engines in use:

Alta Vista	www.altavista.com
America Online	www.aol.com
Ask Jeeves	www.ask.com
Baidu	www.Baidu.com

Bing	www.bing.com
Dogpile	www.dogpile.com
Excite	www.excite.com
Expedia	www.expedia.com
Google	www.google.com
InfoSpace	www.infospace.com
Lycos	www.lycos.com
Mamma	www.mamma.com
Northern Light	www.northernlight.com
Yahoo	www.yahoo.com

Search Tips

- Review the search tips that various search engines provide.
- Use quotation marks around phrases to ensure adjacency of words.
- Use a variety of search engines if you are having difficulty locating a particular topic.
- Domain names describe the location of the server where the information being sought is stored.
- Knowing domain names where files are stored is helpful when conducting random searches for information. Website domains include the following:

  .com: Commercial organizations (businesses)
  .edu: Educational organizations
  .gov: Government agencies
  .mil: Military
  .org: Miscellaneous organizations
  .net: Network providers

A path name follows the domain name and identifies the location of an item on the server.

Medical Library Association

Medical Library Association (MLA) is a nonprofit, educational organization with more than 4,000 health sciences information professional members and partners worldwide. MLA provides lifelong educational opportunities, supports a knowledge base of health information research, and works with a global network of partners to promote the importance of quality information for improved health to the healthcare community and the public. http://www.mlanet.org

User's Guide to Finding and Evaluating Health Information

Millions of Americans search for health information on the Web every year. Millions of health-related webpages are viewed by millions of consumers. Sometimes the information found is just what was needed. Other searches end in frustration or retrieval of inaccurate, even dangerous, information.

This guide outlines the collective wisdom of medical librarians who surf the Web every day to discover quality information in support of clinical and scientific decision making by doctors, scientists, and other health practitioners responsible for the nation's health. This guide is supported by the MLA, the library organization whose primary purpose is promoting quality information for improved health and whose members were the first to realize that not all health information on the Web is credible, timely, or safe.

http://www.mlanet.org/resources/userguide.html

Searching Top 10 Websites

When conducting any search such as ethics or the law, for example, it is helpful to Google the *Ten Top Sites* by specific topic, for example, "10 top health law sites" and "10 top healthcare ethics sites."

■ LEGAL WEBSITES

American Bar Association (ABA): www.abanet.org
[The ABA is the largest voluntary professional association in the world. With more than 400,000 members, the ABA provides law school accreditation, continuing legal education, information about the law, programs to assist lawyers and judges in their work, and initiatives to improve the legal system for the public.]

American Health Lawyers Association (AHLA): www.healthlawyers.org
[The AHLA is the nation's largest, nonpartisan, 501(c)(3) educational organization devoted to legal issues in the healthcare field with more than 10,000 members.]

American Society of Law, Medicine and Ethics (ASLME): www.aslme.org
[The ASLME is a community of colleagues across three major disciplines. The ASLME publishes two nationally acclaimed peer-reviewed journals: *The Journal of Law, Medicine & Ethics* and *The American Journal of Law & Medicine*; the society also sponsors conferences and webinars, as well as research and grants.]

Court Reporters: www.courtreporters.com
[Court Reporters was created to provide legal professionals immediate Internet access to the highest caliber and most reliable court reporters nationwide.]

Courtroom Sciences: www.courtroomsciences.com
[Courtroom Sciences provides litigation solutions to corporations and law firms with a complete set of tools and services.]

FedLaw: www.thecre.com/fedlaw/default.htm
[FedLaw has assembled references of use to people doing federal legal research and that can be accessed directly through "point and click" hypertext connections.]

FindLaw: www.findlaw.com
[FindLaw, a Thomson Reuters business, is a provider of online legal information and Internet marketing solutions for law firms.]

Guide to Law Online: www.loc.gov/law/guide
[*The Guide to Law Online*, prepared by the Law Library of Congress Public Services Division, is an annotated guide to sources of information on government and law available online. It includes selected links to useful and reliable sites for legal information.]

Health Law Resource: www.netreach.net/~wmanning
[Primarily, this page is intended as a resource for healthcare practitioners, professionals, or anyone interested in learning more about the dynamic field of healthcare law and, more specifically, the regulatory and transactional aspects of healthcare law practice.]

HGExperts.com: www.hgexperts.com
[HGExperts.com is a legal experts dictionary with an expert witness directory, litigation support, publications for expert witnesses, forensic science, and more.]

Legal Information Institute (LII): www.law.cornell.edu
[LII is a not-for-profit group that believes everyone should be able to read and understand the laws that govern them, without cost. LII carries out this vision by publishing law online for free, creating materials that help people understand law, and exploring new technologies that make it easier for people to find the law.]

LexisNexis: www.lexisnexis.com
[A leading global provider of content-enabled workflow solutions to professionals in law firms, corporations, government, law enforcement, tax, accounting, academic institutions, and risk and compliance assessment.]

NoLo: www.nolo.com
[NoLo aims to help Americans understand the legal rules and procedures that affect their lives, so they can handle legal matters themselves or seek expert help armed with the knowledge they need. Not only is free law information provided, but the site also includes articles discussing

various law issues including taxes, employment laws, and immigration.]

State Resources, AllLaw.com: www.alllaw.com/state_resources

[AllLaw.com provides state legal links that, when clicked, bring up links for the state with law topics from attorneys to law schools to forms to the state bar.]

Supreme Court Collection: www.law.cornell.edu/supct

[The Supreme Court Collection of LII is a database of all Supreme Court decisions. The decisions can be looked up by case name, topic, or the justices.]

United States Courts.gov: www.uscourts.gov

[United States Courts is the government website for all things related to the U.S. courts, including links to the federal courts, judges, court reporters, and more.]

VersusLaw: www.versuslaw.com

[VersusLaw is a Web-based research site that provides three different law research plans. Each contains both federal and state appellate case law opinions.]

Westlaw: www.westlaw.com

[Although subscription is required, Westlaw has up-to-date legal products and services.]

ETHICS WEBSITES

Advance Directives: www.mindspring.com/~scottr/will.html

[An organized set of links to living will (advance directive) webpages.]

American Association of Tissue Banks (AATB): www.aatb.org

[AATB is a professional, nonprofit, scientific, and educational organization. Among other benefits, the AATB website offers information on the Certification of Tissue Bank Personnel, as well as accreditation processes.]

American Society of Law, Medicine and Ethics (ASLME): www.aslme.org

[With roots extending back to 1911, ASLME is a nonprofit educational organization. Their mission is to provide high-quality scholarship, debate, and critical thought for professionals at the intersection of law, medicine, and ethics. Members come together to examine health questions with far-reaching social ramifications like genetic testing and research, medical record privacy, end-of-life decisions, and the dynamics of informed consent.]

American Society of Transplantation: www.a-s-t.org

[The American Society of Transplantation is an international organization of transplant professionals dedicated to advancing the field of transplantation through the promotion of research, education, advocacy, and organ donation to improve patient care.]

Association of Organ Procurement Organizations (AOPO): www.aopo.org

[AOPO represents and serves organ procurement organizations through advocacy, support, and development of activities that will maximize the availability of organs and tissues and enhance the quality, effectiveness, and integrity of the donation process.]

Bioethics.net: www.bioethics.net

[A leading website on medical ethics; it contains articles, journals, news, jobs, events, and more related to bioethics.]

Center for Bioethics and Human Dignity: www.cbhd.org

[The center exists to equip thought leaders to engage the issues of bioethics using the tools of rigorous research, conceptual analysis, charitable critique, leading-edge publication, and effective teaching.]

Cornell University Law School: www.law.cornell.edu/uscode/

[U.S. Code materials.]

Donate Life America: www.shareyourlife.org

[Donate Life America assists in mobilizing the transplantation community to educate the American public on the need for organ, eye, and tissue donation and motivating the public to make an actionable donor designation. The organization publishes brochures, program kits, and other materials; provides technical assistance and referral services; coordinates the national campaign for organ, eye, and tissue donation; identifies measurable best practices; and leads the Donor Designation Collaborative.]

EthicsWeb.ca: www.ethicsweb.ca/resources/bioethics/

[A collection of ethics-related websites run by philosopher–ethicist Chris MacDonald. Chris has been administering respected ethics-related websites since 1994. The style and function of the various EthicsWeb.ca websites vary, but each strives to present a selected range of high-quality ethics-related resources on a particular topic.]

Eye Bank Association of America (EBAA): www.restoresight.org

[The EBAA champions the restoration of sight through core services to its members, which advance donation, transplantation, and research in their communities and throughout the world. EBAA online has information about donations, awards and grants, and accreditations and certifications.]

Markkula Center for Applied Ethics: www.scu.edu/ethics/practicing/focusareas/medical
[This website contains articles, cases, and links on medical ethics, biotechnology and ethics, clinical ethics, end-of-life decision making, culturally competent health care, and public health policy from the Markkula Center for Applied Ethics at Santa Clara University. Center staff and scholars work with hospitals, public health departments, and other agencies to analyze real-world ethical issues in medicine and biotechnology and to develop innovative tools and programs to address them.]

MedlinePlus: www.nlm.nih.gov/medlineplus/endoflifeissues.html
[Comprehensive review of end-of-life issues.]

National Advisory Board on Social Welfare and Health Care Ethics: www.etene.fi/en
[The National Advisory Board on Social Welfare and Health Care Ethics deals with ethical issues related to health care and the status and rights of patients from the point of view of principle.]

National Center for Biotechnology Information: www.ncbi.nlm.nih.gov/
[The National Center for Biotechnology Information advances science and health by providing access to biomedical and genomic information.]

Planned Parenthold: http://www.plannedparenthood.org
[Planned Parenthood delivers vital reproductive health care, sex education, and information to millions of women, men, and young people worldwide.]

Questia: www.questia.com/Index.jsp
[Questia is an online searching agent with over 70,000 copyrighted books, 2 million articles, and intuitive research tools for organizing, managing, and storing work.]

TransWeb.org: www.transweb.org
[TransWeb.org provides information about donation and transplantation to the general public in order to improve organ and tissue procurement efforts worldwide and to provide transplant patients and families worldwide with information specifically dealing with transplantation-related issues and concern.]

United Network for Organ Sharing (UNOS): www.unos.org
[UNOS is a nonprofit, scientific and educational organization that administers the nation's only Organ Procurement

and Transplantation Network (OPTN), established by the U.S. Congress in 1984. Through the OPTN, the UNOS collects and manages data about every transplantation event occurring in the United States, facilitates the organ matching and placement process using UNOS-developed data technology and the UNOS Organ Center, and brings together medical professionals, transplant recipients, and donor families to develop organ transplantation policy.]

▌GOVERNMENT WEBSITES

Agency for Healthcare Research and Quality (AHRQ): www.ahrq.gov
[The AHRQ is the nation's lead federal agency for research on healthcare quality, costs, outcomes, and patient safety. AHRQ supports improvements in health outcomes, develops strategies to strengthen quality measurement and improvement, and identifies strategies to improve healthcare access, foster appropriate use, and reduce unnecessary expenditures. The website also provides news and events, clinical information, data and surveys, and research findings.]

Centers for Disease Control and Prevention (CDC): www.cdc.gov
[CDC.gov is the CDC's primary online communication channel. Annually, there are close to 500 million page views to the site, averaging 41 million page views per month. CDC.gov provides users with credible, reliable health information on data and statistics, diseases and conditions, emergencies and disasters, environmental health, healthy living, injury, violence and safety, life stages and populations, travelers' health, and workplace safety and health.]

Centers for Medicare and Medicaid Services (CMS): www.cms.gov
[CMS ensures effective, up-to-date healthcare coverage and promotes quality care for beneficiaries. CMS central and regional offices share a common vision and mission as well as a shared commitment to the five key objectives: skilled, committed, and highly motivated workforce; affordable healthcare system; high-value health care; confident, informed consumers; and collaborative partnerships.]

ClinicalTrials.gov: www.clinicaltrials.gov
[A National Library of Medicine (NLM)/National Institutes of Health (NIH) database about clinical research trials that provides information to the public about studies in which new treatments, drugs, diagnostic procedures, vaccines, and other therapies are tested in people to see if they

are safe and effective. A clinical trial can be searched by the name of the disease, the location, type of treatments, or sponsoring institution. The results will show what studies are being conducted, whether a trial is recruiting, the purpose of the study, where and when it will take place, whom to contact, and sources for more information.]

CMS Conditions of Participation: www.cms.gov/CfCsAndCoPs/
[CMS develops conditions of participation (CoPs) and conditions for coverage (CfCs) that healthcare organizations must meet in order to begin and continue participating in the Medicare and Medicaid programs. These minimum health and safety standards are the foundation for improving quality and protecting the health and safety of beneficiaries. CMS also ensures that the standards of accrediting organizations recognized by CMS (through a process called "deeming") meet or exceed the Medicare standards set forth in the CoPs/CfCs.

CoPs and CfCs are the minimum health and safety standards that providers and suppliers must meet in order to be Medicare and Medicaid certified. CoPs and CfCs apply to, for example, hospitals and nursing facilities.]

CMS Interpretive Guidelines: www.cms.hhs.gov/-manuals/downloads/som107_-Appendixtoc.pdf
[The Interpretive Guidelines and Survey Procedures for various providers or suppliers are located in the Appendices to the *State Operations Manual* (SOM).]

CMS Survey and Certification Letters: ww.cms.hhs.gov/SurveyCertificationGenInfo/PMSR/list.asp
[CMS Survey and Certification (S&C) releases information related to survey and certification guidance for various providers and suppliers to its Regional Offices and the State Survey Agencies through communications called Survey and Certification Letters. The letters are released on an ongoing basis. Once a letter is released, it is posted on the CMS website.]

CMS Survey and Certification Home Page: www.cms.hhs.gov/SurveyCertificationGenInfo
[The page provides general information regarding the activities of CMS Survey and Certification. The Interpretive Guidelines and S&C letters may also be accessed from this page.]

CMS AND Electronic CFR (e-CFR): http://ecfr.gpoaccess.gov
[The e-CFR is an electronic version of the Code of Federal Regulations (CFR). The CFR is divided into "Titles," with "Title 42 Public Health," containing CMS regulations. The

Federal Register within the Government Printing Office publishes the CFR of an annual basis. The e-CFR is updated on an ongoing basis.]

Congress: www.congress.org
[A nonpartisan news and information website devoted to encouraging civic participation whose mission is to provide information about public policy issues of the day and tips on effective advocacy so that citizens can make their voices heard.]

Congressional Directory: www.congress.org/congressorg/directory/congdir.tt
[Easy to use directory to find state representatives; also provides demographics, committees, and offices.]

Department of Health and Human Services (HHS): www.hhs.gov
[The Department of Health and Human Services is the U.S. government's principal agency for protecting the health of all Americans and providing essential human services, especially for those who are least able to help themselves. The work of the Department of Health and Human Services is conducted by the Office of the Secretary and by 11 agencies. The agencies perform a wide variety of tasks and services, including research, public health, food and drug safety, grants and other funding, health insurance, and many others.]

Department of Justice (DOJ): www.justice.gov
[DOJ enforces the law, ensures public safety, seeks just punishment, and ensures fair and impartial administration of justice for all Americans. Justice.gov provides information related to the DOJ mission, including forms, publications, news, grants, and an overview of the American Recovery and Reinvestment Act of 2009.]

Department of Labor: www.dol.gov
[The Department of Labor fosters and promotes the welfare of the job seekers, wage earners, and retirees of the United States by improving their working conditions, advancing their opportunities for profitable employment, protecting their retirement and healthcare benefits, helping employers find workers, strengthening free collective bargaining, and tracking changes in employment, prices, and other national economic measurements. In carrying out this mission, the department administers a variety of federal labor laws, including those that guarantee workers' rights to safe and healthful working conditions, a minimum hourly wage and overtime pay, freedom from employment discrimination, unemployment insurance, and other income support.]

Electronic Code of Federal Regulations: http://ecfr
.gpoaccess.gov/cgi/t/text/text-idx?c=ecfr&atpl=%2Findex.tpl
[The Electronic Code of Federal Regulations (e-CFR) is a currently updated version of the Code of Federal Regulations (CFR). It is not an official legal edition of the CFR. The e-CFR is an editorial compilation of CFR material and Federal Register amendments produced by the National Archives and Records Administration's Office of the Federal Register (OFR) and the Government Printing Office. The OFR updates the material in the e-CFR on a daily basis. The current update status appears at the top of all e-CFR webpages.]

Food and Drug Administration (FDA): www.fda.gov
[The FDA is responsible for protecting and advancing public health. FDA.gov offers research and regulatory information on food, drugs, medical devices, vaccines, veterinary drugs, cosmetics, radiation-emitting products, and tobacco products. There is also news, help on reporting problems, and recalls and alerts.]

Government Manual: www.gpoaccess.gov/gmanual
[The U.S. Government Manual provides comprehensive information on the agencies of the legislative, judicial, and executive branches. It also includes information on quasi-official agencies, international organizations in which the United States participates, and boards, commissions, and committees.]

Healthfinder: www.healthfinder.gov
[Healthfinder.gov provides current and reliable health information and tools, including a health topic index, services and information, personal health tools, and the Freedom of Information Act.]

Health Insurance Portability and Accountability Act (HIPAA): www.hhs.gov/ocr/privacy
[HIPAA provides various protections for personal health information. The Department of Health and Human Services provides a wealth of information on HIPAA, including summaries of both the Privacy Rule and the Security Rule, directions in filing complaints, simplification statues and rules, and enforcement actions and results.]

Health Insurance Portability and Accountability Act—Forms: http://hipaa.ucsf.edu/ documentation/default.html
[Forms for patients, staff, data sharing, and more are provided by the University of California, San Francisco. Most forms may be found on state websites.]

Health Resources and Services Administration: www
.hrsa.gov
[The Health Resources and Services Administration, an agency of the U.S. Department of Health and Human Services, is the primary federal agency for improving access to healthcare services for people who are uninsured, isolated, or medically vulnerable. Their goals are to improve access to quality care and services, strengthen the health workforce, build healthy communities, and improve health equity. The website also includes information, for example, about grants, statistics, National Health Services Corps, and the Health Professions Workforce.]

MedlinePlus: www.medlineplus.gov
[MedlinePlus will direct you to information to help answer health questions. MedlinePlus brings together authoritative information from NLM, NIH, and other government agencies and health-related organizations. Preformulated MEDLINE searches are included in MedlinePlus and give easy access to medical journal articles. MedlinePlus also has extensive information about drugs, an illustrated medical encyclopedia, interactive patient tutorials, and latest health news.]

Museum of Medical Research: www.nlm.nih.gov/hmd/
medtour/nih.html
[Founded in 1868 as a part of the NIH, the museum exhibits seek to educate the public about the process of biomedical research, generally focusing on the research of NIH investigators. The museum collects, preserves, and interprets biomedical research instruments and memorabilia, especially those related to the NIH.]

National Cancer Institute: www.cancer.gov
[The National Cancer Institute, part of the NIH, is the federal government's principal agency for cancer research and training. Cancer.gov is comprised of resources such as dictionaries of terms and drugs, funding opportunities, free publications, cancer statistics, and news.]

National Center for Health Statistics: www.cdc.gov/nchs
[The National Center for Health Statistics compiles statistical information to guide actions and policies to improve the health of our people. Information found on the website includes statistics systems, publications, and data access tools about health statistics.]

National Guideline Clearinghouse (NGC): www.guideline
.gov
[A public resource for evidence-based clinical practice guidelines. The NGC provides useful resources such as annotated bibliographies, hospital-acquired conditions, patient resources, and more.]

National Information Center on Health Services Research and Health Care Technology (NICHSR): www
.nlm.nih.gov/nichsr
[NICHSR was created to improve the ". . . collection, storage, analysis, retrieval, and dissemination of information

on health services research, clinical practice guidelines, and on health care technology."]

National Institute of Medicine (IOM): www.iom.edu
[IOM is an independent, nonprofit organization that works outside of government to provide unbiased and authoritative advice to decision makers and the public. IOM.edu has an extensive database of medicinal reports that provide objective and straightforward advice to decision makers and the public and also undertakes many different types of activities, all aimed at improving health.]

National Institutes of Health (NIH): www.nih.gov
[Helping to lead the way toward important medical discoveries that improve people's health and save lives, NIH scientists investigate ways to prevent disease as well as the causes, treatments, and even cures for common and rare diseases. Composed of 27 institutes and centers, the NIH provides leadership and financial support to researchers in every state and throughout the world. NIH.gov gives links to their various institutes and centers, the NIH Almanac, recoveries and reinvestments, and updated news and legislation regarding health.]

National Labor Relations Board: www.nlrb.gov
[The National Labor Relations Board is an independent federal agency created by Congress in 1935 to administer the National Labor Relations Act, the primary law governing relations between unions and employers in the private sector. The statute guarantees the right of employees to organize and to bargain collectively with their employers and to engage in other protected concerted activity with or without a union, or to refrain from all such activity.]

National Network of Libraries of Medicine (NNLM): www.nnlm.gov
[The mission of the NNLM is to advance the progress of medicine and improve public health by providing all U.S. health professionals with equal access to biomedical information and improving the public's access to information to enable them to make informed decisions about their health.]

National Practitioner Data Bank (NPDB): www.npdb-hipdb.hrsa.gov
[The intent of the NPDB is to improve the quality of health care by encouraging state licensing boards, hospitals and other healthcare entities, and professional societies to identify and discipline those who engage in unprofessional behavior; and to restrict the ability of incompetent physicians, dentists, and other healthcare practitioners to move from state to state without disclosure or discovery of previous medical malpractice payment and adverse action history. Adverse actions can involve licensure, clinical privileges, professional society membership, and exclusions from Medicare and Medicaid.]

Occupational Safety and Health Administration: www.osha.gov
[The purpose of the Occupational Safety and Health Administration is to ensure safe and healthful working conditions for working men and women by authorizing enforcement of the standards developed under the act, by assisting and encouraging the states in their efforts to ensure safe and healthful working conditions, and by providing for research, information, education, and training in the field of occupational safety and health.]

PubMed.gov: www.ncbi.nlm.nih.gov/sites/entrez
[PubMed comprises more than 19 million citations for biomedical literature from MEDLINE, life science journals, and online books. Citations may include links to full-text content from PubMed Central and publisher websites.]

■ BEST PRACTICES

Advisory Board Company (ABC): www.advisory.com
[The ABC serves nearly 3,000 progressive organizations worldwide—health care, health benefits, and educational organizations alike—and provides innovative solutions to their most pressing challenges such that they can "hardwire" best-practice performance.]

Association of Cancer Online Resources (ACOR): www.acor.org
[The heart of ACOR is a large collection of cancer-related Internet mailing lists, which deliver millions of e-mail messages to subscribers across the globe. In addition to supporting the mailing lists, ACOR develops and hosts state-of-the-art Internet-based knowledge systems that allow the public to find and use credible information relevant to their illness.]

CancerLinks: www.cancerlinks.org
[CancerLinks.org is a search engine in which you can search for anything cancer related and find relevant websites with answers.]

Careplans.com: www.careplans.com
[Careplans.com provides resources for nursing assessment, planning, implementation, and evaluation. The site

includes articles, links, and libraries to assist caregivers in the care planning process.]

Centre for Evidence-Based Medicine (CEBM): www .cebm.net
[Established in Oxford, CEBM provides free support and resources to doctors, clinicians, teachers, and others interested in learning more about evidence-based medicine through resources such as research and development, training of students and clinicians, and training of the trainers.]

Clinical Pathways: www.openclinical.org/clinicalpathways .html
[The website provides explanation of clinical pathways and their benefits. The website's host OpenClinical.org is designed to be a "one-stop shop" for anyone interested in learning about and tracking developments on advanced knowledge management technologies for health care such as point-of-care decision support systems, "intelligent" guidelines, and clinical workflow.]

Clinical Practice Guidelines: www.ahcpr.gov/clinic/ cpgsix.htm
[This website is under the Agency for Healthcare Research and Quality and provides links to archives and the National Guideline Clearinghouse.]

Institute for Safe Medication Practices (ISMP): www .ismp.org
[The ISMP, based in suburban Philadelphia, is the nation's only 501(c)(3) nonprofit organization devoted entirely to medication error prevention and safe medication use. ISMP represents over 30 years of experience in helping healthcare practitioners keep patients safe and continues to lead efforts to improve the medication use process.]

MD Consult: www.mdconsult.com
[MD Consult offers instant access to full-text articles from over 80 medical journals and clinics, 50 leading medical references across a wide range of specialties, clinically relevant drug information, and over 10,000 patient handouts, MD Consult is truly all you need.]

National Organization for Rare Diseases (NORD): www .rarediseases.org
[NORD provides information about diseases, referrals to patient organizations, research grants and fellowships, advocacy for the rare disease community, and medication assistance programs that help needy patients obtain certain drugs they could not otherwise afford.]

HOSPITAL AND PHYSICIAN FINDERS

American Board of Medical Specialties (ABMS): www .abms.org
[The primary function of ABMS is to assist its member boards in developing and implementing educational and professional standards to evaluate and certify physician specialists. By participating in these initiatives, ABMS also serves as a unique and highly influential voice in the healthcare industry, bringing focus and rigor to issues involving specialization and certification in medicine. ABMS is a designated primary equivalent source of credential information.]

American Medical Association DoctorFinder: www .ama-assn.org/aps/amahg.htm
[The American Medical Association helps doctors help patients by uniting physicians nationwide to work on the most important professional and public health issues.]

Best Hospitals: health.usnews.com/best-hospitals
[*U.S. News & World Report* has ranked over 5,000 hospitals in 16 adult specialties and 10 pediatric specialties to help you find the one that's best for you and your family.]

Besthospitals.com: www.besthospitals.com
[A search engine of the best hospitals in America.]

HealthGrades: www.healthgrades.com
[HealthGrades is the leading healthcare ratings organization, providing ratings and profiles of hospitals, nursing homes, and physicians to consumers, corporations, health plans, and hospitals. HealthGrades provides information and help for consumers, hospitals, health plans, liability insurers, and the community.]

HospitalConnectSearch: www.hospitalconnect.com
[HospitalConnectSearch is a complete source for reliable hospital information, organized by specific areas of interest.]

HospitalLink.com: www.hospitallink.com
[The HospitalLink.com website directory makes it easy to locate hospitals and 1,700 websites by city, state, hospital name, and/or zip code.]

Massachusetts General Hospital: www.mgh.harvard.edu
[The third oldest general hospital in the United States and often ranked among the top five hospitals in the nation by *U.S. News & World Report.*]

Healthcare Resources Alternative Medicine: www
.askdrweil.com
[Dr. Andrew Weil, M.D., answers questions on health care,
aging, vitamins, health plans, and more.]

American Academy of Pain Management: www
.painmed.org
[Founded in 1983 as the American Academy of Algology,
the American Academy of Pain Medicine has evolved as
the primary organization for physicians practicing the specialty of pain medicine in the United States.]

American Hospital Association (AHA): www.aha.org
[AHA is the national organization that represents and
serves all types of hospitals, healthcare networks, and their
patients and communities. Founded in 1898, the AHA provides education for healthcare leaders and is a source of
information on healthcare issues and trends. Close to 5,000
hospitals, healthcare systems, networks, other providers
of care, and 40,000 individual members come together to
form the AHA. The AHA ensures that members' perspec-
tives and needs are heard and addressed in national health
policy development, legislative and regulatory debates, and
judicial matters.]

American Library Association: www.ala.org
[Founded on October 6, 1876, during the Centennial Expo-
sition in Philadelphia, the American Library Association
was created to provide leadership for the development,
promotion, and improvement of library and information
services and the profession of librarianship in order to
enhance learning and ensure access to information for all.]

American Medical Association (AMA): www.ama-assn
.org
[The mission of the AMA is to promote the art and science
of medicine and the betterment of public health. The vision
of the AMA is to be an essential part of the professional
life of every physician. The American Medical Association
helps doctors help patients by uniting physicians nationwide to work on the most important professional and public health issues.]

American Pain Foundation: www.painfoundation.org
[Founded in 1997, the American Pain Foundation is an
independent nonprofit 501(c)(3) organization serving
people with pain through information, advocacy, and
support. Their mission is to improve the quality of life of
people with pain by raising public awareness, providing
practical information, promoting research, and advocating to remove barriers and increase access to effective pain
management.]

Directory of Open Access Journals: www.doaj.org
[This service covers free, full-text, quality-controlled scientific
and scholarly journals, covering all subjects and languages.]

FamilyDoctor.org: www.familydoctor.org/online/famdocen/
home.html
[Health information for the whole family from the American Academy of Family Practitioners.]

Guide to Internet Resources for Cancer: http://www
.cancerindex.org/clinks1.htm
[The Guide to Internet Resources for Cancer is a gateway to
cancer information on the Internet established in 1996. This
nonprofit guide contains over 100 pages and more than 4,000
links to cancer-related information. It is regularly updated
and links are periodically verified using a link-checker.]

HealthWorld Online: www.healthy.net
[HealthWorld Online offers natural solutions to all health-
related questions while providing a community for the
health conscious.]

InteliHealth: www.intelihealth.com
[InteliHealth is one of the nation's leading diversified healthcare benefits companies, serving approximately 37.2 million people with information and resources to help them
make better informed decisions about their health care.]

Library Spot: www.libraryspot.com
[Library Spot is a free virtual library resource center for
educators and students, librarians and their patrons, families, businesses, and just about anyone exploring the Web
for valuable research information.]

Life Extension Foundation: www.lef.org
[The Life Extension Foundation is the world's largest organization dedicated to finding scientific methods for addressing
disease, aging, and death. The Life Extension Foundation is
a nonprofit group that funds pioneering scientific research
aimed at achieving an indefinitely extended healthy human
life span. The fruits of this research are used to develop
novel disease prevention and treatment protocols.]

MayoClinic.com: www.mayoclinic.com
[One of the nation's finest clinics provides information on
diseases and conditions, drugs and supplements, treatment
decisions, and healthy living.]

Medscape: www.medscape.com
[Medscape from WebMD offers specialists, primary care
physicians, and other health professionals robust and integrated medical information and educational tools. Key features consist of selected daily professional medical news
for specialties from Reuters, Medscape Medical News, and

medical news journal publishers and business, financial, managed care, and medical practice information.]

Merriam-Webster On-Line Dictionary: www.merriam-webster.com
[This website offers a full dictionary of all words; resources include the unabridged dictionary, video, and the Britannica Online Encyclopedia.]

National Health Museum (NHM): www.accessexcellence.com
[NHM is a national educational program that provides health, biology, and life science teachers access to their colleagues, scientists, and critical sources of new scientific information via the World Wide Web.]

Telemedicine: www.amdtelemedicine.com
[AMD Global Telemedicine is a supplier of medical technology for telemedicine with over 5,700 installations in 79 countries. This includes medical devices, complete telemedicine encounter management solutions, and application software for both live and store and forward telemedicine.]

Virtual Hospital: www.uihealthcare.com/vh/
[From the University of Iowa (UI), Virtual Hospital provides health content, prepared and reviewed by health professionals, and continues to serve the UI healthcare mission of educating patients and families about their health and informing them about the expert services available at UI hospitals and clinics for maintaining their health and well-being.]

Virtual Library Pharmacy: www.pharmacy.org
[Virtual Library Pharmacy includes all pharmacy-related internet resources compiled by David Bourne, Ph.D., Professor of Pharmaceutics at the University of Oklahoma.]

▌ INTERNATIONAL MEDICAL WEBSITES

Cancer Index: www.cancerindex.org/clinks5o.htm
[The aim of the Cancer Index is to make it easier to find more specific information quickly. This is achieved by providing a directory of some of the key cancer-related sites and pages. Links are sorted into categories (by disease-type, medical specialty, country, etc.), and where possible, annotation is provided to give the reader a brief description of each site or organization. In addition to links, the site presents basic information about cancer-related topics. Also, the site aims to draw the reader's attention to issues about cancer-related information on the Internet, especially those relating to the quality of information.]

Union for International Cancer Control (UICC): www.uicc.org
[The UICC is the leading international nongovernmental organization dedicated to the global prevention and control of cancer. UICC's mission is to connect, mobilize, and support organizations, leading experts, key stakeholders, and volunteers in a dynamic community working together to eliminate cancer as a life-threatening disease for future generations. Founded in 1933, UICC unites over 300 member organizations, specialized and engaged in cancer control, in more than 100 countries across the world. UICC is nonprofit, nonpolitical, and nonsectarian. Its headquarters are in Geneva, Switzerland.]

World Health Network: www.worldhealth.net
[World Health Network is the leading Internet portal for anti-aging medicine.]

World Health Organization (WHO): www.who.int
[WHO is the directing and coordinating authority for health within the United Nations system. It is responsible for providing leadership on global health matters, shaping the health research agenda, setting norms and standards, articulating evidence-based policy options, providing technical support to countries, and monitoring and assessing health trends.

In the 21st century, health is a shared responsibility, involving equitable access to essential care and collective defense against transnational threats.]

World Medical Association (WMA): www.wma.net
[The WMA is an international organization representing physicians. It was created to ensure the independence of physicians and to work for the highest possible standards of ethical behavior and care by physicians, at all times. The WMA provides a forum for its member associations to communicate freely, to cooperate actively, to achieve consensus on high standards of medical ethics and professional competence, and to promote the professional freedom of physicians worldwide. This unique partnership facilitates high caliber, humane care to patients in a healthy environment, enhancing the quality of life for all people in the world.]

✚ Note

1. English author and lexicographer.

Excellence can be attained if you . . .
Care more than others think is wise.
Risk more than others think is safe.
Dream more than others think is practical.
Expect more than others think is possible.

—AUTHOR UNKNOWN

27
Journey to Excellence

Figure 27–1   Pathway to Excellence   © pan_kung/ShutterStock, Inc.

Learning Objectives

The reader upon completion of this chapter will be able to:

- Discuss the meaning of Journey to Excellence.
- Describe a variety ideas for beginning the Journey to Excellence.
- Discuss why a healthcare war room is a valuable tool for organizations.

- Describe several ways in which a project can be funded and a vision become reality.
- Explain the purpose of the Baldrige award.

This chapter is not the end of this text but a beginning of a long journey to excellence. Progress occurs when those of vision see and act on the limitless possibilities for improving patient care. The *Journey to Excellence* begins with a vision by an organization's leadership to continuously improve the way care is provided in multiple settings. To be successful, leadership must be committed charting new waters and improving patient care.

IDEAS FOR GETTING STARTED

The journey to excellence is not an easy path to follow:

 There is nothing more difficult to take in hand, more perilous to conduct, or more uncertain in its success, than to take the lead in the introduction of a new order of things. Because the innovator has for enemies all those who have done well under the old conditions, and lukewarm defenders in those who may do well under the new. This coolness arises partly from fear of the opponents, who have the laws on their side, and partly from the incredulity of men, who do not readily believe in new things until they have had a long experience of them.
—NICCOLO MACHIAVELLI (*THE PRINCE*, 1513)

The ideas presented below are but a few of the many to help healthcare professionals and organizations as they begin their *Journey to Excellence*. They are offered as agenda items, a starting point. Although many practices may have been implemented successfully by various healthcare organizations, they are not an ending—they are merely the means to a new beginning.

Healthcare War Room

The *healthcare war room* is a designated place, a room where healthcare professionals meet to brainstorm ways to improve the quality of patient care. The healthcare war room is not just about doing the right thing, but about doing the right thing well. Every hospital should be encouraged to develop a war room, a place where ideas are generated and agreed upon by leadership to pursue and support. Ideas chosen for pursuit must be assigned to a *rainmaker*, an individual who takes responsibility for a specific project, charting the course and leading the ship to its destination. A rainmaker makes things happen, generates innovative new ideas and new business models, and takes the art of doing business to new levels. A rainmaker is able to carry the torch of success across the finish line with great pride.

The Journey to Excellence requires leadership by an executive who is comfortable in any setting. A successful leader has the passion, creativity, knowledge, and determination to fulfill a project's mission and vision. The leader must be committed to the appointment of those who

believe in the limitless potential to carry a project forward as a team. The visionaries and the innovators need to be identified and their energies given focus and direction.

Telemedicine

Telemedicine is the delivery of healthcare services by means of telecommunications. The use of telemedicine brings modern health care to remote areas of the world. Telecommunications includes *teleradiology*, the interpretation of imaging procedures at a site remote from the patient and where the diagnostic procedure was performed. *Telepathology* involves the interpretation of slides at a location far from where the slides are prepared. Electroencephalograms and electrocardiograms can also be transmitted almost anywhere in the world. *Tele-education* is a tremendous learning tool for linking lectures and formal education programs to multiple sites. "As telecommunication technology has advanced and costs have declined over the past decade, there has been a steady growth in telemedicine."[1]

The possibilities of telemedicine are endless. The benefits include improving access to high-tech care in remote areas of the nation and the world while at the same time reducing the transportation hardships for patients. Patients can remain in their community and still have access to the marvels of modern medicine. Global telemedicine has arrived to provide:

- Worldwide medical consultations conducted by specialty.
- Continual access to updated physiologic data about patients in remote areas.
- Electronic medical records.
- Remote examination of patients at the primary site.
- Remote review of imaging studies, for example, at a secondary site.
- Consultations between the primary and secondary site by means of teleconferencing.

Ambassadors Worldwide

 The structure of world peace cannot be the work of one man, or one party, or one nation. . . . It must be a peace, which rests on the cooperative effort of the whole world.
—ELEANOR ROOSEVELT

Eleanor Roosevelt's words apply to the world of health care. The need for current healthcare information requires a collaborative effort of healthcare professionals from around the world. A first class healthcare system cannot be the work of one man or one nation. It must be a system that depends on the cooperative effort of the world community.

NEWSPAPER CLIPPINGS: Launch of the Global eHealth Ambassador's Program

The International Society for Telemedicine and eHealth (ISfTeH) is engaged in a new and exciting initiative called The Global eHealth Ambassadors Program (GeHAP), with seed funding from the Rockefeller Foundation and the Gulbenkian Foundation.

. . .

The purpose of the program is to raise the profile of eHealth worldwide, through advocacy activities. Advocacy plays a particularly important role within the broad framework of using ICT to strengthen health systems, especially in the Global South.

—Rio de Janeiro, Brazil, *November 11, 2011*

Leaders of healthcare organizations should consider sponsoring an *Ambassadors Worldwide* program that encourages employees to contact other caregivers in their discipline from around the world. Employees could begin their dialogue by inquiring about the way in which another professional in the same discipline addresses a specific issue. From there, a professional relationship may ensue where each professional is able to learn about best practices in each other's country and how to best apply that knowledge in their home countries. Such sharing of information will create worldwide ambassadors for health care, leading to a melding of resources and knowledge for the most effective care of patients.

Hospitals that implement such a program should then share the program's findings with their local community by publishing a hospital newsletter highlighting the most interesting and informative results, including the unique experiences that their employees have had with other caregivers from around the world.

Professional Exchange Program

This concept involves an exchange program whereby international host families would sponsor a healthcare professional in their home for a selected period of time (e.g., 2 or more weeks). The professional would work in a foreign university hospital setting to learn the practices used in that healthcare setting, while also sharing with the host hospital best practices from his or her hospital. Thus, the program would provide a different cultural environment in which caregivers can learn on site each other's best practices.

Partners in Education

 NEWSPAPER CLIPPINGS: San Joaquin Delta and Hospitals Project

This program, initiated by the San Joaquin Delta Community College and funded by a grant through the California Community College System, provides healthcare career exploration in a unique hands-on hospital experience for 600 eighth graders. As students tour the hospitals, they participate in a mock surgery and observe patients and newborns. Additionally, 300 eighth grade classes receive a "Healthcare Career Pathways Resources Binder" to keep students interested.[2]

 NEWSPAPER CLIPPINGS: Education Partnership

Ohio State has developed several programs to inform young people about futures in medicine, encourage interest in the fundamentals of academic medicine—science and mathematics—and expose them to medical scenarios. Here are just a few of the programs that The Ohio State University Wexner Medical Center is proud to offer to students from the local community.

. . .

Participants work diligently to increase student awareness of career opportunities in health care through field trips, speakers, mentoring, shadowing and honors breakfasts. They also aim to increase awareness of OSUMC health services among academically gifted students.[3]

Partners in healthcare education programs, created by hospital–school partnerships, support and enrich student learning by introducing students to opportunities in the healthcare professions. Partners in education can take the form of a school lunch program whereby healthcare professionals (e.g., nurses, pharmacists, physical therapists, physicians) from a local community hospital are matched with students from a local middle school or high school who have an interest in a particular health career. Hospital employee volunteers are matched with one or more students for a semester and have lunch with them during a set day and time each week. Students may even choose to learn about a different discipline the following semester. The earlier this process begins, the greater the opportunity a student has to discover a successful career path.

Information on a wide variety of middle school, high school, and undergraduate college programs can be found by searching "schools partner early for health careers."[4]

Best Practices

The journey to excellence involves searching for best practices worldwide. It is a journey to the far corners of the earth in search of answers to difficult healthcare issues. It is the "worldwide search" to improve the quality of life on a global basis. It involves providing information to those individuals unwilling to accept an end without a fight. It recognizes that the answers to complex disease processes may lead the reader to exotic lands in search of a remedy. Although many issues may seem overwhelming, the answer to many healthcare issues may be a click away.

The sharing of best practices among hospitals should be conducted on a not-for-profit basis. All too often, hospitals spend hundreds of thousands of dollars to implement a hybrid of an idea that is already in the marketplace free of charge. The sharing of information such as job descriptions, performance evaluations, employee handbooks, age-specific educational materials, and infection control PowerPoint presentations should be shared freely among healthcare organizations and tweaked as necessary for the individual organization.

REALITY CHECK: Time to Share

Joe was a healthcare consultant who collected thousands of documents of helpful information that he shared with healthcare organizations. His thinking was this: Why should hospitals have to reinvent the wheel? If organizations were willing to share with others, he was willing to become a conduit for that sharing for the benefit of other hospitals and ultimately for their patients. His hopes were that larger trade organizations would eventually collect the information and freely share with their constituents. Joe provided copies of his CD to fellow consultants and encouraged them to share the information with others. On the second day of a work assignment in Virginia, Joe noticed that one of the consultants to whom he had given a copy of the CD the day before had spread various newspaper clippings about hospitals spread out on the organization's conference room table. Joe thought they looked interesting and asked, "Could I have a copy of your clippings?" The consultant said, "No, these are proprietary information." Joe was thinking to himself, "Wow, I just gave him thousands of pages of documents, and he is unwilling to share four or five newspaper clippings with me."

Discussion

1. Joe never pointed out the fact that he had shared so much the day before. What would you have done if you were Joe? Explain your answer.
2. Should organizations such as the American Hospital Association make greater strides in collecting helpful information that could be shared with others (e.g., innovative pain management centers)? Discuss your answer.

Information Technology

Healthcare organizations need to improve their information technology systems in order to reduce the tremendous amount of paperwork required of caregivers, allowing more time for direct patient care. In addition, physicians should be able to access best practices. Electronic patient information–based technology coupled with computer-assisted diagnosis and treatment options will improve the decision-making process and ultimately patient care outcomes.

The medical record has become a cumbersome compilation of illegible notes from many healthcare disciplines. It has become an unfriendly and far-from-effective communications tool in the care and treatment of patients. Its purpose has shifted from being a useful communications tool between caregivers to becoming a tool for satisfying regulatory bodies. The proverbial wheel is broken, so reinventing the "medical record" wheel is a must, requiring serious attention by the healthcare industry and regulatory bodies in order to provide patients with increased quality of bedside care and time with each patient.

Nurses claim they often spend up to 2 hours or more of an 8-hour shift documenting in-patient records. Getting the nurses and other professionals back to the patient's bedside and away from the computer or pen requires ongoing reengineering of information systems.

Artificial Intelligence

Artificial intelligence (AI)-based medical decision support systems, using the MIR, provide an electronic tool for entering a patient's health information into a computer program to assist in suggesting clinical tests for diagnosing a patient's illness and suggesting alternate treatment plans, including the potential for success of each alternative plan with statistical evidence. The use of AI should involve the following:

- Ensure that the data collected are easily accessible and user friendly to healthcare practitioners, organizations, and consumers of health care, and are used to synergize activities between clinical care, education and training, and research.
- Evaluate computer decision models and continue to improve the value of AI tools.
- Reassure practitioners that AI is designed to be an aide to enhance their knowledge base and skills and, like any other clinical test, to be used as a tool in the decision-making process to diagnose and treat the patient.
- Encourage research to better integrate conventional and traditional medicine in such a way that they complement each other.
- Establish medical field teams (e.g., journalists, physicians, and other healthcare practitioners, as appropriate) who go into the field to investigate what appears to be promising "new medical finds."
- Provide distant learning through worldwide educational conference programming using the conferencing capabilities of major hotel chains, such as Marriott, which have worldwide conferencing center capabilities.

Streamline Data Collection and Evaluation

 It's better to have no data than to have data that leads to the wrong conclusions.

—Author Unknown

Over the years, healthcare organizations have collected an enormous amount of data that have been costly and time consuming to collect and have little clinical value. Collecting data on cesarean section rates for nearly half a century, for example, has done little to improve the quality of health care. The collection of data must be meaningful and lead to improved patient outcomes. With limited financial resources, data gathering should have a recognizable clinical payoff for the patient.

Hospitals should follow the federal government's example and tailor the Paperwork Reduction Act (44 U.S.C. 3501) to their goals for having caregivers spend more time with patients and less with paperwork. The Paperwork Reduction Act reduced the collection of information burden on individuals, ensured the privacy of the information collected and disseminated, and allowed for less time to complete necessary forms and other documents, which, under the act, were mandated to be streamlined.

Medical Information Repository

 The loftier your goals, the higher the risk, the greater your glory.

—Author Unknown

There is a need to develop a comprehensive *medical information repository* (MIR) database for use in computer-assisted diagnosis and treatment. Such a repository should integrate both conventional and traditional medicines.

Conventional medicine is often referred to as evidence-based medicine, meaning that the value of medicine has statistical reliability as to its safety, effectiveness, and efficacy. It is practiced by physicians holding an M.D. (medical doctor) or D.O. (doctor of osteopathy) degree and by their allied health professionals, such as physical therapists, psychologists, nurse practitioners, and physician assistants.

Traditional medicine, as defined by the World Health Organization, "is the sum total of the knowledge, skills, and practices based on the theories, beliefs, and experiences indigenous to different cultures, whether explicable or not, used in the maintenance of health as well as in the prevention, diagnosis, improvement or treatment of physical and mental illness."[5] Traditional medicines include herbal medicine and acupuncture. The safe use of some traditional medicines remains in doubt as a result of the fact that science has yet to substantiate their value, effectiveness, and efficacy. As an example, in herbal medicine, there are a variety of herbal medications that have yet to show value and, in some cases, have contributed to the injury or death of the user. Moreover, there have been reports of drug–herbal interactions; complicating the problem is the fact that herb and vitamin-based over-the-counter "medicines" are not Food and Drug Administration regulated.

The *medical information repository* should be carefully analyzed and verified for reliability. Dissemination of the most current and exhaustive medical information must be continuously updated on a 24-hour, 365-day-per-year basis. The information gathered should be designed to assist and provide clinicians with the most effective curative and rehabilitative regimens to enhance the quality of patient care. Web-based health information should be available and *assessable by the public.*

Focus on Preventative Medicine

Hospitals and physicians are often so busy treating symptoms, diseases, conditions, and injuries that preventative care is often not addressed. By committing more time and resources to preventative medicine, the risks of early onset of disease can be reduced.

The Five Senses

Bedside care involves more than recordkeeping. Imagine for a moment Patient A's and Patient B's experiences through the five senses as described here.

Patient A

See: Your favorite scenes from Africa are on a large, flat-screen television; you have a private room.

Hear: Your favorite music by Enya playing in the background; the corridors are quiet.

Smell: You have fresh flowers, and the bathroom is clean with no harsh chemical odors.

Taste: You have your favorite foods.

Touch: Your pain is controlled, the room is the right temperature, and you have had caring caregivers and family.

Patient B

See: The walls are cracked, the paint is peeling, and mold is growing in the vents.

Hear: The corridor is noisy. You have no visitors, but your roommate has eight of them.

Smell: A sewage plant is nearby, and the wind from its direction is blowing in your open screened window.

Taste: You are on a liquid diet; your water is warm and has a weird taste.

Touch: Your pain is unrelenting, and the room is hot.

Patient A and Patient B are two different patients with two very different experiences. Clearly, the health profession must do more to better address the five senses. Each sense has many components. For example, the sense of touch includes physical, psychological, social, and spiritual elements, each of which needs to be addressed. The physical aspect includes the effective control of a patient's pain. The social aspect involves family, caregivers, visitors, friends, and spiritual guidance. Hospitals may not be able to do everything they would like for their patients, but they can better address their sensory needs.

ADOPT A HOSPITAL

Highways and rivers are adopted, why not *adopt a hospital*? Creating change on a grand scale requires financial backing by mission-driven individuals and corporations willing to adopt hospitals and provide funding for their capital needs for new or expanded programs and services. With fewer than 6,000 hospitals and numerous for-profit corporations in the United States, the healthcare system would be able to continuously grow and provide quality services with an Adopt a Hospital sponsorship from the nation's wealthiest people and corporations such as Apple, General Electric, Johnson and Johnson, Google, IBM, Intel, and Microsoft. In such a program, hospitals would be matched with corporations based on size and needs.

Fundraising is everybody's job, and everybody has a role to play. Seniors can knit, crochet, and have their items sold in a gift or thrift shop. Young people can organize a car wash. Volunteers can have bake sales, sell raffle tickets, or sponsor dinner dances. The possibilities are endless.

FUNDING YOUR DREAMS

 The way to predict the future is to create it. Vision is the gift to see or do what others only dream.
—AUTHOR UNKNOWN

To help make a dream become reality, it is important for others to see and understand the dream. This can be accomplished effectively by visually displaying the vision on an electronic dream board and making it easily visible to all. The dream board could be placed, for example, in high-traffic areas such as the hospital lobby or in the emergency department, intensive care, oncology, and rehabilitation waiting areas. It is important to remember that there can be multiple dreams displayed in various locations within the organization.

Dreams fulfilled should be displayed in what might be termed the "Hall of Dreams," celebrating the successes of those who worked hard to achieve them.

BALDRIGE PERFORMANCE EXCELLENCE PROGRAM

 NEWSPAPER CLIPPINGS: Baldrige and Health Care: New Survey Reaffirms a Proven Partnership for Success

For the second time in two years, Truven Health Analytics, a major healthcare survey research and data analysis organization, has linked hospitals that adopt and use the Baldrige Criteria for Performance Excellence to successful operations, management practices and overall performance.

. . .

"The Baldrige program has long been the gold standard for leadership practices to drive higher quality and organizational performance. Our effort to use the 100 Top Hospitals National Balanced Scorecard to identify the use of these practices is an early step in the establishment of evidence-based management practices," said Jean Chenoweth, senior vice president at Truven Health Analytics, in a Nov. 20, 2012, news release.[6]

—*Micahel E. Newman*, NIST Tech Beat, *December 2012*

The Pathway to Excellence and the accomplishments of an organization's successes are often recognized on a national basis through the *Malcolm Baldrige National Quality Award* (MBNQA). Malcolm Baldrige was Secretary of Commerce from 1981 to July 1987. He was a proponent of quality management. In recognition of his contributions, Congress named the award, which is the highest level of national recognition for performance excellence that a U.S. organization can receive. Congress established the Baldrige Program in 1987 to recognize U.S. companies for their achievements in quality and business performance and to raise awareness about the importance of quality and performance excellence in gaining a competitive edge. Education and healthcare organizations are eligible to quality for the highly competitive award by meeting stringent Health Care *Criteria for Performance Excellence*.[7] To receive the BNQA, an organization must have a role-model organizational management system that ensures continuous improvement in the delivery of products and/or services, demonstrates efficient and effective operations, and provides a way of engaging and responding to customers and other stakeholders.[8]

Notes

1. http://www.ncbi.nlm.nih.gov/pmc/articles/PMC1121135/.
2. http://www.oshpd.ca.gov/HWDD/pdfs/HP_Feb09.pdf.
3. http://medicalcenter.osu.edu/aboutus/community_commitment/education_partnership/pages/index.aspx.
4. http://www.asph.org/userfiles/PartneringWith HealthCareerPrograms.pdf.
5. World Health Organization, Traditional Medicine: Definitions, http://www.who.int/medicines/areas/traditional/definitions/en/index.html.
6. http://www.nist.gov/baldrige/baldrige-120412.cfm?goback=%2Egde_1810424_member_192918450.
7. http://www.nist.gov/baldrige/publications/hc_criteria.cfm.
8. http://www.nist.gov/baldrige/about/baldrige_faqs.cfm.

Glossary

abandonment Unilateral severance by the physician of the professional relationship between himself or herself and the patient without reasonable notice at a time when the patient still needs continuing care.

abortion Premature termination of pregnancy at a time when the fetus is incapable of sustaining life independent of the mother.

accreditation An evaluative process in which a healthcare facility undergoes an examination of its policies, procedures, practices, and performance by an external sector organization ("accrediting body") to ensure that it is meeting predetermined criteria. It usually involves both on and off-site surveys.

admissibility (of evidence) Refers to the issue of whether a court, applying the rules of evidence, is bound to receive or permit introduction of a particular piece of evidence.

advance directives Written instructions expressing an individual's healthcare wishes in the event that he or she becomes incapacitated and is unable to make such decisions for himself or herself.

adverse drug reaction Unusual or unexpected response to a normal dose of a medication; an injury caused by the use of a drug in the usual, acceptable fashion.

affidavit A voluntary statement of facts, or a voluntary declaration in writing of facts, that a person swears to be true before an official authorized to administer an oath.

agent An individual who has been designated by a legal document to make decisions on behalf of another individual; a substitute decision maker.

Americans with Disabilities Act (ADA) Federal act that bars employers from discriminating against disabled persons in hiring, promotion, or other provisions of employment.

appellant Party who appeals the decision of a lower court to a court of higher jurisdiction.

appellee Party against whom an appeal to a higher court is taken.

artificial nutrition and hydration Providing food and liquids when a patient is unable to eat or drink, such as intravenous feedings.

assault A deliberate threat, coupled with the apparent present ability to do physical harm to another.

attestation Act of witnessing a document in writing.

autonomy Right of an individual to make his or her own independent decisions.

battery Intentional touching of one person by another without the consent of the person being touched.

beneficence Describes the principle of doing good, demonstrating kindness, and helping others.

best evidence rule Legal doctrine requiring that primary evidence of a fact (such as an original document) be introduced or that an acceptable explanation be given before a copy can be introduced or testimony given concerning the fact.

bioethics The philosophical study of the ethical controversies brought about by advances in biology, research (e.g., human cloning), and medicine.

borrowed servant doctrine Refers to a situation in which an employee is temporarily placed under the control of someone other than his or her primary employer. It may involve a situation in which an employee is carrying out the specific instructions of a physician. The traditional example is that of a nurse employed by a hospital who is "borrowed" and under the control of the attending surgeon during a procedure in the operating room. The temporary employer of the borrowed servant can be held responsible for the negligent acts of the borrowed servant under the doctrine of respondeat superior. This rule is not easily applied, especially if the acts of the employee are for the furtherance of the objectives of the employer. The courts apply a narrow application if the employee is fulfilling the requirement of his or her position.

cardiopulmonary resuscitation A lifesaving method used by caregivers to restore heartbeat and breathing.

case citation Describes where a court's opinion in a particular case can be located. It identifies the parties in the case, the text in which the case can be found, the court writing the opinion, and the year in which the case was decided. For example, the citation "*Bouvia v. Superior Court (Glenchur),* 225 Cal. Rptr. 297 (Ct. App. 1986)" is described as follows:

- "*Bouvia v. Superior Court (Glenchur)*" identifies the basic parties involved in the lawsuit.
- "225 Cal. Rptr. 297" identifies the case as being reported in volume 225 of the California Reporter at page 297.
- "Ct. App. 1986" identifies the case as being decided in the California Court of Appeals in 1986.

case law Aggregate of reported cases on a particular legal subject as formed by the decisions of those cases.

charitable immunity Legal doctrine that developed out of the English court system that held charitable institutions blameless for their negligent acts.

civil law Body of law that describes the private rights and responsibilities of individuals. The part of law that does not deal with crimes, it involves actions filed by one individual against another (e.g., actions in tort and contract).

clinical privileges On qualification, the diagnostic and therapeutic procedures that an institution allows a physician to perform on a specified patient population. Qualification includes a review of a physician's credentials, such as medical school diploma, state licensure, and residency training.

common law Body of principles that has evolved and continues to evolve and expand from court decisions. Many of the legal principles and rules applied by courts in the United States had their origins in English common law.

complaint In a negligence action, the first pleading that is filed by the plaintiff's attorney. It is the first statement of a case by the plaintiff against the defendant and states a cause of action, notifying the defendant as to the basis for the suit.

Congressional Record Document in which the proceedings of Congress are published. It is the first record of debate officially reported, printed, and published directly by the federal government. Publication of the record began March 4, 1873.

consent See *informed consent.*

consequentialism A moral theory that determines good or bad, right or wrong, based on good outcomes or consequences.

contextualism An ethical doctrine that considers the rightness or wrongness of an action, such as lying, to be based on the particular circumstances of a given situation. The implication is that lying is acceptable in one situation but not in another, even though the situations may be similar. In other words, it depends on the context within which something occurs.

criminal negligence Reckless disregard for the safety of others; the willful indifference to an injury after an act.

decisional capacity Having the mental capacity to make one's own decisions. Mental capacity refers to the ability to understand the risks, the benefits, the alternatives, and the consequences of one's actions. Inferred in this interpretation is knowing that the decision maker can reasonably distinguish right from wrong and good from bad.

defamation Injury of a person's reputation or character caused by the false statements of another made to a third person. Defamation includes both libel and slander.

defendant In a criminal case, the person accused of committing a crime. In a civil suit, the party against whom the suit is brought, demanding that he or she pay the other party legal relief.

demurrer Formal objection by one of the parties to a lawsuit that the evidence presented by the other party is insufficient to sustain an issue or case.

deontological ethics A theory of ethics that focuses on duty, rather than the consequences, when determining the right conduct to be followed.

deposition A method of pretrial discovery that consists of statements of fact taken by a witness under oath in a question-and-answer format, as it would be in a court of law with opportunity given to the adversary to be present for cross-examination. Such statements may be admitted into evidence if it is impossible for a witness to attend a trial in person.

determinism The view that nothing happens without a cause.

directed verdict When a trial judge decides either that the evidence and/or law is clearly in favor of one party or that the plaintiff has failed to establish a case and that it is pointless for the trial to proceed further, the judge may direct the jury to return a verdict for the appropriate party. The conclusion of the judge must be so clear and obvious that reasonable minds could not arrive at a different conclusion.

discharge summary That part of a medical record that summarizes a patient's initial complaints, course of treatment, final diagnosis, and instructions for follow-up care.

discovery To ascertain that which was previously unknown through a pretrial investigation. It includes testimony and documents that may be under the exclusive control of the other party. Discovery facilitates out-of-court settlements.

dogmatic Stubborn refusal to consider challenges to your own ethical point of view.

do-not-resuscitate (DNR) order Directive of a physician to withhold cardio-pulmonary resuscitation in the event a patient experiences cardiac or respiratory arrest.

durable power of attorney A legal instrument enabling an individual to act on another's behalf. In the healthcare setting, a durable power of attorney for health care is a legal instrument that designates and grants authority to an agent, for example, to make healthcare decisions for another.

ethical conduct Conducting oneself in a manner consistent with acceptable principles of right and wrong. Such conduct may relate to one's community, country, profession, and so on.

ethical dilemma A situation that forces a decision to be made that involves breaking some ethical norm or contradicting some ethical value. It involves making a decision between two or more possible actions where any one of the actions can be justified as being the right decision, but whatever action is taken, there always remains some doubt as to whether the correct course of action was chosen. The effect of an action may put others at risk, harm others, or violate the rights of others.

ethicist A person, often with an advanced degree, who specializes in ethics through the application of theory and ethical principles governing right and wrong conduct. Ethicists often serve on hospital ethics committees and are an excellent resource for aid in resolving ethical dilemmas.

ethics A set of principles of right and wrong conduct. A theory or system of moral values, of what is right and what is wrong. Ethics is a system of values that guides behavior in relationships among people in accordance with certain social roles.

ethics committee A committee created to deal with ethical problems and dilemmas in the delivery of patient care.

euthanasia A Greek word meaning "the good death." It is an act conducted for the purpose of causing the merciful death of a person who is suffering from an incurable condition, such as providing a patient with medications to hasten his or her death.

evidence Proof of a fact, which is legally presented in a manner prescribed by law, at trial.

expert witness Person who has special training, experience, skill, and/or knowledge in a relevant area and who is allowed to offer an opinion as testimony in court.

futility Having no useful result. Futility of treatment, as it relates to medical care, occurs when the physician recognizes that the effect of treatment will be of no benefit to the patient. Morally, the physician has a duty to inform the patient when there is little likelihood of success.

Good Samaritan laws Laws designed to protect those who stop to render aid in an emergency. These laws generally provide immunity for specified persons from any civil suit arising out of care rendered at the scene of an emergency, provided that the one rendering assistance has not done so in a grossly negligent manner.

grand jury Jury called to determine whether there is sufficient evidence that a crime has been committed to justify bringing a case to trial.

guardian Person appointed by a court to protect the interests of and make decisions for a person who is incapable of making his or her own decisions.

health According to the World Health Organization, "A state of complete physical, mental, and social well-being and not merely the absence of disease or infirmity."

healthcare proxy Document that delegates the authority to make one's own healthcare decisions to another adult, known as the healthcare agent, when one has become incapacitated or is unable to make his or her own decisions.

hospice Long-term care for terminally ill persons, provided in a setting more economical than that of a hospital or nursing home. Hospice care generally is sought after a decision has been made to discontinue aggressive efforts to prolong life. A hospice program includes such characteristics as support services by trained individuals, family involvement, and control of pain and discomfort.

hydration Intravenous addition of fluids to the circulatory system when the patient is not capable of swallowing.

immoral Behavior that is in opposition to accepted societal, religious, cultural, and/or professional standards.

incapacity An individual's lack of ability to make decisions for himself or herself.

incompetent Individual determined by a court to be incapable of making rational decisions on his or her own behalf.

informed consent Legal concept providing that a patient has the right to know the potential risks, benefits, and alternatives of a medical procedure or treatment before consenting to the procedure or treatment. Informed consent implies that a patient understands a particular procedure or treatment, including the risks, benefits, and alternatives; is capable of making a decision; and gives consent voluntarily.

injunction Court order requiring a person to perform or prohibiting a person from performing a particular act.

in loco parentis Legal doctrine that permits the courts to assign a person to stand in the place of parents and possess their legal rights, duties, and responsibilities toward a child.

interrogatory List of questions sent from one party in a lawsuit to the other party to be answered under oath.

Joint Commission see *The Joint Commission*

jurisdiction Right of a court to administer justice by hearing and deciding controversies.

jurisprudence Philosophy or science of law on which a particular legal system is built.

justice The obligation to be fair in the distribution of benefits and risks.

larceny Taking another person's property without consent with the intent to permanently deprive the owner of its use and ownership.

liability As it relates to damages, an obligation one has incurred or might incur through a negligent act.

libel False or malicious writing intended to defame or dishonor another person and is published so that someone other than the one defamed will observe it.

life support Medical intervention(s) designed to prolong life (e.g., respirator, kidney dialysis machine, tube feedings).

living will A document in which an individual expresses in advance his or her wishes regarding the application of life-sustaining treatment in the event that he or she is incapable of doing so at some future time. A living will describes in advance the kind of care one wants to receive or does not wish to receive in the event that he or she is unable to make decisions for himself or herself. A living will takes effect when a person is in a terminal condition or permanent state of unconsciousness.

malfeasance Execution of an unlawful or improper act.

malpractice Professional misconduct, improper discharge of professional duties, or failure to meet the standard of care of a professional that results in harm to another. It is the negligence or carelessness of a professional person, such as a nurse, pharmacist, physician, or accountant.

mandamus Action brought in a court of competent jurisdiction to compel a lower court or administrative agency to perform—or not to perform—a specific act.

Medicaid Medical assistance provided for by Title XIX of the Social Security Act. Medicaid is a state-administered program for the medically indigent.

Medicare Medical assistance provided for by Title XVIII of the Social Security Act. Medicare is a health insurance program administered by the Social Security Administration for persons aged 65 years and older and for disabled persons who are eligible for benefits. Medicare Part A benefits provide coverage for inpatient hospital care, skilled nursing facility care, home health care, and hospice care. Medicare Part B benefits provide coverage for physician services, outpatient hospital services, diagnostic tests, various therapies, durable medical equipment, medical supplies, and prosthetic devices.

metaethics The study of ethical concepts.

misfeasance Improper performance of an act.

nasogastric tube, insertion of Involves placing a tube through the patient's nose, down the back of the throat into the esophagus, and then into the stomach. Its purpose is to suction out the contents of the stomach.

negligence Omission or commission of an act that a reasonably prudent person would or would not do under given circumstances. It is a form of heedlessness or carelessness that constitutes a departure from the standard of care generally imposed on members of society.

non compos mentis "Not of sound mind"; suffering from some form of mental defect.

nonfeasance Failure to act, when there is a duty to act, as a reasonably prudent person would in similar circumstances.

normative ethics The study of what is right and wrong.

norms Accepted rules and ways of doing things. Without norms, society would be chaotic and unpredictable.

nuncupative will Oral statement intended as a last will made in anticipation of death.

objectivism The belief that morality is based on some universal, external, and unchangeable fact. For example, murder is always wrong.

ombudsman Person who is designated to speak and act on behalf of a patient/resident, especially in regard to his or her daily needs.

paternalism A doctrine that literally means "rule by the father." In health care, it is the concept of physicians making decisions for their patients, whereas the more acceptable approach is autonomy, whereby the physician informs the patient as to the risks, benefits, and alternatives to care and treatment, and then the patient makes the final choice as to what is best.

Patient Protection Affordable Care Act A federal act passed by Congress and signed into law by President Obama in March 2010. Its design and purpose is to provide better health security by putting into place comprehensive health insurance reforms that hold insurance companies accountable, lower healthcare costs, guarantee more choice, and enhance the quality of care for all Americans.

plaintiff Party who brings a civil suit seeking damages or other legal relief.

polytheism Belief and worship in many gods.

probate Judicial proceeding that determines the existence and validity of a will.

probate court A court with jurisdiction over wills. Its powers range from deciding the validity of a will to distributing property.

process A series of related actions to achieve a defined outcome. Ordering and/or administering medications are processes.

prognosis Informed judgment regarding the likely course and probable outcome of a disease.

qui tam action A writ whereby a private individual who assists in a prosecution, such as, a whistleblower who reports healthcare fraud by his employers against the government, can receive a reward for any penalty imposed.

rational Having the capacity to think logically.

real evidence Evidence furnished by tangible things (e.g., medical records and equipment).

relativism The belief that morality is relative to each individual culture. What is right in one culture may be wrong in another culture. In ethics, it is a theory that conceptions of truth and moral values are not absolute but are relative to the persons or groups holding them.

release Statement signed by one person relinquishing a right or claim against another.

remand Referral of a case by an appeals court back to the original court, out of which it came, for the purpose of having some action taken there.

respirator A machine used to assist to keep a patient breathing.

respondeat superior "Let the master answer": an aphorism meaning that the employer is responsible for the legal consequences of the acts of the servant or employee who is acting within the scope of his or her employment.

restraint Can be either "physical" or "chemical" (medication). A physical restraint involves a device (e.g., safety belts, safety bars, geriatric chairs, bed rails) that restricts or limits voluntary movement that cannot be removed by the patient.

slander False oral statement, made in the presence of a third person, that injures the character or reputation of another.

standard of care Description of the conduct that is expected of an individual in a given situation. It is a measure against which a defendant's conduct is compared.

stare decisis "Let the decision stand": the legal doctrine that prescribes adherence to those precedents set forth in cases that have been decided.

statute of limitations Legal limit on the time allowed for filing suit in civil matters, usually measured from the time of the wrong or from the time when a reasonable person would have discovered the wrong.

statutory law Law that is prescribed by legislative enactments.

stipulation An agreement or concession of agreed-upon facts made by the parties in a judicial proceeding relating to the business before the court, which must be in writing unless they are part of the court record. A stipulation of facts is often made to avoid delay judicial proceedings.

subpoena ad testificandum Court order requiring one to appear in court to give testimony.

subpoena duces tecum Court order that commands a person to come to court and to produce whatever documents are named in the order.

subrogation Substitution of one person for another in reference to a lawful claim or right.

summary judgment Generally, an immediate decision by a judge, without jury deliberation.

summons Court order directed to the sheriff or other appropriate official to notify the defendant in a civil suit that a suit has been filed and when and where to appear.

surrogate decision maker An individual who has been designated to make decisions on behalf of another person determined incapable of making his or her own decisions.

terminal condition A medical condition that is incurable and in which death will occur.

testimony Oral statement of a witness given under oath at trial.

The Joint Commission (TJC) A not-for-profit independent organization dedicated to improving the quality of health care in organized healthcare settings. The major functions of The Joint Commission include the development of organizational standards, awarding accreditation decisions, and providing education and consultation to healthcare organizations.

theodicy A vindication of God's goodness and justice in the face of the existence of evil. We often wonder why God allows bad things to happen to good people. The answer often given is that what God allows to happen in the lives of good people is often mysterious to us. We often have difficulty understanding this, and it often provokes anger in us.

tort Civil wrong committed by one individual against another. Torts may be classified as either intentional or unintentional. When a tort is classified as a criminal wrong (e.g., assault, battery, false imprisonment), the wrongdoer can be held liable in a criminal and/or civil action.

tort-feasor Person who commits a tort.

trial court Court in which evidence is presented to a judge or jury for decision.

unethical behavior Character that describes behavior contrary to admirable traits or a code of conduct that has been endorsed by one's society, community, or profession.

utilitarianism A moral theory that treats pleasure and happiness as the only absolute moral good. Acts that bring about happiness and pleasure are good, and acts that bring about pain and suffering are morally bad.

value Worth or usefulness. *Intrinsic values* are those goods that are valuable in their own right. *Instrumental values* are those goods that help us achieve another good.

value judgment A judgment that assigns value to an action.

verdict Formal declaration of a jury's findings of fact, signed by the jury foreperson and presented to the court.

virtue A moral trait that refers to excellence and righteousness.

waiver Intentional giving up of a right, such as allowing another person to testify to information that ordinarily would be protected as a privileged communication.

will Legal declaration of the intentions a person wishes to have carried out after death concerning property, children, or estate. A will designates a person or persons to serve as the executor(s) responsible for carrying out the instructions of the will.

withdrawal of treatment A decision to *discontinue treatment* or medical interventions for the patient when death is imminent and cannot be prevented by available treatment.

withholding of treatment A decision *not to initiate treatment* or medical intervention for the patient when death is imminent and there is no hope of recovery.

witness Person who is called to give testimony in a court of law.

wrongful birth Applies to the cause of action of parents who claim that negligent advice or treatment deprived them of the choice of aborting conception or of terminating the pregnancy.

wrongful life Refers to a cause of action brought by or on behalf of a defective child who claims that but for the defendant (e.g., a laboratory's negligent testing procedures or a physician's negligent advice or treatment of the child's parents) the child would not have been born.

Case Index

Subject Index